# ARTIFICIAL INTELLIGENCE APPLICATIONS AND INNOVATIONS

# IFIP – The International Federation for Information Processing

IFIP was founded in 1960 under the auspices of UNESCO, following the First World Computer Congress held in Paris the previous year. An umbrella organization for societies working in information processing, IFIP's aim is two-fold: to support information processing within its member countries and to encourage technology transfer to developing nations. As its mission statement clearly states,

> *IFIP's mission is to be the leading, truly international, apolitical organization which encourages and assists in the development, exploitation and application of information technology for the benefit of all people.*

IFIP is a non-profitmaking organization, run almost solely by 2500 volunteers. It operates through a number of technical committees, which organize events and publications. IFIP's events range from an international congress to local seminars, but the most important are:

- The IFIP World Computer Congress, held every second year;
- Open conferences;
- Working conferences.

The flagship event is the IFIP World Computer Congress, at which both invited and contributed papers are presented. Contributed papers are rigorously refereed and the rejection rate is high.

As with the Congress, participation in the open conferences is open to all and papers may be invited or submitted. Again, submitted papers are stringently refereed.

The working conferences are structured differently. They are usually run by a working group and attendance is small and by invitation only. Their purpose is to create an atmosphere conducive to innovation and development. Refereeing is less rigorous and papers are subjected to extensive group discussion.

Publications arising from IFIP events vary. The papers presented at the IFIP World Computer Congress and at open conferences are published as conference proceedings, while the results of the working conferences are often published as collections of selected and edited papers.

Any national society whose primary activity is in information may apply to become a full member of IFIP, although full membership is restricted to one society per country. Full members are entitled to vote at the annual General Assembly, National societies preferring a less committed involvement may apply for associate or corresponding membership. Associate members enjoy the same benefits as full members, but without voting rights. Corresponding members are not represented in IFIP bodies. Affiliated membership is open to non-national societies, and individual and honorary membership schemes are also offered.

# ARTIFICIAL INTELLIGENCE APPLICATIONS AND INNOVATIONS

*IFIP 18th World Computer Congress*
*TC12 First International Conference on*
*Artificial Intelligence Applications and Innovations (AIAI-2004)*
*22–27 August 2004*
*Toulouse, France*

Edited by

**Max Bramer**
*University of Portsmouth, UK*

**Vladan Devedzic**
*University of Belgrade, Serbia and Montenegro*

SPRINGER SCIENCE+BUSINESS MEDIA, LLC

**Library of Congress Cataloging-in-Publication Data**

A C.I.P. Catalogue record for this book is available from the Library of Congress.

Artificial Intelligence Applications and Innovations
Edited by Max Bramer and Vladan Devedzic
ISBN 978-1-4757-8025-3          ISBN 978-1-4020-8151-4 (eBook)
DOI 10.1007/978-1-4020-8151-4

© 2004 IFIP International Federation for Information Processing
Originally published by International Federation for Information Processing in 2004
Softcover reprint of the hardcover 1st edition 2004

*Printed on acid-free paper.*

# Contents

**Neural Networks and Fuzzy Systems**

**Agents**

**Applications 2**

**Internet**

**Genetic Algorithms**

**Ontologies and Data Mining**

**Reasoning and Scheduling**

# Foreword

The papers in this volume comprise the refereed proceedings of the First International Conference on Artificial Intelligence Applications and Innovations (AIAI-2004), which formed part of the 18th World Computer Congress of IFIP, the International Federation for Information Processing (WCC-2004), in Toulouse, France in August 2004.

The conference is organised by the IFIP Technical Committee on Artificial Intelligence (Technical Committee 12) and its Working Group 12.5 (Artificial Intelligence Applications). Further information about both can be found on the website at http://www.ifiptc12.org.

A very promising sign of the growing importance of Artificial Intelligence techniques in practical applications is the large number of submissions received this time - more than twice the number for the Artificial Intelligence stream of the last World Computer Congress two years ago. All papers were reviewed by at least three members of the Programme Committee. The best 40 were selected for the conference and are included in this volume. The international nature of IFIP is amply reflected in the large number of countries represented here.

The conference also featured an invited talk by Eunika Mercier-Laurent and a Symposium on Professional Practice in Artificial Intelligence, which ran alongside the refereed papers.

I should like to thank the joint conference chairs, Professor John Debenham and Dr. Eunika Mercier-Laurent and my co-program chair Dr. Vladan

Devedzic for all their efforts in organising the conference and the members of our programme committee for reviewing an unexpectedly large number of papers to a tight deadline. I should also like to thank my wife Dawn for her help in editing this volume of proceedings.

This is the first in a new series of conferences dedicated to real-world applications of AI around the world. The wide range and importance of these applications is clearly indicated by the papers in this volume. Both are likely to increase still further as time goes by and we intend to reflect these developments in our future conferences.

Max Bramer
Chair, IFIP Technical Committee on Artificial Intelligence

The original version of this book was revised.
An erratum to this book can be found at DOI 10.1007/978-1-4020-8151-4_41

# Acknowledgments

## Conference Organising Committee

<u>Conference General Chairs</u>

John Debenham (University of Technology, Sydney, Australia)

Eunika Mercier-Laurent (Association Francaise pour l'Intelligence Artificielle, France)

<u>Conference Program Chairs</u>

Max Bramer (University of Portsmouth, United Kingdom)

Vladan Devedzic (University of Belgrade, Serbia and Montenegro)

## Programme Committee

Agnar Aamodt (Norway)
Luigia Carlucci Aiello (Italy)
Adel Alimi (Tunisia)
Lora Aroyo (The Netherlands)
Max Bramer (United Kingdom)
Zdzislaw Bubnicki (Poland)
Weiqin Chen (Norway)
Monica Crubezy (USA)
John Debenham (Australia)

Yves Demazeau (France)
Vladan Devedzic (Yugoslavia)
Rose Dieng (France)
Henrik Eriksson (Sweden)
Ana Garcia-Serrano (Spain)
Nicola Guarino (Italy)
Andreas Harrer (Germany)
Jean-Paul Haton (France)
Timo Honkela (Finland)
Kostas Karpouzis (Greece)
Dusko Katic (Serbia and Montenegro)
Ray Kemp (New Zealand)
Kinshuk (New Zealand)
Piet Kommers (The Netherlands)
Jasna Kuljis (United Kingdom)
Ilias Maglogiannis (Greece)
Eunika Mercier-Laurent (France)
Antonija Mitrovic (New Zealand)
Riichiro Mizoguchi (Japan)
Enrico Motta (United Kingdom)
Wolfgang Nejdl (Germany)
Erich Neuhold (Germany)
Bernd Neumann (Germany)
Natasha Noy (USA)
Zeljko Obrenovic (Serbia and Montenegro)
Mihaela Oprea (Romania)
Petra Perner (Germany)
Alun Preece (United Kingdom)
Abdel-Badeeh Salem (Egypt)
Demetrios Sampson (Greece)
Pierre-Yves Schobbens (Belgium)
Yuval Shahar (Israel)
Stuart Shapiro (USA)
Derek Sleeman (United Kingdom)
Constantine Spyropoulos (Greece)
Steffen Staab (Germany)
Mia Stern (USA)
Gerd Stumme (Germany)
Valentina Tamma (United Kingdom)
Vagan Terziyan (Finland)

# ARTIFICIAL INTELLIGENCE SYSTEMS IN MICROMECHANICS

Felipe Lara-Rosano, Ernst Kussul, Tatiana Baidyk, Leopoldo Ruiz, Alberto Caballero, Graciela Velasco
*CCADET, UNAM*

Abstract: Some of the artificial intelligence (AI) methods could be used to improve the automation system performance in manufacturing processes. However, the implementation of these AI methods in the industry is rather slow, because of the high cost of the experiments with the conventional manufacturing and AI systems. To lower the experiment cost in this field, we have developed a special micromechanical equipment, similar to conventional mechanical equipment, but of much smaller size and therefore of lower cost. This equipment could be used for evaluation of different AI methods in an easy and inexpensive way. The proved methods could be transferred to the industry through appropriate scaling. In this paper we describe the prototypes of low cost microequipment for manufacturing processes and some AI method implementations to increase its precision, like computer vision systems based on neural networks for microdevice assembly, and genetic algorithms for microequipment characterization and microequipment precision increase.

Key words: artificial intelligence, micromechanics, computer vision, genetic algorithms

## 1. INTRODUCTION

The development of AI technologies opens an opportunity to use them not only for conventional applications (expert systems, intelligent data bases [1], technical diagnostics [2,3] etc.), but also for total automation of mechanical manufacturing. Such AI methods as adaptive critic design [4,5], adaptive fuzzy Petri networks [6,7], neural network based computer vision systems [8-12], etc. could be used to solve the automation problems. To check this opportunity up, it is necessary to create an experimental factory with fully automated manufacturing processes. This is a very difficult and expensive task.

## 2.      MICROEQUIPMENT TECHNOLOGY

To make a very small mechanical microequipment, a new technology was proposed [13,14]. This technology is based on micromachine tools and microassembly devices, which can be produced as sequential generations of microequipment. Each generation should include equipment (machine-tools, manipulators, assembly devices, measuring instruments, etc.) sufficient for manufacturing an identical equipment set of smaller size. Each subsequent equipment generation could be produced by the preceding one. The equipment size of each subsequent generation is smaller than the overall size of preceding generation.

The first-generation microequipment can be produced by conventional large-scale equipment. Using microequipment of this first generation, a second microequipment generation having smaller overall sizes can be produced.

We call this approach to mechanical microdevices manufacturing MicroEquipment Technology (MET) [15].

The proposed MET technology has many advantages:

(1) The equipment miniaturization leads to decreasing the occupied space as well as energy consumption, and, therefore, the cost of the products.

(2) The labor costs are bound to decrease due to the reduction of maintenance costs and a higher level of automation expected in MET.

(3) Miniaturization of equipment by MET results in a decrease of its cost. This is a consequence of the fact that microequipment itself becomes the object of MET. The realization of universal microequipment that is capable of extended reproduction of itself will allow the manufacture of low-cost microequipment in a few reproductive acts because of the lower consumption of materials, energy, labor, and space in MET. Thus the miniaturization of equipment opens the way to a drastic decrease in the unit cost of individual processing.

At a lower unit cost of individual micromachining, the most natural way to achieve high throughput is to parallelize the processes of individual machining by concurrent use of a great quantity of microequipment of the same kind. Exploitation of that great number of microsized machine-tools is only feasible with their automatic operation and a highly automated control of the microfactory as a whole. We expect that many useful and proved concepts, ideas and techniques of automation can be borrowed from mechanical engineering. They vary from the principles of factory automation

(FMS and CAM) to the ideas of unified containers and clamping devices and techniques of numerical control. However automation of micromanufacturing has peculiarities that will require the special methods of artificial intelligence.

# 3. AI BASED CONTROL SYSTEM FOR MICROMECHANICAL FACTORY

Let us consider a general hierarchical structure of the automatic control system for a micromechanical factory. The lowest (first) level of the system controls the micromechanical equipment (the micro machine-tools and assembly manipulators), provides the simplest microequipment diagnostics and the final measurement and testing of production. The second level of the control system controls the devices that transport workpieces, tools, parts, and the whole equipment items; coordinates the operation of the lowest level devices; provides the intermediate quality inspection of production and the more advanced diagnostics of equipment condition. The third control level contains the system for the automatic choice of process modes and routes for parts machining. The top (fourth) level of the control system performs detecting of non-standard and alarm situations and decision making, including communication with the operator.

We proceed from the assumption that no more than one operator will manage the microfactory. It means that almost all the problems arising at any control level during the production process should be solved automatically and that operator must solve only a few problems, that are too complex or unusual to be solved automatically.

Since any production process is affected by various disturbances, the control system should be an adaptive one. Moreover, it should be self-learning, because it is impossible to foresee all kinds of disturbances in advance. AI that is able to construct the self-learning algorithms and to minimize the participation of operator, seem to be especially useful for this task. AI includes different methods for creating autonomous control systems. The neural classifiers will be particularly useful at the lowest level of the control system. They could be used for the selection of treatment modes, checking of cutting tool conditions, control of the assembly processes, etc. They allow to make the control system more flexible. The system will automatically compensate for small deviations of production conditions, such as the change of cutting tool shape or external environment parameters, variations in the structure of workpiece materials, etc. AI will permit to design self-learning classifiers and should provide the opportunity to exclude the participation of human operator at this level of control.

At the second control level, the AI system should detect all deviations from the normal production process and make decisions about how to modify the process to compensate for the deviation. The compensation should be made by tuning the parameters of the lower level control systems. The examples of such deviations are the deviations from the production schedule, failures in some devices, off-standard production, etc. At this level the AI system should contain the structures in which the interrelations of production process constituents are represented. As in the previous case, it is desirable to have the algorithms working without the supervisor.

The third control level is connected basically with the change of nomenclature or volume of the production manufactured by the factory. It is convenient to develop such a system so that the set-up costs for a new production or the costs to change the production volume should be minimal. The self-learning AI structures formed at the lowest level could provide the basis for such changes of set-up by selection of the process parameters, the choice of equipment configuration for machining and assembly, etc. At the third control level the AI structures should detect the similarity of new products with the products which were manufactured in the past. On the basis of this similarity, the proposals about the manufacturing schedule, process modes, routing, etc. will be automatically formed. Then they will be checked up by the usual computational methods of computer aided manufacturing (CAM). The results of the check, as well as the subsequent information about the efficiency of decisions made at this level, may be used for improving the AI system.

The most complicated AI structures should be applied at the top control level. This AI system level must have the ability to reveal the recent unusual features in the production process, to make the evaluation of possible influence of these new features on the production process, and to make decisions for changing the control system parameters at the various hierarchical levels or for calling for the operator's help. At this level, the control system should contain the intelligence knowledge base, which can be created using the results of the operation of the lower level control systems and the expert knowledge. At the beginning, the expert knowledge of macromechanics may be used.

At present many methods of AI are successfully used in the industry [16,17]. They could be used also for micromechanics. But the problems of fully automated microfactory creation can not be investigated experimentally in conventional industry because of the high cost of the experiments. Here we propose to develop low cost micromechanical test bed to solve these problems.

The prototypes of the first generation microequipment are designed and examined in the Laboratory of Micromechanics and Mechatronics,

CCADET, UNAM. The prototypes use adaptive algorithms of the lowest level. At present more sophisticated algorithms based on neural networks and genetic algorithms are being developed. Below we describe our experiments in the area of such algorithms development and applications.

## 4. DEVELOPMENT OF MICROEQUIPMENT PROTOTYPES AND ADAPTIVE ALGORITHMS

### 4.1 Micromachine Tools

The developed prototype of the first generation micromachine tool is shown in Fig. 1. We have been exploiting this prototype for approximately four years for experimental work and student training.

*Figure 1.* The developed second prototype of the first generation of micromachine tool.

This prototype of the micromachine tool has the size 130×160×85 mm$^3$ and is controlled by a PC. The axes $X$ and $Z$ have 20 mm of displacement and the $Y$-axis has 35 mm of displacement; all have the same configuration. The resolution is 1.87 μm per motor step.

### 4.2 Micromanipulators

At present, in the Laboratory of Micromechanics and Mechatronics, CCADET, UNAM the principles, designs and methods of manufacture of micromachine tools and micromanipulators corresponding to the first microequipment generation are developed. All these works are accompanied with of the prototypes development (Fig.2).

*Figure 2.* Sequential micromanipulator prototype

## 4.3    Computer vision system

To obtain a low cost microequipment it is necessary to use low cost components. Low cost components do not permit us to obtain high absolute accuracy of the assembly devices. To avoid this drawback we have developed an adaptive algorithm for microassembly using a technical vision system (Fig. 3).

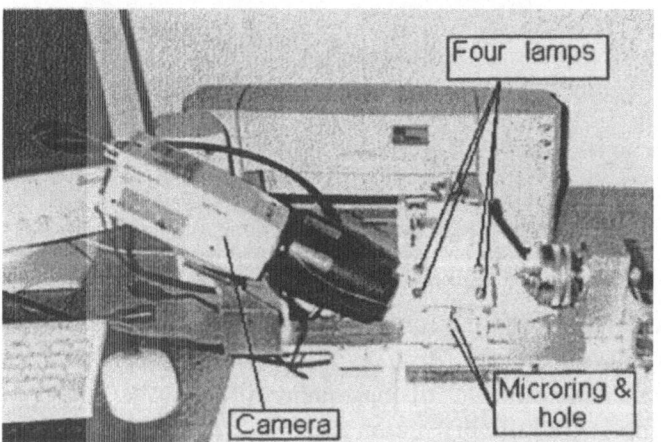

*Figure 3.* The prototype of visual controlled assembly system

The main idea of this approach is to replace the stereovision system, which demands two video cameras, for the system with one TV camera for teleconferences, with a cost of 40 dollars, and four light sources. The shadows from the light sources permit us to obtain the 3-D position of the needle with the microring relative to the hole. The microring is to be inserted into the hole. We use a neural classifier to recognize the relative position.

The problem of automatic microdevices assembly is very important in mechatronics and micromechanics. To obtain the high precision, it is necessary to use adaptive algorithms on the base of technical vision systems. We proposed an approach, that permits us to develop the adaptive algorithms based on neural networks. We consider the conventional pin-hole task. It is necessary to insert the pin into the hole using a low cost technical vision system.

For this purpose it is necessary to know the displacements *(dx, dy, dz)* of the pin tip relative to the hole. It is possible to evaluate these displacements with a stereovision system, which resolves 3D problems. The stereovision system demands two TV cameras. To simplify the control system we propose the transformation of 3D into 2D images preserving all the information about mutual location of the pin and the hole. This approach makes it possible to use only one TV camera.

Four light sources are used to obtain pin shadows. Mutual location of these shadows and the hole contains all the information about the displacements of the pin relative to the hole. The displacements in the horizontal plane *(dx, dy)* could be obtained directly by displacements of shadows center points relative to the hole center. Vertical displacement of the pin may be obtained from the distance between the shadows. To calculate the displacements it is necessary to have all the shadows in one image. We capture four images corresponding to each light source sequentially, and then we extract contours and superpose four contour images. We use the resulting image to recognize the position of the pin relative to the hole. We developed the neural network system which permits us to recognize the pin-hole displacements with errors less than 1 pixel [11,12].

## 4.4    Adaptive Algorithm of the Lowest Level

To compensate for the machine tool errors we have developed a special algorithm for the workpiece diameter measurement using the electrical contact of the workpiece with the measurement disk (Fig. 4). This measurement allows us to develop the algorithm for brass needle cutting. We obtained a brass needle with a diameter of 50 μm and a length of 550 μm (Fig. 5) almost equal to the Japanese needle [18].

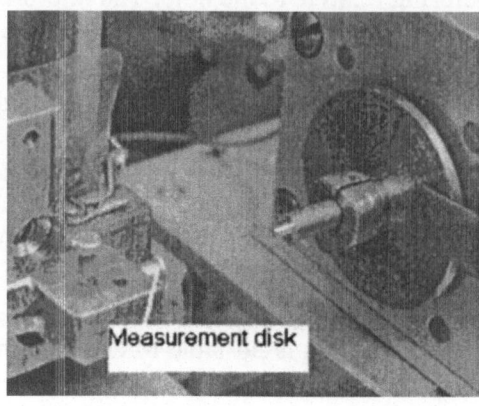

*Figure 4.* The workpiece with measurement disk

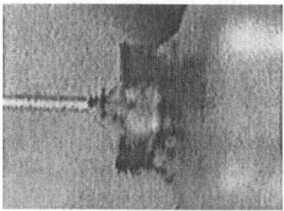

*Figure 5.* The brass needle with 50 μm diameter

## 4.5     Genetic Algorithm for Micromachine Tool Characterization

To improve the micromachine tool precision it is necessary to correct its errors. To obtain the information about the micromachine tools errors, we use a two balls scheme for machine tool parameters measurement. One ball is fixed on the special tool support, which is inserted to the chuck. The second ball is fixed on the machine tool carriage (Fig. 6).

By moving the carriage with the second ball up to the contact with the first ball in different positions it is possible to obtain all the needed information about the geometrical properties of the machine tool. But the geometrical parameters depend on the contact positions in a very complicated manner. To resolve the system of nonlinear equations which represent the mentioned dependence we use a genetic algorithm. This approach permits us to reduce to one third the micromachine tools errors.

## 5.    CONCLUSIONS

AI algorithms could be used to increase the level of manufacturing processes automatization. The experiments with AI algorithms in real industry factories are too expensive. In this article a low cost test bed for AI method examinations is proposed. This test bed is composed of the micromechanical models of conventional industry devices. The prototypes of micromachine tools and micromanipulators were developed and examined with some AI algorithms. The test bed examination results show that AI systems could be proved with low expenses.

*Figure 6.* Ball location in the micromachine tool

## ACKNOWLEDGEMENTS

This work was supported by CCADET, UNAM, projects CONACYT 33944-U, PAPIIT 1112102, NSF-CONACYT 39395-A.

## REFERENCES

1. Eberhart, R.: Overview of computational intelligence [and biomedical engineering applications]. Proceedings od the 20-th Annual International Conference of the IEEE Engineering in Medicine and Biology Society 3 (1998) 1125-1129

2. Hui, T., Brown, D., Haynes, B., Xinxian Wang: Embedded e-diagnostic for distributed industrial machinery. IEEE International Symposium on Computational Intelligence for Measurement Systems and Applications (2003) 156-161
3. Awadallah, M., Morcos, M.: Application of AI tools in fault diagnosis of electrical machines and drives-an overview. IEEE Transactions on Energy Conversion 18, Issue 2 (2003) 245-251
4. Werbos, P.: Advanced Forecasting Methods for Global Crisis Warning and Models of Intelligence. In: General Systems Yearbook 22 (1977) 25-38
5. Prokhorov, D., Wunsch, D.: Adaptive Critic Designs. IEEE Trans. on Neural Networks 8, N 5 (1997) 997-1007
6. Xiaoou Li, Lara-Rosano, F.: A weighted fuzzy Petri net model for knowledge learning and reasoning. International Joint Conference on Neural Networks, IJCNN '99 4 2368 –2372
7. Xiaoou Li, Wen Yu, Lara-Rosano, F.: Dynamic Knowledge Inference and Learning under Adaptive Fuzzy Petri Net Framework. IEEE Transactions on Systems, Man, and Cybernetics 39, N4 (2000) 442-450
8. Bottou, L., Cortes, C., Denker, J., Drucker, H., Guyon L., Jackel L., LeCun J., Muller U., Sackinger E., Simard P., Vapnik V.: Comparison of Classifier Methods: a Case Study in Handwritten Digit Recognition. In: Proceedings of 12$^{th}$ IAPR International Conference on Pattern Recognition 2 (1994) 77-82
9. Fukushima, K. Neocognitron: A hierarchical neural network capable of visual pattern recognition. Neural Networks 1 (1988) 119-130
10. Roska, T., Rodriguez-Vazquez, A.: Toward visual microprocessors. Proceedings of the IEEE 90, Issue 7 (July 2002) 1244-1257
11. Baidyk, T.: Application of Flat Image Recognition Technique for Automation of Micro Device Production. Proceedings of the International Conference on Advanced Intelligent Mechatronics "AIM'01", Italy (2001) 488-494
12. Baidyk, T., Kussul, E., Makeyev, O., Caballero, A., Ruiz, L., Carrera, G., Velasco, G.: Flat image recognition in the process of microdevice assembly. Pattern Recognition Letters 25/1 (2004) 107-118
13. Kussul, E.: Micromechanics and the perspectives of neurocomputing. In: Neuron-like Networks and Neurocomputers, Kiev, Ukraine (1993) 76-82 (in Russian)
14. Kussul, E., Rachkovskij, D., Baidyk, T., Talayev, S.: Micromechanical Engineering: a Basis for the Low-cost Manufacturing of Mechanical Microdevices Using Microequipment. Journal of Micromechanics and Microengineering 6 (1996) 410-425
15. Kussul, E., Baidyk, T., Ruiz-Huerta, L., Caballero, A., Velasco, G., Kasatkina, L.: Development of Micromachine Tool Prototypes for Microfactories. Journal of Micromechanics and Microengineering 12 (2002) 795-812
16. Wenxin Liu, Venayagamoorthy, G., Wunsch, D.: A heuristic dynamic programming based power system stabilizer for a turbogenerator in a single machine power system. 39$^{th}$ IAS Annual Meeting on Industry Applications 1 (2003) 270-276
17. Croce, F., Delfino, B., et al.: Operations and management of the electric system for industrial plants: an expert system prototype for load-shedding operator assistance. IEEE Transactions on Industry Applications 37, Issue 3 (2001) 701-708
18. Okazaki, Yu., Kitahara T.: Micro-Lathe Equipped with Closed-Loop Numerical Control. Proceedings of the 2-nd International Workshop on Microfactories, Switzerland (2000) 87-90

# INTEGRATING TWO ARTIFICIAL INTELLIGENCE THEORIES IN A MEDICAL DIAGNOSIS APPLICATION

Hadrian Peter[1], Wayne Goodridge[2]
[1]*University of the West Indies, Barbados;* [2]*Dalhousie University, Canada*

**Abstract:**     Reasoning Systems (Inference Mechanisms) and Neural Networks are two major areas of Artificial Intelligence (AI). The use of case-based reasoning in Artificial Intelligence systems is well known. Similarly, the AI literature is replete with papers on neural networks. However, there is relatively little research in which the theories of case-based reasoning and neural networks are combined. In this paper we integrate the two theories and show how the resulting model is used in a medical diagnosis application. An implementation of our model provides a valuable prototype for medical experts and medical students alike.

**Key words:**     Medical diagnosis, neural networks, case-based reasoning, reasoning system.

## 1.      INTRODUCTION

Research in Artificial Intelligence (AI) in medicine has relied on progress in research in knowledge bases and reasoning systems (inference mechanisms). Over the years many medical diagnosis systems – MYCIN, Iliad, DXplain, CADIAG-II, INTERNIST, QMR, and MDDB, to name a few – of which MYCIN [1, 2] is arguably the most popular, have been developed. The predominant form of knowledge in MYCIN is represented as a set of rules, and the reasoning system used is *backward chaining*. Iliad and DXplain [3] both use Bayesian reasoning to calculate probabilities of various diagnoses. CADIAG-II [4] – Computer-Assisted DIAGnosis – is a computer-assisted consultation system to support the differential diagnostic process in internal medicine. CADIAG-II uses fuzzy-based reasoning, however, the underlying knowledge base used is not explicitly described in the literature. The knowledge base of INTERNIST, and the strategy used by INTERNIST to address the diagnosis of patients, are described in [5, 6, 7, 8]. QMR (Quick Medical Reference) [9, 10, 11], a reengineering of INTERNIST, is an in-depth information resource that helps physicians to diagnose adult disease. However, again, the underlying reasoning and knowledge systems employed in this diagnosis system are not readily available in the literature. Although MDDB [12] uses case-based reasoning, it uses simple lists as its knowledge base. A disadvantage of most of these methods is that, although they exhibit the capability of making differential diagnoses[1], they do not offer definitive medical consultation[2]. A few earlier attempts at combining the theories of neural networks and case-based reasoning are found in [13, 14, 15].

In this paper we attempt to correct the shortcomings of the above methods by presenting a new approach to medical diagnosis in which we combine a knowledge base, whose underlying structure is the neural network [16, 17, 18], with a Case-Based Reasoning system [19, 20, 21, 22]. We begin by reviewing case-based reasoning (CBR), we identify problems with such reasoning when used in the medical domain, and provide the motivation for our approach. We then examine neural networks, in particular the mathematical underpinnings of *heteroassociative* memory neural networks [23], and how they are incorporated in our model. The architecture of our model – the Case-based Memory Network (CBMN) – is introduced in the next section. We then present the medical diagnosis process in our model, followed by the operational model, a short simulation, and a consultation session. The paper ends with a brief evaluation of the model.


## 2.    MATERIALS AND METHODS

### 2.1    Case-Based Reasoning

Case-based Reasoning (CBR) [19] is an inference mechanism that has found increasing use in expert systems. It consists of the following four stages: retrieve the most similar case or cases; reuse the retrieved case or cases to solve the problem by analogical reasoning; revise the proposed

---

[1] A *differential diagnosis* results when 2 or more diagnoses are possible. These diagnoses are prioritized.
[2] *Definitive medical consultation* between the user and the system leads to a concrete diagnosis.

solution; retain the parts of this experience which are likely to be useful for future problem solving.

When CBR is applied to medical diagnosis systems, the following problems are usually identified:

- There is a concentration on reference rather than on diagnosis.
- There is a lack of intelligent dialog. This may result in "missing information" and therefore a decrease of the accuracy of the diagnosis.
- Inability of most *similarity algorithms* to handle attributes whose values are unknown.
- If the case base contains cases with attributes that take on multiple (rather than just binary) values, then the case base will be quite complex – requiring large numbers of predicates, relations, constraints, and operators [24].
- Updating (revision) of the case base requires complex algorithms and/or highly skilled users.

To overcome these problems, therefore, we developed a variation to the CBR technique called the Case-Based Memory Network (CBMN) model [25]. It was primarily developed to solve medical diagnostic problems and not "pure" classification problems [22]. To simulate the CBMN model we have also designed and implemented an expert system prototype called *CaseB-Pro* - an interactive system that accepts observed findings, generates appropriate questions, and makes conclusions based on the observed findings.

## 2.2    The role of Neural Networks

The attraction of neural networks in our model is that they have the ability to tolerate noisy inputs and to learn – features which are very desirable in a medical diagnosis system. The CBMN uses a special type of neural network called a *heteroassociative* neural network [23]. This neural network provides a mechanism for learning, recording what has been learnt, and identifying stored knowledge. The network stores disease patterns associated with cases, and also recalls cases from memory based on the similarity of those cases to the symptoms of the current case. This technique is different from the similarity measure and retrieval techniques such as kd-trees and Case Retrieval Nets (CRNs) [22] employed in CBR. Related classical works in the field of associative memories are found in [26, 27].

Let the *findings* associated with a *case* be represented by a vector s(p), where p = 1, 2, …,P. Each vector s(p) is an n-tuple. Let the case associated with findings, s(p), be represented by a vector t(p). Each t(p) is an m-tuple.

In our model we store (findings, case) pairs – that is, (s(p),t(p)[3] ), p = 1,…..,P. Here, a "case" is an actual patient, and a "finding" is a symptom, sign, or an investigation. "P" is the maximum number of cases in the database, where

$s(p) = (s_1(p),…,s_i(p),….,s_n(p))$ and
$t(p) = (t_1(p),…,t_j(p),….,t_m(p))$.

We also define a *weight matrix* $W_e = \{w_{ij}\}$, where $w_{ij} = \sum_p s_i(p) \, t_j(p)$.

The heteroassociative neural network can be described as a discrete network where the input and output nodes take values from the set {-1, 0, 1}. We interpret the values as follows: -1 represents the findings that are absent, 0 represents the unknown findings, and 1 represents the findings that are present. Now $E \subseteq \Phi$ (observed findings) can be represented as an n-tuple input vector, say k. Vector k will then be mapped to the $\theta$ domain by the $W_e$ matrix – findings will be mapped onto cases. That is,

$$k \,.\, W_e \subseteq \theta$$
$$\text{or} \quad k \,.\, W_e = t$$

where $t \subseteq \theta$

**Example**

If the output layer of the network contains 3 nodes, then some of the following mappings are possible:

$k \,.\, W_e = (1, 0, 0)$         map 1
$k \,.\, W_e = (0, 1, 0)$         map 2
$k \,.\, W_e = (2, 4, 2)$         map 3

Whenever new findings are presented to the current case, k is changed and, when multiplied with the weight matrix $W_e$ , the vector t(p) is determined. This value of t(p) is then used to determine a set of actual cases from the case base that matches the observed findings.

---

[3] The term *training set* is sometimes used to describe the vector t(p).

If a node in vector t has a positive value, then this node represents a case in which the disorder associated with that case matches the current observed findings. For example, in map 1 the disorder associated with case 1 is a possible candidate.

If a mapped vector t contains nodes with varying positive values, then the node with the largest positive value is most likely to be the case that has the most likely associated disorder for the observed findings. For example, if t = (3,1,-1) then the disorders associated with cases 1 and 2 are likely. However, the disorder associated with case 1 is the more likely candidate.

A disorder, say k, is a part of a definitive diagnosis only if the available findings that will lead to a diagnosis of k exceed the findings that are known. This serves as the point at which we stop posing questions to the system.

Let  $current_j = \sum w_{ij} x_j$,  unknown input nodes not included

and  $unknown_j = \sum |w_{ij}|$, only unknown nodes included

If  $|current_j| > unknown_j$, then k can be a part of the definitive diagnosis.

## 2.3   Architecture of the CBMN

In its simplest form the CBMN structure consists of input information entity (IE) nodes and output (case) nodes. The design goal of the CBMN model is to ensure that a knowledge base, and learning and reasoning mechanisms can be incorporated in the same data structure and be used for diagnostic problem solving. In diagnosing a patient the physician utilizes information from past typical or known exceptional cases that are usually described by a list of symptoms.

To design a medical case base used for diagnostic purposes it is necessary to have two types of cases in the case base [28]:

1. Case Generalizations called *prototypes* **(pure cases)** - these are the "classical" (textbook) cases as viewed by the medical expert.
2. General domain cases – these are actual cases.

The features of disorders – in the input layer of the network - are mapped onto case prototypes (in the hidden layer) which represent the "text book" view of disorders in terms of its identifying features. A case – representing the output layer of the network - is an instance of a prototype, in the same way that an object is an instance of a class in the object oriented programming paradigm [29, 30]. The arrows in the diagram denote weighted links from the input nodes to the case nodes, and the calculation, and adjustment, of these weights is known as training the network.

Cases are actual examples of patients and, in the CBMN model, cannot exist without prototypes, which are the physician's representation of disorders. That is, every case in the case-base must be associated with one and only one known classical medical case (prototype).

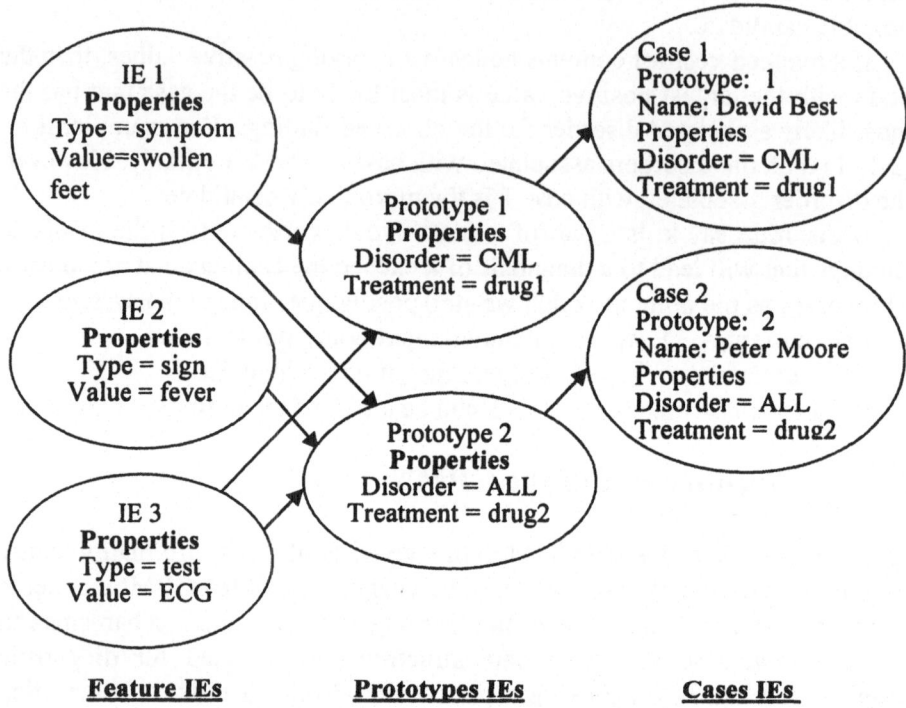

Figure 1. The CBMN Architecture with Prototypes

## 2.4    The Medical Diagnostic Process in the CBMN

A medical consultation consists of the following stages:

- Recording of symptoms and patient history.
- Elicitation / Identification of signs.
- Formulation of notion of diagnosis [31] leading to a hypothesis and differential diagnosis.
- Investigations to narrow down or confirm the diagnosis.

Medical diagnosis depends heavily on known facts about the case in question. The facts are used to form a notion of diagnosis [31], which results in a hypothesis. This hypothesis is strengthened or weakened by discovering more facts about the current case, which in turn invokes a different notion of diagnosis. This process is continued until a definitive diagnosis is found. So, again, making a definitive diagnosis is one of the essential differences between CBMN and many extant medical diagnosis systems.

The new approach to the CBMN model includes a *certainty factor*[4] [18] and a *prevalence factor* for each prototype in the case base. A certainty factor is a number ranging from 0 to 10 that represents the physician's impression of the significance of the presence of a feature with respect to the prototype. A prevalence factor is a number ranging from 0 to 10 that expresses the physician's impression that a patient will have the disorder associated with a given prototype. The certainty factor and prevalence factor may or may not be a scientific measurement since it represents only the physician's notion of the disorder.

The presence or absence of features will affect the physician's belief or disbelief in his hypothesis. Hence the concept of the belief factor is used in the CBMN to "balance" a physician's belief and disbelief in a hypothesis.

We now present the algorithm to find the next best question to be asked at a given stage of the medical consultation process. The system cannot reach any definitive conclusions until it has exhausted each stage.

1.  Find the set, say S, of prototypes that match the observed findings.
2.  Find the prototype, say k, with the highest belief factor in the set S.
3.  Use the unknown feature, say f, of prototype k with the highest certainty factor to generate the next question.
4.  If the certainty factor of f is greater than a question threshold value ($\delta_Q$, set by the experimenter), then the system moves to the next consultation stage until the investigation stage is reached.
5.  When a diagnostic stage is finished the system lists all the prototypes with a confidence measure greater that a threshold value as candidates for the diagnosis of the presented features.
6.  Repeat steps 1-5 above until the investigation stage is completed.

The main objective of this algorithm is to find the optimum diagnostic path that will: (a) Get the correct diagnosis by asking the minimum number of questions and (b) exhaust each diagnostic stage before moving on to the next.

## 2.4.1   Simulation

The simulation of the diagnostic process is implemented in Delphi using a prototype called CaseB-Pro. Its functional specifications can be divided into

---

[4] This model is an example of a truth-functional system for uncertain reasoning.

the following two steps: training the system to identify new cases and using the case base to gain a computer-generated diagnosis.

The two main design goals of the CaseB-Pro prototype - an expert system that combines the theories of neural networks and case-based reasoning – are to implement and test the CBMN model and to develop a computer system that can assist medical students and physicians with the diagnosing of patients. In section 4 we provide an evaluation of the model and an assessment of its "success".

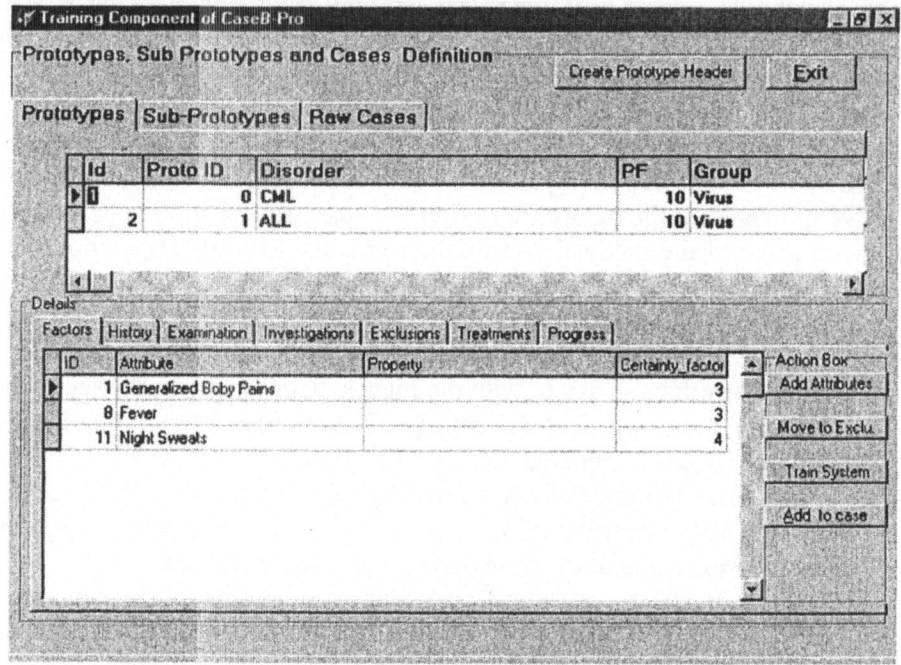

Figure 2. Creating Prototype for CML

The CBMN model uses three types of data structure to represent knowledge. These include: feature information entity data structures, prototype information entity data structures and case information entity data structures.

The training of the model involves adding prototypes to the case base and then, if desired, adding sub-prototypes and actual cases associated with those prototypes. Training also involves the assignment of symptoms, signs, investigations, and exclusions. Training is conducted by using data from classical and actual cases of the disorder in question. The network is trained each time a new case is added to the database, or an existing case is modified. The neural network is used to store and recall cases. Each prototype, sub-prototype, and case, of the case base, has in common a node identification number that uniquely identifies the network node in question.

Figure 2 illustrates how the prototype for the Chronic Myeloid Leukaemia (CML) disorder can be added to the system. Other prototypes can be added in a similar manner.

## 2.4.2     Interacting with the System

Figure 3 provides the interface through which users – namely, medical students, physicians, or other medical experts - interact with the CaseB-Pro system. A typical session (consultation) is invoked when a user types the "consult" command. A list of symptoms is then shown where the user can select major presenting symptoms in the case under consideration. The system then allows the user to enter examination results of the case in question. When the examination stage is exhausted the consultation enters into the investigation stage. An example consultation is provided for illustration.

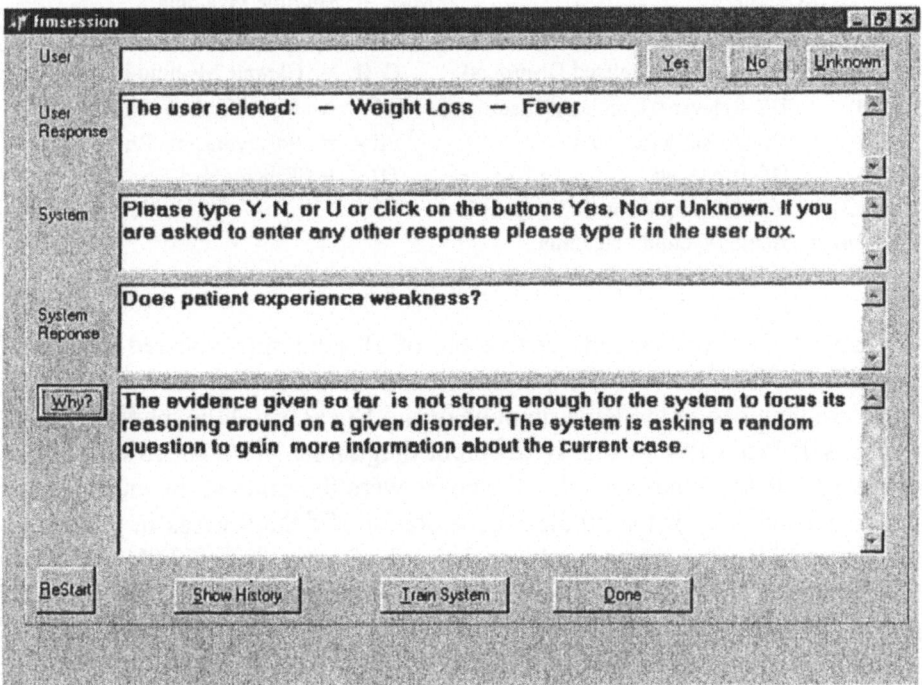

Figure 3. Example of part of consultation session

# 3.      RESULTS

For purposes of testing the system ten cases of Haematological conditions and related disorders were added to the case base. In order to make a preliminary evaluation of CaseB-Pro's diagnostic capabilities, two medical experts who specialize in Haemoncological disorders independently simulated 18 classical Haematological cases within the scope of the system.

*Table 1.* Results of CaseB-Pro. Generated cases based on medical experts' simulations

|   | Case Simulated | Stage 1 | Stage 2 | Opinion-Stage 1 | Opinion-Stage 2 | Comments on DD |
|---|---|---|---|---|---|---|
| 1 | CML | CML | CML | ✔ | ✔ | +++ |
| 2 | MM | MM | MM | ✔ | ✔ | + |
| 3 | PRV | PRV | PRV | ✔ | ✔ | - |
| 4 | ALL | ALL | ALL | ✔ | ✔ | +++ |
| 5 | AA | AA | AA | ✔ | ✔ | +++ |

Key of symbols/abbreviations used in the table:

| | | | |
|---|---|---|---|
| ✔ = Accurate | | MM = | Multiple Myeloma |
| DD = Differential Diagnosis | | NHL = | Non Hodgkins Lymphoma |
| +++ = DD Relevant (Related Disorders) | | CML = | Chronic Myeloid Leukaemia |
| ++ = DD Relevant (Unrelated Disorders) | | MF = | Myelofibrosis |
| + = DD Possibly Relevant | | PRV = | Polycythaemia Rubra Vera |
| - = DD Irrelevant | | TB = | Tuberculosis |
| ALL = Acute Lymphoblastic Leukaemia | | | |
| AML = Acute Myeloid Leukamia | | | |
| AA = Aplastic Anemia | | | |

Table 1 shows the results of five out of 18 randomly selected simulated interactions. It is, however, important to note that although only 5 of the 18 cases are included in the table, in none of the 18 cases did the medical expert and CaseB-Pro arrive at totally different diagnoses. More specifically, in 9 of the 18 (50%) of the cases the diagnoses were the same at the end of stage 2 (see section 2.4) of the medical consultation. Of the 9 cases in which the diagnoses did not match exactly at the end of stage 2, 7 (77.8%) of them resulted in a match after the differential diagnosis (third) stage. The remaining 2 cases, for which concrete results were not possible at the end of stage 3, produced results in concurrence with the medical expert's diagnoses after further investigations were conducted (in stage 4).

As indicated in section 2.4.1 CaseB-Pro was also used as a teaching tool. To test this feature of CaseB-Pro, two students in the advanced stage of their medical studies were encouraged to interact with the system. Initially the students complained that they felt intimidated by the system and feared that the system would expose their lack of knowledge. However, after being persuaded by their medical instructor to use the system as a classroom exercise, the students were noticeably more relaxed. Under the guidance of their medical professor, the students were allowed to conduct an extensive interaction with the system in an effort to diagnose MM, MF, PRV, ALL, and AA (please see the table below). In 80% of the cases the students were able to arrive at the correct diagnoses largely due, they reported, to the ease with which they were able to follow the "trend of thought" used by CaseB-Pro.

## 4. EVALUATION AND CONCLUSION

Many medical diagnosis systems have been designed and are currently in use. The originality of our approach, however, is that we have designed and implemented a system that combines case-based reasoning and artificial neural networks. Because of the restriction placed on the length of our paper, we were unable to provide a more detailed comparison with other approaches. Consistent with our goals we were able to (a) implement and test our model, and (b) to develop a computer system that can assist medical students and physicians with the diagnosing of patients. We have been able to develop a prototype, the CaseB-Pro, based on our new approach, whose authenticity medical experts and medical students were able to test.

It may be too early to make strong pronouncements about the success of our model because it was tested on a small domain. Therefore more research using our approach should be conducted using larger domains and different evaluation strategies. Thus far the feedback from persons who have interacted with our prototype has been encouraging, and therefore we are confident that with further development and testing our prototype can evolve into a useful, full-fledged system.

## REFERENCES

1. Buchanan, B.G., Shortliffe, E.H. (eds.): Rule-Based Expert Systems: The MYCIN Experiments of the Stanford Heuristic Programming Project. Addison-Wesley, Reading, Mass. (1984)
2. Shortliffe, B.G. Computer-Based Medical Consultants: MYCIN. Elsevier/North-Holland, Amsterdam (1976)
3. Bouhaddou, O., Sorenson, D.: Iliad V4.4. Journal of Medical Systems, 15(1) (1991) 93-110

4. Adlassnig, K. –P., Kolarz, G. : Representation and semiautomatic acquisition of medical knowledge in CADIAG-1 and CADIAG-2. Computers and Biomedical Research, **19** (1986) 63-79

5. Miller, R. A., Pople, Jr., H. E., and Myers, J. D. *INTERNIST-I*, an Experimental Computer-Based Diagnostic Consultant for General Internal Medicine, New England J. Med., **307** (August 1982) 468-476.

6. Pople, Jr., H. E. The Formation of Composite Hypotheses in Diagnostic Problem Solving: An Exercise in Synthetic Reasoning, IJCAI **5** (1977)

7. Pople, Jr., H. E. Heuristic Methods for Imposing Structure on Ill-Structured Problems: The Structuring of Medical Diagnostics, in P. Szolovits (ed.), Artificial Intelligence in Medicine, Boulder, CO (1982) 119-185

8. Masserie, F. E., Miller, R.A., and Myers, J.D. INTERNIST-I properties: Representing common sense and good medical practice in a computerized medical knowledge base. Computers and Biomedical Research, **18** (1985) 458-479

9. Arene, I., et al : Evaluation of quick medical reference (QMR) as a teaching tool. MD Comput., **15** (1998) 323-326

10. Aliferis, C.F., et al: A temporal analysis of QMR. J. Am. Med. Inform. Assoc., **3** (1996) 79-91

11. Miller, R.A., Masarie, F.E.,Jr. : Use of the Quick Medical Reference (QMR) program as a tool for medical education, Methods Inf. Med., **28** (1989) 340-345

12.Gierl, L., Stengel-Rutkowski, S. Integrating Consultation and Semi-automatic Knowledge Acquisition in a Prototype-based Architecture: Experiences with Dysmorphic Syndromes. Artificial Intelligence in Med., **6** (1994) 29-49

13. Myllymaki, P., Tirri, H. Bayesian case-based reasoning with neural networks. In Proceedings of the IEEE International Conference on Neural Networks, San Francisco, CA, **1** (March 1993) 422-427

14. Honkela, T. Self-Organizing Maps and Case-based Reasoning. [Electronic Version] retrieved April, 2004 from http://www.mlab.uiah.fi/networks99/honkela.html

15. Agre, G. Koprinska, I. Case-based Refinement of Knowledge-Based Neural Networks. In: Proceedings of International Conference Intelligent Systems: A Semiotic Perspective, Gaithersburg, MD (Oct. 20-23, 1996)

16. Gallant, S.I. : Neural Network Learning and Expert Systems. MIT, Mass. (1993)

17. Goodridge, W. : The Case-Based Memory Network Model and its Use in Medical Expert Systems: MPhil Thesis, University of the West Indies, Barbados (2000)

18. Russell, S.J., Norvig, P. : Artificial Intelligence : A Modern Approach, 2$^{nd}$ ed. Pearson Education, Inc., New Jersey (2003)

19. Aamodt, A., Plaza, P. Case-Based Reasoning: Foundations Issues, Methodological Variations, and Systems Approaches. AI Communications, 7(1) (1994) 39-59

20. Kolodner, J.L. Case-Based Reasoning. Morgan Kaufmann, New York (1993)

21. Koton, P. Evaluating Case-Based Problem Solving. In: Hammond, K.J. (Ed.). Proceedings of the DARPA Workshop on Case-Based Reasoning, Morgan Kaufmann, CA (1989) 260-17022. Lenz, M., et al, (eds.). Case-Based Reasoning Technology: from foundations to

application. In: Lecture Notes in Computer Science, Vol. 1400. Springer-Verlag, New York (1998)

23. Fausett, L. Fundamentals of Neural Networks. Architectures, Algorithms, and Applications. Prentice-Hall International Editions, New Jersey (1994

24. Bergmann, R., Wilke, W. Case-Based Reasoning: Foundations Issues, Methodological Variations, and Systems Approaches. AI Communications, **3** (1995) 53-118

25. Goodridge, W., Peter, H., Abayomi, A. The Case-Based Neural Network Model and Its Use in Medical Expert Systems. In: Lecture Notes in Artificial Intelligence, Vol.1620. Springer-Verlag, Denmark (1999)

26. Anderson, J. A. A simple neural network generating an interactive memory. Mathematical Biosciences, **14** (1972) 197-220.

27. Kohonen, T. Correlation matrix memories. IEEE Transactions on Computers, **21** (1972) 353--359

28. Rainer, S., Pollwein, B., Gierl, L. Experiences with Case-Based Reasoning Methods and Prototypes for Medical Knowledge-Based Systems. In: Lecture Notes in Artificial Intelligence, Vol. 1620. Springer-Verlag, Denmark (1999)

29. Schach, S.R. Object-Oriented and Classical Software Engineering, 5th ed. McGraw-Hill, New York (2002)

30. Booch, G. Object-Oriented Analysis and Design with Applications. Addison-Wesley Publishing Company, California (1994)

31. Lucas, P. A Theory of Medical Diagnosis as Hypothesis Refinement. 6th Conference on Artificial Intelligence, Springer-Verlag, New York (1997) 169-180

# ARTIFICIAL INTELLIGENCE AND LAW

Hugo C. Hoeschl;Vânia Barcellos
*E-Gov, Juridical Intelligence and Systems Institute – Ijuris*

**Keywords:**     Artificial Intelligence (AI); Natural Intelligence (NI), Law; Information of Technology

**Abstract:**     This article intends to make an analysis of the intersection between Artificial Intelligence (AI) and Natural Intelligence (NI) and its application in the scope of Right. The impact caused by the Information Technology, methodologies and techniques used by the main systems developed in the last years and which the elements for the development of intelligent applications in the legal domain, with the aim of demonstrating the capacity to manipulate the knowledge properly and, being so, systemizing its relations, clarifying its bonds, to evaluate the results and applications. There is a real need of new tools that conciliate the best of AI and NI techniques, generating methods and techniques of storage and manipulation of information, what will reflect on law and justice.

## 1.      INTRODUCTION

According to Carnelutti [7] "to discover the rule of legal constructing, science does not have, of course, other ways beyond the senses and intelligence. Intelligence is nothing but the capacity to learn, to apprehend or to understand, to interpret and, mainly to adapt the factual situations. On the one hand, we have all this systematization of Law, using NI, its evolution, its technical, historical and social conditioning; on the other, we have the vertiginous evolution of the technology of the computer sciences, which have an search field dedicated of to the reproduction of human abilities, handicrafts as well as intellectual capacities, which is AI.

The present study intends to start with the elements for the development of intelligent applications in the legal domain (section 2), demonstrating the intersection between AI and the NI, applied to Law (section 3). It intends to evaluate how the research is getting on, in a world-wide context (section 4), we will illustrate (section 5) the application of AI in Law through some empirical procedures adopted by the author and his team (section 5).

## 2.  ELEMENTS FOR THE APPLICATION OF AI TO THE LAW SPHERE

The AI sphere has been studied academically since the 1950s, but it has generated an increasing interest nowadays because of the arising of practical commercial applications.

Researches in AI are related to areas of application that involve human reasoning, trying to imitate it and performing inferences. According to Savory[22], these areas of application that are generally enclosed in the definitions of AI include, among others: specialized systems or systems based on knowledge; intelligent / learning systems; understanding / translation from natural language; understanding / voice generating; analysis of image, scene in real time and automatic programming.

Notice, then, an introductory and superficial vision, about how artificial intelligence can be defined [18]: "Artificial intelligence - The field of the computer sciences that intends to perfect the computers endowing them with some peculiar characteristics of human human intelligence, as the capacity to understand natural language and to simulate the reasoning in uncertainty conditions".

The following are important aspects of AI, as Rabuske [21], among others: development of heuristical methods for the solution of problems; representation of knowledge; treatment of natural language; acquisition of knowledge; artificial reasoning and logics and tools. Amongst its main applications, we have the following: mastering systems; processing of natural language; recognition of standards; robotics; intelligent databases; test of theorems and games.

To make use of intelligent techniques and to try to develop computational tools endowed with logic or structured in cases, in order to assist in the study of legal data, involves another difficult task, which is, to analyze the form chosen by men to communicate and to materialize its norms: the codification of the word in abstract symbols and rigorous grammar rules.

The study and development of any system of automatic and intelligent treatment of the legal information involves, basically, two tasks: the treatment of the natural language and the search of new techniques of storage.

In the first one, the structure of a mechanism, which reads texts and, properly guided, identifies a series of relevant characteristics for the user, in some specific stages. It must search superficial and static references, as dates, names, numbers, etc; to identify subjects, subjects and sub-subjects and, finally, to detect conclusions and lessons, highlighting them, obviously, from other functions.

In the second task, it is good to inquire about the return to the origins of the language. i.e.: the first forms of writing were pictographic, and, in the computational scope, the development of languages and interfaces are in allowing the use of icons (pictographic forms) [12], a more comfortable and practical means of communication than orthography.

This is allowing to idealize a significant advance in communication, according to which "written texts will give place to mental images that present real as well as symbolic objects and emphasize the interaction and the experience in detriment of the passive learning" [12].

## 3.    ARTIFICIAL INTELLIGENCE vs. NATURAL INTELLIGENCE

In the sense of searching, in the practical sphere, this evolution announced, has a powerful referential: the intersection between NI and AI, where it is possible to try to conciliate the processing speed of the second and sophistication of the first one, as pointed by Epstein [11].

Artificial intelligence, in the delimited context - without damage of the already already presented definition - can also be understood, in a still very primary vision, as "the set of techniques used to try to carry through automatons adopting behaviors similar to the ones of human thought", as pointed by Morvan (apud Epstein)[11].

We know that NI is inferior to AI in the capacity of search and the examination of options, but superior in refined and percipient tasks, such as making analogies and to creating metaphors.

Thus, a mechanism that combines NI and AI techniques, intending an adequate manipulation of natural language, allows the identification of ideas of a legal text.

However, it is important to emphasize that a step in the searching direction, the body of a writing piece, in what a person "thought", or either, theirs ideas and conclusions, is teleologically linked to the desire of searching what a person really "felt" when analyzing the subject on which they wrote.

## 3.1      Reasoning's figures

Is important to emphasize that AI it is a figure typical of the information technology, practically molded by it. For the delineation of the intersection pointed, we will soon devote attention to some figures linked to NI, as the analogical reasoning, existing before computers [18]:

Analogical reasoning - A form of knowledge in which the dynamics of a phenomenon of the real world – such as aerodynamics of an airplane which is intended to make - is understood from the study of a model of the phenomenon. One of the biggest contributions of the computer sciences was to reduce costs (and to increase convenience) of analogical reasoning.

The reasoning based on some case is something almost as old as the human habit of "to walking forward". However, we are dealing with a tool of artificial intelligence that uses such nomenclature, being able to be defined as a "methodology", which has as a basic characteristic to search the best solution for a current situation in previous experiences in previous experiences, applying the already consolidated knowledge and whose effectiveness was already validated.

Such procedures, derived from the information technology, has an evident similarity to a traditional figure of the legal reasoning, analogy, one of the most efficient and pertinent instruments for the integration of the commands of law.

According to Bobbio, the analogy can be defined as follows [3]: "we understood by "analogy" the procedure by which a not-regulated case is attributed the same discipline than to a similar regulated case.... The analogy is certainly more typical and the most important interpretative procedures of a certain normative system,: it is the procedure by means of which  the called trend of each legal system to become is explained to enlarge itself beyond the cases expressly regulated."

According to Bobbio, "To be able to come to a conclusion, that is, to make the attribution to the non-regulated case of the same legal consequences attributed to the similar regulated case, there is a need of not any similarity between the two cases, but a relevant similarity, is necessary to ascend from the two cases to a quality that both have in common, that is at the same time the very reason by which those and not other consequences had been attributed to the regulated case".

Other figures resemble the presented context, as the extensive interpretation and the syllogism, with which the analogy cannot be confused. The syllogism has a vertical mechanism of drawing conclusions, while the analogy and the extensive interpretation have a horizontal resource. But, even though analogy and extensive interpretation are next to one another and horizontalized, they are significantly different from each other, pointed also by the very author [3].

This difference causes a strong impact on the construction and modeling of intelligent systems in the legal area, since the proposal is not the construction of systems that generate norms, but that facilitate its application (at least for the time being).

The comparison between institutes demonstrates the importance of the analysis of the structuralized logical processes around the reasoning of a specific area, and demonstrates also, that the logics has much to contribute with artificial intelligence – even in systems based on cases -, being exactly this one of the most favorable aspects of the intersection pointed between AI and NI. This comparison has the purpose of demonstrating that the approach of these institutes tends to produce good results, as well as the viability of the intersections, of AI with the NI, as well as of the figures of reasoning derived from the technology of information with those particular to the legal universe.

## 4. STATE OF ART IN THE INTERNATIONAL SCENERY

We focus on the scientific production in the area of artificial intelligence and law in the International Conference of Artificial Intelligence and Law - ICAIL, edition carried through in Oslo, Norway. In this context, the following works are distinguished:

*Towards adding knowledge to learning algorithms for indexing legal cases*, Bruninghaus[6]. The authors mainly ratify important basic concepts in the scope of the development of intelligent systems for the legal domain - those structured in cases - as, for example the high cost and the slowness of the manual representation of concrete situations. A classification based on boarding was used in the Smile System, constructed by the authors, to locate prompt situations in legal texts, in a automatic way. A controlled vocabulary and linguistic information were integrated to the system with an algorithm of machine learning, important allies in the task of surpassing the traditional difficulties of language.

*Bankruptcy case law: a hybrid IR-CBR approach*, Elhadi and Tibor [10] describe a work of combination between retrieval of information (information retrieval, IR) and CBR, with a modeling based on the procedures according to which the legal operators effect its research techniques as a parcel of the procedural dialectic, suggesting, specifically, that the experiences accumulated by the professionals of the legal domain are used in the modeling of the system.

*Some observations on modeling case based reasoning with formal argument models*, Bench-Capon [2] warns the international community about the importance of conciliating cases and norms in the modeling of a system for this type of application, affirming that "the truth on the subject is that both are essential".

*The evaluation of legal knowledge based system*, Stranieri and Zeleznikow [23] perform important premises on the evaluation of systems based on the legal knowledge, affirming that strategical evaluations of systems that operate in a so complex domain as the legal one are difficult because of the specificity of the systems, considering a model of evaluation with neural nets, referenced by the binoms "structural/functional" and " qualitative/ quantitative" to evaluate the answers emitted by a system.

*Dialectic semantic for argumentation frameworks*. Jakobovits and Vernier [15] proposed a formalist study of dialogues, where a dialogue is seen with a shock between two people, initiated by the proponent who defends the proposed thesis. Carrying through an examination of the argumentative criteria and the different types of dialogues, the authors consider to provide a semantics correspondence allusive to the blocked dialogue.

*Precedent, deontic logic and inheritance*. Horty [14] considers the establishment of some connections between reasoning based on precedents and deontic and monotonic logics He supports that deontic logics acts as a prioritary sensitive reasoning in a norms conflict, reformulating and simplifying a reasoning model based in Ashley's precedents, according to the deontic logics.

*AI techniques for modeling legal negotiation*. Bellucci and Zeleznikow [1], the authors centralize the study in the introduction of the development of an algorithm that uses methods of AI to support the production of a business decision, using a form of cognitive mapping called "bi directed fuzzy cognitive maps".

*The integration of retrieval, reasoning and drafting for refugee law: a third generation legal knowledge based system*. Yeardwood and Stranieri [25]. The authors had developed a structure for the construction of arguments that includes more than 200 arguments, in contribution with the Refugee Review Court of Australia. The process of construction of these arguments requires the integration of retrieval of literal information (IR) with reasoning.

*Justice: A judicial search tool using intelligent concept extraction*. Osborn and Sterling present the modeling of a system based on legal knowledge called "Justice", whose target is to retrieve previous cases. It uses concepts of conceptual retrieval of information, conceptual summarization, analysis automatized statistics and informal document conversion for formalized semi-structured representations.

*A demonstration of a legal reasoning system based on teleological analogies*, text in the which Kakuta and Haraguchi [16], using a structure called GDA (Goal-Dependent Abstraction), the authors analyze an exemplary situation judged by the Supreme Court of Japan, ahead of two consistent doctrinal trends, demonstrating how the system can become an important aid in the task of evaluating and to revise interpretations of norms.

*Agents and norms: how to fill the gap?*, Falcone and Sartor [9] affirm that two specific structural approaches are important to the work described: 1. That of the legal theory and related computational applications, especially in the areas of specialist legal systems, normative reasoning and juridical diagnostic; e 2. That of the theory of the multiagent systems (MAS) and the related computational applications, especially in the areas of computerized cooperative work (to computer supported cooperative work, CSCW). The most important aspects are the following: language and its formalism; reference theories (legal philosophy and deontic philosophy, reverenced by the theory of the agents); targets (models of legal institutions, systems of legal information); rhetoric philosophy and the norm concept.

*Norms in artificial decision making*, Boman [5] effected a study on independent artificial agents programmed to represent and to evaluate vacant or inexact information, with the characterization of agents with a production method of decision in real time, at risk or uncertainty, finishing for presenting a model of "contraining action" using norms.

*Prescribed mental attitudes in goal-adoption and norm-adoption. In this paper, with a theoretical approach*, Castelfranchi [8] affirms that the norms do not only want behavioral conformity, but produces culturing and reassures the authority of the norms, considering that they require submission.

*Approximate syllogisms, on the logic of everyday life*, Philips [19] affirms that, since Aristotle, it is recognized that a valid syllogism cannot have two specific premises, claiming that some rules can be established to similar syllogisms with particular premises, affirming that the lay are correct if it is considered that that these syllogisms do not have strict validity, but similar, having in mind that the premises available in daily life are typically particular.

## 5.    APPLICATION OF AI TO LAW

We will illustrate the application of AI to law through some empirical procedures adopted by the author and his team.

Called methodology CBR is used in parts with techniques of retrieval of literal information, presenting a superior performance to the traditional data bases. For in such a way, had been developed two new technologies for the team the Context Structured Search– CSS and the Dynamically Contextualised Knowledge Representation (DCKR).

CSS® is a methodology that allows the search in natural language through the context of the information contained in the knowledge base, thus breaching, the search paradigm by means of key words and connectors, making it possible for the user to describe a number of characters presented by each consultation, allowing thus, a more elaborated conception of the search. The research is considered ' contextual ' and ' structured ' because of the following reasons: 1. We take into consideration the context of documents stored at the formation of the rhetorical structure of the system 2. This context guides the process of adjustment of the entrance as well as the comparison and election of documents; 3. At the moment of the elaboration of the consultation, the entrance is not limited to a set of words, or the indication of attributes, being able to assume the format of a question structured by the set of a long text is added to the possibility of operating dynamic weights on specific attributes, that work as ' filters ' and make a preliminary election of documents to be analyzed.

DCKR® consists of a dynamic process of analysis of the general context that involves the problem focused. It makes comparisons between the context of documents, enabling the accomplishment of a more precise search and with a better quality. Moreover, the documents are retrieved through pre-determined indexes, that can be valuated by the user when consulting. This technique implies a significant increment in the performance in knowledge structured systems

The Group of intelligence applied to law has been developing researches and implementing systems, involving technology of the legal information. Among the already developed systems, the following ones are distinguished among others:

*Alpha Themis®* - Intelligent software for the retrieval of the knowledge contained in the "resolutions" of the national courts. It is a system of legal technology, one of the first ones in Brazil to unite Artificial Intelligence and Law. It uses techniques of textual Data base and CBR.

*Jurisconsulto®* - Innovative system to retrieve sentences in computerized data bases through CBR. It uses techniques of textual Data Base and CBR.

*Jurisconsulto®* – Sistema inovador para recuperar decisões judiciais em bancos de dados informatizados através de CBR. Utiliza técnicas de Bando de Dados textuais e CBR.

*Olimpo®*- The system has its performance centered in the combination of aspects derived from CBR and from the representation of added literal information to an suitable organization of knowledge the referring to the resolutions of the Security Council of the UN, what allows the retrieval of texts with characteristics similar to the information supplied by the user in natural language. New documents are automatically enclosed in the knowledge base through the extraction of relevant information through a technique called DCKR®. Concepts of CBR and techniques of information retrieval have been applied for a better performance of the system, resulting in the methodology called CSS®.

Such techniques are consolidated through the application in systems and, mainly, by the approval of papers in International Congresses, such as ICAIL (International Conference on Artificial Intelligence and Law), ICEIS (International Conference on Enterprise Information Systems) among others.

## 6. CONCLUSION

The intention is in this work, yet in a synthetic way, to discourse on the intersection between the NI and AI, trying to conciliate them, considering their specificities, in the scope of law. We present some summaries of the activities of international scientific community of artificial intelligence and right, mainly in the development of applications.

The comparison of the institutes demonstrates the importance of the analysis of the logical processes structuralized around the reasoning of a specific area, even in systems based on knowledge, having exactly there, one the strongest favorable aspects of the pointed intersection between AI and NI.

It is possible to conclude that there is a real necessity of attention to the production of tools that emphasize such activity, because, thus, new methods and techniques of storage and manipulation of information will be generated, what it will reflect in a strong way on law and justice, as writing has done.

## REFERENCES

1. BELLUCCI, Emilia, ZELEZNIKOV, John. AI techniques for modeling legal negotiation. In proceedings of the seventh international conference on artificial intelligence and law, p. 108-116, Oslo: Norway, June, 14-18, 1999. 220 p.
2. BENCH-CAPON, T. J. M. Some observations on modeling case based reasoning with formal argument models. In proceedings of the seventh international conference on artificial intelligence and law, p. 36-42, Oslo: Norway, June, 14-18, 1999. 220 p.
3. BOBBIO, Norberto. Teoria do ordenamento jurídico. 4 ed., São Paulo: Unb, 1994.
4. BOBBIO, Norberto. Teoria general del derecho. Bogotá: Temis, 1987.
5. BOMAN, Magnus. Norms in artificial decision making. Artificial intelligence and law, Dordrecht: Netherlands, v 7, n. 1, p. 17-35, march, 1999.
6. BRUNINGHAUS, Stefanie, ASHLEY, Kevin D. Toward adding knowledge to learning algorithms for indexing legal cases. In proceedings of the seventh international conference on artificial intelligence and law, p. 9-17, Oslo: Norway, June, 14-18, 1999. 220 p.
7. CARNELUTTI, Francesco. Metodologia do Direito, 1ª ed., Campinas:Bookseller, 2002.

8.  CASTELFRANCHI, Cristiano. Prescribed mental attitudes in goal-adoption and norm-adoption. Artificial intelligence and law, Dordrecht: Netherlands, v 7, n. 1, p. 37-50, march, 1999.

9.  CONTE, Rosaria, FALCONE, Rino, SARTOR, Giovanni. Introduction: agents and norms: how to fill the gap-. Artificial intelligence and law, Dordrecht: Netherlands, v 7, n. 1, p. 1-15, march, 1999.

10. ELHADI, Mohamed T., VAMOS, Tibor. Bankruptcy case law: a hybrid IR-CBR approach. In proceedings of the seventh international conference on artificial intelligence and law, p. 134-135, Oslo: Norway, June, 14-18, 1999. 220 p.

11. EPSTEIN, Isaac. Cibernética. São Paulo: Ática, 1986.

12. HAMIT, Francis. A realidade virtual e a exploração do espaço cibernético. Rio de Janerio: Berkley, 1993.

13. HOESHL, Hugo Cesar. Tecnologia da Informação Jurídica para o Conselho de Segurança da UNO. Ed. Papel Virtual; Rio de Janeiro; 2002.

14. HORTY, John F. Precedent, deontic logic and inheritance. In proceedings of the seventh international conference on artificial intelligence and law, p. 63-72, Oslo: Norway, June, 14-18, 1999. 220 p.

15. JAKOBOVITS, H., VERMEIR, D.. Dialectic semantic for argumentation frameworks. In proceedings of the seventh international conference on artificial intelligence and law, p. 53-62, Oslo: Norway, June, 14-18, 1999. 220 p.

16. KAKUTA, Tokuyasu, HARAGUCHI, Makoto. A demonstration of a legal reasoning system based on teleological analogies. In proceedings of the seventh international conference on artificial intelligence and law, p. 196-205, Oslo: Norway, June, 14-18, 1999. 220 p.

17. OSBORN, James, STERLING, Leon. Justice. A judicial search tool using intelligent concept extraction. In proceedings of the seventh international conference on artificial intelligence and law, p. 173-181, Oslo: Norway, June, 14-18, 1999. 220 p.

18. PFAFFENBERGER, Bryan. Dicionário dos usuários de micro computadores. Rio de Janeiro: Campus, 1993.

19. PHILIPS, Lothar. Approximate syllogisms – on the logic of everyday life. Artificial intelligence and law, Dordrecht: Netherlands, v 7, ns. 2-3, p. 227-234, march, 1999.

20. PLAZA, Enric (Eds.). Case-based reasoning research and development. Berlin; Heidelberg; New York; Barcelona; Budapest; Hong Kong; London; Milan; Paris; Santa Clara; Singapore; Tokyo: Springer, 1997.

21. RABUSKE, Renato Antonio. Inteligência Artificial. Florianópolis: Ed. Ufsc, 1995.

22. SAVORY, S. E.(editor), "Some Views on the State of Art in Artificial Intelligence" em "Artificial Intelligence and Expert Systems", Ellis Horwood Limited, 1988, pp. 21-34, Inglaterra .

23. STRANIERI, Andrew, ZELEZNIKOV, John. The evaluation of legal knowledge based system. In proceedings of the seventh international conference on artificial intelligence and law, p. 18-24, Oslo: Norway, June, 14-18, 1999. 220 p.

24. WOLKMER, Antônio Carlos. Fundamentos da História do direito.

25. YEARDWOOD, John, STRANIERI, Andrew. The integration of retrieval, reasoning and drafting for refugee law: a third generation legal knowledge based system. In proceedings of the seventh international conference on artificial intelligence and law, p. 117-137, Oslo: Norway, June, 14-18, 1999. 220 p.

# VIRTUAL MARKET ENVIRONMENT FOR TRADE

Paul Bogg and Peter Dalmaris
*Faculty of Information Technology, University of Technology, Sydney, Australia*

Abstract: In today's society, there is a need for greater understanding of activities within electronic market environments and the role information plays in negotiation. Fuelled by greater communication reach and information flow, electronic markets are ever increasingly becoming the primary domain for trade. This paper details a collaborative virtual market environment where participants engaging in trading activities may exploit information refined from both external Internet sources and internal market signals. That information provided is retrieved and distilled using time constrained, data mining techniques.

Key words: Virtual market place, virtual emarket environment,

## 1. INTRODUCTION

What is the future of online trading? What kind of information will a trader require in order to complete a deal? What electronic environment best suits the social dynamic that is the market place of tomorrow?

In an information based society, with an increasingly improving technological infrastructure, there is a need for research into how these new factors will influence electronic markets of the future. Presently, few online environments in a narrow range of online market applications, supply the necessary trade information usually required in order for a buyer and seller to complete a deal. Indeed, what is required in order for a deal to be completed can be seen as an constraint satisfaction problem[1] where objectives are represented as constraints and the strategies used to fulfill them are information based.

It is therefore necessary to investigate environments that enhance the traders and entrepreneurs. If the fulfillment of objectives belonging to these actors is achieved from appropriate information, then environments which facilitate this kind of information in a timely and constrained manner will conduit market stimulation. Information here includes both external (internet) and internal market signals.

There are a number of existing models of electronic market environments around. EBay and ETrade are both examples of present day e-marking trading environments which have been around for a significant number of years. Both provide sufficient trading mechanisms in order to complete deals; however they are not reaching far enough. Their paradigm is suited to well regulated, but simplified buy/sell versions of traditional markets. This paper proposes an alternative: an online collaborative virtual environment, or "virtual e-market place".

Virtual environments are quickly becoming widespread in conjunction with rapidly improving technological infrastructure. Indeed technology seems to be moving so quickly, the potential for virtual environments appearing on hand-held devices, including 3-G mobile devices, in the not too distant future is very real [2]! In an important way, virtual environments complement market environments – market activity is intrinsically social by nature and relies on this communal "look and feel" to generate a buoyant atmosphere on the virtual trading floor. By definition, collaborative virtual environments are social.

Figure 1 details the overall conceptual framework of the e-market virtual environment. This environment incorporates the data mining, e-market and agent activities within a single system. At the *e-market place* layer, basic market transactions are managed as industry processes using a multi-agent business process management system. These transactions include the creation of particular markets, the buying and selling of goods, and the packaging of goods, services, needs and requirements. The basic market transactions take place between a set of 'major actor classes' in the market— the decision-makers. These transactions are monitored by 'supporting actor classes' that include data mining actors. At the *market evolution* layer, the entrepreneurial transactions are also managed by business process management technology. This includes the timely extraction of reliable information and knowledge, as well as entrepreneurial intervention. At the *market information* layer, atomic signals from information bots and other sources feed into the data mining actors, the reliability of these atomic signals is evaluated before the signals are combined by the process management system at the market evolution layer.

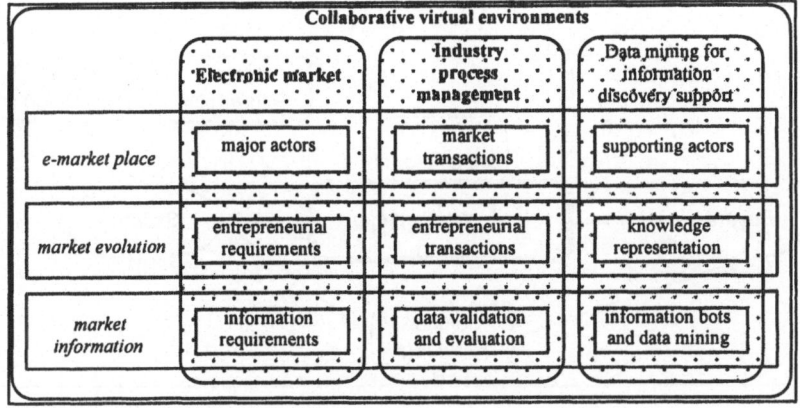

*Figure 1.* Conceptual framework integrating the domains involved

Section 2 will discuss more about present and future e-markets. Section 3 will discuss data mining methodologies and the relevancies in an e-market environment. Section 4 will deal with a brief overview of a process management system for integrating e-market, data mining, intelligent agent and actor activities. Section 5 will cover an exemplar collaborative virtual environment that has been built at UTS, combining the features of constrained information mining with trading.

## 2. ELECTRONIC MARKETS

E-markets are a rich domain of trade and entrepreneurial activity. There is a vast amount of information which resides within the e-markets and the Internet generally which assists market forces and traders alike. Little has been done to harness the rich information flowing through e-markets in order to facilitate negotiation and trade. "[T]he value of the Internet and IT lies in their capacity to store, analyse and communicate information instantly, anywhere at negligible cost" [Economist, 27 Sep. 2000].

The environment of electronic markets is quite different to traditional market environments, and so the scope for trade activity in e-markets cannot be assumed to be the same as their traditional counterpart. Substantial amounts of data may be acquired quickly and cheaply from the electronic markets themselves. Further, valuable signals may be observed by searching the Internet, by reading news feeds, by watching corporate pages, and by reading background market data such as stock exchange data. If all of these individual signals can be distilled into meaningful information, then it may

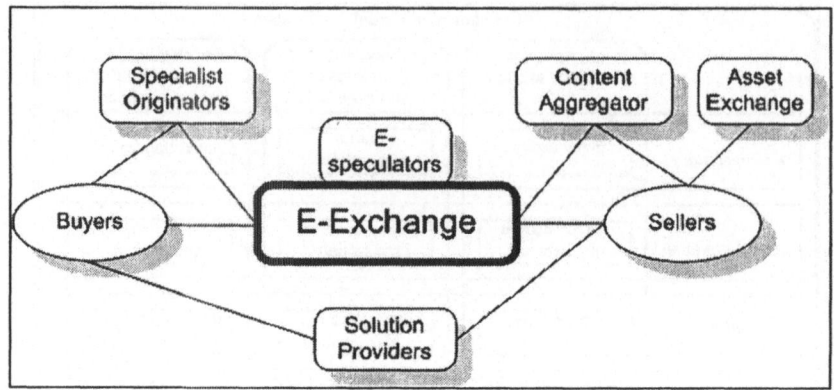

*Figure 2.* Actors interacting in an emerging market landscape

be useful to the trader who relies on "the right information, at the right granularity, at the right time". The scope of possible buying and selling is determined by the range of the support provided by the environment. Trading and the provision of information are intimately interrelated.

In the example model constructed at UTS, the basic market transactions take place in the "e-market place" between a set of *major actor classes*; these are based on an extension of the model given in [3]. There are eight major actor classes—see Figure 2. A central logical component is an "e-exchange" where individual markets are created, within which, subsequent deals are done. This class is essentially an "empty virtual box" for holding markets and for advertising their existence. It contains a collection of pre-packaged market protocols that may be invoked by the creation of a market. The *buyer* and *seller* classes include those wishing to buy or sell a good or service, or any combination of goods or services, in a market. The remaining actor classes are all entrepreneurial in nature, and are instrumental in market evolution. Members of the *content aggregator* actor class act as forward aggregators, they package goods and services and place these packages in markets in the e-exchange. Members of the *solution providers* class act as intermediaries in the negotiation of contracts and the development of long-term business relationships. *E-speculators* take short-term positions in markets in the e-exchange. Sell-side *asset exchanges* exchange or share assets between sellers. *Specialist originators* act as reverse aggregators, they coordinate and package orders for goods and services on behalf of various buyers. The major actors, shown in Figure 2 are all provided with distilled information by the supporting actors, which utilise a variety of data mining and information discovery methods. The buyers, sellers and entrepreneurs are all realised as avatars in the virtual market place.

# 3.    DATA MINING TECHNIQUES

Data mining techniques have successfully been applied to stock, financial market analysis applications [4] and research has been conducted into e-commercial applications of data mining [13]. A variety of structured and unstructured techniques have been developed to mine data from a variety of sources, such as relational databases, web pages and text files. Presently in the e-market environment the main methods have been primarily limited to the B2C framework. This paper describes set of classes which utilise both "classical" and e-commerce based mining methods [5] in order to present timely and essential information to the actors. A set of concurrent mining processes are supported by bots, supported in turn by specialised agents.

The structure for the data-mining task is outlined in Figure 3. An actor in the marketplace requests some kind of information. *Information bots* scour the market place and Internet for relevant information ranging from text in Internet news feeds, to latest stock reports, to price updates and so forth. The information retrieved is stored in a *database* in an unstructured format. *Pre-processors* are separated processes which engage in parsing raw data into formats for data-mining. The *data mining bots* mine the pre-processed data for information discoveries as required by the actor. *Process Agents*, on behalf of the actor, retrieves the information mined by the data mining bots in a constraint enforced manner. Information returned to the agents finally undergoes a visualisation transformation enacted by the *Information Visualiser* in order for the actor to understand its importance.

Delivering relevant information at the right granularity and within tight time constraints are important features of the data mining interactions model. One final feature exists which is important to the information – its visualisation. This will be outlined in section 5. Information is returned in the form most easily digestible by the actor (for humans, natural language, for agent, statistics and numbers are more easily crunched).

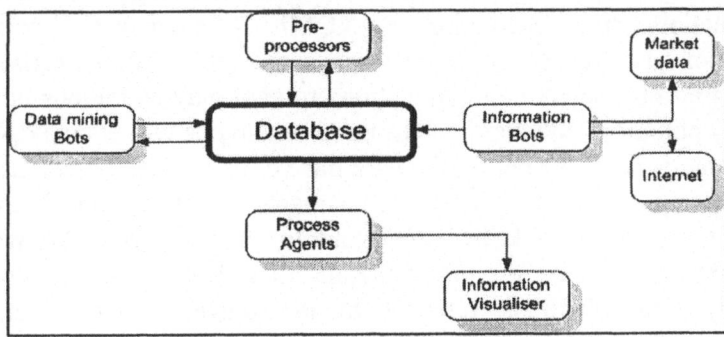

*Figure 3*. Data mining interaction model

# 4.        INDUSTRY PROCESS MANAGEMENT

The term *industry processes* is used here to refer to processes that are triggered by both e-market transactions and entrepreneurial intervention. This is in-line with the term *industry process re-engineering* which concerns the re-engineering of trans-corporate processes as electronically managed processes.    Industry process re-engineering addresses four issues: complexity, interoperability, communication and management.    Of these four issues, complexity, communication and management are particularly relevant here.   Communication and management are dealt with by an agent architecture described below.

All e-market transactions are managed as industry processes.   The problem of delivering information to both traders and entrepreneurs at the right granularity and at the right time is also a process management problem, as is the problem of effecting any intervention that may be triggered indirectly by that information.   A single business process system manages the e-market transactions, the entrepreneurial intervention, and its delivery of information.   The complexity in managing e-market transactions stems from the distributed nature of e-markets and from the complex time constraints that govern the operation of e-markets.   The complexity in information delivery here stems from the unreliable and unpredictable nature of the Internet, and the problem of delivering something useful and reliable in the required time.   This means that a powerful process management system is required, particularly in its capacity to manage heavily constrained and possibly interdependent processes of high value.   The system used is a multi-agent system that is based on a three-layer, BDI (Belief-Desire-Intention) hybrid agent architecture.

Multi-agent technology is an attractive basis for industry process re-engineering [6] [7].   A multi-agent system consists of autonomous components that interact with messages. The scalability issue is "solved"—in theory—by establishing a common understanding for inter-agent communication and interaction.    KQML (Knowledge Query and Manipulation Language) is used for inter-agent communication [8]. Specifying an inter-agent communication protocol may be tedious but is not technically complex.  Standard XML-based ontologies will enable data to be communicated freely [9] but much work has yet to be done on standards for communicating expertise.   Any process management system should take account of the "process knowledge" and the "performance knowledge". *Process knowledge* is the information that has been accumulated, particularly that which is relevant to the process instance at hand. *Performance knowledge* is knowledge of how effective people, agents, methods and plans are at achieving various things.

# 5.     E-MARKET AS A COLLABORATIVE VIRTUAL PLACE

The collaborative market environment should seamlessly integrate the mining and process models with the underlying technology and support both social and negotiation interactions.  Market activities are distributed by nature, so there's also a need to be able to handle all interactions in a single 'logical' location, which in turn allows convenience for research observation and collection of strategies and behaviours within the market place.

Much research and development involved with collaborative virtual environments (CVEs) [10] has been towards the implementation of 'virtual place' models offering ways to handle information, communication and additional functionality [11] [12].  Our approach describes a 'virtual e-market place' that provides 'virtual e-markets' with an environment in which the complete range of market and trade activities are naturally represented.

The model for the e-market place is shown in Figure 4.  The *Virtual environment* is at the centre of all activity.  It is a distributed collaborative environment implemented using Adobe Atmosphere technology and facilitates the 3D representations of actors and markets over the Internet. Within this environment we have built an *e-market place*.  The e-market place is a centralised location for the populations of *e-markets*.  It is essentially the hub for existing markets and for the creation of emerging new markets alike.  An *e-market* is a market area designated for trade and activities. Markets are split into market areas and each e-market describes a set of goods and/or services which are traded within the market.  Fig. 4 shows a screenshot of the implementation of the virtual UTS environment.

The implementation of this virtual environment is divided to three areas. These areas are marked as 1, 2 and 3 in Figure 5. Area 1 displays the 3-D environment in which the user moves and interacts with the various agents. The movement of the user's avatar can be controlled through the keyboard and mouse, and the interaction with the various environmental objects, such as walls, desks etc., is as one would expect in the natural environment. Area 2 is used to display general information about a product (for example, its 3-dimensional representation), comparisons between products in tabular format, and tools that can facilitate the creation of new markets by the user. Area 3 is used for facilitating the actor communications and dialogue and displays the history of the dialog as it continues between a user and a virtual agent. It is through this that the actors can converse with one another.

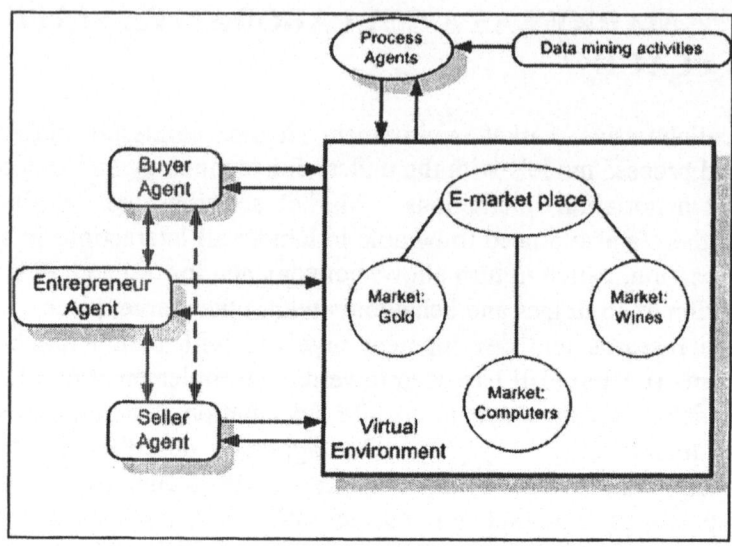

*Figure 4.* E-market model for basic trade in 3 classes of goods

Another aspect of the virtual environment model is establishing a 3D representation of the actors (including traders, etc). In the context of an e-market, the representation should be understandable to all other actors, thus a human who has entered the virtual environment should have an avatar model assigned which shows where they are, the direction they are facing, and any gestures communicated. Avatar models may also be customised to signify specific traits, which may be used to identify individuals from others.

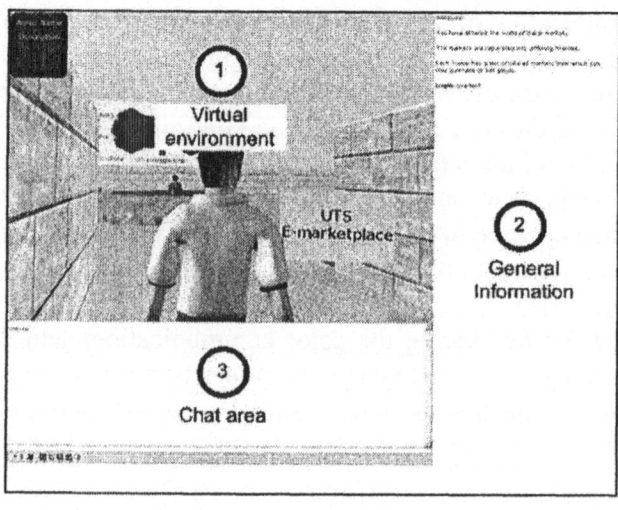

*Figure 5.* The virtual environment market place

Finally, the virtual environment enables *agent* interaction in order to interface *data-mining* information. The process agents described here are the same as those described earlier in the data mining section and have representations in the 3D context. Actors may utilise the mining methods provided by the agents (via an agent avatar visualisation) in order to search for relevant information from many sources across the Internet. They do this in one of the two ways outlined earlier: data driven and hypothesis driven. Agents will seek out information based on the goal and retrieve what is available in a time constrained manner. The results are displayed in a manner that is appropriate to the information to be visualised.

In order to fulfill these, further information will be required. How one may determine whether a product is reasonably priced in this instance might be a combination of comparing Internet prices, market trends for similar products, and being able to negotiate a better price with the seller. The former two would be something an agent might be able to provide visually with data mining techniques, the latter is a social feature inherently tied with markets. How one may determine whether a product is of good quality in this instance might be a combination of Internet published reviews about the product, technical forum views about the seller, and a visual 3D inspection of the product itself.

Precisely what information is required and by when is another matter for further research. Furthermore, there are a wide variety of other e-market scenarios for which the constraints and the satisfying of the constraints become considerably more complex. An example is for a multi-tier auction for e-procurement over the Internet involving steel. In the e-market context, it becomes a much more complex problem of how one would best go about to achieve the best price (as a buyer and seller), however, it is reasonable to suspect that it certainly involves timely, accurate and reliable information, visualisation, and the ability to interact socially with those involved.

## 6.    CONCLUSION

This research has described an implementation of a collaborative virtual environment for e-markets permitting market activities and trade between actors represented as virtual avatars. By enabling a singular virtual location for activity, a smarter way of business is engaged by reducing information overload to well organized visualisations and an environment for interactive decision making and data mining. The merger of e-business with the feeling of 'place' supplied by the 3D virtual context provides for a more coherent and effective way of doing business.

By constructing e-markets in the virtual world context, we are also facilitating further research into what drives trade in the e-market context. Having a centralised market activity centre allows unobtrusive observations to be made about the way business is done, allowing discoveries about the emerging processes between actors to be uncovered.

The reader may enter the UTS e-market place from the following URL (you will need Internet Explorer 6 or newer, and the Adobe Atmosphere plug-in): http://research.it.uts.edu.au/emarkets/tech_vw/demo/demo.html. The e-market is still in prototypical form and consequently no formal evaluations have been made at the time of writing.

# REFERENCES

[1] Sathi, A. and Fox, M., 1989, Constraint-directed negotiation of resource reallocation. In L. Gasser and M. Huhns, editors, Distributed Artificial Intelligence Volume II, San Mateo, California, 1989. Morgan Kaufmann.

[2] Rakkolainen, I., Vainio, T., A 3D City Info for Mobile Users, Tampere University of Technology, Finland

[3] Wise, R. and Morrison, D., 2000. Beyond the Exchange; The Future of B2B. Harvard Business review Nov-Dec 2000, pp86-96.

[4] Kovalerchuk, B. and Vityaev E., 2000, Data Mining in Finance: Advances in Relational and Hybrid Methods. Kluwer, 2000.

[5] Han, J. and Kamber, M., 2001, Data Mining: Concepts and Techniques, Morgan Kaufmann, San Francisco, CA, 2001.

[6] Jain, A.K., Aparicio, M. and Singh, M.P., 1999 "Agents for Process Coherence in Virtual Enterprises" in Communications of the ACM, Volume 42, No 3, March 1999, pp62—69.

[7] Jennings, N.R., Faratin, P., Norman, T.J., O'Brien, P. & Odgers, B. Autonomous Agents for Business Process Management. Int. Journal of Applied Artificial Intelligence 14 (2) 145—189, 2000.

[8] Finin, F. Labrou, Y., and Mayfield, J. "KQML as an agent communication language." In Jeff Bradshaw (Ed.) Software Agents. MIT Press (1997).

[9] Robert Skinstad, R. "Business process integration through XML". In proceedings XML Europe 2000, Paris, 12-16 June 2000.

[10] Capin, T.K., Pandzic, I. S., Magnenat-Thalmann, N. and Thalmann, D. Avatars in Networked Virtual Environments. John Wiley and Sons, Chichester, 1999.

[11] J.A. Waterworth. Spaces, places, landscapes and views: experiential design of shared information spaces. In A. J. Munro, K. Hook and D. Benyon (eds), Social Navigation of Information Space, Springer, London, pp. 132-154, 1999.

[12] T. Manninen. Interaction in Networked Virtual Environments as Communicative Action – Social Theory and Multi-player Games. CRIWG2000 Workshop, Madeira, Portugal, IEEE Computer Society Press, October 18-20 2000.

[13] Jaideep Srivastava and Robert Cooley, Web Mining for E-Commerce: Concepts and Case Studies J.Stefan Institute, Slovenia and Carnegie Mellon University USA

# AN ARTIFICIAL NEURAL NETWORKS APPROACH TO THE ESTIMATION OF PHYSICAL STELLAR PARAMETERS

Rodriguez, Alejandra
*Department of Information and Communication Technologies*
*University of A Coruña. A Coruña. 15071. Spain*
alejandra@udc.es


Carricajo, Iciar
*Department of Navigation and Earth Sciences*
*University of A Coruña. A Coruña. 15011. Spain*
iciar@udc.es


Dafonte, Carlos
*Department of Information and Communication Technologies*
*University of A Coruña. A Coruña. 15071. Spain*
dafonte@udc.es


Arcay, Bernardino
*Department of Information and Communication Technologies*
*University of A Coruña. A Coruña. 15071. Spain*
cibarcay@udc.es


Manteiga, Minia
*Department of Navigation and Earth Sciences*
*University of A Coruña. A Coruña. 15011. Spain*
manteiga@udc.es

**Abstract**

This paper presents an artificial neural networks approach to the estimation of effective stellar temperatures by means of optical spectroscopy.

The present work is included in a global project, whose final objective is the development of an automatic system for the determination of the physical and chemical parameters of stars. In previous works, we designed a hybrid system that integrated neural networks, fuzzy logic and expert systems to obtain the stellar spectral type and luminosity in the MK standard system. Considering those results, we now propose the design of several neural networks for the calculation of stellar temperatures.

The proposed networks have been trained with synthetic spectra that were previously contrasted with statistical clustering techniques. The final networks obtained a success rate of 88% for public catalogue spectra.

Our final objective is to calibrate the MK classification system, obtaining thus a new relation between the temperature and the spectral type.

**Keywords:** Neural Networks, Clustering Techniques, Stellar Physical Parameters, Optical Spectroscopy

# 1.    Introduction

This work is part of a global project that studies the last phases of stellar evolution. Our main objective is to provide an automatic system, based on artificial intelligence techniques, that contributes to the determination of chemical and physical stellar parameters by means of optical spectroscopy.

Spectroscopy is among the most powerful currently available techniques for the study of stars and, in particular, their physical conditions (temperature, pressure, density, etc.) and chemical components (H, He, Ca, K, etc.). In general terms, a stellar spectrum consists of a black body continuum light distribution, distorted by the interstellar absorption and reemission of light, and by the presence of absorption lines, emission lines and molecular bands [Zombeck, 1990].

The stellar spectra are collected from telescopes with appropriate spectrographs and detectors. Observers collect the flux distribution of each object and reduce these data to obtain a one-dimensional spectrum calibrated in energy flux ($erg^{-1}cm^{-2}s^{-1}\text{Å}^{-1}$) and wavelength (Å).

As part of the above-mentioned global project, we have collected a sample of approximately 400 low-resolution stellar spectra from astronomical observations that were carried out at several telescopes. In order to extract useful information from the individual spectra and to study the evolution in the whole sample, we must determine the main stellar parameters, such as spectral type, luminosity, temperature, surface gravity, metallicity, etc.

The estimation of the stellar parameters is often carried out by human experts, who analyse the spectra by hand, with no more help than their own experience. These manual analyses usually lead to a MK classification of the spectra. The MK classification system was firstly proposed in 1943 by Morgan, Keenan & Kellman [Morgan et al., 1943] and has experienced many revisions ever since [Kurtz, 1984]. This bidimensional system is the only one that is widely used for stellar classification. One of its main advantages is that MK classifications are often static, because they are based on the visual study of the spectra and on a set of standard criteria. However, the same spectra can be classified differently by different experts and even differently by the same person at different times.

Any classification system should hold a compromise between maintaining the full information of the spectra and the need for a compact summary of this information. An optimal summary is obviously obtained by a study of the physical parameters.

The manual techniques that are currently used to estimate stellar parameters are very time-consuming and involve a great amount of human resources. It would be highly advisable to dispose of automatic, fast and efficient computational techniques that allow the experts to classify a large number of spectra according to their physical parameters.

In previous works, we developed an expert system for the classification of the stellar spectra of Post-AGB stars in the visible electromagnetic spectral range. The obtained results led us to extend this system to stars of different luminosities and to add new computational techniques, such as fuzzy logic, in order to refine the automatic processing of spectra. We have also tested feed-forward, radial-basis functions (RBF) and self-organising neural networks in order to obtain the spectral type and luminosity of stars through the analysis of their optical spectra. Combining both techniques, we formalised a hybrid system that obtains MK classifications and is able to determine the most appropriate method for each spectrum type. A complete description of these works can be found in [Rodriguez et al., 2003].

Our previous developments have proven that artificial techniques allow researchers to obtain the spectral type and luminosity of stars in a fast, easy and accurate way. Neural networks in particular have given excellent results, which is why this paper proposes the design and implementation of several artificial neural networks to estimate the effective stellar temperature. By carrying out a sensibility analysis of this technique in the estimation of the physical parameters of stars, we can determine the best learning algorithm and network structure for this specific problem.

## 2. Methodology

As mentioned in Sect. 1, we have implemented artificial techniques in order to obtain MK classifications. That first approach combined signal processing [Kalouptsidis, 1997], knowledge-based systems [Buchanan and Shortliffe, 1984], fuzzy logic techniques [Bouchon-Meunier et al., 1991] and artificial neural networks models [Arbib, 1995], integrated by a relational database that stores and structures all the stellar information. Table 1 contrasts the behaviour of the artificial techniques and that of two human experts who collaborated on this project, applied to 100 unclassified spectra belonging to the standard atlas of spectra from [Pickles, 1998].

*Table 1.* Artificial and Manual Techniques for MK Classifications

| Approach | Global | Spectral Type | Luminosity |
|---|---|---|---|
| *Human Expert A* | 99.0% | 92.0% | 81.0% |
| *Human Expert B* | 95.0% | 85.0% | 70.0% |
| *Expert Systems* | 95.6% | 90.3% | 78.2% |
| *Fuzzy Expert Systems* | 98.6% | 93.5% | 79.0% |
| *Backpropagation* | 97.0% | 95.4% | 81.0% |
| *RBF* | 96.2% | 94.6% | 80.0% |
| *Self-Organizing Maps* | 73.0% | 68.0% | 55.0% |

These results led us to develop a final hybrid system based on an expert system that determines the global type of each star and, according to the type, sends the spectra to different neural networks in order to obtain their spectral type as well as their luminosity level. The success rate of that system was very similar to the agreement percentage between experts in the field (about 80%). This paper does not describe the development in detail: a more complete description of the models and stellar parameters used can be found in [Rodriguez et al., 2003]. We only include a brief explanation of the morphological algorithms so as to clarify how the spectral parameters, used as the input layer of most of the proposed neural networks models, are obtained and measured.

## 2.1 Morphological Analysis

Before presenting the spectra to the neural networks, we carry out a morphological analysis of all the spectra in order to obtain the values of the parameters that characterise each spectrum separately. These spectral parameters include the measurement of 25 spectral features that can be divided into three types:

- Absorption and emission lines: including hydrogen, helium and metallic lines (Ca, K, etc.).

- Molecular bands: hydrogen and carbon absorption bands.

- Rates between lines: CH-K rates, He-H rates.

From a morphological point of view, an absorption line is a descending (ascending for emission) deep peak that appears in an established wavelength zone [Zwicky, 1957]. To accurately calculate the intensity of each line, we carry out an estimation of the local spectral continuum. That is

$$C_j = \left( \frac{\sum_{j-n}^{j+n} E_i * X_i}{N} \right) , \tag{1}$$

where $C_j$ is the estimation of the continuum for sample $j$, $E_i$ is the flux in sample $i$, $N$ is the number of values used to calculate the local spectral continuum, and $X$ is a binary vector that indicates the representative fluxes of the spectral continuum in the zone.

A molecular band is a spectral zone in which the flux suddenly decreases from the local continuum during a wide lambda interval [Zwicky, 1957]. For the molecular bands, this means that we only have to measure their energy to decide if they are significant enough. That is

$$B_{lr} = \int_l^r L(\lambda_i) - \int_l^r E(\lambda_i) , \tag{2}$$

where $B_{lr}$ is the flux of the band between the samples $l$ and $r$, $L$ is the projection line, $E$ is the flux function, $\lambda$ the wavelength, $l$ the left limit of the band and $r$ the right limit.

## 2.2 Training and Validation Spectra

In order to build the training set of the artificial neural networks that will be applied to the problem of estimation of stellar effective temperatures, we have chosen a complete and consistent set of synthetic optical spectra. The selected spectra were generated using the SPECTRUM v. 2.56. software written by Richard O. Gray. This software is a stellar spectral synthesis program that allows us to obtain prototype spectra of a chosen effective temperature and surface gravity. SPECTRUM is distributed with an atomic and molecular line list for the optical spectral region 3500 Å to 6800 Å, called luke.lst, suitable for computing synthetic spectra with temperatures between 4000K and 20000K. The details on the physics included in this sofware can be found in [Gray, 2003].

For the generation of synthetic spectra we also used the models calculated by Robert Kurucz [Kurucz, 1979]. The atmospheric model is a tabulation of temperature and pressure at range of mass depths in the stellar photosphere, calculated on the basis of a variety of opacity sources. Each model is characterised by four parameters: effective temperature ($T_{eff}$), metallicity ($[M/H]$), microturbulence velocity ($V_{micro}$) and surface gravity ($log\ g$).

We generated a total of 350 solar metallicity spectra with effective temperatures between 4000K and 20000K and surface gravity from 0.5 to 5.0. This set of synthetic spectra covers the spectral range K-B with luminosity levels I to V (in the MK system). The spectra were generated in the 3500-6800 Å range, which is the wavelength interval where the software is capable of correctly obtaining synthetic spectra.

Before training the neural networks, the synthetic spectra were contrasted with statistical clustering techniques in order to verify their suitability and to avoid dispersions in the whole sample.

Grouping techniques are often used as a tool to verify and test the quality of an established clustering of data: the grouping algorithms make their own division into classes of the input data. Our purpose was to try to discard those spectra that were not similar to any others. We implemented the max-min and K-clustering algorithms [Kaufman and Rousseeuw, 1990]. The data groups obtained by these two techniques prevent us from using some of the initial spectra that could not be included in any of the clusters. We also observed that the algorithms were able to accurately group the spectra of low and medium temperatures (4000K-8000K), although both techniques stored all the spectra with temperatures above 8000K in the same category. Obviously, they are not capable of separating spectra with temperatures higher than 8000K. Finally, we built the training set with 348 synthetic spectra, excluding those that were discarded by the clustering techniques.

As for the test set of spectra, we used the public catalogue of Pickles [Pickles, 1998], choosing only the 79 spectra that match our temperature range.

## 2.3   Artificial Neural Networks Implementation

The neural networks used in this experimentation are based on supervised learning models and backpropagation networks [Rojas, 1996] in particular. In our experiments, we have made use of three different learning algorithms:

- Standard backpropagation: as the most common learning algorithm, it updates the weights after each training pattern.

- Enhanced backpropagation: it uses a momentum term that introduces the old weight change as a parameter for the computation of the new weight change.

- Batch Backpropagation: in standard backpropagation, an update step is performed after each single pattern; in batch backpropagation, all the weight changes are summed over a full presentation of all the training patterns (one epoch). Only then, an update with the accumulated weight changes is performed.

As for the topology, the different networks that were implemented are shown in Table 2. These topologies have been tested for the three backpropagation learning algorithms.

We built the input patterns for the nets with 659 flux values (from 3510 Å to 6800 Å), as well as with the 25 spectral features obtained by means of the morphological algorithms described in Sect. 2.1. The output of all networks is a continuous function that obtains the effective temperature in the form $T_o = ((\log T_{eff} - 3)/2)$.

*Table 2.* Topologies tested for Backpropagation Networks

| *Input Patterns* | *Hidden Layer* |
|---|---|
| 659 flux values | 100:50:10:3 |
| 659 flux values | 10:5:3* |
| 659 flux values | 10:10 |
| 659 flux values | 5:5 |
| 25 Spectral Parameters | 10:5:3 |
| 25 Spectral Parameters | 10:10 |
| 25 Spectral Parameters | 5:5 |

* Best performance topology.

We used the Stuttgart Neural Network Simulator (SNNS v.4.1) [Zell, 2002] to implement the above described networks and to transform them into C code, so they can be integrated into the previously developed tool. In the training phase, the weights were updated in a topological order and initiated randomly with values in the [-1, 1] interval.

During our experiments, we found that the best topology corresponds to an enhanced backpropagation network 659:10:5:3:1; that is, a network with 659 flux values in the input layer, three hidden layers with 10, 5 and 3 neurons respectively, and 1 neuron for the effective temperature in the output layer.

## 2.4    Enhanced Techniques

While analysing the success rates of the implemented neural networks for each different temperature, we observed that all the networks have a higher performance for temperatures between 4000K-8000K (less than 200K mean error). Considering this fact, we separated the input spectra into two sets (4000K-8000K and 8000K-20000K) and trained the best performance network once again, but only with the patterns that correspond to spectra with temperatures in the interval 8000K-20000K. This "overtrained" network resulted in a better performance for all the test spectra.

An additional research consisted in analysing the weights of the output layer units of the best network so as to determine, for each temperature interval, which input parameters have more influence on the output. We were able to reduce the inputs of the network because we considered only the sufficiently significant flux values. This enhanced strategy allowed us to obtain networks that converge sooner, and has resulted in a significant improvement of the performance of the original artificial neural networks (around 2%).

## 3.    Discussion and Results

The best implemented neural networks are able to determine the temperature of the 79 selected spectra from the test catalogue with an error rate below 15% and a mean deviation of 300 K, according to the estimation made by Pickles [Pickles, 1998].

The experts in this field usually work with a mean error of 10% of the correct temperature. Taking this error rate into account, our neural networks approach is able to correctly estimate 88% of the effective temperatures with a minimal mean deviation of 3% (for the coolest stars) and a maximum mean deviation of 7% (for the hottest stars). The final performance is shown in Table 3.

As shown in the results, the best temperature estimations are reached for cooler stars (4000K-8000K), whereas the stars with higher temperatures present a higher error rate; one explanation of this particularity could be that the training set includes few stars of this temperature range, because the models on which we based the generation of the synthetic spectra (Kurucz) can generate only 1 "hot spectrum" for every 4 "cool spectra". Including more spectra for higher temperatures is not meaningful, because the error bar for this interval is established in 1000K. So, for higher temperatures, we can only include one sample spectrum for every 1000K, whereas for cool stars, where the error bar is 250K, we can include four samples. In future extensions, we hope to increase the success rate for hot stars by designing a net of neural networks that includes different trained networks for hot and cool stars.

*Table 3.* ANN Performance for Effective Temperature

| Teff | Spectra number | Success rate | Mean temperature error |
|------|----------------|--------------|------------------------|
| 4000-6000 | 36 | 97.22% | ±230 K |
| 6000-8000 | 19 | 89.47% | ±180 K |
| 8000-10000 | 10 | 60.00% | ±360 K |
| 10000-20000 | 14 | 85.71% | ±580 K |
| Total | 79 | 88.60% | ± 300 K |

## 4.    Conclusions

This paper has presented a computational approach to the estimation of the physical parameters of stars and, in particular, the calculation of effective temperature by means of artificial neural networks.

We have described several models of neural networks and analysed their performance and results to discover the best approach to the estimation of each temperature range. Backpropagation networks were trained with approximately 350 synthetic spectra that were previously contrasted with statistical clustering techniques. In order to obtain the input patterns of the neural networks and extract and measure spectral features, we used the morphological analysis algorithms that were developed in the expert systems approach. Several networks were trained with this parameterisation, and other networks with full flux values; the second strategy yielded the best performance.

The best networks have reached a success rate of approximately 88% for a sample of 79 testing spectra from public catalogues. For the development and evaluation of the system, we can count on the essential collaboration of experts from the area of Astronomy and Astrophysics of the University of A Coruña.

As an additional study, the best implemented networks were analysed to determine the flux values that are more influential in the output for each temperature interval; by training the networks with these small input patterns, we increased the performance of the original networks.

At present, we are analysing other types of neural structures and learning algorithms in order to improve the classification properties. We are also studying the influence of differences in signal to noise ratio in the resulting classification, since our final objective is to obtain a calibration that can determine our own relation between temperature and MK classifications. We are also completing the development of our stellar database, STARMIND (http://starmind.tic.udc.es), to make it accessible through the Internet.

## Acknowledgments

The authors acknowledge support from grants AYA2000-1691 and AYA2003-09499, financed by the Spanish Ministerio de Ciencia y Tecnología.

## References

[Arbib, 1995] Arbib, M. A. (1995). *The Handbook of Brain Theory and Neural Networks*. MIT Press, Cambridge, Massachusetts.

[Bouchon-Meunier et al., 1991] Bouchon-Meunier, R., Yager, R., and Zadeh, L. A. (1991). *Uncertainty in Knowledge Bases*. Springer-Verlag, Berlin.

[Buchanan and Shortliffe, 1984] Buchanan, B. and Shortliffe, E. (1984). *Ruled-based Expert Systems*. Reading MA: Adisson-Wesley.

[Gray, 2003] Gray, R. (2003). Spectrum: A stellar spectra synthesis program. http://www1.appstate.edu/dept/physics/spectrum.

[Kalouptsidis, 1997] Kalouptsidis, N. (1997). *Signal Processing Systems: Theory and Design*. Wiley, New York.

[Kaufman and Rousseeuw, 1990] Kaufman, L. and Rousseeuw, P. J. (1990). *Finding Groups in Data*. Wiley, New York.

[Kurtz, 1984] Kurtz, M. J. (1984). *The MK Process and Stellar Classification of Stars*. David Dunlap Observatory, Toronto.

[Kurucz, 1979] Kurucz, R. L. (1979). Model atmospheres for G, F, A, B and O stars. *The Astrophysical Journal Suppl.*, 40.

[Morgan et al., 1943] Morgan, W. W., Keenan, P. C., and Kellman, E. (1943). *An Atlas of Stellar Spectra with an Outline of Spectral Classification*. University of Chicago Press, Chicago.

[Pickles, 1998] Pickles, A. J. (1998). A stellar spectral flux library. 1150-25000 å. *Publications of the Astronomical Society of the Pacific*, 110:863–878.

[Rodriguez et al., 2003] Rodriguez, A., Dafonte, C., Arcay, B. and Manteiga, M. (2003). An Artificial Neural Network Approach to Automatic Classification of Stellar Spectra. In *Proc. 7TH. Int. Work Conf. on Artificial and Natural Neural Networks (IWANN'03)*, 2: 639–646, Menorca, Spain.

[Rojas, 1996] Rojas, R. (1996). *Neural Networks. A Systematic Introduction*. Springer-Verlag, Berlin.

[Zell, 2002] Zell, A. (2002). Stuttgart neural network simulator. http://www-ra.informatik.uni-tuebingen.de/SNNS/.

[Zombeck, 1990] Zombeck, M. V. (1990). *Handbook of Astronomy and Astrophysics*. Cambridge University Press, Cambridge, second edition.

[Zwicky, 1957] Zwicky, F. (1957). *Morphological Astronomy*. Springer, Berlin.

# EVOLUTIONARY ROBOT BEHAVIORS BASED ON NATURAL SELECTION AND NEURAL NETWORK*

Jingan Yang[1,2], Yanbin Zhuang[2], Hongyan Wang[1]

[1]*Institute of Artificial Intelligence, Hefei University of Technology*
*Hefei 230009, Anhui, P. R. China*
*jayang@mail.hf.ah.cn*

[2]*School of Computer Science & Engineering, Changzhou Institute of Technology*
*Changzhou 213002, Jiangsu Province, P. R. China*
*zhuangyb@czu.cn*

**Abstract**    The methodology of artificial evolution based on the traditional fitness function is argued to be inadequate for constructing the entities with behaviors novel to their designers. Evolutionary emergence via natural selection(without an explicit fitness function) is a promising way. This paper primarily considers the question of what to evolve, and focuses on the principles of developmental modularity based on neural networks. The connection weight values of this neural network are encoded as genes, and the fitness individuals are determined using a genetic algorithm. In paper we has created and described an artificial world containing autonomous organisms for developing and testing some novel ideas. Experimental results through simulation have demonstrated that the developmental system is well suited to long-term incremental evolution. Novel emergent strategies are identified both from an observer's perspective and in terms of their neural mechanisms.

**Keywords:**    Natural selection, development neural network, evolutionary algorithm, novel behavior.

## Introduction

The goal of artificial life presents us with the problem that we do not understand natural life well enough to specify it to a machine. Therefore we must either increase our understanding of it until we can, or create a system which outperforms the specifications we can give it. The first possibility includes the traditional top-down methodology, which is clearly as inappropriate for ALife as it has been proved to be for artificial intelligence. It also includes man-

*Partial funding provided by the Internatioanl Centre for Theoretical Physics, Trieste, Italy ual incremental(from bottom to up) construction of autonomous systems with the aim of increasing our understanding and ability to model life by building increasingly impressive systems, retaining functional validity by testing them within their destination environments. The second option is to create systems which outperform the specifications given them and which are open to produce behaviors comparable with those of (albeit simple) natural life. Evolution in nature has no(explicit) evaluation function. Through organism-environment interactions, including interactions between similarly-capable organisms, certain behaviors fare better than others. This is how the non-random cumulative selection works without any long-term goal. It is why novel structures and behaviors emerge.

As artificial evolution is applied to increasingly complex problems, the difficulty in specifying satisfactory evaluation functions is becoming apparent–see [1], for example. At the same time, the power of natural selection is being demonstrated in prototypal systems such as Tierra and Poly-World[2]. Artificial selection involves the imposition of an artifice crafted for some cause external to a system beneath it while natural selection does not. Natural selection is necessary for evolutionary emergence but does not imply sustained emergence (evermore new emergent phenomena) and the question "what should we evolve?" needs to be answered with that in mind[3]. This paper sets out to answer that question. Further discussion concerning evolutionary emergence can be found in [4], along with evaluations of other natural selection systems. Note that an explicit fitness landscape is not a requirement for artificial selection and so an implicit fitness landscape does not imply natural selection.

General issues concerning long-term evolution have been addressed by Harvey's Species Adaptation Genetic Algorithm'(SAGA) theory[5]. He demonstrates that changes in genotype length should take place much more slowly than crossover's fast mixing of chromosomes. The population should be nearly-converged, evolving as species. Therefore the fitness landscape (actual or implicit) must be sufficiently correlated for mutation to be possible without dispersing the species in genotype space or hindering the assimilation by crossover of beneficial mutations into the species.

## 1. Designing Evolutionary Robot

Neural networks are the straightforward choice because of their graceful degradation (high degree of neutrality). But how should the network structure be specified? The evolutionary emergence of novel behaviors requires new neural structures. We can expect most to be descended from neural structures that once have different functions. There are many known examples of neural structures that serve a purpose different from a previous use. Evidence from gene theory tells us that genes are used like a recipe, not a blueprint. In any cell, at any stage of development, only a tiny proportion of the genes will be in use. Further, the effect that a gene has depends upon the cell's local environment–its neighbors.

Two sections above are related: for a type of module to be used for a novel function(and then to continue to evolve from there), without loss of current function, either an extra module must be created or there must be one spare' (to alter). Either way, a duplication system is required. This could be either by gene duplication or as part of a developmental process.

Gene duplication can be rejected as a sole source of neural structure duplication, because the capacity required to store all connections in a large network without a modular coding is genetically infeasible. Therefore, for the effective evolutionary emergence of complex behaviors, a modular developmental process is called for. For the sake of research validity (regarding long-term goals), this should be included from the outset.

**Gruau's cellular encoding**: Gruau used genetic programming(GP) to evolve his cellular programming language' code for developing modular artificial neural networks[6, 7]. The programs used are trees of graph-rewrite rules whose main points are cell division and iteration. The crucial shortcoming is that modularity can only come from either gene duplication (see objections above) or iteration. But iteration is not a powerful enough developmental backbone. Consider, for example, the cerebral cortex's macro-modules of hundreds of mini-columns. These are complicated structures that cannot be generated with a repeat one hundred times: mini-column' rule. There are variations between modules.

**Cellular automata**: Many researchers have used conventional cellular automata (CA) for the construction of neural networks. However, such work is more at the level of neuron growth than the development of whole networks. Although CA rules are suited to the evolution of network development in principle, the amount of work remaining makes this a major research hurdle.

**Diffusion models**: while there are a number of examples of work involving the evolution of neural networks whose development is determined by diffusion along concentration gradients, the resulting network structures have (to date) been only basic. So as to concentrate on the intended area of research, these models have also been passed over.

**Lindenmayer systems**: Kitano used a context-free L-system[8, 9] to evolve connectivity matrices. The number of rules in the genotype was variable. Boers and Kuiper used a context-sensitive L-system to evolve modular feed-forward network architecture[10, 11]. Both these works used backpropagation to train the evolved networks. Also, the resulting structures were fully-connected clusters of unconnected nodes(i.e. no links within clusters and if one node in cluster $A$ is linked to one node in cluster $B$ then all nodes in $A$ are linked to all in $B$). It may be that the results achieved reflect the workings of backpropaga-

58

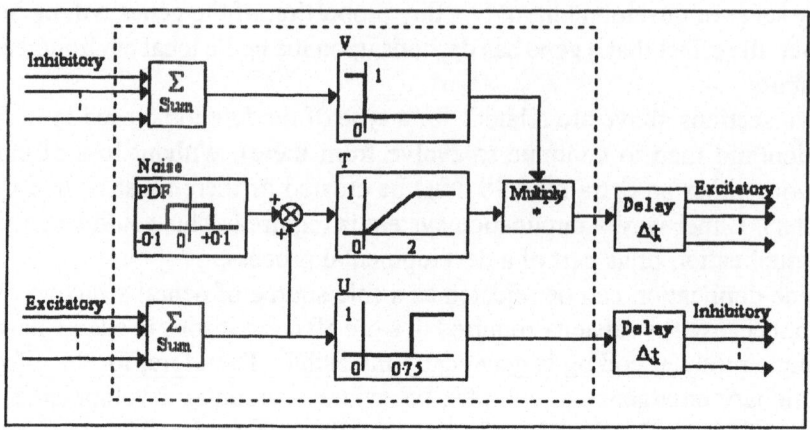

*Figure 1.* Schematic block diagram of a neuron (from Cliff, Harvey and Husbands, 1992).

tion more than evolution. However, these works demonstrated the suitability of L-systems to 'non-iterative modular' network development.

## 2. The Neural and Development Systems

The artificial neural networks used here are recurrent networks[12, 13]. Let the current node be $N_i$, and $N_i's$ excitatory output at time $t$ is $OE_i(t)$, inhibitory output is $OI_i(t)$. Let the node which links to the current node be $N_{ik}$, $k=0,\cdots, K$, and the value of noise be $V_{noise}$, then

$$OE_i(t + \Delta t) = V(-\sum_{k=0}^{k} OI_{ik}(t) \times T(\sum_{k=0}^{k} OE_{ik}(t) \pm V_{noise}$$

$$OI_i(t + \Delta t) = U(\sum_{k=0}^{k} OE_{ik}(t))$$

Where

$$V(x) = \begin{cases} 1 & \text{if } x > 0 \\ 0 & \text{otherwise} \end{cases}$$

$$U(x) = \begin{cases} 1 & \text{if } x > 0.75 \\ 0 & \text{otherwise} \end{cases}$$

$$T(x) = \begin{cases} 1 & \text{if } x > 2 \\ \frac{1}{2}x & \text{if } 0 < x < 2 \\ 0 & \text{otherwise} \end{cases}$$

**Developmental system**: A context-free $L$-system was designed for the evolution of networks of these neurons. Specific attention was paid to producing a system in which children's networks resemble aspects of their parents'. Each node has a bit-string 'character'(label) associated with it, initialized at construction and modifiable during development. These characters may be of any non-zero length. A node may be network input, network output, or neither, as determined by an axiom(birth) network and development.

A production rule matches a node if its predecessor is the start of the node's character. The longer the matching predecessor, the better the match; the best matching rule (if any) is applied. Thus ever more specific rules can evolve from those that have already been successful. The production rules have the following form:

$$P \rightarrow S_r, S_n; b_1, b_2, b_3, b_4, b_5, b_6$$

Where:

$P$   Predecessor (initial bits of node's character)

$S_r$   Successor 1: *replacement* node's character

$S_n$   Successor 2: *new* node's character bits link details [0=no,1=yes]

$(b_1, b_2)$ reverse types [inhibitory/excitatory] of (input, output) links on $S_n$

$(b_3, b_4)$ (inhibitory, excitatory) link from $S_r$ to $S_n$

$(b_5, b_6)$ (inhibitory, excitatory) link from $S_n$ to $S_r$

If a successor has no character (0 length) then that node is not created. Thus this predecessor node may be replaced by 0, 1 or 2 nodes. The 'replacement' successor (if it exists) is just the old (predecessor) node, with the same links but a different character. The *new* successor (if it exists) is a *new* node. It inherits a copy of the old node's input links unless it has a link from the old node ($b_3$ or $b_4$). It inherits a copy of the old node's output links unless it has a link to the old node ($b_5$ or $b_6$). New network input nodes are (only) produced from network input nodes and new network output nodes are (only) produced from network output nodes. Character-based matching of network inputs and outputs ensures that the addition or removal of nodes later in development or evolution will not damage the relationships of previously adapted network inputs and outputs.

**Genetic decoding of production rules**: The genetic decoding is loosely similar to that in [10]. For every bit of the genotype, an attempt is made to read a rule that starts on that bit. A valid rule is one that starts with 11 and has enough bits after it to complete a rule.

To read a rule, the system uses the idea of 'segments'. A segment is a bit string with its odd-numbered bits ($1^{st}$, $3^{rd}$, $5^{th}$,···) all 0. Thus the reading of a segment is as follows: read the current bit; if it is a 1 then stop; else read the next bit–this is the next information bit of the segment; now start over, keeping track of the information bits of the segment. Note that a segment can

*Table 1.* The six link-details bits represented by the binary strings

| | | | | | | | | | | | | | | | | | | |
|---|---|---|---|---|---|---|---|---|---|---|---|---|---|---|---|---|---|---|
| Genotype: | 1 | 1 | 1 | 0 | 1 | 1 | 0 | 0 | 1 | 0 | | 1 | | 1 | | 1 0 1 1 0 0 |
| Decoding: | + | + | + | → | _1_ | * | _0_ | * | 0 | | 1 | | 1 | | 1 0 1 | |
| | | + | + | + | _1_ | → | _0_ | * | .0 | | 1 | | 1 | | 1 0 1 1 0 0 | |
| Rule 1: | | $P$ | | → | $S_r$ | , | $S_n$ | , | | link bits | | | | | | |
| | | Any | | → | 1 | , | 0 | , | 0 | 1 | | 1 | | 1 0 1 | | |
| Rule 2: | | | | | $P$ | → | $S_r$ | , | $S_n$ | , | | link bits | | | | |
| | | | | | 1 | → | 0 | , | 1 | 1 | | 0 | | 1 1 0 0 | | |

be empty (have 0 information bits). The full procedure to (try to) read a rule begins with reading a segment for each of the predecessor, the first successor (replacement node) and the second successor (new node). Then the six link-details bits represented by the binary strings are read, if possible. This example is represented in table 1.

## 3. Experimental Scheme

To develop and validate the method above, a simple ALife system has been created. 'Life' is a two-dimensional world of artificial organisms each of which controlled by a neural network using the developmental system above. Evolution is strictly controlled by natural selection. There are no global system rules that delete organisms; this is under their own control.

The experimental world (Figure 2) is divided into a grid of squares; usually $20 \times 20$ of them. No two individuals may be within the same square at any time. This gives the organisms a 'size' and puts a limit on their number. They are otherwise free to move around the world, within and between squares. As well as a position, each organism has a forward (facing) direction, set randomly at birth.

## Algorithm

*Initialization*
Every square in the world has an individual with a single-bit genotype '0' born into it.

*Main Loop*
In each time step (loop), every individual alive at the start of the cycle is processed once. The order in which the individuals are processed is otherwise random. These are the steps involved for each individual:

- Network inputs are updated.

- Development—one iteration.

- Update all neural activations including network outputs.

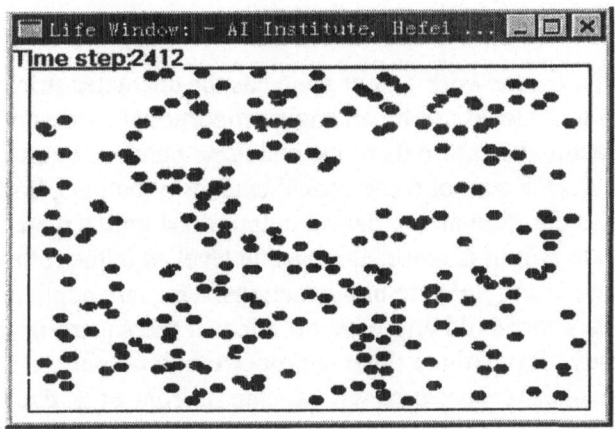

*Figure 2.* The experimental world (a two-dimensional toroidal virtual world containing autonomous organisms).

- Actions associated with certain network outputs are carried out according to those outputs. These actions are: *"reproduce"*, *"fight"*, *"turn clockwise"*, *"turn anti-clockwise"*, and *"move forward"*.

## Neural Network Details

The axiom network consists of three nodes with two excitatory links:

Network input: 001→000→01→network output

The network output node's character (01) matches reproduction. The network input node's characters(left input 01) match this, without matching any of the other action characters. Finally, the hidden node's characters neither match other node's characters or the action characters nor are matched by the other nodes' or the action characters. Development takes place throughout the individual's life, although necessary limits on the number of nodes and links are imposed.

## Interactions Between Organism and Environments

Five built-in actions are available to each organism. Each is associated with network output nodes whose characters start with a particular bit-string:

**01\***   Try to reproduce with organism in front

**100\***   Fight: Kill organism in front (if there is one)

**101\***   Turn anti-clockwise

**110\***   Turn clockwise

**111*** Move forward (if nothing in the way)

For example, if a network output node has the character string 1101001, the organism will turn clockwise by an angle proportional to the node's excitatory output. If an action has more than one matching network output node then the relevant output is the sum of these nodes' excitatory outputs, bounded by unity as within any node. If an action has no output node with a matching character, then the relevant output is noise, at the same level as in the (other) nodes.

Both *reproduce* and *fight* are binary actions. They are applied if the relevant output exceeds a threshold and have no effect if the square in front is empty. To turn and move forward are done in proportion to output.

When an organism *reproduce* with a mate in front of it, the child is placed in the square beyond the mate if that square is empty. If it is not, the child replaces the mate. An organism cannot reproduce with an individual that is fighting if this would involve replacing that individual. Reproduction involves crossover and mutation. Life's crossover always offsets the cut point in the second individual by one gene, with equal probability either way–which is why the genotype lengths vary. Mutation at reproduction is a single gene-flip(bit-flip). An organism's network input nodes have their excitatory inputs set to the weighted sum of ' matching' output nodes' excitatory outputs from other individuals in the neighborhood. If the first bit of an input node's character is 1 then the node takes its input from individuals to the right hand side (including forward-and back-right), otherwise from individuals to the left. An input node 'matches' an output node if the rest of the input node's character is the same as the start of the character of the output node. For example, an input node with character 10011 matches(only) output nodes with character's starting with 0011 in the networks of individuals to the right. Weighting is inversely proportional to the Euclidean distances between individuals. Currently the input neighborhood is a 5×5 area centered on the relevant organism.

## 4.  Experimental Results

**Kin similarity and convergence:** When two Life organisms (with networks developed from more than just a couple of production rules each) reproduce, the child's network almost always resembles a combination of the parents' networks. Examination of networks from Life's population at any time shows similarities between many of them. The population remains nearly converged, in small numbers of species, throughout the evolution. The criterion of a sufficiently correlated (implicit) fitness landscape has been met by the developmental system, making it suitable for long-term evolution.

**Emergence of increasing complexity:** Once Life has started, there is a short period while genotype lengths increase until capable of containing a production rule. For the next ten to twenty thousand time steps (in typical runs),

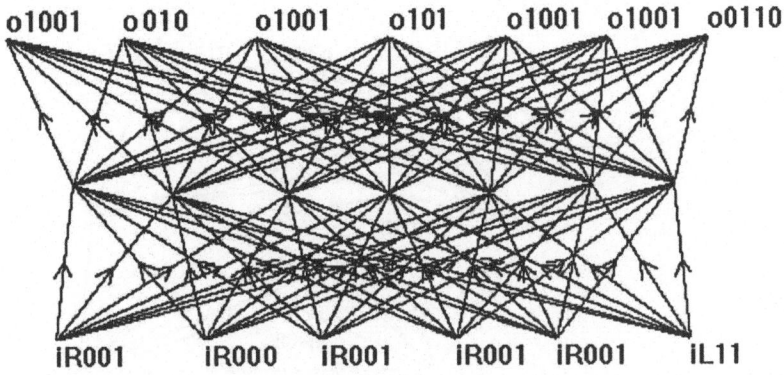

*Figure 3.*    A neural network of a dominant organism.

networks resulting in very simple strategies such as '*do everything*' and '*always go forwards and kill*' dominate the population. Some networks do better than others but not sufficiently well for them to display a dominating effects. In every run to date, the first dominant species that emerges has been one whose individuals turn in one direction while trying to fight and reproduce at the same time. Figure 3 shows an example of such an individual, after the user dragged the nodes apart to make detailed examination possible. Note the outputs o101, o01 and o100 (*turn anti-clockwise, reproduce* and *fight*). Note also the large number of links necessary to pass from inputs to outputs, and the input characters which match non-action output characters of the same network (o000, o00). Individuals of this species use nearby members, who are also turning in circles, as sources of activation (so keeping each other going).

Although this is a very simple strategy, watching it in action makes its success understandable. Imagine running around in a small circle stabbing the air in front of you. Anyone trying to attack would either have to get his timing exactly right or approach in a faster spiral–both relatively advanced strategies. These individuals also mate just before killing. The offspring (normally) appear beyond the individual being killed, away from the killer's path. Because of the success of this first dominant species, the world always has enough space for other organisms to exist. Such organisms tend not to last long; almost any movement will bring them into contact with one of the dominant organisms. Hence these organisms share some of the network morphology of the dominant species. However, they can make some progress: Individuals have emerged that are successful at turning to face the dominant species and holding their direction while trying to *kill* and *reproduce*. An example of such a 'rebel' (from the same run as Figure 3 is shown in Figure 4.

Running averages of the number of organisms reproducing and killing (Figure 5) suggest that further species emerge. However, organisms have proved

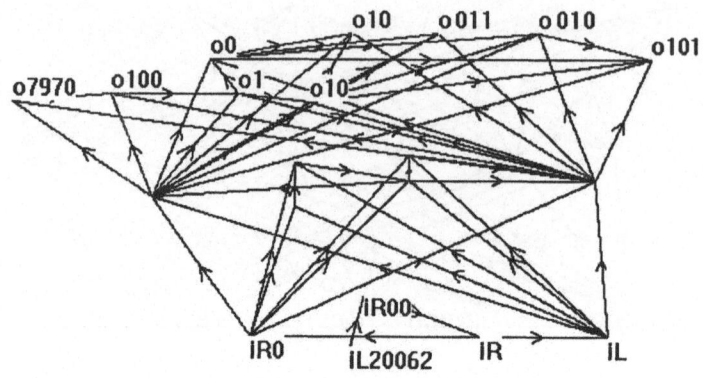

*Figure 4.* A neural network of a rebel organism.

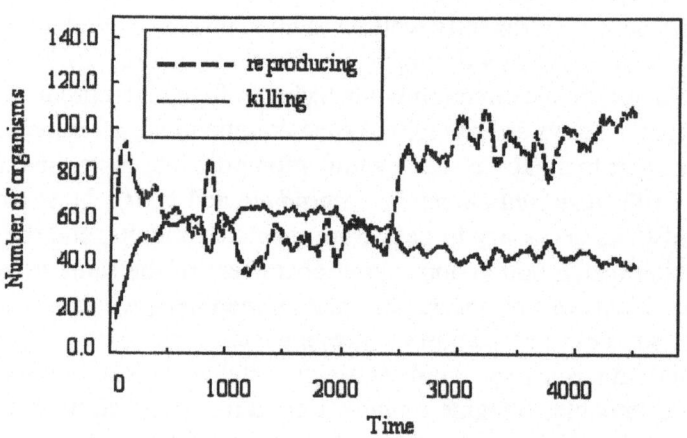

*Figure 5.* Typical running averages of the number of organisms reproducing and killing.

difficult to analyze beyond the above, even at the behavioral level. All that can currently be said is that they share characteristics of the previous species but are different.

## 5. Conclusions

The algorithm proposed in this paper is novel, feasible. Although the behaviors that emerged are very low-level, they are encouraging nonetheless, for the increases in complexity were in ways not specified by the design. It is difficult to evaluate any ongoing emergence because of the difficulty in analyzing later organisms. Either tools to aid in such analysis will have to be constructed, or a more transparent system should be created.

In work involving pure natural selection, the organisms' developmental and interaction systems are analogous to the fitness functions of conventional genetic algorithms. While the general aim involves moving away from such comparisons, the analogy is useful for recognizing how the epistasis of fitness landscape issue transfers across: Certain ontogenetic and interaction systems can result in individuals with similar genotypes but very different phenotypes. The results show that Life's developmental system does not suffer from this problem, making it suitable for long-term incremental evolution. This is a significant result for a modular developmental system.

This work has made it clear that the specification of actions, even at a low-level, results in the organisms being constrained around these actions and limits evolution. Alternatives in which the embodiment of organisms is linked to their actions that need to be further investigated.

1 The evolutionary robots can learn and integrate the visual behaviors and attention autonomously with biologically motivated visual behaviors cooperated as parallel, complementary and "highly coupled processes" in the tracking systems, simplifying the acquisition of perceptual information and system modeling and control;

2 Combining competitive coevolutionary genetic programming with evolutionary learning, and creating evolutionary robotics with advanced complex vision systems, performing more complex obstacle avoidance behavior and target approach activity;

3 Evolutionary robots can solve out problems on obstacle avoidance and target approach autonomously by self-learning environments knowledge based on competitive coevolutionary genetic programming.

## Acknowledgements

Authors would like to thank the reviewers for their helpful revising suggestions and comments.

## References

[1] Zaera N., Cliff D., and Bruten J.(1996). *Evolving collective behaviours in synthetic fish.* Proceedings of SAB96, MIT Press Bradford Books, 635–644.

[2] Ray, T. S.(1991). *An approach to the synthesis of life.* In Langton, C.; Taylor, C.; Farmer, J.; and Rasmussen, S. eds., Artificial Life II, 371–408. Redwood City, CA: Addison-Wesley.

[3] Yaeger, L.(1993). *Computational genetics, physiology, metabolism, neural systems, learning, vision, and behavior or polyworld: Life in a new context.* In Langton, C. G., ed., Artificial Life III, 263–298.

66

[4] Malrey Lee(2003). *Evolution of behaviors in autonomous robot using artificial neural network and genetic algorithm.* International Journal of Information Sciences, Vol.155, Issue 1-2, pp.43-60.

[5] Harvey, I.(1993). *Evolutionary robotics and SAGA: the case for hill crawling and tournament selection.* In Langton, C. G., ed., Artificial Life III.

[6] Koza, J. R.(1992). *Genetic Programming.* Cambridge, MA: MIT Press/Bradford Books.

[7] Gruau, F.(1996). Artificial cellular development in optimization and compilation. Technical Report, Psychology Department, Stanford University, Palo Alto, CA.

[8] Lindenmayer, A.(1968). Mathematical models for cellular interaction in development. *Journal of Theoretical Biology (Parts I and II)*, 18: 280−315.

[9] Kitano, H. (1990). Designing neural networks using genetic algorithms with graph generation system. *Complex Systems*, 4: 461−476.

[10] Boers, E. J. and Kuiper, H.(1992). Biological metaphors and the design of modular artificial neural networks. Master's thesis, Departments of Computer Science and Experimental Psychology, Leiden University.

[11] Yang, J. A. and Wang, H. Y.(2002). Research on combined behavior method for evolutionary robot based on neural network. *Journal of Shanghai Jiao Tong University*, Vol.36, Sup. pp.89−95.

[12] Wang, H. Y. and Yang, J. A.(2000). Research on evolutionary robot behavior using developmental network, *Acta Electronica Sinica*, 28(12): 41−45.

[13] Wang, H. Y., Yang, J. A. and Jiang, P.(2000). Research on evolutionary robot behavior using developmental network [J]. *Journal of Computer & Development*, 37(12): 1457−1465.

# CONTROL OF OVERHEAD CRANE BY FUZZY-PID WITH GENETIC OPTIMISATION

A. Soukkou1, A. Khellaf2, S. Leulmi1
*1Department of Electrotechnics, University of Skikda 21000, Algeria. 2Department of electronics, University Ferhat Abbas-Sétif 19000, Algeria soukkou_a@yahoo.fr; khellaf_a@yahoo.fr; leulmi_salah@yahoo.fr*

**Abstract:**    A fuzzy logic controller with the fuzzy knowledge base: scaling factors of the input/output variables, membership functions and the rules are optimized by the use of the genetic algorithms, is presented in this work, and its application in the highly nonlinear systems. The fuzzy structure is specified by a combination of the mixed Sugeno's and Mamdani's fuzzy reasoning. The mixed, binary-integer, coding is utilized to construct the chromosomes, which define the set of necessary prevailing parameters for the conception of the desired controller. This new controller stands out by a non standard gain (output scaling factor) which varies linearly with the fuzzy inputs. Under certain conditions, it becomes similar to the conventional PID controller with non-linearly variable coefficients. The results of simulation show, well, the efficiency of the proposed controller.

**Key words:**    Genetic algorithms, fuzzy controller, PID

## 1. INTRODUCTION

The control of complex systems, that are nonlinear or contains an unknown dynamics, is a difficult task. In addition, the desired performances become more and more severe. It is one of the raisons that lead to the apparition of new control methods that are more sophisticated.

The apparition of the fuzzy logic formalism [1] gave birth of a new approach, where the control laws are replaced by a set of linguistic rule, determines the control strategies and objectives. This approach requires the knowledge of the human appraisal (experience). The fuzzy systems performances depend on the exactness of the obtained knowledge's. These problems have lead to the development of hybrid systems that could unite the training capacities of the neural networks and the decision capacities of fuzzy systems. The main objective of hybrid systems is the design of fuzzy controllers with optimum parameters.

In this hybridization, the network topology is specified by the type of the inference and by the fuzzy rules used (Sugeno's or Mamdani reasoning).

The training allows us to adjust the weights of the network, that constitute the base of the fuzzy knowledge, by the minimization of a given cost function that depends on the performances and the desired control strategy.

The backpropagation, based upon the usual gradient method, suffers from convergence problems. This constitutes a constraint that degrades the efficiency degrees of the fuzzy neural controllers.

The genetic algorithms (GA), inspired from the natural genetics [2], become a powerful competitor in the parameter optimisation domain necessary for the design of optimal fuzzy controllers.

Designing an optimal fuzzy controller is, then, a selection of an optimal vector of parameters or variables that will minimize a certain cost function subject to some constraints. Then, we can expect that simultaneous use of the combined fuzzy-genetic approaches lead to the construction of a fuzzy inference system whose structural parameters (its fuzzy knowledge base) are optimized by the GA. The main objective is to exploit the effectiveness of each to build more flexible and efficient controllers.

This article is divided in two main parts:

Description of the methodology of conception of the fuzzy neural controller.

Simulation and results of the application of the new controller on an example of nonlinear systems.

## 2.    METHODOLOGY OF CONCEPTION

Mamdani's and Sugeno's models are the basis of the majority of the fuzzy controllers used in the literature of the domain of the fuzzy logic control. The main difference between the two reasonings resides in the way of assessment of the consequences of the fuzzy rules. In the method of Mamdani [3-4], every rule is represented by a conjunction (MIN) and the aggregation of the rules by a disjunction (MAX). In this model, the consequences are independent of the controller's entries. The link between the conditions and the actions is achieved, solely, by operators.

Takagi-Sugeno and Kang [5] proposed a model to develop a systematic approach for a generation of fuzzy rules from the data set of input-output (I/O). A rule of this type has the following shape:

$$Ri: IF\ (x_1\ is\ A_{1i})\ AND\ ...\ AND\ (x_m\ is\ A_{mi})\ THEN$$
$$Y_i = F_i\ (x_1,\ x_2,\ ...,\ x_m) \tag{1}$$

Generally $F_i(-)$ possesses a polynomial form of $x_1, x_2,...$ and $x_m$.

$$F_i(x_1,...,x_m) = a_{0i} + a_{1i}x_1 + ... + a_{mi}x_m \tag{2}$$

This form is called the model of Sugeno of order one. In some cases, $F_i(-)$ must be constant (Sugeno of order zero). The determination of the coefficients of the consequences must be made by a parametric identification method [6].

The methods of defuzzification adapted to this form of rules are based on the approach: *Defuzzify Without Combining (DWC)*. The more used is the one weighted-average defuzzification, given by:

$$y = \frac{\sum_{i=1}^{M} \mu_i F_i(x_1, x_2,..., x_m)}{\sum_{i=1}^{M} \mu_i} \tag{3}$$

Where M is the number of the rules and μi is the degree of activation of the ith rule calculated either by the operator of conjunction (MIN) or the arithmetic product.

$$\mu_i = \mu_i(x_1) \times \mu_i(x_2) \times \mu_i(x_3)....\times \mu_i(x_m) \tag{4}$$
$$\mu_i = MIN(\mu_i(x_1), \mu_i(x_2), \mu_i(x_3),...., \mu_i(x_m))$$

The simplicity and the reduced execution time present two advantages of the Sugeno's approach. Its simplicity of implementation has attractes the attention of several researchers [7-8]. The main goal is to develop new technics to reduce the number of parameters of the consequences that burdens the Sugeno's method.

Hao Ying [9] proposed an analytical method of treatment of the Sugeno controller's. The output polynomials are proportional one of the other. While introducing some modifications to the level of the form of the rules, one gets:

$$R_1 : IF\ (x_1\ is\ A_{11})\ AND\ ...\ AND\ (x_m\ is\ A_{1m})\ THEN$$
$$f_1 = R_1 f(x_1,...,x_m)$$
$$R_2 : IF\ (x_1\ is\ A_{21})\ AND\ ...\ AND\ (x_m\ is\ A_{2m})\ THEN$$
$$f_2 = R_2 f(x_1,...,x_m)$$

$$\vdots \qquad (5)$$

$$R_M : IF\ (x_1\ is\ A_{M1})\ AND\ ...\ AND\ (x_m\ is\ A_{Mm})\ THEN$$
$$f_M = R_M f(x_1,...,x_m)$$

Where,

$$f(x_1,...,x_m) = a_0 + a_1 x_1 + ... + a_m x_m \qquad (6)$$

Using the weighted-average defuzzification method, the digital output for a set of entries $x_1, x_2, ...$ and $x_m$ is given by:

$$U = \frac{\sum_{i=1}^{M} \mu_i f_i}{\sum_{i=1}^{M} \mu_i} = \frac{\sum_{i=1}^{M} \mu_i R_i}{\sum_{i=1}^{M} \mu_i} \cdot f(x_1,...,x_m) \qquad (7)$$

Where M is the number of the rules and $\mu_i$ is the degree of activation of the $i^{th}$ rule calculated either by the operator of conjunction (MIN) or the arithmetic product. $R_i$ represents the center of gravity of the fuzzy set output (singleton) of the $i^{th}$ rule.

Under the vectorial form:

$$\vec{R} = (R_1, R_2, R_3,...,R_M)\ ;\ \vec{\mu} = (\mu_1, \mu_2, \mu_3,...,\mu_n)\ ;\ \vec{x} = (x_1, x_2, x_3,...,x_n)$$

The expression (7) becomes:

$$U = G(\vec{x}, \vec{\mu}, \vec{R}) f(\vec{x}) \qquad (8)$$

Where,

$$G(\vec{x}, \vec{\mu}, \vec{R}) = \frac{\sum_{i=1}^{M} \mu_i R_i}{\sum_{i=1}^{M} \mu_i} \qquad (9)$$

The expression $a_0+a_1x_1+ ... +a_mx_m$ represents an association of the linear controllers, which contain the linear PID controller as a special case ($a_0 = 0$). The following three-input variables are used by the discrete-time PID control in incremental form:

$$x_1(n)= y_r(n)- y(n) \; ; \; x_2(n)= x_1(n)- x_1(n-1); \; x_3(n)= x_2(n)- x_2(n-1)$$

Where $y_r(n)$ and $y(n)$ are a set-point/reference signal for process output and the process output at sampling time $n$, respectively.

According to data of the problem to treat, the output variable can be the action of control or its variation. It is sometimes discriminating to formulate the rules of inference so that the response signal intervenes like increment of the control signal between the instants $n$ and $n-1$:

$$U(n)= U(n-1)+\Delta U(n) \tag{10}$$

With respects of the saturation regions:

$$U_{min} \leq U(n) \leq U_{max} \tag{11}$$

The increment permits to introduce an integral behaviour to the global controller level. In the rest of this paper, we denote the output and the change in output as $U(n)$ and $\Delta U(n)$ at time $n$, respectively.

In the case of the direct action control, the controller's output form will be given by:

$$\begin{aligned} U(n) &= G(\vec{x}, \vec{\mu}, \vec{R})f(\vec{x}) = G(-)(K_{OP} x_1(n)+ K_{OD} x_2(n)) \\ &= (G(-)K_{OP})x_1(n)+ (G(-)K_{OD})x_2(n) \end{aligned} \tag{12}$$

The law of PD controller in its incremental or discreet form is given by:

$$U_{PD}(n)= \overline{K_P} \; x_1(n)+ \overline{K_D} \; x_2(n) \tag{13}$$

Where, $\overline{K_P}$ and $\overline{K_D}$ are constant gains named proportional-gain, and derivative-gain, respectively. It returns the controller equivalent to a PD with gains $K_P$ and $K_D$ variables and non-linear, since the output of a fuzzy system is non-linear in relation to these entries.

$$\overline{K_P} \rightarrow G(-)K_{OP} \; ; \; \overline{K_D} \rightarrow G(-)K_{OD}$$

In the case of the control variation, the output controller's will be:

$$\Delta U(n) = G(-)(a_1 x_1(n) + a_2 x_2(n) + a_3 x_3(n)) \qquad (14)$$

By analogy with a PI and a PID in the discrete-time form, the control variation is:

$$\Delta U_{PI}(n) = \overline{K_P}\, x_2(n) + \overline{K_I}\, x_1(n) \qquad (15)$$

$$\Delta U_{PID}(n) = \overline{K_P}\, x_2(n) + \overline{K_I}\, x_1(n) + \overline{K_D}\, x_3(n) \qquad (16)$$

The relation (14) can write itself as follows:

$$\Delta U(n) = (a_1 G(-))\, x_1(n) + (a_2 G(-))\, x_2(n) + (a_3 G(-))\, x_3(n) \qquad (17)$$

This last is similar to the one of the expression (16), only the constant gains $K_P$, $K_I$ and $K_D$ are replaced by nonlinear factors: $(a_2.G(-))$, $(a_1.G(-))$ et $(a_3.G(-))$, respectively.

Generally, the control of the complex systems by a PID presents a delicate task. The solution of the problem comes back to choose or to develop an efficient method for the determination of the gains of different actions, or the combination of the PID with other more sophisticated methods very adapted to the complexity and to the nature of the industrial processes.

The controller so developed presents a way of this hybridization, whose goal is to take advantage on the one hand of the precision of the mathematical model of the PID, on the other hand, of the suppleness of the elements manipulated by the fuzzy logic. What drives to the realization of a fuzzy controller to one degree of autonomy.

## 3.    CONTROL STRUCTURE

Figure 1 shows the structure of the command system that contains four blocks:
- Optimization block characterized by GA.
- Structural block representing the fuzzy controller.
- Decisions block defining the performances criteria.
- System block to be controlled.

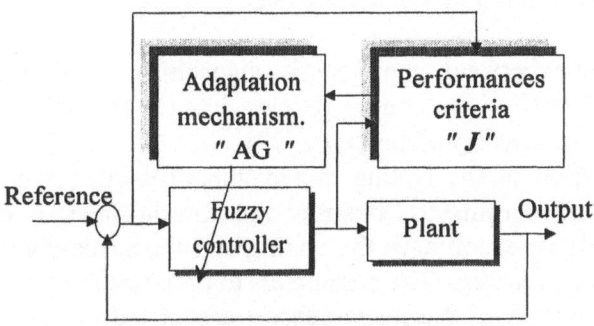

*Figure 1*. Control structure.

The interaction between these four blocks is summarized by the flow chart represented by figure 2.

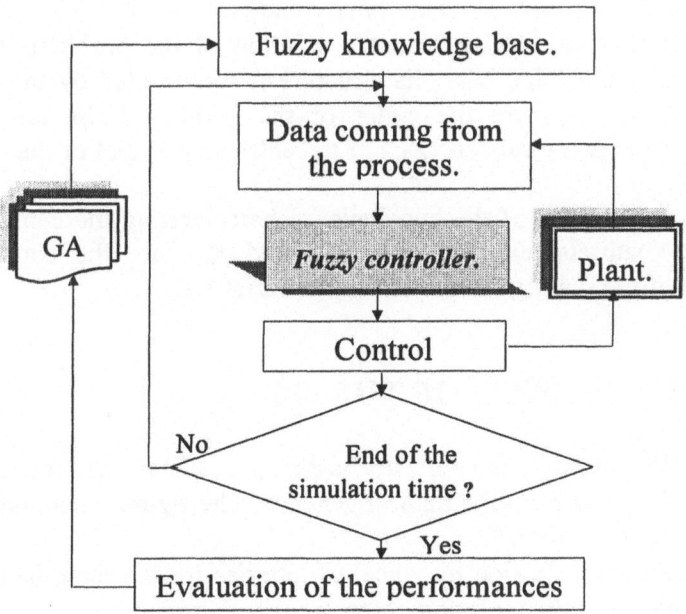

*Figure 2*. Interaction between the different blocks of the control structure.

## 4.    PARAMETERS CODING

The difference between the genetic algorithms used in the literature resides to the levels of the coding (binary, integer or real) and the genetic operators adapted to every coding type [13].

The introduction of the coding mixed, binary-integer, multiparametered and concatenated permits to construct the chromosome of the GA. This technique allows or encourages the coding and the successive juxtaposition of the different parameters. The parameters to optimize are:

- The widths of the fuzzy subsets associated to the spaces of I/O, binary-coded.
- The rules or the centers of the fuzzy subsets of the consequences are coded in integer. Every center is coded by a number included between 1 and the maximal number N of the fuzzy subsets of the output space [10-12].
- The coefficients $K_{XI}$, $K_{X2}$, $K_{OP}$, $K_{OI}$ and $K_{OD}$, associated to the scaling factors of I/O are binary-coded.

Every chromosome can represent a solution of the problem, that is, a fuzzy optimal knowledge base. Its structure is represented by the figure 3. $L_{ZEX1}$, $L_{ZEX2}$ and $L_{ZEU}$ are the codes of the widths of the universes of discourses of the fuzzy subsets (ZE) of the entries $x_1$, $x_2$ and of the output $U$, respectively.

The $R_i$ are the codes of the conclusions characterizing the centers of the output fuzzy subsets and $K_{XI}$, $K_{X2}$, $K_{OP}$ and $K_{OD}$ are the codes of the coefficients of the scaling factors of the I/O variables.

## 5.    MECHANISM OF THE GA

The genetic algorithms are stochastic procedures of research and exploration, inspired from the natural genetics. The figure 4 summarizes the principle of the standard GA.

The GA uses the selection by wheel of lotteries for the reproduction, two points crossover and the mutation operators.

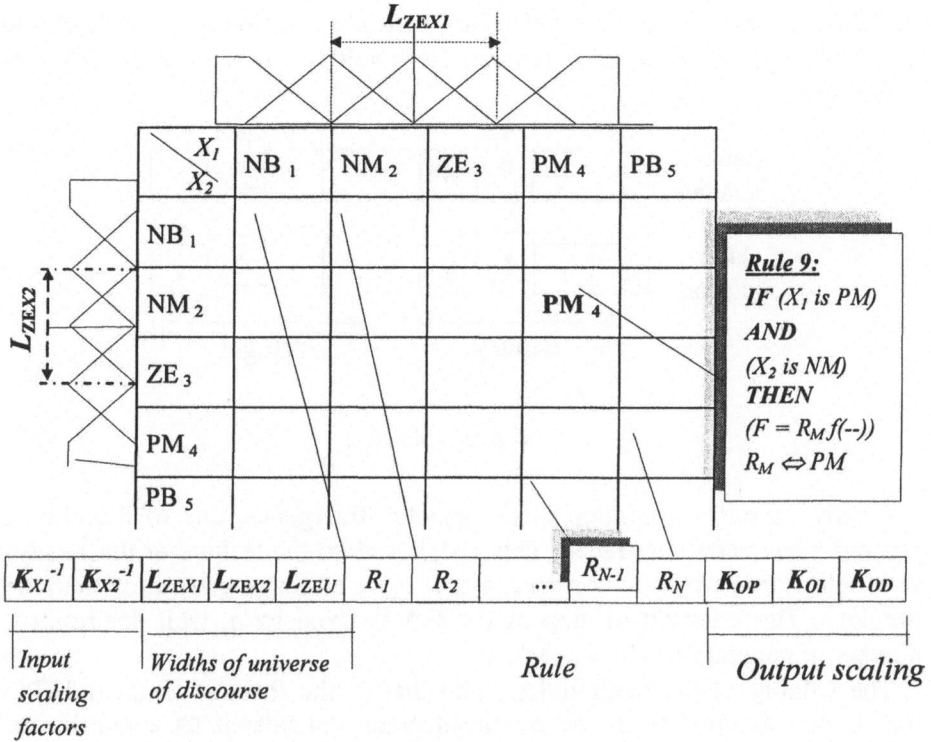

*Figure 3.* Structure of the chromosome.

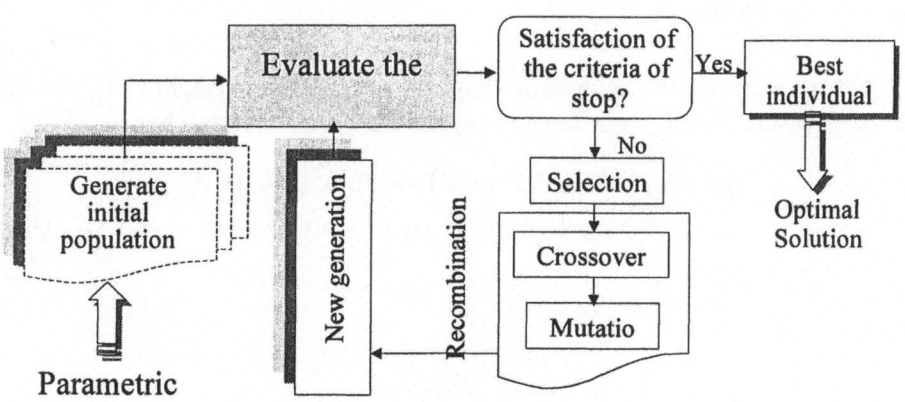

*Figure 4.* Execution process of the GA.

If the mutation, takes place in the binary-coded part, the operator of mutation has the same principle that the one of the standard mutation. If the mutation takes place in the integer part, instead of changing a 1 in 0 or 0 in 1, we change the allele by a random from value 1 to N different from its actual value.

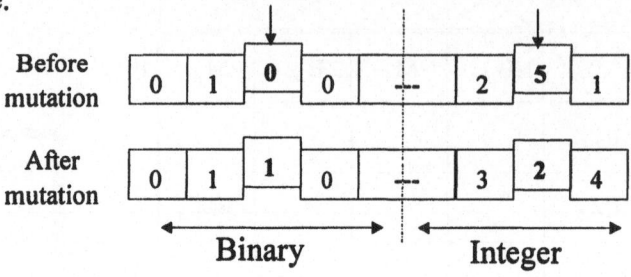

*Figure 5.* Mutation.

Finally, to put a limitation to the genetic divergence, one of the elitism strategies has been introduced. This last, based on the technic of the steady-state selection, permits to construct a new more effective generation than the previous. The criterion of stop of the GA is fixed by a, well determined, number of generations (Max-Gen).

The validity of the methodology and that of the form of command (PD non linear) are tested on the overhead crane considered as a non-linear, single input / multi-output system (SIMO).

## 6.    SIMULATION

Figure 6 shows the schematic diagram of the crane system [14], as well as its structure. The dynamics of the system are characterized by:

$$
\begin{aligned}
(m_1 + m_2)\ddot{x} + m_2 L\ddot{\theta}\cos(\theta) - m_2 L\dot{\theta}^2\sin(\theta) &= F \\
m_2 L^2\ddot{\theta} + m_2 L\ddot{x}\cos(\theta) + m_2 gL\sin(\theta) &= 0
\end{aligned}
\tag{18}
$$

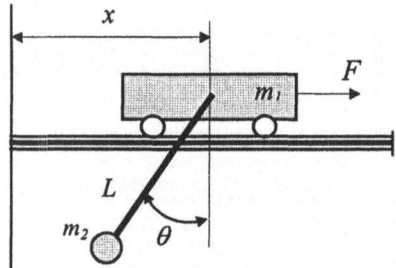

*Figure 6.* Overhead crane structure.

Where, $m_1$, $m_2$, $x$, $L$, $\theta$ and F are the mass of the wagon, load mass, crane position, the angle of the segment in respect to the vertical axis, and driving force, respectively. The numerical used data in the simulation are: $L = 1m$, $m_1 = 1kg$, $m_2 = 1kg$, $g = 9.8m/s^2$.

The objective of the control is to generate a sequences of actions $F$(in Newton) permitting to consolidate the system in a desired state from a predetermined initial state.

The overhead crane system has four state variables $(x, \dot{x}, \theta, \dot{\theta})$. If the fuzzy controller has $N$ inputs, there will be $M^N$ items of rules even if every variable has $M$ fuzzy subsets. It becomes difficult to design the fuzzy controller. The solution is to divide the system in sub-systems.

Liu Diantong in [14] proposed one controller with two fuzzy sub-controllers: displacement fuzzy controller is used to control load displacement and anti-swing fuzzy controller is used to damp load swing. Figure 7 is the schematic diagram of the control system.

The adapted chromosome structure for this system has the same form of the figure 3, but doubled. A part for $FLC_1$ and the other for $FLC_2$. The control system will be the superposition of the two outlays of the two controllers.

In this application the objective function responsible for the ordering of the chromosomes in the population is:

$$F_{it} = \left(1 + \sum_{k=1}^{500} \left(10^{-4}|x_{err}(k)| + 10^{-4}|\theta_{err}(k)| + 10^{-5}|F(k)|\right)\right)^{-1} \quad (19)$$

The controller thus developed ($FLC_1$, $FLC_2$) for this application is characterized by: (5×5×5, 5×5×5), i.e., five fuzzy subsets for each I/O variables. What gives to the total 25×2 rules.

Every chain of the population will contain 95×2 alleles (10 bits for each of the widths of the universe of discourses, 25×2 integers for the rules and 10 bits for every coefficient of the gains). The parameters of the GA are presented in table 1.

*Tab 1.* Parameters of the GA.

| Parameter | Value |
|---|---|
| The size of the population. | 40 |
| The probability of mutation. | 0.03 |
| The crossover probability. | 0.8 |
| The maximal number of generation. | 500 |

- The parameters, $K_{X1}$ and $K_{X2} \in [5, 40]$, $K_{OP}$ and $K_{OD} \in [1, 500]$.

The initial conditions used in this simulation are: $\left(x, \dot{x}, \theta, \dot{\theta}\right) = \left(10m, 0m/\text{sec}, 30^0, 0^0/\text{sec}\right)$.

Figure 8 indicates the evolution of the objective function. The rule base gotten at the end of execution of the GA is:

( *511114455524135213121313115 , 43351335245422133512345* )

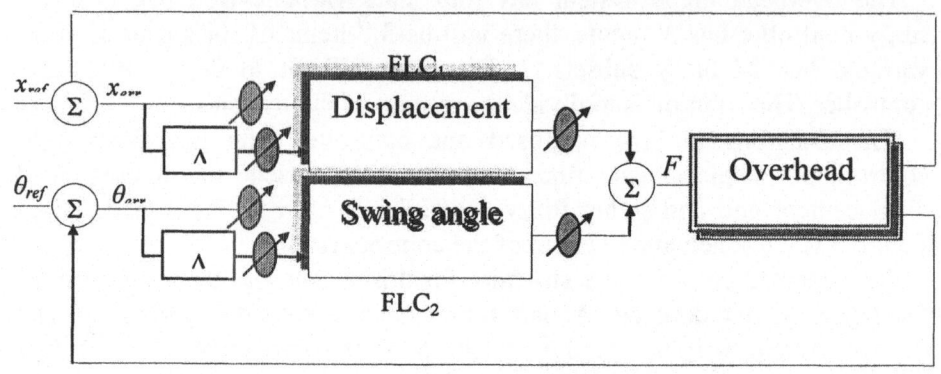

*Figure 7*. Schematic diagram of the control

*Figure 8*. Evolution of the objective function.

Simulation results from initial state (10, 0, 30, 0) to target state (10, 0, 0, 0) are shown in figure 9. The generated force is presented by the figure 10.

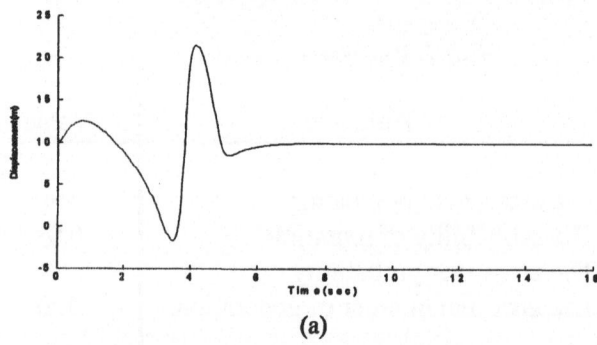

(a)

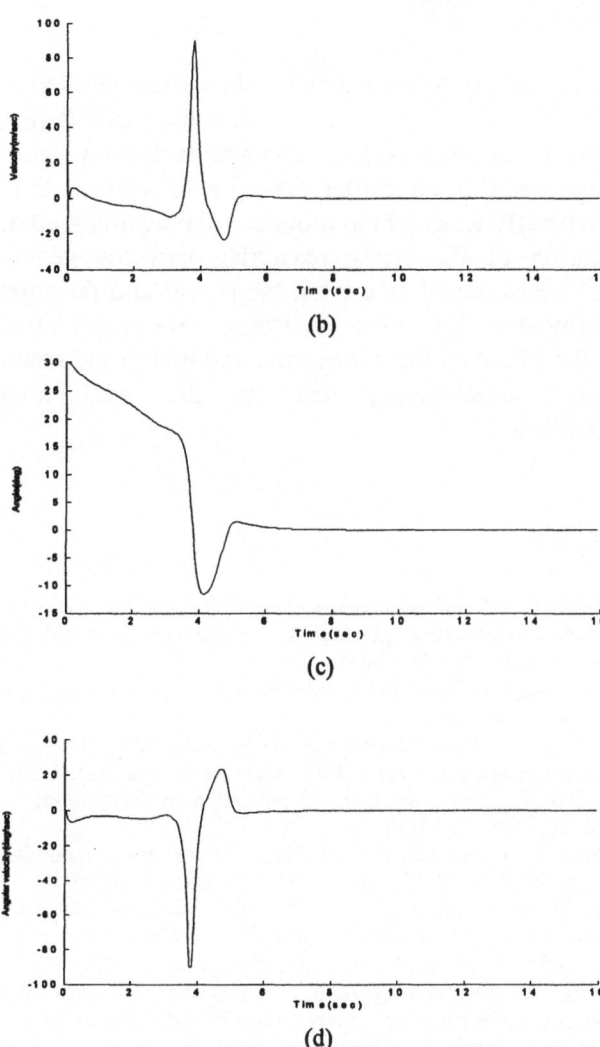

*Figure 9.* Evolution of the state variables.

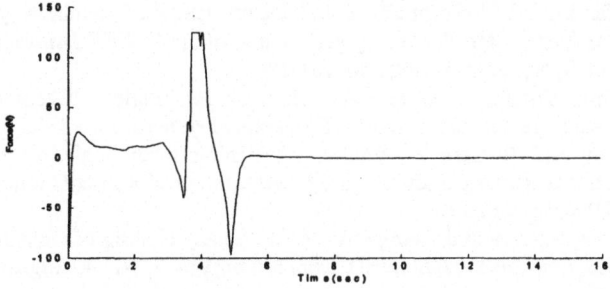

*Figure 10.* Output control.

## 7.    CONCLUSION

In this work, the proposed controller has been applied to control the overhead crane system. The efficiency of this approach is measured by the controller's capacity to bring back the crane to its desired state.

One can say that this controller manages to achieve the desired task, which justifies the efficiency of the proposed conception method.

The association of the fuzzy reasoning and the genetic algorithms constitute an efficient means to exploit the power and the suppleness of the elements manipulated by these different procedures and approaches intervening in the phase of the conception and add to the resulted controller an «intelligent" functionality that is the goal aimed by the intelligent controllers.

## REFERENCES

[1] L. A. Zadeh, "Fuzzy sets", *Information and Control*, Vol. 8, 1965, pp. 338-353.

[2] David E. Goldberg, *'Algorithmes génétiques: exploration, optimisation et apprentissage automatique'*, Addison-Wesley, 1994.

[3] Mamdani, E. H., "Application of fuzzy algorithms for simple dynamic plant", *Proc. IEE*, D-121, 1974, pp. 1558-1588.

[4] Mamdani, E. H., and Assilian, "An experiment in linguistic synthesis with a fuzzy logic controller", *International Journal of Man- Machine Studies*, Vol. 7, 1975, pp. 1-13.

[5] M. Sugeno and G. T. Kang, "Structure identification of fuzzy model", *Fuzzy sets and systems*, Vol. 28, 1988, pp.15-33.

[6] Jhy-Shing Roger Jang and Chuen-Tsai Sun, "Neuro fuzzy modeling and control", *Proceedings of the IEEE*, Vol. 83, No. 3, March 1995, pp. 378-406.

[7] X. W. Yan, Z. D. Deng and Z. Q. Sun, "Genetic Takagi-Sugeno-fuzzy reinforcement learning", *Proceeding of the 2001 IEEE, International Symposium On Intelligent Control*, September 5-7, 2001, Mexico city, Mexico, pp. 67-72.

[8] Chia-Feng Juang and Yuan-Chang Liou, "A TSK-type recurrent fuzzy network for dynamic systems processing via supervised and reinforcement learning", *2001 IEEE International Fuzzy Systems Conference*, pp. 240-243.

[9] Hao Ying, "Constructing nonlinear variable gain controllers via the Takagi-Sugeno fuzzy control", *IEEE Transactions On Fuzzy Systems*, Vol. 6, No. 2, May 1998, pp. 226-234.

[10] A. Homaifar and Ed McCormick, "Simultaneous design of membership functions and rules sets for fuzzy controllers using genetic algorithms", *IEEE Transactions On Fuzzy Systems*, Vol. 3, No. 2, May 1995, pp. 161-176.

[11] Jinwoo Kim, Yoonkeon Moon, and Bernard P. Zeigler, "Designing fuzzy net controllers using genetic algorithms", *IEEE control systems*, June 1995, pp. 66-72.

[12] Jinwoo Kim, and Bernard P. Zeigler, "Designing fuzzy logic controllers using a multiresolutional search paradigm", *IEEE Transactions On Fuzzy Systems*, Vol. 4, No. 3, August 1996, pp. 213-226.

[13] Sanjay Kumar Sharma and George W. Irwin, "Fuzzy Coding of Genetic Algorithms", *IEEE Transactions on Evolutionary Computation*, Vol. 7, No. 4, August 2003, pp 344-355.

[14] Liu Diantong, YI Jianqiang, TAN Min, "Proposal of GA-based two-stage fuzzy control of overhead crane", *Proceeding of IEEE TENCON'02*, 2002, pp. 1721-1724.

# CREATIVE DESIGN OF FUZZY LOGIC CONTROLLER

Lotfi Hamrouni, Adel M. Alimi
*REGIM: Research Group on Intelligent Machines, University of Sfax, ENIS, Tunisia.*
*lotfi.hamrouni@hotpop.com , adel.alimi@ieee.org*

**Abstract:** The present paper proposes a novel idea used to conceive a proper fuzzy logic controller for an industrial application. Generally, the design of fuzzy logic controller is treated as numerical optimisation problem. Genetic algorithms and neural networks are the main techniques used to adjust the values of fuzzy logic controller parameters. The majority of approaches start with an empty fuzzy logic controller, having default parameters, and make improvement over the previous one. This operation is not really a design activity; it's better called a learning process. In this work we regard the conception of a fuzzy logic controller as creative designing problem. We import from AI-creative-design community three methods: decomposition, co-evolution and emergence; we apply these techniques to combine elementary components in order to generate a fuzzy logic controller.

**Key words:** Fuzzy Logic Controller, Artificial Intelligence, Creative Designing.

## 1.  INTRODUCTION

As we attempt to solve real-world problems, we realize that they are typically ill-defined systems, difficult to model and with large-scale solutions spaces.   In these cases precise models are impractical, too expensive, or non-existent. The relevant available information is usually in the form of empirical prior knowledge and input-output data representing instances of the system's behavior. Therefore, we need approximate reasoning systems capable of handling such imperfect information.

In an industrial textile company called SITEX, for example, we have to develop a fuzzy logic controller (FLC) to control the color shading (nuance) of yarns to produce denims with specific shading. The shading of the denims is the change in appearance due to the color, the distortion and the orientation of the yarns. The shading is basically a difference in light reflection not a change in color or hue, therefore quantitative evaluation of the correlation between the shading of the yarns and the shading of the fabrics is virtually impossible to achieve. In addition, the available parameters of this problem do not define the solution directly; they define a set of components from which the solution is constructed. The only available parameters are: the shading of the yarns, the recipe of the washing and the shading of the fabrics.

Manually designing an FLC to satisfy such requirements is difficult if not impossible to do. Instead, we used to apply two professional learning methods: ANFIS and FuzzyTech [11][12] . Unfortunately, the results are not satisfied. We guess that the system is highly ill-defined.

In the next we propose our experience considering a fuzzy system as a creative object. We explain shortly three techniques used to model the creative design phenomena. Section two deals with the general model of co-evolution process in design, section three explains the hierarchical decomposition of an FLC, section four presents the computational modeling of emergence, section five presents the co-evolution of fuzzy logic controller and finally a conclusion.


## 2.      FRAMEWORK OF CO-EVOLUTIONARY DESIGN

The AI-Design community regards the design as a state-space search where problem leads to solution. To be more practical, there are many versions of solution generated during the course of design, where each current one is, in general, an improvement over the previous one. This kind of synthesis of solutions can be viewed as an evolutionary system over time.

In effect, this simplified view faces a lot of challenges: (1) evolutionary design systems explore new ways to construct solutions by changing the relationships between components; (2) It can vary the dimensionality of the space by adding and removing elements; (3) It can explore alternatives instead of optimising a single option. However, the major criticism is on the assumption that the problem "or fitness function" is defined once-and-for-all. This is definitely not true for design. The central principle behind the opposing views is that design should be considered as an iterative process where there is interplay between fitness reformulation and solution generation. The evolution of both the solution and the fitness lead to the so-called co-evolutionary design (figure 1).

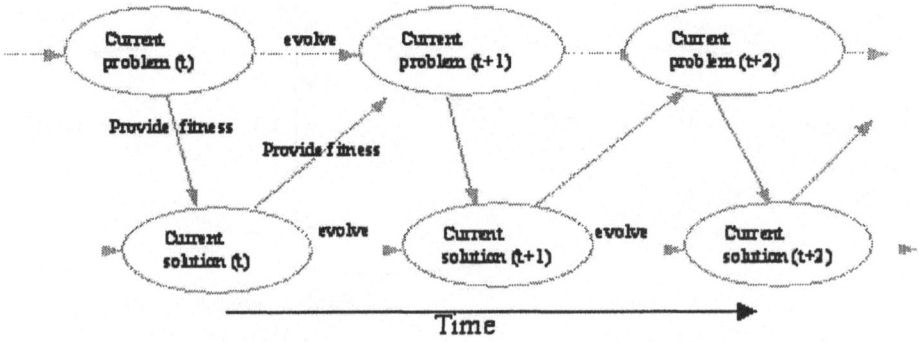

*Figure 1.* General framework of co-evolutionary design

## 3. EMERGENCE IN CREATIVE DESIGN

Emergence is another issue that recently drawn the attention of research workers in the *design community*, e.g. Gero & Yan [13], Gero, Damski & Jun [14], Edmonds & Soufi [15] etc. It is an important research issue in biology as well as in creative design. The definitions offered from the *design community* are usually applied to shape only. Hence, attempts are made to borrow definitions of emergence from other research communities to enrich our understanding. Since the *ALife* (Artificial Life) research community has also put emergence high on its research agenda.

Emergence is defined as a recognition of collective phenomena resulting from local interactions of low level units. A complex evolving representation can thus be classified as an emergent representation. In general, the methods of Gero & Schnier [16] do not specify whether the evolving representation is structure or behaviour. In figure 2, we consider the evolution of the two first level.

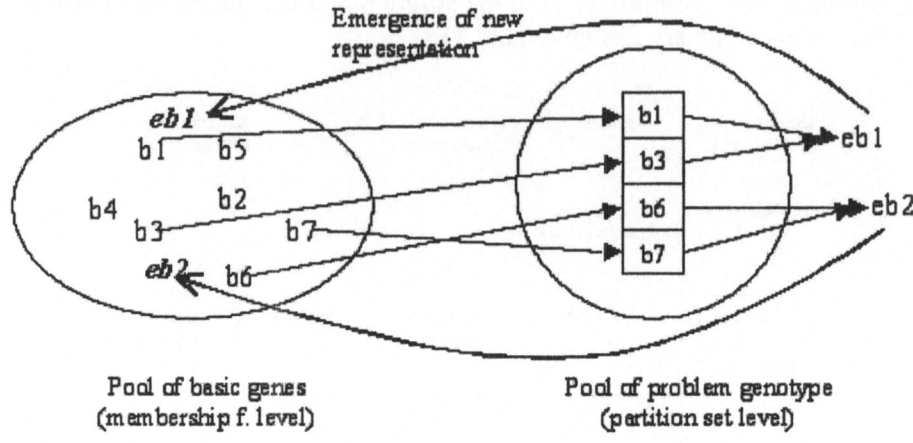

Pool of basic genes                                        Pool of problem genotype
(membership f. level)                                      (partition set level)

*Figure 2.* Direct application of evolving representation  (Emergence in level 1 and 2)

## 4.    HIERARCHICAL DECOMPOSITION OF FUZZY LOGIC CONTROLLER

Another important agenda follow, which is the decomposition of one problem into hierarchical structure, Simon [9] points out that it is only possible for complex organisms to evolve if their structure is organised hierarchically. Indeed, the generation of an object can be achieved through the recursive generation of its components until a level is reached where the generation becomes one of generating an element which is composed of basic units (Figure 2). The advantages of such a hierarchical approach are that only those factors relevant to the design of that component are considered and factors relevant to the relationships between components are treated at their assembly level. According to the evolutionary design process model offered by Gero [10], each two successive levels in the hierarchy can be considered as two state-spaces (solution-space and problem-space), the solution space can be considered to contain structure elements where the design process is to search the right combination of structure elements to satisfy the required behaviour. Co-evolutionary design process is suitably applied to model this problem design exploration; this is graphically illustrated in section 5.

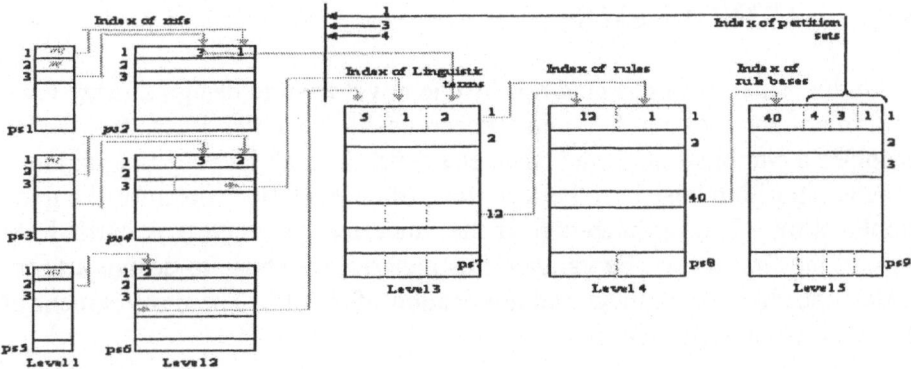

*Figure 3.* Multi-level decomposition of three variable fuzzy logic controller  (combination and propagation)

## 5.  CO-EVOLUTIONARY DESIGN OF FUZZY LOGIC CONTROLLER

The previous co-evolution model is applied to evolve the five levels of the decomposed FLC.

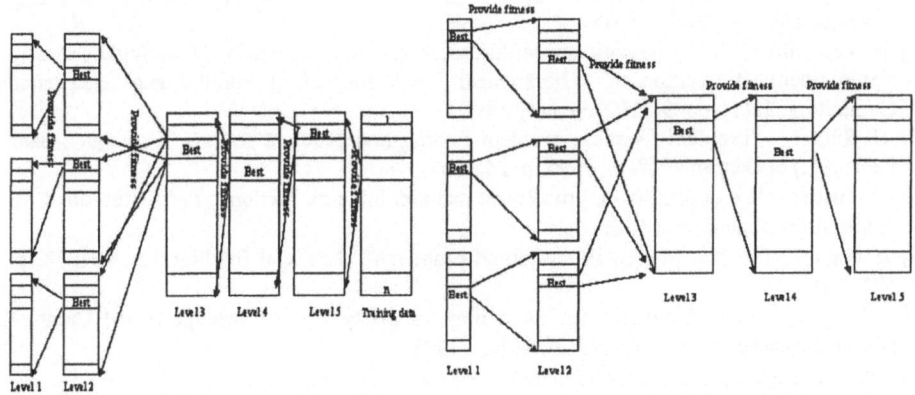

*Figure 4.* "Problem leads to Solution" or synthesis

*Figure 5.* "Solution refocuses the Problem" or reformulation

## 6.      CONCLUSION

In this paper, we presented briefly one novel form to design a fuzzy logic controller. By making the good decomposition of the FLC, the design becomes a combination of the basic elements. In each level of abstraction, a genetic algorithm based on the technique of co-evolution looks for the good combination. The optimization of the numerical parameters is carried out only in the first level. To validate this method, we chose to design a fuzzy logic controller for an industrial application of textile. The development of this application is in progress.

## REFERENCES

[1] S. Mitra and Y. Hayashi, "Neuro-fuzzy rule generation: survey in soft computing framework," IEEE Transactions on Neural Networks, Vol. 11, 2000, pp. 748-768.

[2] M. M. Gupta and D. H. Rao, "On the principles of fuzzy neural networks," Fuzzy Sets and Systems, Vol. 61, 1994, pp. 1-18.

[3] C. Karr, "Genetic algorithms for fuzzy controllers," AI Expert, Vol. 6, 1991, pp.26-33.

[4] C. L. Karr and E. J. Gentry, "Fuzzy control of pH using genetic algorithms," IEEE Transaction on Fuzzy Systems, Vol. 1, 1993, pp. 46-53.

[5] M. Regattieri Delgado, F. Von Zuben, and F. Gomide. "Hierarchical Genetic Fuzzy Systems". Information Sciences - Special Issue on Recent Advances in Genetic Fuzzy Systems, 136(1-4):29-52, 2001.

[6] Jinwoo Kim – "A Framework for Multiresolution Optimization in a Parallel/Distributed Environment: Simulation of Hierarchical GAs" Journal of Parallel and Distributed Computing, 32(1), pp. 90-102, January 1996.

[7] H. Simon – "Problem forming, problem finding and problem solving in design", dans Collen(A.) et Gasparski (W), , 1995, p. 245-257.

[8] M. Fustier – 'La résolution de problèmes: méthodologie de l'action' , Paris, Editions ESF et Librairies Techniques, 1989.

[9] H. Simon "The structure of ill structured problems", Artificial Intelligence, 4, 1973, p. 181- 201.

[10] Gero, J. S. and Maher, M. L. "Modeling Creativity and Knowledge-Based Creative Design", Lawrence Erlbaum, Hillsdale, NJ. (1993)

[11] Inform Software Corp., fuzzy-TECH User's Manual, 1996.

[12] Jyh-Shing Roger Jang "ANFIS: Adaptive-Network-Based Fuzzy Inference System", IEEE Transactions on Systems, Man, and Cybernetics 1993

[13] Gero, J. & Yan, M. (1994). Shape emergence by symbolic reasoning, Environment and Planning B: Planning and Design 21: 191–218.

[14] Gero, J., Damski, J. & Jun, H. (1995). Emergence in caad systems, in M. Tan & R. Teh (eds), The Global Design Studio, Centre for Advanced Studies of Architecture, National University of Singapore, pp. 423–438.

[15] Edmonds, E. & Soufi, B. (1992). The computational modelling of emergent shapes in design, in J. S. Gero & F. Sudweeks (eds), pp. 173–189.

[16] Gero, J. & Schnier, T. (1995). Evolving representation of design cases and their use in creative design, in J. Gero & F. Sudweeks (eds), pp. 343–368.

# ON-LINE EXTRACTION OF FUZZY RULES IN A WASTEWATER TREATMENT PLANT

J. Victor Ramos[1,3], C. Gonçalves[2] and A. Dourado[3]

*[1]School of Technology and Management, Polytechnic Institute of Leiria; Morro do Lena – Alto do Vieiro, 2411-901 Leiria, Portugal; [2]Soporcel – Sociedade Portuguesa de Papel, S.A., Apartado 5 – Lavos, 3081-851 Figueira da Foz, Portugal; [3]Adaptive Computation Group – CISUC, Departamento de Engenharia Informática; Pólo II –Universidade de Coimbra, 3030-290 Coimbra, Portugal*

**Abstract:**     Fuzzy systems have an important role in knowledge extraction from the huge amount of data acquired by the industrial distributed computer control systems. The paper presents a work concerning the building of a computational model of the WasteWater Treatment Plant (WWTP) in Soporcel mill (pulp and paper). Clustering of data is developed and from clusters a set of fuzzy rules describing the process behaviour is obtained, building up simple and applicable models with reasonable accuracy. Due to the time-varying dynamics of the process, on-line learning algorithms are necessary. Evolving Takagi-Sugeno (eTS) fuzzy models are used to predict the pH values in the plant. The approach is based on an on-line learning algorithm that recursively develops the model structure and parameters during the operation of the process. Results for the second stage of the effluent neutralization process are presented and, despite the complexity, non-linear characteristics and time-varying dynamics of the process, the results show that the eTS fuzzy models are computationally very efficient and have practical relevance.

**Key words:**     On-line learning; TS fuzzy models; eTS fuzzy models; subtractive clustering algorithm; recursive fuzzy clustering; pulp and paper industry.

## 1.     INTRODUCTION

Modern information technology allows the collection, store and analysis of huge amounts of data that can be used to construct models. Each day more decisions are made based on the analysis of data; however exploiting the information contained in database systems in an intelligent way turns out to be fairly difficult since there is a lack of tools to transform data into useful information and knowledge.

Several methods and tools are used in intelligent data analysis, including soft computing techniques. Fuzzy systems can be used to create accurate predictive models from data but it is also important that these models should be interpretable and therefore useful to describe in words the underlying data in order to support efficiently the human decision process (Setnes, 2001).

Construction of a computational model for the WWTP presents several difficulties and in the absence of a first-principles model, fuzzy modelling, and particularly Takagi-Sugeno (TS) fuzzy models, seems to be the most appropriate approach. TS fuzzy models provide a powerful tool for modelling complex nonlinear systems because of its representational power, possibility of using learning algorithms to identify its parameters, gain insights into the local behaviour of the sub-models and its interpretability (Yen et al., 1998).

A variety of methods and architectures has emerged to determine the structure and parameters of TS fuzzy models. It is interesting to observe the progress in the field, particularly the evolution from a seminal knowledge-driven approach towards a data-driven approach. One of the main reasons for this is the permanent growth of available data from real-world applications and the increasing demands for effective decisions in real-time or almost real-time. These applications demand a new kind of admissible on-line learning algorithms in order to extract knowledge from data in a quick and efficient way.

The paper is organised in five sections. In section 2 the effluent neutralization process is described and some aspects related with its modelling are explained. Section 3 introduces the basic notions of the applied fuzzy modelling techniques. Experimental results for the second stage of the neutralization process are shown in section 4 and section 5 presents the conclusions.

## 2.     EFFLUENT NEUTRALIZATION PROCESS

Three different stages compose the mill effluent treatment plant: primary, secondary and tertiary stage. The primary treatment consists in the effluent neutralization and suspended solids removal, the secondary or biological treatment uses activated sludge for the degradation of dissolved organic matter and the tertiary treatment consists in colour removal and effluent equalization, regarding the quality and temperature.

In this work we focus on the primary treatment, more particularly on the study of the effluent neutralization process.

## 2.1  Description of the neutralization process

The acid effluent, the north alkaline effluent and the south alkaline effluent compose the plant effluent, Fig.1. Before the acid effluent enters the WWTP it is partially neutralised in two stages. The first stage consists in the addition of dust collected by the electro filter of the limekiln and the second stage consists in the addition of hydrated lime.

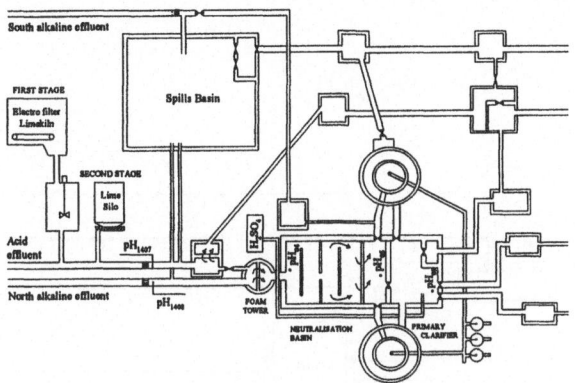

*Figure 1.* Plant of the effluent neutralization process.

The second stage has a much higher neutralization capacity than the first stage, though with associated cost, since hydrated lime has to be bought. The correct neutralization of the industrial effluent is vital for the functionality of the secondary treatment and the quality of the final effluent. The goal is to achieve at the end of the primary treatment a pH in the interval [6.0; 8.0] and simultaneously minimizing the consumption of neutralization materials.

## 2.2  Modelling of the neutralization process

### 2.2.1  Hierarchical structure

A hierarchical structure is proposed to deal with the high number of variables that influence the values of pH. Five sub-models are considered: first stage, second stage, foam tower, neutralization basin and primary clarifier. The hierarchical structure was created based on knowledge obtained from process engineers and operators. Only the most relevant variables have been considered. Fig. 2 represents the input and output variables for the different models.

## 2.2.2      Structure of the models

One of the goals of this work is to construct fuzzy models that are interpretable, simple and applicable. In order to achieve this goal, each sub-model will be a first-order model with time transport delay: the output $y_k$ will depend only on one past value of each of the inputs, $u^p_{k-T_{d_p}}$, and one past value of the output, $y_{k-1}$, Eq. (1).

$$y_k = f\left(u^1_{k-T_{d_1}}, u^2_{k-T_{d_2}}, \ldots, u^p_{k-T_{d_p}}, y_{k-1}\right) \tag{1}$$

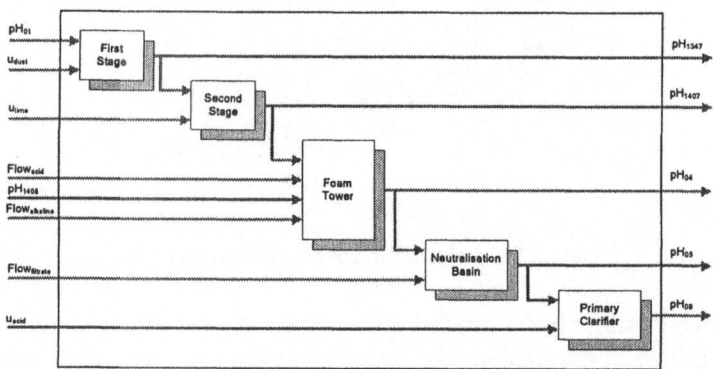

*Figure 2*. Hierarchical structure for the effluent neutralization process.

## 2.2.3      Input selection

The time transport delay for each variable was estimated based on process knowledge, completed with experimental data using ANFIS (Adaptive Network-based Fuzzy Inference System). ANFIS employs an efficient hybrid learning method that combines gradient descent and least-squares method to minimize the mean square modelling error (Jang, 1996).

For instance, in the second stage, the input variables are the pH of the acid effluent ($pH_{1347}$) and the addition of hydrated lime ($u_{lime}$). The output variable is the pH of the acid effluent ($pH_{1407}$), Fig. 2.

The dynamical model of the second stage can be expressed by:

$$y_k = f\left(u^1_{k-T_{d_1}}, u^2_{k-T_{d_2}}, y_{k-1}\right) \tag{2}$$

where the output $y_k$ is a function of the two inputs, respectively at instants $k - T_{d_1}$ and $k - T_{d_2}$, and the output at instant $k-1$. To determine the time transport delay associated with the input variables ($pH_{1347}$ and $u_{lime}$) several fuzzy models were constructed, each with a different combination of past entries of these two inputs. For each input variable 10 candidate inputs $\left(u_{k-1}^1, u_{k-2}^1, \ldots, u_{k-10}^1; u_{k-1}^2, u_{k-2}^2, \ldots, u_{k-10}^2\right)$ were considered. The objective was to find the most influential two inputs, i.e., the ANFIS model with the smallest modelling error, using only a single epoch of training. Fig. 3 presents the values of the MSE (Mean Square Error) for each model. These values were calculated for the data set represented in Fig. 4.

The time transport delay for the two input variables is 2 minutes and 30 seconds, i.e., $T_d = 5$, since the sampling interval was $T = 30$ seconds.

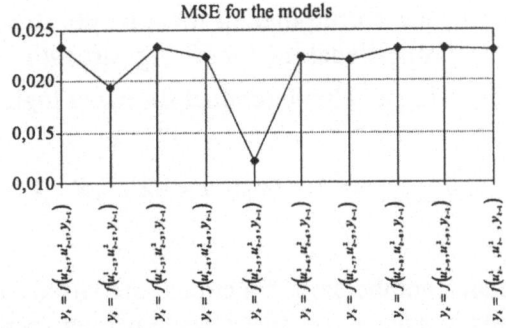

*Figure 3.* Time transport delay in the second stage of the process.

The dynamical model of the second stage can now be expressed by:

$$y_k = f\left(u_{k-5}^1, u_{k-5}^2, y_{k-1}\right) \tag{3}$$

The two input variables have the same time transport delay because it is impossible to dissociate the load of the process on the second stage, represented by the input variable pH1347, from the addition of hydrated lime.

## 3.  FUZZY MODELLING TECHNIQUES

This section briefly describes the two approaches used for modelling the effluent neutralization process: TS fuzzy models and eTS fuzzy models.

## 3.1    TS fuzzy models for off-line learning

TS fuzzy models were proposed in an effort to formalize a systematic approach to generate fuzzy rules from an input-output data set. The basic idea is to decompose the input space into fuzzy regions and to approximate the system in every region by a simple model (Takagi and Sugeno, 1985). A typical if-then rule in a first-order TS fuzzy model has the following format:

$$\Re_i : If \; x_1 \; is \; X_{i1} \ldots and \; x_n \; is \; X_{in} \; then \; y_i = a_{i0} + a_{i1}x_1 + \cdots + a_{in}x_n; \; i = 1,2,\ldots,R \; (4)$$

where $R_i$ denotes the $i^{th}$ fuzzy rule; $R$ is the number of fuzzy rules; $X_{ij}$ denotes the antecedent fuzzy sets, $j = 1,\ldots,n$; $y_i$ is the output of the $i^{th}$ linear subsystem and $\pi_i = [a_{i0}, a_{i1}, \ldots, a_{in}]^T$ are its consequent parameters.

The contribution of the corresponding local model to the overall output of the TS model is proportional to the firing strength $\tau_i$ of each rule, computed by Eq. (5), using algebraic product for fuzzy logic conjunction:

$$\tau_i = \mu_{i1}(x_1) \times \cdots \times \mu_{in}(x_n) = \bigcap_{j=1}^{n} \mu_{ij}(x_j); \; i = 1,2,\ldots,R; \; j = 1,2,\ldots,n \qquad (5)$$

Usually Gaussian membership functions are used to represent the antecedent fuzzy sets in such a way that a trade-off between complexity and precision of the model is obtained.

The TS model output is calculated by weighted averaging of the individual contribution of each rule:

$$y = \sum_{i=1}^{R} \lambda_i y_i = \sum_{i=1}^{R} \lambda_i x_e^T \pi_i \qquad (6)$$

where $\lambda_i = \dfrac{\tau_i}{\sum\limits_{i=1}^{R} \tau_i}$ is the normalized firing strength of the $i^{th}$ rule and $x_e^T$ is

the extended input vector, $x_e^T = [1, x^T]$, allowing the free parameter in $\pi$.

The problem of identification of a TS fuzzy model is divided into two sub-tasks: learning the antecedent part of the model (consisting on the determination of the centres and spreads of the membership functions), and learning the parameters of the consequents. The identification on the antecedent part was solved by subtractive clustering the input-output space. This approach can be used for initial estimation of the antecedent parameters and the resulting cluster centres are used as parameters of the antecedent parts, defining the centres of the rules of the TS fuzzy model (Chiu, 1994). The estimation of the parameters of the consequents is a least squares problem for fixed antecedent parameters. The vector of linear sub-model is made locally optimal in least squares sense (Angelov and Filev, 2004).

## 3.2    eTS fuzzy models for on-line learning

eTS fuzzy models have been recently introduced by Angelov and Filev and the approach is based on an on-line learning algorithm that recursively develops the model structure and parameters (Angelov and Filev, 2004). Structure identification includes estimation of the antecedent parameters by recursive fuzzy clustering and the consequent parameters are obtained by applying the modified Recursive Least Squares (w)RLS estimation algorithm. In the following the basics of the algorithm are briefly recalled.

### 3.2.1    On-line estimation of the antecedent parameters

The recursive fuzzy clustering algorithm uses the notion of the informative potential (accumulated spatial proximity measure), introduced in the mountain clustering algorithm and then refined in the subtractive clustering algorithm, to compute the potential of each new data point in order to select the cluster centres (focals).

The algorithm starts with the first data point established as the focal point of the first cluster. Its coordinates are used to form the antecedent part of the fuzzy rule using Gaussian membership functions and its potential is assumed equal to 1. Starting from the next data point onwards the potential of the new data points is calculated recursively. In contrast with the subtractive clustering algorithm there is not a specific amount subtracted from the highest potential, but update of all the potentials after a new data point is available on-line. The potential of the new data sample $z_k$ is recursively calculated as Eq. (7) (Angelov and Filev, 2004),

$$P_k(z_k) = \frac{k-1}{(k-1)(\vartheta_k + 1) + \sigma_k - 2v_k} \tag{7}$$

where $\vartheta_k = \sum_{j=1}^{n+1}(z_k^j)^2$, $\sigma_k = \sum_{l=1}^{k-1}\sum_{j=1}^{n+1}(z_l^j)^2$, $v_k = \sum_{j=1}^{n+1} z_k^j \beta_k^j$ and $\beta_k^j = \sum_{l=1}^{k-1} z_l^j$.

Parameters $\vartheta_k$ and $v_k$ are calculated from the current data point, $z_k$, while $\beta_k^j$ and $\sigma_k$ are recursively updated by Eq. (8) (Angelov and Filev, 2004).

$$\sigma_k = \sigma_{k-1} + \sum_{j=1}^{n+1}\left(z_{k-1}^j\right)^2 \; ; \; \beta_k^j = \beta_{k-1}^j + z_{k-1}^j \tag{8}$$

After the new data are available they influence also the potentials of the centres of the clusters $(z_l^*, l=1,...,R)$, which are respective to the focal points of the existing clusters $(x_l^*, l=1,...,R)$. The reason is that by definition the potential depends on the distance to all data points, including the new ones. The potential of the focal points of the existing clusters is recursively updated by Eq. (9) (Angelov and Filev, 2004).

$$P_k\left(z_l^*\right)= \frac{(k-1)P_{k-1}\left(z_l^*\right)}{k-2+P_{k-1}\left(z_l^*\right)+P_{k-1}\left(z_l^*\right)\sum_{j=1}^{n+1}\left(d_{k(k-1)}^j\right)^2} \tag{9}$$

where $P_k(z_l^*)$ is the potential of the cluster $z_l^*$ at time k, which is a prototype of the $l^{th}$ rule, $d_{k(k-1)}^j = z_k^j - z_{k-1}^j$, denotes the projection of the distance between two data points, $z_k^j$ and $z_{k-1}^j$, on the axis $z^j$ ($x^j$ for $j=1,2,...,n$ and on the axis y for $j=n+1$).

Further developing the previous algorithm, if the potential of the new data point is higher than the maximum potential of the existing centres or lower than the minimum then the new data point is accepted as a new centre as Eq. (10):

$$\text{If } P_k(z_k) > \overline{P}_k \text{ or } P_k(z_k) < \underline{P}_k \text{ then } R = R+1; x_R^* = x_k; P_k(x_R^*) = P_k(x_k) \tag{10}$$

where $\overline{P}_k = \max_{l=1}^{R} P_k(z_l^*)$ and $\underline{P}_k = \min_{l=1}^{R} P_k(z_l^*)$.

If in addition to the previous condition the new data point is close to an old centre then the new data point replaces this centre, instead of being accepted as a new one, Eq. (11):

$$\text{If } \left(P_k(z_k) > \overline{P}_k \text{ or } P_k(z_k) < \underline{P}_k\right) \text{ and } \delta_{min} < \frac{r}{2} \text{ then}$$
$$z_j^* = z_k; P_k(z_j^*) = P_k(z_k) \tag{11}$$

where $\delta_{min} = \min\limits_{l=1}^{R}\|z_k - z_l^*\|$, $r$ is the constant radii and $j$ is the index of the replaced centre (closest cluster centre to the new data point).

### 3.2.2   On-line estimation of the consequent parameters

The problem of increasing size of the training data is handled by the RLS algorithm for the globally optimal case and by the weighted RLS algorithm for the locally optimal case. Under the assumption of a constant/unchanged rule base the optimization problems are linear in parameters.

In eTS fuzzy models, however, the rule base is assumed to be gradually evolving. Therefore, the number of rules as well as the parameters of the antecedent part will vary. Because of this evolution, the normalized firing strengths of the rules will change. Since this affects all the data (including the data collected before time of the change) the straightforward application of the RLS or wRLS algorithm is not correct. A proper resetting of the covariance matrices and parameters initialization of the algorithms is needed at each time a rule is added to and/or removed from the rule base. The modified RLS algorithm for global and local parameter estimation is described in the reference (Angelov and Filev, 2004).

### 3.2.3   Rule base evolution in eTS fuzzy models

The recursive procedure for on-line learning of eTS fuzzy models includes the following stages:
1. Initialization of the rule base structure (antecedent part of the rules);
2. Reading the next data sample at the next time step;
3. Recursive calculation of the potential of each new data sample, Eq. (7);
4. Recursive update of the potentials of old centres, Eq. (9);
5. Possible modification or upgrade of the rule base structure, Eqs. (10)-(11);
6. Recursive calculation of the consequent parameters;
7. Prediction of the model output for the next time step.
   The algorithm continues from stage 2 at the next time step.


## 4.      EXPERIMENTS

This section describes the experiments done in the second stage of the effluent neutralization process to predict the pH values.

## 4.1      Experiment 1

In the first experiment, two plant data sets from consecutive days are used, the first one, Fig. 4, for training, and the second one, Fig. 5, to determine the generalisation capability of the fuzzy models (validation). Each data set has 2880 samples and the data is normalized into de domain [0, 1] to avoid negative influence in clustering results from variations in the numerical ranges of the different features (Babuska, 1998).

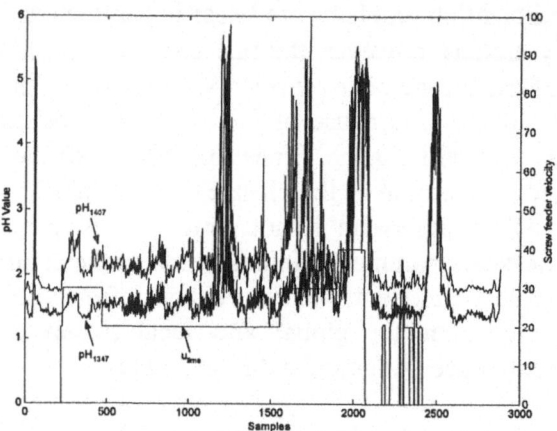

*Figure 4.* Training data set for the second stage of the effluent neutralization process.

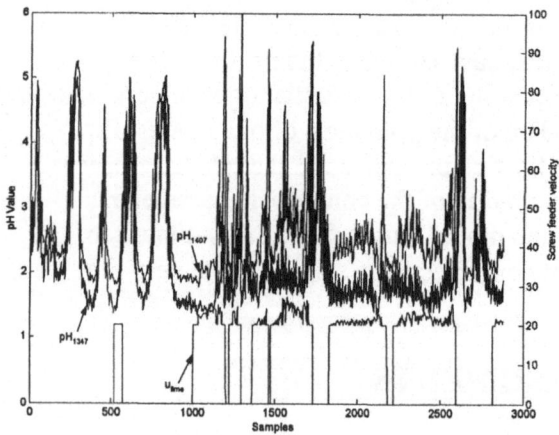

*Figure 5.* Validation data set for the second stage of the effluent neutralization process.

### 4.1.1 TS fuzzy model

The TS fuzzy model approach is applied for off-line learning. The value for the constant radii was, $r = 0.3$.

Fig. 6 shows the evolution of the process and model output for training (left) and validation (right). Table 1 presents the parameters of the TS fuzzy model acquired from data, namely information about the centres of the Gaussian membership functions and the parameters of the linear sub-models. The width of the membership functions is the same for all the fuzzy sets, $\sigma_{ij} = 0.1061$.

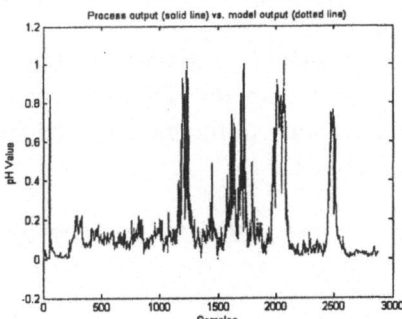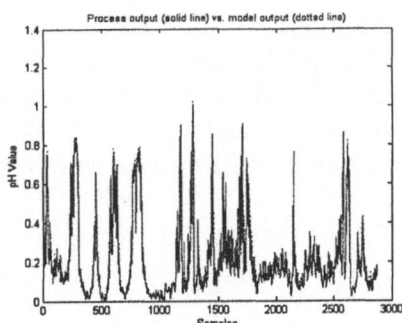

*Figure 6.* Off-line learning with TS fuzzy model approach.

Even with a small number of fuzzy rules, only 3, the performance of the TS fuzzy model is satisfactory both for training and validation data. It must be stated that the structure and parameters of the TS fuzzy model obtained from training data remain unchanged when the model is tested with the validation data. The accuracy of the model can be improved if a smaller value for radii is considered since this parameter can be used to control the number of fuzzy rules and inherently the model complexity and precision.

*Table 1.* TS fuzzy model parameters, off-line learning.

| Rule | $u^1_{k-5}$ | $u^2_{k-5}$ | $y_{k-1}$ | $y_k$ |
|------|------|------|------|------|
| $R_1$ | 0.0746 | 0.4989 | 0.1045 | $y^1 = 0.7207 - 0.4268u^1_{k-5} + 0.636\,1u^2_{k-5} + 0.1909y_{k-1}$ |
| $R_2$ | 0.0565 | 0 | 0.0296 | $y^2 = 0.4170 - 0.1545u^1_{k-5} + 0.5513\,1u^2_{k-5} - 0.0108y_{k-1}$ |
| $R_3$ | 0.0847 | 0.7496 | 0.1348 | $y^3 = 0.2721 - 0.1682u^1_{k-5} + 0.7526\,1u^2_{k-5} + 0.1443y_{k-1}$ |

### 4.1.2 eTS fuzzy model

The eTS fuzzy model approach is applied for on-line learning. The value for the constant radii was $r = 0.5$ and the initialization parameter for RLS was $\Omega = 750$. Fig. 7 shows the evolution of the process and model output for training (left) and validation (right). Table 2 presents the parameters of the eTS fuzzy model at the end of the learning process for training data.

The structure and parameters of the eTS fuzzy model, at the end of the training, were exactly the same with which the eTS fuzzy model was initialized for validation. The number of rules at the end of training was 8, and it remains the same after validation, but some fuzzy rules were replaced and the parameters of the model were constantly updated. In practice what happens is that at every instant a new model is constructed and even though the structure (number of fuzzy rules) does not change the model parameters are varying.

The performance of the eTS fuzzy model is satisfactory but the complexity of the eTS fuzzy model is higher than the TS fuzzy model. Another important aspect is the poor interpretability of the model since there are a lot of similar membership functions, Table 2.

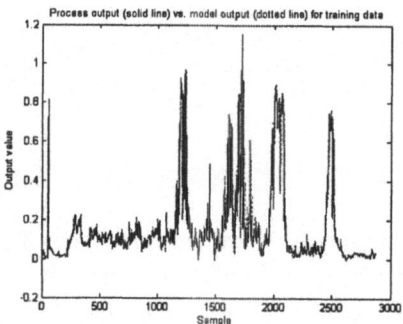 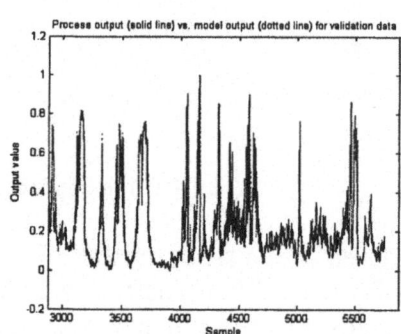

*Figure 7.* On-line learning with eTS fuzzy model approach.

*Table 2.* eTS fuzzy model parameters, on-line learning.

| Rule | $u_{k-5}^1$ | $u_{k-5}^2$ | $y_{k-1}$ | $y_k$ |
|------|------|------|------|------|
| $R_1$ | 0.0795 | 0 | 0.0264 | $y^1 = -0.0067 + 0.4768u_{k-5}^1 + 0.0183u_{k-5}^2 + 0.3773y_{k-1}$ |
| $R_2$ | 0.5232 | 0 | 0.0433 | $y^2 = -0.0471 + 0.4566u_{k-5}^1 + 1.3214u_{k-5}^2 + 0.5224y_{k-1}$ |
| $R_3$ | 0.8962 | 0 | 0.1145 | $y^3 = 0.6906 - 0.6354u_{k-5}^1 - 0.6062u_{k-5}^2 + 1.4509y_{k-1}$ |
| $R_4$ | 0.9545 | 0 | 0.3133 | $y^4 = -1.1746 + 1.4509u_{k-5}^1 + 0.7195u_{k-5}^2 + 1.4558y_{k-1}$ |
| $R_5$ | 0.9809 | 0 | 0.8124 | $y^5 = -0.2341 + 0.0694u_{k-5}^1 + 0.0401u_{k-5}^2 + 1.2025y_{k-1}$ |
| $R_6$ | 0.0635 | 0.7486 | 0.1169 | $y^6 = 0.0899 + 0.1542u_{k-5}^1 - 0.1045u_{k-5}^2 + 0.8327y_{k-1}$ |
| $R_7$ | 0.0922 | 0.4961 | 0.1261 | $y^7 = -0.0107 + 1.0377u_{k-5}^1 - 0.0803u_{k-5}^2 + 0.5816y_{k-1}$ |
| $R_8$ | 0.9933 | 0.9956 | 0.8806 | $y^8 = 0.1300 + 0.3535u_{k-5}^1 + 0.0630u_{k-5}^2 + 0.3808y_{k-1}$ |

## 4.2 Experiment 2

In order to more effectively test the generalisation capabilities of the fuzzy models a second validation data set, from a third day, was considered, Fig. 8. This data set is from a different month and it can be observed that the input variables present a quite different behaviour.

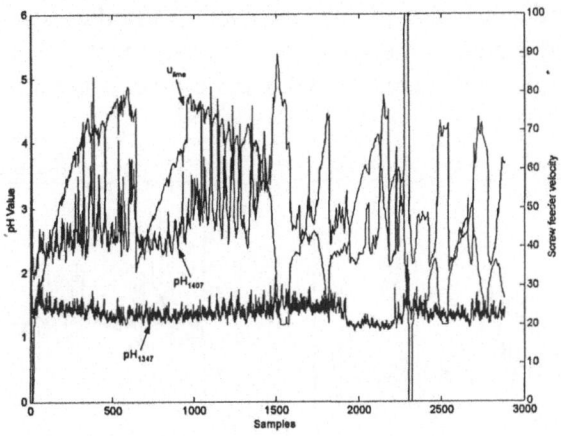

*Figure 8.* Validation data set (2) for the second stage of the effluent neutralization process.

### 4.2.1 TS fuzzy model

The behaviour of the TS fuzzy model is presented in Fig. 9 and it is clear that the error between the process and model output has increased considerably. This is because the dynamics of the process has changed and the structure and parameters of the model remained fixed (the same as in experiment 1).

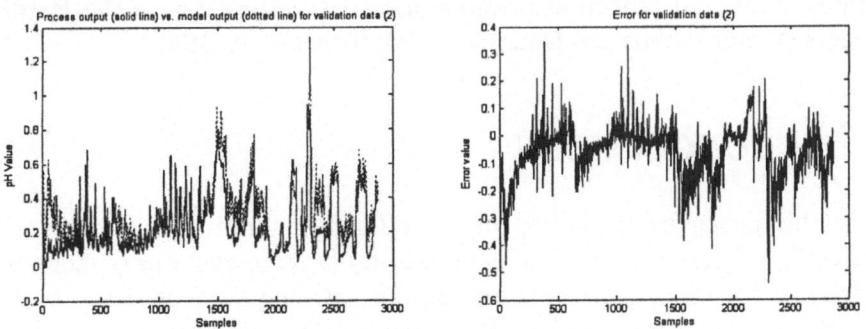

*Figure 9.* Off-line learning with TS fuzzy model approach for validation data set (2).

This confirms what we already know, process dynamics change with time and for off-line learning the only way to improve on this is to use more representative data or models must be build for different operating points.

### 4.2.2    eTS fuzzy model

Fig. 10 presents the behaviour of the eTS fuzzy model and it is satisfactory, particularly for the second half of the data set. The number of fuzzy rules at the end is the same as in experiment 1 but the number of replaced fuzzy rules has increased, with some rules being replaced more than once.

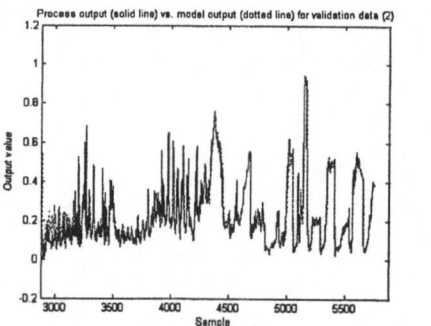 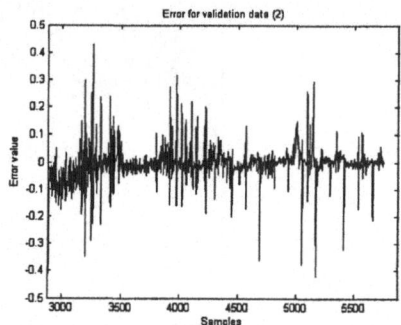

*Figure 10.* On-line learning with eTS fuzzy model approach for validation data set(2).

With on-line learning even if the training data is not representative of all the operating points of the process it is possible to achieve satisfactory results since the approach can evolve the structure and parameters of the model, according with the current dynamics of the process. The interpretability of the model remains poor and to improve on this rule base simplification and reduction methods must be applied during the learning process (Victor Ramos and Dourado, 2004; Setnes et al., 1988).

## 5.    CONCLUSIONS

In this paper the modelling of the effluent neutralization process of a WasteWater Treatment Plant in pulp industry is presented. Fuzzy modelling techniques for off-line learning and on-line learning were used and on-line learning of fuzzy rules proves to be an efficient technique for building up predictive models, particularly when processes present non-linear characteristics and time-varying dynamics. These models will be used for monitoring and for synthesizing automatic closed-loop controllers.

Although some improvements on the interpretability of the models are necessary their adaptive nature makes them a useful tool for on-line modelling of real-world applications of AI in decision, monitoring and control.

## ACKNOWLEDGEMENTS

This work is supported by PRODEP III – Acção 5.3, and partially supported by POSI – Programa Operacional Sociedade de Informação of Portuguese Fundação para a Ciência e Tecnologia under Project ALCINE (POSI/EEI/14155/2001). Soporcel company gave the data for this work. The authors also express their gratitude to Prof. Plamen Angelov, Lancaster University, UK, for the fruitful collaboration concerning recursive clustering.

## REFERENCES

Angelov, P.; Filev, D., 2004, An Approach to Online Identification of Takagi-Sugeno Fuzzy Models, *IEEE Transactions on Systems, Man, and Cybernetics*. **34**(1): 484-498.

Babuska, R., 1988, Fuzzy Modeling for Control, *International Series in Intelligent Technologies*, Kluwer Academic Publishers.

Chiu, S., 1994, Fuzzy Model Identification Based on Clustering Estimation, *Journal of Intelligent and Fuzzy Systems*, **2**: 267-278.

Jang, J.-S. R, 1996, Input Selection for ANFIS Learning. in: *Proceedings of the IEEE International Conference on Fuzzy Systems*, New Orleans.

Setnes, M., 2001, Complexity Reduction in Fuzzy Systems, *PhD Thesis*, Delft University of Technology.

Setnes, M, Babuska, R., Kaymak, U., and van Nauta Lemke, H.R., 1988, Similarity Measures in Fuzzy Rule Base Simplification, *IEEE Transactions on Systems, Man, and Cybernetics*, **28**(3): 376-386.

Victor Ramos, J., and Dourado, A., 2004, On-Line Interpretability by Fuzzy Rule Base Simplification and Reduction, *EUNITE Conference*, Aachen, Germany.

Takagi, T., and Sugeno, M., 1985, Fuzzy Identification of Systems and Its Applications to Modeling and Control, *IEEE Transactions on Systems, Man, and Cybernetics*, **15**(1):116-132.

Yen, J., Wang, L., and Gillespie, W., 1998, Improving the Interpretability of TSK Fuzzy Models by Combining Global and Local Learning, *IEEE Transactions on Fuzzy Systems*, **6**(4):530-537.

# AN AUTONOMOUS INTELLIGENT AGENT ARCHITECTURE BASED ON CONSTRUCTIVIST AI

Filipo Studzinski Perotto, Rosa Vicari and Luís Otávio Alvares
*Universidade Federal do Rio Grande do Sul, Caixa Postal 15.064, CEP 91.501-970, Porto Alegre, RS, Brasil*

**Abstract:**    This paper intends to propose an learning agent architecture based on Constructivist AI approach. First we show how Artificial Intelligence can incorporate some concepts from Jean Piaget's psychology to form Constructivist AI as a branch of Symbolic AI. Then we present details about the proposed architecture, discussing the provided agent autonomy. Eventually, we report experimental results.

**Key words:**    Artificial Intelligence, Constructivism, Agents.

## 1.    INTRODUCTION

Over the last decade, Artificial Intelligence has seen the emergence of proposals of new paradigms, new techniques (many of them born from the hybridization of classical techniques), and a search for new theoretical conceptions, coming from the contact with other disciplines. Exploration on these AI borders may make possible to overcome some current limitations of conventional AI systems.

From these new ways of conceiving AI, we highlight the Constructivist Artificial Intelligence. In general lines it comprises all works on this science that refer to the Constructivist Psychological Theory, essentially represented by Jean Piaget. The constructivist conception of intelligence was brought to the scientific field of Artificial Intelligence in the early 90's, and it has not occupied the desirable space among researchers, who are mostly linked to the classical paradigms. But even as an alternative proposal, still searching for legitimacy and consolidation, Constructivist AI has shown to be able of contributing to the discipline. Theoretical discussions on the meaning of the incorporation of piagetian concepts by AI are present in [Drescher 1991], [Boden 1979], [Inhelder & Cellerier 1992] and [Rocha Costa 1989, 1995].

Following the proposal of Constructivist AI, our work proposes a model of intelligent agent which implements some of Jean Piaget's-conceived intelligence and learning mechanisms. There are some models that are already implemented [Drescher 1991], [Wazlawick 1993] and [Muñoz 1999] which are our basic reference, both for the initial inspiration and as a parameter to see which limits need to be surmounted.

## 2.        JEAN PIAGET'S PSYCHOLOGICAL THEORY

Piagetian Psychology is also known as Constructivist Theory. According to Piaget, the human being is born with a few cognitive structures, but this initial knowledge enables the subject to build new cognitive structures through the active interaction with the environment [Becker 2001], [Montangero 1997].

Piaget sees intelligence as adaptation, which is the external aspect of an internal process of organization of cognitive structures, called "schemas". So, the subject's schemas are transformed, but the functions that regulate the construction of new schemas do not vary during life [Piaget 1953]. A schema is all that, in an action, can be differentiated, generalized and applied to other situations [Montangero 1997]. It is the elementary cognitive structure, and represents a world's regularity observed by the subject. The schema comprises perception, action and expectation.

The subject realizes all of his experiences by his schemas. Sometimes the subject's expectation fails, and compels to a modication in schemas. There is, thus, a process of interactive regulation between the subject and the environment. The subject is all the time making "accommodations" and "assimilations". Assimilation is the process through which the subject uses his schemas to interact with the world. Accommodation occurs when his schemas are not able of responding to some situation, and is the process through which the subject modifies his schemas trying to adapt himself to the environment. In this game of assimilations and accommodations the subject progressively differentiates its schemas in order to deal with reality [Piaget 1978].

Accommodation is the transformation of schemas starting from the experience aiming at making the system more adapted to the environment. As accommodation happens in a schema the subject already has, the new structure arises molded by structures that already exist. Thus, at the same time that the schemas integrate novelties, they also maintain what they already know. The system reaches a stable point because each accommodation widens its ability of assimilating. Thus, novelties will less and less affect the system equilibrium, and the system will be more prepared to deal with novelties [Piaget 1953].

Initially, the psychological subject counts only on "sensorial boards" (instant perceptions of the visual, auditory, tactile, cinestesic, tasting fields …). These boards do not maintain any implicit logic relation, and they are, a priori, disconnected. From this universe of "sensorial boards", intelligence will build elementary notions, set relations, find regularities and eventually will build an objective, substantial, spatial, temporal, regular, external universe, independently of intelligence itself. The "real" will be composed in this adaptation movement by the increasing coherence between schemas [Piaget 1957].

## 3.    CONSTRUCTIVIST AGENT: MODEL

The Constructivist Agent model we are proposing uses basically the concepts of Piaget's Constructivist Theory. Previous models had already tried this accomplishment, each one using some type of computational technique to implement the mechanisms described by Piaget. The first model is presented in [Drescher 1991], and uses statistical calculation to find correlations between the agent's observation, actions and results.

Other important model is presented in [Wazlawick 1993], and is inspired by genetic algorithms [Holland 1992] and in the model of self-organized neural network [Kohonen 1989]. In this architecture, the agent has a population of schemas, and each generation preserves the best schemas, that represents the correct relations between observation, action and results, based on the own agent experience.

Other constructivist agent architectures are presented in [Muñoz 1999], that inserts planning to Wazlawick Agent, [Balpaeme, Steels & Looveren 1998], that uses the same strategy to reach emergence of catergories and concepts in a multiagent environment, [Birk & Paul 2000], which inserts genetic programming in Drescher Agent, and [De Jong 1999], using schemas that reinforces itself to form concepts.

The model we are proposing differs from previous ones because they are based only in assimilation-accomodation mechanisms, without statistical aproachs, or selectionist regulations, or reinforcement learnings.

An autonomous agent, in Artificial Intelligence, is a system able to choose its actions independently and effectively through its sensors and effectors in the environment. [Davidsson 1995]. The constructivist agent is an embodied agent. Agent's body acts as a mediator between environment and mind through its external sensors (inputs) and external effectors (outputs). Body also has internal (somatic) states and metabolisms that serve as basis to an internal organic motivational sense. Agent's mind interacts with body by internal sensors and internal effectors. The mind has two systems: cognitive and emotional. Figure 1 shows the agent's structure, with a body mediating the mind and the environment, and with an emotional system interacting with the cognitive system.

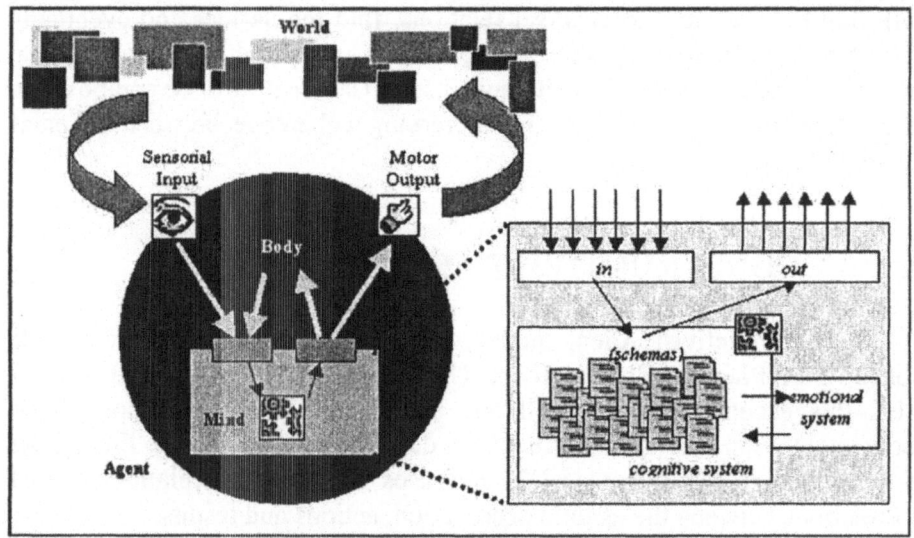

*Figure 1.* Architecture of Agent (on the left, the agent interacts with the environment through its body; on the right, details of mental structure)

The constructivist agent's mind receives sensorial inputs and activates action outputs. The cognitive system has a set of schemas (its cognitive constructions) representing agent's beliefs. For each situation the agent experiences, and depending on the desire of changing this situation, the agent will select and activate one of these schemas. Cognitive system also has a mechanism to build schemas. The set of agent's schemas may be initially empty because the mechanism proposed is able to build all its knowledge by interacting with the environment, while it carries out its activity not needing any pre-programming.

A schema is composed of a triple {Context, Action, Expectation}. The *Context* is the representation of situations that the schema is able to assimilate. *Action* represents the action that the agent will carry out in the environment if the schema is activated. *Expectation* represents the result expected after the action. A schema is represented in Figure 2.

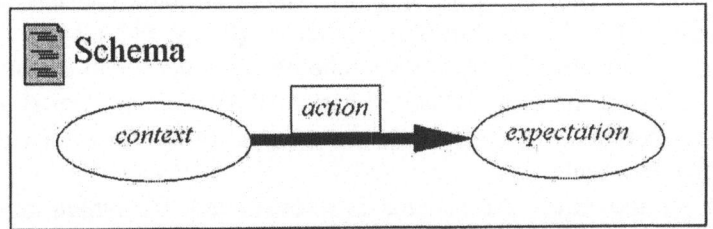

*Figure 2.* Structure of Schema (Context, Action, Expectation)

The situation in which the agent is at every moment (context realized through sensors) is compared with the context of the schema, and it will be excited if there is compatibility. When an excited schema is activated, the cognitive system makes it to perform its Action (through the agent's effectors). Regulation happens because the cognitive mechanism checks if the result (context realized at the instant following the action) is according to the expectation of the schema, where the difference serves as a parameter for adjusting and evaluating the schema.

At every instant (execution step), the agent's cognitive system verifies the context of all schemas, exciting those that are compatible with the situation realized through sensors. The mechanism consults, then, the emotional system, which will choose among the schemas excited the one that will be activated.

The mind's emotional system interacts with cognitive system and it is the responsible for guiding the agent's actions, conferring an affective meaning to knowledge and enabling the agent to have its own goals. Emotions can be seen as the subject's presence of internal states correlated to structures of the cognitive system that evaluate it. There is no space here in the present paper to deepen this discussion, but it is opportune to say that our own experiments showed the need for an emotional system that serves as the motor for the agent's actions. According to [Rocha Costa & Graçaliz 2003], internal motivation is the basis to real autonomy of agents. This result is according to recent studies of cognitive research where it is claimed the mutual dependence between knowledge and affectivity in the intelligent behavior. Body and emotional system are fundamental elements to guarantee the autonomy of our constructivist agent, thus all intentionality is an emergent result of its own mechanisms. This claim have support in [Bercht 2001], [Sloman 1999], [LeDoux 1996] and [Damásio 1994].

The triple {Context, Action, Expectation} is composed of vectors of elements that may undertake three values: true, false or don't care (represented, respectively, by '1', '0' and '#'). A true value indicates the presence of an element, a false value indicates absence and the third value is to make a generalization of the element in the schema, don't care indicates no matter if it is present or not. For example, a schema that has the context vector = (0,1,#) is able to assimilate situations (0,1,0) e (0,1,1).

There is compatibility between a schema and a certain situation when the context vector of the schema has all true or false elements equal to those of the agent's perception vector. Note that compatibility does not compare the 'don't care' elements.

After an activation, the schema is re-evaluated. Its evaluation measures the prediction ability of the system. A schema has a good capacity of predicting if its expectations are fully corresponded after the execution of its action, and can then be called 'adequate schema'. Evaluation happens by the analysis of compatibility between the expectation vector of the schema applied at the previous instant, and the agent's perception vector. As this fitness is historic, and accumulates during the several applications of the schema, it is expected that it tends to a value that describes its real prediction ability.

## 4.     CONSTRUCTIVIST AGENT: ALGORITHMS

Schemas are always re-evaluated after each activation. The new fitness of a schema should be equal to some ponderation between its previous fitness and the expectation compatibility of the schema with the current situation. For instance, as indicated:

```
RE-EVALUATION Method
  S := ActivatedScheme;
  S.NewFitness := (S.OldFitness + Compat(Scheme.Expect))/2;
```

The learning process of our constructivist agent happens through the refinement of the set of schemas, this means making it more adapted to its environment. This learning happens through four basic methods, named: Guided Creation, Expectation Generalization, Context Generalization and Differentiation.

When the agent faces a situation where it does not have compatible schemas (or if those that it has are, in some way, rejected by the emotional system) then it activates the Guided Creation method, with the aim of widening its repertoire of schemas and dealing specifically with the situation it is at that very moment. The method works as it follows:

```
GUIDED CREATION Method
  if Agent.ActivatedScheme = null then
    S := Tscheme.Create;
    S.Context := Agent.Perception;
```

```
S.Action := NewActionForContext;
Agent.AddScheme(S);
Agent.Execute(S);
S.Expect := Agent.Perception;
S.Fitness := 0.5;
```

The whole new schema created by the Guided Creation method has the vector of context and Expectation totally specific, created after the situation experienced and after the result directly observed after the action. The cognitive mechanism of the agent has methods to find the most generic schemas as possible after these initial specific schemas, adjusting the expectations and integrating analogue contexts. In more complex environments, the number of sensations the agent realizes is huge, and, in general, from these, only a few of them are relevant in the context of a schema. In the same way, an action the agent performs will generally modify only a few aspects of the environment.

Expectation Generalization modifies an existent schema in order to make it more adequate, that is, more precise in its expectations. It works as a kind of accommodation, once the schema adjusts itself according to its last application. The method simply compares the activated schema's expectation and the agent's perception after the application of the schema and changes the elements that are not compatible to each other for the indefinite value '#'. As the Guided Creation method always creates the schema with expectations totally determined and equal to the result of its first application, the walk the schema performs is a reduction of expectations, up to the point it reaches a state where only those elements that really represent the regular results of the action carried out in that context remain.

```
EXPECTATION GENERALIZATION Method
  S := Agent.ActivatedScheme;
  For i := 0 to Agent.Perception.Size-1 do
    if S.Expect[i] <> Agent.Perception[i] then
      S.Expect[i] := #;
```

When the agent finds two similar schemas to approach different contexts, the Integration algorithms come into action. These two schemas only trigger the procedure if they have high fitness (being considered reliable) and if they have the same action and expectation (action and expectation vectors must be completely compatible). As all schemas are born with their context very well specified, the mechanism needs to find the state with the higher level of generalization as possible, without loosing adequacy. The algorithm operates as it follows:

```
INTEGRATION Method
  if (S1.Action = S2.Action) and (S1.Expect = S2.Expect)
then
    if (S1.Fitness = 1) and (S2.Fitness = 1) then
      S := TScheme.Create;
      S.Action := S1.Action;
      S.Expect := S1.Expect;
      For i := 0 to S.Context.Size-1 do
        if S1.Context[i] <> S2.Context[i] then
          S.Context[i] := S1.Context[i]
        else
          S.Context[i] := #;
      Agent.SubstituteSchemes(S1, S2, S);
```

Differentiation becomes a necessary mechanism because Generalization may make inapropriate generalizations, occasionally. If a generalized schema does not work well, it creates a new schema. It acts as it follows:

```
DIFFERENTIATION Method
  S := Agent.ActivatedScheme;
  if (S.Fitness = 1) and (S.InstantFitness < 1) then
    NewS := TScheme.Create;
    NewS.Context := Agent.LastPerception;
    NewS.Action := S.Action;
    NewS.Expect := Agent.ActualPerception;
```

Thus, the algorithm that chooses the schema that will be activated at each turn in the agent should be prepared to choose always the compatible schema that has the most specific context.


## 5.     MODEL SIGNIFICATION

The problem can be stated in the following form: the environment has certain regularities that the agent may check during interaction. Considering that these regularities are stable, there will be, for an agent which is in this environment, a set of valid schemas that the agent should be able to build.

If we consider context, action and expectation as a triple search space, then the problem solving means, for the constructivist agent, to find the set of valid schemas in this search space. Thus, after some time, each schema of the set of schemas that the agent has built should represent a valid correlation between a context, an action and an expectation in the given environment. The set of built schemas defines adaptation of agent to its environment.

The agent model we have mentioned here has a reactive profile: although it learns with experience, it does not have temporality (it does not take into consideration past through any kind of historic memory, and does not plan the future), thus limiting itself to understand only instant relations; it does not count on a symbolic capacity nor abstraction, that is, it is not able to formulate concepts that go beyond the perception level, sensorimotor.

The whole new schema is generated through a process of Guided Creation. This method creates a schema absolutely specific, because its Context vector is only able to assimilate this unique situation, and its expectation vector expects to find always the same exact result after the action application. The cognitive mechanism finds an adequate generalization of this schema through the Expectation Generalization, Integration and Differentiation methods.

## 6. PRELIMINARY RESULTS

We have made an experience of implementation of the Constructivist Agent, inserted in a simple virtual environment. In the simulation, the agent should learn how to move in a plane without colliding with obstacles. The plane is a bidimensional grid. The cells of grid may contain an empty space or a wall. At each time, the agent can do one of three possible actions: give a step ahead, turn to left or turn to right. The agent walks freely across empty spaces, but collides when tries to step against the wall. Figure 3 shows the simulation environment, where dark cells are walls, clear cells are empty spaces, and the blue cell is the agent, seeing one cell ahead.

Initially the agent does not have any schema and it also did not distinguish the obstacles from the free ways. The agent had only one external perception: the vision of what was in front of it, and the sensation of pain when there happened a collision. The agent's body has four properties: *pain, fatigue, exhaustion* and *pleasure*. All of these properties have corresponding internal perceptions. Pain ocurrs when the agent collides with a wall, and lasts just one instant. Agent's corporal metabolism eliminates the sensation of pain at the next instant. When the agent repeats much times the action of walk, then fatigue is activated, and if the walk continues, sensation of exhaustion is finnaly activated. These sensations disappear after a few instants when the action of walk ends. Pleasure occurs when the agent walks, during only one instant too.

Agent's emotional system implements three emotional triggers: pain and exhaustion define negative emotional values, whereas pleasure defines a positive value. At the end of a period of interaction with the environment, we hope the agent had been able of building a set of schemas that prevented it of making the moves that leads to pain in each visual context, and prevent it of exhaustion when fatigue appears. In addition, the agent prefers walking in other situations, because it feels pleasure.

*Figure 1.* Simulation Environment

After some experiments, we may consider our results were successful. The agent, after some time in interaction with the environment, learns about the consequences of its actions in different situations. This knowledge is used by the agent to avoid emotionally negative situations, and to pursue emotionally positive situations. In Table 1 we show the main schemas built by the agent in the simulation.

*Table 1.* Main schemas built by the agent during the simulation

| Context | Action | Expectation |
|---|---|---|
| * vision = wall | * walk ahead | * pain = true |
| | | * vision = wall |
| * (any context) | * turn left | * pain = false |
| | * turn right | |
| * fatigue = true | * walk ahead | * exhaustion = true |
| * fatigue = false | * walk ahead | * pleasure = true |
| * vision = empty space | | |

# 7.     CONCLUSIONS AND NEXT STEPS

The constructivist models in AI are interesting as they make possible to develop architectures of intelligent agents that adapt themselves to the environment without the programmer's intervention in the construction of its cognitive structures. The agent, although programmed to accomplish certain tasks, is free to build its knowledge in the interaction with the environment, and thus, finding alone the solutions for problems that may arise. This autonomy of cognitive construction is associated to a motivational autonomy, given by the corporal and emotional sensations.

The model presented hitherto is an alternative that follows these guidelines. The achieved experimental results show that the constructivist agent is able to learn regularities of its environment. After some time, the agent behaviour becomes coherent with its emotional values because a set of adapted schemas was constructed through the continual interaction with the environment.

However, it is limited to a too reactive agent (without memory, nor planning, nor conceptual abstraction). We hope, as a continuation of this work, to point a way for the implementation of a more cognitive constructivist agent that has temporality and conceptualization. Everything indicates that the next step means to make possible that the agent builds multiple sets of schemas related to each other, making the meaning of perception and acting vary in a way that these also make reference to their own cognitive activity.

Constructivist Psychology is in accordance with this systemic perspective of the mind. Furthermore, the idea of a modular mind operation (where each module works in a specific domain, but in constant interaction with other modules) is postulated by several researchers in neuropsychology [Rapp 2001], [Luria 1979], [Pinker 1997], [Damasio 1996]. Also in AI, this Idea can be found, somehow, in [Minsky 1985].

In this way, the agent architecture will be extended to integrate the following capabilities:

- temporal perception: the agent must be able to perceive time distributed contexts, in addition to the capability of identifying regularities in the instantaneous perception. Thus, the agent will observe sequenciated events; this capability is requirement to emergence of  planning and factual memories.

- abstract concept formation: the agent must be able to overpass the sensorial perception constructing abstract concepts; forming this new knowledge elements, the agent aquires new forms to structure the comprehension of its own reality in more complex levels.

- multiple knowledge systems: the agent must be able to construct subsets of perceptions or concepts, which represent specific knowledge domains; a domain is a dynamic knowledge system. In the interaction, these domains represent proper significances mediating the specific agent adaptation.

- operatory transformation: the agent must be able to create operations that change among different systems or schemes, preventing that knowledge remains as a database of cases, and enabling the agent to understand further phenomenon regularities, systematic transformation regularities in the world.

- non-modal logics: the agent cannot have only deductive inference. A hypothesis inference mechanism is required, as well as uncertainty and inconsistency treatment.


# REFERENCES

Becker, Fernando. Educação e Construção do Conhecimento. Porto Alegre: ArtMed, 2001.

Belpaeme, T., Steels, L., & van Looveren, J. The construction and acquisition of visual categories. In Birk, A. and Demiris, J., editors, Learning Robots, Proceedings of the EWLR-6, Lecture Notes on Artificial Intelligence 1545. Springer. 1998.

Bercht, Magda. Em direção a agentes pedagógicos com dimensões afetivas. Porto Alegre: UFRGS, 2001. (Tese de Doutorado)

Birk, Andreas & Paul, Wolfgang. Schemas and Genetic Programming. Ritter, Cruse, Dean (Eds.), Prerational Intelligence: Adaptive Behavior and Intelligent Systems without Symbols and Logic, Volume II, Studies in Cognitive Systems 36, Kluwer, 2000.

Boden, Margaret. Piaget. Glasgow: Fontana Paperbacks, 1979.

Coelho, Helder. Sonho e Razão. 2.a. ed. Lisboa: Editora Relógio d'Água, 1999.

Damasio, António. Descartes' Error: Emotion, Reason and the Human Brain. New York: Avon Books, 1994.

Davidsson, Paul. On the concept of concept in the context of autonomous agents. II World Conference on the Fundamentals of Artificial Intelligence. p85-96, 1995.

De Jong, E. D. Autonomous Concept Formation. In: Proceedings of the Sixteenth International Joint Conference on Artificial Intelligence IJCAI, 1999.

Drescher, Gary. Mide-Up Minds: A Construtivist Approach to Artificial Intelligence. MIT Press, 1991.

Holland, John. Genetic Algorithms. Scientific American, 1992.

Inhelder B. & Cellerier G. Le cheminement des découvertes de l'enfant. Neuchâtel: Delachaux et Niestlé, 1992.

Kohonen, Teuvo. Self-Organization and Associative Memory. Berlin: Springer-Verlag, 1989.

LeDoux, J.E. The Emotional Brain. New York: Simon and Schuster, 1996.

Luria, Aleksandr. The Making of Mind. Harvard University Press, 1979.

Minsky, Marvin. The Society of Mind. New York: Simon & Schuster, 1985.

Montangero, J., & Maurice-Naville, D. Piaget or the advance of knowledge. New York: Lawrence. Erlbaum Associates, 1997.

Muñoz, Mauro H. S. Proposta de Modelo Sensório Cognitivo inspirado na Teoria de Jean Piaget. Porto Alegre: PGCC/UFRGS, 1999. (Dissertação de Mestrado)

Piaget, Jean. Play, Dreams and Imitation in Childhood. London: Heinemann, 1951.

Piaget, Jean. The Origins of Intelligence in the Child. London: Routledge & Kegan Paul, 1953.

Piaget, Jean. Construction of Reality in the Child. London: Routledge & Kegan Paul, 1957.

Piaget, Jean. A Epistemologia Genética; Sabedoria e Ilusões da filosofia; Problemas de Psicologia Genética; Vida e Obra. (Os Pensadores). São Paulo: Abril Cultural, 1978.

Steven Pinker. How the Mind Works. W. W. Norton, New York, NY, 1997.

Rapp, B. (Ed.). The Handbook of Cognitive Neuropsychology. Hove, UK: Psychology Press, 2001.

Rocha Costa, Antônio Carlos da, & Dimuro, Graçaliz Pereira. Needs and Functional Foundation of Agent Autonomy. 2003. (http://gmc.ucpel.tche.br/imqd/artigos/needs-03-04-06.pdf, 21/1/04)

Rocha Costa, Antônio Carlos da. Inteligência Artificial Construtivista: princípios gerais e perspectivas de cooperação com a informática na educação. Porto Alegre: Instituto de Informática UFGRS, 1995.

Sloman, Aaron. Review of Affective Computing. AI Magazine 20 (1): 127-133, 1999.

Wazlawick, Raul. Um Modelo Operatório Para a Construção do Conhecimento. Florianópolis, PPGEP/UFSC, 1993. (Tese de Doutoramento)

# FINDING MANUFACTURING EXPERTISE USING ONTOLOGIES AND COOPERATIVE AGENTS

Olga Nabuco [1], Mauro F. Koyama [1], Francisco Edeneziano D. Pereira [1] and Khalil Drira [2]

[1] Centro de Pesquisas Renato Archer, 13081-970 Campinas, SP, Brazil; [2] LAAS –CNRS 7, Av. Colonel Roche 31077 Toulouse, France

**Abstract:**    The new product development process, in its early phases, congregates knowledge from diverse domains and sources, spread among specialists that usually are not aware of each other's research interests. This work presents a tool designed to make the establishment of new communities or teams easier. The tool organizes their informal vocabulary into formal domain categories, in order to correlate them, and advises its users of potential networks they could belong to. An approach based on ontologies and machine learning is used to structure and make knowledge acquisition / retrieval, together with agents that cooperate and coordinate the access to the knowledge. The tool automatically updates its knowledge base relieving the user from tasks she/he is unfamiliar with. Initial experiments demonstrated the potential of this kind of tool. A test case is being developed encompassing members of a scientific network in the manufacturing area. Results will be analyzed envisaging its broader use and application to different knowledge domains.

**Key words:**    knowledge sharing tools, ontology, knowledge acquisition, agents, manufacturing recommendation system.

## 1.    INTRODUCTION

The design and conception phase of a product congregates knowledge from various domains. This knowledge is spread among people who have their own jargon and are possibly not aware of each other's vocabulary, even if they belong to the same technological chain. In order to truly cooperate people need to share a vocabulary, even minimal, so that they can exchange information that have the same meaning for each other.

This work addresses the cooperation among specialists mainly in the early phase of peer recognition. It introduces Sharing Engineering Information and Knowledge - SHEIK Tool - a system based on software agents that proactively retrieves and presents contextualized information based on user's vocabulary.

The approach was to develop a distributed architecture that permits to find manufacturing expertise by means of specialists recommendation in selected domains of manufacturing, in a way that can lead to establishment of new development teams. The early phases of product development were targeted, as it is the time a new community can emerge.

This article is organized as follows: section 2 discusses cooperation in manufacturing virtual enterprise; section 3 presents a functional description of SHEIK system; section 4 describes an initial prototype evaluation; section 5 shows the importance of knowledge and ontologies to recommendation systems; section 6 concludes the paper.


## 2.     COOPERATION IN A MANUFACTURING VIRTUAL ENTERPRISE

Manufacturing is an area that is facing drastic transformations due especially to the production paradigm change: from mass to customized production. Such change entails transformations in the productive processes, that are increasingly automated, as well as in the organizational processes that are changing from functional to business process view.

Product development is a key process for industrial enterprises. A survey carried out by Harmsen et al. (2000) in 513 Danish industrial companies showed that managers ranked the perceived importance of product development competence in fourth place in a 10 items list; sales, market responsiveness, production management were ranked number one to three.

Concurrent Engineering (CE) is the current paradigm for product development. Its purpose is to overlap product development phases. Willaert et al. (1998) discuss CE and shows that it can not lead to maximum benefits if it were considered alone, being necessary to consider it in a wider context called Collaborative Engineering.

Early phases of product development are those ones in which concepts are being studied, searching for fitness for the development problem in hand. In these phases the specialists may not have a complete idea for solutions, they are screening concepts against their criteria. This is a moment when specialists profit from their social network, asking questions as who knows about the product and who knows others that know about it.

## 3. SHARING ENGINEERING INFORMATION AND KNOWLEDGE - SHEIK - OVERVIEW

SHEIK is a tool for enhancing cooperation among members (potential or actual) of a community of practice (competence network) in a particular knowledge domain. The idea is that specialists could connect themselves to the network (local or global) and subscribe to a recommendation service the output of which would be specialists' profiles, containing their technical areas of interest, mapped from an ontology related to their main knowledge domain.

The purpose of this tool is to ease community establishment. Users can recognize potential peers from answers delivered from system and they can contact these potential peers to verify their skills and will to cooperate.

After communities are set up, SHEIK will serve as a maintenance tool and as a warehouse of knowledge and specialists' profiles. Also, it is a known fact that information needs of specialists vary in time so SHEIK could aid by recommending new profiles as needed.

## 3.1 Sheik requirements

The SHEIK requirements were presented in (Nabuco et al., 2001), together with a requirements modeling framework which is shortly summarized as follows: it encompasses three generic requirements (or dimensions) – cooperation, coordination and communication – and two views – system (technological) view and user (human) view.

Knowledge is the central element in all dimensions. **Cooperation** among team's members needs those members to share part of their knowledge. **Coordination** mutually identifies producers and consumers of information/knowledge. **Communication** locates and clarifies the path among producers and consumers.

Views are related to gather physical system requirements. **System view** considers technological and economical constraints, allowing a feasible solution to be defined; **user view** regards how to facilitate interaction between user and system.

To meet these requirements it was designed a technological solution that combines multi-agent systems and ontologies. Characteristics as system distribution and autonomy to act on behalf of its users were some of the reasons that led to the multi-agent solution. Enhancing the multi-agent systems capabilities ontologies were added, in which the core recommender system is based on and, machine-learning algorithms, performing the "intelligent" side of the agents. The Sheik multi-agent system has three functional elements: Multi-Agent System (MAS), Sheik meta-model, and Intelligent Modules.

## 3.2     Sheik multi-agent system

As shown by Figure 1, the Multi-Agent System is formed by two types of agents:   Sheik - an interface agent that runs in each user's machine, monitoring user activities in a timely basis, and Erudite - a matchmaker agent that interfaces with a Knowledge Base (KB) whose knowledge is related to a specific (sub) domain of Manufacturing.

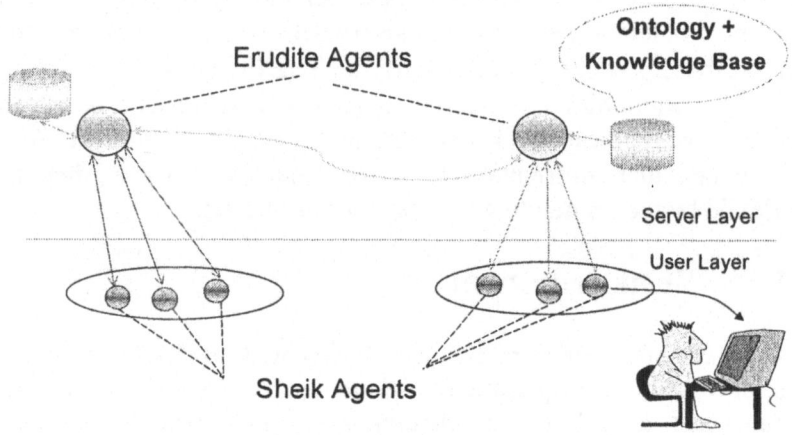

*Figure 1.* SHEIK Architecture

SHEIK architecture (see Figure 1) is organized into two layers: User Layer, composed of a colony of Sheik agents each one running in a user's machine and Server Layer, composed of a federation of Erudite agents running on server machines.

Each Sheik agent automatically updates users' profiles information relative to its user's knowledge domain, asks the Erudite agent for a recommendation containing specialists in domains related (or coincident) to his own domain. After Sheik had received a response, it e-mails its content to his user.

Each Erudite agent is related to a particular knowledge domain and contains an associated ontology relating person's profiles to a knowledge domain. Erudite agents, upon receiving a request from one Sheik agent, perform a search in its local KB, and if they find data about the referred knowledge domains they respond immediately to the Sheik agent. In case data is not found locally by an Erudite agent, it queries other Erudite agents to get pertinent data and if successful it forwards the data (knowledge domains and profiles) to the requesting Sheik agent.

The system was designed considering an open system perspective, so it could be easily replicated, and capable of executing in heterogeneous environments. As part of this philosophy the reutilization of existing tools and code was emphasized, as a manner of shortening development cycle and collaborating in others efforts in disciplines related to the project.

It was used a MAS prototyping tool (MASPT), created at "Renato Archer" Research Center – CenPRA. MASPT is based on a MAS Development Methodology (MASDM) that was developed for dealing with the modeling and development of architectures for shop floor control (Koyama, 2001). Results from the requirements phase (Nabuco et al., 2001), based on the GAIA methodology for agent-oriented analysis and design (Wooldridge et al., 1999), were used as a starting point for the design, that proceeded using MASDM.

Today, a set of systems for developing MAS exists (www.fipa.org/resources/livesystems.html). At the time the detailed design (2002) was done system's designers considered existent systems inadequate for the project development because designers required the projected system to be lightweight and low-cost. Some of the existing systems required either a RMI / CORBA server or compliance to FIPA or MASIF specifications, adding unnecessary complexity to the system. Also features for Java code generation, that could ease rapid prototyping were lacking or were not effective at that time, so designers opted for using CenPRA's MASPT that generates a MAS using *ad hoc* performatives declared by users and exchanged as Java serialized objects in a TCP-IP environment.

## 3.3    Sheik intelligent modules and meta-model

Intelligent Modules are used to accomplish required agents' functionalities. Figure 2 shows the basic models for both the Erudite agent and the Sheik agent. KA means Knowledge Acquisition and KB means Knowledge Base, the Intelligent Modules for each agent. This approach of making intelligent modules explicit provides great flexibility to the system that can be upgraded by changing them.

Sheik agent was designed to act on behalf of its user, acquiring data on his/her interests and consulting the Erudite agent to verify who are the possible peers (specialists with compatible / similar profiles) to consult, aiming at cooperation. To perform Sheik's KA functionality, the Kea tool

(Witten et al., 1999) was selected. It is based on a bayesian networks approach for keyword extraction and analysis and is available in Java.

The Erudite agent is responsible for answering requests from Sheik agents on behalf of their users. It must use its KB functionality. A KB based on ontology was selected; such an approach allows one to relate specialist's profiles (characterized by keywords, and working areas) to knowledge domains (for instance, manufacturing, software engineering, artificial intelligence).

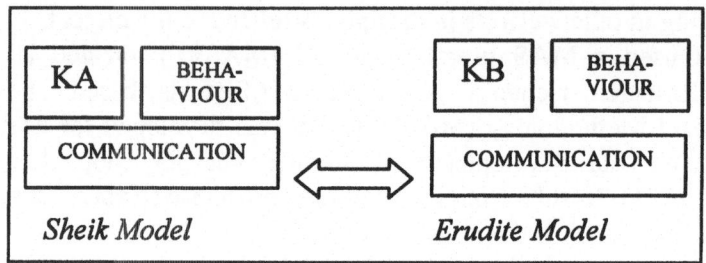

*Figure 2.* Sheik & Erudite models

To implement KB functionality, the Protégé System (Gennari et al., 2001) was selected as it is both an ontology editor and a knowledge base editor. It is available in Java as well and has been extended, having a large community of users and plug-ins developed (http://protege.stanford.edu).

An ontology can be considered as having been formed as a combination of a taxonomy and a set of rules. Such a set can be conceptualized through a knowledge meta-model.

A meta-model, named Sheik meta-model, that relates a manufacturing taxonomy (IMTI, 2000) and a conceptual class named Profiles (person's profiles) was developed to be used in SHEIK. Those elements were entered into Protégé, Figure 3, and the resulting knowledge base was populated with initial data concerning mainly profiles from researchers working on the SHEIK project.

## 4.      PROTOTYPE EVALUATION

The SHEIK prototype, using Kea tool and Protégé KB, was tested in a research environment composed of two laboratories: one at CenPRA and the other at Campinas State University - Unicamp, School of Mechanical Engineering. These laboratories are located in the same city but physically separated (10 Km). They are connected to the Internet and have Manufacturing as their main research area.

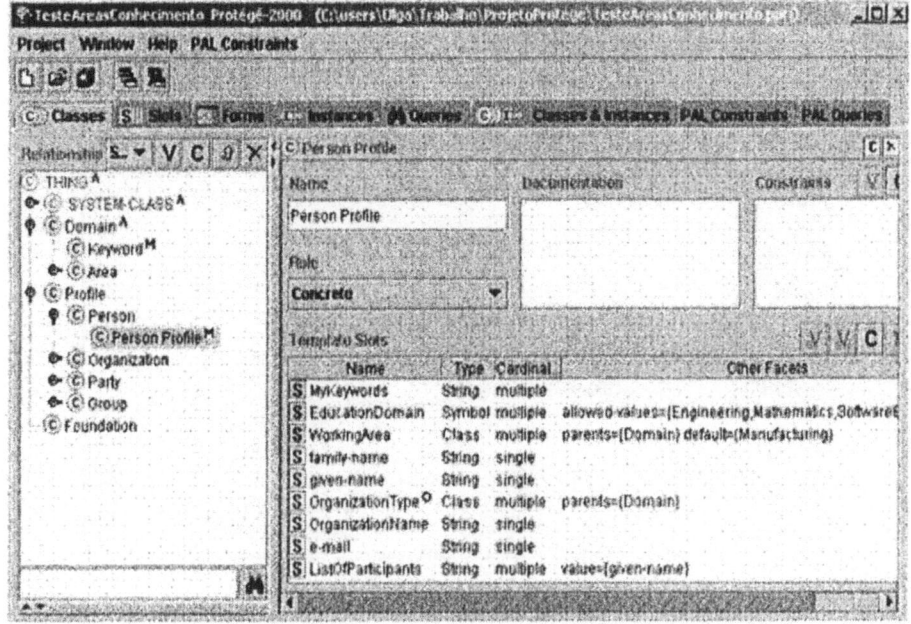

*Figure 3.* Sheik meta-model mapped into Protégé.

An Erudite agent was installed at Unicamp, containing the related Protégé system and acting as a server in the Internet. Researchers' profiles were manually populated in order to avoid the cold-start problem.

Sheik agents were installed at CenPRA. They gathered local user's data by means of their KA functionality. Local presentation of the data was done using an optional (Sheik agents do not use it) external module, as shown in Figure 4. It was tested the Sheik's ability to request related researcher's profiles from Erudite.

Figure 4 (left side) shows an user profile, defined locally at user's machine. In the future, it can be used to automatically feed the KB when the user subscribes the Erudite services, meaning the system could be capable of fully automatic start-up and operation. Figure 4 (right side) shows the output of Kea tool. These data are combined with local user's profile and sent to Erudite agent.

Two aspects were verified in the evaluation: if the system met the specifications and the users' acceptance.

The specification constrained Sheik agent to be light in terms of memory use and memory occupation, profiling the users and "learning" with them. Learning means that the agent searches new keywords increasing its accuracy as time passes by. Communication with Erudite agent was made using an *ad hoc* protocol. Erudite used the Protégé Axiomatic Language application program interface to query the database about keywords and the people related to them. Considering the specifications it was concluded that the system worked properly, according to the expected behavior.

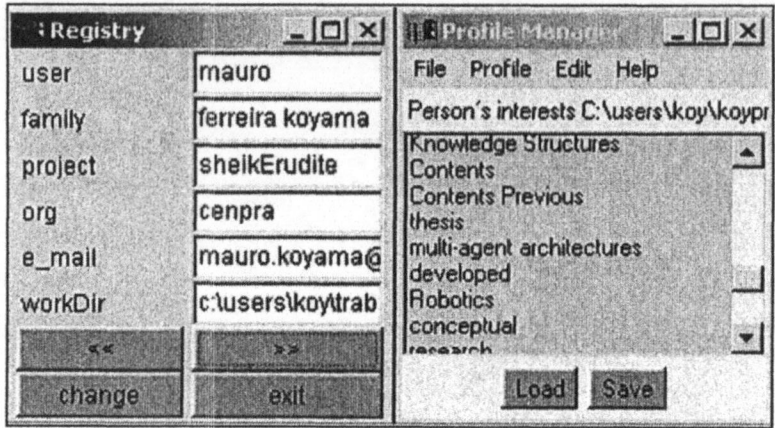

*Figure 4.* Sheik's user interface.

Regarding users' acceptance the system was considered well-behaved. Users disliked Kea's characteristic of acquiring keywords only from text files. is unable to gather information from other sources than text files. After this evaluation, other format conversions (PDF to TXT, PS to TXT and DOC to TXT) were added to the Sheik agent.

To date no system has been found in the literature with similar objectives and structure and having enough published information to make an effective benchmarking effort possible. Table 1 summarizes systems listed in section 5. The table shows that SHEIK is a recommendation system based on multi-agent system, knowledge sharing and ontologies that recommends specialists with compatible profiles.

## 5.    RELATED SYSTEMS

During an innovation process, people inside teams need to exchange information and share knowledge. There is an evolution in the way knowledge exchange is viewed (McLure and Faraj, 2000), from "knowledge as object" to "knowledge embedded in people" and finally as "knowledge embedded in the community" view.

Recommendation Systems search and retrieve information according to users' needs; they can be specialized on users profile or on the user's instantaneous interests (e.g., when users browse the web). They can be classified as collaborative filtering with and without content analysis and knowledge sharing. This kind of system is usually based on artificial intelligence techniques such as multi-agent systems, machine learning algorithms and ontologies. These techniques can be used separately or combined in different ways to find information and deliver it to the people who need it.

*Table 1.* Recommendation Systems comparison

| | Collaborative filtering | | Knowledge sharing | Multi-agent | Re-commends | Uses ontology |
|---|---|---|---|---|---|---|
| | With content analysis | Without content analysis | | | | |
| Yenta | y | | | y | Scientific papers | |
| GroupLens | y | | | | Usenet news | |
| Referral Web | y | | | y | Scientists | |
| Phoaks | | y | | | Scientists | y |
| OntoShare | | | y | | Opinions | y |
| QuickStep | | | y | y | Web pages | y |
| OntoCoPI | | | y | | Communities of practice | y |
| Sheik | | | y | y | Similar profiles | y |

Collaborative filtering with content analysis is based on information from trusted people which the system recognizes and also recommends. Examples of this kind of system are: The GroupLens Research Project (Konstan, 1997), The ReferralWeb (Kautz, 1997) and Yenta (Foner, 1999).

Collaborative filtering without content analysis examines the meta-information and classifies it according to the user's current context. It can recommend multimedia information that otherwise could be too complex to be analyzed. PHOAKS (Terveen et al., 1997) is an example of a system that associates scientific profiles by chaining bibliographic references with no comprehension of the article's contents.

Shared Knowledge Systems aim to construct a knowledge base according to a previous specialists know-how or best practice memories. Ontologies are well-suited for knowledge sharing as they offer a formal base for describing terminology in a knowledge domain (Gruber, 1993; McGuiness, 2001). Examples of recommendation systems that use ontologies are: OntoShare (Davies et al., 2002), OntoCoPI - Ontology Communities of

Practice Identifier (Alani et al., 2002) and the QuickStep system (Middleton et al., 2002).


## 6.    CONCLUSION

SHEIK integrates many concepts from distributed systems and artificial intelligence having as target product development in manufacturing that is a strongly team-based process. The literature review revealed a lack of systems as SHEIK which supports teams establishment in the early phases of product development and with the cross-functional profiles of the specialists involved in this process.

In the initial evaluation, despite the fact that the set of users was small, it was verified that the SHEIK prototype worked satisfactorily. Technically, the concept's feasibility was verified. An agreement is in course between SHEIK developers and one Brazilian non-governmental organization, in the manufacturing area, encompassing around 100 researchers, to setup an scalable experiment.

The problem of interoperation with other systems was not studied at an application level, but this was not a priority as, to date, there are no standards defining ontological descriptions of manufacturing systems and subsystems and as the idea was toward team establishment where the principle of minimal ontological commitment applies.

The underlying MAS can be upgraded to be compatible with emerging agents communication protocols standards, if necessary, preserving the intelligent modules (knowledge base and knowledge acquisition).

Validations of the used tools were done. Both Kea tool from Waikato University, New Zealand, and Protégé from Stanford University School of Medicine, USA, proved useful.

It is expected that the new test-case being set will enable unveiling new and existing problems and  will permit to enhance SHEIK and put it to reliable use in the manufacturing.


## REFERENCES

Alani, H., O'Hara, K. and Shadbolt, N. ONTOCOPI: methods and tools for identifying communities of practice' Proceedings of 2002 World Computer Congress, Intelligent Information Processing Stream (Montreal) 2002.

Davies, J., Dukes, A. and Stonkus, A. OntoShare: Using ontologies for knowledge sharing. Proceedings of the www2002 International Workshop on the Semantic Web. Hawaii, May 7, 2002.

Foner, L. N.. Political Artifacts and Personal Privacy: The Yenta Multi-Agent Distributed Matchmaking System. Boston: Media Arts and Sciences, Massachusetts Institute of Technology, 1999. 129p. PhD Thesis.

J. Gennari, M. A. Musen, R. W. Fergerson, W. E. Grosso, M. Crubézy, H. Eriksson, N. F. Noy. The Evolution of Protégé: An Environment for Knowledge-Based Systems Development. *International Journal of Human-Computer Studies*, in press, http://faculty.washington.edu/gennari/#pubs.

Gruber, T. R., Towards principles for the design of ontologies used for knowledge sharing, *International Journal of Human-Computer Studies*, v.43 n.5-6, p. 907-928, Nov./Dec. 1995

Harmsen, H., Grunert, K. G., and Bove, K., Company Competencies as a Network: the Role of Product Development, Journal of Production Innovation Management, pp194-207, v. 17, 2000

IMTI - Integrated Manufacturing Technology Initiative. 21st Century, Manufacturing Taxonomy A Framework for Manufacturing Technology Knowledge Management. V1.0. Dec. 2000, http://www.IMTI21.org.

Kautz, H., Selman, B., Shah, M.. The hidden web. *American association for artificial intelligence.* Summer 1997. p 27-36.

Konstan, Joseph A., Miller, B. N., Hellocker, J.L., Gordon, L. P., Riedl, J. Applying collaborative filtering to Usenet News. Communications of ACM. Vol 40. N°3. March 1997.

Koyama, Mauro F., Arquitetura de Supervisão e Controle de Chão de Fábrica baseada em componentes genéricos, School of Mechanical Engineering, State University of Campinas, Brazil, PhD Thesis, 2001.

McGuinness, D. L., Ontologies and online commerce. IEEE Intelligent Systems. V. 16. N° 1 p. 8-14. 2001.

Middleton, S., De Roure, D., Shadbolt, N. Capturing Knowledge of user preferences: ontologies in recommender systems. *Proceeding of First International Conference on Knowledge Capture, KCAP2001.*

McLure M. W., Faraj, S., "It is what one does": why people participate and help others in electronic communities of practice. *Journal of Strategic Information Systems.* N°. 9, p. 155-173. 2000.

Nabuco, O., Drira, K., Dantas E., A Layered Design Model for Knowledge and Information Sharing Cooperative Systems, in *Proceedings of tenth IEEE International Workshops of Enabling Technologies: Infrastructure for Collaborative Enterprises*, p. 305-310, MIT, Cambridge, Massachusetts, USA, June 2001.

Terveen, L., Hill, W., Amento, B., McDonald, D., Creter, J. PHOAKS: A system for sharing recommendations. Communications of the ACM. Vol. 40, N. 3. March 1997.

Witten, I.H., Paynter, G.W., Frank, E., Gutwin, C. and Nevill-Manning, C.G., "Kea: practical automatic keyphrase extraction, " *Proc Digital Libraries '99.* 254-265, Berkeley, CA, USA, August 1999.

Willaert, Stephan S.A., Graaf, Rob de, and Minderhoud, S., Collaborative engineering: A case study of Concurrent Engineering in a wider context, *Journal of Engineering an Technology Management*, JET-M, v. 15, pp. 87-109, 1998

Wooldridge, M., Jennings, N., Kinny, D. A methodology for agent-oriented analysis and design. *Proc. 3rd Int. Conf. On Autonomous Agents*, pp 68-76, Seattle, WA, 1999.

# USING AGENTS IN THE EXCHANGE OF PRODUCT DATA

Udo Kannengiesser and John S. Gero
*Key Centre of Design Computing and Cognition, University of Sydney*

Abstract:     This paper describes using agents in the exchange of industrial product data
              when predefined translators are not available. A major problem with standard
              translators is that a seamless data transfer instantly fails when not every
              translator implements a mapping into or from the standard format. This is
              frequently the case for large design projects that involve the use of a multitude
              of heterogenous tools, possibly in evolving configurations over time. This
              approach to using agents aims to flexibly provide product models in a form
              adapted to the need of the particular tools when a common data format is not
              readily available. Experiments show the feasibility of this approach as well as
              its efficacy and efficiency.

Key words:     product data exchange, product modelling, interoperability

## 1        INTRODUCTION

There has been an increased use of computational tools to support
various tasks in product development. Examples include computer-aided
drafting (CAD) and manufacturing (CAM) systems and a number of
specialised tools for analyses such as finite element analysis (FEA) and
spreadsheet analysis. Most computational systems have been developed
independently from one another to address the specific needs of each task
and use different product data representations. However, industrial product
development is a process that involves a complex network of interrelated
activities, each of which needs information produced or manipulated by the
other. Interoperability – the ability to move data from one representation of a
product to another to allow other computational processes to operate on it

has become an area of growing concern as the cost of such interchanges increases (NIST 1999).

Most approaches to the exchange of product data (today commonly subsumed in the notion of product modelling) are founded on a standard data model that is used to translate between the different native formats of the tools. Any object that needs to be made interoperable must be pre-defined in this model and encoded into a standard form. One of the best-known product models is the ISO 10303 standard, informally known as STEP (STandard for the Exchange of Product model data).

Despite the growing use of STEP some practical issues remain. One of them is that interoperability between a set of tools is solely determined by the intersection of their translation capabilities. As many translators have been specialised to implement only certain subsets of the standard data model, in practice a completely seamless data transfer is often not possible (Pratt 2001). Especially large design projects involving a highly diverse set of tools are affected. This problem is aggravated when technological or organisational changes over the duration of a project necessitate the integration of new tools or new exchanges among present tools. In addition, the pace at which ISO standards are developed and implemented is generally very slow and often lags behind the needs and developments in industrial practice (Eisenberg and Melton 1998).

Updating the set of translators for every modification in the tool environment is time-consuming, costly and not always possible within the time constraints of a project. There is a need for a more flexible approach, one that is able to quickly achieve interoperability when a common product model is not readily available. We have developed an agent-based system that can exchange product data among tools that do not share a common format. Experimental results show that this approach can be an effective and efficient way to provide the needed flexibility in the transfer of product data when pre-defined translators are not available. Our conceptual assumptions draw from research in cognitively-based situated agents.

## 1.    SITUATED AGENTS

A characteristic that allows a system or agent to adapt its behaviour to changes in its environment is situatedness, an idea from cognitive science. A situated agent does not simply react reflexively in its environment but uses its interpretation of its current environment and its knowledge to produce an action (Clancey 1997). As a consequence, a situated agent can be exposed to different environments and produce appropriate responses.

Gero and Fujii (2000) have developed a modular architecture for a situated agent, Figure 1. The agent's sensors monitor the environment to produce sense-data relevant for the agent. The sensors receive biases from the perceptor, which "pulls" the sense-data to produce percepts. Percepts are grounded patterns of invariance over interactive experiences. Perception is driven both by sense-data and biases from the conceptor, which "pulls" the percepts to produce concepts. Concepts are grounded in the percepts as well as possible future interactions with the environment. The hypothesizor identifies mismatches between the current and desired situation and decides on actions that when executed are likely to reduce or eliminate that mismatch. Based on the hypothesized action, the action activator decides on a sequence of operations to be executed on the environment by the effectors.

This architecture provides a framework for different modes of cognition and consequently different degrees of flexibility in the agent's actions: A *reflexive* agent uses the raw sensory input data from the environment to generate a pre-programmed response. A *reactive* agent uses percepts to activate its actions, which can be viewed as a limited form of intelligence constrained by a fixed set of concepts and goals. A *reflective* agent constructs concepts based on its current goals and beliefs and uses them to hypothesize possible desired external states and propose alternate actions that will achieve those desired states through its effectors. The agent's concepts may change as a consequence of its experience.

Situated, reflective agents are especially useful in dynamic environments characterised by high heterogeneity and frequent change. One such environment is the fragmented world of industrial design software.

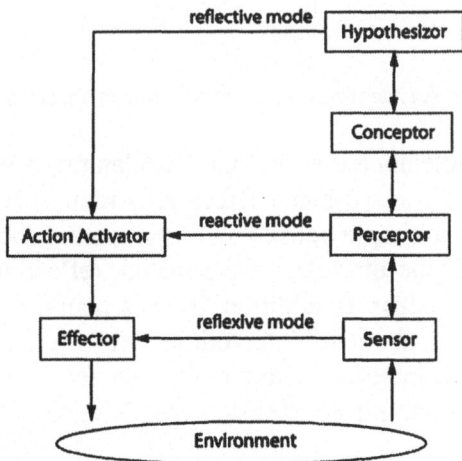

*Figure 1.* A modular architecture for a situated agent allowing different modes of reasoning.

## 2.      IMPLEMENTATION

We have implemented a system consisting of a situated, reflective agent (which we call the product modelling (PM) agent) and a number of tools, each of which is "wrapped" by a simple, reactive agent, Figure 2. The PM agent maintains all the data of a particular product throughout the different design stages from the initial specification to the released design description. The individual design stages are carried out by the tool agents that modify or add to the product data. The PM agent knows about the tool agents' roles and the current state of the design with respect to a given project plan and accordingly manages all data transfers to and from the tool agents. Cutkosky et al. (1993) have used a similar architecture using agents wrapping design tools and facilitators to exchange their data; however their approach is based on pre-defined standard translators.

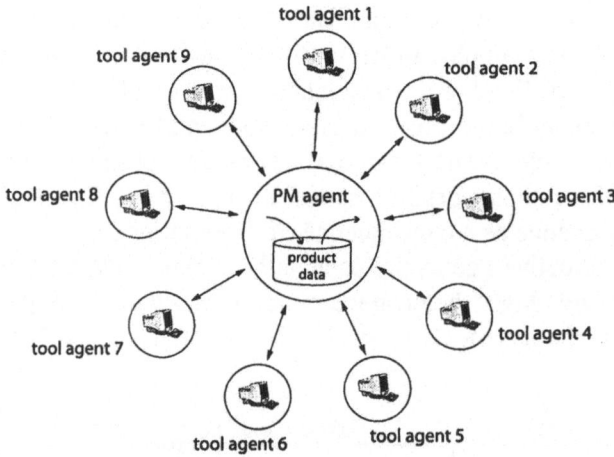

*Figure 2.* An agent-based system for product data exchange.

All agents are implemented in the rule-base language Jess[1] and connected to their environment by sensors and effectors written in Java. While the tool agents, here, are rather simple consisting of perceptors and action activators, the PM agent has all the modules of a situated, reflective agent, including conceptor and hypothesizor. In addition, it has a neural network (in Java) to represent its memories about its interactions with the tool agents, which it uses to bias the way it interacts with its environment. The neural network is an interactive activation and competition (IAC) network that has the same

---

[1] Java Expert System Shell (http://herzberg.ca.sandia.gov/jess/)

architecture as the one proposed by McClelland (1981) and includes an unsupervised learning algorithm. In addition, we have given the agent the capability to add new neurons to the IAC network as well as to reorganise the connections among the neurons to update its memory according to its current interpretation of its interactions. This allows the agent to integrate new experiences such as previously unknown formats or new associations between the formats and the tool agents (in case a tool agent replaces its tool by one that uses a different format). The PM agent can construct new formats from interpreting messages represented in unfamiliar formats using a set of generative rules and semantic knowledge.

The messages exchanged among the agents are structured according to specifications developed by the Foundation for Intelligent Physical Agents (FIPA 2004). There are two types of messages: strings representing product models, and propositions or requests to clarify their meanings when an agent fails to understand a product model. The latter type is based on synonyms and hypernyms (super-names) as a means to explain unknown data. This has been inspired by the conceptual foundations of WordNet (Miller 1995). Figure 3 shows all possible agent interactions using the AUML[2] notation.

Failure of the PM agent to provide a tool agent with product data that is represented in the correct format necessitates help from the human user who then has to translate the data manually. Similarly, if the PM agent fails to understand the product data produced by a tool agent, human intervention is required to fill the data into the PM agent's product database. We will use the number of times that human intervention occurs during the design project as an indicator for our system's efficacy.

As the PM agent can learn from its interactions with the tool agents, we expect it to transfer the product data with less and less effort among the same set of tool agents. As a result, there will be fewer messages in the system dealing with expressing lack of understanding or clarifying meanings. We will refer to this type of messages using the linguistic term *repair*. The number of times that repair occurs during the design project will serve as an indicator for our system's efficiency.

Figure 4 shows a possible result of the PM agent learning (parts of) formats and thus increasing interoperability through its interactions. Commencing with a limited amount of knowledge that is sufficient to allow interoperability with some tool agents (tools T3 and T6), we expect the PM agent to construct new knowledge over time to exchange product data with other tool agents, either completely automated (tools T1, T2 and T4) or semi-automated (tool T5). The PM agent might not be able, however, to

---

[2] AGENT UML (http://www.auml.org/)

learn a tool agent's format if that format is completely different from its previous experiences (tool T7).

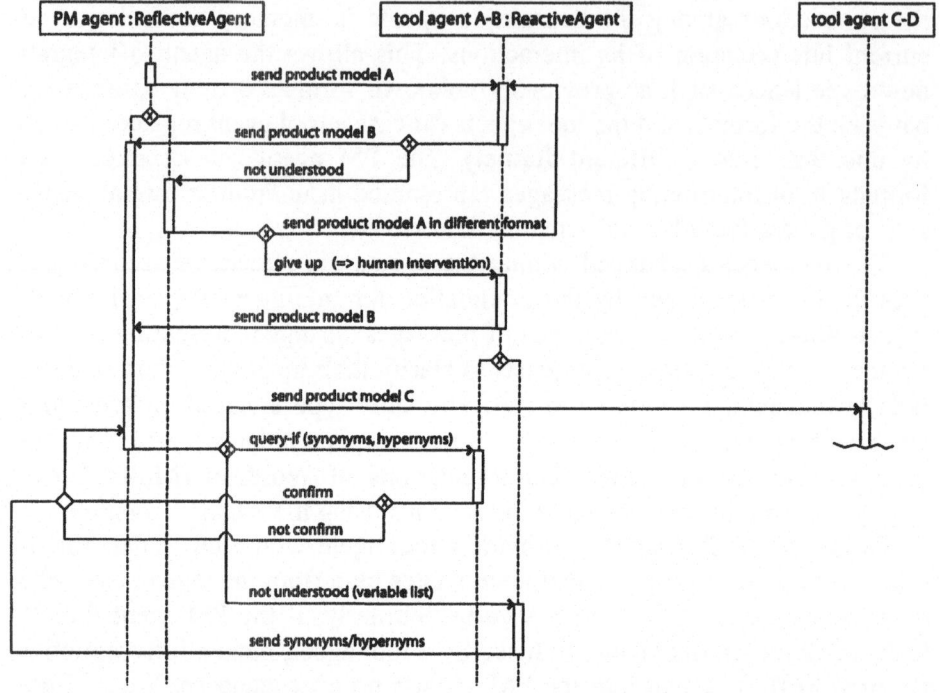

*Figure 3*. Possible interactions between the PM agent and a tool agent that needs a product model A as its input to produce product model B as its output (tool agent A-B). After the PM agent has successfully parsed product model B (eventually using human intervention), it sends a product model C to tool agent C-D.

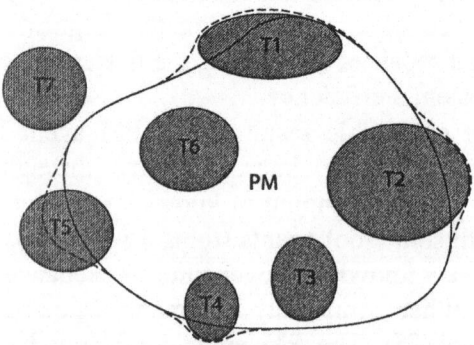

*Figure 4*. The PM agent's knowledge (PM) covering some of the formats of tool agents (T1 - T7). The dashed line indicates new knowledge gained over a series of interactions.

# 3.        EXAMPLE: DESIGN OF A TURBOCHARGER

Our product example whose design data is to be exchanged among the agents is an exhaust-gas turbocharger for passenger cars, Figure 5. This product is quite complex with a large amount of data describing its structure and behaviour. For reasons of illustrative simplicity we have reduced this complexity to only 268 variables, without limiting the validity of the model.

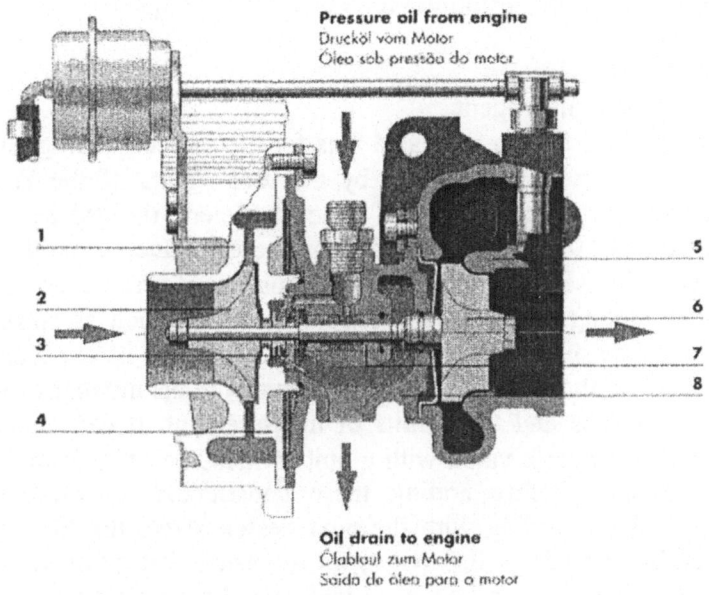

*Figure 1.* A turbocharger for passenger cars (Source: BorgWarner Turbo Systems): 1. Compressor housing, 2. compressor wheel, 3. thrust bearing, 4. compressor backplate, 5. turbine housing, 6. shaft & turbine wheel assembly, 7. bearing bushing, 8. centre housing.

All data is represented by content, specifically in the form of:

< variable name >   < value >   < unit of measure >

Different formats can be distinguished by different sets of variable names describing the same set of concepts. For example, depending on the format, the compressor air flow of 0.176 m$^3$/s at an engine speed of 5500 rpm may be represented as "AF1000 0.176 m$^3$/s", "AF_1000 0.176 m$^3$/s" or "V_RED_1000 0.176 m$^3$/s". We have defined 7 different formats covering each of the 268 product variables.

We have implemented 16 tool agents, each of which has (hard-coded) knowledge about at most two of the 7 formats: one format must be used to represent the tool's input data and one to represent the tool's output data (these formats can also be identical). Although a tool agent does not have the possibility to swap or mix its input and output format, it can communicate its knowledge about mappings among them (as synonyms or hypernyms) to the PM agent if requested. The PM agent uses its knowledge about the tool agents to provide each of them with the correct product model represented in the correct form. This knowledge is stored in its IAC network as associations between tool agents and the following types of properties:

- function or role in the design project
- behaviour (as an input-output view) of the tool or agent
- input format
- output format
- vendor of the tool or agent

This knowledge is also used as a bias for the correct parsing template to interpret product models produced by the tool agents. If the PM agent's knowledge about the correct format is not sufficient, the PM agent uses its knowledge about other, similar formats or about product semantics to parse the message. Its semantic knowledge consists of pre-coded qualitative relationships among some of the product variables, such as "nozzle inner diameter < nozzle outer diameter". The agent also uses its expectations and perceptions about the product model with respect to the number of variables, their type of values and their units of measurement. It can conclude, for example, that a numeric value with a unit of measure of "$N/mm^2$" possibly indicates "stress". Before adding these constructed assumptions to its knowledge and proceeding with the next design stage, the PM agent first seeks reconfirmation from the tool agent to ensure that its assumptions are correct. If the PM agent is unable to understand a product model using its semantic knowledge, it tries to receive help from the tool agent by communicating with it.

Figure 6 shows the project plan we have established for simulating a part of the design of a turbocharger. Every task is carried out by a different tool agent. We have set up a scenario that includes two iterations that represent necessary reformulation for optimising the product's performance after evaluating the prototype. This permits us to examine if the PM agent becomes more successful and efficient when interacting with the same agents for a second or third time. These are the agents carrying out the tasks 2 to 11 after the 1$^{st}$ iteration and 3 to 12 after the 2$^{nd}$ iteration. We have also set up some tool agents to modify their formats to simulate the integration of new tools during the design project and to test the PM agent's ability to adapt to these changes by quickly reorganising its memory.

The scenario requires a total of 68 product data transfers between the PM agent and the tool agents. We have given the PM agent some initial translation knowledge that is sufficient to cover 41 of them, while the remaining 27 data exchanges will require either additional effort of interpretation and communication by the agents or intervention by the human user. This potential lack of interoperability concerns the input and/or output formats of 7 of the 16 tool agents.

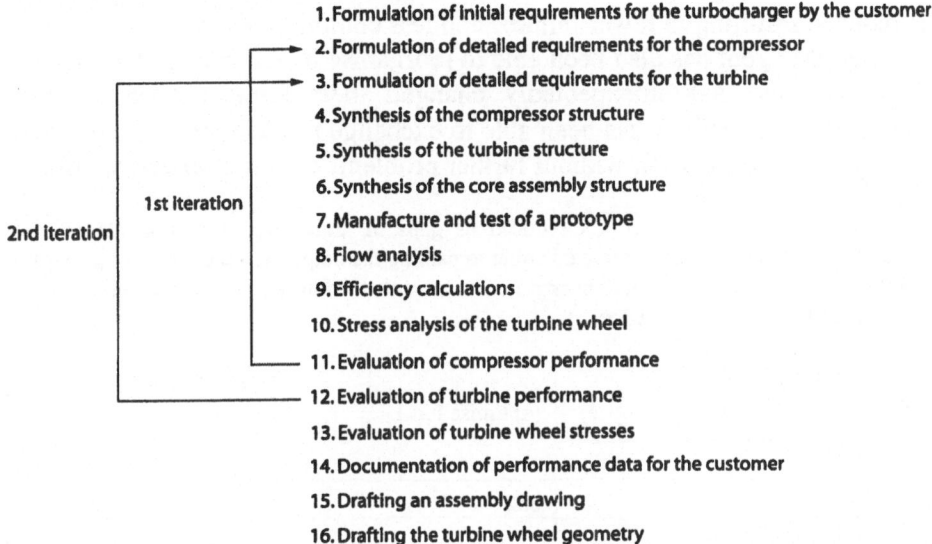

1. Formulation of initial requirements for the turbocharger by the customer
2. Formulation of detailed requirements for the compressor
3. Formulation of detailed requirements for the turbine
4. Synthesis of the compressor structure
5. Synthesis of the turbine structure
6. Synthesis of the core assembly structure
7. Manufacture and test of a prototype
8. Flow analysis
9. Efficiency calculations
10. Stress analysis of the turbine wheel
11. Evaluation of compressor performance
12. Evaluation of turbine performance
13. Evaluation of turbine wheel stresses
14. Documentation of performance data for the customer
15. Drafting an assembly drawing
16. Drafting the turbine wheel geometry

*Figure 2.* A project plan and scenario for simulating the design of a turbocharger.

## 4.    RESULTS

*Table 1.* Interoperability characteristics of the agent-based system compared to a static system using pre-defined translators.

| total no. data trans-fers | Static system using pre-defined translators | | | | Agent-based system | | | Increase in interoper-ability with the agent-based system |
| --- | --- | --- | --- | --- | --- | --- | --- | --- |
| | no. auto-mated trans-fers | no. manual trans-fers | Interoper-ability rate | | no. auto-mated transfers | no. manual trans-fers | Interoper-ability rate | |
| 68 | 41 | 27 | 60 % | | 60 | 8 | 88 % | 46 % |

Table 1 summarises the results of the simulation with regard to its efficacy. The agent-based system has raised the potential rate of interoperability by nearly 50% compared to what a static system would be able to achieve under the same initial conditions.

Table 2 gives an overview of the failures and repairs occurring in exchanging product data throughout the two iterations in the scenario. It also shows the PM agent's knowledge gaps regarding the formats of 7 of the 16 tool agents (labelled A-1 to A-16). As some of these gaps are gradually eliminated through agent interaction, the (potential) lack of interoperability is reduced resulting in fewer failures and less communication.

The PM agent has also been able to reorganise its knowledge after agents A-4, A-5 and A-8 unexpectedly changed their formats after the first iteration. As a result, it has been able to exchange product models with them after the second iteration without further problems or communicative effort.

*Table 2.* Failures and repairs get reduced as gaps of knowledge are eliminated during interaction. Failures/repairs are related either to parsing the output of a tool agent or providing it with the correct input. The dark background represents the knowledge gaps pertaining at the beginning of the current sequence.

| | 1st sequence (designing 1st prototype) | 2nd sequence (optimisation 1) | 3rd sequence (optimisation 2) |
|---|---|---|---|
| A-1 | 1.1 | | |
| A-2 | 2.1 | 2.2 | |
| A-3 | 3.1 failed input output repair | 3.2 | 3.3 |
| A-4 | 4.1 input repair * | 4.2 input repair ** | 4.3 |
| A-5 | 5.1 | 5.2 output repair | 5.3 |
| A-6 | 6.1 | 6.2 | 6.3 |
| A-7 | 7.1 failed input failed output | 7.2 failed input failed output | 7.3 failed input failed output |
| A-8 | 8.1 | 8.2 output repair | 8.3 |
| A-9 | 9.1 output repair | 9.2 | 9.3 |
| A-10 | 10.1 | 10.2 | 10.3 |
| A-11 | 11.1 | 11.2 | 11.3 |
| A-12 | | 12.2 | 12.3 |
| A-13 | | | 13.3 failed input |
| A-14 | | | 14.3 |
| A-15 | | | 15.3 |
| A-16 | | | 16.3 |

\* This input repair was due to an over-generalisation of the neural network giving the PM agent an incorrect bias, which led to constructing the product data in an inappropriate format.
\*\* This input repair was due to A-4 changing its input format without informing the PM agent of this change.

# 5. CONCLUSION

Our experiments have shown that an agent-based approach to product data exchange can provide interoperability without pre-defined translators. It can allow design projects to choose the computational tools appropriate for the needs of the actual design tasks and worry less about the availability of a standard translator. This would make these projects more adaptable to technological and organisational changes. Although our implementation has demonstrated to some extent how using agents in product modelling can increase interoperability, we expect better results when more than one situated agent is used. Our current work focuses on extending the tool agents (which to date are only reactive) to be situated.

Letting situated agents negotiate a shared product model on the fly can potentially constitute a method for pushing future standardisation. After a product model has been agreed upon and successfully used by a set of agents, this model can be used later as the prototype version of a new part of the standard model. Such a method would ground the standard in practice and accelerate its development and implementation.

# ACKNOWLEDGEMENTS

This work is supported by a University of Sydney Sesqui Research and Development grant and by an International Postgraduate Research Scholarship.

# REFERENCES

Clancey, W.J., 1997, *Situated Cognition*, Cambridge University Press, Cambridge.

Cutkosky, M.R., Engelmore, R.S., Fikes, R.E., Genesereth, M.R., Gruber, T.R., Mark, W., Tenenbaum, J.M. and Weber, J.C., 1993, PACT: An experiment in integrating concurrent engineering systems, *IEEE Computer* 26(1): 28-37.

Eisenberg, A. and Melton, J., 1998, Standards in practice, *SIGMOD Record* 27(3): 53-58.

FIPA, 2004, FIPA ACL Message Structure Specification, *Document No. SC00061G* (April 24, 2004); http://www.fipa.org/specs/fipa00061/SC00061G.pdf.

Gero, J.S. and Fujii, H., 2000, A computational framework for concept formation for a situated design agent, *Knowledge-Based Systems* 13(6): 361-368.

McClelland, D.E., 1981, Retrieving general and specific information from stored knowledge of specifics, *Proceedings of the Third Annual Meeting of the Cognitive Science Society*, pp. 170-172.

Miller, G.A., 1995, WordNet: A lexical database for English, *Communications of the ACM* 38(11): 39-41.

NIST, 1999, Interoperability cost analysis of the US automotive supply chain, *Planning Report #99-1*, NIST Strategic Planning and Economic Assessment Office, Gaithersburg, MD.

Pratt, M.J., 2001, Practical aspects of using the STEP standard, *Journal of Computing and Information Science in Engineering* 1(2): 197-199.

# A PERVASIVE IDENTIFICATION AND ADAPTATION SYSTEM FOR THE SMART HOUSE

Paulo F. F. Rosa[1], Sandro S. Lima[1], Wagner T. Botelho[1], Alexandre F. Nascimento[2] and Max Silva Alaluna[1]

[1]Military Institute of Engineering,Systems Eng. Dept, Rio de Janeiro, Brazil; [2] 6th Military Region, Salvador, Brazil

**Abstract**: The smart house is a system composed of several cooperating agents, which make it possible to act autonomously in performing tasks, that in conventional houses are done by their inhabitants. The current work proposes a smart house capable: (a) of identifying the inhabitants in the house, (b) to adapt itself to the inhabitants preferences, as well as to modify itself to changes on these preferences, and (c)to maintain optimal levels of safety, energy saving and comfort. This work develops an identification and adaptation system for the smart house, based on a multiagent methodology. This approach simplifies the implementation of the communication policy among the agents; besides, it gives more flexibility to the system, by delegating to each agent a specific job in the house. New jobs are added to the system by simply developing the necessary agents to execute them. The system is built through the definition of all the tasks for the house; at this point, the agents and their relationships are defined, in order to properly execute the tasks. This system uses a pervasive human footstep sensor capable of recognizing the inhabitants of the house, through their weights and the characteristics of their locomotion. A neural network is used to learn and adapt to the daily habits of each individual, as well as to properly negotiate the changes in these patterns of behavior. In order to validate our idea, experiments were done with a room's lighting system, the results of which show a very reliable system, capable to perform personalized actions in the house.

**Key words**: smart house; domotics; pervasive computing; footstep sensor; sensor network; multiagent systems; neural network; consumer electronics.

# 1.    INTRODUCTION

The smart house is a system composed of several cooperating agents that make it possible to act autonomously in performing tasks that in conventional houses are done by their inhabitants. The house is composed of several environments, in which local agents are used to perform cooperatively many tasks. Furthermore, two global agents are defined: *water* and *energy agents*, which represent the main resources in the house. The current work proposes a smart house capable: (a) of identifying the inhabitants in the house, (b) to adapt itself to the inhabitants preferences, as well as to modify itself to changes on these preferences, and (c) to maintain optimal levels of safety, energy saving and comfort.

This work develops an identification and adaptation system for the smart house, based on a multiagent methodology. This approach simplifies the implementation of the communication policy among the agents; besides, it gives more flexibility to the system, by delegating to each agent a specific job in the house. New jobs are added to the system by simply developing the necessary agents to execute them. There are several methodologies that facilitate the construction of multiagent systems, for example: MaSE[1,2], Gaia[3,4], Message/UML[5,6], Prometheus[7-10] and Tropos[11,12]. This work combines the MaSE methodology and UML (Unified Modelling Language). This approach describes all the available services in high level just to broke them down in more details; so, all the necessary agents to the construction of the system can be identified, as well as the their relationships to each other.

The MaSE methodology uses graphic models and consists in two phases: analysis and design. The analysis identifies subgoals necessary to accomplish the main goals - to each goal is asserted a rule and a group of agent class. This phase includes three steps: capturing goals, applying use cases and refining roles. Initially, we define and structure the main goal as a collection of subgoals to be accomplished. Next, use cases translates the goals into rules and association of tasks. Finally, the roles are defined using sequence diagrams, it is necessary to assure that all roles had been identified; so, we will be able to develop the tasks that define their behavior and the communication pattern. In the design phase, the system is implemented, indeed. It consists on three steps: creating agent classes, constructing conversations and assembling agent classes. The first step consists on the creation of the agent's class diagrams that describe the system as a whole, showing its functioning and relationships. The second step defines a coordination protocol for the agents. The third step is necessary to define the agent architecture and its components. The final step of the design phase is the system design that involves building a deployment diagram which specifies the locations of the agents within a system. In the next section, the system is explained in more details.

## 2.     THE SMART HOUSE PROJECT

In order to develop the system, it is necessary to identify all of its performable tasks. The identification of these tasks is facilitated through use case diagrams that depict a general view of all the available services in the house. However, this diagram presents no further details regarding how and by whom such tasks will be performed. At this phase of the project, the house might be able to: identify its inhabitants; to adapt the room to the preferences of its occupants; to learn new preferences delivered by the residents; to react to external influences disturbing the environment settings; and, to detect toxic gases and fire. From now on, we present the description of the tasks performed by the house.

*Identification*: A person entering in a room, activates the footstep sensor[13,14]. This event starts data acquisition by the sensor, that will inputs to the footstep algorithms, in order to determine the person's walking features. An ART1 (Adaptive Resonance Theory) neural network uses the results from the footstep algorithm to learn and associate the way of walking to a specific individual. Ergonomic studies[15] point to the uniqueness of footstep features within a group of persons. This system is capable to recognize new users in real time, as well as to detect slight variations on the locomotion patterns of the usual inhabitants.

*Adaptation*: after receiving the identification from the resident, the room makes a research on the resident's preferences and sends them to the agents that control the services supplied by the house. As soon as the tasks are concluded, the agents send a warning to the room; finally, the service will be finished when all the agents conclude their jobs.

*Lighting settings*: unsatisfied with the luminosity, the resident will be able to adjust the dimmer, causing the system to do a new reading of a light sensor, and the new preference of the resident is updated.

*Temperature settings*: when the resident modifies the temperature of a room, the system updates his/her preference in the profile databank.

*Lighting compensation*: weather variations can influence the luminosity of a room. This event is not done by the resident (resident's interference are done using the dimmer), so the system compensates the luminosity changes accordingly to the person's profile.

*Gas protection*: gas sensors are constantly monitoring the rooms. When dangerous levels are reached, the gas supply is interrupted, the alarm is turned on and the exhaustion begins working, until normality is reached.

The details of the services previously presented can be graphically represented, through activity diagrams. In these diagrams, we can view all the stages of a service, the decision points and the alterations that occur in the elements of the system, during the task. Figure 1 and Figure 2(a) shows the use cases diagrams and the activities diagram for the use case Identification. From this activity diagram we can see that we need to implement 2 (two) agents: the *Identification Agent* and the *Security Agent*.

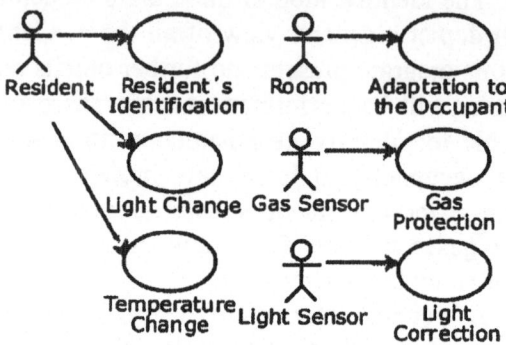

*Figure 1.* The use cases

The agents that are necessary to achieve the required functionality are obtained through the analysis of all the diagrams of the system activity, and will be addressed in the next section.

## 2.1    Defining the agents

Is this section, we present the agents that execute the system's tasks. The *id agent* recognizes the resident, permitting the house to act in a personalized way. The *room agent* receives the resident's identification and starts the adaptation process, by sending messages to the agents that control the equipments in the room. The *temperature agent* is responsible for keeping the room temperature accordingly to its occupant's preference, and also for updating the person changing profile. The *lighting agent* and the *noise agent* act just like the temperature agent, but in the illumination and noise fields. The *security agent* acts together with the id agent protecting the house against burglars; it is also responsible for detecting toxic gases and fire. The *electricity* and *water agents* control the use of these resources in the house; they can also be used in consumption's control policies. In order to allow for personalized actions, the room agent adapts the room to the resident's preferences, after his identification. These information are supplied by the *resident agent* [see Figure 2(b)]. We can verify that there is a group of preferences for each room (i.e., temperature, light and noise levels), but due to the system's construction methodology, new preferences can be included as the system grows.

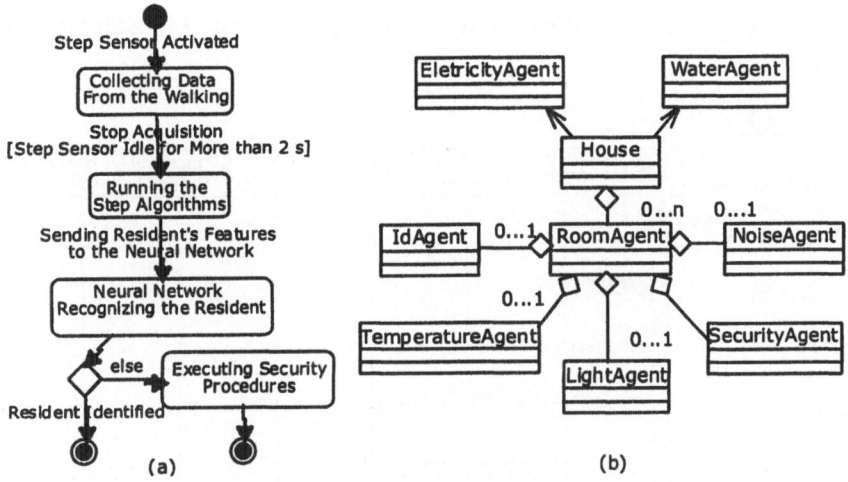

*Figure 2.* (a) Activity diagram of the resident identification. (b) The intelligent house agent

The agents that adapt the room to its occupant make sensors reading to define their actions, such as to send appropriate commands to the actuators. It can be verified that the system interacts with several equipments, such as: dimmers, thermostats in the cooler, sensors and home appliances in general. These equipments usually do none direct communication with a computer; consequently, it is necessary to develop an *Interface Class*, that will be composed of devices, such as: acquisition data boards and X-10 standard control panels.

After defining the agents of the house and their roles in the execution of the tasks, the next section will present the agents' control policies.

## 2.2     The control policy

The policy adopted by the system, for the communication among the agents, considers that the resident is identified by the id agent, when the resident agent enters a room in the house. The id agent informs the room the identity of the resident. The room agent gets the information about the residents' preferences with the resident agent, so it will be able to adapt the room. After getting the residents' preferences, the room agent asks the lighting, temperature and noise agents to allocate the necessary resources to the levels accepted by the resident.

When some non-identified person enters a room, the security agent is informed and it takes the proper action against the burglar. Besides, this agent, in conjunction with the temperature agent, is responsible for protecting the house against fire. As an example of the control policies, Figure 3 shows the communication among agents during the adaptation of a room.

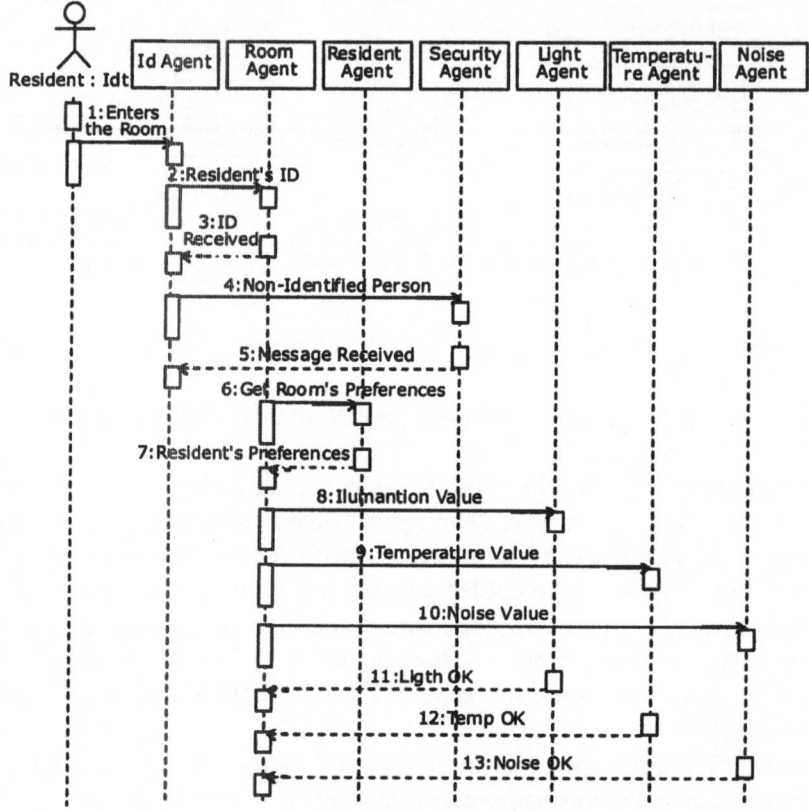

*Figure 3.* Room adaptation.

Finally, the house has to identify the residents, in order to act in a personalized way. In the next section, we will present, in detail, the id agent. Based on its work, every other agent in the house performs their job.

## 2.3     The id agent

The distinction of the persons living in the house might be done in the most natural and non-invasive way, in order to take into account concerns such as privacy and system's user friendlessness. We use a footstep sensor developed by Nascimento[13,15], which is capable to identify the residents on a house based on the features of their walking. The id agent is formed by three parts: (1) a sensor network; (2) a footstep algorithm; and (3) a neural network for classification and identification.

The sensor network collects data, in order to obtain the physical features to uniquely identify the resident, such as: $f$ (footstep frequency), $p$ (person's weight), $\delta_d$ (angle of the right foot), $\delta_e$ (angle of the left foot) and $s$ (footstep length).

The sensor network is composed of load cells, the locations of which are described with (X, Y) cartesian coordinates. The load cells are disposed such as we can see in Figure 4. The distance $d$ between the sensors has to be chosen carefully, since its value should permit the correct identification of a resident with a minimum data amount and computational effort. The value $d$ = 2cm was chosen, because it provided the best results with the minimum efforts, considering an adult's foot characteristics. In order to track the residents inside the house, a sensor network is placed in the transition zones for each room and in the house's entrances. The sensor network is able to identify several residents at a time, due to the fact that for a distance between two footsteps greater than 90cm, they are considered to be from different persons. Footsteps laying within 90cm from each other might belong to a single person, and are known as *correlate group*.

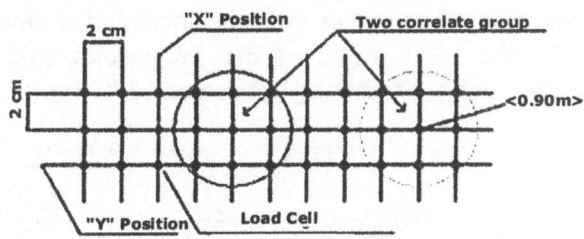

*Figure 4.* The sensor net.

The second part of the id agent is composed of the footstep algorithms: (1) footstep angle algorithm; and (2) the footstep frequency algorithm. In this paper, we work with variations of the the algorithms presented in works[13,15]. These algorithms receive the data collected by the sensor network and calculate the walking features of the resident.

The parameter $p$ is an output from the load cell. The parameters $\delta_d$ and $\delta_e$ are determined by the footstep position and the direction of the person's locomotion. The parameter $s$ is obtained by the distance between the right and left feet. We can observe that, as we walk, our feet accomplishes three phases: the support phase, the sustaining phase, and the impulse phase[1]. Let $T_a$, $T_s$ and $T_i$ be the time period for the support, sustain and impulse phases, respectively. Experimentally, it was observed that these phases demand the same amount of time; i.e., $Ta = Ts = Ti = T/3$. In this work, we considered these three phases with length $D=3$, where $D$ is the footstep length. To calculate the footstep angle, we must find the last and the first sensors, that have been activated in that footstep. Then, we calculate the middle point between them, and the supporting points that are located in the first and second parts of the same footstep. The angle of the foot (right or left) is discovered using two equations for concurrent straight lines in any point. Then, we find the points ($A$, $P_1$ and $P_2$) for the footstep. The footstep direction is given by the line between the points $P_2$ and $P_1$. The straight line between the points $A$ and $A'$ shows the direction of the movement. The angle $\delta_d$ is given by the direction of movement and the footstep direction of the right foot. The data acquisition system works with a data structure ($X$, $Y$, $p$, $T$, $E$), where: ($X$, $Y$) are the cartesian coordinates of the footstep sensor; $P$ is the weight; $T$ indicates the time, in which the sensor was activated or deactivated (0-deactivated and 1-activated). In order to obtain the frequency $f$, the algorithm calculates the time interval between the first sensors activated on footstep $i$ and $i+1$. Furthermore, to determine the frequency, the algorithm uses the structure ($X$, $Y$, $T$), that can find the coordinates and the time of activation of the first sensor in each footstep. The final value of the frequency will be the mean value of the frequencies calculated in this process. The characteristics of walking are presented in Figure 5.

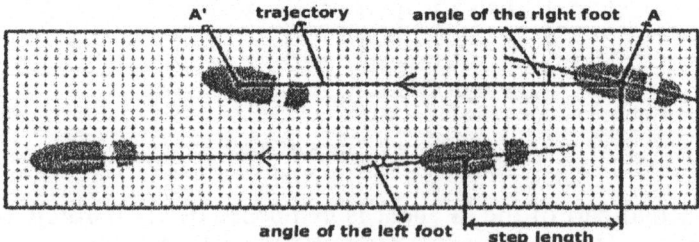

*Figure 5.* The resident's walking features.

The neural network is used to identify the home's resident using his/her walking features calculated by footstep algorithms. The ART1 neural

---

[1] Here is a brief explanation of the three phases of a person's walk: *(a) Support phase:* when the swing foot reachs the ground; *(b) Sustaining phase:* the entire foot is placed on the floor, preparing for an impulse; and *(c) Impulse phase:* the foot propels the body forward and the leg loses contact with the ground.

network is used because its training algorithm is non-supervised, which eliminates the need of previous presentation of the residents' walking patterns; and also, for being capable to recognize a resident that presents variations in his/her walking.

In order to validate the id agent, we have to show that it is capable of recognizing new individuals (as well as, being aware of that in future), even if they present variations of their walking features. The footstep patterns of some individuals were collected as experimental data, using a plane ground surface covered with paper. So, during the people's walk, the footsteps (the shoes were marked with ink) were registered in the paper, allowing us to collect the data needed for the footstep algorithms, that is summarized in Table 1.

*Table 1.* Features extracted from 10 persons.

| Individual | $\delta_e[^\circ]$ | $\delta_d[^\circ]$ | s[cm] |
|:---:|:---:|:---:|:---:|
| 1 | -27.6 ± 1.7 | 22.7 ± 1.8 | 52.7 ± 1.3 |
| 2 | -35.8 ± 2.4 | 28.2 ± 1.2 | 55.7 ± 1.1 |
| 3 | -34.7 ± 1.9 | 28.4 ± 3.1 | 78.1 ± 1.7 |
| 4 | -26.6 ± 2.1 | 25.1 ± 2.3 | 65.0 ± 1.6 |
| 5 | -24.2 ± 1.7 | 21.4 ± 1.5 | 70.2 ± 2.1 |
| 6 | -42.4 ± 2.7 | 31.5 ± 2.6 | 59.6 ± 1.9 |
| 7 | -31.7 ± 2.6 | 23.8 ± 1.8 | 72.5 ± 1.5 |
| 8 | -16.5 ± 2.4 | 12.5 ± 3.2 | 68.0 ± 1.0 |
| 9 | -21.2 ± 2.9 | 18.8 ± 2.7 | 59.5 ± 1.8 |
| 10 | -33.2 ± 1.6 | 30.3 ± 2.4 | 75.4 ± 1.5 |

The ART1 neural network uses binary input, so we have to make some considerations. The input variable $p$ ranges from $20kg$ to $147kg$, so it is represented using a vector of 7 bits. The input variable f ranges from $1Hz$ to $2.2Hz$. If the precision used is $0.10Hz$, then we will have 13 possible frequency levels, so it is represented with a vector of 4 bits. The input variables $\delta_d$, $\delta_e$ and s follow no specific pattern. From the data collected, we can see that the angle of the left foot presents a variation of -25.9° (-42.4° < $\delta_e$ < -16.5°) and the angle of the right foot presents a variation of 19.0° (+12.5° < $\delta_d$ <+31.5°). If the precision adopted is 0.1°, we need a vector of 9 bits for the angle of the left foot, and a vector of 8 bits for the angle of the right foot. The footstep length s presented a variation of $25.4cm$ ($52.7cm < s$ $< 78.1cm$). Consequently, an 8-bit vector is enough, for a 0.1cm precision. If the output variable Idt can be represented by a vector of 4 bits, we can identify up to 16 people - a more than reasonable number of persons in a house.

Let us suppose the existence of a house with the residents with the features displayed in Table 2.

*Table 2.* Residents features.

| Idt | f [Hz] | P [Kg] | $\delta_e$ [°] | $\delta_d$ [°] | s [cm] |
|-----|--------|--------|----------------|----------------|--------|
| 1 | 2.2 | 80 | -27.6 | 22.7 | 52.7 |
| 2 | 1.2 | 65 | -35.8 | 28.2 | 55.7 |
| 3 | 2.0 | 45 | -34.7 | 28.4 | 78.1 |
| 4 | 1.7 | 50 | -26.6 | 25.1 | 65.0 |
| 5 | 1.8 | 70 | -24.2 | 21.4 | 70.2 |
| 6 | 1.4 | 75 | -42.4 | 31.5 | 59.6 |
| 7 | 2.1 | 95 | -31.7 | 23.8 | 72.5 |
| 8 | 1.6 | 85 | -16.5 | 12.5 | 68.2 |

Since the ART1 neural network works with binary data, we convert the features in Table 2, and each person is now represented by a 36 bits vector. This vector contains all the studied features and will be the input for the neural network and are shown in Table 3.

*Table 3.* Residents features input for the ART1 neural network.

| Idt | f [Hz] | p [Kg] | $\delta_e$ [°] | $\delta_d$ [°] | s [cm] |
|-----|--------|--------|----------------|----------------|--------|
| 1 | $1100_2$ | $0111100_2$ | $001101111_2$ | $01100110_2$ | $00000000_2$ |
| 2 | $0010_2$ | $0101101_2$ | $011000001_2$ | $10011101_2$ | $00011110_2$ |
| 3 | $1010_2$ | $0011001_2$ | $010110110_2$ | $10011111_2$ | $11111110_2$ |
| 4 | $0111_2$ | $0011110_2$ | $001100101_2$ | $01111110_2$ | $01111011_2$ |
| 5 | $1000_2$ | $0110010_2$ | $001001101_2$ | $01011001_2$ | $10101111_2$ |
| 6 | $0100_2$ | $0110111_2$ | $100000011_2$ | $10111110_2$ | $01000101_2$ |
| 7 | $1011_2$ | $1001011_2$ | $010011000_2$ | $01110001_2$ | $11000110_2$ |
| 8 | $0110_2$ | $1000001_2$ | $000000000_2$ | $00000000_2$ | $10011011_2$ |

For a better visualization, each individual pattern will be represented by a block formed by small white and black squares. A white square represents a bit 1 (one) an a black square a bit 0 (zero). The blocks should be read from the top to the bottom, from left to right.

First, we will show that the id agent is capable of recognizing the residents of the house; so, we developed a matlab function that implements the ART1 neural network. This function takes as parameters the output of the footstep algorithms. Figure 6 shows the final configuration of the neural network after the residents features being presented; in the top of the figure, we can see the patterns from each resident and in the bottom we can see the clusters formed for each pattern recognized by the agent.

Now, we have to show that the id agent is capable of identifying a resident, even if there are variations in his/her walking features. These variations should be saved in the resident's cluster. Suppose, for example, that the resident 1 is carrying a bag, so his/her weight changes from 80 to $90kg = 1000110_2$ and his/her footstep length, s, goes from 52.7cm to 54.0 cm $= 00001101_2$. Imagine also that resident 7 is going on a diet, and now, s/he is weighting $82kg = 0111110_2$ and his/her footstep frequency now is $1.7Hz = 0111_2$.

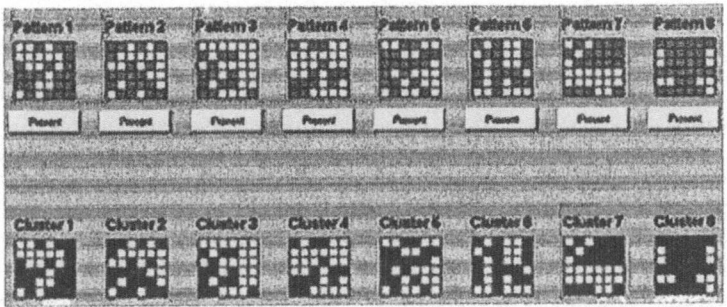

*Figure 6.* Recognition of the residents.

Figure 7 shows the final configuration of the neural network after the presentation of the new features of residents 1 and 7, the ART1 neural network has learned the new patterns of the residents and saved them to their clusters.

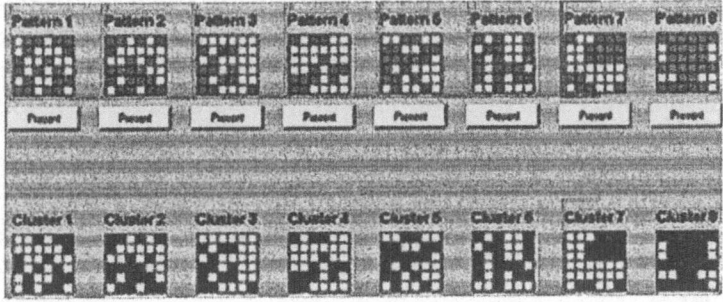

*Figure 7.* Recognition of the residents with variation on walking patterns in residents 1 and 7.

We have proved that the id agent accomplished its role very well, being able to identify new users, creating new clusters for them; and recognizing variations on patterns already presented to the network, making the necessary changes on the clusters in order to learn these new characteristics.

In the next section, we introduce the lighting agent, which uses the information provided by the resident agent to adjust the lights of a room based on the occupant's preferences.

## 3.　　LIGHTING AGENT

The lighting agent that we propose sets the level of the lights of each room based on the preferences of the resident recognized by the id agent. The system consists of a photoresistor and a dimmer, which can be operated manually or through a microcontroller. Hereafter, we make a description of the learning process. As soon as an identified resident enters for the first time in a room, and stays there for 10 seconds at least, the system should keep the last value informed by the photoresistor. The system will track the person all over the house for a certain time, in order to pick up a report of his/her light setting preferences. This period of $10s$ is enough to the person to change the light level of a room. For the very first 3 times of a person in a room, the illumination will be activated in 60% of its maximum value and it will be reduced until the user changes the position of the dimmer. Besides, if a person increased the dimmer's set 3 (three) times, the next time the light level will be set in 100%.

The total luminous flux of a room is given by: $\Phi T = \Phi 1 + \Phi 2 + \Phi 3$, where they are, respectively: the flux of the controlled room, the flux from the natural source and the flux from neighboring rooms.

To test our lighting agent, we modeled a room using the matlab. In the simulation we considered resident's illumination level preference of 3.780 lumens, and that the lamps installed in the room are capable to produce a maximum luminous flux of 5.400 lumens. During all day, variations of the luminous flux occurred in the room, see Table 4.

*Table 4.* [Variation of the Liminous Flux of a Room During a Day.]

| $\Phi TA$ | 70% PmaxA=3.780lumens | Constant |
|---|---|---|
| $\Phi T1A$ | $(5.400xNdA) / 20$ | $NdA$-dimmer's position A |
| $\Phi T2A$ | 0 | $0h < t \leq 7h$ |
| | $[ ((1000x17) - (tx1000)) / 3 ]$ | $7h < t < 10h$ |
| | 1000 | $10h \leq t \leq 14h$ |
| | $[ ((1000x17) - (tx1000)) / 3 ]$ | $14h < t < 17h$ |
| | 0 | $17h \leq t \leq 0h$ |
| $\Phi T3A$ | 0 | $0h < t \leq 7h$ |
| | $[(120xt - 7x\,120)/3] + 100$ | $7h < t < 10h$ |
| | $220 \sin 1.57xt + 220$ | $10h \leq t \leq 14h$ |
| | $[((120x7)-(tx120))/3]+100$ | $14h < t < 17h$ |
| | 0 | $17h \leq t \leq 0h$ |

The lighting agent has to maintain the luminous flux of the room constant during all day, despite the action of the natural source and neighbor rooms. We can see, in Figure 8, that the agent reduces or increases the lights of the room according to the external sources of light.

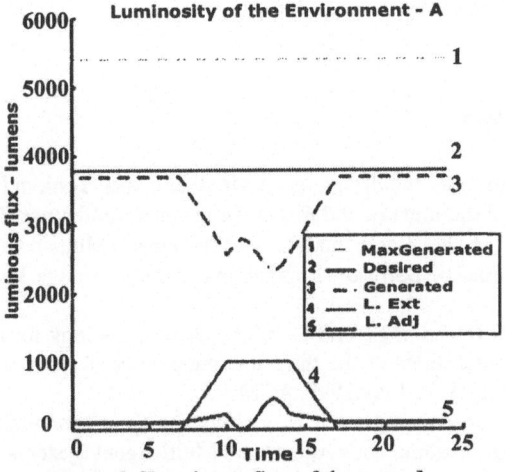

*Figure 8.* [Luminous flux of the room.]

Using fluorescent lamps in the room we achieved an energy saving of 707*Wh* in 24 hours, which means a reduction of 36.8%. Therefore, the lighting agent presented here accomplished its goal of recognizing the individual, and most of all, the agent saved energy keeping the comfort levels stable, what is one of the objectives of the smart home.

## 4.     FINAL COMMENTS

The current work proposed a smart house capable of identifying the inhabitants in the house, adapting itself to the inhabitants daily preferences, as well as to modify itself to changes on these preferences, and maintaining optimal levels of safety, energy saving and comfort. This work developed an identification and adaptation system for the smart house, based on a multiagent methodology. This approach simplifies the implementation of the communication policy among the agents; besides, it gives more flexibility to the system, by delegating to each agent a specific job in the house. The system uses a pervasive human footstep sensor capable of recognizing the inhabitants of the house, through their weights and the characteristics of their locomotion. A neural network is used to learn and adapt to the daily habits of each individual, as well as to properly negotiate the changes in these patterns of behavior. In order to validate our idea, experiments were done with a room light system, the results of which show a very reliable system, capable to perform personalized actions in the house. As a next approach to this research, we intend to build a prototype for the entire system and implement features of other multiagent modeling methodologies to optimize the performance of our smart house project.

# REFERENCES

1. S. A. DeLoach. Analysis and design using MaSE and agentTool, in Proceedings of the 12th Midwest Artificial Intelligence and Cognitive Science Conference (MAICS 2001), 2001.
2. S. A. DeLoach, M. F. Wood, and C. H. Sparkman, Multiagent systems engineering, International Journal of Software Engineering and Knowledge Engineering, 11(3): 231-258, 2001.
3. M. Wooldridge, N.R. Jennings, and D. Kinny, A methodology for agent-oriented analysis and design, In Proceedings of the third international conference on Autonomous Agents (Agents-99), Seattle, WA, May 1999, ACM.
4. M. Wooldridge, N.R. Jennings, and D. Kinny. The Gaia methodology for agent-oriented analysis and design. Autonomous Agents and Multi-Agent Systems, 3(3), 2000.
5. G. Caire, F. Leal, P. Chainho, R. Evans, F.G. Jorge, G. Juan Pavon, P. Kearney, J. Stark, and P Massonet. Project p907, deliverable 3, Methodology for agent-oriented software engineering. Technical Information Final version, European Institute for Research and Strategic Studies in Telecommunications (EURESCOM), 09 2001.
6. Giovanni Caire, Francisco Leal, Paulo Chainho, Richard Evans, Francisco Garijo, Jorge Gomez, Juan Pavon, Paul Kearney, Jamie Stark, and Philippe Massonet, Agent oriented analysis using MESSAGE/UML, In Michael Wooldridge, Paolo Ciancarini, and Gerhard Weiss, editors, Second International Workshop on Agent-Oriented Software Engineering (AOSE-2001), pages 101-108, 2001.
7. L. Padgham and M. Winiko, Prometheus: A methodology for developing intelligent agents, In 3$^{rd}$ International Workshop on Agent-Oriented Software Engineering, July 2002.
8. L. Padgham and M. Winiko, Prometheus: A pragmatic methodology for engineering intelligent agents, In Proceedings of the OOPSLA 2002 Workshop on Agent Oriented Methodologies, pages 97108, Seattle, November 2002.
9. L. Padgham and M. Winiko, Prometheus: Engineering intelligent agents, tutorial notes, available from the authors, October 2002.
10. L. Padgham and M. Winiko, Prometheus: A brief summary, technical note, available from the authors, January 2003.
11. F. Giunchiglia, J. Mylopoulos and A. Perini, The Tropos software development methodology: Processes, Models and Diagrams, in Third International Workshop on Agent-Oriented Software Engineering, July 2002.
12. P. Bresciani, P. Giorgini, F. Giunchiglia, J. Mylopoulos, and A. Perini, Troops: An agent-oriented software development methodology. Technical Report DIT-02-0015, University of Trento, Department of Information and Communication Technology, 2002.
13. A. F. Nascimento, Dynamic system of Residential Automation, Master Thesis in Systems and Computation, Military Institute of Engineering - IME, Rio de Janeiro, Brazil, 2002.
14. P. F. F. Rosa, A. F. Nascimento, S. S. Lima, "Domotic: A Pervasive Identification System for the Smart House". World Congress on Engineering and Technology Education, 2004 WCETE, pp. 1233-1238.
15. R. J. Orr, and G. D. Abowd, The Smart Floor: A Mechanism for Natural User Identification and Tracking, in Proceedings of the CHI 2000 Conference on Human Factors in Computing Systems: Extended Abstracts, ACM Press, New York (2000), pp. 275-276.

# DEDUCTIVE DIAGNOSIS OF DIGITAL CIRCUITS*

J. J. Alferes[1], F. Azevedo[1], P. Barahona[1], C. V. Damásio[1], and T. Swift[2]

[1] *Centro de Inteligência Artificial (CENTRIA), FCT/UNL, 2829-516 Caparica, Portugal.*
*{jja\fa\pb\cd}@di.fct.unl.pt;* [2] *Dept. of Computer Science, State University of New York at Stony Brook, NY 11794-4400, USA, tswift@cs.sunysb.edu*

**Abstract:**     In this paper we present an efficient deductive method for addressing combinational circuit diagnosis problems. The method resorts to bottom-up dependencies propagation, where truth-values are annotated with sets of faults. We compare it with several other logic programming techniques, starting with a naïve generate-and-test algorithm, and proceeding with a simple Prolog backtracking search. An approach using tabling is also studied, based on an abductive approach. For the sake of completeness, we also address the same problem with Answer Set Programming. Our tests recur to the ISCAS85 circuit benchmarks suite, although the technique is generalized to systems modelled by a set of propositional rules. The dependency-directed method outperforms others by orders of magnitude.

**Key words:**  Fault Diagnosis, Logic Programming, Abduction

## 1.     INTRODUCTION

Because of its simplicity and applicability, model-based diagnosis has proven an important problem in artificial intelligence. Simply put, model-based diagnosis can be seen as taking as input a partially parameterized structural description of a system and a set of observations about that system. Its output is a set of assumptions which, together with the structural

* This work was partially supported by Praxis XXI Project TARDE.

description, logically imply the observations, or that are consistent with the observations. This corresponds to the *Matching-Abnormal-Behaviour* (MAB) diagnosis conceptual model[1].

A problem-solving system for model-based diagnosis can be used to diagnose faulty behaviour of systems from their specifications, and may be valuable in the manufacture of electrical circuits, engine components, copier machines, etc. However, such a system could also be used to allow deliberative agents revise their plans, to parse natural language in the presence of errors and other tasks.

As stated, model-based diagnosis bears a strong resemblance to satisfiability in first-order logic. Accordingly, the implementation of model-based diagnosis has most often been based on general problem-solving systems, such as truth maintenance systems (TMS[2]) or belief revision systems[3]. However, given its logical flavour, model-based diagnosis should be amenable to logic programming (LP) techniques, such as abduction or default logic. For diagnosis, the power of an LP approach, if it can be made successful, is that the search of problem space can be made by an optimized general purpose engine rather than using a specially designed diagnoser or TMS.

Here we explore various LP approaches to model-based diagnosis, and apply them to the *c6288* digital circuit from the ISCAS'85 set of benchmarks[4]. *C6288* (Fig. 1) is a 16-bit multiplier, which can be seen as a grid-like pattern of 240 half and full adders, consisting of 2406 logical gates in all.

*C6288* is of special interest in that it has traditionally proven difficult to diagnosis system. It is reported[5] that several special-purpose diagnosers could not reliably detect faults in this circuit. However, the best LP approaches reliably detect all faults, and appear superior in the execution times. Moreover, LP approaches, when compared to the special-purpose ones, also have the advantage of requiring a very small amount of code – often less than a hundred lines.

In our experiments, we adopt the usual *stuck-at* fault model, where faulty circuit gates can be either *stuck-at-0* or *stuck-at-1*, respectively outputting value 0 or 1 independently of the input. We first experimented with two naïve approaches that use a generation mechanism to identify possible sets of faults and then a test mechanism to test whether the faults are consistent with a given set of observations. We then experimented an approach that uses tabling to abduce faults consistent with observations. Here, for lack of space, we only briefly mention them, though details can be found in a report[6]. We then present an approach based on generating diagnoses as a stable model (SM) of a program, an approach that uses a novel mechanism of grounding the input to the SM generator via tabling. We next show how a deductive dependency-directed technique can be adapted to efficiently derive diagnoses and be advantageously implemented in Prolog in a backtrack-free manner. Finally, we compare the performance of all techniques and analyse their strengths and weaknesses.

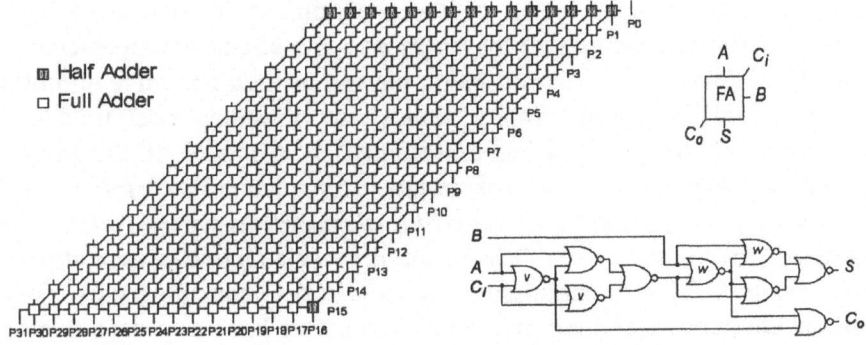

*Figure 1*. High-level Model of c6288 Multiplier Circuit and full adder module (images obtained from http://www.eecs.umich.edu/~jhayes/iscas/ ).

## 2. NAÏVE APPROACHES AND TABLING

Perhaps the simplest, even naïve, method to test a circuit for a diagnosis is a simple *generate-and-test* method. Essentially, for each faulty gate that we intend to test, we simply replace its model by fixing its output to the appropriate faulty value which, in our running example is the negation of the correct value – generate phase. We then compare the output produced by the faulty model with the observed output. If they are the same, the (possible) fault is accepted, otherwise rejected – test phase. A slightly different method (that we call *generate-and-check*) consists in, rather than only comparing to the output vector in the end, to force the output vector in the test phase.

An alternative is a *backtracking* approach, making use of the in-built depth-first search strategy of Prolog engines. Instead of taking as input the faulty state of the gate, this approach simply models all the possible states of the gate, and returns either a list with the faulty state or an empty list.

The use of tabling is natural for handling the grid-like structure of *c6288*, which can require a huge amount of recomputation of circuit values, if a top-down approach (such as each of the two above) is used. In the *tabling* approach, that we implemented in XSB[7], we represent the faulty behaviour of a gate as an assumption, and a diagnosis as a consistent set of assumptions.

## 3.       STABLE MODEL PROGRAMMING

A new, and growing in importance, LP paradigm is that of Stable Models (or Answer-set) Programming[8,9]. In it, solutions to a problem are represented by the stable models[10] of the corresponding program, rather than by answer substitutions of a single model of the program, as in traditional LP. In traditional LP (as in the above) the diagnoses of a circuit are represented by terms, the clauses of the program being viewed as their recursive definition. In stable model (SM) programming, clauses are viewed as constraints on the diagnoses, each diagnosis being represented by a model of the program defined in terms of those constraints. As claimed[8], *"stable model programming is especially well suited for all problems where solutions are subsets of some universe, as each solution can be modelled by a different stable model"*. This is definitely the case of circuit diagnosis, where solutions are subsets of abnormal gates, and so we have also used this new approach to solve the circuit problem.

To represent our circuit diagnosis problem in SM programming, all we have to define is a suitable set of constraints over the predicates that define the circuit and the diagnoses. An important constraint in this domain is that each gate is either normal or abnormal, and cannot be both. This is easily coded by the following two rules:

```
abnormal(X) :- gate(X), not normal(X).
normal(X) :- gate(X), not abnormal(X).
```

i.e. if *X* is a gate that is not normal then it must be abnormal, and vice-versa.

Moreover, if some, e.g., AND-gate is normal, then its output value must be the conjunction of its inputs. If it is abnormal, its output is the negation of the conjunction. Rules imposing exactly this are:

```
val(out(and2,G), V):- normal(G), val(in(and2,G,1), I1), val(in(and2,G,2), I2), and(I1,I2,V).
val(out(and2,G),V):- abnormal(G), val(in(and2,G,1), I1), val(in(and2,G,2), I2), nand(I1,I2,V).
```

It remains to be imposed that: *a)* no point can simultaneously have 2 different values; *b)* all values of a given output vector are observed; and *c)* only single-faults occur:

```
inconsistent :- val(P,V1), val(P,V2), V1 \= V2.
explains :- val(out(and2,c545gat),V1), ..., val(out(nor2,c6288gat),V32).
nonsingle :- abnormal(G1), abnormal(G2), G1 \= G2.
goal :- explains, not inconsistent, not nonsingle.
:- not goal.
```

where each *Vi* in the *explains/0* clause is replaced by the output value of the corresponding gate in a given output vector. This clearly resembles the formulation of an abduction problem: our goal is that all observed output values are explained, there are is inconsistency and no diagnoses with more than one abnormal gate. And we are only interested in SM's in which our goal is satisfied (i.e. it is not false). The SM's of this program, restricted to predicate *abnormal/1*, exactly correspond to the diagnosis of the circuit.

For computing the SM's of the described program (i.e. the single-fault diagnoses of the circuit) we have used the *smodels* system[11] version 2.26 for Windows. For dealing with the grounding of the program, required by *smodels*, and for pre-processing away the function symbols *out/2* and *in/3* used in the representation of the circuit, we have developed an XSB-Prolog program. Although this is all that is required of the XSB-Prolog for this circuit diagnosis problem, the program does more. The additional functionality of the mentioned XSB-Prolog program might be crucial for other diagnosis problems and, in general, for other problems that can be coded as abduction.

Our XSB-Prolog program starts by running the query *goal* in a program with the representation of the problem having the above clause for *goal/0*, without the last clause (*:- not goal*), and where all predicates are tabled. In this execution, all calls that depend on loops over negation are suspended. Note that, in the above representation, the only loop over negation is the one between predicates *abnormal/1* and *normal/1*. After the execution, the tables of the various predicates contain the so-called *residual program*[11], which has, for each predicate, the (non-failing) rules used during execution, simplified by removing all body literals proven true (and not suspended). It is well known[11] that the SM's of the residual program are the same as those of the part of the original program relevant to the query. Moreover, if all the calls during the execution are ground (which is the case for our representation) the residual program is also ground. Thus, this residual program, after some simple pre-processing that eliminates the function symbols *out/2* and *in/3*, is what is passed to *smodels* for computing the diagnoses. This method is now easy to implement, due to the recent XAsp package of XSB 2.6, which already provides special predicates for this purpose and linking to *smodels*. Its main advantage over a direct usage of *smodels* is that only the part of the program relevant to the query has to be considered when computing the SM's. Besides gains in efficiency, this is also important for general abduction problems: in this way, the obtained abductive solutions come only in terms of abducibles relevant to the query (i.e. only relevant abductive solutions are computed).

# 4.      DEPENDENCY-DIRECTED DIAGNOSIS

As an alternative to model the circuit diagnosis problem, we represent digital signals with sets and Booleans. A deductive dependency-directed technique[13,14] is used to simulate the circuit behaving normally, as well as to deduce the behaviour of all faulty circuits. This technique has been used by the Electronic CAD community for fault simulation, but in this section we show how to apply it to our diagnosis problem.

Since the faulty behaviour of a circuit can be explained by several sets of faults, we represent a signal not only by its normal value but also by the set of diagnoses it depends on. More specifically, a signal is denoted by a pair $L$-$N$, where $N$ is a Boolean value (representing the Boolean value of the circuit when there are no faults) and $L$ is a set of diagnoses, that might change the signal into the opposite value. For instance, for single faults, $X=\{g/0,i/1\}$-$0$ means that signal $X$ normally is $0$ but if gate $g$ is *stuck-at-0*, or gate $i$ is *stuck-at-1*, then its actual value is $1$. $\varnothing$-$N$ represents a signal with constant value $N$, independently of any fault. For generality, we need to explicitly represent the fault modes in the set of faults. In the following we assume that any gate in a circuit may be faulty.

A gate $g$, that can either be normal, *stuck-at-0* or *stuck-at-1*, may be modelled by means of a normal gate to which a special buffer, an **S-buffer**, is attached to the output. As such, all gates are considered normal, and only S-buffers can be faulty. The modelling of S-buffers is as in Table 1:

*Table 1*. S-buffer logic table

| In | $\varnothing$-0 | $\varnothing$-1 | $L_i$-0 | $L_i$-1 |
|---|---|---|---|---|
| Out | $\{g/1\}$-0 | $\{g/0\}$-1 | $\{g/1\} \cup L_i$ - 0 | $\{g/0\} \cup L_i$ - 1 |

When the input is $0$ and independent of any fault, the S-buffer output would normally be also $0$, but if it is *stuck-at-1* then it becomes $1$. More generally, if the normal input is $0$ but dependent on $L_i$, the output depends not only on $g/1$ but also on input dependencies $L_i$. The same reasoning can be applied to the case where the normal input signal is $1$, and the output of an S-buffer $g$ with input $L_i$-$N$ can be generalised to $\{g/\overline{N}\} \cup L_i$-$N$, where $\overline{N}$ stands for the complement of Boolean value $N$.

Normal gates fully respect the Boolean operation they represent. We discuss the behaviour of NOT and AND-gates as illustrative of these gates. All other gates can be modelled as combinations of these. Given the above explanation of the encoding of digital signals, for a normal NOT-gate whose input is signal $L$-$N$, the output is simply $L$-$\overline{N}$, since the set of faults on which it depends is the same as the input signal.

For an AND-gate, in the absence of faults, the output is the conjunction of the normal inputs. The set of faults that may change the output signal into the opposite of the normal value is less straightforward to determine. When both normal inputs are 1 (1st case of the table below), a fault in set $L_1$ or set $L_2$ justifies a change in the output. In the second case (two 0s), to invert the output signal, a fault in both $L_1$ and $L_2$ must exist. So, the set of faults that justify a change in the gate's output is the intersection of the input sets. In the last two cases, to obtain an output different from the normal 0 value, it is necessary to invert the normal 0 input, and not to invert the normal 1 input (justifying the set difference in the output), as in Table 2:

*Table 2.* AND-gate logic table

| In1 | $L_1$-1 | $L_1$-0 | $L_1$-0 | $L_1$-1 |
|-----|---------|---------|---------|---------|
| In2 | $L_2$-1 | $L_2$-0 | $L_2$-1 | $L_2$-0 |
| Out | $L_1 \cup L_2$-1 | $L_1 \cap L_2$-0 | $L_1 \backslash L_2$-0 | $L_2 \backslash L_1$-0 |

To model the diagnosis problem and find the possible single faults that explain the faulty output vector $F$, a bit-wise comparison between $F$ and the deduced simulated logic output must be performed. Let $r_o$ and $s_o$ denote, respectively, the real and simulated value of output bit $o$, where $r_o$ is a Boolean value $B_o$ and $s_o$ is a set-Boolean pair $L_o$-$N_o$. When $B_o \neq N_o$, the only possible single faults are in $L_o$ and any such fault explains $B_o$. When $B_o = N_o$, none of the faults in $L_o$ occur. Hence, the set of faults that justify the full incorrect output vector $F$ is given by $\{f: \forall_o ((B_o \neq N_o \Rightarrow f \in L_o) \wedge (B_o = N_o \Rightarrow f \notin L_o))\}$ where $o$ ranges over all the output bits. The diagnostic solution is then given by intersecting all the dependency sets $L_o$ where $r_o$ is incorrect and removing the union of $L_o$ where $r_o$ is as expected.

The LP implementation of the dependency-directed fault diagnosis is immediate: we simply propagate bottom-up the signals over the circuit (as in the generate-and-test, and backtracking approaches), making use of logical variables and unification. In contrast with the *generate-and-test* implementation, Boolean values representing 0/1 circuit values are now substituted by a term *Value-ListOfGates*, and the gates' behaviours are as described above. To implement the set operations, we resorted to the *ordsets* library for operations over sorted lists of SICStus Prolog[15]. Of all the approaches in this paper, it turns out that this is the most efficient one. This is as expected, since with this approach only one pass in the circuit is needed to extract the information needed to compute all the faults for all the output vectors.

This method can be extended to handle multiple fault diagnoses. The major problem is the representation of all the possible diagnoses. In the single fault case, our sets may have at most $2*G$ gates, where $G$ is the number of gates in the circuit (2406 for *c6288*). However, for double faults the lists may expand to $4*G^2$ (around 23 million elements for *c6288*!). A better representation is needed in order to avoid this explosion. We tried to encode sets of double faults by sets of pairs of the form *(f,ListOfFaults)* or *(f,-ListOfFaults)*. For instance, the pair (10/1,[20/0,40/1,50/1]) represents the set of faults {(10/1,20/0), (10/1,40/1), (10/1,50/1)}, while (10/1,-[20/0,40/1,50/1]) stands for the set of all double faults, containing 10/1, minus the above ones. We have extended the ordinary set operations to pairs of this form and tested it with *c6288*. All double faults for *c6288* could be determined in a reasonable amount of time (see the conclusions section).

## 5.     RESULTS AND CONCLUSIONS

In this paper we addressed several approaches to the circuit diagnosis problem. The implementations were tested using the same input vector, 01001000000100010001000110100000, corresponding to the multiplication of 34834 by 1416, returning 49324944, represented in binary by (least significant bit first) 00001001110001010000111101000000. From this correct output we flipped a bit at a time, obtaining 32 incorrect output vectors. The results for the various approaches were as shown in Table 3 (all tests run on a Pentium III 733 MHz; for *Test, Check, BT* and *Dependency*, SICStus 3.8.5 was used; for *Tabling*, XSB-Prolog 2.2; for *Smodels*, SModels 2.26).

Timings should be looked with some care. Note that we are using different Prolog systems, with possible impact on the performance. In the last column of the table, only the total time appears since, for the dependency-directed approach, the information needed to obtain the diagnoses is computed in a single propagation over the circuit (this phase takes 220ms). The diagnoses for each test are then obtained by set operations on the results, this phase taking a total of 610ms. On average, for a single test vector, diagnoses can be found in around 20ms, after propagation. Thus, total execution time reduces to 240ms. This is by far the best method presented here. The main reason is that, contrary to previous methods, this one is backtrack-free. The method can also be generalized to multiple faults. When computing all double faults, the propagation phase took approximately 780 seconds. Note that the operations on sets of faults are now more complex and therefore we have a 3500-fold slowdown. An implementation for larger cardinality of faults is an open research problem. Notice that a similar technique can be used in Abductive LP, widening the applications of the method.

*Table 3.* Diagnosis results (in seconds) for 32 incorrect ouput vectors of c6288.

| Vector | #Sols | Test | Check | BT | Tabling | Smodels | Dependency |
|--------|-------|------|-------|-----|---------|---------|------------|
| 1 | 1 | 19.05 | 0.92 | 0.00 | 0.06 | 5.23 | - |
| 2 | 9 | 19.67 | 3.41 | 0.33 | 0.22 | 42.13 | - |
| 3 | 18 | 19.94 | 4.39 | 0.44 | 0.45 | 47.00 | - |
| 4 | 27 | 19.11 | 5.44 | 0.66 | 0.73 | 50.61 | - |
| 5 | 11 | 19.11 | 6.37 | 0.83 | 0.36 | 53.30 | - |
| 6 | 45 | 19.50 | 8.08 | 1.20 | 1.44 | 65.00 | - |
| 7 | 54 | 20.11 | 9.77 | 1.60 | 1.85 | 72.18 | - |
| 8 | 23 | 19.05 | 9.94 | 1.81 | 1.08 | 65.86 | - |
| 9 | 11 | 19.06 | 10.77 | 2.20 | 1.14 | 67.50 | - |
| 10 | 11 | 19.28 | 11.81 | 2.63 | 3.40 | 70.67 | - |
| 11 | 90 | 20.32 | 12.80 | 3.30 | 7.35 | 126.31 | - |
| 12 | 80 | 19.06 | 13.73 | 3.79 | 5.46 | 125.97 | - |
| 13 | 87 | 19.06 | 15.65 | 4.34 | 7.01 | 140.56 | - |
| 14 | 10 | 19.23 | 16.04 | 4.89 | 6.91 | 76.44 | - |
| 15 | 91 | 20.37 | 16.26 | 5.38 | 10.68 | 157.05 | - |
| 16 | 21 | 19.06 | 16.42 | 5.60 | 8.92 | 77.63 | - |
| 17 | 135 | 19.06 | 16.59 | 6.26 | 14.13 | 225.12 | - |
| 18 | 127 | 19.23 | 17.90 | 6.54 | 13.95 | 103.67 | - |
| 19 | 101 | 20.26 | 16.48 | 5.71 | 11.48 | 136.01 | - |
| 20 | 104 | 18.95 | 16.59 | 5.71 | 10.81 | 132.96 | - |
| 21 | 33 | 19.01 | 16.59 | 5.66 | 8.94 | 81.26 | - |
| 22 | 31 | 20.43 | 17.96 | 5.71 | 10.22 | 80.13 | - |
| 23 | 37 | 19.00 | 16.53 | 5.72 | 11.56 | 86.38 | - |
| 24 | 33 | 19.01 | 16.59 | 5.71 | 12.73 | 84.83 | - |
| 25 | 64 | 19.44 | 16.64 | 5.71 | 15.54 | 87.10 | - |
| 26 | 25 | 19.99 | 17.96 | 5.77 | 6.92 | 75.09 | - |
| 27 | 46 | 19.01 | 16.59 | 5.71 | 7.45 | 73.20 | - |
| 28 | 37 | 18.95 | 16.59 | 5.77 | 3.42 | 64.35 | - |
| 29 | 28 | 20.43 | 16.80 | 6.59 | 2.05 | 57.79 | - |
| 30 | 19 | 19.00 | 17.91 | 6.31 | 1.07 | 52.32 | - |
| 31 | 1 | 19.01 | 16.64 | 5.77 | 0.11 | 9.98 | - |
| 32 | 10 | 19.33 | 16.59 | 5.77 | 0.51 | 46.61 | - |
| Total Time | | 621.09 | 432.75 | 133.42 | 187.95 | 2640.24 | 0.83 |

As expected, *generate-and-test* takes constant time. *Generate-and-check* is a little better, but its performance degrades as the wrong bit becomes more and more significant, since incorrect assumptions fail later. The backtracking version performs quite well, but shows the same problem of *generate-and-check*, for the same reasons.

The tabling approach is very good at solving problems with a small number of faults, the running times being almost independent of the wrong bit. The justification is a dynamic ordering of inputs and dependencies checking used to direct the search. It gets worse for greater number of faults since more memory is required to store the tabled predicates. Also notice that XSB Prolog is much slower than SICStus.

The SM programming approach is, among those presented, the least efficient. However, this approach has been specially tailored for solving NP-complete problems, which is not the case for our single-fault circuit diagnosis. Nevertheless, we were impressed with the robustness of the *smodels* system, which was capable of handling the very large files resulting from the residual program for each test in this circuit. In fact, for each output vector, the (ground) logic program, generated by the XSB-Prolog program, that served as input to *smodels* has, on average, 31036 clauses and around 2.4 MB of memory. On the other hand, the representation of the circuit and of the problem is (arguably) the most declarative and easier one.

We have also tried to implement a solution resorting to SICStus library of constraints over Booleans. Our efforts proven useless, since SICStus was unable to handle the constraints we generated (usually, ran out of memory).

Although we did not run specialized diagnosis systems in the same platform, we can compare our times with the ones presented by those systems some years ago, and take into account the hardware evolution. The results of the shown LP approaches are then quite encouraging. For example, the results of the DRUM-II specialized system[16] seem worse than ours: it can take 160 seconds to diagnose all single faults in *c6288* for a specific output vector. We dare to say that this system, even if ported to an up-to-date platform, would still be less efficient than our dependency-directed approach (which takes 0.83s to produce the diagnoses for the 32 output vectors), and would possibly be comparable to our general approaches of backtracking and tabulation (which, for the worst case take, respectively, 6.59 and 15.54 seconds).

# REFERENCES

1. P. Lucas, Symbolic Diagnosis and its Formalisation, *The Knowledge Engineering Review* **12**(2), (1997), pp. 109–146.
2. J. Doyle, A Truth Maintenance System, *Artificial Intelligence* **12**(3), (1979), pp. 231-272.
3. J. de Kleer and B. C. Williams, Diagnosing Multiple Faults, *Artificial Intelligence* **32**(1), (April 1987), pp. 97-130.
4. ISCAS. Special Session on ATPG, *Proceedings of the IEEE Symposium on Circuits and Systems*, Kyoto, Japan, (July 1985), pp. 663–698.

5. P. Fröhlich, *DRUM-II Efficient Model-based Diagnosis of Technical Systems*, PhD thesis, University of Hannover, (1998).
6. J. J. Alferes, F. Azevedo, P. Barahona, C. V. Damásio and T. Swift, Logic Programming Techniques for Solving Circuit Diagnosis; ssdi.di.fct.unl.pt/~fa/papers/diagnosis_ps.zip.
7. *The XSB Programmer's Manual: version 2.1*, Vols. **1-2** (2000); http://xsb.sourceforge.net
8. M. Marek and M. Truszczyński, Stable models and an alternative logic programming paradigm, *The Logic Programming Paradigm: a 25-Year Perspective*, (Springer, 1999), pp. 375–398.
9. I. Niemelä, Logic programs with stable model semantics as a constraint programming paradigm, edited by I. Niemelä and T. Schaub, *Computational Aspects of Nonmonotonic Reasoning*, (1998), pp. 72–79.
10. M. Gelfond and V. Lifshitz, The stable model semantics for logic programming, in: *ICLP'88*, edited by R. Kowalski and K. Bowen (MIT Press, 1988), pp. 1070–1080.
11. I. Niemelä and P. Simons, Smodels - an implementation of the stable model and well-founded semantics for normal logic programs, in: *4th LPNMR*, (Springer, 1997).
12. W. Chen and D. S. Warren, Computation of stable models and its integration with logical query evaluation, *IEEE Trans. on Knowledge and Data Engineering* (1995).
13. D. B. Armstrong, A Deductive Method of Simulating Faults in Logic Circuits, *IEEE Trans. on Computers* **C-21**(5), 464–471 (May 1972).
14. H. C. Godoy and R. E. Vogelsberg, Single Pass Error Effect Determination (SPEED), *IBM Technical Disclosure Bulletin* **13**, 3443–3344 (April 1971).
15. Programming Systems Group of the Swedish Institute of Computer Science. *SICStus Prolog User's Manual*, (1995).
16. Peter Fröhlich and Wolfgang Nejdl, A static model-based engine for model-based reasoning, in: *Proceedings of IJCAI97* (1997), pp. 466–473.

# VERIFICATION OF NASA EMERGENT SYSTEMS

Christopher Rouff[1], Amy KCS Vanderbilt[1], Walt Truszkowski[2] James Rash[2]
and Mike Hinchey[2]
*SAIC[1]; NASA Goddard Space Flight Center[2]*

**Abstract:**     *NASA is studying advanced technologies for a future robotic exploration mission to the asteroid belt. This mission, the prospective ANTS (Autonomous Nano Technology Swarm) mission, will comprise of 1,000 autonomous robotic agents designed to cooperate in asteroid exploration. The emergent properties of swarm type missions make them powerful, but at the same time are more difficult to design and assure that the proper behaviors will emerge. We are currently investigating formal methods and techniques for verification and validation of future swarm-based missions. The advantage of using formal methods is their ability to mathematically assure the behavior of a swarm, emergent or otherwise. The ANT mission is being used as an example and case study for swarm-based missions for which to experiment and test current formal methods with intelligent swarms. Using the ANTS mission, we have evaluated multiple formal methods to determine their effectiveness in modeling and assuring swarm behavior.*

**Key words:**    emergent behavior; formal methods; spacecraft; swarms; verification

## 1.     INTRODUCTION

NASA is studying advanced technologies for a future robotic exploration mission to the asteroid belt.   One mission, the prospective ANTS (Autonomous Nano Technology Swarm) mission, will comprise 1,000 autonomous robotic agents designed to cooperate in asteroid exploration. Since the ANTS and other similar missions are going to consist of autonomous spacecraft which may be out of contact with the earth for extended periods of time, and have low bandwidths due to weight constraints, it will be difficult to observe improper behavior and to correct any errors after launch. Because of this proper verification of these kinds of missions is extremely important. One of the highest possible levels of assurance comes from formal methods[1]. Once written, a formal specification can be used to prove properties of a system (e.g., the underlying system will go from one state to another or not into a specific state) and check for particular types of errors (e.g. race conditions). The authors have investigated a collection of formal methods techniques for verification and validation of spacecraft using swarm technology. Multiple formal methods were evaluated to determine their effectiveness in modeling and assuring the behavior of swarms of spacecraft[2, 3]. The ANTS mission was used as an example of swarm intelligence for which to apply the formal methods.

The ANTS mission[4, 5] will have swarms of autonomous pico-class (approximately 1kg) spacecraft that will search the asteroid belt for asteroids that have specific characteristics (Figure 1). To implement this mission a high degree of autonomy is being planned, approaching total autonomy. A heuristic approach is being considered that uses a social structure to the spacecraft in the swarm. Artificial intelligence technologies such as genetic algorithms, neural nets, fuzzy logic and on-board planners are being investigated to assist the mission to maintain a high level of autonomy. Crucial to the mission will be the ability to modify its operations autonomously to reflect the changing nature of the mission and the distance and low bandwidth communications back to Earth.

Approximately eighty percent of spacecraft, called workers, will have a single specialized instrument (e.g., a magnetometer, x-ray, visible/IR, neutral mass spectrometer). Other spacecraft are called rulers that have rules that decided the types of asteroids and data the mission is interested in and will coordinate the efforts of the workers. Messengers will coordinate communications between the workers, rulers and Earth. Each worker spacecraft will examine asteroids they encounter and send messages back to a ruler that will then evaluate the data and form a team to investigate it that contains the appropriate spacecraft with specialized instruments.

One of the most challenging aspects of using swarms is how to verify that the emergent behavior of such systems will be proper and that no undesirable behaviors will occur. In addition to emergent behavior in swarms, there are also a large number of concurrent interactions between the agents that make up the swarms. These interactions can also contain errors, such as race conditions, that are difficult to detect until they occur. Once they do occur, it can be difficult to recreate the errors since they are usually data and time dependent. Verifying intelligent swarms are even more difficult since the swarms are no longer made up of homogeneous members with limited intelligence and communications. Verification will be difficult not only due to the complexity of each member, but also due to the complex interaction of a large number of intelligent elements.

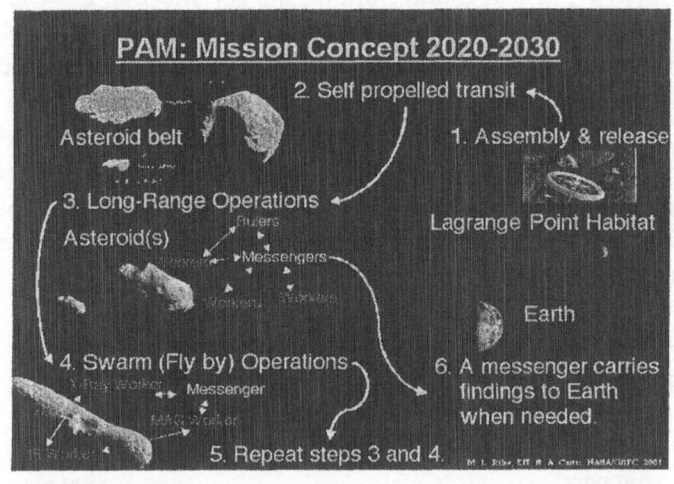

2003-0604 NASA/RASC ANTS        M. Rilee, P. Clark, L-3; S. Curtis, G. Marr,W. Truszkowski, NASA/GSFC

*Figure 1.* ANTS Mission concept.

## 2.    FORMAL APPROACHES AND ASSURANCE

As mission software becomes increasingly more complex, it also becomes more difficult to test and find errors. Race conditions in these systems can rarely be found by inputting sample data and checking if the results are correct. These types of errors are time-based and only occur when processes send or receive data at particular times, in a particular sequence or after learning occurs. To find these errors, the software processes involved have to be executed in all possible combinations of states (state space) that the processes could collectively be in. Because the state space is exponential (and sometimes factorial) to the number of states, it becomes untestable with a relatively small number of processes. Traditionally, to get around the state explosion problem, testers have artificially reduced the number of states of the system and approximated the underlying software using models.

Formal methods are proven approaches for assuring the correct operation of complex interacting systems[6, 7]. Verifying emergent behavior is an area that most formal methods have not addressed. We surveyed a number of formal methods techniques to determine if there existed formal methods that have been used or would be suitable for verifying swarm-based systems and their emergent behavior[8, 9]. Formal methods were surveyed based on whether they had currency support, were based on a formal model, had tool support, and had been used to specify and verify agent-based or swarm-based systems. What was found from the survey was that there are a number of formal methods that support either the specification of concurrency or algorithms. It was also found that in recent years there have been a large number of hybrid or combination formal methods that have been developed with the hope of specifying both concurrency and algorithms with the same method. Table 1 shows part of the results of the survey for mainstream formal methods, Table 2 shows the results for hybrid formal methods and Table 3 shows a comparison of formal methods that have been used to specify swarm-based systems.

*Table 1.* Comparison of candidate formal methods for intelligent swarms.

| Name | Con-currency Support | Algorithm Support | Tool Support | Formal Basis | Used in Agent-Based Specs. | Used in Swarm-Based Specs. |
|------|----------------------|-------------------|--------------|--------------|----------------------------|----------------------------|
| Artif. Physics | Yes | Yes | Yes | Mathem. | Yes | limited |
| B | No | Yes | Yes | Set Theory/ Pred. Log. | Yes | No |
| BDI Logic | Yes | No | Yes | Logic | Yes | limited |
| CSP | Yes | No | Yes | Algebraic | Yes | No |
| F/State Machs | No | Yes | Yes | Form. Lang | Yes | No |
| Game Theory | Yes | No | Yes | Mathem. | Yes | Yes |
| I/O Automata | Yes | Yes | Yes | Form. Lang | Yes | No |
| KARO | Yes | No | limited | Logic | Yes | No |
| Mat.Analysis | Yes | No | Yes | Mathem. | Yes | Yes |
| Petri Nets | Yes | No | Yes | Yes | Yes | No |
| Pi Calculus | Yes | No | Yes | Algebraic | Yes | No |
| Real Tm Logic | Yes | No | Yes | Logic | No | No |
| SCR | No | Yes | Yes | Form. Lang | No | No |
| Statecharts | Yes | No | Yes | Form. Lang | Yes | No |
| UML | Yes | Yes | Yes | No | Yes | No |
| X-Machines | No | Yes | limited | Form. Lang | Yes | No |
| Z | No | Yes | Yes | Set Theory/ Pred. Calc. | Yes | No |

Table 1 summarizes the results of mainstream formal techniques and their use on swarm and agent-based systems. The formal methods were evaluated for concurrency support, algorithm support, tool support, their formal basis, whether they had been used in specifying agent-based systems and whether they had been used in specifying swarm-based systems.

Table 2 compares hybrid or combination formal methods surveyed. This table also lists support for concurrency, algorithms, tool support, whether it is based on a formal foundation, has been used to specify agent-based systems and if it has been used to specify swarm-based systems. For the tool support, a yes is entered only if there was integrated tool support for the combined languages.

*Table 2.* Comparison of hybrid formal methods.

| Name | Concurrency Support | Algorithm Support | Tool Support | Formal Basis | Used in Agent-Based Specs. | Used in Swarm-Based Specs. |
|------|------|------|------|------|------|------|
| Commun. X-Machines | Yes | Yes | No | Yes | Yes | Yes |
| CSP-OZ | Yes | Yes | No | Yes | Yes | No |
| Object-Z and Statecharts | Yes | Yes | No | Yes | Yes | No |
| Temporal B | Yes | Yes | No | Yes | Yes | No |
| Temporal Petri Nets | Yes | No | No | Yes | Yes | No |
| Timed Comm. Object Z | Yes | Yes | No | Yes | Yes | No |
| Timed CSP | Yes | No | Yes | Yes | Yes | No |
| ZCCS | Yes | Yes | No | Yes | Yes | No |

Table 3 compares methods that have been used for modeling or specifying swarm-based systems (computer or biological based). It lists whether each method provides support for concurrency, algorithms, has tool support, is based on a formal foundation, and if it supports the analysis of emergent behavior and whether it has been used to specify swarm-based systems (software or biological).

The following is a summary of specification techniques that have been used for specifying social, swarm and emergent behavior:

- Weighted Synchronous Calculus of Communicating Systems (WSCCS), a process algebra, was used by Tofts to model social insects[10]. WSCCS was also used in conjunction with a dynamical systems approach for analyzing the non-linear aspects of social insects[11].

- X-Machines[12] have been used to model cell biology[13] and modifications, such as Communicating Stream X-Machines[14], also have potential for specifying swarms.
- Dynamic Emergent System Modeling Language (DESML)[15], which is a variant of UML, has been suggested for modeling emergent systems.
- Cellular automaton[16] has been used to model systems that exhibit emergent behavior (such as land use).
- Artificial Physics[17] is based on using properties from physics to model constraints and interaction between agents.
- Simulation approaches that use a modeling technique to model the behavior.   These approaches do not model emergent behavior beforehand, only after the fact.

Though there were a few formal methods that have been used to specify swarm-based systems, only two had been used to analyze the emergent behavior of swarms.  One of these formal methods was WSCCS and the other was artificial physics.  In addition, it was also discovered that the majority of the work in specifying swarm-based systems has been done on biological systems by biologist with the help of computer scientists that used modified formal methods[10, 11, 13].

*Table 3*. Comparison of formal methods used for swarm specifications.

| Name | Concurr-ency Support | Algorithm Support | Tool Support | Formal Basis | Emergent Behavior Anal. | Used in Swarm-Based Specs. |
|------|------|------|------|------|------|------|
| Cellular Automaton | Yes | Yes | Yes | FSM | No | Yes |
| Com. X-Machines | Yes | Yes | No | Formal Lang. | No | Yes |
| Unity Logic | Yes | No | (limited) | Logic | No | Yes |
| WSCCS | Yes | No | (Prob. workbench) | (Process Alg.) | (Markov Chain) | Yes |

## 3.     EVALUATION OF SPECIFICATION METHODS

Based on the results of the survey, four formal methods were selected to do sample specification of part of the ANTS mission.  These methods were: the process algebras CSP[18] and WSCCS[10], X-Machines[12], and Unity Logic[19]. DESML, Cellular Automata, artificial physics and simulation approaches were not used even though they had been used for specifying or analyzing emergent behavior. DESML was not selected because it had not been used to analyze emergent behavior. Cellular Automata was not selected because it did not have any built in analysis properties for emergent behavior and because it has been primarily used for simulating emergent systems. Though not used for the specification, it too may be revisited to examine its strengths. Artificial physics, though again has possibilities, was not used due to its early stages of development and use. Lastly, simulation techniques were not used because verification can not be done only using simulation. This is because there could be emergent or other undesirable behaviors occurring that are not visible or come out in a simulation, but may be there none the less. A formal technique is designed to find exactly these kinds of errors.

The following describes the results of the sample specifications and the evaluation of the methods used.

CSP is very good at specifying the process protocols between and within the spacecraft and analyzing the result for race conditions. Being able to evaluate a system for race conditions is very important in systems, particularly swarm-based systems which are highly parallel. From a CSP specification, reasoning about the specification can be done to determine race conditions as well as converted into a model checking language for running on a model checker. Though the above is important and process algebras have been widely used for specifying agent-based systems, there is no facility for evaluating emergent behavior of the end system.

WSCCS is a process algebra that takes into account the priorities and probabilities of actions performed. It further provides a syntax and large set of rules for predicting and specifying the choices and behaviors of the Leader, as well as a congruence and syntax for determining if two automata are equivalent. All of this in hand, WSCCS can be used to specify the ANTS spacecraft and to reason about and even predict the behavior of one or more spacecraft. This robustness affords WSCCS the greatest potential for specifying emergent behavior in the ANTS swarm. What it lacks is an ability to track the goals and model of the ANTS mission in a memory.

Unity Logic has a syntax equivalent to simple Propositional Logic for reasoning about predicates and the states they imply as well as for defining specific mathematical, statistical and other simple calculations to be performed. However, it does not appear to be rich enough to allow ease of specification and validation of more abstract concepts such as mission goals. This same simplicity, however, may make it a good tool for specifying and validating the actual Reasoning portion of the ANTS Leader spacecraft, when the need arises. In short, specifying emergent behavior in the ANTS swarm will not be accomplished well using Unity Logic, though logic does provide many useful properties for reasoning about systems.

X-Machines provide a highly executable environment for specifying the ANTS spacecraft. It allows for a memory to be kept and it allows for transitions between states to be seen as functions involving inputs and outputs. This allows us to track the actions of the ANTS spacecraft as well as write to memory any aspect of the goals and model. This ability makes X-Machines highly effective for tracking and affecting changes in the goals and model. However, X-Machines do not provide any robust means for reasoning about or predicting behaviors of one or more spacecraft, beyond standard propositional logic. This will make specifying or analyzing emergent behavior difficult or impossible.

Based on the above evaluation, the following are some of the properties of a formal method needed for specifying swarm-based systems:

- Ability to model and reason about aggregate behavior based on future actions of the individual agents of a swarm (such as provided by WSCCS)
- Ability to model and reason about concurrent processes for detection of race conditions (such as provided by CSP and Unity Logic)
- Ability to model states of an agent of the swarm to assure correctness (such as provided by statecharts, X-Machines or Z)
- Ability to model and reason about persistent information so adaptive behavior can be verified (such as provided by X-Machines).

A blending of the above methods seems to be the best approach for specifying swarm-based systems and analyzing emergent behavior of these systems. Blending the memory and transition function aspects of X-Machines with the priority and probability aspects of WSCCS may produce a specification method that will allow all the necessary aspects for specifying emergent behavior in the ANTS mission and other swarm-based systems. The idea of merging the above methods is currently being furthered studied as well as adding some of the properties of logic and cellular automata.

## 4.    CONCLUSION

Swarm-based missions are becoming more important to NASA and other government missions so new science can be performed. These types of missions have many positive attributes but represent a change in paradigm from current types of single spacecraft missions. Due to this, swarms require new types of verification and validation techniques to assure their correct operation. To overcome their non-deterministic nature, high degree of parallelism, intelligent behavior and emergent behavior, new kinds of verification methods need to be used.

This paper gave the results of an investigation into formal method techniques that might be applicable to future swarm-based missions and that can verify their correctness. It also analyzed the properties of these methods to determine the needed attributes of a formal specification language to predict and verify emergent behavior of future NASA swarm-based systems.

We are currently working on developing a new formal method based on blending aspects of the above formal method as well as adding additional mathematical techniques from other areas of mathematics that might prove fruitful for predicting the emergent behavior of swarms. From this new formal method we will use the ANTS and another NASA swarm-based mission to test the capabilities of the resulting formal method. We expect that the resulting formal method could become the basis of other specification languages to support specification and analysis of future swarm-based systems.

# REFERENCES

1. E. Clare and J. Wing. Formal Methods: State of the Art and Future Directions. Report by the Working Group on Formal Methods for the ACM Workshop on Strategic Directions in Computing Research, ACM Computing Surveys, vol. 28, no. 4, Dec. 1996, pp. 626-643.
2. E.G. Bonabeau, G. Theraulaz, et al. Self-organization in Social Insects, Trends in Ecology and Evolution, 1997, vol. 12, pp. 188-193.
3. G. Beni. and J. Want. Swarm Intelligence. In Proceedings of the Seventh Annual Meeting of the Robotics Society of Japan, pp 425-428, Tokyo, Japan, 1989, RSJ Press.
4. ANTS team. Protocol for ANTS Encounters. NASA GSFC, Code 695.
5. S.A. Curtis, J. Mica, J. Nuth, G. Marr, M. Rilee, and M. Bhat. ANTS (Autonomous Nano-Technology Swarm): An Artificial Intelligence Approach to Asteroid Belt Resource Exploration. International Astronautical Federation, 51st Congress, October 2000.
6. P. Nayak, P. Pandurang, et. al. 1999. Validating the DS1 Remote Agent Experiment. In Proceedings of the 5th International Symposium on Artificial Intelligence, Robotics and Automation in Space (iSAIRAS-99).
7. C. Rouff, J. Rash, M. Hinchey. Experience Using Formal Methods for Specifying a Multi-Agent System. Sixth IEEE International Conference on Engineering of Complex Computer Systems (ICECCS 2000) September 11-15, 2000.
8. C. Rouff, W. Truszkowski, J. Rash and M. Hinchey. Formal Approaches to Intelligent Swarms. IEEE/NASA Software Engineering Workshop, Greenbelt, MD. December 2003.
9. C. Rouff, A. Vanderbilt, W. Truszkowski, J. Rash and M. Hinchey. Verification of NASA Emergent Systems. Ninth International Conference on Engineering of Complex Computer Systems (ICECCS 2004), Florence, Italy, April 14-16, 2004.
10. C. Tofts. Describing social insect behaviour using process algebra. Transactions on Social Computing Simulation. 1991. 227-283.

11. D.J.T. Sumpter, G.B. Blanchard and D.S. Broomhead. Ants and Agents: A Process Algebra Approach to Modelling Ant Colony Behaviour. Bulletin of Mathematical Biology. 2001, 63, 951-980.

12. S. Eilenberg. Automat, Languages and Machines, Vol. A. Academic Press, 1974.

13. M. Holcombe. Mathematical models of cell biochemistry. Technical Report CS-86-4. 1986. Dept of Computer Science, Sheffield University, United Kingdom.

14. J. Barnard, J. Whitworth and M. Woodward. Communicating X-machines. Journal of Information and Software Technology, 38(6), 1996.

15. J.R. Kiniry. The Specification of Dynamic Distributed Component Systems. Masters' Thesis, CS-TR-98-08 1998 California Institute of Technology, Comp. Sci. Depart.

16. J. von Neumann. Theory of Self-Reproducing Automat. University of Illinois Press, Urbana, Illinois. 1996. Edited and completed by Q.W. Burks.

17. W. Spears and D. Gordon. (1999) Using artificial physics to control agents. Proceedings of the IEEE Conference on Information, Intelligence, and Systems (ICIIS'99).

18. C.A.R. Hoare. Communicating Sequential Processes. Communications of the ACM, 21(8):666-677, August, 1978.

19. K. Chandy and J. Misra. Parallel Program Design: A Foundation. Addison-Wesley. 1988.

# KNOWLEDGE BASE STRUCTURE
*Understanding maintenance*

John Debenham
*University of Technology, Sydney*

Abstract: In a unified conceptual model for first-order knowledge bases the data and knowledge are modelled formally in a uniform way. A knowledge base is maintained by modifying its conceptual model and by using those modifications to specify changes to its implementation. The maintenance problem is to determine which parts of that model should be checked for correctness in response a change in the application. The maintenance problem is not computable for first-order knowledge bases. Two things in the conceptual model are joined by a maintenance link if a modification to one of them means that the other must be checked for correctness, and so possibly modified, if consistency of the model is to be preserved. A characterisation is given of four different kinds of maintenance links in a unified conceptual model. Two of these four kinds of maintenance links can be removed by transforming the conceptual model.

Key words: KBS methodology, expert systems, intelligent systems

## 1.    INTRODUCTION

In a unified conceptual model for first-order knowledge bases the data and knowledge are modelled formally in a uniform way. The conceptual model is used to drive the maintenance process. The maintenance problem is to determine which parts of that model should be checked for correctness in response a change in the application. The maintenance problem is not computable for first-order knowledge bases. Maintenance links join two things in the conceptual model if a modification to one of them means that the other must be checked for correctness, and so possibly modified, if consistency of that model is to be preserved. If that other thing requires modification then the links from it to yet other things must be followed, and so on until things are reached that do not require modification.  If node A is linked to node B which is linked to node C then nodes A and C are *indirectly* linked.  In a *coherent* knowledge base everything is indirectly linked to everything else.  A good conceptual model for maintenance will have a low density of maintenance links [1].  The set of maintenance links should be *minimal* in than none may be removed.

Informally, one conceptual model is "better" than another if it leads to less checking for correctness.  The aim of this work is to generate a good conceptual model.  A classification into four classes is given here of the maintenance links for conceptual models expressed in the unified [2] knowledge representation.

Approaches to the maintenance of knowledge bases are principally of two types [3].  First, approaches that take the knowledge base as presented and then try to *control* the maintenance process [4].  Second, approaches that *engineer* a model of the knowledge base so that it is in a form that is inherently easy to maintain [5] [6].  The approach described here is of the second type because maintenance is driven by a maintenance link structure that is simplified by transforming the conceptual model.

The majority of conceptual models treat the "rule base" component separately from the "database" component.  This enables well established design methodologies to be employed, but the use of two separate models means that the interrelationship between the things in these two models cannot be represented, integrated and manipulated naturally within the model [2].

The terms data, information and knowledge are used here in the following sense.  The *data* things in an application are the fundamental, indivisible things.  Data things can be represented as simple constants or variables.  If an association between things *cannot* be defined as a succinct, computable rule then it is an *implicit* association.  Otherwise it is an *explicit* association.  An *information* thing in an application is an implicit association between data things.  Information things can be represented as tuples or relations.  A *knowledge* thing in an application is an explicit association between information and/or data things.  Knowledge can be represented either as programs in an imperative language or as rules in a declarative language.

## 2.    CONCEPTUAL MODEL

Items are a formalism for describing all data, information and knowledge things in an application [2].  Items incorporate two powerful classes of constraints, and a single rule of decomposition is specified for items. The key to this unified representation is the way in which the "meaning" of an item, called its *semantics*, is specified. The semantics of an item is a function that *recognises* the members of the "value set" of that item. The value set of an item will change in time $\tau$, but the item's semantics should remain constant. The value set of a data item at a certain time $\tau$ is the set of labels that are associated with a population that implements that item at that time. The value set of an information item at a certain time $\tau$ is the set of tuples that are associated with a relational implementation of that item at that time. Knowledge items have value sets too. Consider the rule "the sale price of parts is the cost price marked up by a universal mark-up factor"; this rule is represented by the item named *[part/sale-price, part/cost-price, mark-up]* with a value set of corresponding quintuples. The idea of defining the semantics of items as recognising functions for the members of their value set extends to complex, recursive knowledge items too.

An *item* is a named triple $A[\, S_A, V_A, C_A\,]$ with *item name A*, $S_A$ is called the *item semantics* of $A$, $V_A$ is called the *item value constraints* of $A$ and $C_A$ is called the *item set constraints* of $A$. The item semantics, $S_A$, is a $\lambda$-calculus expression that recognises the members of the value set of item A. The expression for an item's semantics may contain the semantics of other items $\{A_1,..., A_n\}$ called that item's *components*:

$$\lambda\, y_1^1...y_{m_1}^1...y_{m_n}^n \cdot [\, S_{A_1}(y_1^1,...,y_{m_1}^1)\, \wedge......\wedge$$
$$S_{A_n}(y_1^n,...,y_{m_n}^n)\, \wedge\, J(y_1^1,...,y_{m_1}^1,...,y_{m_n}^n)\, ]\cdot$$

The item value constraints, $V_A$, is a $\lambda$-calculus expression:

$$\lambda\, y_1^1...y_{m_1}^1...y_{m_n}^n \cdot [\, V_{A_1}(y_1^1,...,y_{m_1}^1)\, \wedge......\wedge$$
$$V_{A_n}(y_1^n,...,y_{m_n}^n)\, \wedge\, K(y_1^1,...,y_{m_1}^1,...,y_{m_n}^n)\, ]\cdot$$

that should be satisfied by the members of the value set of item A as they change in time; so if a tuple satisfies $S_A$ then it should satisfy $V_A$ [8]. The expression for an item's value constraints contains the value constraints of that item's *components*. The item set constraints, $C_A$, is an expression of the form:

$$C_{A_1} \wedge C_{A_2} \wedge...\wedge C_{A_n} \wedge (L)_A$$

where L is a logical combination of:

- Card lies in some numerical range;
- Uni($A_i$) for some i, $1 \le i \le n$, and
- Can($A_i$, X) for some i, $1 \le i \le n$, where X is a non-empty subset of $\{A_1,..., A_n\} - \{A_i\}$;

subscripted with the name of the item $A$, "Uni($a$)" means that "all members of the value set of item $a$ must be in this association".

"Can($b$, A)" means that "the value set of the set of items A functionally determines the value set of item $b$". "Card" means "the number of things in the value set". The subscripts indicate the item's components to which that set constraint applies.

For example, each *part* may be associated with a *cost-price* subject to the "value constraint" that parts whose part-number is less that 1,999 should be associated with a cost price of no more than \$300. A set constraint specifies that every part must be in this association, and that each part is associated with a unique cost-price. The information item named *part/cost-price* then is:

$part/cost\text{-}price[$ $\lambda xy\bullet[$ $S_{part}(x) \wedge S_{cost\text{-}price}(y) \wedge costs(x, y)$ $]\bullet$,

$\lambda xy\bullet[$ $V_{part}(x) \wedge V_{cost\text{-}price}(y) \wedge ((x < 1999) \rightarrow (y \leq 300))$ $]\bullet$,

$C_{part} \wedge C_{cost\text{-}price} \wedge$

$(Uni(part) \wedge Can(cost\text{-}price, \{part\}))_{part/cost\text{-}price}$ $]$

Rules, or knowledge, can also be defined as items, although it is neater to define knowledge items using "objects". "Objects" are item building operators. The knowledge item *[part/sale-price, part/cost-price, mark-up]* which means "the sale price of parts is the cost price marked up by a uniform markup factor" is:

*[part/sale-price, part/cost-price, mark-up]*[

$\lambda x_1 x_2 y_1 y_2 z\bullet[($ $S_{part/sale\text{-}price}(x_1, x_2) \wedge S_{part/cost\text{-}price}(y_1, y_2) \wedge$

$S_{mark\text{-}up}(z)$ $) \wedge ((x_1 = y_1) \rightarrow (x_2 = z \times y_2))]\bullet$,

$\lambda x_1 x_2 y_1 y_2 z\bullet[$ $V_{part/sale\text{-}price}(x_1, x_2) \wedge V_{part/cost\text{-}price}(y_1, y_2) \wedge$

$V_{mark\text{-}up}(z)$ $) \wedge (( x_1 = y_1 ) \rightarrow ( x_2 > y_2 ))]\bullet$,

$C_{[part/sale\text{-}price, part/cost\text{-}price, mark\text{-}up]}$ $]$

Two different items can share common knowledge and so can lead to a profusion of maintenance links. This problem can be avoided by using objects. An n-adic *object* is an operator that maps n given items into another item for some value of n. Further, the definition of each object will presume that the set of items to which that object may be applied are of a specific "type". The *type* of an m-adic item is determined both by whether it is a data item, an information item or a knowledge item and by the value of m. The type is denoted respectively by $\mathbf{D}^m$, $\mathbf{I}^m$ and $\mathbf{K}^m$. Items may also have unspecified, or free, type which is denoted by $\mathbf{X}^m$. The formal definition of an object is similar to that of an item. An *object* named $A$ is a typed triple $A[E,F,G]$ where E is a typed expression called the *semantics* of $A$, F is a typed expression called the *value constraints* of $A$ and G is a typed expression called the *set constraints* of $A$. For example, the *part/cost-price* item can be built from the items *part* and *cost-price* using the *costs* operator:

$part/cost\text{-}price = costs(part, cost\text{-}price)$

$costs[\lambda P:X^1 Q:X^1 \cdot \lambda xy \cdot [\ S_P(x) \wedge S_Q(y) \wedge costs(x,y)\ ]\cdot\cdot,$

$\lambda P:X^1 Q:X^1 \cdot \lambda xy \cdot [V_P(x) \wedge V_Q(y) \wedge ((1000<x<1999) \to (y \le 00))\ ]\cdot\cdot,$

$\lambda P:X^1 Q:X^1 \cdot [\ C_P \wedge C_Q \wedge (Uni(P) \wedge Can(Q, \{P\}))_{V(costs,P,Q)}\ ]\cdot]$

where $V(costs, P, Q)$ is the name of the item $costs(P, Q)$.

Data objects provide a representation of sub-typing. Rules are quite clumsy when represented as items; objects provide a far more compact representation. For example, consider the *[part/sale-price, part/cost-price, mark-up]* knowledge item which represents the rule "parts are marked-up by a universal mark-up factor". This item can be built by applying a knowledge object **mark-up-rule** of argument type $(I^2, I^2, D^1)$ to the items *part/sale-price, part/cost-price* and *mark-up*. That is:

*[part/sale-price, part/cost-price, mark-up]* =

   **mark-up-rule**(*part/sale-price, part/cost-price, mark-up*)

Objects also represent value constraints and set constraints in a uniform way. A decomposition operation for objects is defined in [7].

A *conceptual model* consists of a set of items and a set of maintenance links. The items are constructed by applying a set of object operators to a set of fundamental items called the *basis*. The *maintenance links* join two items if modification to one of them necessarily means that the other item has at least to be checked for correctness if consistency is to be preserved. Item join provides the basis for item decomposition. Given items $A$ and $B$, the item with name $A \otimes_E B$ is called the *join* of $A$ and $B$ on E, where E is a set of components common to both $A$ and $B$. Using the rule of composition $\otimes$, knowledge items, information items and data items may be joined with one another regardless of type. For example, the knowledge item:

*[cost-price, tax]* $[\lambda xy \cdot [S_{cost-price}(x) \wedge S_{tax}(y) \wedge x = y \times 0.05] \cdot,$

   $\lambda xy \cdot [V_{cost-price}(x) \wedge V_{tax}(y) \wedge x < y] \cdot, C_{[cost-price,\ tax]}\ ]$

can be joined with the information item *part/cost-price* on the set *{cost-price}* to give the information item *part/cost-price/tax*. In other words:

*[cost-price, tax]* $\otimes_{\{cost-price\}}$ *part/cost-price* =

*part/cost-price/tax*$[\ \lambda xyz \cdot [\ S_{part}(x) \wedge S_{cost-price}(x) \wedge$

   $S_{tax}(y) \wedge costs(x,y) \wedge z = y \times 0.05\ ]\cdot,$

$\lambda xyz \cdot [\ V_{part}(x) \wedge V_{cost-price}(x) \wedge V_{tax}(y) \wedge$

   $((1000<x<1999) \to (0<y \le 300)) \wedge (z<y)\ ]\cdot,$

$C_{part/cost-price/tax}\ ]$

In this way items may be joined together to form more complex items. The $\otimes$ operator also forms the basis of a theory of decomposition in which each item is replaced by a set of simpler items. An item $I$ is decomposable into the set of items D = $\{I_1, I_2,..., I_n\}$ if: $I_i$ has non-trivial semantics for all i, $I = I_1 \otimes I_2 \otimes ... \otimes I_n$ , where each join is monotonic; that is, each term in this composition contributes at least one component to $I$. If item $I$ is decomposable then it will not necessarily have a unique decomposition. The $\otimes$ operator is applied to objects in a similar way [7]. The rule of decomposition is: "Given a conceptual model discard any items and objects which are decomposable". For example, this rule requires that the item *part/cost-price/tax* should be discarded in favour of the two items *[cost-price, tax]* and *part/cost-price*.


## 3.        MAINTENANCE LINKS

A *maintenance link* joins two items in the conceptual model if modification of one item means that the other item must be checked for correctness, and maybe modified, if the consistency of the conceptual model is to be preserved [9]. The number of maintenance links can be very large. So maintenance links can only form the basis of a practical approach to knowledge base maintenance if there is some way of reducing their density on the conceptual model.

For example, given two items $A$ and $B$, where both are n-adic items with semantics $S_A$ and $S_B$ respectively, if $\pi$ is permutation such that:
$$(\forall x_1 x_2...x_n)[ S_A(x_1,x_2,...,x_n) \leftarrow S_B(\pi(x_1,x_2,...,x_n)) ]$$
then item $B$ is a *sub-item* of item $A$. These two items should be joined with a maintenance link. If $A$ and $B$ are both data items then $B$ is a *sub-type* of $A$. Suppose that:

$$X = E D; \text{ where } D = C A B \tag{1}$$

for items $X$, $D$, $A$ and $B$ and objects $E$ and $C$. Item $X$ is a sub-item of item $D$. Object $E$ has the effect of extracting a sub-set of the value set of item $D$ to form the value set of item $X$. Item $D$ is formed from items $A$ and $B$ using object $C$. Introduce two new objects $F$ and $J$. Suppose that object $F$ when applied to item $A$ extracts the same subset of item $A$'s value set as $E$ extracted from the "left-side" (ie. the "$A$-side") of $D$. Likewise $J$ extracts the same subset of $B$'s value set as $E$ extracted from $D$. Then:

$$X = C G K; \text{ where } G = F A \text{ and } K = J B \tag{2}$$

so $G$ is a sub-item of $A$, and $K$ is a sub-item of $B$. The form (2) differs from (1) in that the sub-item maintenance links have been moved one layer closer to the data item layer, and object C has moved one layer away from the data item layer. This is illustrated in Fig. 1. Using this method repeatedly sub-item maintenance links between non-data items are reduced to sub-type links between data items.

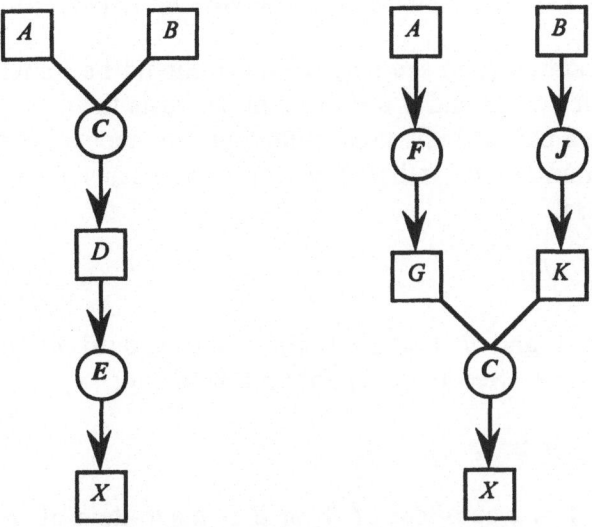

Figure 1. Reducing sub-item relationships

It is shown now that there are four kinds of maintenance link in a conceptual model built using the unified knowledge representation. Consider two items $A$ and $B$, and suppose that their semantics $S_A$ and $S_B$ have the form:

$$S_A = \lambda y_1^1 \ldots y_{m_1}^1 \ldots y_{m_p}^p \cdot [S_{A_1}(y_1^1, \ldots, y_{m_1}^1) \wedge \ldots \wedge$$
$$S_{A_p}(y_1^p, \ldots, y_{m_p}^p) \wedge J(y_1^1, \ldots, y_{m_1}^1, \ldots, y_{m_p}^p)] \cdot$$
$$S_B = \lambda y_1^1 \ldots y_{n_1}^1 \ldots y_{n_q}^q \cdot [S_{B_1}(y_1^1, \ldots, y_{n_1}^1) \wedge \ldots \wedge$$
$$S_{B_q}(y_1^q, \ldots, y_{n_q}^q) \wedge K(y_1^1, \ldots, y_{n_1}^1, \ldots, y_{n_q}^q)] \cdot$$

$S_A$ contains $(p + 1)$ terms and $S_B$ contains $(q + 1)$ terms. Let $\mu$ be a maximal sub-expression of $S_{A \otimes B}$ such that:

*both* $S_A \rightarrow \mu$ *and* $S_B \rightarrow \mu$         (a)

where $\mu$ has the form:

$$\lambda y_1^1 \ldots y_{d_1}^1 \ldots y_{d_r}^r \cdot [S_{C_1}(y_1^1, \ldots, y_{d_1}^1) \wedge \ldots \wedge S_{C_r}(y_1^r, \ldots, y_{d_r}^r) \wedge$$
$$L(y_1^1, \ldots, y_{d_1}^1, \ldots, y_{d_r}^r)] \cdot$$

If $\mu$ is empty, ie. 'false', then the semantics of $A$ and $B$ are independent. If $\mu$ is non-empty then the semantics of $A$ and $B$ have something in common and $A$ and $B$ should be joined with a maintenance link.

Now examine $\mu$ to see *why* $A$ and $B$ should be joined. If $\mu$ is non-empty and if both $A$ and $B$ are items in the basis then:

$A$ and $B$ are a pair of basis items with logically dependent semantics    (b)

If $\mu$ is non-empty and if $A$ is *not* in the basis then there are three cases. First, if:

$$S_A \leftrightarrow S_B \leftrightarrow \mu \tag{c}$$

then items $A$ and $B$ are equivalent and should be joined with an *equivalence link*. Second if (c) does not hold and:

$$either\ S_A \leftrightarrow \mu\ or\ S_B \leftrightarrow \mu \tag{d}$$

then either $A$ is a sub-item of $B$, or $B$ is a sub-item of $A$ and these two items should be joined with a *sub-item link*. Third, if (c) and (d) do not hold then if $\Delta$ is a minimal sub-expression of $S_A$ such that $\Delta \rightarrow \mu$. Then:

$$either\ S_{A_j}(y_1^j,...,y_{m_j}^j) \in \Delta,\ for\ some\ j \tag{e}$$

$$or\ J(y_1^1,..,y_{m_j}^1,...,y_{m_p}^p) \in \Delta \tag{f}$$

Both (e) and (f) may hold. If (e) holds then items $A$ and $B$ share one or more component items to which they should each be joined with a *component link*. If (f) holds then items $A$ and $B$ may be constructed with two object operators whose respective semantics are logically dependent. Suppose that item $A$ was constructed by object operator $C$ then the semantics of $C$ will imply:

$$\Phi = \lambda Q_1 {:} X_1^{i_1}\, Q_2 {:} X_2^{i_2} ... Q_j {:} X_j^{i_j} \cdot \lambda y_1^1\, ... y_{d_1}^1 ... y_{d_r}^r \cdot [$$
$$S_{P_1}(y_1^1,...,y_{d_1}^1)\, \wedge\ .....\ S_{P_r}(y_1^r,...,y_{d_r}^r)\, \wedge\ \ L(y_1^1,..,y_{d_1}^1,...,y_{d_r}^r)]\cdot$$

where the $Q_i$'s take care of any possible duplication in the $P_j$'s. Let $E$ be the object $E[\,\Phi,\, T,\, \emptyset\,]$ then $C$ is a sub-object of $E$; that is, there exists a non-tautological object $F$ such that:

$$C \simeq_w E \otimes_M F \tag{g}$$

for some set M and where the join is not necessarily monotonic. Items $A$ and $B$ are *weakly equivalent*, written $A \simeq_w B$, if there exists a permutation $\pi$ such that:

$(\forall x_1 x_2 ... x_n)[S_A(x_1,x_2,...,x_n) \leftrightarrow S_B(\pi(x_1,x_2,...,x_n))]$

where the $x_i$ are the $n_i$ variables associated with the i'th component of $A$. If $A$ is a sub-item of $B$ and if $B$ is a sub-item of $A$ then items $A$ and $B$ are weakly equivalent.

If (g) holds then the maintenance links are of three different kinds. If the join in (g) *is* monotonic then (g) states that $C$ may be decomposed into $E$ and $F$. If the join in (g) is *not* monotonic then (g) states that either $C \simeq_W E$ or $C \simeq_W F$. So, if the join in (g) is not monotonic then *either E* will be weakly equivalent to *C, or C* will be a sub-object of *E*.

It has been shown above that sub-item links between non-data items may be reduced to sub-type links between data items. So if:

- the semantics of the items in the basis are all logically independent;
- all equivalent items and objects have been removed by re-naming, and
- sub-item links between non-data items have been reduced to sub-type links between data items

then the maintenance links will be between nodes marked with:

- a data item that is a sub-type of the data item marked on another node, these are called the *sub-type links*;
- an item and the nodes marked with that item's components, these are called the *component links*, and
- an item constructed by a decomposable object and nodes constructed with that object's decomposition, these are called the *duplicate links*.

If the objects employed to construct the conceptual model have been decomposed then the only maintenance links remaining will be the sub-type links and the component links. The sub-type links and the component links cannot be removed from the conceptual model.

Unfortunately, decomposable objects, and so too duplicate links, are hard to detect. Suppose that objects $A$ and $B$ are decomposable as follows:

$A \simeq_W E \otimes_M F$

$B \simeq_W E \otimes_M G$

Then objects $A$ and $B$ should both be linked to object $E$. If the decompositions of $A$ and $B$ have not been identified then object $E$ may not have been identified and the implicit link between objects $A$ and $B$ may not be identified.

## 4. CONCLUSION

Maintenance links are used to maintain the validity of first-order knowledge bases. Maintenance links join two items in the conceptual model if modification of one of these items could require that the other item should be checked for correctness if the validity of the conceptual model is to be preserved. The efficiency of maintenance procedures depends on a method for reducing the density of the maintenance links in the conceptual model. One kind of maintenance link is removed by applying the rule of knowledge decomposition [7]. Another is removed by reducing sub-item relationships to sub-type relationships [2]. And another is removed by re-naming.

## REFERENCES

1.  Mayol, E. and Teniente, E. (1999). "Addressing Efficiency Issues During the Process of Integrity Maintenance" in *proceedings Tenth International Conference DEXA99*, Florence, September 1999, pp270-281.
2.  Debenham, J.K. (1998). *"Knowledge Engineering"*, Springer-Verlag, 1998.
3.  Katsuno, H. and Mendelzon, A.O. (1991). "On the Difference between Updating a Knowledge Base and Revising It", in *proceedings Second International Conference on Principles of Knowledge Representation and Reasoning, KR'91*, Morgan Kaufmann, 1991.
4.  Barr, V. (1999). "Applying Reliability Engineering to Expert Systems" in *proceedings 12th International FLAIRS Conference*, Florida, May 1999, pp494-498.
5.  Jantke, K.P. and Herrmann, J. (1999). "Lattices of Knowledge in Intelligent Systems Validation" in *proceedings 12th International FLAIRS Conference*, Florida, May 1999, pp499-505.
6.  Darwiche, A. (1999). "Compiling Knowledge into Decomposable Negation Normal Form" in *proceedings International Joint Conference on Artificial Intelligence, IJCAI'99*, Stockholm, Sweden, August 1999, pp 284-289.
7.  Debenham, J.K. (1999). "Knowledge Object Decomposition" in *proceedings 12th International FLAIRS Conference*, Florida, May 1999, pp203-207.
8.  Johnson, G. and Santos, E. (2000). "Generalizing Knowledge Representation Rules for Acquiring and Validating Uncertain Knowledge" in *proceedings 13th International FLAIRS Conference*, Florida, May 2000, pp186-2191.
9.  Ramirez, J. and de Antonio, A. (2000). "Semantic Verification of Rule-Based Systems with Arithmetic Constraints" in *proceedings 11th International Conference DEXA2000*, London, September 2000, pp437-446.
10. Debenham, J.K. "The Degradation of Knowledge Base Integrity", in *proceedings 13th International FLAIRS Conference FLAIRS-2000*, Orlando, Florida, May 2000, pp113-117.

# LEARNING BAYESIAN METANETWORKS FROM DATA WITH MULTILEVEL UNCERTAINTY

Vagan Terziyan[1], Oleksandra Vitko[2]
*[1]University of Jyväskylä, Finland, vagan@it.jyu.fi [2]Kharkov National University of Radioelectronics, Ukraine, vitko@kture.kharkov.ua*

**Abstract:**     Managing knowledge by maintaining it according to dynamic context is among the basic abilities of a knowledge-based system. The two main challenges in managing context in Bayesian networks are the introduction of contextual (in)dependence and Bayesian multinets. We are presenting one possible implementation of a context sensitive Bayesian multinet – the Bayesian Metanetwork, which implies that interoperability between component Bayesian networks (valid in different contexts) can be also modelled by another Bayesian network. The general concepts and two kinds of such Metanetwork models are considered. The main focus of this paper is learning procedure for Bayesian Metanetworks.

**Key words:**     Bayesian Metanetworks, Bayesian learning, multilevel uncertainty, context

## 1.     INTRODUCTION

Creating and managing knowledge according to different levels of possible context – are among the basic abilities of an intelligent system. Multilevel representation of a context allows reasoning with contexts towards solution of the following problems [9]:
– to derive knowledge interpreted using all known levels of its context;
– to derive unknown knowledge when interpretation of it in some context and the context itself are known;
– to derive unknown knowledge about a context when it is known how the knowledge is interpreted in this context;

– to transform knowledge from one context to another one.

Metanetwork-based models (e.g. the Semantic Metanetworks, the MetaPetrinets, etc.) have proved to be more powerful tools for knowledge representation in the presence of multiple contexts [8, 9].

A Bayesian network is known to be a valuable tool for encoding, learning and reasoning about probabilistic (casual) relationships. The Bayesian network for a set of variables $X = \{X_1, ..., X_n\}$ is a directed acyclic graph with the network structure S that encodes a set of conditional independence assertions about variables in X, and the set P of local probability distributions associated with each variable [4].

The two main challenges in utilizing context in Bayesian networks are the introduction of contextual independence [1] and Bayesian multinets. A recursive Bayesian multinet was introduced by Pena et al. [6] as a decision tree with component Bayesian networks at the leaves. The key idea was to decompose the learning Bayesian network problem into learning component networks from incomplete data.

The main goal this research is to study another multiple Bayesian model – the Bayesian Metanetwork, which implies that interoperability between component Bayesian networks (valid in different contexts) can be also modelled by another Bayesian network. Such models suit well to e.g. user profiling applications where different probabilistic interrelations within predictive features from user's profile can be controlled by probabilistic interrelations among the contextual features, and other applications that require the formalism to manage two-level uncertainty or even multilevel uncertainty. The combination of the ideas of Metamodels and Bayesian network resulted to a refined and powerful formalism of a Bayesian Metanetwork.

The rest of the paper is organised as follows. In Section 2 we briefly introduce the formalism of Bayesian Metanetwork. In Section 3 we suggest the learning procedure for Bayesian Metanetwork. We conclude in Section 4.


## 2.    THE BAYESIAN METANETWORKS

In our previous work [10], Bayesian Metanetwork formalism was used to model user preferences in mobile electronic commerce. Specific features and constraints of the mobile commerce environment demand the new flexible models of knowledge management. Such models assume to deal with the causal probabilistic relations in the cases when changes of a context occur. It was also shown that the Bayesian Metanetwork provides enough flexibility to be a powerful formalism also for many other data mining tasks [12].

***Definition.*** The Bayesian Metanetwork is a set of Bayesian networks, which are put on each other in such a way that the elements (nodes or conditional dependencies) of every previous probabilistic network depend on the local probability distributions associated with the nodes of the next level network.

The Bayesian Metanetwork is a triplet: $MBN = (BN, R, P)$, where $BN = \{BN_1, BN_2, ...BN_n\}$ is a set of Bayesian networks, each of which is considered on the appropriate level according to the index; $R = \{R_{1,2}, R_{2,3}...R_{n-1,n}\}$ is a set of sets of interlevel links; P is a joint probability distribution over the Metanetwork.

Each $R_{i,i+1}$ is a set of interlevel links between $i$ and $i+1$ levels. We have proposed 2 types of links:

– $R_{v-e}$ is a link "vertex-edge" meaning that stochastic values of vertex $v_{ik}$ in the network $BN_i$ correspond to the different conditional probability tables $P_k(v_{i-1,j} | v_{i-1,pj})$ in the network $BN_{i-1}$;

– $R_{v-v}$ is a link "vertex-vertex" meaning that stochastic values of vertex $v_{ir}$ in the network $BN_i$ correspond to the different relevance values of vertex $v_{i-1,r}$ in the network $BN_{i-1}$.

According to the introduced two types of interlevel links we consider two models of the Bayesian Metanetwork:

– *C*-Metanetwork, which has interlevel links of $R_{v-e}$ type used for managing conditional dependencies (Conditional Dependencies Metanetwork);

– *R*-Metanetwork, which has interlevel links of $R_{v-v}$ type used for modelling relevant feature selection (**Relevance Metanetwork**).

## 2.1     Bayesian C-Metanetwork for Managing Conditional Dependencies

In a C-Metanetwork the context variables are considered to be on the second (contextual) level to manage the conditional probabilities associated with the predictive level of the network [10, 12]. The sample of C-Metanetwork projected to 2-D space is presented in Figure 1.

Standard Bayesian inference is applied in the Bayesian network of each level. The examples and rules of propagation through the whole C-Metanetwork we have presented in [10, 12].

The two-level Metanetwork can be easily extended to the multilevel (multicontext) Metanetwork. In principle, we can assume that a Bayesian Metanetwork may have as many levels as necessary.

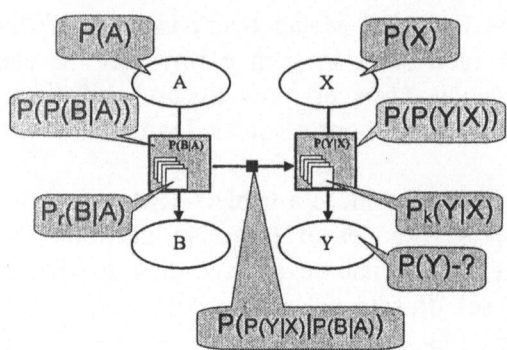

*Figure 1.* The sample of a Bayesian C-Metanetwork. The nodes of the 2nd-level network correspond to the conditional probabilities of the 1st-level network P(B|A) and P(Y|X). The directed arc in the 2nd-level network corresponds to the conditional probability P(P(Y|X)|P(B|A))

## 2.2    The Bayesian R-Metanetwork for Modelling Relevant Feature Selection

The Bayesian Metanetwork can be also used as a tool for the relevant feature selection. In R-Metanetwork the context variables are again considered as the higher-level control upon the basic network with predictive variables [10, 12]. Values of the context variables are assumed to have an influence to the relevancies of the variables on the predictive level.

We consider relevance value as a probability of importance of the variable to the inference of target attribute in the given context.

Contextual relevance network can be defined over the given predictive probabilistic network as it is shown in Figure 2.

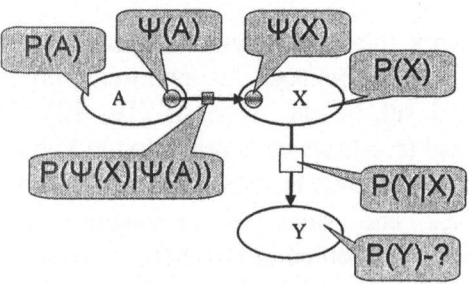

*Figure 2.* The simple relevance network with the attributes ψ(A), ψ(X) and the conditional probability P(ψ(X)| ψ(A)) defined over the predictive network with the attributes A, X, Y and the conditional probability P(Y|X)

The Bayesian R-Metanetwork in Figure 2 encodes the conditional dependencies over the relevancies and contains:

- the relevance predicate: $\psi(X) = $ "yes", if parameter X is relevant; $\psi(X) = $ "no", if parameter X is not relevant;
- the relevance value: $\psi_X = P(\psi(X) = $ "yes").

Standard Bayesian inference is applied to the Bayesian network of each level. The examples and rules of propagation through the whole R-Metanetwork we have presented in [10, 12].

## 3.  LEARNING BAYESIAN METANETWORKS

In this Section we suggest the learning procedures for Bayesian Metanetworks. Both structure learning and parameter learning are considered.

A number of methods for learning a Bayesian network were developed and are in use, see e.g. [2, 4, 5]. Such methods can be applied for learning component Bayesian networks on each level of the Metanetwork. The main challenge of this work was the extension of the standard learning procedures for the case of multilevel probabilistic Metanetworks to enable learning interlevel relationships.

Let's consider the following learning task:

**Given** training set *D* of training examples $<X_1, X_2, ... X_n, Y>$,

**Goal** to restore:

- the set of levels of Bayesian Metanetwork $\{l_1, l_2, ... l_L\}$, each level is a Bayesian network;
- the interlevel links for each pair of successive levels $\{l_r, l_{r+1}\}$;
- the network structure and parameters at each level, particularly probabilities $P(v_i)$ and $P(v_i|parents(v_i))$ for each variable $v_i$.

We suggest the following learning procedure for Bayesian Metanetworks consisting of four stages; the last three of them are iteratively repeated at each level of the Metanetwork.

**Stage 1.** Division of attributes among the levels. The task of this stage is to divide the input vector of attributes $<X_1, X_2, ... X_n>$ into the predictive, contextual and perhaps metacontextual attributes. According to this division the levels of the Metanetwork will be built. Research in the context learning is rather active nowadays. Several fundamental works are published in this field and suggest the criteria for detecting the contextual variables, e.g. [11, 13]. We are using these criteria as they are presented in these works. We consider metacontextual variables as contextual variables for contextual variables.

**Stage 2.** Learning the network structure at the current level can be made by existing methods [2, 4, 5]. If the node ordering is known then the method of Cheng and Greiner is rather attractive and easy [2]. We used this method in our experiments.

It is worth to mention that for the R-Metanetwork the stage 2 returns only the maximal size model. Later, when the Metanetwork will be in use, the smaller substructure can be used according to the learned relevancies of attributes.

**Stage 3.** Learning the interlevel links between the current and subsequent levels. This is a new stage that has been added specifically for a Bayesian Metanetwork learning. This stage is described below both for the C-Metanetwork and for the R-Metanetwork.

**Stage 4.** Learning the parameters in the network at the current level is made by the standard procedure just taking into account the dynamics of parameters' values in different contexts.

If the context level is not empty, then the stages 2, 3 and 4 are repeated for the next-level network.

## 3.1     Learning Interlevel Links in C-Metanetwork

In Section 2, we have noticed that the vertex of every next level in a Bayesian C-Metanetwork is associated with the possible conditional probability matrix of the Bayesian network from the previous level. We will describe the establishment of such interlevel links in a C-Metanetwork.

Consider the fragment of the C-Metanetwork from Figure 3. If the standard parameter learning algorithm knows the causal relationships between the variables it will return the single conditional probability table $P(B|A)$: $P_{ik} (B = b_i \mid A = a_k )$ for the arc $A{\rightarrow}B$ and the single conditional probability table $P(Y \mid X)$: $P_{rs}(Y = y_r \mid X = x_s )$ for the arc $X{\rightarrow}Y$. The standard algorithm processes the whole training set $<A, B, X, Y>$.

Assume there are several contexts in which this network fragment is observed. The parameters of the network in different contexts most probably will be different as well. In such a case it is reasonable to study each context separately and to calculate the more accurate parameters in each context instead of "averaging" probabilities over all the contexts.

Divide the whole vector $<A, B, X, Y>$ of the training set into $n$ clusters $<A, B, X, Y>_1$, $<A, B, X, Y>_2$, ...,$<A, B, X, Y>_n$ according to the values of context attributes for the causal dependence $A{\rightarrow}B$. Applying the learning procedure in each data cluster $<A, B, X, Y>_j$ we get separately $n$ conditional probability matrixes $P_j (B \mid A)$: $P_{jik}(B = b_i \mid A = a_k )$, $j = 1, n$.

In the same way we divide the vector $<A, B, X, Y>$ into $m$ clusters $<A, B, X, Y>_1$, $<A, B, X, Y>_2$, ...,$<A, B, X, Y>_m$ according to the values of context attributes for causal dependence $X \to Y$ and get separately $m$ conditional probability matrixes $P_t(Y|X)$: $P_{trs}(Y = y_r | X = x_s)$, $t = \overline{1,m}$.

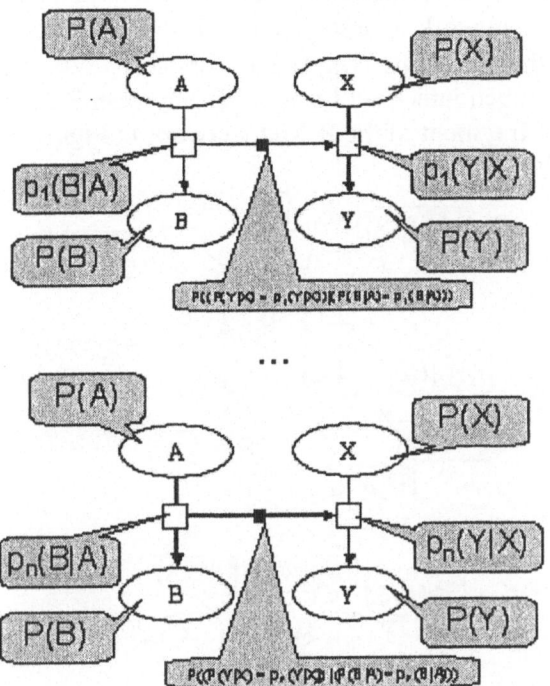

*Figure 3.* Different probability tables corresponding to different contexts are associated with vertexes of the second-level Bayesian network

Thus in each context the Bayesian network gets different parameters (Figure 3) and will be managed by the second-level contextual network.

The second level of the Metanetwork is entered for management of the probability tables in the first-level network. The sets of matrixes $\{P_j(B|A)\}$ and $\{P_t(Y|X)\}$ can be considered as the random variables $U$ and $W$ at the second level of the Metanetwork. The variable $U$ will have as many values, as we consider contexts for the causal dependence $A \to B$. Each value $u_j$ will correspond to the probability matrix $P_j(B|A)$. In the same way we define the variable $W$ with the values $w_t$ which correspond to $P_t(Y|X)$.

If the causal probabilistic dependence occurs between the contextual variables, then we learn Bayesian dependence $W \to U$ at the second level of the Metanetwork. The learning procedure will result in composing the (meta)matrix $P(W|U)$, i.e. the matrix of matrixes:

$$P(W|U) = \{P((W = P_j(Y|X)) | (U = P_t(B|A))\}, j = \overline{1,n}, t = \overline{1,m}.$$

## 3.2    Learning interlevel links in R-Metanetwork

In Section 2, we have mentioned that the vertex of each next level in the Bayesian R-Metanetwork is associated with the possible relevancies of the attributes of the previous Bayesian network. We will describe the establishment of such interlevel links in the Bayesian R-Metanetwork.

Consider the fragment of the R-Metanetwork in Figure 4.

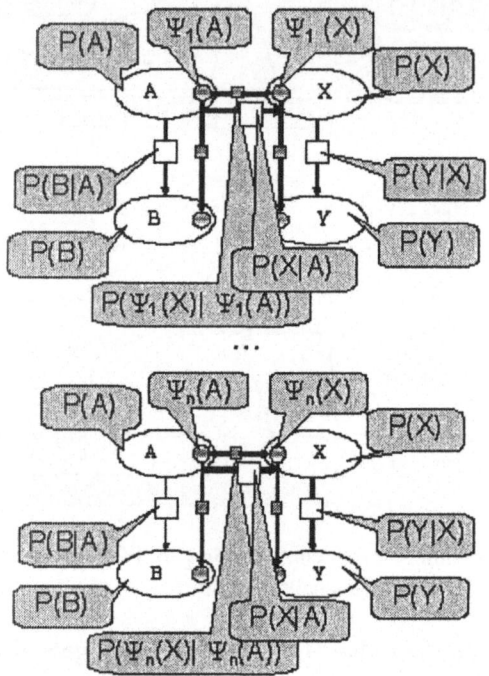

*Figure 4.* Different relevancies corresponding to different contexts are associated with vertexes of the second-level Bayesian network

Assume $Y$ is a target attribute. The standard feature selection method will process the whole training set $<A, B, X, Y>$ and will return some relevance estimations for each predictive attribute: $\Psi(A)$, $\Psi(B)$, $\Psi(X)$. The good overview of the existing feature selection methods is given in [3, 7]. We consider the relevance of the target attribute $\Psi(Y)$ is equal to 1.

Assume there are several contexts in which this network fragment is observed. It is possible that relevancies of attributes will be different in different contexts. As it was done in the case of C-Metanetwork, here it is also reasonable to study each context separately and to calculate the more accurate relevancies in each context instead of "averaging" relevancies

$\Psi(A)$, $\Psi(B)$, $\Psi(X)$ over all contexts. Different relevancies can lead to different network structures in different contexts.

Divide the whole vector $<A, B, X, Y>$ of the training set into $n$ clusters $<A, B, X, Y>_1$, $<A, B, X, Y>_2$, ...,$<A, B, X, Y>_n$ according to the values of context attributes. Applying the learning procedure in each data cluster $<A, B, X, Y>_j$ we get separately $n$ values of relevancies $\Psi_j(A)$, $\Psi_j(B)$, $\Psi_j(X)$.

Thus we get in each context the Bayesian network with different relevancies of attributes (Figure 4). The second level of the Metanetwork is entered for management of the feature selection in the first-level network. The sets of matrixes $\{\Psi_j(A)\}$, $\{\Psi_j(B)\}$, $\{\Psi_j(X)\}$ can be considered as the random variables $U$, $V$ and $W$ at the second level of the Metanetwork.

If the causal probabilistic dependence occurs between the contextual variables, then we learn the Bayesian dependence $W{\rightarrow}U$ at the second level of the Metanetwork. The learning procedure will result in composing the (meta)matrix $P(W|U)$ as follows:

$$P(W|U) = \{P((W = \psi_j(X)) | (U = \psi_t(A)) = \psi_{jt}(X|A)\}, \; j = \overline{1, n}, \; t = \overline{1, m}.$$

## 4. CONCLUSIONS

The general concept and the two types of a Bayesian Metanetwork are considered as tools to present the second order uncertainty. C-Metanetwork allows managing the conditional dependencies of the Bayesian network and assumes context-based conditional dependencies between conditional dependencies. R-Metanetwork assumes that the relevancies of predictive variables in the Bayesian network are random variables themselves. This metanetwork provides a tool for recalculating attributes' relevancies depending on context change. Generally a Bayesian Metanetwork is a multilevel structure of component Bayesian networks. The controlling extra level(s) in a Metanetwork is used to select the appropriate parameters or substructure from the basic network based on the contextual attributes. The accent in this paper is done to the learning procedure for Bayesian Metanetworks. Both structure learning and parameter learning are considered. The main challenge of this work is the extension of the standard Bayesian learning procedures with the algorithm of learning the interlevel links. The experiments (made outside the scope of this paper due to the domain specifics) on the data from the highly-contextual domain have shown the effectiveness of the proposed models and learning procedures. The multiple-factor concept of radiation risk for population has been modelled, and the leaning procedure has shown quite good correlation of the predicted results with expert estimations. The subjective (social) factors, which influence the radiation risk distribution, have been modelled at the contextual level of the Metanetwork. Still more experiments are needed to support the concept of a Bayesian Metanetwork and to specify concrete areas where its implementation will be reasonable. Just now we have some evidence to assume Bayesian Metanetwork to be a powerful tool in cases where structure (or strengths) of causal relationships between observed parameters of an object essentially depends on a context. Also it can be a useful diagnostic model for such an object, which diagnosis depends on different set of observed parameters depending on a context.

# REFERENCES

[1]   Boutiler, C., Friedman, N., Goldszmidt, M., Koller, D., Context-Specific Independence in Bayesian Networks, In: Proceedings of the 12-th Conference on Uncertainty in Artificial Intelligence (UAI-96), 1996, 115-123.

[2]   Cheng J., Greiner R.. Learning Bayesian Belief Network Classifiers: Algorithms and System, In: Proceedings of the Fourteenth Canadian Conference on Artificial Intelligence (AI-2001), 2001, 141-151.

[3]   Dash, M., Liu, H., Feature Selection for Classification, Intelligent Data Analysis 1 (3) 1997, 131-156.

[4]   Heckerman, D., A Tutorial on Learning with Bayesian Networks. Technical Report MSR-TR-95-06, Microsoft Research, March, 1995.

[5]   Madigan D., Raftery A., Volinsky C., Hoeting, J. Bayesian Model Averaging, In: Procs. AAAI Workshop on Integrating Multiple Learned Models, Portland, 1996, 77-83.

[6]   Pena, J., Lozano, J.A., Larranaga, P., Learning Bayesian Networks for Clustering by Means of Constructive Induction, Machine Learning, 47(1), 2002, 63-90.

[7]   Siedlecki W., Skalansky J., On Automatic Feature Selection, International Journal of Pattern Recognition and Artificial Intelligence, 2, 1988, 197-220.

[8]   Terziyan V., Multilevel Models for Knowledge Bases Control and Automated Information Systems Applications, Doctor of Technical Sciences Degree Thesis, Kharkov State Technical University of Radioelectronics, 1993.

[9]   Terziyan V., Puuronen S., Reasoning with Multilevel Contexts in Semantic Metanetworks, In: P. Bonzon, M. Cavalcanti, R. Nossun (Eds.), Formal Aspects in Context, Kluwer Academic Publishers, 2000, 97-126.

[10]  Terziyan V., Vitko O., Bayesian Metanetworks for Modelling User Preferences in Mobile Environment. In: Proceedings of the German Conference on Artificial Intelligence, Hamburg, 15-18 September 2003 , LNCS, Vol. 2821, Springer, 370-384.

[11]  Turney P. The identification of context-sensitive features: a formal definition of context for concept learning, In: Proceedings of the Workshop on Learning in Context-Sensitive Domains at the Thirteenth International Conference on Machine Learning (ICML-96), 1996, 53-59.

[12]  Vitko O., The Multilevel Probabilistic Networks for Modelling Complex Information Systems under Uncertainty. Ph.D. Thesis, Kharkov National University of Radioelectronics, 2003.

[13]  Widmer G. Tracking Context Changes through Meta-Learning, Machine Learning, 27(3), 1997, 259-286.

# USING ORGANIZATIONAL STRUCTURES EMERGENCE FOR MAINTAINING FUNCTIONAL INTEGRITY IN EMBEDDED SYSTEMS NETWORKS

Jean-Paul Jamont
*Laboratoire de Conception et d'Intégration des Systèmes*
*Institut National Polytechnique de Grenoble*
*F-26000 Valence, France*

jean-paul.jamont@esisar.inpg.fr


Michel Occello
*Université Pierre-Mendès France*
*Laboratoire de Conception et d'Intégration des Systèmes*
*Institut National Polytechnique de Grenoble*
*F-26000 Valence, France*

michel.occello@iut-valence.fr

**Abstract**      This paper deals with the application of multiagent self-organization techniques for giving adaptive features to distributed embedded systems evolving in agressive environments. Interesting results are presented, showing how functionnal integrity maintenance of artificial complex systems can take advantage of a collective decentralized approach.

**Keywords:** Structure emergence, self-organization, multiagent system, wireless sensor network.

## Introduction

Multiagent systems are especially adapted for designing complex (open, distributed) systems. We propose an innovative approach for open multiagent systems in the context of wireless networks of intelligent sensors.

Such networks are composed by automonous hybrid hardware/software entities ensuring measuring tasks and information routing tasks. The sensor wireless nodes have to adapt their behavior according to their independant energy resources and their position in the organization.

We describe how we improve both management of communication and management of energy resources including a strong fault tolerant feature through a totally decentralized approach and inherent multiagent emergence features.

We give finally an insight to the experimental intelligent wireless sensor network architecture used for the EnvSys Project[1] of instrumentation of an underground river system.

## 1. Emergence and Multiagent systems

**Multiagent system.** An agent is a software entity embedded in an environment which it can perceive and in which it acts. It is endowed with autonomous behaviors and has objectives. Autonomy is the main concept in the agent issue: it is the ability of agents to control their actions and their internal states. The autonomy of agents implies no centralized control.

A multiagent system is a set of agents situated in a common environment, which interact and attempt to reach a set of goals. Through these interactions a global behavior, more intelligent than the sum of the local intelligence of multiagent system components, can emerge. The emergence process is a way to obtain, through cooperation, dynamic results that cannot be calculated in a deterministic way.

A multiagent system can have several characteristics. It is *open*, as opposed to *closed*, if its structure is capable of dynamical changes: in other words, the system tolerates that the agents enter and leave freely the multiagent system. A multiagent system can be *homogeneous*, as opposed to a *heterogeneous*, if it is constituted of homogeneous agents from the point of view of their theory (representation and properties) and their architecture (particular methodology of agent design).

**Emergence.** The emergence talks about the not programed and irreversible sudden appearance of phenomena in a system (maybe multiagent) confirming that "the whole is more than the sum of each part".

It is difficult to qualify the emergent characteristic of a phenomenon, however Muller and Parunak, 1998 proposes an interesting definition of it. Falling under the prolongation of the work reported in (M.R. Jean, 1997), it affirms that a phenomenon is emergent if:

---

[1]This project is funded by the FITT program (Incitative Fund for Technological Transfert) of the French Rhône-Alpe Regional Council.

- there is a set of agents interacting via an environment whose state and dynamic cannot be expressed in terms of the emerging phenomenon to produce in a vocabulary or a theory D,

- the dynamic of the interacting agents produces a global phenomenon such as, for example, an execution trace or an invariant,

- The global phenomenon is observable either by the agent (strong sense) or by an external observer (weak sense) in different terms from the subjacent dynamics i.e. another vocabulary or another theory D '.

To give to an agent's system a particular functionality, the tradionnal method consists in carrying out a functional decomposition of the problem in a set of primitives which will be established in the agents. The alternative suggested by (Steels, 1990) aims to make this functionality emerge from the interactions between the agents. The advantages of the "emergent functionality" approach are first of all a reinforcement of the robustness of the system : it is less sensitive to the changes of the environment. The reason is that, unlike to the case of a programmed functionality (traditional approach), the designer doesn't need to consider all the possibilities for the system reacts according to each situation.

## 2. Communication management of wireless sensor networks

In this part we expose our pratical problem (the Envsys project), the main difficulties of this type of application and the traditional solution to solve this problem.

## 2.1 Our practical case: the EnvSys project

The purpose of the ENVironment SYStem project is to monitor an underground river network. Let us present the origin of this project and the problems occurring in such an application (Jamont et al., 2002).

**Origin of the project.** The ENVSYS project finds its origin in a statement: the measurement of the various parameters in an underground river system is a complex task. In fact, the access to this type of underground galleries is difficult: it requires help from speleologists. Besides, the installation of wire communication networks is difficult, especially because the structure of hydrographic systems is very often chaotic. Finally, in the case of a radio communication network, the underground aspect complicates wave propagation and for the moment the techniques which are used are not totally mastered.

The general idea of the project is to study the feasibility of a sensor network from the existing physical layer. This will allow wireless instrumentation of a subterranean river system. Such a network would present an important interest in many domains: the study of underground flows, the monitoring of deep collecting, flooding risk management, river system detection of pollution risks, etc.

**The issue.**     In a subterranean river system, the interesting parameters to measure are numerous: temperature of air and water, air pressure and if possible water pressure for the flooded galleries, pollution rate by classical pollutants, water flow, draft speed, etc. All this information will be collected at the immediate hydrographic network exit by a work station like a PC. These data will be processed to activate alarms, study the progress of a certain pollution according to miscellaneous measuring parameters, determine a predictive model of the whole network by relating the subterranean parameters measures of our system with the overground parameter measures more classically on the catchment basin.

We do not wish to carry out this instrumentation with a wire network for obvious reasons of convenience. We shall use electromagnetic waves with low frequencies as a carrier. These waves have an interesting property: they are able to go through rock blocks. Every sensor has a limited transmission range.

Having defined the role of sensors, we can represent the structure of our communication network. It consists of a set of sensors and a listening station as illustrated on the following figure (see fig 1):

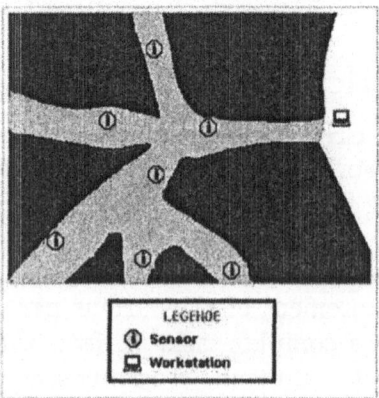

*Figure 1.*    The monitored cave

Here is a non-exhaustive list of problems which one needs to address:

- How to carry out the physical layer and what level of protocol connection to choose above such layer?

- How to route the information in the best way? Each of the sensors cannot physically communicate with the workstation which collects the information. Which sensor should thus make the decision to repeat the information?

- How to monitor such a complex environment?

- What kind of intelligence to give the network?

The main contribution of the work presented in this paper is situated at a logical level, concerning especially the last three points of the problems listed before.

Generally these devices have autonomous energy sources. These constraints must be taken into account in order to optimize the communication management (the energy devoted to communication constitutes an important part of the sensor energetic cost). The energetic parameter is important in the sense that it can create internal faults or that it can influence other parameters like the emission range. Furthermore the environment can be hostile (temperature, pressure, water flood environment...) and can cause internal faults.

The open nature of these networks can be another source of important errors. In fact, insertion and departure of the nodes occur randomly and often unpredictably. Furthermore, in the case of mobile devices the infrastructure of sytems are not persistant and the global data monitoring must be organized from local observation.

## 2.2    Wireless network routing protocols

Networks of wireless autonomous sensors for monitoring physical environments are a recent but very active application and research area. These networks, where the routing process is distributed to all the hosts, are called ad-hoc networks. If the hosts are mobile they can be called MANET networks for Mobile Ad-hoc NETwork. The associated routing protocols are centered on the flooding techniques which consist in sending messages to all the members of the network to be sure the receiver gets the message: the associated power cost is very high.

There are different routing protocols to solve the problem of routing in (mobile) wireless networks. Generally they are a compromise between the control traffic reduction and the latency in finding the route to a destination. These protocols are divided into different families.

The *reactive* families are the on-demand protocols. These protocols never try to find a route to a destination before a message requires transmission. A reactive protocol attempts to discover routes only on demand. One of the major advantage of this routing technique family is that the bandwidth is mainly used for data transmission. The Dynamic Source Routing protocol (DSR Johnson and Maltz, 1996), that we can see after, is one of the more popular and simplest protocol.

The *proactive* protocols use periodically updated routing tables and for those it is necessary to exchange many types of control messages for creating a "network model". These messages enable a node to discover its neighborhood for example. The Destination Sequence Distance Vector protocol (DSDV Perkins et al., 1994) for example is one of the first protocols of this family specified by the MANET work group and it takes the RIP functionning principle. The Optimized Link State Routing protocol (OLSR Clausen et al., 2001) and Clusterhead Gateway Switch Routing protocol (CGSR Chiang et al., 1997) agregate the different hosts in clusters.

*Hybrid* protocols adopt the reactive protocol behavior and, if necessary, use routing tables for increasing efficiency. The majority of these protocols use a proactive or reactive scheme depending on the type of requirements.

## 3. Our solution based on the emergence

### 3.1 What should emerge?

Our objective is to decrease the energy expense induced by the inherent floodings techniques. For that we will use a group structure inspired by the clusters of the CGSR protocol. Our organizational basic structures are constituted by (see fig 2):

- one and only one *group representative agent* (r) managing the communication in its group,

- some *connection agents* (c) which know the different representative agents and can belong to several groups,

- some *simple members* (s) which are active in the communication process only for their own tasks (They don't ensure information relay).

With this type of organizational structure, the message path between the source (a) and the receiver (b) is $((a, r),^* [(r, c), (c, r)], (r, b))$. If the source is a representative agent the first term doesn't exist. If the receiver is a representative agent the last term doesn't exist.

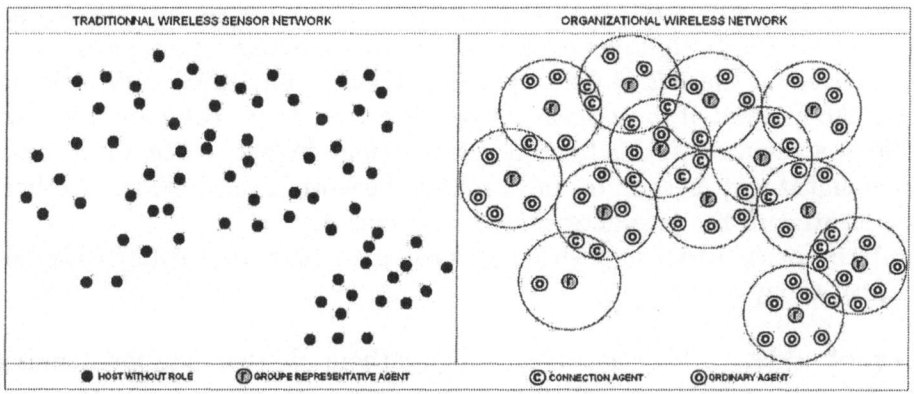

*Figure 2.* Our organizational structure

The energy saving comes owing to the fact that the flooding is only directed to the representative agent of the groups and to some connection agent. To give an order of idea, a receiver path research with flooding techniques will cost, in the case of a traditionnal wireless network, a number of emissions equal to the number of stations. In the case of a clustered wireless network, the number of transmitted messages are about twice the numbers of representative agent (all the representative agents are contacted via one connection agent ). In our example (fig 2) the cost would be in the first case of 74 messages and in the second of 26 messages is an economy.

However, the networks with an organizationnal structure must take care of the maintenance of their routing table. Generally, the adaptive features of these tables come from periodical exchanges between the different nodes. In our approach we do not wish to use this technique to ensure the maintenance of coherence. Indeed, our principle will be "if we do not need to communicate, it is useless to spend energy to ensure the coherence maintenance". However, we will thus use eavesdropping of surrounding agent communications. We extract from these messages exchange knowledge to update our beliefs about our neighboors. Moreover, our self-organization mechanism will integrate a energy management policy. These structures will thus emerge.

## 3.2 How to make the solution emerge?

It is necessary for us to wonder now how we will make emerge these structures. The multiagent methods aim at decreasing the complexity of system design by a decentralized analysis. There are several multiagent system methods (Iglesias et al., 1998). We are thereafter going to be interested in the AEIO decomposition (Demazeau, 1995). We will follow the method of multiagent design discussed in (Occello and Koning, 2000), associated to this MAS decomposition. In fact, we chose to apply this multiagent method for our problem because it privileges an explicit description of the interactions and the environment.

It proposes a decomposition according to four axes collectively accepted today.

**Agent axis.** The *agent axis* (A) gathers all elements for defining and constructing these entities. It concerns the agent's know-how and knowledge, its model and its architecture. In our problem we use the ASTRO hybrid architecture (Occello and Demazeau, 1998).

**Environment axis.** The *environment axis* (E) deals with elements necessary for the multiagent system realization such as the perception of this environment and the actions one can do on it.

**Interaction axis.** The *interaction axis* (I) includes all elements which are in use for structuring the external interactions among the agents (agent communication language, interaction protocols).We defined thirteen different types of small messages.

- *WhoAreMyNeighbors* is used by an agent to know who its neighbors are. This message is transmitted when an agent is created (the first goal of a new agent is to know its neighbors) or when an agent feels that its neighbor table is not coherent with reality.

- *IAmOneOfYourNeighbors* : It makes it possible for an agent to answer the preceding request. With this message, it thus provides its identifier, its role and its membership group.

- *IChangeMyRole* : It is used by any agent to inform its neighbors that it decides to change its role. This message contains the agent identifier, its role and its membership group.

- *AskConnectionAgentGroup* : It is used by representative agents which want to update their knowledge on the close groups. It obliges the connection agent to answer.

- *AnswerConnectionAgentGroup* : It is used by a connection agent to announce to a representative agent the other representative agent that it can contact.

- *VerifyNeighborGroupConsistency* : It is sent by an agent, to its representative, which believes to have detected an inconsistency with a close group. There is an inconsistency between two groups when two agents of different groups see themselves and their representative cannot communicate with a short path (fixed by a time-to-live).

- *ConflictRepresentativeResolution* : It is used by a representative agent, in conflict with one or more other reprentative agents, for communicating its score. There are conflicts when two neigbors have a representative role.

- *ISuggestYouToBeRepresentative* : It is a suggestion given by a representative to one of the agents of its group. It can give this order for correct an inconsistency problem.

- *FindPacketPath* is used by a representative agent which wants to know the path (list of representative agents) to join another agent.

- *PacketPathResult* : It is the answer of the representative of the recipient of the *FindPacketPath* message.

- *ACKMessage* : It is a configuration message used to confirm to the transmitter that its message has arrived to its destination. These messages play a role in the coherence of the organization.

- *BadWay* : It is a message sent by a representative who has noticed a problem. This message takes the erroneous road and the organization verifies its consistency.

- *EncapsuledData* : It is a message which encapsulates data.

**Organization axis.** The *organization axis* (O) allows to order agent groups in organization determined according to their roles. We have identified eleven different self-organization techniques.

The adaptation of our whole multiagent system is obtained through the emergence of organizational structures by self-organization based on role allocation modifications. The organization is built according to an exchange of messages between agents. The decision algorithm is very simple, in case of conflict a mechanism of election is applied according to some criteria (energetic level, number of neighbors...).

Relations between agents are going to emerge from the evolution of the agents'states and from their interactions. We are only going fix the organization parameters, i.e. agents'tasks, agents'roles.

The ideal representative agent is the one having the most important number of neighbors and the most important level of energy. The level of energy is an important parameter in the sense that the representative agent is the most sollicited agent in the group from a communication point of view. We use role allocation based self-organization mechanisms involving the representative agent election. Our election function integrates some data on neigbors and energy levels. This function estimates the adequation between its desire to be the boss and its capacity to access to this position. The organization is modified only when a problem occurs. We do not try to maintain it if we have no communication. In addition to the configuration messages, all agents use eavesdropping. In fact, when some communicating entities (humans, robots etc.) share a common environment they might intercept some messages (broadcasted or not). From this eavesdropping message they can extract some authorised information like the receiver, the sender, the type of message and the packet's path.

Our algorithm, presented below, can be adjusted by other agents' suggestions such as an organization inconsistency. Moreover, an agent can give up its role because its power level quickly fall or fall under a limit that the agent thinks dangerous for its integrity. So it can become a simple member.

```
IF neighnorNumber¿0 THEN
  * One has neighbors
  IF neighnorRepresentativeNumber=0 THEN
      * None of our neighbors is representative: one decides to become to it. This
      * case intervenes when one has just created the agent or when he is isolate.
      * One does not proceed to a vote because one make the system unstable (the
      * sensor goes surely to carry on its path)
      myRole = REPRESENTATIVE;
  ELSE IF myRole = REPRESENTATIVE THEN
      * I am a representative agent too: I enter in conflict with the other applicants
      * to this role an election will take place and the agent with the best score will
      * remain in place.
      RepresentativeElectionProcedure()
  ELSE IF neighnorRepresentativeNumber=1 THEN
      * One of our neighbors is representative: one subjects oneself to its authority
      * and his even if the organization is less effective than otherwise. One privi-
      * leges, for the moment, stability to performance in the organization. One will
      * await a failure or its wish to leave its mandate.
      myRole = SIMPLEMEMBER;
  ELSE
      * There are, in our vicinity, several representatives: one becomes connection
      * agent for these representatives
      myRole = CONNECTION
  ENDIF
ELSE
  * One does not have a neighbor: one has any more no role
  myRole = NOTHING
ENDIF
```

# 4.    Results of our approach

It is significant when one is interested in self-organizing systems to think to the results evaluation problems. Indeed, as we noted previously, the self-organized systems are essentially fault tolerant and thus are particularly suited when one cannot plan all the situations which will occur. It is thus difficult to evaluate a self-organization method whose power is precisely to adapt to unforeseen situations.

In this part, we are thus going to give elements which will be used as a basis for the evaluation of self-organized system. We will initially be interested in the observability of these systems then, in the analysis of these observations.

## 4.1    Observation

We can distinguish three observation levels for agents organization: An external level of the multiagent system (case 1, picture 5) considering the system as a black box (we can observe only input/output), an internal level of the multiagent system (case 2, picture 5) if we focus on interactions between agent society, an internal level agent (case 3, picture 5) considering the agent and its architecture.

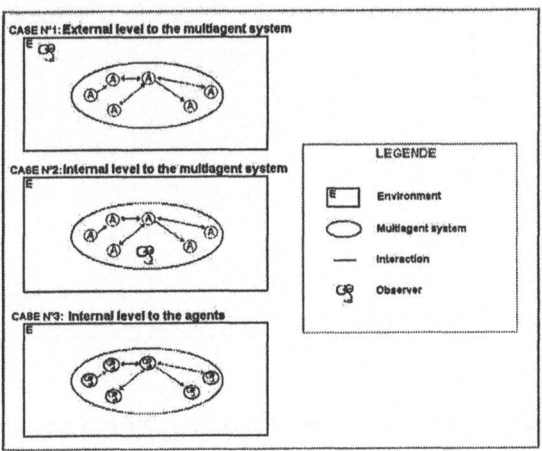

*Figure 3.*    Observation of agent organization

In self-organized multiagent systems, the stable states are an emergence of structure: we want to identify, to observe, these structures. We want to focus on global energy expence generated by messages exchange : the adapted level of observation is so the internal level of the multiagent system (case 2).

## 4.2    Results analysis of self-organization

First, we want to evaluate the self-organization without taking our application into account. Generally, a process of self-organization must be stable, sensitive and convergent (Groupe MARCIA, 1996) at the same time to be interesting and exploitable:

- Stable: the stability of a system refers to its constancy in time. The system must thus be stable in order to highlight persistent structures which would change only under the influence of internal or external disturbances.

- Sensitive: the sensitivity refers to its capacity to make a structure evolve into a partial or total recognition state according to whether all the selected criteria were satisfied or not. It is thus necessary that the process of self-organization be sensitive, so that it is possible for the emerging structures to be questionned.

- Converges: the convergence of a system reflects its capacity to evolve to known structures. The system must thus be convergent so that one leads to new structures.

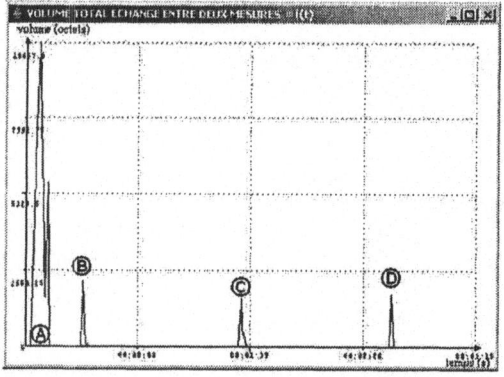

*Figure 4.*    Message volume exchanged for self-organization

Figure 5 shows the stability, the sensitivity and the the convergence of our self-organization process. The stable state are between the 4 evenements (A: Self-organization of 300 sensors, B: Re-organization to correct inconsistensy, C: Adding 10 sensors, D: re-organisation to correct an error detected by eavesdropping in a receiver search).

In a second time we take into account our application to quantify the correlation between our aim and the result of the self-organization process.

As we saw previously, this part of the analysis consists in quantifying the adequacy between the process of car-organization conceived and the results which were expected. It will thus be necessary for us to determine if the system is *valide* and/or *pertinent*. These two properties will be correlated with *interest* and the *simplicity*. Let us clarify these terms:

- the system is known as *valid* if the result produced by the self-organized process is in conformity with the expected one.

- the system is known as *pertinent* if the structure can be observed as easily as its implementation and as the comprehension that an observer would have of it.

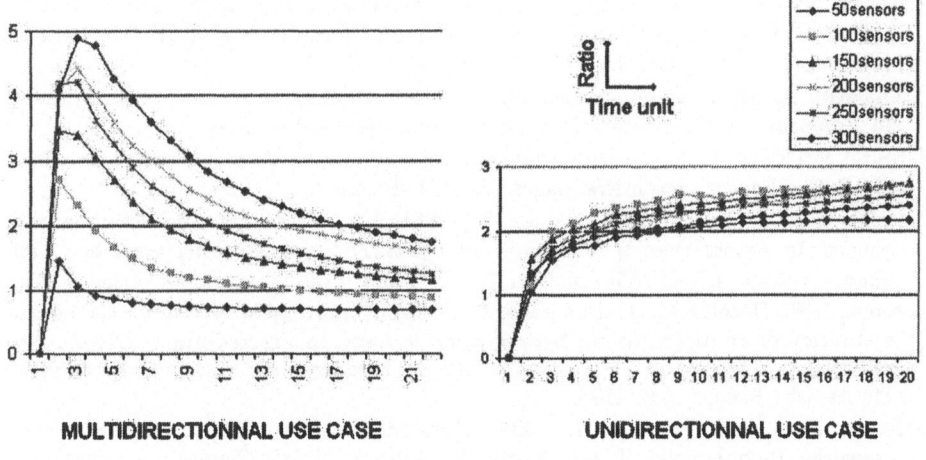

MULTIDIRECTIONNAL USE CASE        UNIDIRECTIONNAL USE CASE

*Figure 5.*    Ratio ASTRO efficiency divided by DSR-ROUTAGE efficiency

Figure 5 shows that in most of case our approach is efficient as expected, the validity is so prooved.

Each agent local algorithm managing the role selection presents a very low complexity due to the decentralization. The global structure constituted by the agent's localization can be easily observed and understood. The approach can be qualified of pertinent according to the definition given previously.

## Conclusion

We presented in this paper a hybrid software/hardware application for the management of an environmental sensor network. We proposed a multiagent analysis of this system and detailled how we use collective features to make the system adaptive. The innovative aspect of this work stands in the use of self-organization techniques based on emergence of structure. The concept of emergence is usually quite difficult to defend in an applicative real world context. We have made an effort to show through quantitative results the validity and the pertinence of the approach. This paper wants to contribute, by this way, to show that artificial intelligence mechanisms as self-organization can lead to interesting results and can improve classical techniques.

# References

Chiang, C., Wu, H.-K., Liu, W., and Gerla, M. (1997). Routing in clustered multihop, mobile wireless networks. In *Proceedings of IEEE Singapore International Conference on Networks*, pages 197–211, Singapore.

Clausen, T., Jacquet, P., Laouiti, A., Muhlethaler, P., Qayyum, A., and L.Viennot (2001). Optimized link state routing protocol. In *Proceedings of IEEE International Multitopic Conference - INMIC'2001*, Pakistan.

Demazeau, Y. (1995). From interactions to collective behavior in agent-based systems. In *European Conference on Cognitive Science*, Saint-Malo France.

Groupe MARCIA (1996). Auto-organisation := évolution de structure(s). In *PRC-GDR Intelligence artificielle*, pages 139–152. Hermes.

Iglesias, C., Garrijo, M., and Gonzales, J. (1998). A survey of agent oriented methodologies. In *Proceedings of Workshop on Agent Theories, Architectures, and Languages*, volume LNAI 1555, pages 163–176, Paris, France. Springer-Verlag.

Jamont, J.-P., Occello, M., and Lagrèze, A. (2002). A multiagent system for the instrumentation of an underground hydrographic system. In *Proceedings of IEEE International Symposium on Virtual and Intelligent Measurement Systems - VIMS'2002*, Mt Alyeska Resort, AK, USA.

Johnson, D.-B. and Maltz, D.-A. (1996). Dynamic source routing in ad hoc wireless networks. In Imielinski, T. and Korth, H., editors, *Mobile Computing*, pages 153–181. Kluwer Academic Publishers.

M.R. Jean (1997). Emergence et sma. In *JFIADSMA'1997 - Journée Francophones IAD et SMA*, Nice. Hermes.

Muller, J.-P. and Parunak, V. D. (1998). Vers une méthodologie de conception de systèmes multi-agents de résolution de problème par émergence. In *JFIADSMA - Journée Francophones IAD et SMA*, Pont--Mousson, France. Hermes.

Occello, M. and Demazeau, Y. (1998). Modelling decision making systems using agents for cooperation in a real time constraints. In *Proceedings of 3rd IFAC Symposium on Intelligent Autonomous Vehicles*, volume 1, pages 51–56, Madrid, Spain.

Occello, M. and Koning, J.-L. (2000). Multi-agent based software engineering: an approach based on model and software reuse. In *From Agent Theory to Agent Implementation II - EMCSR 2000 Symposium*, pages 645–657, Vienna.

Perkins, C.-E., Royer, E.-M., and Das, S. (1994). Highly dynamic destination-sequenced distance-vector (dsdv) routing for mobile computers. In *Proceedings of Special Interest Group on Data Communication conference- ACM SIGCOMM'94*.

Steels, L. (1990). Cooperation between distributed agents through self-organisation. In Demazeau, Y. and Muller, J.-P., editors, *Decentralized AI*. Elsevier Science Publishers B.V. (North Holland).

# EFFICIENT ATTRIBUTE REDUCTION ALGORITHM

Zhongzhi Shi, Shaohui Liu, Zheng Zheng
*Institute Of Computing Technology,Chinese Academy of Sciences, Beijing, China*

**Abstract:** Efficiency of algorithms is always an important issue concerned by so many researchers. Rough set theory is a valid tool to deal with imprecise problems. However, some of its algorithms' consuming time limits the applications of rough set. According to this, our paper analyzes the reasons of rough set algorithms' inefficiency by focusing on two important factors: indiscernible relation and positive region, and analyzes an equivalent and efficient method for computing positive region. And according to our research on the efficiency of some basic issues of rough set, a complete algorithm for the reduction of attributes is designed and its completeness is proved. Theoretical analysis and experimental results illustrate that our reduction algorithm is more efficient than some other algorithms.

**Key words:** Rough set, Positive region, Attribute Core, Attribute reduction algorithm, Discernibility matrix

## 1. INTRODUCTION

The classical rough set developed by Professor Pawlak is a valid mathematical theory, which has the ability to deal with imprecise, uncertain and vague information. In recent years, it has been applied in machine learning, data mining, knowledge acquiring successfully and has a great improvement of its theory and applications [2-7, 20].

At present, the research about rough set is mainly about mathematical properties, extended models, effective sub-algorithms and the relationship between rough set and other uncertain methods, etc. Rough set's effective algorithms include the algorithms about indiscernible classes, upper approximation, lower approximation, positive region, attribute reduction and attribute core, etc. In rough set, attribute reduction is one of the most important parts and there are several algorithms for it at present [8-17,20]. Hence, computation of attribute reduction is the key for rough set.

Attribute reduction is a process for reducing the redundant attributes, under keeping the classifying and decision ability of an information system. Skowron presented a discernibility matrix that is a useful tool for attribute reduction. Most of the disernibility matrix based algorithms first collect a decision table's discernibility information into a matrix, thus we can get the attribute core of an information system from the matrix easily. Because of the explicit presentation of discernibility information by discernibility matrix, it is simple for the computation of attribute core and attribute reduction sets, etc. Thus, many algorithms for computing attribute reduction are based on discernibility matrix. Unfortunately, there are also some problems about discernibility matrix, one of which is that the time complexity of computing discernibility matrix is so high that, when the data set is huge, it is time consuming to find the attribute reduction sets.

The inefficiency of attribute reduction algorithms limits the application of rough set. So, it is important to find efficient algorithms and algorithms for attribute reduction. For solving the problem, we first analyze the reason leading to these algorithms' high time complexity. Then, based on the concept of indiscernible relation and positive region, we research the properties of indiscernible relation and present a new method for computing positive region. Moreover, we present an incremental algorithm for computing positive region and at last, an attribute reduction algorithm is developed. We compare our attribute reduction algorithm with other attribute reduction algorithms and the results show that our algorithm is more efficient.

In section 2, we introduce some basic notions of rough set. In section 3, we analyze the properties of indiscernible relation and present an algorithm for computing positive region. In section 4, we discuss the incremental computation of positive region and design an efficient and complete attribute reduction algorithm. In section 5, we test our attribute reduction algorithm's validity and ability, and compare it with other attribute reduction algorithms. The last section is the conclusion and future work of this paper.

## 2.      BASIC NOTIONS OF ROUGH SET

For the convenience of description, we introduce some basic notions of rough set at first.

**Definition 1** A decision information system is defined as $S=<U,A,V,f>$, where $U$ is a finite set of objects and $A=C\cup D$ is a finite set of attributes. $C$ is the condition attribute set and $D$ is the decision attribute set. With every attribute $a \square A$, set of its values $V_a$ is associated and $V = \bigcup_{a \in A} V_a$. Each attribute has a determine function $f: U \times A \rightarrow V$.

**Definition 2** Given an information system $S$ and an attribute subset $B \subseteq A$, we can define an indiscernible relation by the following:

$IND(B) = \{(x,y) \in U \times U \square \forall \ b \in B, \ b(x) = b(y)\}$.

It is obvious that $IND(B)$ is an indiscernible relation and an object $x$'s indiscernible class $[x]_{IND(B)}$ in $B$ can be defined as follows

$[x]_{IND(B)} = \{y: y \in U, \ yIND(B)x\}$.

For the convenience of description, we use $B$ to replace $IND(B)$ where there isn't any confusion.

**Definition 3** Given a partition $R$, and a subset $X \subseteq U$, we can define a $B$-lower approximation of X in U and a $B$-upper approximation of $X$ in $U$ by the following:

$$\underline{B}X = \{x \in U : [x]_B \subseteq X\},$$

$$\overline{B}X = \{x \in U : [x]_B \cap X \neq \phi\}.$$

**Definition 4** $POS_P(Q) = \bigcup_{x \in U/Q} \underline{P}X$ is the P positive region of $Q$, where $P$ and $Q$ are both attribute sets of an information system and $\underline{P}X$ is the $P$ lower approximation of an object set $X$.

**Definition 5** An attribute $r$ of an information system is said to be relatively dispensable or superfluous if $POS_P(Q) = POS_{(P-\{r\})}(Q)$, otherwise, relatively indispensable. A relative reduction of $P$ is a set of attributes $S \subseteq P$ such that all attributes $a \square P-S$ are relatively dispensable, all attributes $a \square S$ are relatively indispensable and $POS_S(Q) = POS_P(Q)$. We use term $Red_D(B)$ to denote the family of relative reducts of $B$. $Core_D(B) = \cap Red_D(B)$ is called the $D$-core of attribute set B.

# 3. BASIC ALGORITHMS OF ROUGH SET

## 3.1 Indiscernible Relation

Indiscernible relation is one of the most important concepts in rough set. It is the basis to define some other basic concepts, such as upper approximation and lower approximation, etc. Consequently, the complexity of computing indiscernible relation influences other algorithms' executing time directly.

The general method of computing indiscernible relation $IND(B)$ is that: compare each object in $U$ with all of the other objects one by one. And the objects with the same values of attributes in $B$ belong to the same indiscernible class and the objects with different values of attributes in $B$

belong to different indiscernible classes. At the worst case, the method need to compare two objects with $|U|^2$ times, i.e., the time complexity of the method is $O(|B||U|^2)$[2,17].

Based on the definition of $IND(B)$, indiscernible class has the following property:

**Property 1:** The two objects belong to the same indiscernible class, iff they have the same values of the attributes in $B$.

Based on this property, we can improve the general algorithm for computing $IND(B)$. Before calculating the indiscernible relation, we list the objects in $U$ according to the values of attributes in $B$ first. The algorithm is as follows:

**Algorithm1:** Algorithm for computing all indiscernible classes of $IND(B)$

Input: $S=<U, A, V, f>$, $U=\{u_1, u_1, \dots, u_{|U|}\}$, and $B\subseteq A$;

Output: $U/B$.

Step 1 Arrange the objects in $U$ based on the values of attributes in $B$;

Step 2 $s=1, j=1, B_1=\{u_1\}$;

Step 3 for $i=2$ to $|U|$ do

   if $u_i$ and $u_j$ have the same values of attributes in $B$,

    then $B_s=B_s\cup\{u_i\}$;

  else $s=s+1, B_s=\{u_i\}, j=i$.

The time complexity of ordering the objects in $U$ is $O(|B||U|log|U|)$. In step 3, each object in $U$ needs to be searched only once, so the complexity of step 3 is $O(|B||U|)$. Therefore, the complexity of algorithm 1 is $O(|B||U|log|U|)$, which is lower than the general algorithm.

If $IND(B)$ is known, we can calculate the $B$-lower approximation or $B$-upper approximation of object set $X\subseteq U$ only by searching whether the $B$ indiscernible classes are included in $X$ or have intersections with $X$. The number of $B$ indiscernible classes is $|U|$ at the worst case. Thus, when the $B$ indiscernible classes are known, the time complexities of lower and upper approximations are both $O(|U|)$.

Given an information system $S$, supposing $B\subseteq A$ and $X\subseteq U$, we can deduce from the time complexity of algorithm 1 that the time complexities of calculating $X$'s lower approximation, $X$'s upper approximation, the attribute core of $B$ and $Red_D(B)$ are $O(|A||U|log|U|)$, $O(|A||U|log|U|)$, $O(|A|^2|U|log|U|)$ and $O((2^{|A|}|A||U|log|U|)$ respectively. They are lower than the corresponding algorithms' complexities in [16,20], which are $O(|A||U|^2|)$, $O(|A||U|^2|)$, $O(|A|^2|U|^2|)$ and $O((2^{|A|}|A||U|^2)$.

## 3.2 Positive Region

Because the definitions of attribute core and relative attribute reduction are based on positive region, computation of positive region is the key of rough set.

According to the definition of $POS_P(Q)$, the general method of computing $POS_P(Q)$ is that: first, compute the indiscernible classes based on $Q$, and suppose the result is $U/Q=\{Q_1, Q_2, \ldots Q_n\}$, $0<n\leq|U|$; then, calculate $\underline{P}(Q_i)$ respectively($i=1,2,\ldots,n$). When $U/P$ and $U/Q$ are known, the time complexity of computing $\underline{P}(Q_i)$ is $O(|U|)$, so the time complexity of computing $POS_P(Q)$ is $O(|U|^2)$[16,20].

Based on the definition of positive definition, we can develop a new algorithm for computing positive region. We introduce a theorem as follows at first.

**Theorem 1:** $POS_P(Q) = \bigcup_{Y \in U/P \text{ and } |Y/Q|=1} Y$

Proof.

Suppose $U/P=\{P_1, P_2, \ldots P_m\}(0<m\leq|U|)$, $U/Q=\{Q_1, Q_2, \ldots Q_n\}(0<n\leq|U|)$ and $x \in POS_P(Q)$.

Because $POS_P(Q) = \bigcup_{X \in U/Q} \underline{P}(X) = \underline{P}(Q_1) \cup \underline{P}(Q_2) \cup \ldots \underline{P}(Q_n)$,

there is an indiscernible class $Q_k \in U/Q(1\leq k\leq n)$ that satisfies $x \in \underline{P}Q_k$. In similar way, because $\underline{P}Q_k = \bigcup_{P_i \subseteq Q_k} P_i$, there is an indiscernible class $P_l \in U/P(1\leq l\leq m)$ that satisfies $x \in P_l$. Because $P_l \subseteq Q_k$, for all objects that belong to $P_l$, they not only have the same values of attributes in P, but also have the same values of attributes in Q. So $P_l/Q=\{P_l\}$, that is $|P_l/Q|=1$. And since $P_l \in U/P$, we know $P_l \subseteq \bigcup_{Y \in U/P \text{ and } |Y/Q|=1} Y$, thus $x \in \bigcup_{Y \in U/P \text{ and } |Y/Q|=1} Y$. So,

$POS_P(Q) \subseteq \bigcup_{Y \in U/P \text{ and } |Y/Q|=1} Y$

Suppose $x \in \bigcup_{Y \in U/P \text{ and } |Y/Q|=1} Y$, then there is an indiscernible class $P_l \in U/P$ $(1\leq l\leq m)$ that satisfies $|P_l/Q|=1$ and $x \in P_l$. And since $|P_l/Q|=1$, thus $P_l/Q=\{P_l\}$, that is, for all objects in $P_l$, they have the same values of the attributes in Q. And because $P_l \subseteq U$, there is an indiscernible class $Q_k \in U/Q$ $(1\leq k\leq n)$ such that $P_l \subseteq Q_k$. According to the definition of lower approximation, we know $\underline{P}P_l \subseteq \underline{P}Q_k$, and since $\underline{P}P_l=P_l$, thus $P_l \subseteq \underline{P}Q_k \subseteq POS_P(Q)$, so $x \in POS_P(Q)$. Therefore, $\bigcup_{Y \in U/P \text{ and } |Y/Q|=1} Y \subseteq POS_P(Q)$.

Based on all above, theorem 1 holds.

According to theorem 1, we develop a new algorithm for computing positive region.

**Algorithm 2:** Improved algorithm for computing positive region

Input: $S=<U, A, V, f>$, and $P$, $Q \subseteq A$;

Output: $POS_P(Q)$.

Step 1: Compute the indiscernible classes based on $P$ and suppose the result is $\{P_1, P_2, \dots P_m\}$, $0 < m \leq |U|$;

Step 2: $POS_P(Q) = \phi$;

Step 3: For $i=1$ to $m$ do

Computing the $Q$ indiscernible classes of $P_i$. And if there is only one resulting indiscernible class, then $POS_P(Q) = POS_P(Q) \cup P_i$.

The time complexity of step 1 is $O(|P||U|\log|U|)$. The time complexity of the $i$th loop in step 3 is $O(|Q||P_i|\log|P_i|)$, so the time complexity of step 3 is $O(|Q||P_1|\log|P_1|) + O(|Q||P_2|\log|P_2|) + \dots + O(|Q||P_m|\log|P_m|)$. Since $|P_i| \leq |U|$ and $|P_1| + |P_2| + \dots + |P_m| = |U|$, we have $O(|Q||P_1|\log|P_1|) + O(|Q||P_2|\log|P_2|) + \dots + O(|Q||P_m|\log|P_m|) \leq O(|Q||U|\log|U|)|$.

Because $|Q| \leq |A|$ and $|P| \leq |A|$, the time complexity of computing positive region is reduced to $O(|A||U|\log|U|)$ using algorithm 2. We can deduce from above analysis that the complexity of computing attribute core, and attribute reduction is decreased to $O(|A|^2|U|\log|U|)$, $O((2^{|A|}|A|^2||U|\log|U|)$.

# 4.     EFFICIENT ALGORITHMS FOR ATTRIBUTE     REDUCTION

Since computing attribute reduction sets is a NP hard problem, we often use heuristic methods to find the optimal or hypo-optimal attribute reduction sets. One of the common features of these methods is that they use the importance degree of attributes as the heuristic information. By taking different importance degrees of attributes, there exist different kinds of attribute reduction algorithms, such as the positive region based attribute reduction algorithm [9,10,16], the discernible matrix and attribute frequency based attribute reduction algorithm[12,15], and information entropy based attribute reduction algorithm[14], etc.

Unfortunately, most of the algorithms[9,10,12,14] are not complete. As a result, it is not assured to acquire the attribute reduction set. For example, Table 1 is a decision table, $\{a,b,c,d,e\}$ is the condition attribute set and $\{f\}$ is the decision attribute set. Using the algorithms [9,10,12,14] we mentioned before, the resulting condition attribute reduction set is $\{a,b,c\}$. However, $a$ is an attribute that can be ignored and $\{b, c\}$ is the result in deed.

*Table1 A Decision System DS*

| U | a | b | c | d | e | f | U | a | b | c | d | e | f | U | a | b | c | d | e | f |
|---|---|---|---|---|---|---|---|---|---|---|---|---|---|---|---|---|---|---|---|---|
| 1 | 1 | 1 | | 1 | 1 | 1 | 13 | 13 | 13 | 13 | 13 | 13 | 13 | 25 | 25 | 25 | 25 | 25 | 25 | 25 |
| | 2 | 2 | 1 | 1 | 1 | 2 | 14 | 14 | 13 | 14 | 13 | 13 | 14 | 26 | 25 | 26 | 26 | 25 | 25 | 26 |
| 3 | 3 | 3 | 3 | 3 | 3 | 3 | 15 | 15 | 15 | 15 | 15 | 15 | 15 | 27 | 27 | 27 | 27 | 27 | 27 | 27 |
| 4 | 4 | 4 | 3 | 3 | 3 | 4 | 16 | 16 | 15 | 16 | 15 | 15 | 16 | 28 | 27 | 28 | 27 | 28 | 27 | 28 |
| 5 | 5 | 5 | 5 | 5 | 5 | 5 | 17 | 17 | 17 | 17 | 17 | 17 | 17 | 29 | 29 | 29 | 29 | 29 | 29 | 29 |
| 6 | 6 | 6 | 5 | 5 | 5 | 6 | 18 | 18 | 17 | 18 | 17 | 17 | 18 | 30 | 29 | 30 | 29 | 30 | 29 | 30 |
| 7 | 7 | 7 | 7 | 7 | 7 | 7 | 19 | 19 | 19 | 19 | 19 | 19 | 19 | 31 | 31 | 31 | 31 | 31 | 31 | 31 |
| 8 | 8 | 8 | 7 | 7 | 7 | 8 | 20 | 20 | 19 | 20 | 19 | 19 | 20 | 32 | 31 | 32 | 31 | 32 | 31 | 32 |
| 9 | 9 | 9 | 9 | 9 | 9 | 9 | 21 | 21 | 21 | 21 | 21 | 21 | 21 | 33 | 33 | 33 | 33 | 33 | 33 | 33 |
| 10 | 10 | 10 | 9 | 9 | 9 | 10 | 22 | 22 | 21 | 22 | 21 | 21 | 22 | 34 | 33 | 33 | 34 | 34 | 33 | 34 |
| 11 | 11 | 11 | 11 | 11 | 11 | 11 | 23 | 23 | 23 | 23 | 23 | 23 | 23 | 35 | 35 | 35 | 35 | 35 | 35 | 35 |
| 12 | 12 | 11 | 12 | 11 | 11 | 12 | 24 | 23 | 24 | 24 | 23 | 23 | 24 | 36 | 35 | 35 | 36 | 35 | 36 | 36 |

Besides, The time complexities of the algorithms[9,10,12,14] are all $O(|A|^2|U|^2)$. Reference 15 presented an attribute reduction algorithm based on attribute sequence and discernible matrix. Its time complexity is also $O(|A|^2|U|^2)$ and its spatial complexity is $O(|A||U|^2)$; Reference 16 presented an attribute reduction algorithm, but having a relatively high time complexity, $O(|A|^3|U|^2)$.

## 4.1 The Incremental Computation Of Positive Region

How to calculate the attributes' importance degree is the key problem in heuristic attribute reduction algorithms. Also, it is important for improving the efficiency of algorithms. In the remainder of our paper, we mainly discuss the algorithms for the condition attribute reduction of a decision system $S=<U, C\cup D, V, f>$. In these algorithms, the importance degree of an attribute $a\in C-R\square R\subset C\square$to the decision attribute set $D$, $SGF(a,R,D)$, is defined as follows:

$SGF(a,R,D)=\gamma_{R\cup\{a\}}-\gamma_R$, where $\gamma_R=|POS_R(D)|/|U|$.

From the formula, we know positive region is the key for computing $SGF(a,R,D)$. According to algorithm 2, the time complexity of computing $\gamma_{R\cup\{a\}}$ is $O((|R|+|D|+1)|U|\log|U|)$.

Based on the definition of indiscernible relation, we can prove the following property easily.

**Property 2:** Suppose $S=<U, C\cup D, V, f>$ is a decision system, $R\subset C$, $a\in C-R$, and $U/R=\{R_1,R_2,...,R_m\}$ $0<m\leq|U|$, thus, $U/(R\cup\{a\})=R_1/\{a\}\cup R_2/\{a\}\cup...\cup R_m/\{a\}$, that is $U/(R\cup\{a\})=\underset{X\in U/R}{\cup}X/\{a\}$.

According to theorem 1 and property 2, it is easy to conclude that:
**Corollary 1:**

$$POS_{R\cup\{a\}}(Q) = \bigcup_{Y\in U/(R\cup\{a\})\ and\ |Y/Q|=1} Y = \{\cup Y : Y \in \bigcup_{X\in U/R} X /\{a\},$$

and $|Y/Q|=1\}$.

Based on corollary 1, we present an incremental algorithm for computing positive region as follows:

**Algorithm 3:** Incremental algorithm for computing positive region
Input: $S=<U, C\cup D, V, f>$, $U/R=\{R_1, R_2, \dots R_m\}$, $0<m\leq|U|$;
Output: $POS_{R\cup\{a\}}(D)$.
Step 1: Calculate the indiscernible classes $U/R\cup\{a\}$ according to $U/R$ and suppose the result is $W_1, W_2,\dots W_n$, $0<n\leq|U|$;
Step 2: $POS_{R\cup\{a\}}(D)=\phi$;

Step 3: For $i=1$ to $m$ do
        Classify $W_i$ based on $D$ and if the resulting indiscernible relation has only one indiscernible class, then $POS_{R\cup\{a\}}(D) = POS_{R\cup\{a\}}(D)\cup W_i$.

Similar with the analysis of algorithm 2's complexity, when $U/R$ is known, we can deduce that the time complexity of algorithm 3 is $O((|D|+1)|U|\log|U|)$. It is obviously that the complexity is irrelevant with $|R|$. Therefore, when we incrementally compute positive region $POS_{R\cup\{a\}}(D)$, we can save the result of $U/R$ first to reduce the complexity.

In the similar way, when $U/R$ and $POS_R(D)$ are known, the complexity of computing $SGF(a,R,D)$ is $O((|D|+1)|U|\log|U|)$.

## 4.2    A New Attribute Reduction Algorithm

Based on the above understanding, we develop an efficient attribute reduction algorithm.

**Algorithm 4:** A new attribute reduction algorithm
Input: $S=<U, C\cup D, V, f>$;
Output: the D-attribute reduction set of C, i.e., *RED*.
Step 1: Compute the D-attribute core of C, $CORE_D(C)$ ;
Step 2: $RED= CORE_D(C)$;
Step 3: Compute $POS_C(D)$, $U/RED$ and $POS_{RED}(D)$;
Step 4: While $|POS_C(D)|\neq| POS_{RED}(D)|$, do
        1) Find the attribute $a$ that the value of $SGF(a,RED,D)$ is maximal;
        2) $RED=RED\cup\{a\}$ and add $a$ to the tail of *RED*;
        3) Use algorithm 3 to compute $U/RED$ and $POS_{RED}(D)$;
Step 5: Get the last attribute $a$ from *RED* and if $a\in CORE_D(C)$,
        then *RED* is the result and the algorithm is end
        else if $|POS_C(D)|=| POS_{RED-\{a\}}(D)|$
                $RED=RED\square\{a\}$; go to step 5.

Relative attribute core is the start point of algorithm 4 and with step 4 it is assured to find a subset $RED$ of $C$ that satisfies $|POS_C(D)|=|POS_{RED}(D)|$. The condition attributes are arranged in $RED$ with their importance degrees. The attributes arranged in the frontal part of $RED$ are core attributes, and the less importance degree of the attributes, the latter positions the attributes locate. In step 5, if some attributes are ignorable, the attributes with less importance degree are reduced first. At last, the attributes remained in $RED$ are all that can't be deleted. Therefore, the resulting $RED$ is the attribute reduction set we want. Based on the above, we can conclude that our algorithm is complete for finding condition attribute reduction set.

## 4.3    Analysis Of Algorithm 4's Complexity

The time complexity of step 1 is $O((|C|+|D|)^2|U|\log|U|)$ and the time complexity of step 3 is $O((|C|+|D|)|U|\log|U|)$. In each loop of step 4, the first step need to compute $SGF(a,RED,D)$ with $|C-RED|$ times, and the complexity of the third step is $O(((|D|+1)|U|\log|U|)$. In the worst case, it need $|C|$ times to execute step 4, that is, in total, it need to compute the importance degree of attributes $|C|+(|C|-1)+...+1=|C|(|C|+1)/2$ times. Since the time complexity of computing $SGF(a,R,D)$ is $O((|D|\Box1)|U|\log|U|)$, the time complexity of step 4 is $O(|C|^2 (|D|+1)|U|\log|U|)$.

Using the method mentioned in [24], any decision table can be transformed to a decision table with only one decision attribute, so we might as well suppose $D=\{d\}$, i.e., $|D|=1$, and according to the above analysis the time complexity of algorithm 4 is $O(|C|^2|U|\log|U|)$.

Based on the above analysis, we can know the spatial complexity of algorithm 4 is $O(|C||U|)$.

## 5.    RESULTS OF EXPERIMENT

*Table 2* Comparison of The Three Attribute Reduction Algorithms

| Decision table | $n$ | $m$ | $A_1$ | | $A_2$ | | $A_3$ | |
|---|---|---|---|---|---|---|---|---|
| | | | $m'_1$ | $t_1$(sec) | $m'_2$ | $t_2$(sec) | $m'_3$ | $t_3$(sec) |
| Table 1 | 36 | 5 | 3 | 0.001 | 2 | 0.01 | 2 | 0.001 |
| BUPA Liver Disorders | 345 | 6 | 3 | 0.06 | 3 | 0.12 | 3 | 0.02 |
| Voting Records Database | 435 | 16 | 9 | 0.16 | 10 | 0.94 | 9 | 0.05 |
| Tic-Tac-Toe Endgame database | 958 | 9 | 8 | 0.86 | 8 | 0.93 | 8 | 0.17 |
| Chess End-Game | 3196 | 36 | 29 | 789.5 | 29 | 265.1 | 29 | 0.52 |
| Mushroom Database | 8154 | 22 | 4 | 7603.6 | 5 | 470.8 | 5 | 3.92 |

In order to test the validity and ability of algorithm 4, we use the data of table 1 and also collect some data sets from UCI database, then we program based on our algorithm. Our experiment is carried on the computer whose frequency is PIII 800, EMS memory is 128M, and operating system is WIN2000. We compare the algorithms in reference [12] and [16] with our algorithm. $A_1$ is the algorithm in [12], $A_2$ is the algorithm in reference [16] and $A_3$ is ours (algorithm 4). We suppose $n$ is the number of the objects, $m$ is the number of condition attributes before reduced, $m'_i$ is the number of condition attributes after reduced using $A_i$ and $t_i$ is the executing time of $A_i$. The results are shown in table 2.

From table 2, it is obvious that $A_3$ is more efficient than $A_1$ and $A_2$. With the increasing of objects' number, the improving of $A_3$'s efficiency is greater. In the same case, the efficiency of $A_1$ decreases due to its high spatial complexity, $O(|A||U|^2)$. The results of experiments are consistent with our analysis. It proves our algorithm's validity and efficiency, and shows that our algorithm is more suitable to huge data set.

# 6.      CONCLUSION AND FUTURE WORK

In rough set, fuzzy problems are discussed by upper and lower approximation and we can use some relevant mathematical formula to get results. Rough set is objective and based on original data set totally. Nowadays, because of rough set's unique feature, more and more scholars devoted into the research on it and made a great success. However, a lot of problems are needed to be resolved. Now, there are so little applications of rough set theory that have obvious benefits in industry[5], so it is important to find faster and more efficient algorithms to advance it.

In this paper, the properties of indiscernible relation are discussed and a new algorithm computing positive region is presented and proved. Based on these, we analyze the incrementally computing of positive region. Then, we develop an attribute reduction algorithm, which is complete and efficient with time complexity $O(|C|^2|U|\log|U|)$. Our simulation results show that our algorithm is better than many existed attribute reduction algorithms. In addition, due to the efficiency of our algorithm, it is useful to the application of rough set and helpful to apply it in dealing with huge data set. The future work of this paper includes feature selecting with rough set, constructing a better classifier that is suitable to decision support and using other uncertain methods to improve the classifying ability.

## ACKNOWLEDGMENT

This work is supported by the National Science Foundation of China (No.6007319, 60173017, 90104021) and the Nature Science Foundation of Beijing (No. 4011003).

## REFERENCE

1. Z. Pawlak. Rough Sets, International Journal of Computer and Information Science, 1982, 11(5): 341~356
2. Z. Pawlak. Rough Sets: Theoretical Aspects of Reasoning about Data, Dordrecht: Kluwer Academic Publishers, 1991
3. A. Skowron. Rough Sets and Boolean Reasoning, In: W. Pedrycz ed. Granular Computing: An emerging Paradigm, New York : Physica-Verlag, 2001
4. Q. Liu, Rough Set and Rough Reasoning, Scientific Press, 2001
5. W. Ziako. Rough Sets: Trends, Challenges, and Prospects, In: W. Ziarko, Y. Y. Yao ed. Rough Sets and Current Trends in Computing(RSCTC 2000), Berlin: Springer-verlag, 2001
6. Q.Liu, S.H. Huang, L.W Yao, Rough Set Theory: Present State And Prospects, Computer Science, 1997, 24(4): 1~5
7. J. Wang, D.Q.Miao, Rough Set Thoery and Its Application: A Survey, Pattern Recognition And Artificial Intelligence, 1996, 9(4): 337~344
8. A. Skowron, C. Rauszer. The Discernibility Matrics and Functions in Inforamtion System. In: R.Slowinski ed□Intelligent Decision Support Handbook of Applications and Advances of the Rough Sets Theory. Dordrecht: Kluwer Academic Publishers, 1992, 331~362
9. X.H. Hu, N. Cercone, Learning in Relational Databases: A Rough Set Approach., International Journal of Computational Intelligence, 1995, 11(2): 323~338
10.   J. Jelonek, K. Krawiec, R. Slowinski. Rough Set Reduction of Attributes and Their Domains for Neural Networks, International Journal of Computational Intelligence, 1995, 11(2): 339~347
11.Q.Liu, S.H. Liu, F. Zheng, Rough Logic And Its Applications, Journal of Software, 2001, 12(3): 415□419
12.J. Wang, R. Wang, D.Q. Miao, Data Enriching Based on Rough Set Theory, Chinese Journal of Software, 1998, 21(5): 393~399
13.D. Pan, Q.L. Zheng, An Adaptive Searching Opima: Algorithm for The Attribute Reducts, Journal of Computer Research & Development, 2001, 38(8)□904~910
14.D.Q. Miao, G.R. Hu,A Heuristic Algorithm for Reduction of Knowledge, Journal of Computer Research & Development, 1999, 36(6): 681~684
15.J. Wang, J. Wang. Reduction Algorithms Based on Discernbility Matrix: The Ordered Attributes Method, Journal of Computer Science & Technology, 2001, 16(6): 489~504
16.J.W. Guan, D.A. Bell. Rough Computational Methods for Information Systems, Artificial Intelligences, 105(1998): 77~103
17.L.Y. Chang, G.Y. Wang, Y. Wu, An Approach for Attribute Reduction and Rule Generation Based on Rough Set Theory, Journal of Software, 1999, 10(11): 1206~1211
18.N. Zhong, A. Skowron, S. Ohsuga (Eds.) New Directions in Rough Sets, Data Mining, and Granular-Soft Computing(RSFDGrC'99), Berlin: Springer-Verlag, 1999

19. E. Orlowska. (Ed.) Incomplete Information: Rough Set Analysis, New York : Physica-Verlag, 1998
20. W.X. Zhang, W.Z. Wu, J.Y. Liang, D.Y. Li, Rough Set Theory And Methods, Scientific Press, 2001
21. J. Wroblewski, Finding Minimal Reducts Using Genetic Algorithm, ICS Research report 16/95, Warsaw University of Technology
22. W. Ziarko, The Discovery, Analysis, and Representation of Data Dependencies In Database, in G. Piatesky-Shapiro, W. Frawley (eds), Proceedings of the IJCAI Workshop On Knowledge Discovery, AAAI Press, 1991, 195~212
23. S.K.M. Wong, W. Ziarko, On Optimal Decision Rules in Decision Tables, Bulletin, Polish Academy of Sciences, 1985, 33(11-12): 693~696
24. G.Y. Wang, Rough Set Theory and Knowledge Acquisition, Press of Xi'an Jiaotong University, 2001

# USING RELATIVE LOGIC FOR PATTERN RECOGNITION

Juliusz L. Kulikowski
*Institute of Biocybernetics and Biomedical Engineering PAS, Warsaw, Poland, e-mail jlkulik@ibib.waw.pl*

**Abstract:** It is presented an approach to pattern recognition in the case of extremely poor primary information about the properties of patterns that are to be recognized. In such case algorithms based on reference sets of objects are widely used. However, in some situations experts cannot assign the names of patterns to the reference objects in an unique way. It is shown here that in such cases an approach based on topological logic can be used for relative logical evaluation of statements formulated by the experts. There is described a method of relative reference sets construction and of using them in an algorithm of pattern recognition admitting relative logical evaluation of statements concerning the recognized patterns.

**Key words:** pattern recognition, relative objects' similarity assessment, topological logic

## 1. INTRODUCTION

Pattern recognition is, generally speaking, an art of giving reasonable answers to the questions like: *"What does the given sign (image, object, string of data, etc.) represent?"* assuming that the answer should indicate the name of a class of objects the observed one belongs to and that there is at least one alternative class it might belong to as well. The *pattern* is thus a synonym of a *class of similar objects*. The principles that are used as a basis of solution of a pattern recognition problem depend on primary assumptions and information about the objects under observation, the patterns, and the criteria of pattern recognition quality. We call the set of such primary assumptions and information a *pattern recognition model*. In literature pattern recognition models based on deterministic, probabilistic and/or statistical assumptions have been described [1]. Another class of models form those based on potential functions [2], artificial neural networks [3], "*k Nearest Neighbors*" (*k-NN*) approach and other learning concepts [4]. The aim of this paper is presentation of a pattern recognition approach useful in situation of extremely poor primary information concerning the recognized classes of objects. The approach is based on a concept of *topological logic*, originally formulated by C.G. Hempel [5].

## 2.    PATTERN RECOGNITION METHODS UNDER PRIMARY INFORMATION DEFICIENCY

Let us start with consideration of the *k-NN* pattern recognition method as a one having opinion of being based on very wide primary assumptions. In fact, it can be used if the below-given conditions are satisfied:

*a/* there is given an observation space $X$ whose elements are some real $n$-component vectors $\xi$;

*b/* $X$ is a metric space i.e. there is defined a distance function:

$$d: X \times X \rightarrow R^+ \tag{1}$$

where $\times$ stands for a Cartesian product, $R^+$ denotes a non-negative real half-axis, and $d$ satisfies the reciprocity, symmetry and triangle-inequality conditions;

*c/* the number $K$ of recognized patterns is fixed, finite and a priori known;

*d/* each pattern is a random vector $\Xi_\kappa$, $\kappa = 1,2,...,K$, whose conditional probability distribution is a priori unknown; however, $1^\circ$ its mean value and variance are finite, $2^\circ$ the mean values of the random vectors are significantly different.

In addition, it is assumed that there is given a family of *reference sets* $S_1, S_2,...,S_K \subset X$ such that:

*e/* they are finite and mutually disjoint;

*f/* each reference set corresponds to a given pattern;

*g/* the elements (vectors $\xi$) of any reference set are observed and correctly classified values of a random vector corresponding to the given pattern;

*h/* the cardinal numbers (numbers of elements) $|S_\kappa|$, $\kappa = 1,2,...,K$, of the reference sets can be increased so that the sets become representative for the corresponding statistical populations.

The classical *k-NN* method is thus based on strong assumptions which in practice are not obviously satisfied. In particular:

*A/ X* may be not a metric space;

*B/* assignment of the reference set elements $\xi$ to the patterns may be not univocally given;

*C/* a similarity between the new-observed objects $x$ and those of the reference set $S$ may be evaluated with a limited accuracy.

Therefore, it arises the problem: how in the above-mentioned situation the pattern recognition problem could be solved. A solution based on a generalized similarity concept will be proposed below.

## 3. THE NOTION OF *RELATIVE SIMILARITY*

The notion of *similarity* in pattern recognition is a crucial one. For a given object $x$ its pattern is recognized if a class $\Xi_x$ of objects similar to the given one is indicated. However, an interpretation of the notion of *similarity* in classical sets [6], *fuzzy sets* [7], *rough sets* [8] theory etc. is different. In the $k$-$NN$ method the distance measure $d$ is used as a decreasing function of objects' similarity. In [9] an extension of the similarity concept and a method of pattern recognition method, called "*k Most Similar Objects*" ($k$-$MSO$) has been proposed.

A new situation arises when stating: "Budapest *reminds* me of Vienna *more than* Prague". In this case no numerical similarity measure is used; two pairs of objects: [Budapest, Vienna] and [Budapest, Prague] are taken into account and their similarities are compared. This leads to a below described concept of *relative similarity*. For this purpose let us take into account a non-empty set $A$ and a Cartesian product $F = A \times A$. A similarity of the elements of $A$ can be defined as a sort of ordering of the elements of $F$. Any two elements of $F$ in the sense of similarity can be: *a/* equivalent, *b/* one may be dominating with respect to the other one or *c/* mutually incomparable (this is not admitted if similarity is evaluated by a numerical similarity measure). Then the model is specified by the below-given definitions:

For any $a, b, c, d, e, f \in A$ and for any their unordered pairs:

Definition 1.

A *relative similarity equivalence between the pairs of elements of* a set $A$ is a relation $\approx_{sim}$ (read: „*are similar equivalently to*") described on a Cartesian product $F \times F$ (i.e. on the pairs of pairs of the elements of $A$) satisfying the following conditions:

1/ $\{a,a\} \approx_{sim} \{a,a\}$ (reciprocity),

2/ if $\{a,b\} \approx_{sim} \{c,d\}$ then $\{c,d\} \approx_{sim} \{a,b\}$ (strong symmetry),

3/ if $\{a,b\} \approx_{sim} \{c,d\}$ and $\{c,d\} \approx_{sim} \{e,f\}$ then $\{a,b\} \approx_{sim} \{e,f\}$ (transitivity),

4/ $\{a,a\} \approx_{sim} \{b,b\}$ (equivalence of similarities of identical elements).

Any subset $\Phi_k \subseteq F$ consisting of all pairs of elements satisfying the relation $\approx_{sim}$ will be called a *class of relative similarity*.

Definition 2.
A *relative similarity between the pairs of elements of A* is a relation $\leq_{sim}$ (read: *„are similar at most like"*) described on a Cartesian product $F \times F$ and satisfying the following conditions:
1/ $\{a,a\} \leq_{sim} \{a,a\}$ (reciprocity),
2/ $\{a,b\} \leq_{sim} \{c,d\}$ and $\{c,d\} \leq_{sim} \{a,b\}$ if and only if $\{a,b\} \approx_{sim} \{c,d\}$ (weak symmetry),
3/ if $\{a,b\} \leq_{sim} \{c,d\}$ and $\{c,d\} \leq_{sim} \{e,f\}$ then $\{a,b\} \leq_{sim} \{e,f\}$ (transitivity),
4/ there are no $\{a,a\}$ and $\{c,d\}$ such that $\{a,a\} \leq_{sim} \{c,d\}$ and not $\{a,a\}$ $\approx_{sim} \{c,d\}$ (maximality of self-similarity).

Definition 3.
A *relative incomparability of the pairs of elements of A* is a relation $\neq_{sim}$ (read: *"are incomparable in similarities to"*) described on a Cartesian product $F \times F$ such that
$\{a,b\} \neq_{sim} \{c,d\}$ if and only if it is neither $\{a,b\} \leq_{sim} \{c,d\}$ nor $\{c,d\}$ $\leq_{sim} \{a,b\}$.

The above-defined relations can be illustrated by a directed graph $G = [Q, L, \varphi]$, where $Q$ denotes a set of nodes, $L$ is a set of arcs and $\varphi$ is a function assigning arcs to ordered pairs of nodes. The graph, called a *relative similarity graph* (*RSG*), should satisfy the conditions:
*a/* all its nodes in an unique way have been assigned to the subsets $\Phi_k \subseteq F$ forming classes of relative similarity,
*b/* the function $\varphi$ in an unique way assigns an arc $\lambda_{kl}$ to an ordered pair $[\Phi_k, \Phi_l]$ such that for each element $\{a,b\} \in \Phi_k$ and each element $\{c,d\} \in \Phi_l$ it is $\{a,b\} \leq_{sim} \{c,d\}$ (but not the reverse),
*c/* $G$ is contourless.
It follows from the definition that to any pair $\{\{a,b\},\{e,f\}\}$ satisfying the condition $\{a,b\} \leq_{sim} \{e,f\}$ it will be assigned in *RSG* a path $\Lambda_{km}$ from $\Phi_k$ to $\Phi_m$ such that $\{a,b\} \in \Phi_k$ and $\{e,f\} \in \Phi_m$. Any pair $\{\{a,b\},\{e,f\}\}$ such that in *RSG* it can not be represented in the above-described way is relatively incomparable. A *RSG* is thus a representation of relative similarities among the elements of $A$.

It also follows from the definition of *RSG* that $Q$ contains a subset $Q_{max}$ of *maximum nodes* such that no arc $\lambda_{kl}$ starting from a node in $Q_{max}$ connects it with another node outside $Q_{max}$.

## 4. RELATIVE REFERENCE SETS

The reference sets used in learning pattern recognition algorithms are usually collected under the recommendations of experts given in the form of statements:

$$\Theta_\kappa(\xi) : \text{``}\xi \text{ represents } \Xi_\kappa\text{''}$$

which means that $\xi$ being an observation (an object) from $\Sigma$ should be included into $S_\kappa$, where $S_\kappa$ is a reference set representing the $\kappa$-th pattern.

A problem arises when the experts are not convinced that the given objects can be assigned to reference sets in an unique way. The below-presented notion of *relative reference sets* based on *topological logic* [5] (see also [10], [11], [12]) is a solution of the problem.

The statements that should be logically assessed are: $\Theta_1(\xi)$, $\Theta_2(\xi)$,..., $\Theta_\kappa(\xi)$,..., $\Theta_K(\xi)$. It is admitted that for a given $\xi$ not only one of the statements is "true" and the logical values of the statements can not be evaluated but by relative comparisons. For this purpose let us assume that the expert has his intuitive concept of "typical" representatives $\xi^*_1$, $\xi^*_2$,..., $\xi^*_\kappa$,..., $\xi^*_K$ of the corresponding patterns. Then, for any $\xi^*_\kappa$, $\kappa = 1,2,...,K$, he takes into consideration a pair $\{\xi^*_\kappa, \xi\}$, and he establishes a semi-ordering relation among the pairs:

$\{\xi^*_\kappa, \xi_1\} \approx_{sim} \{\xi^*_\lambda, \xi_2\}$ meaning that the similarity between $\xi^*_\kappa$ and $\xi$ is equivalent to the one between $\xi^*_\lambda$ and $\xi$, or

$\{\xi^*_\kappa, \xi\} \leq_{sim} \{\xi^*_\lambda, \xi\}$ meaning that the similarity between $\xi^*_\kappa$ and $\xi_1$ is at most like the one between $\xi^*_\lambda$ and $\xi$, etc.

In practice, the relation can be established as follows.

1. For a given number $K$ of patterns and for a given reference object $\xi$ the expert is asked to assign to $\xi$ a string of *rank position markers*:

$$n(\xi) = [\nu_1, \nu_{2,...}, \nu_\kappa,..., \nu_K] \qquad (3)$$

where $\nu_\kappa \in [0,1,...,K-1]$, denoting the length of the shortest path connecting $\xi$ with $\xi^*_\kappa$ in a *RSG*. For example, if $K = 5$ and $n(\xi) = [2,1,2,3,4]$, then *RSG* will have the form shown in Fig. 1.

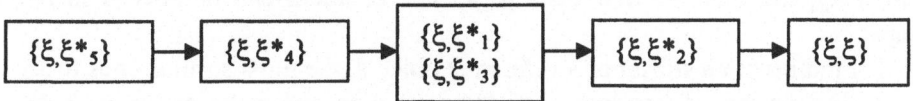

Fig. 1. A graph $G(\xi)$ representing relative similarities between objects.

$G(\xi)$ thus illustrates a ranking of patterns, as seen by the expert: the shorter is the path in $G(\xi)$ between the nodes containing $\{\xi,\xi^*_\kappa\}$ and $\{\xi,\xi\}$, the more representative is $\xi$ as a member of $S_\kappa$.

Similar relationships should be established for all other members of $\Sigma$.

2. For the given $\Sigma$ and a $\kappa \in [1,2,...,K]$ there will be denoted by $\Phi^\kappa_0$, $\Phi^\kappa_{1,...}$, $\Phi^\kappa_{K-1}$ the subsets of $\Sigma$ consisting of reference objects $\xi$ such that the distance in the *RSG* between $\{\xi,\xi^*_\kappa\}$ and $\{\xi,\xi\}$ is equal, correspondingly, 0, 1,...,$K$-1. So defined subsets form a partition of $\Sigma$:

$$\Sigma = \bigcup_{\lambda=0}^{K-1} \Phi^\kappa_\lambda \qquad (4)$$

For each $\kappa$ the partition is, in general, different. The subsets $\Phi^\kappa_0$, $\Phi^\kappa_{1,...}$, $\Phi^\kappa_{K-1}$ form a semi-ordered family of sets that can be also represented by a graph.

3. The above-described operation of the reference set $\Sigma$ partition into a semi-ordered family of subsets $\Phi^\kappa_\kappa$ should be performed for all $\kappa \in [1,2,...,K]$. This leads to the following definition:

Definition 4.

Let $\Sigma$ be a finite subset of the elements of observation space $X$ in which the relations $\approx_{sim}$ and $\leq_{sim}$ have been defined. Then for any fixed $\kappa \in [1,2,...,K]$ a partition of $\Sigma$ into a semi-ordered family of subsets $\{\Phi^\kappa_\lambda\}$, $\lambda \in [0,1,...,K-1]$, induced by the relations $\approx_{sim}$ and $\leq_{sim}$ will be called *a relative reference set (RRS)* corresponding to the pattern $\Xi_\kappa$.

A membership of a reference object $\xi$ in the *RRS* is thus characterised by its relative similarity to the given patterns, as indicated by the expert.

## 5. PATTERN RECOGNITION

Let us assume that for the given observation space $X$ it is given a family of *RRS*s corresponding to $K$ patterns. Let it be also given a new object $x \in X$, $x \notin \Sigma$. It arises the problem of assigning $x$ to a pattern which means: indication of a pattern $\Xi_\kappa$ whose members are, in the sense of relative similarity, the most similar ones to $x$. The problem can be solved in two steps:

1. Finding out a subset of $k$ reference objects, the most similar ones to $x$;

2. Evaluation of relative similarity of $x$ to the patterns through the relative similarity of reference objects the most similar ones to $x$.

The problem consists in logical evaluation of the pairs of statements:

$\Theta_\kappa(x)$: "*x is similar to $\xi_p$*" $\wedge$ "*$\xi_p$ is similar to $\xi^*_\kappa$*",

$\Theta_\lambda(x)$"*x is similar to $\xi_q$*" $\wedge$ "*$\xi_q$ is similar to $\xi^*_\lambda$*",

where $\xi_p$, $\xi_q \in \Sigma$ and $\kappa$, $\lambda \in [1,2,...,K]$. This can be done using the general principles of topological logic ([5], [10], [11]), stating, in particular, that if $A$ and $B$ are some statements then

$1°$ $A \leq_{log} B$ (read: "*A is logically valuable at most as B*") then $(A \wedge B) \leq_{log} A$ and $(A \wedge B) \leq_{log} B$;

$2°$ $A \approx_{log} B$ (read: "*A is logically as valuable as B*") then $(A \wedge B) \approx_{log} A$ and $(A \wedge B) \approx_{log} B$;

$3°$ $A \leq_{log} B$ then $A \leq_{log} (A \vee B)$ and $B \leq_{log} (A \vee B)$;

$4°$ $A \approx_{log} B$ then $A \approx_{log} (A \vee B)$ and $B \approx_{log} (A \vee B)$.

We are thus able to compare logically the pairs of statements like:
"*x is similar to $\xi_p$*", "*$\xi_p$ is similar to $\xi^*_\kappa$*",

etc. for various $x$, $\xi_p$, $\xi^*_\kappa$, as well as composite statements like:

"*x is similar to $\xi_p$*"$\wedge$ "*$\xi_p$ is similar to $\xi^*_\kappa$*".

This leads, finally, to the following pattern recognition rule:

Algorithm:

For the given reference set $\Sigma$, set $R$ of scaling objects and an object $x \in X$:

Using the scaling objects $R$ find in $\Sigma$ a subset $\xi_1$, $\xi_2$, ..., $\xi_k$, of $k$ reference objects the most similar to $x$;

For each $\xi_p$, $p = 1,2,...,k$, if $\xi_p \in \Phi^\kappa_\lambda$, formulate the statement:

$\Theta_\kappa(x)$: "*x is similar to $\xi_p$*" $\wedge$ "*$\xi_p$ is similar to $\xi^*_\kappa$*",

Evaluate relatively the so obtained statements $\Theta_\kappa(x)$ according to the logical rules $1°$, $2°$;

Select the statements of the highest logical value: if it is $\Theta_\kappa(x)$ then $\Xi_\kappa$ is the recognized pattern, if there are more than one statement of the highest value, than all the corresponding patterns are logically mutually equivalent.

## 6.    CONCLUSIONS

The methods of relative logical assessment of statements based on topological logic can be used in pattern recognition in the case of extremely poor primary information about the patterns being to be recognised. In such case relative similarities of observed objects can be used instead of exact numerical similarity scales.

## ACKNOWLEDGEMENTS

I would like to express my deep thanks to the Reviewers of this paper for their valuable comments and critical remarks.

## REFERENCES

1. G.J. McLachlan, *Discriminant Analysis and Statistical Pattern Recognition* (John Wiley and Sons, Inc., New York, 1992).
2. E.M. Braverman, *Experiments on Machine Learning of Recognition of Visual Pattern* (in Russian, Avtomatika i telemechanika, No 3, 1962).
3.  C.M. Bishop, *Neural Networks in Pattern Recognition* (Clarendon Press, Oxford, 1997).
4. E. Fix, J.L. Hodges, *Discriminatory Analysis: Nonparametric Discrimination Small Sample Performance* (Project 21-49-004, Rep. No 11, USAF School on Aviation Medicine, Randolph Field, Texas, 1952, pp. 280-322, ).
5. C.G. Hempel, *A purely topological form of non-Aristotelian logic* (Journ. Symb. Logic, 2(3), 1937).
6. H. Rasiowa, R. Sikorski, *The Mathematics of Meta-Mathematics* (PWN, Warsaw, 1968).
7. L.A. Zadeh, *Fuzzy Sets.* (Inf. and Control, vol. 8, 1965, pp. 338-353,).
8. Z. Pawlak, *Rough Sets. Theoretical Aspects of Reasoning About Data"* (Dordrecht, Kluwer Academic Publishers, 1991).
9. J.L Kulikowski, *Pattern Recognition Based on Ambiguous Indications of Experts* (in: Mat. Konferencji n.t. „Komputerowe Systemy Rozpoznawania KOSYR'2001", Wyd. Politechniki Wroclawskiej, Wroclaw, 2001, pp. 15-22).
10. Ch. A. Vessel, *"On the topological logic* (in Russian, in: "Non-classical Logic", Nauka, Moscow, 1970, pp. 238-261).
11. J.L. Kulikowski, *Decision Making in a Modified Version of Topological Logic* (in: Proc. of the Seminar on „Non-conventional Problems of Optimization", Part 1, Prace IBS PAN, No 134, Warszawa, 1984, pp. 24-44).
12. J.L. Kulikowski, *Topological logic and rough sets. A comparison of methods* (in Polish, in: „Zbiory rozmyte i ich zastosowania, Wyd. Politechniki Slaskiej, Gliwice, 2001, pp. 195-216).

# MATHTUTOR: A MULTI-AGENT INTELLIGENT TUTORING SYSTEM

Janétte Cardoso
*Institut de Recherche Informatique de Toulouse (IRIT) - UT1*
jcardoso@univ-tlse1.fr


Guilherme Bittencourt, Luciana B. Frigo, Eliane Pozzebon
and Adriana Postal
*Departamento de Automação e Sistemas (DAS) - UFSC*
{ gb | lu | eliane | apostal }@das.ufsc.br

**Abstract**

In this paper we propose a multi-agent intelligent tutoring system building tool that integrates different formalisms in order to facilitate the teacher task of developing the contents of a tutorial system and at the same time to provide adaptiveness and flexibility in the presentation. The adopted formalisms are ground logic terms for the student model, data-bases for the domain model and object Petri nets for the pedagogical model. The interaction between the student and each agent of the system is controlled by an object Petri net, automatically translated into a rule-based expert system. The object Petri net tokens are composed by data objects that contain pointers to the student model and to the domain knowledge, stored into a data-base of texts, examples and exercises. The object Petri net transitions are controlled by logical conditions that refer to the student model and the firing of these transitions produce actions that update this student model.

**Keywords:** Intelligent Tutoring Systems, Intelligent Agents, E-Learning, Expert Knowledge-based Systems, Design Methodologies

## Introduction

The field of Artificial Intelligent in Education (AI-ED) includes several paradigms, such as Intelligent Computer Aided Instruction (ICAI), Micro-world, Intelligent Tutoring Systems (ITS), Intelligent Learning Environment (ILE) and Computer Supported Collaborative Learning conference (CSCL), that originated many systems [12],[15],[14],[4]. Moreover, innovative computer technology, such as hyper-media, Internet and virtual reality, had an important impact on AI-ED [3],[2].

Nevertheless, the task of building ITSs that cover a rich domain and at the same time are adaptive to user level and interests continue to be a very complex one. On the one hand, the domain knowledge must be structured and its presentation planned by a human teacher in an attractive and interesting way. On the other hand, differences among the students, such as background knowledge, personal preferences and previous interactions with the system, must be taken into account.

In [11], Mizoguchi and Bourdeau identifies several drawbacks of current AI-ED tutoring systems, e.g. the conceptual gap between authoring systems and authors, the lack of intelligent authoring methodologies, the difficulty of sharing and reusing components of ITS, the gap between instructional planning and tutoring strategy for dynamic adaptation of the ITS behavior. Furthermore, they note that all these drawbacks are content-related and do not depend directly on issues such as representation and inference formalisms.

In this paper we propose a multi-agent ITS building tool, called MathTutor, that integrates different formalisms in order to facilitate the teacher task of developing the contents of a tutorial system and at the same time to provide adaptiveness and flexibility in the presentation. Multi-Agent Systems (MAS) technology have been of great help in reducing the distance between ideal systems and what can really be implemented, because it allows to simplify the modeling and structuring tasks through the distribution, among different agents, of the domain and student models. The proposed tool is based on a conceptual model, called MATHEMA [6], that provides a content-directed methodology for planning the domain exposition and teaching strategies. The main contribution of the paper, besides instantiating the MATHEMA model into a working tool, is to propose an original way of integrating the student and pedagogical models using *Object Petri Net (OPN)* [16].

The MathTutor tool has been implemented using the Java programming language environment. The expert systems included in the system were implemented using Jess [9], a Java Expert System Shell based on the widely used Clips system. The multi-agent society is supported by Jatlite [10], a Java platform that implements the KQML agent communication language [8]. The interface is based on Servlets and uses the HTTP protocol and can be accessed through any browser, what allows the use of the system as a distance learning tool. Using this tool, a prototype of an Intelligence Tutor System, aimed to teach *Information Structure* was implemented. The course is based on the programming language Scheme [1, 7] and covers the program of an undergraduate discipline of the Control and Automation Engineering course at the University of Santa Catarina, Brazil.

The paper is organized as follows. In Section 1, the ITS building tool architecture is described. In Section 2, the architecture of the agents that compose the multi-agent society and the tutor systems that they contain are presented. In Section 3, the authoring mechanism that allow the design of new courses to be included into the system is described. In Section 4, some related work is presented. Finally, in Section 5, we present some conclusions and future work.

# 1. Tool Architecture

The tool architecture is based on the conceptual model MATHEMA [6] and consists basically of three modules: the society of tutorial agents (TAS), the student interface and the authoring interface. The interface provides access to the system through any Internet browser. The authoring interface module allows the definition of the course structure and contents and is discussed in more detail in Section 3. Finally, the society of tutorial agents consists of a multi-agent system where each agent, besides communication and cooperation capabilities, contains a complete intelligent tutorial system focused on a sub-domain of the target domain. The fact that the system consists of a multi-agent society allows the distribution of domain contents and student modeling data among the several agents that cooperate in the tutoring task.

The MATHEMA conceptual model [6] provides a partitioning scheme, called the *external view*, leading to sub-domains. This partitioning scheme is based on epistemological assumptions about the domain knowledge and consists of a three dimensional perspective. The proposed dimensions are: *context*: along the context dimension the domain knowledge is partitioned according to a set of different points of views about its contents; *depth*: given one particular context, the associated knowledge can be partitioned according to the methodologies used to deal with its contents; *laterality*: given one particular context and one particular depth, complementary knowledge can be pointed to in order to allow the student to acquire background knowledge not in the scope of the course or to reach related additional contents. Each sub-domain defined according to this scheme is under the responsibility of a different agent, that contains a complete ITS specialized in the sub-domain. This fact facilitates the specification of the course contents, because the teacher can concentrate in each sub-domain. During the execution of the system, if one agent concludes that the next tutoring task is out of its capabilities, it asks the other agents of the society for cooperation.

In the case of the implemented ITS prototype, the domain knowledge – Information Structure – is divided into two contexts – theoretical and practical –, and each of these contexts is worked out in two depths – procedural abstraction and data abstraction. Therefore, the tutorial agent society consists of four agents, each one responsible for one of the following sub-domains: *TP* - theoretical procedural abstraction; *PP* - practical procedural abstraction; *TD* - theoretical data abstraction; *PD* - practical data abstraction. Lateral knowledge includes computer architectures, programming languages courses, in particular about the Scheme language [7], complexity analysis, software engineering techniques, among other.

According to the *internal view* of the MATHEMA conceptual model, the knowledge associated with each sub-domain (TP, PP, TD and PD in the case of the ITS prototype) is organized into one or more curricula. Each *curriculum* consists of a set of pedagogical units and each *pedagogical unit* is associated to a set of *problems*. In the first interaction of a new student with the system, the interface module asks for identification data, basic preferences and background knowledge, and builds the initial student model. The control is then passed to one of the TAS agents. In the first interaction, typically this agent would be the one that is responsible for the initial pedagogical unit of the course, the *theoretical procedural abstraction (TP)*, in the case of the implemented ITS prototype.

## 2.    Agent Architecture

Each agent in the TAS has the architecture shown in fig. 1. The behavior of the agent is controlled by the *Coordinator* module and consists of the following activities: (i) According to the information in the student model, one predefined curriculum is chosen. (ii) The rules that implement the pedagogical model of the chosen curriculum are loaded and the expert system shell inference engine is started. (iii) The inference engine, based on the rules and on the information in the student model, infers which pedagogical unity should be used next. (iv) The coordinator extracts the appropriate interaction data associated with the inferred pedagogical unity, typically a HTML page, from the domain knowledge data base and sends it to the interface. (v) If the pedagogical unity does not need any interaction with the Scheme program, the result of the interaction with the student is used to directly update the student model. (vi) If some interaction with the Scheme program is

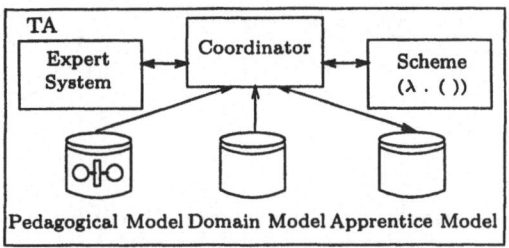

*Figure 1.* Tutorial Agent

needed, the Coordinator performs it and returns the results to the interface, that would typically show to the student these results in the same HTML page. (vii) When the interface finishes the interaction with the student, the coordinator runs again the inference engine and the process is repeated.

Two special events may stop the above behavior: (i) the present curriculum ends, or is interrupted by the student, and in this case either a new curriculum is chosen or the session is terminated; (ii) the present curriculum rules infer that the next interaction should be controlled by another agent, e.g., to switch between theoretical and practical contexts, or to change the depth of the present context, and in this case, the coordinator uses its communication and cooperation capabilities to inform the other agent that it should take the control. In the following subsections the three models (see fig. 1) are presented in detail.

## 2.1 Domain Model

The adopted formalism for the domain model is a data base of Servlets definitions, i.e. interactive HTML pages, structured according to the pedagogical approach proposed in the MATHEMA conceptual model [6]. This approach is inspired both by the constructivism [13] and by the Vygotsky's theory of social knowledge [17]. The idea is to allow the student to acquire and construct knowledge through the interaction with the tutor system, that is designed with the aim of reinforcing the active participation of the student in the learning process. To achieve this goal, the interaction is based on cooperative problem solving activities, combining *learning by doing* and *learning by being told* [5].

According to the internal view of the MATHEMA conceptual model, the knowledge associated with each sub-domain (TP, PP, TD and PD in the case of the ITS prototype) is organized into one or more curricula. Each curriculum consists of a set of pedagogical units ordered according to prerequisites. For instance, in the Information Structure ITS prototype, the pedagogical units associated with the sub-domains

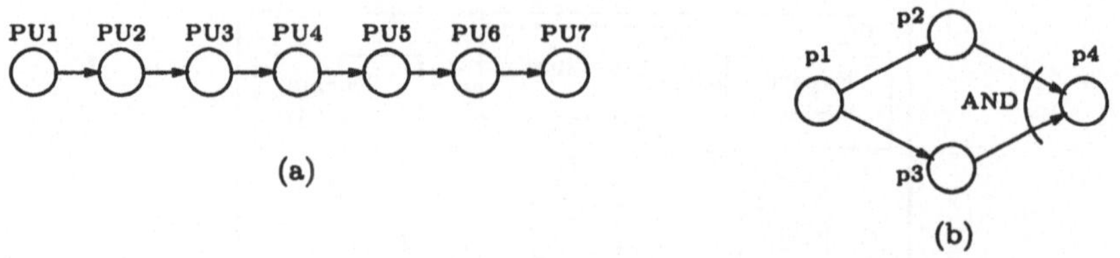

236

*Figure 2.*    Prerequisite graphs: (a) Curriculum CV1, (b) Pedagogical Unit PU1

TP and PP (Procedural abstraction) are: PU1 - Primitive procedures; PU2 - Compound Procedures; PU3 - Interaction and recursion; PU4 - Higher-Order Procedures; PU5 - Procedures as Arguments; PU6 - Procedures as General Methods; PU7 - Procedures as Returned Values. In this example, both contexts – theoretical and practical – have the same pedagogical units, what changes is the point of view about the subject.

A possible curriculum prerequisite graph for the "theoretical procedural abstraction" domain is represented in fig. 2(a). Each pedagogical unit is associated with a set of problems, in the sense that, if the student is able to solve the problems associated with a given pedagogical unit, the system considers that the contents of the unit have been learned. The problems are also ordered according to prerequisite. The prerequisite order graph is defined by the teacher using the authoring interface (see Section 3). A possible prerequisite graph for the problems in pedagogical unit "primitive procedures" (UP1) is represented in fig. 2(b). Note that $p_4$ has two prerequisites – $p_2$ and $p_3$ – and they can be done in any order. Each problem is associated with a set of interactive HTML pages that support the problem solving activities. These pages are of three types – explanations, examples and exercises – and the pages of each type are ordered by difficulty.

The interactive pages that implement a problem have a standard format with some navigation controls, such as *exit, proceed, repeat,* etc. Explanations and examples are just HTML text pages to be read by the student and typically would be available in different levels of complexity for each content. Exercises can be (multiple) choice questions, questions that ask for some symbolic or numerical answers or questions asking for some Scheme implementation, that need the interaction with the Scheme program to be tested. Below, we present a fragment of the domain model structure for the pedagogical unit "primitive procedures" of the TP and PP sub-domains, in the Jess knowledge base syntax:

```
(deffacts domain
(ped-unit (name ped-unit1)
          (title "Primitive procedures")
          (problems (p1 p2 p3 p4))) ...
(problem (name p1)
          (ped-unit ped-unit1)
          (question "What are computers and programming languages?")
```

```
           (explanations (p1-exp1 p1-exp2 p1-exp3))
           (examples (p1-exa1 p1-exa2 p1-exa3))
           (exercices(p1-exe1 p1-exe2 p1-exe3))) ...
(page (name p1-exe1)
      (type exercice)
      (title "Fibonacci number")
      (location "/var/www/mathtutor/exercises/p2/e1.html")
      (return number)) ...)
```

The system knowledge base is represented by Jess *unordered facts* with the following structure: $(\langle object \rangle \ (\langle slot \rangle \ \langle value \rangle) \cdots (\langle slot \rangle \ \langle value \rangle))$, where $\langle object \rangle$ is the type of the fact, $\langle slot \rangle$ the name of an attribute and $\langle value \rangle$ its associated value. The three levels of the domain model structure can be clearly seen in the representation: a pedagogical unit contains a set of problems and each problem is associated with sets of explanations, examples and exercises objects, represented by **page** objects, where a pointer to the associated interactive HTML page is stored.

## 2.2 · Student Model

The adopted formalism for the student model is the subset of first-order logic supported by the Jess knowledge base mechanism. This mechanism consists of a base of facts containing ground logic terms and a query language that may contain terms with variables. The model contains static and dynamic information. The static information consists of identification data (name, origin, background knowledge, etc.) and preferences (theoretical oriented, practical oriented, first overview than detail, step by step, etc.). The dynamic information consists of descriptions of the student activities during all the interaction sessions of the student with the system. The dynamic information is stored into a distributed knowledge base, where each one of the TAS agents stores the details of its own interactions with the student and just summaries of the interactions of the other agents. These summaries contains basically which pedagogical units have been visited and the degree of advance in each of them.

Below, we present a fragment of the student model in the Jess knowledge base syntax:

```
(defglobal ?*app* =
 (assert (student (name "Maria")...(doing pu1-p1)(what examples))))
(deffacts student
(problem (student ?*app*)
         (ped-unit ped-unit1)
         (name p1)
         (to-be-done-explanations (p1-exp2 p1-exp3))
         (to-be-done-examples (p1-exa3))
         (to-be-done-exercices (p1-exe2 p1-exe3))) ...
(explanations (student ?*app*)
              (name p1-exp1)
```

238

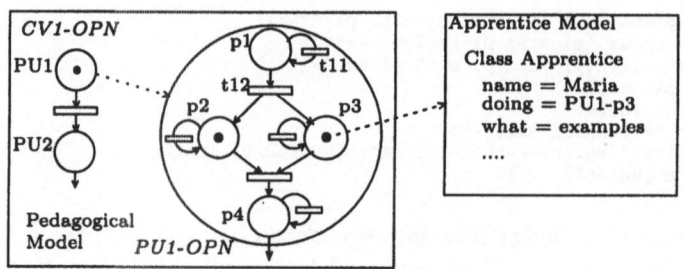

*Figure 3.* Object Petri Net

```
            (session 1)) ...
(example (student ?*app*)
         (name p1-exa1)
         (session 1)) ...
(exercice (student ?*app*)
          (name p1-exe1)
          (session 2)
          (result ok)) ...)
```

The student identification data is stored in a fact assigned to a global variable (?*app*). In particular, this fact contains the present interaction situation of the student: in the slot **doing**, the current pedagogical unit/problem and, in the slot **what**, the current activity. The student model consists of objects of type **problem**, **explanation**, **example** and **exercise**, linked to the student identification data by the **student** slot, where the details of the interaction, such as the session number in which the object was accessed, the result obtained, etc, are stored.

## 2.3    Pedagogical Model

The pedagogical model controls the interaction between the student and each agent of the system and is implemented by an object Petri Net (OPN) [16], automatically translated into a rule-based expert system. The OPN and its associated expert system are generated by the Authoring Interface (see Section 3) based on the description, provided by the teacher, of courses sequences (curricula and prerequisite order of pedagogical units and problems) and contents (explanations, examples and exercises, ordered by difficulty). An important point in the proposed approach is that the teacher does not need to specify the interaction with the student model, this interaction is automatically included in the OPN using the prerequisite and difficulty orders defined by the teacher.

In an OPN, the tokens are object instances. A OPN is defined by a control structure (places, transitions and arcs connecting places to/from transitions) and by the data structure of its tokens. In our case, all places and tokens have the same class (type): student. The generated OPN is hierarchical, because nodes of the curriculum graph are pedagogical units, and each pedagogical unit is itself a graph whose nodes are problems (see fig. 3). The tokens are instances of the student class whose associated data structures are defined in Section 2.2. A token in a place $PU_i$ of the curriculum OPN represents that the student is doing pedagogical unity $PU_i$. Each place $PU_i$ is *exploded* in a $PU_i$-OPN whose places are problems $p_i$. A student token in a place $p_i$ means that the student *can* do it. If the token attribute `doing` is set to $PU_i$-$p_j$, the student is actually *doing* problem $p_j$ of pedagogical unit $PU_i$. Considerer fig. 3, the student is doing $PU_1$ (m($PU_1$)=Maria), can do $PU_1$-$p_2$ and $PU_1$-$p_3$ (m($p_2$)=m($p_3$)=Maria) and is actually doing $p_3$ (`Maria.doing=`$PU_1$-$p_3$), in particular doing an example associated with problem $p_3$, because `Maria.what` = examples.

The arcs represent the prerequisite order between pedagogical units, in curriculum OPN, and between problems, in the problem OPN. Besides these prerequisite conditions, transitions have also extra firing conditions controlled by the student model. The firing of transitions produce actions that update the student model. These extra conditions, predefined into the OPNs, are not specified by the teacher and allow the system to be adaptive with respect to the different students.

Below, we present a fragment of the pedagogical model in the Jess knowledge base syntax, in the situation shown in fig. 3:

```
(deffacts pedagogical
(place (name pu1-p1)(ped ped-unit1)(probl p1))
(place (name pu1-p2)(ped ped-unit1)(probl p2)(token ?*app*))
(place (name pu1-p3)(ped ped-unit1)(probl p3)(token ?*app*))
(place (name pu1-p4)(ped ped-unit1)(probl p4))
(place (name pu2-p1)(ped ped-unit2)(probl p1))
...
(trans (name t11)(place-in pu1-p1)
                 (place-out pu1-p1)
                 (condition repeat))
(trans (name t12)(place-in pu1-p1)
                 (place-out pu1-p2) (place-out pu1-p3)
                 (condition continue)) ...)
```

Places and transitions are represented by Jess objects (classes `place` and `trans`). The tokens are the global variables associated with students and are stored in the slot `token` of the class `place`. Conditions are functions that access the student model to determine whether the transition should fire or not and are stored in the slot `condition` of class `trans`.

## 3. Authoring Interface

The complexity of the MathTutor architecture is a consequence of the intended goal of presenting the domain knowledge in an attractive and interesting way and, at the same time, to provide adaptiveness to

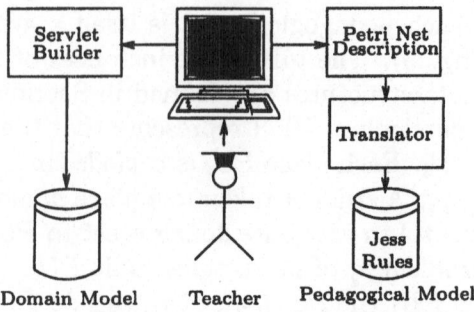

*Figure 4.*   Authoring Mechanism

user level and interests. Nevertheless, this complexity makes the task of designing a course for the system equally complex.

To facilitate this task, an authoring mechanism is proposed (see figure 4). This mechanism, following the internal view of the MATHEMA conceptual model, has three levels. At the first level, the teacher specifies the curricula of the course. Each curriculum is composed by a set of pedagogical units and their possible sequences of execution. To specify each curriculum the teacher disposes of a graphical interface that allows the construction of graphs (see fig. 2(a)). Each graph is associated with a curriculum and each node of a graph is associated with a pedagogical unit. An edge from node $pu_1$ to node $pu_2$ means that pedagogical unit $pu_2$ has pedagogical unit $pu_1$ as prerequisite. Each node may have the following input edges: (i) none: the pedagogical unit has no prerequisite and can be executed anytime; (ii) one: the pedagogical unit has only one pedagogical unit as prerequisite and this one must be executed before it is available for execution; (iii) two or more *necessary* edges: the pedagogical unit has several prerequisite pedagogical units and all must be executed, in any order, before it is available for execution; (iv) two or more *alternative edges*: the pedagogical unit has several prerequisite pedagogical units but only one of them must be executed before it is available for execution.

Nodes and the different types of edges may be combined in a complex graph, according to the intended course sequences. The output of the interface first level consists of a graph represented as an expression in a pre-defined formal language.

The interface second level allows the definition of the pedagogical units. Each pedagogical unit consists of a set of problems whose definitions are specified through a specific interface. The problem definition includes a question that the student should be able to answer, after the interaction with the problem, and the specification of the number of explanations, examples and exercises that will be associated with the problem. The prerequisite ordering among the problems of the same pedagogical unit is defined through the same graphical interface used to define the ordering of pedagogical units (see fig. 2(b)) and is represented by an expression in the same formal language.

Based on the information obtained in these two first levels, the interface generates an object Petri net (OPN) description of the course sequences, taking into account the defined prerequisites. In this OPN, each problem is associated with a place and each pedagogical unit with a sub-net. The use and update mechanisms of the apprentice model are automatically integrated into the OPN, leaving to the teacher only the task of providing the associated explanations, examples and exercises. The OPN is automatically translated into Jess expert system rules that implement it.

The interface third level is where these explanations, examples and exercises are specified by the teacher. They can be directly typed into the interface or copied from previously prepared files. The texts are incorporated into Servlets HTML pages in a standard format that already include the navigation controls. Presently, the exercise pages that include interaction with the Scheme system must be defined manually.

## 4. Conclusion

We presented MathTutor, a multi-agent tool for building intelligent tutoring systems based on a principled model for content exposition and learning strategy planning. The tool also includes a three level authoring interface, through which the structure of on-line courses can be defined. It was used to implement a prototype ITS to teach Information Structure as an undergraduate course. The implemented ITS prototype consists of a multi-agent society composed by four ITSs, each one specialized on a sub-domain.

Future work includes the refinement of the student model use and update mechanisms embedded into the object Petri net control. Future work also includes the development of other courses based on the same architecture and the evaluation of the implemented ITS prototype by the students of the discipline of Information Structure of the Control and Automation Engineering course at the University of Santa Catarina.

## References

[1] H. Abelson and G. J. Sussman. *Structure and Interpretation of Computer Program*. The Mit Press, 1996.

[2] S. R. Alpert, M. K. Singley, and P. G. Fairweather. Deploying intelligent tutors on the web: An architecture and an example. *J. of AI in Education*, 10:183–197, 1999.

[3] P. Brusilovsky. Adaptive hypermedia: From intelligent tutoring systems to web-based education. *LNCS 1839*, June 2000. ITS 2000, Montreal, Canada.

[4] W.J. Clansey. *Knowledge-Based Tutoring: The GUIDON Program*. The MIT Press, 1987.

[5] E. Costa. Artificial intelligence and education: the role of knowledge in teaching. In *Machine and Human Learning*, pages 249–258. 1991.

[6] E. de B. Costa, M.A. Lopes, and E. Ferneda. MATHEMA: A learning environment based on a multi-agent architecture. In *LNAI*, volume 991, pages 141–150, October 1995.

[7] Matthias Felleisen, Robert Bruce Findler, Matthew Flatt, and Shriram Krishnamurthi. *How to Design Programs An Introduction to Computing and Programming*. The MIT Press, 2001.

[8] T. Finin, Y. Labrou, and J. Mayfield. *KQML as an Agent Communication Language*. MIT Press, 1995.

[9] Ernest J. Friedman-Hill. *Jess, The Rule Engine for the Java Platform*. Sandia National Laboratories, Livermore, CA, distributed computing systems edition, September 2003. http://herzberg.ca.sandia.gov/jess/.

[10] JATLite. Java agent template lite. Technical report, Stanford University, 1997.

[11] R. Mizoguchi and J. Bourdeau. Using ontological engineering to overcome common AI-ED problems. *J. of AI in Education*, 11(2):107–121, 2000.

[12] T. Murray. Authoring intelligent tutoring systems: An analysis of the state of the art. In *J. of AI in Education*, volume 10. 1999.

[13] Jean Piaget. *The Psychology of Intelligence*. Routledge Classics, Sept. 2001.

[14] John Self. *Artificial intelligence and human learning : intelligent computer-aided instruction*. Chapman and Hall, 1988.

[15] John Self. Theoretical foundations for intelligent tutoring systems. *J. of AI in Education*, 1990.

[16] C. Sibertin-Blanc. High-level Petri nets with data structures. In *European Workshop on Application and Theory of Petri nets*, pages 141–170, Helsinki, Finland, June 1985.

[17] Lev Semyonovich Vygotsky. *Mind in Society: The Development of Higher Psychological Processes*. Harvard University Press, 1978.

# ANALYSIS AND INTELLIGENT SUPPORT OF LEARNING COMMUNITIES IN SEMI-STRUCTURED DISCUSSION ENVIRONMENTS

Andreas Harrer
*Universität Duisburg-Essen, Germany*

Abstract: Conventional discussion environments provide the technical platform for distributed discussion and collaboration, but apart from some statistical data collected, rarely provide information about the collaborative interactions taking place within the environement or even support the discussion by stimulating the learning setting according to the current situation. In this article we present our approach for intelligent support of groups of learners in distributed web-based discussion environments. First we show how the state of a conversation can be monitored using a classification of the respective contributions and describe the design of a user interface specifically tailored for that end. Then we present an implementation of this type of interface and of a proof-of-concept agent supporting the discussion processes actively. That agent analyses the current state of a conversation and makes contributions acording to the current situation.

## 1. INTRODUCTION

A typical characteristic of intelligent tutoring systems (ITS) is the ability to adapt the system's behaviour in the learning process to the learner's needs and the given learning situation. This is possible, because ITS create learner models as a source for making decisions that influence the learning process. The construction of a learner model is achieved by analysing the user's input to the ITS.

With the spreading of computer networks and both technical and software-related possibilities to build distributed systems (such as wireless networking facilities and middleware platforms like CORBA) in the last years research in learning environments focussed on a type of systems called CSCL-systems (Computer Supported Collaborative Learning) that made it possible to learn together in (spatially or temporarilly) distributed groups. These systems at first provided the technical facilities for networked learning, i.e. a distributed learning environment. The analysis of the group work itself wasn't topic of research and therefore the systems were not able to support the learning processes of groups as ITS do for single users.

In I-CSCL (intelligently CSCL) systems or, as we call it, Intelligent Distributed Learning Environments (IDLE) the analysis of learning processes which was typical for ITS is extended also on collaborative and cooperative learning processes in distributed learning communities. With mechanisms for such an analysis of interactions, taking place during group learning, the collaborative processes can be supported intelligently by the system.

An IDLE's potential to support learning processes in groups depends heaviliy on the richness of the information about learning situations and processes. Typically collaborative activities can be distinguished into *domain-related activities* and *coordination-oriented interactions*. Collaborative modelling tools, such as Cool Modes (Pinkwart et al. 2002) tend to rely more on domain-related activities, such as creating/modifying/deleting domain objects. In these systems information about the learning process is inferred by analysis of domain level activities and states resulting by a stream of activities. A classification for analysis methods in these systems can be found in (Gaßner, Jansen, Harrer, Herrmann, Hoppe 2003). On the other side coordination-oriented interactions take place when learners make plans for solving tasks and coordinating their efforts, which are then conducted as activities on domain level. Discussion Environments such as web-based discussion boards provide an infrastructure for this coordination level, but at the moment have scarce facilities for analysing and stimulating the learning processes taking place in the discussion boards. In this paper we present our approach for analysis of interactions and intelligent support in distributed learning communities using such discussion environments.

## 2.     ANALYSIS OF CONVERSATIONS

For the approach of interaction analysis we base our considerations on speech act theory (Searle 79) and conversational theory (Winograd & Flores

86). Speech act theory classifies the type of utterances according to the purpose, called *illocutionary act*, the speaker has in mind. For example if the speaker wants to bring the hearer to do something, the illocutionary act is called *Directive*, because the speaker wants to direct the hearer. Conversational theory investigates in typical patterns and sequences of speech acts in conversations. These patterns seem to be domain-independent in most cases and therefore are usable in IDLEs regardless of different domains of knowledge. Typically those conversations can be represented as conversational networks as the one shown as a finite automaton in Figure 1. That one is a model of a conversation, where one actor requests an explanation and another actor reacts to that request. At the moment the conversation is in state 6, a situation reached by a request for an explanation by student A (state 1 to 2), a commitment of student B for an explanation (state 2 to 3), and then the explanation of B (state 5 to 6).

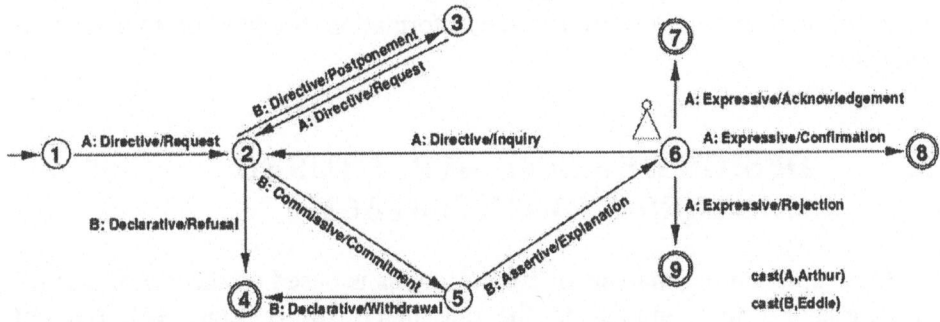

**Figure 1**: Conversational Network

To use the concept of conversational networks in IDLEs we have to generalize the networks in such a way that they can model interaction between the members of a learning community (usually more than the two participants in conversational networks). Therefore we developed a two-tier-model for interactions on coordination level for learning communities. Our model consists of

- a tier with *conversational networks* each for a pair of participants of the learning community, which represent the individual parts of the interaction; these networks are of the type shown in Figure 1.

- a tier for the community level; represented in a so-called *group network* we describe information at group level explicitly. Events taking place in individual conversational networks can have effect on group level and therefore also on other individual networks: for example if there is a transition in a individual network as in Figure 1 from state 2 to state 5 the learner who committed herself for an explanation should make her explanation before other students commit themselves also. So at group level we can specify the results of such an event and coordinate the networks for a proper flow of interactions (in this example we could move all the other students into a state, where they cannot commit themselves at the moment, for example state 3). So we have interdependence between individual level and group level.

To use our model of interactions at coordination level for the analysis of interactions taking place in IDLE, we have to find a way to trace the flow of conversations and therefore to diagnose current states at individual and group level. In the next section we present the design of a type of user interface that enables us to get the information needed for this kind of analysis.

## 3.    DESIGN OF A SEMI-STRUCTURED CONVERSATION INTERFACE

Our approach for analysis of conversations is based on the use of a semi-structured interface, similar to the one in (Baker & Lund 96), but not restricted to sentence openers. A complete diagnosis of the content of the messages sent in conversations, is either to obstrusive for the user when using a formal input language or has to use quite sophisticated and reliable methods of natural language processing and text understanding, which are hardly available nowadays. So we chose to have some parts of the message that can be interpreted automatically, which can give us enough information to trace the states in conversations and thus get models of interactions in distributed learning environments.

For our user-interface we have three different kinds of building blocks for a message:

*predefined phrases*, which have assigned to them specific information usable for learner modeling and that is interpretable for the IDLE

*choices*, where the user can modify and parameterize the contents; these elements have also some machine-interpretable information in it

*free user input*, which provides full potential to let the user express herself; these parts are considered unstructured for the further course of this paper and are therefore not machine-interpretable.

Combining these three types of building blocks, we get a more flexible format of messages than in a pure sentence-opener interface, where the user chooses a phrase beginning the sentence and then continuing the message with free input. In Figure 2 we present an example for a sentence template in our semi-structured interface:

Could you $Style explain to me $FillWord $Keyword
in more detail $Intensity? $Problem

**Figure 2**: Example for a sentence template in the interface

In this sentence we have all the three types of building-blocks in use. The parts for *$Style*, *$Intensity* and *$Keyword* are choices for the user, where he can choose a more polite form, a degree of urgency ("... explain to me ... in more detail [*now/soon/some time*]...') and an object (knowledge-unit) the meassage refers to. The slot with *$Explanation* is free user input, where he can give details what isn't clear to him. The rest of the message is a predefined phrase, to which we assign some information about the phrase usable for construction of learner models.

In Figure 3 we give an example for speech act informations assigned to the predefined phrase to give a message a machine-interpretable meaning, if a user chooses that phrase. In that way the user does not have to classify his message explicitly but the classification can be done implicitly without burdening the user with details of the used conversational theory.

Could you ... explain to me ... in more detail?
>     Category: Directive
>     Subcategory:  Inquiry

**Figure 3**: Predefined phrase with speech act informations

Now we give a detailed example for the kind of information regarding the interactions in learning communities that can be produced with the help of our semi-structured interface: We assume a learning community with the two learners Arthur and Eddie taking place in a conversation represented in our conversational network in Figure 1. The current state for conversation is state 6, actor A is Arthur and actor B is Eddie. The previous explanation (now called e1) didn't help actor A to understand his problem, so he chooses the message template in Figure 2 and produces the following message with the help of the semi-structured interface:

"Could you please explain the Markov-Algorithm to me

in                               more                          detail?

That is more difficult to understand than I expected."


The IDLE uses the speech act information of the predefined phrase shown in Figure 3 to trace the state transition in the conversational network from state 6 to 2 caused by the diagnosed speech act (Directive/Inquiry) and constructs an entry for the learner models with information about the interaction that happended by that speech act. This information unit is shown in Table 1.

```
Speech-Act: i1
Sender:     Arthur
Receiver:   Eddie
Category:   Directive
Subcategory:  Inquiry
Intensity:  normal
Context:   refers to Explanation e1
Propositional Content:
  (interpreted)    DomainConcept(Markov-Algorithm)
  (uninterpreted)    "That is more difficult to
understand than I expected."
  Style:    polite
```

**Table 1**: example for group model content created within the interface

Some of the information is gained directly by the predefined phrase (category, subcategory of the speech act), some by the choices ("please" for a polite style, no specific choice of [now|soon|some time] for a normal intensity) and some by the conversational network (reference to explanation e1). There is also some propositional content in the message that can be interpreted by the system (the choice for *$Keyword*) and some that is not interpreted, that is the free user input part of the message. We can also make further inferences about that information entry that could give us hints about the roles the two participants have in that conversation. The interactions in that network could imply that Arthur is the student and Eddie is the teacher in the learning community.

The information that we get with our approach of using a semi-structured interface to trace the flow of interactions in learning communities can be a valuable ressource for the intelligent support of groups in IDLE (Harrer & Herzog 1999). For example it can be used to diagnose special situations in the group work, where an articificial intelligent tutor gives some hints because the participants are stuck with the problem. The information in learner models can also be used to support the formation of proper learning groups as the approach of Opportunistic Group Formation (Ikeda, Go, Mizoguchi 1997) suggests. For that end the information gained with our interaction analysis can be further processed by other components of IDLE to make intelligent support adapted to the current learning situation feasible. This processing can be based on the analysis of traces/logfiles of interactions at coordination level.

Our mechanism for interaction analysis combined with domain level editors would produce a trace which can be processed to gain further information of higher abstraction level (Barros & Verdejo 1999). For example we can infer a high level of coordination, when we analyze frequent interaction between learners which produced a common problem solution. A large amount of actions and interaction from one specific learner is a strong indication for high participation in collaborative processes. So our interaction analysis is not only usable for tracing interaction processes but also a resource for processing high level contents of learner models such as effort, participation, coordination, dominance and so on, which can be used to adapt the learning process in IDLEs to the given situation. In future work we plan to bring together the two kinds of user inputs, domain level actions and coordinative interactions together in one integrated learning environment.

## 4. SPREKON - IMPLEMENTATION OF THE SEMI-STRUCTURED INTERFACE

Our approach of a semi-structured interface for conversations is prototypically implemented in the SPREKON interface: It is a web-based conversation system with group management facilities similar to regular threaded dicussion boards, but with the underlying principles for classification of contributions according to speech act categories and subcategories as we presented in the preceding section. The implementation of a client-server architecture was done using the web technologies Java Servlets and Java Server Pages to provide a platform-independent environment with minimal installation effort on users' (clients) side. A screenshot of the english version of SPREKON (a testsite is available under

*http://blonskij.informatik.uni-duisburg.de:8080/sprekon_english*)   can   be
seen in Figure 4.

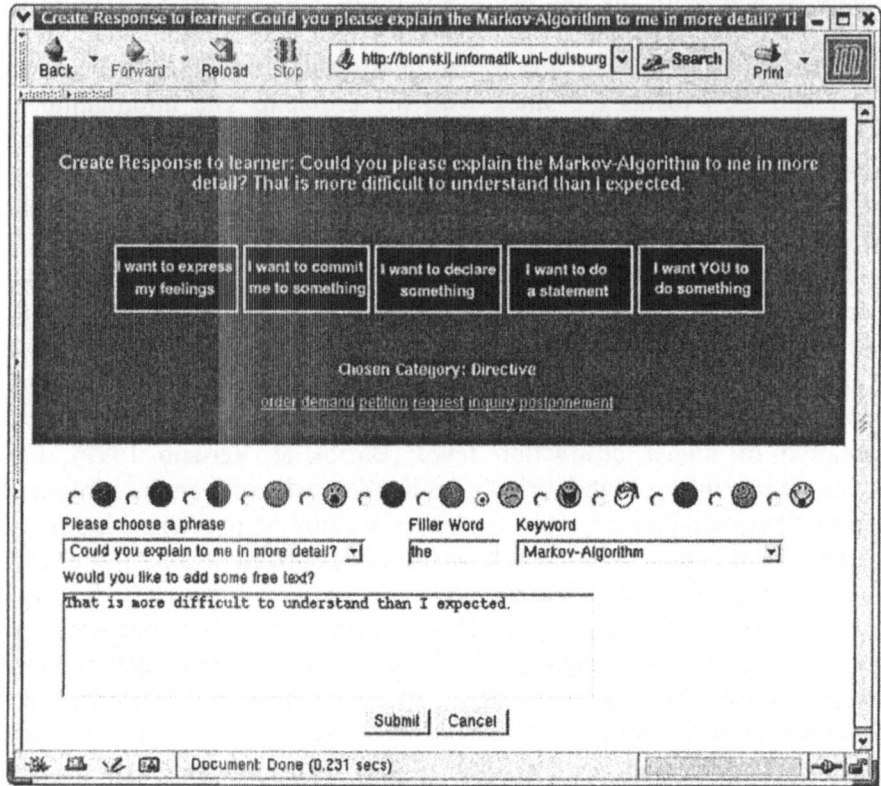

**Figure 4**: Screenshot of SPREKON interface: creation of semi-structured
contribution

In the figure above you can see a window for the creation of a
conversational contribution. Following the examples from the preceding
section the user has an inquiry to a previously given explanation and
therefore chooses a predefined phrase which characterises a directive/inquiry
(in the upper part of the window) in speech act categories. Since he
specifically has problems with the domain concept Markov-Algorthm, he
chooses that keyword from the domain glossary (a choice list on the right
side) and finishes his contribution by formulating the problem in a free text
area (on the lower part). Other attributes of the resulting speech act can be
inferred from the use of respective emoticons and similar UI elements. When
the user submits his contribution to the SPREKON-server the contribution is
integrated into the conversation thread and internally stored as an XML-
document complying to the format demonstrated in the previous section with

some augmentations, such as time stamp, unambigious references to previous contributions. A simplified example for such an XML-document can be seen in Figure 5.

```
<message id="46711293231602">
  <name>
    <username>Arthur</username>
    <account>arthur@somewhere.org</account>
  </name>
  <date><day>8</day></date>
  <content domain="basicCourse">
  <phrasetext>Could you $ explain to me $ in more
   detail?</phrasetext>
  <fillerword>the</fillerword>
  <keyword>Markov-Algorithm</keyword>
  <freetext>That is more difficult than I expected.
  </freetext>
  </content>
  <speechAct category="directive">
    <subcategory>inquiry</subcategory>
    <phrase>Could you explain that in more detail?</phrase>
  </speechAct>
  <reference>
    <predecessor>46759182731502</predecessor>
    <successor>not yet available</successor>
  </reference>
</message>
```

**Figure 5**: XML document representing a SPREKON contribution

SPREKON is designed for flexibility of application domains, underlying conversational theories, and components interacting with the interface, e.g. for analysis of conversations and intelligent support:

- the glossary of the terms within the specific application domain SPREKON should be used for can be exchanged easily by using another text-based glossary description
- predefined phrases can be exchanged and accustomed to suit the users needs
- categories of the contributions can be exchanged according to the conversational model used (such as Questions-Options-Criteria QOC for handling design rationale conversations)
- the contributions which are stored as XML-files can be used by external applications for analysis purposes, such as statistical

analysis of the types of contributions or more complex analyses (we did this in a classroom experiment and computed collaboration features of a discussion inspired by the procedure in (Barros & Verdejo 1999)).

## 5.        ANAKON - AGENT-BASED SUPPORT OF CONVERSATIONS

To show the potential of intelligent support in learning environments possible with our conversational analysis approach, we designed the ANAKON framework for integration of artificial agents into our discussion environment. These agents can take specific roles for the learning community (Harrer 1999), such as co-learner or learning companion (Chan & Baskin 1988), mediator or observer.

The main components of such an agent are:
- conversational models representing, which high-level actions are appropriate to the current state of the conversation
- detailed plans how the high-level actions can be conducted in atomar steps
- domain knowledge base, if the agent's task is to contribute to the domain level discussion (this would not be necessary for a mediator agent exclusively responsible for the flow of interaction)
- building blocks to create the text of the agent's contributions

As proof-of-concept for our agent-based approach, we implemented a learning companion agent that has some kind of domain knowldege and thus in some situations can provide helpful domain level comments and in some cases cannot, a typical form of a learning companion with "mediocre abilities". We parameterized this agent in respect to the components from above as following:
- the agent has as conversational model the typical conversational network for requests, explanations, and inquiries as shown in Figure 1, where the agent is taking the role of actor B
- detailed plans for each action the agent may take in the conversational model, for example before commiting to an explanation the agent first checks, if he has information about a keyword useful for the explanation, and if it has information it selects a text phrase for the commitment. A plan for this short example is specified in an XML document like this:

```
<commitmentPlan>
  <action>lookupKeyword</action>
  <phrases>
    <text>That is easy, listen:</text>
    <text>I will explain that to you.</text>
    <text>OK, I'll tell you.</text>
  </phrases>
</commitmentPlan>
```

- the agent has a part of the domain glossary with keywords, definitions and explanations to use in its explanations
- the agent has some phrases as building blocks for the contributions but could as well use the building blocks learners use in the SPREKON interface to create the text messages.

An example for a dialogue between a learner (learner) and the agent learning companion (compie) looks like in Figure 6:

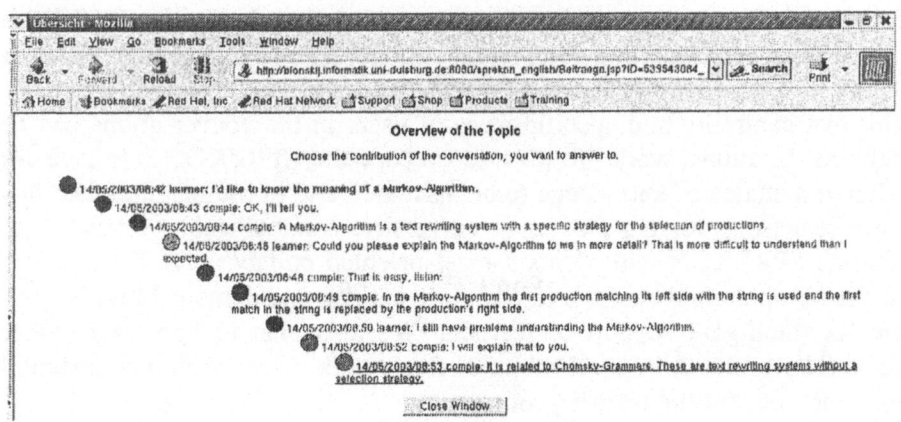

**Figure 6**: Example dialogue between learner and artificial learning companion

In the dialogue you can find the typical pattern of speech acts (request/inquiry, commitment, explanation) represented in Figure 1. The learning companion twice has some information about the keyword *Markov-Algorithm*, but the third time it just has a crossreference that may or may not be helpful to the other learner. Adding more conversational models and generic parameterizable phrases in the future will improve the credibility of the agents behaviour.

## 6.  CONCLUSIONS

In this article we presented our approach for analysis and intelligent support of distributed learning communities using discussion environments. The analysis of the flow of interaction in conversations is based on speech act theory and conversational theory. We designed a semi-structured user interface that produces the output needed for this mechanism of analysis and implemented this interface type as the web-based SPREKON conversational interface. This interface has been used in a seminar and in the exercises to a lecture both in computer scienec at our university. We also described our framework for integration of artificial agents into the discussion environment. These agents can support the collaboration by giving hints, explanations or providing other types of help based on their respective roles. A learning companion agent has already been implemented as proof-of-concept of this support. We plan to test the agent's impact on learning scenarios in future experiments. Recent development within the SPREKON context has been done in a component conducting Social Network Analysis (SNA) (Wassermann & Faust 1994) in the structured discussion threads. With that centrality and specific roles of users in the conversations can be analyzed. In future work we plan to prepare the SPREKON interface for different domains of knowledge to be discussed and to use this interface in a larger scale, e.g. for big classes at university. Another goal we have is to integrate SPREKON with domain-level oriented collaborative tools and to use the rich potential analysis of both interactions and domain activities will give for intelligent support of learners. We also plan to implement other agents (Harrer 2000) in the ANAKON framework which shall take different functions/roles for the learning community.

## ACKNOWLEDGEMENTS

My thanks go to my students Margret Bauer, Jörg Geiger, Angelika Müller for their implementation work in SPREKON and ANAKON, and my colleague Clemens Harlfinger for his support in the supervision of these projects.

# REFERENCES

Baker, M., & Lund, K. (1996). Flexibly structuring the interaction in a CSCL environment. In P. Brna, A. Paiva, and J. Self, (eds.). Proceedings of the European Conference on Artificial Intelligence in Education EuroAIED'96, Lisbon.

Barros, B. & Verdejo, M.F. (1999). An approach to analyse collaboration when shared structured workspaces are used for carrying out group learning processes. In Lajoie, S.P. & Vivet, M., (eds), Proc. of the World Conference on Artificial Intelligence in Education AI-ED 99, 449-456, IOS Press Amsterdam.

Chan, T.W. & Baskin, A.B. (1988). ``studying with the prince''. In Frasson, C. et al. (editors), Intelligent Tutoring Systems, Montreal.

Gaßner, K., Jansen, M., Harrer, A., Herrmann, K., Hoppe, H.-U. (2003). Analysis Methods for Collaborative Models and Activities. In Proceedings of Computer Support for Collaborative Learning CSCL2003, Kluwer Academic Publishers, Dordrecht.

Harrer, A. (1999). Group learning in hybrid communities in intelligent tutoring systems. In Lajoie, S.P. & Vivet, M., (eds), Proc. of the World Conference on Artificial Intelligence in Education AI-ED 99, 708-710, IOS Press, Amsterdam..

Harrer, A. (2000). Unterstützung von Lerngemeinschaften in verteilten intelligenten Lehrsystemen. PhD thesis, Technische Universität München, Institut für Informatik, 2000.

Harrer, A., & Herzog, C. (1999). SYPROS going IDLE - from a classical ITS to an intelligent distributed learning environment. In Cumming, G. et al. (eds). Proceedings of ICCE '99, 7th International Conference on Computers in Education, 836-839, IOS Press, Amsterdam.

Ikeda M., Go, S., Mizoguchi, R. (1997). Opportunistic group formation. In du Boulay, B., & Mizoguchi, R. (eds.) Proceedings of the World Conference on Artificial Intelligence in Education AI-ED 97, 167-174, Kobe, IOS Press, Amsterdam.

Pinkwart, N., Hoppe, H.U., Bollen, L. & Fuhlrott, E. (2002). Group-oriented modelling tools with heterogeneous semantics. In Proceedings of Intelligent Tutoring Systems ITS-2002 . Springer, Berlin.

Searle, J.R. (1979). Expression and Meaning. Cambridge Univ. Press, Cambridge, UK.

Wassermann, S., & Faust, K. (1994). Social Network Analysis: Methods and Application. Cambridge University Press, Cambridge.

Winograd, T., & Flores, F (1986). Understanding Computers and Cognition. Ablex Publishing Corporation, Norwood, New Jersey.

# AN ADAPTIVE ASSESSMENT SYSTEM TO EVALUATE STUDENT ABILITY LEVEL

Antonella Carbonaro, Giorgio Casadei, Simone Riccucci
*University of Bologna, Italy*

Abstract:    The experience from years of development and use, the advance of technology, and the development of authoring tools for questions and tests has resulted in a sophisticated, computer based assessment system. However, there is still a lot of room for further development. Some of the current ideas for development are discussed in the remainder of this work. A primary aim of assessment, both formative and summative, is provide the necessary information to improve future educational experiences because it provides feedback on whether the course and learning objectives have been achieved to satisfactory level. Yet, it is important that the assessment data be accurate and relevant to effectively make informed decisions about the curriculum. Moreover, formative assessment can also be used to help bridge the gap between assessment and learning. This may be achieved particularly where assessment strategies are combined with useful feedback, and integrated within the learning process. The answers to the described objectives are enhanced if we could integrate adaptive testing techniques; accurate and fitted assessment data may improve both the curriculum and the student ability level. The idea behind a computerized adaptive testing (CAT) is quite forward: to apply to each examinee only those items useful to know his proficiency level. As a consequence of this, CAT is more efficient than conventional (i.e., fixed-item) tests. It provides more precise measurements for same-length tests or shorter tests for same-precision measurements.

Key words:    Assessment, Item Response Theory, Computerized Adaptive Testing, Ability

## 1.    SYSTEM DESCRIPTION

The systems used to deliver our tests, have approximately the same functions even if they have been developed in two different architectures. The first one, "Examiner", was developed using ASP (Active Server Pages)

technologies and Access as Database Management System, the second one, "XTest", following the experience of the first system, was developed in Java/JSP (Java Server Pages) and mySQL as DBMS to make it platform independent. The task performed by these systems is to create and manage questions of various types, create randomized test for an exam given some constraints on contents, deliver the test created to a client application. For Examiner, the questions are delivered as HTML text to a web browser that render them on the screen, while for XTest a Java Applet receives data from a server application launched from a machine that acts as control console. The main advantage of first solution is the minimal requirements of client system resources so that only a browser HTML 1.0 compatible is needed to run the client application. The second solution need to install a JRE (Java Runtime Environment) on the client machine, but a Java Applet has more potential in creating new questions type and in a large distributed environments, it allows to have less computational loading on the server.

In such systems, the teacher has to create and insert some question that is grouped by their subject topics and in a successive phase, they will decide how to build the test for the session. The courses concern base competences on Computer Science and Prolog programming. The courses have been divided in six topics:

-    GLOSSARY: the questions belonging to this topic, ask for the meaning of some word or the functions of some objects of the computer world;
-    FOUNDAMENTALS: this topic concerns basic knowledge on calculability, algorithms, complexity, computer architecture, compiler and programming languages;
-    PROLOG: question that ask to interpret or complete some pieces of Prolog source code;
-    PROLOG01: this topic is about the Prolog syntax;
-    PROLOG02: this topic is about the problem formalization in prolog;
-    TURING: exercises on turing machine;

The item type chosen for student assessment was closed answer type. In particular, even if the systems are able to manage more than one item type, the multiple response questions have been used. This kind of question consists in a text representing the question itself and a list of $n$ possible answers that the examinee has to check if the answer is right. For each answer is associated a score that is positive if the answer is right and negative otherwise. A zero score is assigned for not checked answer. The sum of the single score, gives the exercise result. The questions are sequentially presented to the student and if they are checked, the student is not allowed to review question. Otherwise, he can review it once again.

Furthermore, the questions are randomly presented to give the feeling that each test is different from each other.

## 2.     THEORETICAL FUNDAMENTS

Item Response Theory is used as mathematical model providing necessary framework to our system. In this measurement theory, there is an attempt to relate some unobservable characteristics, like getting good grades, learning new material easily, relating various sources of information, and using study time effectively, to observable variables like test results. For the purpose of this work, we assume that there an underlying arbitrary characteristic associated to the examinee that we call ability. This is the unidimensional assumption, that is only one kind of unobservable characteristic is needed to complete the test.

The relation between item examinee performance and his ability can be expressed by a monotonic increasing function called Item Response Function or Item Characteristic Curve.

Such a function states that the probability of correct answer grows as the underlying ability grows. Starting from these assumptions we can mathematically model our system, with this theory.

Each model has its own set of parameters (constants) to associate with item. Typical parameters are difficulty level and a discrimination power. The main advantage of this theory, is that the scale to measure ability is unique regardless both the item and person sample.

It is possible to estimate such parameters starting from a sample of responses given in real exam sessions, through a procedure called EM algorithm, so we can associate the parameters to the items and setup the adaptive system.

### 2.1     Item Information Function

Item Information Function (IIF) is a powerful tool to evaluate and construct a test, either in fixed or adaptive way. Intuitively this function tells us the amount of information given by an item about an examinee with a given ability. This function evaluates the utility of an item to estimate an examinee that is supposed to have certain ability. Analyzing the function shape, in particular its peak, we can have a visual appealing of the item difficulty.

As an example, the more the difficulty level is closer to the examinee ability, the bigger IIF value is (it is desirable to assess high skill students with very difficult question and low prepared students with easy question).

IIF allow us to estimate the error made in evaluating examinee ability by computing its inverse square root.

## 2.2    Generalized Partial Credit Model

The choice of model for our system is the Generalized Partial Credit Model [MUR1992] because of the multi-category nature of the items belonging to item bank. In this IRT model a score $X_i = 0, 1$ ,.., $m_i$ can be obtained on item $i =1$,.., $B$ from an item bank with $B$ items. A higher score indicates a better performance and $m_i$ indicates the maximum score on item $i$.

The probability of obtaining a score $k$ on item $i$, given the value of the ability $\theta$, is denoted by

$$P_{ik}(\theta) = \frac{e^{\sum_{v=0}^{k} a_i(\theta - b_{iv})}}{\sum_{c=0}^{m_i} e^{\sum_{v=0}^{c} a_i(\theta - b_{iv})}} \qquad k = 0,1,\ldots,m_i \ \ b_{i0}=0$$

where $a_i$ is the discrimination parameter and $b_{iv}$ is the item step parameters.

Note that instead of the ICC, here we have a set of $m_i$ *Item Category Response Function* that correlates the ability level with the category response probability.

The IIF for this model is given by the following equation

$$I_i(\theta) = a_i^2 \left[ \sum_{k=0}^{m_i} k^2 P_{ik}(\theta) - \left( \sum_{k=0}^{m_i} k \ P_{ik}(\theta) \right)^2 \right]$$

## 2.3    Computerized adaptive testing

The base idea of this assessment technique, is that during the test, the ability of an examinee can be estimated and the useful item for the current ability be chosen from item bank (generally the item that will mostly reduce the ability estimation error at the test end).

Testing process can be divided in the following phases:

1 – How to start a test:

if we have no information about the examinee, we suppose that he has a medium ability usually corresponding to value 0. Upon this consideration the system chooses the most suitable item for the ability 0. Another strategy is to deliver two or three items randomly chosen in order to obtain initial ability estimation.

2 – How to continue a test:

many strategies can be applied to item selection. The most common is based on Item Information Function (IIF). As mentioned before, this function represents the amount of item information at a certain point on the ability scale. The more high information is, the more accurate will be the ability estimation. The item selection algorithm based on this function, at each step of the test, estimates the examinee ability and gets the most informative item, for such ability, from the item bank. In this way it attempts to reduce at minimum the estimation error.

3 – How to stop a test:

the stopping rule is based on three conditions: reaching of prefixed estimation precision, maximum test length and maximum time to finish the test.

The selection algorithm described above, it's not efficient in terms of item exposure rate. In fact, for some reasons due to the IRT, it always tends to choose the best quality items in terms of discrimination power (as mentioned above more discrimination power correspond to more information given by an item), making necessary the need of some control mechanisms. The adopted mechanism for our system are the "SH algorithm" for overexposure rate control and the "progressive method for exposure control" [EGG2001] for underexposure control. The system also need for a content balancing mechanism, due to the need of specify the test content. The "Constrained CAT" algorithm [LCH2001] was implemented.

## 2.4    System setup

To make operative our system, we need for item parameters estimate, from real data collected during exam sessions. Data used was collected in various exam sessions (about 1400 tests done) of Italian Bologna University in first year undergraduate courses of faculty "Economia di internet" in Forlì department, "Economia del turismo" in Rimini and finally "Psicologia" in Cesena.

To make operative this system, we have collected and analyzed the exam results we have done in the following way:

-   the items are in Multi Response form, where to each answer is associated a score stating the correctness level. The final score is expressed by the selected answer score sum.
-   each question is allowed to be reviewed once and it is not possible to change the answer once the student confirms it. A time limit was imposed depending on the number of item.

Now we have a minimum and a maximum score for each question (item) answered by the examinees. We need to transform this data in a format according to Generalized Partial Credit Model. The choice was to model the items with a five category GPCM by dividing the items score range in five intervals. Thus for the first interval we have assigned the value 0, for the second the value 1 and so on. The data obtained is a matrix of integer number where in each row we have the result of an exam and in each column the result for each question. Once we have done this transformation, we have used ICLWin software [HAN2002] for the item calibration phase.

The adaptive approach for testing can now be used taking advantage of IRT paradigm (Computerized Adaptive Testing [WAI2002]). During the test the ability of examinee can be estimated and the useful item for the current ability be chosen from item bank (generally the item that will mostly reduce the ability estimation error at the test end).

## 3.     SIMULATION STUDIES AND RESULTS

To evaluate the system efficiency, in term of estimation error and item exposure rate, we have simulated some exam sessions with the adaptive method and compared the results with the fixed test mode used upon now.

In real exam sessions, teacher chooses which arguments to include in the test and how much items for each argument include in the test and the system gets the items randomly from the item bank, with respect to specified topic constraint.

For simulation studies, we assume that the number of items is equally distributed around the arguments and the arguments are randomly chosen for every simulated session. For each simulation run, the system generates 200 exam session composed by $n$ examinees with $n$ from a uniform distribution in the range [30-200], so we have about 23000 examinees for each simulation. Each examinee has associated an ability value from a Gaussian normal distribution with mean 0 and variance 1. With a random mechanism, $k$ arguments are chosen for each session. An additional constraint is that a minimum length for a test is 10 items. The stop rules for adaptive test is a maximum length of 30 items and a maximum error of 0.3 on ability scale.

First simulation was conducted by turning off all the control on content balancing and exposure to evaluate the need of such control mechanism. From the first simulation, we have obtained that item exposure rate is quite uniform across the entire item pool and the maximum exposure rate is lower than 8%. This is an acceptable upper bound for exposure rate so the overexposure control will be disabled in next simulation. There will be the need for underexposure control, because some of the item has not been used at all. Figures 1-3 show the result of a more realistic situation, where both content balancing and underexposure rate control is applied. The figures show a substantial enhancement in item exposure rate with an acceptable loss of performance. The test length is increased of about five items, on average, while the estimation error is almost the same. To complete the system evaluation, we now compare the estimation error made with the past real exams, with that of computerized adaptive testing system developed.

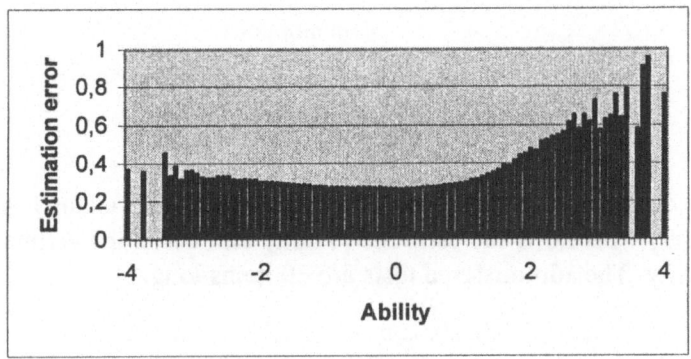

*Figure 1.* Estimation error as the ability function

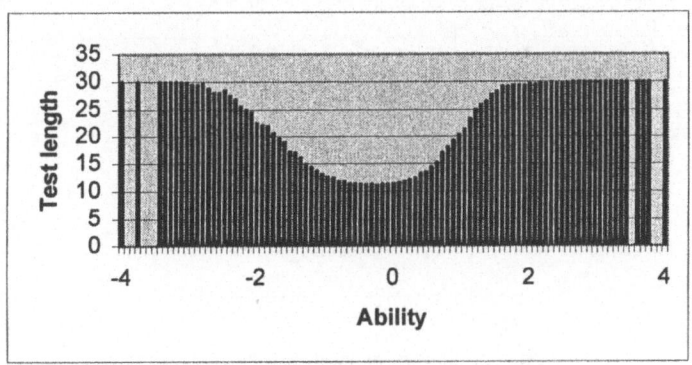

*Figure 2.* Test length as ability function

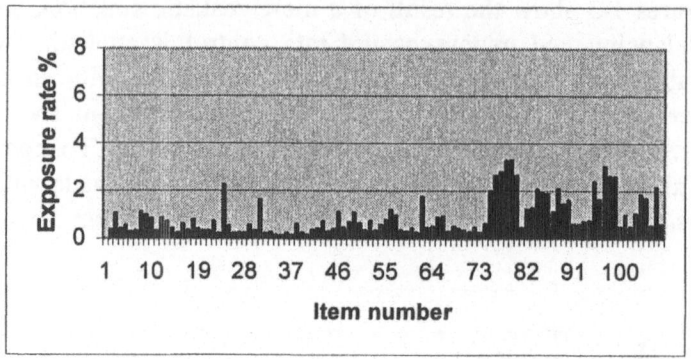

*Figure 3.* Item exposure rate for each item

Figure 4 shows a scattered graphic where for each exam *i* we draw a point ($\theta_i$,*Err*) where $\theta$ is the estimated ability and Err is the estimation error for the ability. The administered tests are 30 items long.

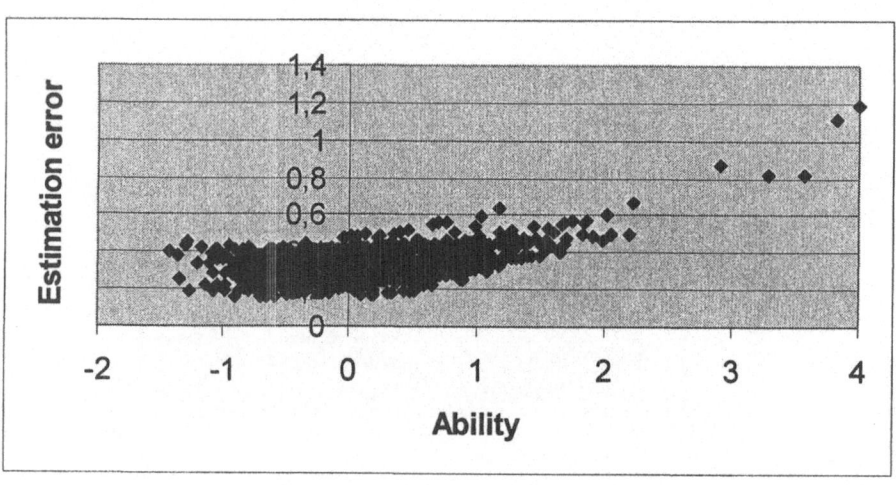

*Figure 4.* Scatter chart of estimation error for real exams

# 4.      CONCLUSION AND FUTURE WORK

We have seen that the IRT framework gives us a powerful tool to evaluate student proficiency and it allow to build, on solid mathematical bases, a dynamic system that understand the ability level during the test delivery phase.

Computerized adaptive testing is about twice more efficient than the fixed-item test and a further development is needed. On the other side, this kind of system needs a relatively complex process of setup (pre-test data collection, item evaluation and calibration). Next step of our work is to make the system capable to learn from its experiences, automating this phase.

Very interesting is to introduce the new IRT models that include more than one characteristic to evaluate. Such a models are object of intensive research and in the next few years, they can be utilized to develop systems that are more complex.

Another important problem is the need for very large amount of data in calibration phase to make item parameters reliable. The introduction of artificial intelligence techniques like neural networks should be useful both in the calibration process and to help manipulating more complicated models.

# REFERENCES

[EGG2001]  T.J.H.M. Eggen, "Overexposure and underexposure of items in computerized adaptive testing", 2001, http://download.citogroep.nl/pub/pok/reports/Report01-01.pdf

[HAN2002]  Bradley A. Hanson, IRT Command Language (ICL), 2002, http://www.b-a-h.com/software/irt/icl/

[LCH2001]  Chi-keung Leung, Hua-hua Chang, Kit-tai Hau, "Making    a-Stratified Computerized Adaptive Testing Design More Practical: Imposing Non-statistical Constraints", 2001, http://www.fed.cuhk.edu.hk/GCJCE/gcjce04/gcjce04.html

[HSR1991]  Hambleton R.,Swaminathan H., Rogers J., *Fundamentals    of Item Response Theory*, NewBury Park, SAGE Publications, 1991.

[MUR1992]  Muraki, E. (1992). A generalized partial credit model: Application of an EM algorithm. *Applied Psychological Measurement, 16*, 159-176.

[REHS2000] P.W. van Rijn ,T.J.H.M. Eggen ,B.T. Hemker ,P.F. Sanders ,"A Selection Procedure for Polytomous Items in Computerized Adaptive Testing", 2000, http://download.citogroep.nl/pub/pok/reports/Report00-05.pdf

[WAI2000]  Wainer H. and other, *Computerized Adaptive Testing: A Primer*, 2° edizione, Mahwah, Lawerence Erlbaum Associates, 2000.

# FORMING THE OPTIMAL TEAM OF EXPERTS FOR COLLABORATIVE WORK

Achim P. Karduck and Amadou Sienou
*University of Applied Sciences, Furtwangen*
*Robert-Gerwig-Platz 1, 78120 Furtwangen, Germany*

**Abstract**      The "networked economy" challenges organizations to reconsider their business models. The aim of our work is to assist organizations dealing with challenges concerning team building. In order the deal with questions related to the formation of the best team, we have defined team formation as the process of allocating the set of experts that best fulfils team requirements.

Focusing on how to support the selection of experts for collaborative work, we have formulated team formation as a constraints satisfaction optimization problem solved by extending the iterated hill-climbing search strategy.

**Keywords:**      Resource allocation, constraints satisfaction optimization, Decision support, Ad-hoc team formation, Collaborative work

## 1.      Introduction

Suppose *SAM & associates systems, Inc.*, an organization of experts, is member of a worldwide heterogeneous network of financial consultants. Michael M., employee of this company, is expert on insurance questions. The consultant is now in conference with a customer in order to process questions concerning insurances. Because of the complexity of the problem, Michael M. has decided to connect to the headquarter in order to have support in some fields. In this case, the later have to form a team of experts that will assists him. For this purpose, an environment for Computer Supported Collaborative Work (CSCW) is required. It should allow the (1) creation of a shared workspace, provide (2) assistance for the team formation process, support (3) content management and enable (4) community support for synchronous and asynchronous collaboration processes. These requirements lead to scenarios for knowledge intense services that require seamless and spontaneous use of expertise in the back-office of an organization.

In this paper, we will explain how to form the best team in order to support this kind of scenarios. Our approach to team formation is based on Intellectual Asset Management (IAM). Intellectual Assets are the tacit assets of an organization, such as expert profiles or the results of an advice process. Derived from Modern Portfolio Theory (Fabozzi and Markowitz, 2002), the target is to optimize return versus risk of an asset allocation strategy.

## 2. Forming teams

### 2.1 What is team formation

As supported in to the group development theory (Tuckman and Jensen, 1977), a team goes through the phases forming, storming, norming, performing and adjourning to get performed while producing results. During the "forming" step, members are brought together for the first time for a particular task.

We call, team formation the process anterior to the forming stage of the group development theory. It consists in the identification and the selection of candidates. The decision to select a candidate is based on how well his/her profile fulfills the requirement specification. This supposes the existence of criteria to be considered while analysing the profiles. Since the focus is on the formation phase, factors essential to start the "forming" stage of team development are those that really matter. In the literature, some factors have been empirically evaluated or applied to other teams (Anderson, 1996; Deborah and Nancy, 1999; Lipnack and Stamps, 2000; Tuckman and Jensen, 1977; Schutz, 1955). In previous investigations we have considered the following factors (Karduck and Sienou, 2004):

| Factors | Description |
|---|---|
| Competencies | Skills and experiences of experts |
| Interest | Skills that experts want to improve in teams |
| Risk | The financial risk of having an expert in a team |
| Availability | Time frame, when an expert is available for a team |
| Commitment | Financial attachment of an expert to a team |
| Budget | Amount of money available for a project |
| Constraints | Constraints related to skills, availability and budget |

*Table 1.* Factors affecting team formation.

### 2.2 A model for team formation

In order to carry out a project, this one is subdivided into tasks able to be carried out by single experts. A task, in order to be performed, requires a set of competencies and interests. Experts are entities with interests and competencies who are looking for positions. Team brokerage consists of finding the right expert for a task. Assigning a set of tasks defined in the context of a project to a set of experts is a Resource Allocation Problem (RAP). There are different approaches to solve RAP. Constraint programming is one of the successful approaches (Tsang, 1993). Key concepts of constraint programming are variables, their domains and constraints. Here, constraints are restrictions on the values to which a variable may be instantiated. The goal is to find an instantiation of all variables that satisfy all constraints.

Team formation is the Constraint Satisfaction Problem (CSP) $(Z, D, C)$ defined as follows:

**Variables Z:** $Z = \{z_1, .., z_n\}$ is the set of variables, each standing for a task which should be assigned to an expert.

**Domains D:** $D = \{d_1, .., d_n\}$ is the set of domains of values to which variables $z_i$ can be instantiated. Let us call elements of $d_i$ instances denoted $I$. An Instance is the assignment of a task to an expert. Instances are conceptualized as follows:

- **Budget.** Amount of money planned for the task to be assigned; denoted $B(I)$.

- **Cost.** A value representing the cost of assigning a task to an expert. Denoted $C(I)$, this value is the product of the hourly wage required by the expert and the number of hours planned for the task.

- **Level of Commitment.** The *commitment breaking cost* is the amount that a partner will have to pay if he leaves the organization before the achievement of goals (Petersen and Divitini, 2002). The level of commitment is denoted $L(I) \in [0, 1]$.

- **Performance.** A value, denoted $P_{instance}$ that expresses the performance value of an instance.

**Constraints C:** $C$ is a set of constraints in $Z$ and $D$. Constraints have been classified into availability constraint, position constraint, instance constraints and team constraints.

- **Availability constraint.** An expert is eligible for a team if he/she is available during the executing time of the task for which he/she is applying.

- **Position constraint.** An expert applying for a task will be considered only if the position posted in the context of this task is the one that he/she is looking for.

- **Instance constraints.** These constraints are restrictions to the level of interest, level of skill and experience. An expert is considered having an interest, skill or experience only if his/her levels of skills or experience are at least equal to the level defined in the constraints.

- **Team constraints.** In contrast to instance constraints, which refer only to single experts, team constraints affect the whole team.

  Let us introduce a binary variable $x_I \in \{0, 1\}$ expressing whether an instance is activated; i.e. if the task $z_i$ is assigned to a given expert, the value $x_I = 1$; otherwise $x_I = 0$. Based on the properties of single resource allocation we have defined the following constraints:

**$C_1$.** The total budget planned for a project should not be exceeded:

$$\sum_i^n \sum_{I \in z_i} C(I) \times x_I \leq \sum_i^n \sum_{I \in z_i} B(I) \times x_I \qquad (1)$$

For convenience, let us define the quotient

$$\Delta_{budget} = \frac{\sum_i^n \sum_{I \in z_i} C(I) \times x_I}{\sum_i^n \sum_{I \in z_i} B(I) \times x_I} \qquad (2)$$

and specify this constraint as follows:

$$\Delta_{budget} \leq 1 \qquad (3)$$

**$C_2$.** All tasks must be assigned and each only once:

$$\forall z_i \in Z, \quad \sum_{I \in z_i} x_I = 1 \qquad (4)$$

Like any constraint satisfaction problems, this one will also have one, none or multiple solutions $X = \langle I_1, ..., I_n \rangle$. A solution is a n-dimensional vector representing a team. A solution is valid if both constraints $C_1$ and $C_2$ hold. The search space has a size of $\prod_{i=1}^n |d_i|$. Therefore, we need to support the selection of a team by introducing the concept of team performance value $P$, which maps each solution $X$ to a value $P(X)$. The value $P(X)$ depends on single performance values of the experts involved in the team $X$.

## 3. Evaluating performance values

Selecting an expert for a given task is a decision problem depending on multiple criteria. The decision is based on the performance of an instance which is an aggregate value of the factors cost, synergy, skills, experiences, commitment and risk interpreted as the following non-dependant criteria:

- **Cost.** The cost of assigning a task to an expert denoted $i$ is $C(i)$. In order to express this factor in term of positif values, we will consider the function $\Delta_{cost}$ expressing how expensive is an expert in comparison with the worst case.

- **Level of commitment.** Value defined in the previous section as $L(I)$.

- **Synergy.** The *value of synergy* is the similarity $V_s$ between candidate interests and the interests required for the task in question. Here, interest is defined as list of attributes-values pairs with a level of interest.

- **Competency (skills and experience).** Let $V_c$ be the aggregate value of the competency of an expert. This value is defined as the similarity between his/her competencies with the ones required for the task. The competency of an expert is the set $\{(A_i, \ell_i, expe_i), i = 1...n\}$ where $A_i$ is an attribute-value pair representing the skill, $\ell_i$ the level of skill and $expe_i$ the experience expressed in number of months.

Let $\omega_i, i = 1...4$ be weighting factors representing the initiator's relative preferences for the criteria $\Delta_{cost}$, $V_s$, $V_c$ and $L(I)$ respectively. We define the performance $P_{instance}$ of an instance $I$ as follows:

$$P_{instance}(I) = \sum_{i=1}^{4} \omega_i \times I_i^{value} \qquad (5)$$

where

$$I_{i=1..4}^{value} = \langle \Delta_{cost}, V_s, V_c, L(I) \rangle$$

This value expresses "how well" the profile of an expert fulfills the requirement specification of a given task. Similarly, we define the performance value $P(X)$ of the whole team as follows:

$$P(X) = \sum_{i=1}^{n} \omega_i \times \sum_{I \in z_i} P_{instance}(I) \times x_I \qquad (6)$$

Here $\omega_i \in [0, 1]$ is a weight representing the relative importance of the instance $I$ and $\sum_{i=1}^{n} \omega_i = 1$. At this stage of the formation process, the main problem to deal with is to find the team with the highest performance value so that all tasks are assigned to exactly one expert and the total cost does not exceed the total budget.

## 4. Finding the optimal team

### 4.1 Problem statement

Finding the optimal team is the following single resource allocation and Constraint Satisfaction Optimization Problem (CSOP)(see eq. 6 for $P(X)$):

$$find \qquad X = \langle I_1, ..., I_n \rangle$$
$$s.t. \qquad maximize \; P(X)$$
$$subject \; to$$
$$\Delta_{budget}(X) \leq 1 \qquad\qquad (7)$$
$$\forall z_i \in Z, \; \sum_{I \in z_i} x_I = 1$$
$$\forall I \in z_i, \; x_I \in \{0, 1\}$$

Notice that $\forall I \in z_i, i = 1...n, \omega_i \geq 0$ and $\omega_i$ is constant.

Since $\sum_{I \in z_i} P_{instance}(I) \times x_I \geq 0$, $\forall I \in z_i$, the value $P(X)$ is maximal if the values $P_{instance}(I)$ are maximal; i.e. the team performance is maximal if tasks are assigned always to experts having the highest performance value. We claim that it is possible to find the best team without executing an exhaustive search. For this purpose, consider the following search problem.

**Objective.** The objective consists in maximizing the team performance $P$, not exceeding the total budget, and assigning each task only once. Since it is algorithmically possible to satisfy the last constraint ($\forall z_i \in Z$, $\sum_{I \in z_i} x_I = 1$) by instantiating each variable exactly once, this one is no longer relevant to the solution if the control of the algorithm forces single allocations. The objective consists henceforth in maximizing the team utility without exceeding the total budget.

Formally, a state $X = \langle I_1, ..., I_n \rangle$ is a solution if

$$maximized_k(P(X)) \wedge C(X) = true$$

where the constraint $C$ is $C(X) : \sum_i^n C(I_i) \leq \sum_i^n B(I_i)$.
Here $maximized_k(P(X)) = true$ if $X$ is a solution and $P(X) \geq P(x_k)$ for the $k$ first potential solutions.

**Representation.** We have defined a state as a vector of instances. A state $X = \langle I_1, ..., I_n \rangle$ represents a team consisting of the $I_i^{th}$ candidate of the $i^{th}$ task.

**Evaluation function.** A state $X_1$ is better than another one $X_2$ if $P(X_1) > P(X_2)$. A state $X_1$ is however a solution only if the *cost constraint* is satisfied; i.e. $\Delta_{budget}(X_1) \leq 1$. Notice that this evaluation metric does not provide any information about the satisfiability of the *cost constraint*.

**Operators.** Let us suppose that experts are ranked according to the decreasing order of the values of $P_{instance}$. In case that the best team is not a valid solution, one will examine the next best team. This one is formed by replacing exactly one candidate for a task by the next best candidate for the same task. This process is a 1-flip operation used to expand the search space. We say that a state $X'$ is a neighbor of the state $X$ if the former is obtained by flipping the value of only one variable of $X$.

## 4.2    Search strategy

Given that we intend to maximize the profit
$P(X) = \sum_{i=1}^{n} \omega_i \sum_{I \in z_i} P_{instance}(I) \times x_I$ and given that the operands $\omega_i \geq 0$
and $\sum_{I \in z_i} P_{instance}(I) \times x_I \geq 0$ for all instances $I \in z_i$, the best state is
without any doubt the set of the best instances; i.e. $max(P(X)) = \sum_i \omega_i \times max(\sum_{I \in z_i} P_{instance}(I) \times x_I)$. The best state is however not necessarily a
valid solution since the *cost constraint* must be satisfied. In case that the best
state is not a valid solution, one will examine the next best one, and so on, until
a valid solution is found.

In order to find solutions without systematically searching the whole space,
we have considered the iterated hill-climbing strategy. The Hill-climbing search
is a local search strategy, which starts from an initial point of the search space.
While iterating, the strategy selects a new point from the neighborhood of the
current point, and replaces the current point by the new one if this one is better
than the current. If a maximum number of iterations is reached or no more improvements are possible, the algorithm terminates. The iterated hill-climbing
consists in searching the space until a given maximum number of iterations is
reached (Michalewicz, 1999). The basic concepts of this algorithm are applicable to our search problem.

Let us consider the table 2. Let $\Omega = \langle 0.32, 0.26, 0.42 \rangle$ be weights expressing the relative preference for the variables $z_1$, $z_2$ and $z_3$ respectively. The state
$\langle 0, 1, 1 \rangle$ is interpreted as the instantiation of the variable $z_1$, $z_2$, $z_3$ to the instances having the indexes 0, 1, 1 respectively. This state is actually the team
formed by selecting the best candidate for $task_1$ and the second best for $task_2$
and $task_3$. The numbers in columns 2, 3 and 4 are performance values of the
corresponding instances (candidates' scores regarding to tasks). The value at
$(z_1, 0) = 0.528$ is for instance the score of allocating $task_1$ to the candidate at
the index 0.

| | Variables and domains | | |
|---|---|---|---|
| | $z_1$ | $z_2$ | $z_3$ |
| 0 | 0.528 | 0.618 | 0.53 |
| 1 | 0.471 | 0.593 | 0.452 |
| 2 | 0.443 | 0.404 | 0.351 |
| $\Omega$ | 0.320 | 0.260 | 0.420 |

*Table 2.*   Scenario: variables and domains

The best initial state is $P(000) = 0.552$. The iterated hill-climbing algorithm suggests the generation of neighbors and the selection of the best one. The current state becomes therefore better with each iteration. As outlined in table 3, in this case, neighbors of the initial state $P(000) = 0.552$ are $(010)$, $(100)$, $(001)$. Let us suppose that the initial state is not a valid solution (i.e. it does not satisfy the *cost constraint*), the next best neighboring state to be examined is therefore $P(010) = 0.546$. If the state $(010)$ in turn is not a solution, the algorithm has to select its next best neighbor which is $(000)$ since the 1-flip operator expanding states always chooses the best values. Given that the state $(000)$ has been already visited, the algorithm sticks around this one. In order to avoid this, we will introduce a *tabu list* which is a memory where already visited states are stored (algorithm 3). In the reminder of this section, the expressions "tabu state" or "is tabu" means that the state is in the *tabu list*.

Let us suppose once again that the current state $P(010) = 0.546$ does not satisfy the *cost constraint*; according to the iterative hill-climber, its best neighbor $P(110) = 0.528$ should become the current state. However, notice that there is one already computed state neighboring the predecessor of $P(010) = 0.546$ which is better than $P(110) = 0.528$ (the best neighbor of the current state). Actually, the neighbor $P(100) = 0.534$ of the initial state $(000)$ is better than $P(110) = 0.528$. Given that we intend to visit best states first, the next state should be $(100)$. Since the classic iterated hill-climbing algorithm does not support this case, we will introduce a concept similar to the best-first search which consists in defining a second memory called *open list* (algorithm 3) to store generated neighbors of the current state. The new algorithm should henceforth always select the best state of the *open list*. The current state becomes therefore $P(100) = 0.534$ while $P(110) = 0.528$ becomes the next in case that this former has to be invalid. The state next to $P(110) = 0.528$ is $P(200) = 0.525$ which has only two neighboring states since all states able to be its third neighbor are in the *tabu list*. The algorithm terminates if all states are in the *tabu list* or the objective of finding the best of the next $k$-states satisfying the *cost constraint* is reached. The whole algorithm called *team-former* is listed in algorithm 3. Here the best team is the state $(000)$ that corresponds to the instances $\langle I_0, I_1, I_1 \rangle$; i.e. the best candidate for $task_1$, the second best for $task_2$ and $task_3$.

| Path | State | Neighbors | | |
|------|-------|-----------|---|---|
| 1 | (000) | P(010)=0.546 | P(100)=0.534 | P(001)=0.519 |
| 2 | (010) | P(110)=0.528 | P(011)=0.513 | P(020)=0.497 |
| 3 | (100) | P(110)=0.528 | P(200)=0.525 | P(101)=0.501 |
| 4 | (110) | P(210)=0.519 | P(111)=0.495 | P(120)=0.478 |
| 5 | (200) | P(210)=0.519 | P(201)=0.492 | |
| 6 | (001) | P(011)=0.513 | P(101)=0.501 | P(002)=0.477 |
| | | ... | | |
| 27 | (222) | | | |

*Table 3.* Sample states and neighbors.

```
Team-Former ( Z, D, k):
    space: Z = {z_i,   i = 1...n}, D = {d_i, i = 1..n}
    tabu, open, result, counter
    s_best ⇐ best state
    s_c ⇐ s_best
    while ( open is not empty )
        add s_c to tabu
        if ( Δ_budget(s_c) ≤ 1)     /** s_c is a solution **/
            add s_c to result
            if ( s_best not solution )
                s_best ⇐ s_c
            end if
            if ( counter ≥ k )
                return result
            end if
        end if
        if ( s_best is a solution )
            counter ⇐ counter + 1
        end if
        open ⇐ open ∪ neighbors(s_c) /** expands the space **/
        s_c ⇐ best state from open
        remove s_c from open
    end while
```

To exemplify the *team-former* algorithm, consider Figure 1 illustrating the search path with the parameter $k = 10$. Points represent performance values of all states of the space whereby circles are performance values of the k-best solutions states. States which should be visited if no solutions were available are also represented by points. As outlined in figure 1, states with high performance values are visited first and the algorithm will stop at the $10^{th}$. Given

276

that no state after the $10^{th}$ state is better than the best of the k-first, our outgoing assumption concerning the possibility to find the best solution without an exhaustive search of the state holds for this scenario. Notice that the strategy

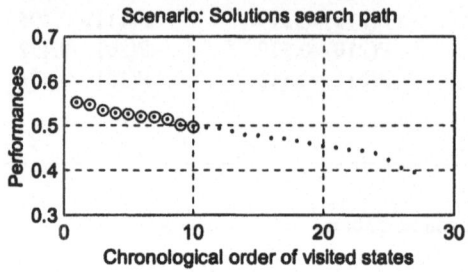

*Figure 1.* Scenario: team-former solutions and path

does an exhaustive search if no solution is available. In addition, if solutions have low performance values, they will be visited late. That is because the algorithm searches by decreasing the value of performance and believes that the great part of solutions is high performed. This is an optimistic approach to forming teams since we make the assumption that teams with hight performances may not exceed the total budget.

Comparing the *team-former* algorithm with the iterated hill-climber, it is necessary to notice some points.

The *team-former* algorithm does not repeat until a maximum depth of iteration is reached. In contrary, it runs until the $k^{th}$ state after the first solution has been visited or the whole space has been expanded. When the domain is completely expanded, the algorithm becomes an exhaustive search. The concept of k-states solution is however similar to the iteration's depth of the iterated hill-climber. The factor $k$ has not a particular role concerning the outcome of the search. It is rather a concept introduced in order to satisfy the statement (relative maximization) of the problem.

In contrast to the iterated hill-climber, which does not have any memory, the *team-former* is able to manage two lists in order to avoid local maxima, to prevent local maxima and to improve the search by generating and visiting only opened states. It encloses features from tabu-search and best-first search. Unlike *iterated hill-climbing*, the *team-former* strategy always select the best state by merging the neighborhood of the current state with all previously processed non-tabu states. In addition, each state is visited only once.

While having reasoned about performances of states, one should have noticed that the values $P$ are decreasing from state to state instead of increasing as intended while formulating the problem as a maximization one. In fact, the objective is to find the solution(s) with the optimal performance in a given range of values (k) rather than absolutely maximizing the performance function.

## 5. Related Work

Concerning the area of the formation of teams, works related to our project are the ones from (Rub and Vierke, 1998; Petersen and Gruninger, 2000; Petersen and Divitini, 2002). In contrast to the first concept which supports the configuration of virtual enterprizes, we have emphasized the formation of virtual teams of humans. Both concepts share the aspects of optimal resource allocation. Unlike the second approach, where the virtual team initiator is the entity evaluating partners, we have adopted a brokerage approach. The approaches differs deeply in the metrics and the aggregation procedures used to process performances values.

## 6. Conclusion

The work on team formation support will be extended according to the *"3C Collaboration Model (Communication, Coordination, Cooperation)"* (Fuks and de Lucena; C. J., 2004). Especially coordination will be investigated in two aspects: *awareness* of the team members concerning the individual activities and *commitment* in terms of the delegation of individual responsibilities.

The model developed will be extended in the future concerning IAM with respect to risk/result-correlations, as applied in Modern Portfolio Theory in Finance (Fabozzi and Markowitz, 2002). We expect, that transferring these concepts will lead to new perspectives in requirement analysis and project management in general, in team formation in particular. One aspect we plan to investigate further is the correlation between the team size and the effectiveness of team work. Even we believe that this research question is difficult to quantify, we believe it to be an important measure due to the correlation of team size and coordination cost.

In the context of TeamBroker, we have (1) conceptualized factors and performance values affecting the formation of teams, (2) formalized constraints imposed by the project that a team has to carry out, (3) transformed the problem of forming teams into a resource allocation problem and (4) solved it by using methods of constraints programming. We have developed the Team-Former algorithm, which is an extension of the iterated-hill climbing search strategy. The algorithm guarantee to find the best solution first if any one exists.

A successful application of our concept to team formation requires the definition of performances metrics for competencies and interests by processing the similarity between vectors representing experts' competencies or interest and the one representing task requirements.

278

Because of the similarity between the team-former algorithm and the A* algorithm, in the future, we plan to discuss the team-former algorithm in relation to this one and to explain under which conditions the team-former becomes an A* algorithm.

# References

Anderson, W. (1996). Human resource development challenges in a virtual organization. In *IEMC Proceedings: Managing the Virtural Enterprise*, Vancouver, B.C.: IEMC.

Deborah, L. D. and Nancy, T. S. (1999). *Mastering Virtual Teams : Strategies, Tools, and Techniques That Succeed*. 0787941832. Jossey-Bass Pub, San Francisco.

Fabozzi, F. J. and Markowitz, H. N. e. (2002). *The Theory and Practice of Investment Management*. Wiley, 1 edition.

Fuks, H.; Raposo, A. B. G. M. A. and de Lucena; C. J., P. (2004). Applying the 3c model to groupware engineering. *Monografias em Ciência da Computação*, (1).

Karduck, A. P. and Sienou, A. (2004). Teambroker: Constraint based brokerage of virtual teams. In *Proceedings of the sixth International Conference on Enterprise Information Systems (ICEIS 2004)*, Porto, Portugal.

Lipnack, J. and Stamps, J. (2000). *Virtual Teams*. John Wiley & Sons, 2 edition.

Michalewicz, Z. / Fogel, D. B. (1999). *How to Solve It: Modern Heuristics*. 3540660615. Springer Verlag.

Petersen, S. A. and Divitini, M. (2002). Using agents to support the selection of virtual enterprise teams. In *Proceedings of Fourth International Bi-Conference Workshop on Agent-Oriented Information Systems (AOIS-2002)*, Bologne, Italy. AAMAS 2002.

Petersen, S. A. and Gruninger, M. (2000). An agent-based model to support the formation of virtual enterprises. In *International ICSC Symposium on Mobile Agents and Multi-agents in Virtual Organisations and E-Commerce (MAMA'2000)*, Woolongong, Australia.

Rub, C. and Vierke, G. (1998). Agent-based configuration of virtual enterprises. In Holsten, A. e. a., editor, *Proc. of the Workshop on Intelligent Agents in Information and Process Management KI'98*, volume 9.

Schutz, W. (1955). What makes groups productive? *Human Relations*, 8:429–465.

Tsang, R. (1993). *Foundations of Constraint Satisfaction*. Academic Press.

Tuckman, B. and Jensen, N. (1977). Stages of small-group development revised. *Group and Organizational Studies*, 2(4):419–427.

# IMPACT ON PERFORMANCE OF HYPERTEXT CLASSIFICATION OF SELECTIVE RICH HTML CAPTURE

Houda Benbrahim and Max Bramer
*University of Portsmouth, UK {houda.benbrahim, max.bramer}@port.ac.uk*

Abstract: Hypertext categorization is the automatic classification of web documents into predefined classes. It poses new challenges for automatic categorization because of the rich information in a hypertext document. Hyperlinks, HTML tags, and metadata all provide rich information for hypertext categorization that is not available in traditional text classification. This paper looks at (i) what representation to use for documents and which extra information hidden in HTML pages to take into consideration to improve the classification task, and (ii) how to deal with the very high number of features of texts. A hypertext dataset and three well-known learning algorithms (Naïve Bayes, K-Nearest Neighbour and C4.5) were used to exploit the enriched text representation along with feature reduction. The results showed that enhancing the basic text content with HTML page keywords, title and anchor links improved the accuracy of the classification algorithms.

Key words: Machine Learning; Hypertext classification.

## 1. INTRODUCTION

It has been estimated that the World Wide Web comprises more than 3 billion pages and is growing at a rate of 1.5 million pages a day [1]. A recent study [2] showed that users prefer to navigate through directories of pre-classified content, and that providing a categorized view of retrieved documents enables them to find more relevant information in a shorter time. The common use of the manually constructed category hierarchies for navigation support in Yahoo [3] and other major web portals has also demonstrated the potential value of automating the process of hypertext categorization.

Automated hypertext categorization poses new research challenges because of the rich information in a hypertext document. Hyperlinks, HTML tags, and metadata all provide rich information for classifying hypertext that is not available in traditional text categorization. Researchers have only recently begun to explore the issues of exploiting rich hypertext information for automated categorization.

There is a growing volume of research in the area of learning over web text documents. Since most of the documents considered are in HTML format, researchers have taken advantage of the structure of those pages in the learning process. The systems generated differ in performance because of the quantity and nature of the additional information considered.

Oh et al. [4] reported some observations on a collection of online Korean encyclopedia articles. They used system-predicted categories of the linked neighbors of a test document to reinforce the classification decision on that document and they obtained a 13% improvement over the baseline performance when using local text alone.

Furnkranz [5] used a set of web pages from the WebKB university corpus to study the use of anchor text and the words near the anchor text in a web page to predict the class of the target page pointed to by the links. By representing the target page using the anchor words on all the links that point to it, plus the headlines that structurally precede the sections where links occur, the classification accuracy of a rule-learning system improved by 20%, compared with the baseline performance of the same system when using the local words in the target page instead.

Slattery and Mitchell [6] used the WebKB university corpus, but studied alternative learning paradigms, namely, a First Order Inductive Learner which exploits the relational structure among web pages, and a Hubs and Authorities style algorithm exploiting the hyperlink topology. They found that a combined use of these two algorithms performed better than using each alone.

Yang, Slattery and Ghani [7] have defined five hypertext regularities which may hold in a particular application domain, and whose presence may significantly influence the optimal design of a classifier. The experiments were carried out on 3 datasets and 3 learning algorithms. The results showed that the naïve use of the linked pages can be more harmful than helpful when the neighborhood is noisy, and that the use of metadata when available improves the classification accuracy.

Attardi et al. [8] described an approach that exploits contextual information extracted from an analysis of the HTML structure of Web documents as well as the topology of the web. The results of the experiments with a categorization prototype tool were quite encouraging.

Chakrabarti et al. [9] studied the use of citations in the classification of IBM patents where the citations between documents were considered as hyperlinks, and the categories were defined on a topical hierarchy. Similar experiments on a small set of pages with real hyperlinks were also conducted. By using the system-predicted category labels for the linked neighbors of a test document to reinforce the category decision on that document, they obtained a 31% error reduction, compared to the baseline performance when using the linked documents, treating the words in the linked documents as if they were local. This approach increased the error rate of their system by 6% over the baseline performance.

This paper deals with web document categorization. Two issues will be considered in depth: (i) the choice of representation for documents and the extra information hidden in HTML pages that should be taken into consideration to improve the classification task, and (ii) how to deal with the very high number of features generated when processing text. Finally, data collected from the web will be used to evaluate the performance of the different classification methods with different choices of text representation and feature selection strategy.

Document representation is described in Section 2. Some classification algorithms used for hypertext are reviewed in Section 3. Section 4 presents experiments and results, comparing different classification algorithms with different webpage representation techniques.

## 2. TEXT REPRESENTATION

In order to apply machine-learning methods to document categorization, consideration first needs to be given to a representation for HTML pages. A pre-processing stage is used to remove potentially distracting information before a document is presented to a classifier. First, HTML tags, digits and punctuation marks are removed.

Next, an indexing procedure that maps a text into a compact representation is applied to the dataset. The most frequently used method is a *bag-of-words* representation where all words from the set of documents under consideration are taken and no ordering of words or any structure of text is used.

There are two ways in which the words (features) can be chosen in order to classify a set of documents. The words can be selected to support classification under each category in turn, i.e. only those words that appear in documents in the specified category are used (the *local dictionary* approach). This means that the set of documents has a different feature representation (set of features) for each category. Alternatively, the words can be chosen to support classification under all categories, i.e. all the words that appear in any of the documents are used (*global feature selection*). In this paper, the local dictionary approach is adopted, as it has been reported to lead to better performance [10] and [11].

Assuming there are N features for a particular classification, the documents are represented using a vector space model (VSM) [12]. The i[th] document $O_i$ is represented as an N-dimensional vector $O_i = (X_{i1}, X_{i2}, X_{i3}, \ldots X_{iN})$, where $X_{ij}$ stands for the *weight* of word $t_j$, and measures the importance of $t_j$ in the document.

There are a number of ways to compute the weights of words. The most commonly used methods are *binary* (where 1 denotes presence and 0 absence of the term in the document), *term frequency* in the document, and *Term Frequency-Inverse Document Frequency* (TF-IDF). The TF-IDF method has been reported to lead to better performance [13] and has been used in this paper.

The weights $X_{ij}$ are computed using the formula:

$(TF\_IDF)_{ij} = tf_{ij} * idf_i$ where $idf_i * \log_2 (n / df_j)$

$tf_{ij}$ is the number of times term $t_j$ occurs in document $O_i$

$df_j$ is the number of training documents in which word $t_j$ occurs at least once

$n$ is the total number of training documents.

This weighting function encodes the intuitions that the more often a term occurs in a document, the more it is representative of the document's content, and that the more documents in which a term occurs, the less discriminating it is. In order to make weights fall in the [0,1] interval and for documents to be represented by vectors of equal length, the weights resulting from the function $(TF\_IDF)_{ij}$ are normalized by 'cosine normalization', given by:

$$X_{ij} = \frac{(TF\_IDF)_{ij}}{\sqrt{\sum_{j=1}^{N} (TF\_IDF)_{ij}^2}}, \quad 1 \le i \le n \text{ and } 1 \le j \le N$$

where N is the number of terms that occur at least once in the set of training documents.

With the bag-of-words approach for text representation, it is possible to have tens of thousands of different words occurring in a fairly small set of documents. Using all these words is time consuming and represents a serious obstacle for a learning algorithm. Moreover many of them are not really important for the learning task and their usage can degrade the system's performance. Many approaches exist to reduce the feature space dimension, the most common ones are: (i) the use of a stop list containing common English words, (ii) or the use of stemming, that is keeping the morphological root of words, or (iii) the use of feature selection algorithms such as information gain.

In the experiments reported here, stop words are removed and IG (information gain) criterion is used as it has been reported to outperform many of the common existing feature selection methods [14]. The IG criterion measures the number of bits of information gained for category prediction by knowing the presence or absence of a feature in a document. The IG of a term t and for a class $C_k$ ( $1 \leq k \leq c$, where c is the number of target classes) is defined as:

$$IG(t,C_k)=-P(C_k)\log P(C_k)+P(t)P(C_k/t)\log P(C_k/t)+P(\bar{t})P(C_k/\bar{t})\log P(C_k/\bar{t})$$

$P(C_k)(or P(\overline{C}_k))$ is the probability of having class $C_k$ (or not having $C_k$).
$P(t)(or P(\bar{t}))$ is the probability of having term t (or not having term t).
$P(C_k/t)$ is the probability of having class $C_k$ given that term t is observed in the document.
$P(C_k/\bar{t})$ is the probability of having class $C_k$ given that term t is not in the document

These probabilities are estimated by counting occurrences in the training set of documents. The IG function captures the intuition according to which the most valuable terms for categorization under $C_k$ are those that are distributed most differently in the sets of positive and negative examples of the category.

In this work a procedure according to which all terms are ranked based on their IG(t, $C_k$) is used for feature selection. For every class $C_k$, only the features (from the training documents belonging to $C_k$) with the highest (say) 20, 50 or 100 values of IG(t, $C_k$) are selected. The other features are ignored.

# 3.    CLASSIFICATION ALGORITHMS

## 3.1    Naïve Bayes (NB)

Naïve Bayes (NB) is a widely used model in machine learning and text classification. The basic idea is to use the joint probabilities of words and categories in the training set of documents to estimate the probabilities of categories for an unseen document. The term 'naïve' refers to the assumption that the conditional probability of a word is independent of the conditional probabilities of other words in the same category.

A document is modeled as a set of words from the same vocabulary, $V$. For each class, $C_j$, and word, $w_k \in V$, the probabilities, $P(C_j)$ and $P(w_k|C_j)$ are estimated from the training data. Then the posterior probability of each class given a document, D, is computed using Bayes' rule:

$$P(C_j \mid D) = \frac{P(C_j)}{P(D)} \prod_{i=1}^{|D|} P(a_i \mid C_j)$$

where $a_i$ is the $i^{th}$ word in the document, and $|D|$ is the length of the document in words. Since for any given document, the prior probability $P(D)$ is a constant, this factor can be ignored if all that is desired is ranking rather than a probability estimate. A ranking is produced by sorting documents by their odds ratios, $P(C_1|D) / P(C_0|D)$, where $C_1$ represents the positive class and $C_0$ represents the negative class. An example is classified as positive if the odds are greater than 1, and negative otherwise.

## 3.2    K-Nearest Neighbor (KNN)

K-Nearest Neighbor (KNN) is a well-known statistical approach in pattern recognition. KNN assumes that similar documents are likely to have the same class label. Given a test document, the method finds the $K$ nearest neighbors among the training documents, and uses the categories of the $K$ neighbors to weight the category candidates. The similarity score of each neighbor document to the test document is used as the weight of the categories of the neighbor document. If several of the K nearest neighbors share a category, then the per-neighbor weights of that category are added together, and the resulting weighted sum is used as the likelihood score of that category with respect to the test document. By sorting the scores of candidate categories, a ranked list is obtained for the test document. By thresholding on these scores, binary category assignments are obtained. The decision rule in KNN can be written as:

$$y(\vec{x}, c_j) = \sum_{\vec{d_i} \in KNN} sim(\vec{x}, \vec{d_i}) y(\vec{d_i}, c_j) - b_j$$

where $y(\vec{d_i}, c_j) \in \{0,1\}$ is the classification for document $\vec{d_i}$ with respect to category cj (y = 1 for Yes, and y = 0 for No); $sim(x, d_i)$ is the similarity between the test document $x$ and the training document $d_i$; and $b_j$ is the category specific threshold for the binary decisions.

## 3.3 Decision Tree Classification (C4.5)

C4.5 is a decision tree classifier developed by Quinlan. The training algorithm builds a decision tree by recursively splitting the data set using a test of maximum gain ratio. The tree is then pruned based on an estimate of error on unseen cases. During classification, a test vector starts at the root node of the tree, testing the attribute specified by this node, then moving down the tree branch corresponding to the value of the attribute in the given example. This process is then repeated for the subtree rooted at the new node until a leaf is encountered, at which time the pattern is asserted to belong to the class named by that leaf.

# 4.     EXPERIMENTS

## 4.1     Dataset

To test the proposed algorithms for hypertext classification, datasets were needed that reflected the properties of real world hypertext classification tasks.

The major practical problem in using web document datasets is that most of the URLs become unavailable. The well-known dataset WebKB project at CMU [15] is outdated since most of its web pages are no longer available.

*Table 1.* Dataset Summary

| Category' ID | Category' Name | Associated Theme |
|---|---|---|
| A | Commercial Banks | Banking and Finance |
| B | Building Societies | Banking and Finance |
| C | Insurance Agencies | Banking and Finance |
| D | Java | Programming Languages |
| E | C/C++ | Programming Languages |
| F | Visual Basic | Programming Languages |
| G | Astronomy | Science |
| H | Biology | Science |
| I | Soccer | Sport |
| J | Motor Sport | Sport |
| K | Sport | Sport |

The data used for the experiments comprises a set of HTML web documents. The dataset was provided by Reading University, UK [16]. The Open Directory Project and Yahoo! categories were used to provide web pages that have already been categorized by people. The considered dataset consists of 11,000 pages. The web pages were distributed over 11 different categories under 4 distinct themes. The dataset consists of some sets of categories that are quite distinct from each other, as well as other categories that are quite similar to each other. Table 1 gives a summary of the dataset.

## 4.2    Performance Measures

The evaluation of the different classifiers is measured using four different measures: recall (R), precision (P), accuracy (Acc), and F1 measure [17]. These can all be defined using the 'confusion matrix' shown as Table 2.

*Table 2.* Confusion Matrix

|                              | Correct Class is $C_k$ | Correct Class is $\overline{C_k}$ |
|------------------------------|:---------------------:|:--------------------------------:|
| Assigned class is $C_k$      | a                     | b                                |
| Assigned class is $\overline{C_k}$ | c               | d                                |

$$R = \frac{a}{(a+c)} \ if\,(a+c) > 0 \ otherwise \ R = 1$$

$$P = \frac{a}{(a+b)} \ if\,(a+b) > 0 \ otherwise \ P = 1$$

$$Acc = \frac{(a+d)}{n} \ where \ n = a+b+c+d > 0$$

$$F1 = \frac{2PR}{(R+P)} = \frac{2a}{(2a+b+c)} \ if\,(a+c) > 0 \ otherwise \ undefined.$$

Recall (R) is the percentage of the documents for a given category that are classified correctly. Precision (P) is the percentage of the predicted documents for a given category that are classified correctly. Accuracy (Acc) is defined as the ratio of correct classification into a category $C_k$.

Neither recall nor precision makes sense in isolation from the other. In fact, a trivial algorithm that assigns class $C_k$ to all documents will have a perfect recall (100%), but an unacceptably low precision. Conversely, if a system decides not to assign any document to $C_k$ it will have a perfect precision but a low recall. The F1 measure has been introduced to balance recall and precision by giving them equal weights.

Classifying a document involves determining whether or not it should be classified in any or potentially all of the available categories. Since the four measures are defined with respect to a given category only, the results of all the binary classification tasks (one per category) need to be averaged to give a single performance figure for a multiple class problem.

In this paper, the 'micro-averaging' method will be used to estimate the four measures for the whole category set. Micro-averaging reflects the per-document performance of a system. It is obtained by globally summing over all individual decisions and uses the global contingency table.

## 4.3    Design of Experiments

The classification algorithms NB, KNN and C4.5 were applied to the dataset to address the different binary classification problems. The full set of 11 categories was used. The dataset was randomly split into 70% training and 30% testing.

*Table 3*. Number of features for each class and for each choice of text representation

|   | Ct | CtStm | Mt | MtStm | CtMt | CtMtStm |
|---|-----|-------|-----|-------|------|---------|
| A | 8587 | 5649 | 1957 | 1513 | 11350 | 8478 |
| B | 8667 | 5972 | 1820 | 1427 | 11173 | 8673 |
| C | 11533 | 7649 | 2232 | 1827 | 13943 | 10282 |
| D | 20444 | 15231 | 7108 | 5922 | 23271 | 18118 |
| E | 26429 | 20407 | 6375 | 5265 | 27675 | 21968 |
| F | 15805 | 12154 | 5394 | 4397 | 18562 | 14972 |
| G | 29165 | 20722 | 9198 | 7681 | 32015 | 23636 |
| H | 69181 | 54713 | 9068 | 7644 | 70762 | 57117 |
| I | 27928 | 23108 | 5064 | 4409 | 29080 | 25718 |
| J | 21955 | 16327 | 5703 | 4970 | 23224 | 18099 |
| K | 36569 | 28352 | 8491 | 7026 | 38606 | 30824 |

Cell abbreviation
*Ct (Content):* basic text content with the stemming option turned off.
*Ctstm (ContentStem):* basic text content with the stemming option turned on.
*Mt (Meta):* metadata + title + link anchors with the stemming option turned off.
*Mtstm (MetaStem):* metadata + title + link anchors with the stemming option turned on.
*Ctmt (ContentMeta):* basic text content + metadata + title + link anchors with the stemming option turned off.
*Ctmtstm (ContentMetaStem):* basic text content + metadata + title + link anchors with the stemming option turned on.

Two local dictionaries were then built for each category after stop word removal (using a stop list of 512 words provided by David Lewis [18]), with the option of stemming turned either on or off. Documents were represented by VSM where the weights were computed using TF-IDF. Information Gain (IG) was used to select the best features.

Three series of experiments were conducted. The documents are represented by (i) the basic content of HTML documents or (ii) the metadata (keywords and description), title and link anchors, or (iii) a combination of basic html content, metadata, title and link anchors, with the consideration of extra weight assigned to metadata, title and link anchors. Table 3 gives the number of features for each of the eleven classes (A to K) and for each choice of text representation.

For all 11 classes, the 'metadata + title + link anchors' representation (with or without stemming) requires considerably fewer features than the other representations, which all include 'basic text content', and the processing time required to construct the local dictionary is correspondingly far less. Thus, if all other factors were equal, the preferred choice of representation would be Meta or MetaStem.

## 4.4     Results and Interpretation

The different algorithms result in different performance depending on the features used to represent the documents.

The first set of experiments evaluates C4.5, NB and KNN, for texts represented using either (i) the basic content with the stemming option turned on or off, or (ii) meta data, title and link anchors with stemming option turned on or off, or (iii) a combination of basic content, metadata, title and link anchors with extra weight assigned to metadata, title and link anchors, with stemming option turned on or off.

Figure 1 and Figure 2 in Appendix 1 report, respectively, the performance accuracy and F1 measure on the test set of C4.5, NB and KNN for the different text representation options. They show that the use of stemming improves the performance of C4.5, NB and KNN for all the options of text representation. They also show that C4.5 outperforms NB and KNN for texts represented by basic content or metadata in both cases of stemming switched on or off. C4.5 and KNN do closely well for text represented by basic text content and metadata. Further, enhancing the basic content of texts with metadata improves the performance of all the classifiers. Figures 3, 4 and 5 in Appendix 1 report the average accuracy of C4.5, NB and KNN (respectively) on the test set for the different text representation options and different feature numbers. Information gain has been used to select the best 20, 50, and 100 words that have the highest IG in each local dictionary. The figures show that, for the different vector space model sizes, stemming improves the accuracy of the considered learning algorithms. They show also that choosing the best 20 features from the metadata representation for text degrades the performance of C4.5, NB and KNN considerably. However, choosing the best 100 features from the different text representations is competitive with the accuracy of the classifiers used with all the features. Also, using feature selection to reduce the feature space model gives a huge reduction in the learning time of the classifiers. Figures 6, 7 and 8 in Appendix 1 report the F1 measure of C4.5, NB and KNN (respectively) on test set with the different options of text representation and different feature numbers. They report similar conclusions to those of figures 3, 4 and 5.

## 5. CONCLUSION AND FUTURE WORK

In summary, a number of experiments were conducted to evaluate the performance of some well-known learning algorithms on hypertext data. Different text representations have been used and evaluated. We applied C4.5, NB and KNN to a dataset of HTML documents. Basic text content or metadata, title, and link anchors, or basic text content along with metadata, title and link anchors were used for text representation. Information Gain was used for feature selection to reduce the feature space dimension. The following conclusions can be drawn.

- The use of stemming helps C4.5, NB and KNN improve their performance over the testing set.
- The use of basic text content enhanced with weighted metadata (metadata + title + link anchors) improves the performance of the 3 classifiers.
- The use of IG as a feature selection technique did not improve the accuracy of the classifiers, but instead helped reduce the text processing and learning time needed.
- C4.5 outperforms NB and KNN for the different text representation options.
- The accuracy of C4.5 used with the stemmed metadata for text representation (case1) is competitive with that of C4.5 used with basic text content enhanced with weighted metadata as text representation (case 2). In particular, the processing and learning time for case 1 is much less than that of case 2.

The use of the extra information hidden in HTML pages improved the performance of the different classifiers. In future work, this extra information will be extended by including the information in the 'linked neighborhood' of each web page. As a next step, features from outgoing and ingoing links will be used to enhance the text representation and evaluate the classifiers. Experiments with different datasets should also be conducted before final conclusions can drawn.

# REFERENCES

[1] K.Bharat and A. Broader. A technique for measuring the relative size and overlap of public web search engines. In Proc. Of the 7$^{th}$ World Wide Web Conference (WWW7), 1998.

[2] H. Chen and S. Dumais. Bringing order to the web: automatically categorizing search results. In proceedings of CHI-00, ACM International Conference on Human Factors in Computing Systems, p 145-152, Den Haag, NL, 2000. ACM Press, New York, US.

[3] http://www.yahoo.com

[4] H. Oh, S. Myaeng, and M. Lee. A practical hypertext categorization method using links and incrementally available class information. In proceedings of the Twenty Third ACM SIGIR Conference, Athens, Greece, July 2000.

[5] J. Furnkranz. Exploiting structural information for text classification on the WWW. Proceedings of IDA-99, Third Symposium on Intelligent Data Analysis, pp 487-497, Amsterdam, NL, 1999.

[6] S. Slattery and T. Mitchell. Discovering test set regularities in relational domains. In Seventeenth International Conference on Machine Learning, June 2000.

[7] Y. Yang, S. Slattery and R. Ghani. A study of approaches to hypertext categorization. Journal of Intelligent Information Systems (Special Issue on Automatic Text Categorization) 18 (2-3) 2002, pp. 219-241.

[8] G.Attardi, A. Gulli, and F.Sebastiani. Automatic web page categorization by link and context analysis. In Proceedings of THAI'99, European Symposium on Telematics, Hypermedia and Artificial Intelligence, 1005-119, 1999.

[9] S.Chakrabati, B. Dom, and P. Indyk. Enhanced hypertext categorization using hyperlinks. Proceedings ACM SIGMOD International Conference on Management of Data, pages 307-318, Seattle, Washington, June 1998. ACM Press.

[10] C. Apte, F. Damereau, and S. Weiss. Automated learning of decision rules for text categorization. ACM trans.Information Systems, Vol.12, No.3, July 1994, pp. 233-251.

[11] A.Bensaid and N. Tazi. Text categorization with semi-supervised agglomerative hierarchical clustering. International Journal of Intelligent Systems, 1999.

[12] G. Salton and McGill. Introduction to Modern Information Retrieval. McGraw Hill, 1983.

[13] G. Salton and C. Buckley. Term weighting approaches in automatic text retrieval. Information Processing and Management, 24 (5), pp 513-523, 1988.

[14] Y.Yang and J.Pederson. A Comparative study on feature selection in text categorization. International Conference on Machine Learning (ICML), 1997.

[15] http://www-2.cs.cmu.edu/afs/cs.cmu.edu/project/theo-20/www/data/

[16] http://www.pedal.rdg.ac.uk/banksearchdataset/

[17] Y. Yang. An evaluation of statistical approaches to text categorization. Journal of Information Retrieval, 1999.

[18] D. Lewis. Feature selection and feature extraction for text categorization. Proceedings of Speech and Natural Language Workshop, 1992, pp. 212-217.

# Appendix 1

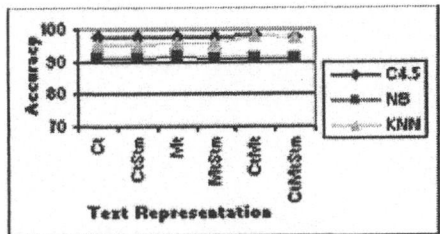

*Figure 1. C4.5, NB and KNN accuracy for different choices of text representation*

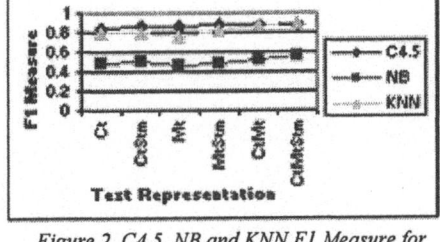

*Figure 2. C4.5, NB and KNN F1 Measure for different choices of text representation*

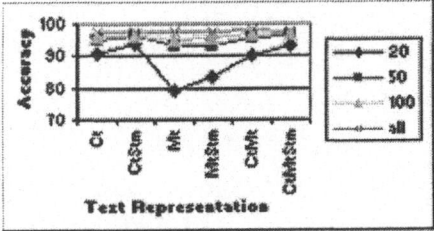

*Figure 3. C4.5 accuracy for different choices of text representation*

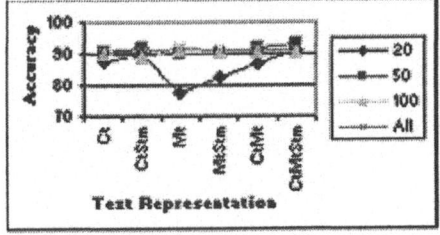

*Figure 4. NB accuracy for different choices of text representation*

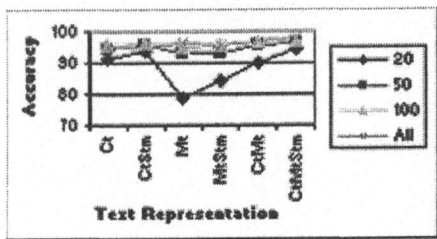

*Figure 5. KNN accuracy for different choices of text representation*

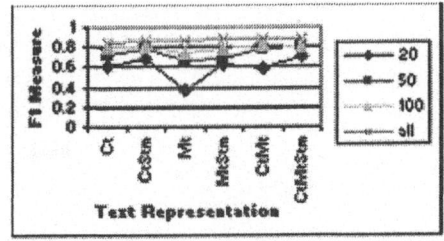

*Figure 6. C4.5 F1 Measure for different choices of text representation*

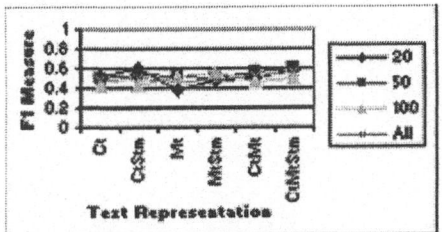

*Figure 7. NB F1 Measure for different choices of text representation*

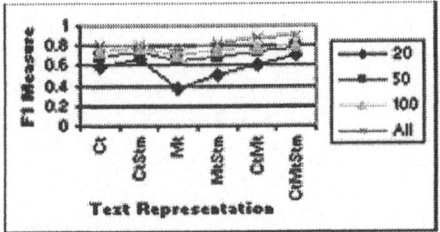

*Figure 8. KNN F1 Measure for different choices of text representation*

# INTRODUCING A STAR TOPOLOGY INTO LATENT CLASS MODELS FOR COLLABORATIVE FILTERING

Gabriela Polčicová
*Faculty of Informatics and Information Technologies*
*Slovak University of Technology, Ilkovičova 3, 81219 Bratislava, Slovakia*
polcicova@fiit.stuba.sk


Peter Tiňo
*School of Computer Science*
*University of Birmingham, Birmingham, B15 2TT, UK*
P.Tino@cs.bham.ac.uk

**Abstract**    Latent class models (LCM) represent the high dimensional data in a smaller dimensional space in terms of latent variables. They are able to automatically discover the patterns from the data. We present a topographic version of two LCMs for collaborative filtering and apply the models to a large collection of user ratings for films. Latent classes are topologically organized on a "star-like" structure. This makes orientation in rating patterns captured by latent classes easier and more systematic. The variation in film rating patterns is modelled by multinomial and binomial distributions with varying independence assumptions.

**Keywords:** collaborative filtering, latent variable models, visualization

## Introduction

When deciding which book to read, which film to watch, or which website to visit, people often rely on advise given by other people [3]. This is possible only inside small communities, where people know each other. In many situations we would like to automate that process. The method addressing the problem of making recommendations is collaborative filtering (CF) that leverages the existing preferences (ratings/profiles) of users in large comunities.

One approach to CF uses probabilistic modeling (e.g. LCM) to infer new recommendations. The main advantage of this approach is that it is able to automatically discover preference patterns in user profile data.

Besides producing new recommendations, the CF system can be used to understand the principal taste trends in the rating data by careful analysis of preference patterns extracted by LCM. Unfortunately, detailed examination of all latent classes is a very tiring and time consuming process. In this paper we suggest a way of addressing this problem: the latent space is endowed with a topological organization that enables us to visualize the common interest patterns in an easily accessible way. We study latent class models for user ratings with star topology.

The paper is organized as follows. In section 1 we describe LCMs for user ratings and in Section 2 we endow them with star topology. Section 3 is devoted to Expectation-Maximization (EM) algorithm for training the models. The experiments are described in section 4. The paper is concluded in section 5.

## 1. Latent Class Models for User Ratings

In this section we briefly describe latent class approach to modeling user ratings introduced in [3, 4]. We work with three sets: the set $\mathcal{U}$ of users, the set of films (items), $\mathcal{Y}$, and the set $\mathcal{V}$ of rating values that are used by users to evaluate films.

We would like to predict the rating $v_{u,y} \in \mathcal{V}$ given by a user $u \in \mathcal{U}$ to a film $y \in \mathcal{Y}$. With each triplet $(u, y, v_{u,y})$, either observed or just hypothetical, we associate a latent variable (class) $z_{u,y} \in \mathcal{Z} = \{1, 2, \ldots, K\}$ that "explains" why the user $u$ rates the film $y$ by $v_{u,y}$.

The latent variables $z \in \mathcal{Z}$ index "abstract" classes of users in two types of models:

- **Type I** – given a film $y$, all users from class $z$ tend to adopt the same rating pattern expressed through $P(v|y, z)$ over evaluations from $\mathcal{V}$. Given a user $u$ and a film $y$, the probability of vote $v$ is modeled as $P(v|y, u) = \sum_{z \in \mathcal{Z}} P(v|y, z)P(z|u)$, where $P(z|u)$ is the probability that the user $u$ "participates" in class $z$.

- **Type II** – all users from class $z$ tend to adopt the same preferences over the [rating, film] pairs $(v, y)$. Given a user $u$, the probability of a pair $(v, y)$ is modeled as $P(v, y|u) = \sum_{z \in \mathcal{Z}} P(v, y|z)P(z|u)$.

Classes $z$ express "common interest patterns" among the users found in the ratings [3] and $P(z|u)$ then represents to what extend the user $u$ participates in the common interest pattern $z$.

Given a set of observation triplets, free parameters of the model, $P(z|u)$ and $P(v|y,z)$, are determined by an EM procedure [3].

## 2. Introducing a Topology into Latent Class Models

We endow the latent classes with a topographic organization. In [5] we presented topographic organization of latent classes on a grid. In this paper we introduce a less tight star topology that organizes latent classes such that similar classes lie close to each other (on the same branch).

Topology is introduced into the latent space via the channel noise methodology [2]: for latent classes $z_1$ and $z_2$ lying close to each other, the probability $P(z_2|z_1) = P(z_1|z_2)$ of corrupting one into the other in the transmission process through a communication channel is high.

Latent classes are placed on the nodes of a hierarchical star (Figure 1 (a)). Star can be completely described by a triple $(L, b, \gamma)$, where $L$ is the number of levels of the star, $b = (b_1, \ldots, b_{L-1})$ is a vector of branching degrees $b_l$ for nodes on non-leaf levels $l = 1, \ldots, L - 1$. $\gamma \in (0, 1)$ is a parameter determining the strength of the connection between two connected nodes (channel noise). The channel noise probabilities $P(z_1|z_2)$ are shown in Figure 1 (b). Probabilities between non-connected nodes are 0.

It is convenient to work with two copies $\mathcal{Z}_Y$ and $\mathcal{Z}_Z$ of the latent space $\mathcal{Z}$. For each user $u \in \mathcal{U}$, the film-conditional ratings $v$ (type I) or pairs $(v, y)$ (type II) are generated as follows:

1  randomly generate a latent class index $z_Y \in \mathcal{Z}_Y$ by sampling the user-conditional probability distribution $P(\cdot|u)$ on $\mathcal{Z}_Y$.

2  transmit the class identification $z_Y$ through a noisy communication channel, and receive (a possibly different) class index $z_Z \in \mathcal{Z}_Z$ with probability $P(z_Z|z_Y)$.

3  randomly generate a film-conditional rating $v$ with probability $P(v|y, z_Z)$ (type I) or a pair $(v, y)$ with probability $P(v, y|z_Z)$ (type II).

The models for user ratings have now the following form:

$$P(z_Z|u) = \sum_{z_Y \in \mathcal{Z}_Y} P(z_Z|z_Y)P(z_Y|u), \tag{1}$$

$$P(v|y, u) = \sum_{z_Z \in \mathcal{Z}_Z} P(v|y, z_Z)P(z_Z|u) \qquad \text{[type I]} \tag{2}$$

$$P(v, y|u) = \sum_{z_Z \in \mathcal{Z}_Z} P(v, y|z_Z)P(z_Z|u) \qquad \text{[type II]} \tag{3}$$

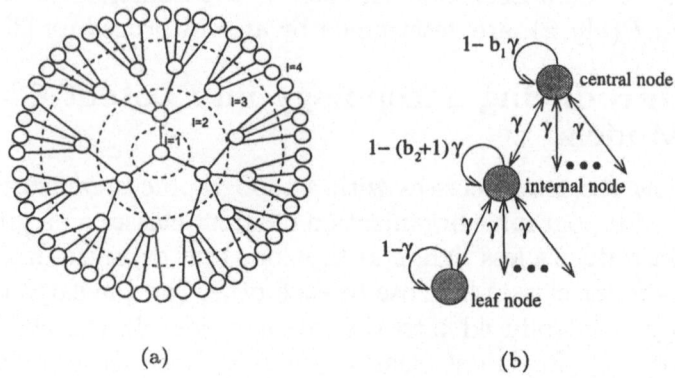

*Figure 1.* (a) An example of star topology of latent classes with four levels ($L = 4$). $b = (3, 4, 4)$. (b) Channel noise probabilities defining the star topology.

## 3. Parameter Estimation

Following [3], we denote by $\rho(v, y, z_Z)$ the probabilities $P(v|y, u)$ and $P(v, y|u)$ in type I and type II models, respectively.

To fit model parameters $P(z_Y|u)$ and $\rho(v, y, z_Z)$ to the observed data $\mathcal{D} = \{(u_1, y_1, v_1), ..., (u_N, y_N, v_N)\}$, we use EM algorithm [1] that maximizes likelihood of data $\mathcal{D}$ and iterates two steps - Expectation (E) and Maximization (M) - until convergence.

### 3.1 E-step

In the E-step, the algorithm computes the expected values of latent variables using the current values of the model parameters:

$$P(z_Y|\, y, u, v) = \frac{P(z_Y|u) \sum_{z_Z} \rho(v, y, z_Z) P(z_Z|z_Y)}{\sum_{z_Y'} P(z_Y'|u) \sum_{z_Z} \rho(v, y, z_Z) P(z_Z|z_Y')}, \tag{4}$$

$$P(z_Z|\, y, u, v) = \frac{\rho(v, y, z_Z) \sum_{z_Y} P(z_Z|z_Y) P(z_Y|u)}{\sum_{z_Z'} \rho(v, y, z_Z') \sum_{z_Y} P(z_Z'|z_Y) P(z_Y|u)}. \tag{5}$$

### 3.2 M-step

In the M-step, the algorithm re-estimates the model parameters by maximizing the expected complete data log-likelihood evaluated in the E-step. To derive the update equations, we need to determine the types of distributions for $P(z_Y|u)$ and $\rho(v, y, z_Z)$. It is natural to assume multinomial $P(z_Y|u)$. However, for $\rho(v,y,z_Z)$ we use either multinomial, or binomial distribution. Multinomial distribution simply models probabilities of occurrence of ratings $v$. In the other hand, binomial distribution respects the ordering of rating values $v^1$ and imposes the assumption of unimodal rating distribution. We work with the following models:

- type I

    - I-Mult: multinomial $P(v|y, z_Z)$,

    - I-Bin: binomial $P(v|y, z_Z)$ (respects ordering of ratings).

- type II

    - II-Mult: joint multinomial $P(v, y|z_Z)$,

    - II-IndM: we assume conditional independence of $v$, $y$ given $z_Z$: $P(v, y|z_Z) = P(v|z_Z)P(y|z_Z)$; both $P(y|z_Z)$ and $P(v|z_Z)$ are multinomials,

    - II-IndB: $P(v, y|z_Z) = P(v|z_Z)P(y|z_Z)$; $P(y|z_Z)$ is multinomially and $P(v|z_Z)$ is binomially distributed (respects ordering of ratings).

Update equation for $P(z_Y|u)$ is the same for all types of models:

$$P(z_Y|u) = \frac{\sum_{y \in \mathcal{Y}_u} P(z_Y|\, y, u, v_{u,y})}{|\mathcal{Y}_u|}. \tag{6}$$

### 3.2.1    I-Mult and II-Mult.    Update equations are:

$$P(v|\, y, z_Z) = \frac{\sum_{u \in \mathcal{U}_{v,y}} P(z_Z|\, y, u, v)}{\sum_{v'} \sum_{u \in \mathcal{U}_{v',y}} P(z_Z|\, y, u, v')} \qquad \text{[type I]} \tag{7}$$

$$P(v, y|\, z_Z) = \frac{\sum_{u \in \mathcal{U}_{v,y}} P(z_Z|\, y, u, v)}{\sum_{v',y'} \sum_{u \in \mathcal{U}_{v',y'}} P(z_Z|\, y', u, v')} \qquad \text{[type II]} \tag{8}$$

where $\mathcal{U}_{v,y} = \{u \in \mathcal{U}|\ (u, y, v) \in \mathcal{D}\}$ is the set of users that evaluated film $y$ with rating $v$.

### 3.2.2    II-IndM.    Update equations are given by:

$$P(y|z_Z) = \frac{\sum_{u \in \mathcal{U}_y} P(z_Z|\, y, u, v_{u,y})}{\sum_{y'} \sum_{u \in \mathcal{U}_{y'}} P(z_Z|\, y', u, v_{u,y'})}, \tag{9}$$

---

[1]i.e. it takes into account that ratings 4 and 5 are closer to each other than 1 and 5

$$P(v|z_Z) = \frac{\sum_y \sum_{u\in\mathcal{U}_{y,v}} P(z_Z|\ y,u,v)}{\sum_{v'} \sum_y \sum_{u\in\mathcal{U}_{yv'}} P(z_Z|\ y,u,v')}. \tag{10}$$

**3.2.3    II-IndB.**    Update equation for $P(y|z_Z)$ is the same as in eq. (9). $P(v|z_Z) = \binom{V}{v}p_{z_Z}{}^v(1-p_{z_Z})^{V-v}$ is a binomial distribution with mean $p_{z_Z}|\mathcal{V}|$ and shape parameter $p_{z_Z}$. Update equation for parameter $p_{z_Z}$ is given by:

$$p_{z_Z} = \frac{\sum_y \sum_{u\in\mathcal{U}_y} P(z_Z|\ y,u,v_{u,y})v_{u,y}}{V\ \sum_y \sum_{u\in\mathcal{U}_y} P(z_Z|\ y,u,v_{u,y})}. \tag{11}$$

**3.2.4    I-Bin.**    If $P(v|y,z_Z)$ is binomially distributed, then parameter $p_{z_Z,y}$ of the distribution is updated according to:

$$p_{z_Z,y} = \frac{\sum_{u\in\mathcal{U}_y} P(z_Z|\ y,u,v_{u,y})v_{u,y}}{V\sum_{u\in\mathcal{U}_y} P(z_Z|\ y,u,v_{u,y})}. \tag{12}$$

## 4.    Experiments

In this section we demonstrate latent class models with $K = 64$ latent classes and either star topology (STop) described by ($L = 4$, $b = (3,4,4)$, $\gamma = 0.15$) or no topology (NTop) with 64 independent latent classes. Models of types I and II are trained with different distribution models for $\rho(v,y,z_Z)$, as described in Section 3.2.

We experimented with *EachMovie dataset*[2] containing ratings for films. User ratings are expressed on a 6-point scale. We selected a set of 100 most rated films. The number of users that rated at least one film from the selected set was 60, 895.

We partitioned the set of ratings into two sets – training and test sets. The training set $\mathcal{D}$ is used to train the models and visualize the data. The test set $T$ is used for evaluation of generalization capabilities of the models *within the set of users contained in* $\mathcal{D}$. Similarly to [3], we applied *all but one protocol*: 1 randomly selected rating from each user having at least 10 ratings was assigned to the test set.

The rating models are trained on the training set $\mathcal{D}$. To initialize model parameters we run SOM with the same star topology on the data $\mathcal{D}$ (see [5]). After the initialization, models are trained with the EM algorithm[3] and data are visualized. We use perplexity $P =$

---

[2]http://www.research.compaq.com/SRC/eachmovie/
[3]typically the data likelihood given by the models leveled up after 50 iterations

$\exp\left[-\frac{1}{|T|}\sum_{(u,y,v_{uy})\in T}\log\rho(u,y,v)\right]$ of ratings on the training and test sets to compare the models.

## 4.1 Results

Tables 1 and 2 show perplexities of the models on training and test sets. For models of both types, perplexity of training data is smaller for multinomial distribution than for the binomial. In contrast, binomial distribution beats multinomial distribution on test data. This indicates that binomial distribution better regularizes the models by introducing less degrees of freedom (free parameters) and by imposing a unimodal structure on ordered rating values $v$. Models with unconstrained latent space (NTop) fit the training data better, but tend to overfit, as evidenced by better test set perplexities of models with imposed latent space topology (STop).

*Table 1.* Perplexity for training data.

|        | I-Mult | I-Bin | II-Mult | II-IndM | II-IndB |
|--------|--------|-------|---------|---------|---------|
| STop   | 2.86   | 3.62  | 159.28  | 157.79  | 191.04  |
| NTop   | 2.64   | 3.50  | 134.90  | 140.18  | 170.70  |

*Table 2.* Perplexity for test data.

|        | I-Mult | I-Bin | II-Mult  | II-IndM  | II-IndB |
|--------|--------|-------|----------|----------|---------|
| STop   | 6.77   | 4.25  | 1636.92  | 1245.50  | 517.11  |
| NTop   | 10.73  | 4.29  | 77243.87 | 33807.27 | 2353.47 |

## 4.2 Visualization

In this section we present some visualization plots of "common interest patterns" found by the models with star topology.

**4.2.1 Models of Type II.** Models of type II are suitable for visualizing the most probable films for each abstract class, i.e. films with largest $P(y|z) = \sum_v P(v,y|z)$. In order to understand to what degree are the films in particular classes similar, we present genre codes for latent classes in a hierarchical tree. Genre code for each class is made up from genres of 5 most probable films for that class. Genres[4] for films are taken from Internet Movie Database[5] and they are represented by abbreviations shown in Table 3. The size of each genre abbreviation in genre codes for classes is proportional to the number of films (among the 5 most probable films) of that genre.

*Table 3.*   Genre abbreviations.

| A: Action | C: Comedy | D: Drama | E: Western | F: Family |
|---|---|---|---|---|
| H: Horror | L: Classic | M: Musical | N: Animation | P: Crime |
| R: Romance | S: Sci-Fi | T: Thriller | U: Mystery | V: Adventure |
| W: War | Y: Fantasy | | | |

Figure 2 shows genre codes for classes of a model *STop II-IndB*. Topological organization of the classes according to the genres is clearly visible. The genre organization emerges naturally from the rating patterns in the data set and the imposed star (tree) topology on the latent classes.

**4.2.2    Models of Type I.**    For models of type I, it is possible to visualize the rating distribution $P(v|y, z)$ for each fixed film $y$, given the latent class $z$. By inspecting the latent-class-conditional rating distributions $P(\cdot|y, z)$, we can demonstrate that "similar" films tend to have similar rating distributions. For illustration purposes, we choose four films: two are *romantic comedies – Ghost* and *Pretty Woman*, one film is a *criminal horror – Silence of the Lambs*, the last film is a *criminal drama – Pulp Fiction*.

Figure 3 visualizes rating patterns for those films as modeled by *STop I-Bin*. They are almost identical for the two *romantic comedies* (Figures 3(a) and 3(b)) and very different from *criminal drama* in Figure 3(c). The two *crime* films lead to both similar and dissimilar patterns on parts of the tree (Figures 3(c) and 3(d)).

For example, users concentrated in class 3 of the fourth level[6] enjoy romantic comedies. In contrast, users represented by class 2 of the third level and classes 5-8, 25 and 27 of the fourth level tend to dislike them. Classes 2, 9, 20 and 33 of the fourth level represent users that like crimes. Class 22 on the fourth level represents a mixture of users that are attracted to both comedies and crimes.

---

[4]The film genres were not explicitly used in training the models.
[5]http://www.imdb.com
[6]All classes of each level are counted from the left to right.

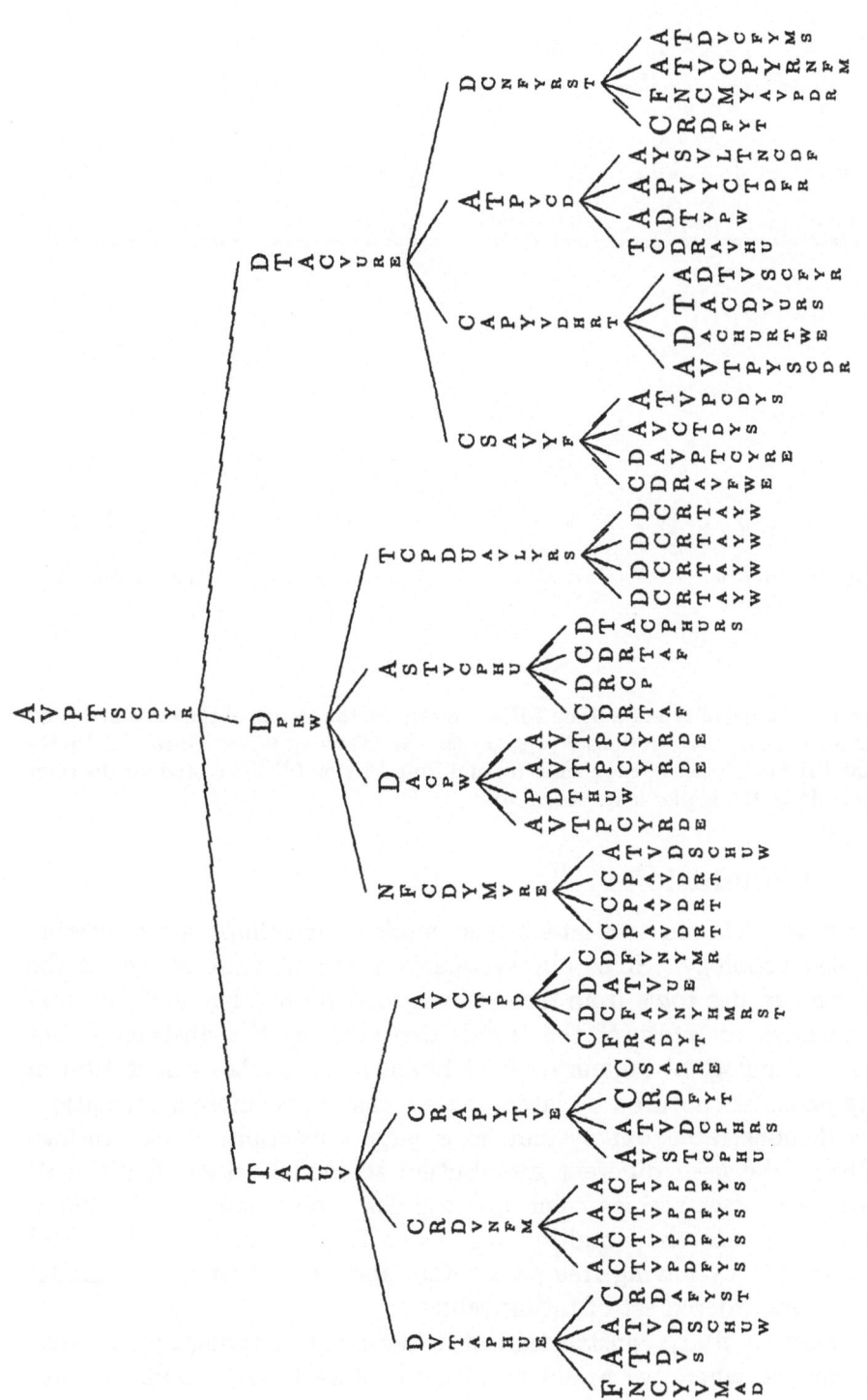

*Figure 2.* Model STop II-IndB: genre codes for latent classes.

302

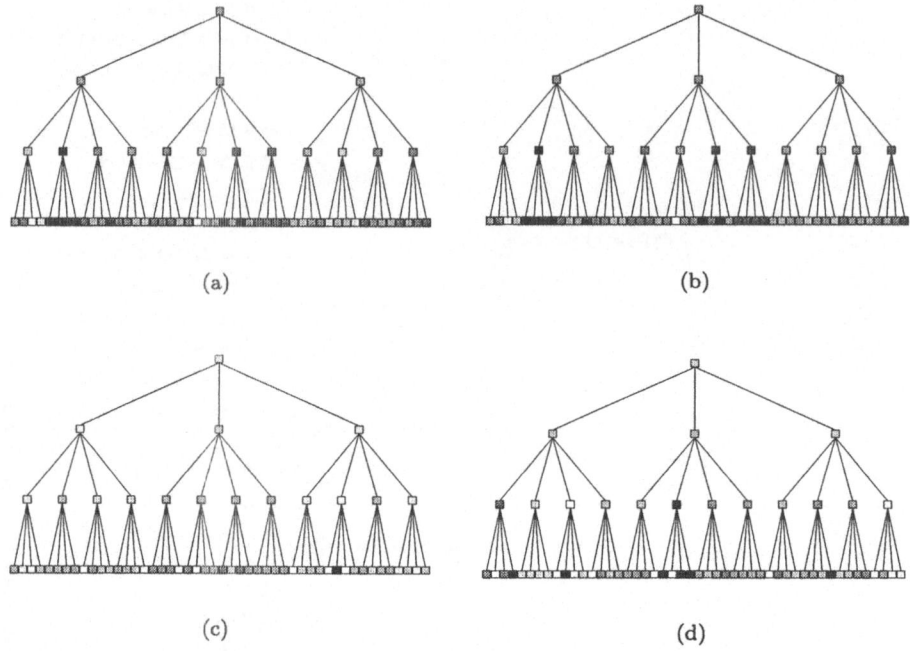

*Figure 3.* Model of type I – STop I-Bin. Shown are the means of the class-and-film-conditional rating distributions $P(v|y_*, z)$ for the following films: Ghost (a) Pretty Woman (b) The Silence of the Lambs (c) and Pulp Fiction (d). The brighter the color of the node is, the higher is its mean rating.

## 5.   Conclusions

We have endowed two latent class models for collaborative filtering with star topology. Since our system is a probabilistic model of the data, we can use tools from data mining and probability and information theories to interpret the trends captured by the abstract latent classes. Topological organization of latent space makes orientation in rating patterns captured by latent classes easier and more systematic.

We demonstrated our system on a large collection of user ratings for films. We used different distribution to model (class conditional) variations in user ratings. For star topology, binomial distribution is more appropriate than multinomial, since it adds an extra degree of regularization by having free parameters and by imposing a unimodal structure on ordered set of rating values.

We plan to study construction of a hierarchy of topographic latent class models, where we would be able to interactively "zoom in" into interesting user groups and rating patterns.

# Acknowledgments

This work was supported by the Slovak Grant Agency VEGA under under Grant No. VG 1/0162/03.

# References

[1] A.P. Dempster, N.M. Laird, and D.B. Rubin. Maximum likelihood from incomplete data via the EM algorithm. *Journal of the Royal Statistical Society, B,* 39(1):1–38, 1977.

[2] T. Hofmann. Probmap - a probabilistic approach for mapping large document collections. *Journal for Intelligent Data Analysis,* 4:149-164, 2000.

[3] T. Hofmann. Learning what people (don't) want. In L. De Raedt and P. Flach, editors, *12th European Conference on Machine Learning (ECML),* pages 214–225. Springer, 2001.

[4] T. Hofmann, and J. Puzicha Latent Class Models for Collaborative Filtering. *Proceedings of the International Joint Conference in Artificial Intelligence,* 1999.

[5] P. Tiňo, and g. Polčicová. Topographic organization of user preference patterns in collaborative filtering. *Neural Network World,* 13(3):311–324, 2003.

# DIALOGUING WITH AN ONLINE ASSISTANT IN A FINANCIAL DOMAIN: THE VIP-ADVISOR APPROACH

Josefa Z. Hernandez[1], Ana Garcia-Serrano[1] and Javier Calle[2]
[1]Technical University of Madrid, Spain; [2]Carlos III University, Madrid, Spain

Abstract: Virtual assistants are a promising business for the near future in the web era. This implies that the supporting applications have to be endowed with advanced capabilities to service offerings and to communicate with the users in a more direct and natural way. This paper presents the agent-based architecture of the virtual assistant and focuses on the dialogue module. The content exchange between the agents is based on *communicative acts* to cope with the complexity of unrestricted language used by human users communicating with online assistants. The assistant is capable to interact with users and to provide the right output through the exploitation of different information sources. The approach was applied and tested on the insurance field in the frame of the European research project VIP-Advisor[1].

Key words: Applications of Artificial Intelligence, Integration of AI with other Technologies, Speech and Natural Language Interfaces

## 1. INTRODUCTION

The work described in this paper is related with the development and deployment of a virtual assistant that advices the user for risk management in the insurance and finance field. With the aim of perform a satisfactory interaction with the user, the VIP-ADVISOR assistant main features are:

- *competent* by reasoning with a rule-based for financial knowledge and an additional case based knowledge source for information retrieval support
- *user-adapted*, given that automatically adopts to the user's needs

---

[1] VIP-ADVISOR project IST-2001-32440 (www.vip-advisor.fi.upm.es)

- *reactive and easy to use* through the use of natural language speech (translated into text with technologies from Linguatec GmbH)

The virtual assistant is capable of interacting with the user in natural language, adapt its recommendations to the requirements and characteristics of the customers and provide explanations along the interaction.

One of the main aspects of the interaction in the web is the capability of the web site of generating some kind of trust feeling in the user, just like in a person-to-person interaction. Things like understanding the aspects that influence the degree of the different risks identified, assisting the user in the final decision to get a product are not easy things to achieve in an online advisor site. Dialogue models and related techniques can play a crucial role in providing this kind of enhancement.

The paper is structured as follows: next section focuses on the design and deployment of the dialogue management performed by the Interaction Agent of the assistant; section 3 includes a brief description of the VIP-ADVISOR project. Section 4 is devoted to explain the semantic and pragmatic agents communication language that cover specific peculiarities of the dialogue and the domain. In section 5 is included some related work and, finally, in section 6 some conclusions are presented.

## 2. THE VIP-ADVISOR PROJECT

The virtual assistant developed in the VIP-Advisor project was conceived to support users on risk management. An existing 'conventional' online application for risk management was embedded in the virtual assistant as one of the information sources.

The architecture of the online assistant using an agent-based approach includes:

- An *Interface agent* responsible for the multimedia interaction with the users, supported by a graphical user interface, including a 3D avatar, speech recognition and synthesis, eventually with online translation, and natural language processing.
- *Intelligent agents,* identifying the information sources exploitable by the assistant, which are responsible for generating the information required by the user.
- An *Interaction agent* or interaction manager responsible for the coherent evolution of the user-system interaction, i.e. what to say and how to say it according to the context of the conversation and the recent dialogue.

The communication between the different agents performs briefly as follows: User demand is received by the Interface Agent through mouse clicks or with a spoken or written sentence. If this sentence is in German it is translated to English and delivered to the natural language processor.

The NL interpreter analyses the English sentences to extract both the content and the intention of the input and deliver it to the Interaction agent. In the case the input is given through mouse clicks the content and intention of these clicks is also extracted and delivered to the Interaction agent.

According to the input, the Interaction agent decides how to proceed with the conversation, identifying what kind of answer needs to be provided and which is the Intelligent Agent that has to generate it. In the VIP-Advisor system two Intelligent Agents are used: the existing risk management application and a case-based reasoner to deal with unexpected situations/queries. Once the response from the corresponding Intelligent Agent is received it is recorded –for future interactions- and delivered to the Interface Agent together with indications on how to provide it to the user (e.g. the kind of language to be used, the gestures of the 3D avatar). The Interface Agent distributes the output information among the different modules involved –the NL generator, the speech synthesizer, the 3D avatar and the graphical interface- and the response is displayed to the user.

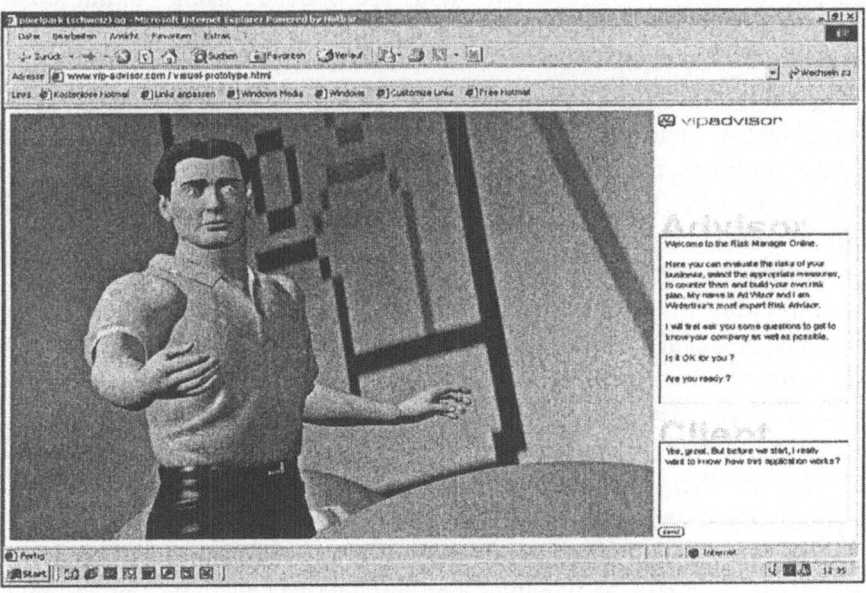

*Figure 1.* Screenshot of the VIP-Advisor prototype

The two prototype versions of the VIP-Advisor intelligent assistant have been developed with an agent-based architecture, where all agents are web services and the inter-agent communication is based upon SOAP protocol and the exchange of XML files. Single platforms for implementation and programming languages used are varied. In particular, the Interaction agent and the natural language modules of the Interface Agent were developed in Java and Ciao Prolog (www.clip.dia.fi.upm.es). Figure 1 shows a snapshot of the VIP-Advisor prototype.

From the previous description it can be guessed that a powerful language for the communication between all the agents has to be involved in this process. In the next section a detailed description of the communicative acts role in the semantic and pragmatic agents communication language is included.

## 3.    SEMANTIC AND PRAGMATIC AGENTS COMMUNICATION LANGUAGE

The system has to be able to manage the meaning of the user actions and the intentions that he/she has when performing those actions (clicking, speaking, writing, ...). These two items are encoded using communicative acts, an adapted and extended version of the Searle's theory of speech acts[1,2] to the e-services environment.

The communication between the agents is based on a set of communicative acts consisting in a set of fourteen of these structures distributed into six categories:

1. *Representative*, the emitter shows a link with the reality, sharing with his interlocutor;
2. *Directive*, the emitter should direct his interlocutors next actions;
3. *Authorizative*, the emitter wants his interlocutor to perform some action;
4. *Courtesy*, social conventions that both interlocutors should observe just for protocol, tuning, or politeness;
5. *Non-verbal*, Required for non-verbal social conventions such us connection; and
6. *Null*, when there is no effective communication but imply an intervention (such content empty discourses and pauses).

Several parameters characterise the occurrence of each dialogue act in a way that can be shown as 'labelled' communicative acts to be handled by the agents. A detailed description is provided in Garcia-Serrano and Calle[3].

The dialogue-based interaction approach applied is supported by a discourse model with a twofold dimension: informational and intentional. The informational approach establishes that the coherence of the discourse follows from semantic relationships between the information conveyed by successive utterances (inference-based approach as major computational tool). The intentional approach claims that the coherence of discourse derives from the communicative intention of both speakers and that mutual understanding depends on the capability to recognise those intentions (following speech act theories). The dialogue-based interaction applied also supports a genuine integration of semantics and pragmatics, since a good analysis of dialogue requires semantic representation (representation of the content of what the participants are saying) and pragmatic information (what kinds of communicative acts they are performing - asking/answering a question, making a proposal, ....-, what information is available to each speaker, what is the purpose behind their various utterances, etc.)

*Table 1*. Example of representative acts

| Parameters: | [t]: | type | Data: objective information |
| | | | Confirmation: bivaluated |
| | | | Suggest: subjective opinions |
| | [m]: | matter | Approve: confirms the subject |
| | | | Deny: negates the subject |
| | | | Identity: identifies the subject |
| | | | Feature: marks an attribute |
| | | | Has: ownership |
| | | | Interest: aim |
| | [s]: | subject | Product, User, System, Offer... |
| | [c]: | content | [ value | var=value ] |
| Inform | I'm AI: | | inform(data,identity,user,AI) |

According to the previous considerations, the Interaction Manager has three main responsibilities: (1) managing the evolution of the conversation in a coherent way which means keeping track of the on-going dialogue and deciding how to proceed next, (2) asking the corresponding Intelligent Agent to perform the necessary task to generate the information required by the user, and (3) delivering to the Interface Agent the required information together with indications on how to provide it.

Three modules support the Interaction Agent to undertake these responsibilities:

- *Dialogue manager* for controlling the evolution of the conversation. It records the state of the dialogue according to the active dialogue strategy, through a dialogue state component, and the intention or communicative goal that needs to be satisfied next, through a thread joint stack component.
- *Session model* for handling the static information of the interaction
- *Discourse maker* for generating the next intervention of the system, i.e. the stream of communicative acts to be delivered to the Interface Agent. It contains a task model for determining what the effects of a discourse

should be and how the external modules (i.e. the risk manager and/or case-based reasoner results) should contribute to the dialogue.

The general performance of the interaction agent is summarized in the following. During user's turn (in a dialogue), the interaction agent will be waiting for his action. Then, a stream of communicative acts (or several of them) will be delivered to the agent. If it is only a null act informing of a pause, or an act derived from the G.U.I. (if the user clicked on a menu, for example), or some verbal intervention interpreted by the Natural Language Interpreter. Anyway, the information carried by these communicative acts will be interpreted all the same.

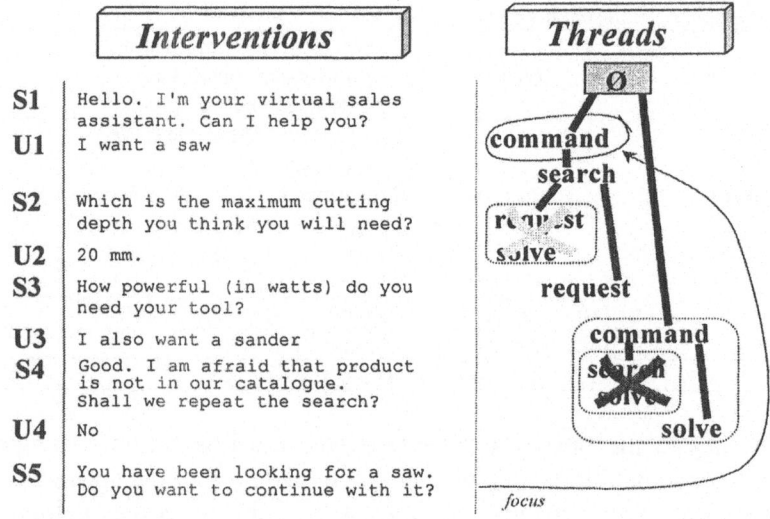

*Figure 2.* Threads management in an interaction example

Regarding the threads management, the intervention can follow the focused thread, any other previous thread, or originate a new one (initiative threads, or just 'initiatives'). Threads are arranged as a tree like structure, and leaf nodes should be closed with the inclusion of a 'solve' thread, which means that the thread of that branch has been satisfied (of course, the thread won't be erased, but 'faded'). Any interlocutor might at any moment 'jump' to a branch in the thread tree different than the focused one (a previous thread or a new one that is not a descendent of the focused thread, as example in figure 2).

In the example before intervention (S2) the intelligent agent has to provide a product identification. Since there were several of them, the discourse maker decides to create a new thread to obtain from the user more information (particularly, the desired cutting depth for that product) in order to refine the solution. So, entry point of the discourse maker changes (new focused thread), and this time, it has no need of external help for obtaining all needed contents, hence chooses some patterns for expressing its desired discourse.

Notice that the two intelligent agents are not the only ones that might pose an initiative. In fact, almost every component in the interaction could need to introduce initiatives. For example, the session model could need to reinforce the credibility of a context piece (whenever the use of the piece determines a certain threshold, and the credibility is under that minimum required). Then, this component should introduce an initiative for reinforcing the 'quality' of the information (that will probably lead to a subdialogue starting with the question 'this feature has this value, hasn't it?'). Even the very thread model could pose initiatives (when the 'quality' of a thread is under a predefined threshold).

The evaluation of the second prototype was performed using several scenarios, with different situations and related aspects to be addressed during Main results of the evaluation focusing on the dialogue management are:

- Only the 1 % of total interventions were buggy ones (cause user and system not to be attuned into the same plane of interpretation) and are always recovered through only the 1,52 % of total interventions.
- 9 % of total interventions were of no use (most of them due to doubts)
- The average number of steps performed through any intervention was 0,84 for the user and 1,51 for system's interventions. These results reveal quick progress of any dialogue.

Finally, some remarks about future improvements suggested by the evaluation are included. Although there were a few buggy interventions, intentional commitment should be attained for avoiding these situations. Even if the system directed dialogues were not very aggressive, the dialogue should be reinforced (avoiding user's 'acts of faith').

## 4. RELATED WORK

Much of the research in the area has been restricted to task oriented dialogue domains. However, even most advanced systems in interaction are far from achieving good pragma-linguistic levels. Different systems were implemented according a few of most relevant theories on pragmatics, with remarkable results.

Current approaches in dialogue modeling[4] have assumed goal related to introducing system participation in the dialogue. Thus user and system have 'autonomous' role in the interaction yet they need to be suitable attuned for success in attaining their common goals through joint action. In this regard three approaches for dialogue modelling are applied: dialogue grammars, plan-based models, and joint action theories applied to dialogue.

Late research on dialogue grammars for task-oriented dialogues try to combine conversational games models with powerful reasoning tools. An example provided by Pulman[5] proposes combining this technique with the reasoning power of the Bayesian networks either for the recognition/interpretation of the user moves, the planning of next moves (tactics) and the planning of next games (strategy).

In the plan-based models the system is endowed with the capability to interpret/understand user' action plans to achieve goals. One approach considers plans as long-term intentions the system aims to accomplish. Hence, the dialogue management will maintain a stack of system goals to attain, the so-called agenda proposed in Boye et al.[6]. Changing the plan for this agenda could pose different dialogue strategies. Another approach for plan-based models considers a plan always focused on a fixed task. Hence, interaction should be seen as a way for acquiring some information needed for the task and the state of the dialogue that determined by the information already acquired (or 'information state'). Satisfactory results have being obtained within this approach, being the more representative those from the IST projects Trindi and Siridus[7,8].

Finally, joint-action models are based upon the premise that a dialogue is feed by both talking entities, and that they have at least one common reference point, a commitment. Those joints have to be kept 'alive' by both entities with an acceptable level of certainty and efficiency, so they can refer to it. The previously mentioned IST projects Trindi and Siridus claim for the goodness of including such a "common ground" between user and system, and the Advice project applied it with satisfactory results.

Another example on the use of these models is the IBM MIND[9] (Multimodal Interpretation for Natural Dialog), with features as in the previous project NLSA system: multimodality, architectural, semantic structures. But the discourse level analysis is more complex, mainly based upon Grosz and Sidner[10] theories of intention and attention. It differentiate between two main discourse elements: the unit (intention partially developed within a turn) and the segment (full intention, developed through several turns, at least one). The segment will be composed of five attributes: Intention, Attention, Initiator, Addressee, and State. Also two types of discourse relations can be observed: structural relations (intention-sub intention structures), and transitional relations (transitions between conversation segments and between conversation units; they can be further sorted in two types, intention switch and attention switch respectively). These intentional structures (segments) will help to handle the dialogue structure, as observed in the figure, for attaining coherent dialogues.

Multimedia based systems are very well spread, and there exist several examples of successful use of agent-based technology as QuickSet[11]. This system stands for improving HCI by posing very efficient interfaces, using for example a pen on a tactile screen, but also quicker human interfaces to deal with verbal expression or pointing using a gesture recognizer.

Regarding the tasks a user might ask through interaction, they are always defined by the domain (often knowledge based). In anticipation of the forthcoming growth of the number of these tasks for most systems, an organization of them should be modeled along with the consequences their results could have for the interaction. Another open issue is the standardization of the activation of tasks (often performed by external agents), and the interpretation of the task results and the mechanisms to introduce them into the dialogue.

## 5. CONCLUSIONS

For attaining natural interaction with the user, specialized agents are needed to perform mayor tasks: the interface ones, the dialogue management and the intelligent decision making in order to generate/interpret the content of the communication. The proposed architecture is successful in this direction also for multi-user performance[12].

The development of an Interaction Agent able of performing any complete interaction within an specific domain is a very difficult task, so is necessary to separate, as in this work, the knowledge of how-to-interact and the rest of the (domain dependent) knowledge. The proposal for the interaction agent is based on the three components presented at section 3.

Next step should be done is the adaptability of the assistant to the different kind of users. A final open problem is to attain the independence of the domain and then the learning of the assistant from the available domain knowledge and available dialogue corpus.

## ACKNOWLEDGEMENTS

We would like to thank the ISYS research group at the Technical University of Madrid for their support during the design, development and deployment of the interaction agent and NL components of the interface agent, and everyone involved in the project VIP-ADVISOR.

# REFERENCES

1  N. Asher and A. Lascarides, 2003, *Logics of conversation* Cambridge University Press.
2  J. R. Searle, 1969, *Speech Acts: An Essay in the Philosophy of Language.* Cambridge University Press
3  A. García-Serrano, J. Calle, 2002, *A Cognitive Architecture for the Design of an Interaction Agent.* In: Cooperative Information Agents VI, LNAI 2446. Springer Verlag.
4  Cohen, P.R. *Dialogue Modeling.* Survey of the state of the art in Human Language Technology, 1997; chap. 6, pp. 234-240.
5  Pulman, S.G. *Conversational Games, Belief Revision, and Bayesian Networks.* In CLIN VII (7$^{th}$ Computational Linguistics in the Netherlands), 1997.
6  Boye, J., Wirén, M., Rayner, M., Lewin, I., Carter, D., Becket, R. *Language Processing Strategies and Mixed-Initiative Dialogues.* In IJCAI-99 Workshop on Knowledge and Reasoning in Practical Dialogue Systems, 1999.
7  Cooper, R., Larsson, S., 1998. *Dialogue Moves and Information States.* In Proceedings of the third IWCS. Tilburg, 1999.
8  Amores, J.G., Quesada, J.F. *Dialogue Moves for Natural Command Languages.* Procesamiento del Lenguaje Natural, 27, pp. 81-88. Jaén (Spain), 2001.
9  Chai, J. Pan, S., Zhou, M. MIND: *A Context-based Multimodal Interpretation Framework in Conversational Systems.* In Natural, Intelligent and Effective Interaction in Multimodal Dialogue Systems, Eds. O. Bernsen , L. Dybkjaer and J. van Kuppevelt; Kluwer Academic Publishers, 2003.
10 Grosz B. and Sidner C. *Attention, intention and the structure of discourse,* Computational linguistics, V12, N3, 1986
11 Cohen, P.R., Johnston, M., McGee, D.R., Oviatt, S.L., Pittman, J., Smith, I., Chen, L., and Clow, J. (1997) QuickSet: Multimodal interaction for distributed applications, in the Proceedings of the Fifth International Multimedia Conference (Multimedia '97), ACM Press: Seattle, WA, pp. 31-40
12 J. Correas, F. Bueno, D. Teruel, A. García-Serrano, An Agent-based Architecture for Multi-user Applications. In: Challenges in Open Agent Systems, AAMAS'02, Bologna, Italy, July 2002.

# AN AGENCY FOR SEMANTIC-BASED AUTOMATIC DISCOVERY OF WEB-SERVICES

Simona Colucci,[1] Tommaso Di Noia,[1] Eugenio Di Sciascio,[1] Francesco M. Donini,[2] Marina Mongiello,[1] Giacomo Piscitelli,[1] and Gianvito Rossi[1]

[1] *Politecnico di Bari. Via Re David, 200, 70125 Bari. Italy*\*
{ s.colucci, t.dinoia, disciascio, mongiello, gv.rossi, piscitel } @poliba.it

[2] *Università della Tuscia. Via S. Carlo 32, 01100 Viterbo. Italy*
donini@unitus.it

**Abstract**     With the evolution of Web service technology, services will not only become increasingly sophisticated, but also move into the area of business-to-consumer and peer-to-peer interactions. Because of todays wide variety of services offered to perform a specific task, there is a need for mediation infrastructures able to support humans or agents in the eventual selection of appropriate services. It is a common opinion that such issues should be solved adopting semantically rich unambiguous descriptions. Hence, ontologies should be used to describe services, to ease their discovery and selection. In order to perform such a selection, a matchmaking procedure, based on semantic descriptions similarity, is needed. Technologies developed for the Semantic Web based on theoretical studies on Artificial Intelligence, particularly on Description Logics, can help in this sense. As the Semantic Web is conceived as an extension of the current one, technologies developed explicitly for they both must be used synergically in order to provide a semantic layer to approaches such as UDDI registries, using OWL formatted descriptions. In this paper we present a framework for discovery of services, stored in an UDDI registry, which exposes a description whose semantic can be modeled using OWL-DL based formalism. In order to perform this task, methodologies to compute semantic differences between two descriptions and non-standard inference services have been investigated and exploited in an implemented system.

## 1.     Introduction

The discovery process of a Web Service can be defined as: "The act of locating a machine-processable description of a Web service that may have been

\*Partial funding provided by projects PON CNOSSO and MS3DI

previously unknown and that meets certain functional criteria" [Web Services Glossary, 2003]. The previous definition points out that finding a web service requires the identification through a description modeled using a machine-processable language. It is also emphasized that the only constraint needed on the description semantics is a functional one. In [OWL-S overview, 2003] automatic web service discovery is introduced as: "Automatic Web service discovery involves the automatic location of Web services that provide a particular service and that adhere to requested constraints. [...] Currently, this task must be performed by a human who might use a search engine to find a service, read the web pages, and execute the service manually, to determine if it satisfies the constraints". In the latter definition, the human interposition required to prune the searching space, is highlighted: "read the web pages". During such a pruning process, a user has to decide how good the service is with respect to what s/he is looking for. In other words, the user bears the burden to decide how the meaning (semantics) of the available services description is similar to the searched one, and in the presence of several available services sort them some way.

Automation of the web services discovery process requires as a first step providing service descriptions –what the service actually offers– that have to be well defined, machine understandable and processable. It is a common opinion that such issues should be solved adopting semantically rich clear descriptions, so ontologies should be used to describe services to ease their discovery and selection [S.A.McIlraith and Martin, 2003].

Because of todays wide variety of services offered to perform a specific task, there is a need for mediation infrastructures able to support humans or agents in the eventual selection of appropriate services. A semantic-based matching mechanism is then needed, based on the automatic analysis of descriptions similarity. This process is usually called *matchmaking*. Several recent works formalize with Description Logics (DLs) the matchmaking of descriptions (see the Realted work section for more detail). DLs, in fact, allows to model structured descriptions of supplies and demands as concepts, usually sharing a common ontology. Furthermore DLs allow for an open-world assumption. Incomplete information is admitted, and absence of information can be distinguished from negative information.

Usually, standard reasoning services of a DL system — subsumption and (un)satisfiability — are employed to determine a match. In brief, if a supply is described by a concept $S$ and a demand by a concept $D$, unsatisfiability of the conjunction of $S$ and $D$ noted as $S \sqcap D$ identifies the incompatible proposals, satisfiability identifies potential partners — that still have to agree on underspecified constraints — and subsumption of $S$ and $D$ noted as $S \sqsubseteq D$ means that requirements on $D$ are completely fulfilled by $S$.

As a matter of fact the flat classification into compatible and incompatible matches can be of little help in the presence of, say, some hundred compatible proposals. In previous works [Di Noia et al., 2003b; Di Noia et al., 2003c; Di Noia et al., 2003a] we introduced a logic-based formal framework and reasonable algorithms to classify and rank matches into classes, *i.e.*, *Exact match:* all requested characteristics are available in the description examined;*Potential match:* some part of the request is not specified in the description examined;*Partial match:* some part of the request is in conflict with the description examined.

The algorithms are modified versions of the structural subsumption algorithm originally proposed in [Borgida and Patel-Schneider, 1994] and compute a distance between each description w.r.t. a requested service according to the following criteria. *Potential match*: how much of the request is not specified in the description examined. *Partial match*: how much of the request is in conflict with the description examined. Notice that an *Exact match* can obviously be considered a special case of potential match where subsumption is true.

In this paper we present our semantic-based framework, based on Description Logics formalization and reasoning, and its deployment in a prototype, which overcomes simple subsumption matching of services descriptions, providing information on their similarity and allowing services classification and ranking with reference to a given service request.

The system embeds an adapted NeoClassic system, which communicates via DIG, and carries out service discovery through matchmaking of the exposed service descriptions with requested ones. With reference to the well-known triangle diagram for web-services interaction our system plays the role of *Discovery Agency*.

The remaining of the paper is organized as follows. Next Section recalls some of the relevant literature. In Section 3 we briefly revise basics of description logics and our approach to description matching using description logics. In Section 4 we present our Discovery Agency and its operating mode. Concluding remarks close the paper.

## 2. Related Work

The Retsina Multiagent infrastructure [Sycara et al., 2003] includes a matching agent [Sycara et al., 2002] and [Paolucci et al., 2002b] with a language, LARKS, specifically designed for agent advertisement. No ranking is presented but for what is called relaxed match, which basically reverts again to a free-text similarity measure. So a basic service of a semantic approach, such as inconsistency check, seems unavailable with this type of match. Standard Information retrieval techniques have been also used in the GRAPPA matchmaking framework [Veit et al., 2001]. An extension to the approach in [Paolucci et al., 2002b] is proposed in [Li and Horrocks, 2003] where two new levels for service profiles matching are introduced. JADE agent platform for semantic web services discovery is used there on a test ontology based on DAML-S. The approach presented does not introduce a ranking method to measure proximity of service descriptions. In [Di Sciascio et al., 2001] an initial setting for logical matchmaking was presented in a person-to-person framework, based on sub-sumption matchmaking. In [Gonzales-Castillo et al., 2001] and [Trastour et al., 2002] an initial matchmaking framework was proposed, which operated on ser-vice descriptions in DAML+OIL and was based on the FaCT reasoner. IBM's Websphere-SilkRoad matchmaking environment is based on a matchmaking engine that describes supplies / demands as properties and rules. Matching is accomplished by simply comparing properties and verifying rules. No no-tion of distinction between full, partial potential and inconsistent matches are present [Hoffner et al., 2000]. A similar approach, with descriptions defined in XML and again a rule based decision system is in [Casati and Shan, 2001]. In [Ströbel and Stolze, 2002] an extension to the original Websphere match-maker is proposed, which introduces users' specification of negotiable con-straints when no total match is available. Also in [Benatallah et al., 2003] web services matchmaking was tackled. An approach was proposed, which is based on the Difference operator in DLs, followed by a set covering op-eration optimized using hypergraph techniques. Anyway, to the best of our knowledge there is no algorithm able to compute an exact Concept Differ-ence in a DL endowed of the negation constructor. In [Di Noia et al., 2003c] a logic based approach to matchmaking in an e-marketplace, which allows to categorize and rank matches is presented. Its initial deployment also in a web-service-oriented system is reported in [Colucci et al., 2003b]. In [Di Noia et al., 2003a; Colucci et al., 2003a] novel DL services, namely Concept Abduc-tion and Concept Contraction are proposed in the framework of e-marketplaces matchmaking to overcome limitations of presently available inferences.

## 3.    Description Logics for Semantic Discovery

Description Logics (DLs) [Baader et al., 2002] are a family of logic for-malisms for knowledge representation. We assume readers be familiar with them and just provide some insight into the specific constructs and system we adopt. Several DL-based reasoning systems have been implemented, such as Loom, Kris, FAcT, Racer, among others. Our system embeds a modified version of CLASSIC system [Borgida and Patel-Schneider, 1994]. Although CLASSIC DL is not very expressive w.r.t. other proposed systems, its lan-guage has been designed with the goal to be as expressive as possible while still admitting polynomial-time inferences. It manages an $\mathcal{ALN}$ (Attributive Language with unqualified Number restrictions) DL. Constructs allowed in an

$\mathcal{ALN}$ DL are:

A *atomic concepts*.Sets of objects.

$\top$ *universal concept*. All the objects in the domain.

$\bot$ *bottom concept*. The empty set.

$\neg A$ *atomic negation*. All the objects not belonging to the set represented by $A$.

$C \sqcap D$ *intersection*. The objects belonging both to $C$ and $D$.

$\forall R.C$ *value restriction*. All the objects participating to the $R$ relation whose range are all the objects belonging to $C$.

$(\geq n R)|(\leq n R)$ *unqualified number restrictions*. Respectively the minimum and the maximum number of objects participating in the relation $R$.

The CLASSIC system uses a $simple - TBox$ in order to express the relations among objects in the domain. With a $simple - TBox$ in all the axioms (for both inclusion and definition) the left side is represented by a concept name. As for each atomic concept only one axiom is allowed, in the CLASSIC system, it is possible to use a normal form and each $C$ concept has an equivalent normal form as $C_{names} \sqcap C_{\sharp} \sqcap C_{all}$, in which $C_{names}$ is a conjunction of names, $C_{\sharp}$ of number restrictions, and $C_{all}$ of universal role quantifications. Thanks to the normal form, the management of the hierarchical structure of an ontology, within its nested levels, is possible without traversing the semantic graph represented by the axioms.

Matchmaking is a process by which given an object ($O$) belonging to a set, a sub-set is searched, whose elements share some characteristics with $O$, *i.e.*, match $O$. Obviously, in our setting, objects to be found are web-services descriptions, based on a request submitted to a facilitator. In previous works [Di Noia et al., 2003b; Di Noia et al., 2003c] we introduced a logic-based formal framework to classify and rank matches into classes, *i.e.*, *Exact match:* all characteristics in the requested object are available in the offered one; *Potential match:* some characteristics in the requested object are not specified in the offered one; *Partial match:* some characteristics in the requested object are in conflict with the offered ones. In order to perform the matchmaking process, we identified some properties a facilitator should have.

*[Open-world descriptions]* The absence of a characteristic in the description of an offered or requested object should not be interpreted as a constraint of absence, instead it should be considered as a "don't care for the moment".

*[Non-symmetric evaluation]* A matchmaking system may give different evaluations depending on whether it is trying to match $O$ with $R$, or $R$ with $O$ — *i.e.*, depending on who is going to use this evaluation.

If requested and offered objects are modeled using a logic, then objects with the same meaning should have the same ranking, independently of their syntactic descriptions.

*[Syntax independence in ranking matches]* A ranking of matches is *syntax independent* if for every pair of offered objects $O_1$ and $O_2$, requested object $D$,

and ontology $\mathcal{T}$, when $O_1$ is logically equivalent to $O_2$ then $O_1$ and $O_2$ have the same ranking score for $R$, and the same holds also for every pair of logically equivalent requested object $R_1$, $R_2$ with respect to every available one $O$. In order to show the relation between ranking and implications, let us consider a description with sets of words. Let $R$ be a requested object and $O_1$, $O_2$ be two offered objects defined as follows:

$$R \quad = \quad \{computer, intel, hard\_disk, LCDmonitor\}$$
$$O_1 \quad = \quad \{computer, intel, browser, linux\}$$
$$O_2 \quad = \quad \{computer, intel, browser, linux, word\_processor\}$$

In this case, the characteristics that $O_2$ adds to $O_1$ are irrelevant for $R$. Hence, whatever the rank for $O_1$, the one for $O_2$ should be the same. If instead we let

$$O_3 = \{computer, intel, browser, linux, LCDmonitor\}$$

then $O_3$ should be ranked better than $O_1$ since it adds a characteristic required by $R$.

*[Monotonicity of ranking potential matches over subsumption]* A ranking of potential matches is *monotonic over subsumption* whenever for every requested object $R$, for every pair of offered objects $O_1$ and $O_2$, and ontology $\mathcal{T}$, if $O_1$ and $O_2$ are both potential matches for $R$, and $\mathcal{T} \models (O_2 \sqsubseteq O_1)$, then $O_2$ should be ranked either the same, or better than $O_1$, and the same should hold for every pair of requested objects $R_1$, $R_2$ with respect to an offered one $O$. The point of view is flipped over when turning to partial matches. In such matches we already have some characteristics in conflict between $R$ and $O$; adding new characteristic to $R$ may only make the match worse than before (introducing new conflicting characteristic) or keep it the same (if new characteristic are not in conflict).

*[Antimonotonicity of ranking partial matches over implication]* A ranking of partial matches is *antimonotonic over implication* whenever for every requested object $R$, for every pair of offered objects $O_1$ and $O_2$, and ontology $\mathcal{T}$, if $O_1$ and $O_2$ are both partial matches for $R$, and $\mathcal{T} \models (O_2 \sqsubseteq O_1)$, then $O_2$ should be ranked either the same, or worse than $O_1$, and the same should hold for every pair of requested objects $R_1$, $R_2$ with respect to an offered one $O$.

In the following we briefly illustrate the behavior of the algorithms we adopt in our system (for a complete description see [Di Noia et al., 2003c]). Given a requested object $R$ and an offered one $O$ we have a *potential* match if $R \sqcap O$ is satisfiable in $\mathcal{T}$, *i.e.*, the properties of neither concepts exclude the other. The *rankPotential* algorithm takes as inputs two concepts to be matched *i.e.*, $R$ vs. $O$, in normal form, such that $R \sqcap O$ is satisfiable and returns a score $n$. The algorithm adds to $n$ the number of concept names in $R$ that are not among the concept names of $O$ and number restrictions of $R$ that are not implied by those of $O$ and for each universal role quantification in $R$ adds to $n$ the result of a recursive call. A total match, *i.e.*, concept implication, yields a $n = 0$ score, while $n \geq 0$ of $O$ w.r.t. $R$, *i.e.*, the score increases (worsens) as the two descriptions are, though still compatible, more different. Notice the rationale of the approach, which penalizes generic descriptions, which in simple subsumption matching would be unfairly advantaged, as the algorithm ranks better more specific descriptions of $O$ matching $R$. It can be proved the algorithm is syntax independent, and monotonic over subsumption. Also notice that *rankPotential* can be used to compute a metric for the length of a concept. In fact the length of a concept $R$ can be weight up as the score returned by *rankPotential* algorithm when $O = \top$. Given a requested object $R$ and an offered one $O$ we have a *partial* match if $R \sqcap O$ is unsatisfiable in $\mathcal{T}$, *i.e.*, some of the properties of concepts are in conflict. In the *rankPartial* algorithm we are hence looking for inconsistencies. Also this time the algorithm takes as input two concepts in normal form, but this time the score accounts for inconsistencies.

The basic idea of the Semantic Web initiative is to structure information with the aid of markup languages, based on the XML language, such as RDF and RDFS (http://www.w3.org/RDF/), DAML+OIL (www.daml.org/2001/03/)and more recently OWL [McGuinness et al., 2002]. These languages have been conceived to allow for representation of machine understandable, unambiguous, description of web content through the creation of domain ontologies, and aim at increasing openness and interoperability in the web environment. A subset of the OWL-DL language is the obvious candidate for a framework based on DLs, as we propose in the following section.

## 4.    Discovery Agency

The theoretical framework summarized in the previous section has been deployed in a complete Discovery Agency. The agency, which is a web service itself, exposes a SOAP over HTTP interface.

The system carries out two main activities: publication of web-services and semantic search on published web-services. To this aim it exploits available standards such as UDDI (Universal Description, Discovery and Integration) (www.uddi.org), which defines a facilities set supporting description and discovery of Web Services providers, Web Services, and technical access interfaces to Services trough a structured registry and UNSPSC (United Nations Standard Products and Services Code) (www.unspsc.org), a wide openstandard developed and maintained by *Dun & Bradstreet* to categorize families of services (and consequently, in our approach, domain ontologies). UDDI aims to define a facilities set supporting description and discovery of Web Services providers, Web Services itself, and technical access interfaces to Services. UDDI uses widespread standards such as HTTP, XML, XML Schema and SOAP, providing a set of functions allowing one to register companies, services and their access information, to modify or cancel registrations and to search in the registrations database. The deployment of a Web Service is made up of three phases: *registration of the provider as company*; *deployment of a description of provided service*; *deployment of service invocation information*. These information are usually grouped in categories: *white pages*(Businesses), *yellow pages*(Services), *green pages*(technical information). User may search a Service, then, by company or by capability. UDDI Registries are available on the Web and are themselves Web Services: the user have to know access information to a given UDDI to use it. Business UDDI Registries store in their records four types of knowledge: *businessEntity*: non technical information about providers (white pages); *businessService*: non technical information about provided capabilities (yellow pages); *bindingTemplate*: technical information about services (green pages); *tModel*: Service access details (depending on *bindingTemplate*). UDDI provides also API(Application Programming Interfaces) for information and Services search(Inquiry API) and deployment(Publishing API). UNSPSC provides a product classification, for E-commerce purpose, useful to identify the category of a selling item (and then of the selling item web service). It helps us to search and localize Services identifying suppliers of given product or service. Searching by code avoids the shortcomings of textual retrieval: results of searching process are Services providing capabilities classified under the given code and not irrelevant Services whose name contains the searched product. UNSPSC is a hierarchical classification made up of four levels. Each level include a two digits numeric code and a textual description, as follows: *Segment: identifies the market segment of a product*; *Family: identifies a universally recognized product category*; *Class: identifies a group of products with the same functionality or usage; Commodity: identifies a group of equivalent products*.

Obviously the added value we pursue is that, having obtained a subset of the search space using UNSPSC categorization, a semantic match of users request with available web-services description is possible.

## MAMAS

The core module of the discovery agency is the MAtchMAker Service: MAMAS. It embeds a version of the original NEOCLASSIC the C++ version of CLASSIC modified in order to perform the matchmaking functionalities. The interface exposed by MAMAS is based on DIG 1.0 specifications [Bechhofer et al., 2003] for an $\mathcal{ALN}$ Description Logic. Hence, through a *tell* and *ask* mechanism it is able to dynamically load an ontology, request web service description and offered web service description stored in the UDDI registry, as DL individuals, and return the matchmaking results.

MAMAS behavior can be simply explained with the aid of an example. Suppose to have two published web services offering rental service:

$ws1 = rent \sqcap \forall related\_to.(bedroom \sqcap \forall contains\_bed.wedding\_bed$
$\sqcap \forall is\_contained.sea\_house) \sqcap \forall available.summer \sqcap$
$\forall has\_price.((\geq 200\ euro) \sqcap (\leq 350\ euro))$
$ws2 = rent \sqcap \forall related\_to.(bedroom \sqcap \forall is\_contained.mountain\_house \sqcap$
$\forall has\_appliances.TV \sqcap VCR \sqcap Internet)$

$ws1$ could be a good choice for room finding if you want to spend your summer holiday in a site near the sea; on the other hand $ws2$ offers rooms with accessories in houses sited on the mountains. Now we present two possible users of rental services: a human being looking for a double room in a site near the sea

$hb = rent \sqcap \forall related\_to.(double\_room \sqcap \forall is\_contained.$
$(house \sqcap \forall is\_located.sea)) \sqcap \forall available.august$
$\sqcap \forall has\_price.(\leq 300\ euro)$

and the personal software agent of a touristic agency looking for particular rooms available in June in order to compose "all inclusive" supplies:

$sa = rent \sqcap \forall related\_to.(bedroom \sqcap \forall is\_contained.apartment$
$\sqcap \forall has\_appliance.fully\_furnished) \sqcap \forall available.june$
$\sqcap \forall has\_price.(\leq 300\ euro)$

It is easy to observe that in both cases, $ws1$ and $ws2$ do not completely satisfy $hb$ and $sa$. Nevertheless, $ws1$ is a good solution for $hb$, and both $ws1$ and $ws2$ are good solutions for $sa$, while $ws2$ offers a service which is in conflict with the one serched by $hb$. MAMAS catches this behavior and, computing both $hb$ and $sa$ lengths, provides the following results:

- for $hb$:
  $ws1$ is a **potential** match with a *8%* of mismatch degree
  $ws2$ is a **partial** match with a *2%* of incompatibility degree

- for $sa$:
  $ws1$ is a **potential** match with a *21%* of mismatch degree
  $ws2$ is a **potential** match with a *15%* of mismatch degree

The DIG interface for NeoClassic is provided by the NEODIG Java servlet. The DIG standard is basically an XML Schema describing the language used to interact with a DL reasoner, in order both to introduce new knowledge and to query a DL knowledge base, using HTTP POST requests. The DIG standard allows only qualified number restriction ($\mathcal{Q}$) and not unqualified number restriction ($\mathcal{N}$), such as the one supported by CLASSIC, in the <language> TAG there are generic <atMost/ > and <atLeast/ >. It is well known that an unqualified number restriction is reducible to a qualified number restriction. In fact $(\geq 2 R) = (\geq 2R).\top$ and $(\leq 2 R) = (\leq 2R).\top$.

As DIG was thought for standard DL inference we added auxiliary TAG to perform the **matchMake** ask. A matchmaking request, identified by an id, of a description *I1* versus another description *I2* is:

```
<matchMake  id="q">
          <individual name="I1"/>
          <individual name="I2"/>
</matchMake>
```

where *I1* is the description of an offered web service, stored in the registry, and *I2* is the description of the searched one. The reply includes the category type of match obtained, *i.e.*, potential –no conflict– or partial –elements in conflict– and the score determined for the match. For potential match:

```
<matchMake  id="q">
          <type name="rankPotential"/>
          <result num="potentialScore"/>
</matchMake>
```

for a partial match:

```
<matchMake  id="q">
          <type name="rankPartial"/>
          <result num="partialScore"/>
</matchMake>
```

The Knowledge Bases (Kbs) Repository contains ontologies, written using a subset of OWL-DL, representing knowledge domains corresponding to UN-SPSC items. A classification of services within a taxonomy is useful to limit the searching space of the requested service, *i.e.*, the domain of the service. An issue that arose was whether to build an ontology for each item in the taxonomy or to build a single ontology embedding the whole taxonomy. In the former case there would be about 10'000 ontologies related to each other, in the latter one there would be one ontology with a huge number of concepts and roles. Both cases are not easily manageable. Trading-off pros and cons in our approach, we assume the development of an ontology for each *Family* level in UNSPSC.

## Web Service Publication

A typical problem in knowledge management systems is how to expose the knowledge to a human user, in a way as friendly as possible in order to keep a high degree of flexibility. To face this issue, once the domain has been identified via the UNSPSC code, if the user interacts using a browser, the system sends an applet to guide the composition of the description both to publish or

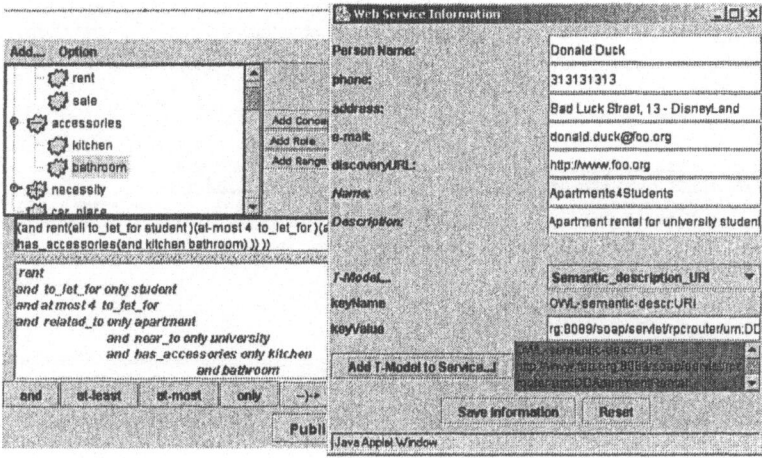

*Figure 1.*    Graphical User Interface during web service publication.

to search a service description. The applet loads the corresponding domain ontology and the user is guided in the description of the service. The composition area of the GUI is divided in: 1. an area diplaying the whole concepts taxonomy; 2. a list which is dynamically populated as soon as a concept is selected (The list items are the role whose domain is the selected concept); 3. a list populated by the concept which are the range of the selected role. The description composition is supported by a translation of the DL expression into a format closer to the human language, as shown in Figure 1. Each Web Service published in the UDDI registry, must expose both *setDescription()* and *getDescription()* methods. These methods are invoked via a SOAP RPC. With the former method, the OWL-DL formatted version of the description is binded to the Web Service, with the latter one such description is returned. The publication of a web-service in our system goes through various steps. The publisher provides first the UNSPSC code of the service application domain; then with the aid of the above described applet s/he is guided in the description of the service and in the definition of service location and interface parameters. The activities that can be requested to the system in the publication stage are hereafter summarized. *Publication of an OWL-DL ontology to be classified within UNSPSC taxonomy.* As the CLASSIC reasoner used in the agency manages an $\mathcal{ALN}$ DL, the ontology has to be modeled using only the constructors allowed by such a logic. The file name representing the ontology must be in the form XX.XX.owl, where the two groups of digits represent the UNSPSC *family* level.

*Search of an item in the UNSPSC taxonomy and of its corresponding level within the taxonomy.* It is possible to surf the UNSPSC taxonomy in order to

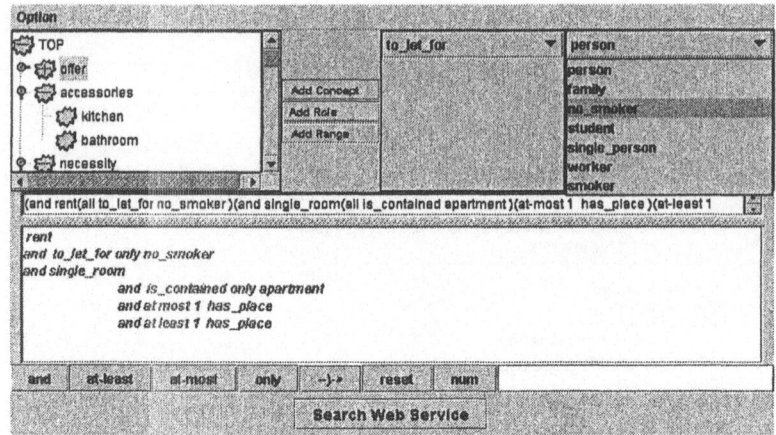

*Figure 2.* Graphical User Interface during a service request composition.

find the exact code representing the service to be published.

*Publication of a web service, in the UDDI registry, whose semantic description is built based on a published ontology.* The publication consists of both an instantiation of two tModels in the registry and the RPC of the *setDescription()* method for the Web Service being published. The first tModel represents UNSPSC information, the second one is related to the URI of the OWL-DL formatted semantic description.

We would like to point out that, although our framework is generic, a simple mapping between UDDI and OWL-S is possible and a semantic description can be well embedded into an OWL-S (formerly DAML-S) [OWL-S overview, 2003] based description of the publishing service. The semantic description can be interpreted as the **effect** part of the IOPE (Input, Output, Precondition, Effect) model proposed in OWL-S for the *Service Profile* class. Using the mapping proposed in [Paolucci et al., 2002a] the UDDI tModel representing the semantic description field of the service is formatted as a part of OWL-S description of the service.

## Web Service Discovery

The search process also goes through various stages and it is initiated again providing the UNSPSC code of the searched service, which can be evoked also using a keyword based approach, and defined up to the commodity level navigating through the hierarchical structure of the classification levels. Having selected a code the applet again guides the user in the description of the requested service, in accordance with the domain ontology. Once the user has found the UNSPSC code corresponding to the search domain, the ontology corresponding to the family level of the code is selected and its class taxonomy and roles constraints are sent back to the user. Again the user is helped by an applet that guides her/him in the request description composition, see figure 2. Both the description and the reference domain ontology ID are sent to the Communication Service that provides interaction with MAMAS and finally returns a ranked list of services matching the request, and corresponding service invocation information. The discovery process of a web service can be hence summarized as:

*Search a UNSPSC code (ID) using a keyword-based approach;*

*Build a semantic description of the web service to be searched, using the ontology identified by ID;*

*Send the description to the Discovery Agency;*

*Find in the UDDI registry all the services with a semantic description identified by ID;*

*Call the getDescription() for all the Web Services identified in the previous step;*

*Match services OWL-DL descriptions with the requested one;*

*Send back to the user the ranked list of services information.*

Computing the length of the requested description, the ranked list is expressed in terms of percentage degree of mismatch (for *rankPotential* results) or of incompatibility (for *rankPartial* results).

## 5. Conclusion

We have investigated web-services advertisement and discovery in a framework based on DLs formalization and reasoning, which overcomes simple subsumption matching, providing information on service similarity and allowing match ranking and classification. Based on the theoretical work we have implemented a fully functional agency for semantic-based web-service discovery, which exploits state of art technologies and protocols.

## References

Baader, F., Calvanese, D., Mc Guinness, D., Nardi, D., and Patel-Schneider, P., editors (2002). *The Description Logic Handbook.* Cambridge University Press.

Bechhofer, S., Mller, R., and Crowther, P. (2003). The DIG Description Logic Interface. In *Proc. DL'03,* volume 81 of *CEUR Workshop Proceedings.*

Benatallah, B., Hacid, M.-S., Rey, C., and Toumani, F. (2003). Request Rewriting-Based Web Service Discovery. In *Proc. ISWC,* volume 2870 of *LNCS,* pages 242–257.

Borgida, A. and Patel-Schneider, P. F. (1994). A Semantics and Complete Algorithm for Subsumption in the CLASSIC Description Logic. *J. of Artificial Intelligence Research,* 1:277–308.

Casati, F. and Shan, M. C. (2001). Dynamic and Adaptive Composition of E-Services. *Information Systems,* 26:143–163.

Colucci, S., Di Noia, T., Di Sciascio, E., Donini, F., and Mongiello, M. (2003a). Concept Abduction and Contraction in Description Logics. In *Proc. DL'03*, volume 81 of *CEUR Workshop Proceedings*.

Colucci, S., Di Noia, T., Di Sciascio, E., Donini, F., and Mongiello, M. (2003b). Logic Based Approach to web services discovery and matchmaking. In *Proc. E-Services Workshop at ICEC'03*.

Di Noia, T., Di Sciascio, E., Donini, F., and Mongiello, M. (2003a). Abductive matchmaking using description logics. pages 337–342, Acapulco. MK.

Di Noia, T., Di Sciascio, E., Donini, F., and Mongiello, M. (2003b). Semantic matchmaking in a P-2-P electronic marketplace. In *Proc. Symposium on Applied Computing (SAC '03)*, pages 582–586. ACM.

Di Noia, T., Di Sciascio, E., Donini, F., and Mongiello, M. (2003c). A system for principled Matchmaking in an electronic marketplace. In *Proc. WWW '03*, pages 321–330, Budapest. ACM Press.

Di Sciascio, E., Donini, F., Mongiello, M., and Piscitelli, G. (2001). A Knowledge-Based System for Person-to-Person E-Commerce. In *Proc. KI-2001 Workshop ADL-2001*, volume 44 of *CEUR Workshop Proceedings*.

Gonzales-Castillo, J., Trastour, D., and Bartolini, C. (2001). Description Logics for Matchmaking of Services. In *Proc. KI-2001 Workshop ADL-2001*, volume 44. CEUR Workshop Proceedings.

Hoffner, Y., Facciorusso, C., Field, S., and Schade, A. (2000). Distribution Issues in the Design and Implementation of a Virtual Market Place. *Computer Networks*, 32:717–730.

Li, L. and Horrocks, I. (2003). A Software Framework for Matchmaking Based on Semantic Web Technology. In *Proc. WWW '03*, pages 331–339, Budapest. ACM Press.

McGuinness, D., Fikes, R., Hendler, J., and Stein, L. (2002). DAML+OIL: An Ontology Language for the Semantic Web . *IEEE Intelligent Systems*, 17(5):72–80.

OWL-S overview (2003). www.daml.org/services/owl-s/1.0/.

Paolucci, M., Kawamura, T., Payne, T., and Sycara, K. (2002a). Importing the semantic web in uddi. In *Proc. of Web Services, E-business and Semantic Web Workshop*.

Paolucci, M., Kawamura, T., Payne, T., and Sycara, K. (2002b). Semantic Matching of Web Services Capabilities. In *Proc. ISWC*, number 2342 in LNCS, pages 333–347.

S.A.McIlraith and Martin, D. (2003). Bringing Semantics to Web Services. *IEEE Intelligent Systems*, pages 90–93.

Ströbel, M. and Stolze, M. (2002). A Matchmaking Component for the Discovery of Agreement and Negotiation Spaces in Electronic Markets. *Group Decision and Negotiation*, 11:165–181.

Sycara, K., Paolucci, M., Van Velsen, M., and Giampapa, J. (2003). The RETSINA MAS infrastructure. *Autonomous agents and multi-agent systems*, 7:29–48.

Sycara, K., Widoff, S., Klusch, M., and Lu, J. (2002). LARKS: Dynamic Matchmaking Among Heterogeneus Software Agents in Cyberspace. *Autonomous agents and multi-agent systems*, 5:173–203.

Trastour, D., Bartolini, C., and Priest, C. (2002). Semantic Web Support for the Business-to-Business E-Commerce Lifecycle. In *Proc. WWW '02*, pages 89–98. ACM.

Veit, D., Muller, J., Schneider, M., and Fiehn, B. (2001). Matchmaking for Autonomous Agents in Electronic Marketplaces. In *Proc. Agents '01*, pages 65–66. ACM.

Web Services Glossary (2003). http://www.w3.org/TR/2003/WD-ws-gloss-20030808/.

# GESOS: A MULTI-OBJECTIVE GENETIC TOOL FOR PROJECT MANAGEMENT CONSIDERING TECHNICAL AND NON-TECHNICAL CONSTRAINTS

Claude Baron[1], Samuel Rochet[1], Daniel Esteve[2]
[1] LESIA, INSA, 135 av. de Rangueil, 31077 Toulouse cedex 04, France
[2] LAAS, CNRS, 7 av. du colonel Roche, 31077 Toulouse cedex 04, France
claude.baron@insa-tlse.fr, rochet@insa-tlse.fr, daniel.esteve@laas.fr

Abstract:     Project managers have a difficult issue to deal with: identify tasks to plan during project management, with their technical and non-technical parameters, determine a target to reach, and effectively reach it to avoid financial penalties. This paper presents a tool able to join system design and project management. We think thus facilitate the construction of an architecture of planning and the optimization of this one according to methods that we propose to develop. Our main motivation is to prevent the obvious incompatibilities between technical objectives and socio-economical requirements in the enterprise. Thus, we want to help decision makers to chose a project skeleton, called scenario, at the launching of the project, but also during its management, in order to quickly react in case of the occurrence of any perturbation. A method using evolutionary algorithms seemed adapted. We will see the benefits that result from this approach and concludes on the perspectives of larger applications we can envisage thanks to the tool that supports it, GESOS.

Key words:    evolutionary computing, genetic algorithms, metaheuristic optimization, system design, project management, multi-criteria decision making

## 1.    INTRODUCTION

Our work takes place in the domain of development of methodologies for the project management. The originality of our approach is to couple this domain with the one of system design. In a simplified way, the question is to succeed in making simultaneously evolve the organization of the project and design. With the process of project management we associate some mechanisms of robustness and adaptability related to external disturbances of technical, social or economic nature, in order to respect the laid down objectives.

The problem thus becomes a question of minimization of the distance between the objective effectively achieved by the scenario (in terms of costs, times, quality...) and the laid down initial objective. However, the choice of the various tasks to be carried out during a project is a complex optimization problem. Only some heuristic methods can enable us to find a solution that is close to the optimum in a reasonable time, like evolutionary algorithms. Indeed, considering this problem, we could note that such methods seemed best adapted because these research algorithms allow taking into account multiple parameters of which they seek many combinations simultaneously. We validated our approach using a tool based on the use of the genetic algorithms, GESOS (Genetic Evaluation, Selection and Optimization of Scenarios).

## 2.         GENERAL CONTEXT OF THE PROJECT

### 2.1      Objective: reach the targets

On one side, the objectives of a system design process consist in obtaining an exact conformance of the system to technical requirements: performances, quality, reliability, testability, etc. On the other side, the project manager has to deal with a project management process : define targets to reach (in terms of costs, duration, resources...), then define tasks and their associated means and suppliers, that have to be scheduled in order, precisely, to reach the target within the previously defined constraints : duration, means (financial, manpower, machines, suppliers, etc.).

So the project's objectives consist in reaching a group of technical or economical targets. In order to measure how precisely these targets are reached, we have decided to use the Taguchi's approach in which quality should be measured by the deviation from a specified target value. This concept will be developed in section 3.4.2.

### 2.2      The notion of scenario

We are convinced that the first description level for tasks can be derived from the functional components description obtained at the preliminary design step [Bar04b]. This operation is processed on the base of technical considerations, has to consider non technical objectives relative to the project management: costs, market, supply constraints, supplying delays, quality, certification, any types of risks...

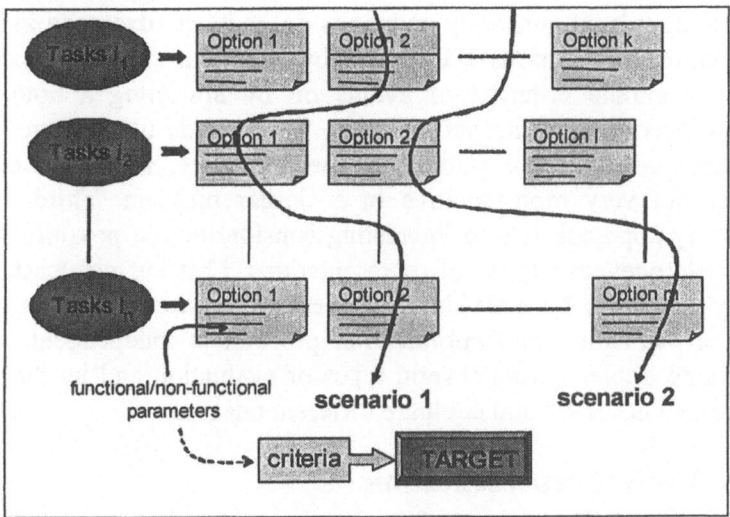

*Figure 1.* Generation of scenarios

The intersection between the tasks' content and the technical and non-technical objectives leads to establish several possibilities for the project organization which are coherent with general specifications of products, as illustrated on figure 1; we call them *scenarios*. Scenarios are deduced from the options attached to each task they correspond to global solutions respecting both technical specifications and strategic project requirements. In a simplified way, we can say that a scenario is a combination of options and the main point of this paper is to present a procedure to define the best appropriated combination.

## 3. THE TOOL GESOS

### 3.1 Why an evolutionary choice?

Choosing various options associated to project's tasks is an optimization problem for which no exact polynomial algorithm is known. The use of an exact method of optimization is then not very realistic for large-sized problems; that's why we need to use a heuristic method. The evolutionary algorithms seemed interesting for several reasons. First, the research algorithms are well adapted to multiple parameters of which they consider many combinations at the same time, which allows offering the decision maker a range of solution at each step. One thus lay out with each stage of calculation a unit of available solutions and not a single solution, as the method of simulated annealing or taboos do. It is an advantage in our case where a choice of solutions will have to be offered at the user. Second, they use a very simple criterion of evaluation by allocating a note to each individual according to its performance. This avoids using more complex mathematic tools like the gradient or the derivative, which are not easily usable or not very representative in a similar problem. Third, using an evolutionary approach is also interesting considering the possibility it offer to treat heterogeneous types of representations. Last but not least, the fact that only one mark by individual is necessary in the evolutionary process makes the evaluation and optimization procedures independent. One can thus imagine implementing several types of evaluation and let the decision maker chose one, or try and compare different ones...

## 3.2 Project representation

Our work take place in a more ambitious project [Bar04a] where several research and industrial partners are involved. For instance, data for GESOS will provide from two other programs developed at the LAAS. The first one, HILES [Ham03], realizes a product formal description and the second, LORA [Bri04] allows representing temporal relations between project's tasks and in particular the sequence and resources allocation. In a simplified way, we can consider that the information coming from HILES, which provides technical elements, completed by LORA's project management information, permits a complete representation of the project. GESOS will use these resources to construct one complete project representation before determining the optimal scenario. After this step of optimization, solutions can be re-introduced at HILES and LORA in order to permit the decision maker to respectively simulate the operations of the product and project scheduling.

The first constraints types treated by GESOS are the temporal relations between tasks and more precisely the precedence relations between them which traduce the case, when one action can't be done before the end of the others. It's the main relation type behind the project tasks. We represent tasks to realize by numbered squares and precedence relations by arrows. We can with this representation use a graph to visualize task's sequencing.

This last relation allows treating classical problems of scheduling in which project structure doesn't have any alternatives. But in our problematic, options associated to each tasks are unknown as well as the project architecture. For instance, the choice of one material affects the machining steps and only machining steps compatible with this one can be used. That's why we need to introduce one element representing a choice in the project sequence; it's what we call decision nodes. To represent the choices that appear in the project we add two numbered circles into the tasks graph. Each one represents a node and it's the ensemble of these two nodes which forms a decision. Thus, we have an initial node and a final node. The first circle on figure 2 with a double line is the initial node. Only one way will be activated after one initial node, all the others will be deactivated. The final node has a single line and all the relations after him must be realized.

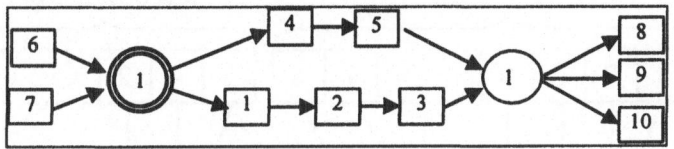

*Figure 2.* Project's structure with decision nodes

Thus, only one task sequence is possible between an initial and final node. For example, on figure 2 two ways are possible. As showed on figure 3, the tasks 1, 2 and 3 can be active and 4 and 5 inactive or tasks 4 and 5 actives and 1, 2 and 3 inactive.

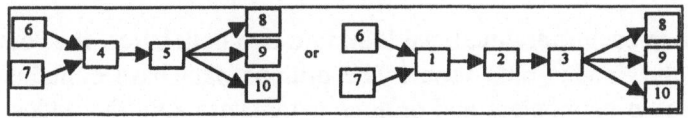

*Figure 3.* Possible Structures issues to Figure 2

Nodes allow the representation of the mutual exclusion of certain tasks by others and we can then combine nodes to represent complex scenarios structures.

## 3.3     Individual coding

This section presents the individual representation. The choice of an appropriated representation allows obtaining an efficient operation of the algorithm.

Our objective is to determine the best way into the options to reach the fixed target. This means select for each task an option and for each node a way. Parameters linked to tasks and options being determined, remain two object types which can vary into the individual selected: to each task, the option selected and to each node, the decision chose. Our coding is very simple, on the first chromosome part will be coded the options associated to each tasks and on the second chromosome part, the way of each nodes as showed on figure 4.

For a problem with n tasks with $i_n$ options each and m nodes with $i_m$ choices, on the n first genes, gene i correspond to task i and on genes n+1 to n+m, gene i correspond to node i-n. In each of themes, one integer between 1 and $i_n$ or $i_m$, function of the case, does reference to the option or way chosen.

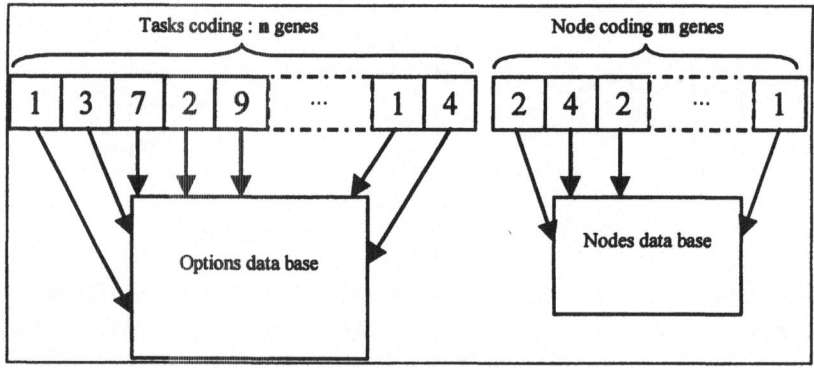

*Figure 4.* Chromosome signification

To decode each individual, we look into two data bases, the "options data base" and the "nodes data base". The options data base contains all tasks with these own parameters and options parameters and, the nodes data base all information needed too define the way between each group of two nodes which corresponds to each project's choice.

This representation using only integers allow to manipulated individuals with restricted size and can easily be decoded before the individual evaluation step. In addition, this coding allows using directly classical methods of crossover and mutation without reconstruct non-viable individuals. This is due to the fact that we use a coding in which an object does not depends of a gene chain but only of one gene; so a gene modification can not change all the meaning of the chromosome but only the object corresponding to the modified gene.

## 3.4    Genetic procedure

In this section will be described the genetic procedure implemented in GESOS. It's a strictly classical algorithm. After a random population initialization, we apply the classical sequence of evaluation, selection, crossover, mutation as shown on figure 5. The point requiring to be developed is the evaluation process. It will be explained in the following paragraphs. The other algorithms used, roulette wheel method for the selection, single point crossover and one gene mutation are the standards methods [Gol94] and don't need to be explain in details in this paper.

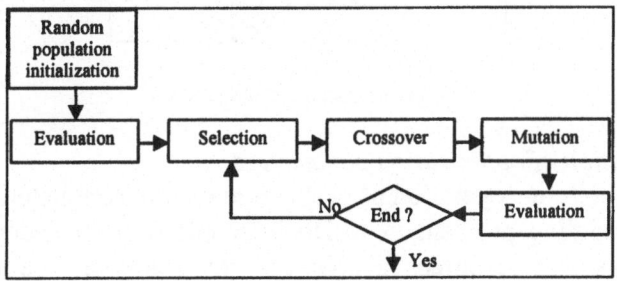

*Figure 5.* Genetic procedure

In the following paragraph we will detail the evaluation process. The different steps of its decomposition will be explained before the criteria used and to finish we will explain the method of fitness attribution.

### 3.4.1 Evaluation steps

The evaluation implies to:
- determine the individuals projects sequences starting from a complex project in which all tasks aren't activated
- and find an efficient multi-objective algorithm in order to valorize the apparition of good schemata and keeping the solutions diversity.

For that, the following steps are successively realized:
*1. Problem reduction :*
For each individual, the choices done during the project are known during the evaluation. In function of the individual's chromosome, we know what options and ways have been chosen. However, in function of the choices linked to nodes, certain tasks or others nodes will be inactive. These ones will be absent from the scenario realized, that's why it's useless to keep them during the rest of evaluation. So, a second scenario is generated in which all inactive tasks and nodes are removed.

For instance, on figure 6 we can see the second scenario obtained of one chromosome. Stay only tasks 1, 2, 6, 7 and 8 with respectively the $3^{rd}$, $5^{th}$, $8^{th}$, $5^{th}$ and $2^{nd}$ of their associated options.

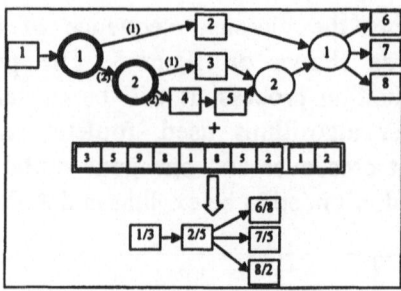

*Figure 6.* Scenario reduction

*2. Determination of optimization parameters*

Once the previous operation of problem reduction completed, we obtain a classical scheduling problem in which intervene only precedence relations between tasks and resources availability. In this case, we could easily determine a project sequence by classical methods, and by the same occasion evaluate parameters; this last point is detailed in the paragraph 3.4.2.

Presently, we use distance between cost and budget and distance between project duration and desired duration for parameters. The first is determined by the summation of the cost of each realized task. The second using a PERT method variant in which is introduce moreover tasks antecedence relations, constraints linked to resources availability.

*3. Multi-criteria evaluation:*

In our problem we try to minimize the distance of all parameters by report there respecting objectives (see 3.4.2); it's a typically multi-criteria problem. To make our selection, we have developed a method based on the Strength Pareto Evolutionary Algorithm. The selection process will be developed in paragraph 3.4.3.

### 3.4.2    Evaluation criteria

We have seen on paragraph 2.1 that the objective is to reach the technical and economical targets. In order to measure how precisely the targets are reached, we decided to use the Taguchi's approach. Taguchi methods, developed by Dr. Genichi Taguchi [War89], can be described in a basic idea: Quality should be measured by the deviation from a specified target value, rather than by conformance to preset tolerance limits.

Taguchi believes that the customer becomes increasingly dissatisfied as performance departs farther away from the target. He suggests a quadratic curve to represent a customer's dissatisfaction with a product's performance. The curve is centered on the target value, which provides the best performance in the eyes of the customer. This is a customer-driven design rather than an engineer's specification. There is some financial loss incurred at the upper consumer tolerance. This could be a warranty charge to the organization or a repair expense for example.

This synthetic and very attractive approach invites us to represent in terms of costs every consequence of the product requirements. Indeed, originally, the Taguchi's loss function establishes a financial measure of the user dissatisfaction with a product's performance as it deviates from a target value. In our context, the project manager has to define a target considering technical as well as financial objectives. He thus has to simultaneously lead a product development and a pure project management processes.

Value of each optimization parameters will be the value of loss function associated to the objective which permits us to work on a minimization problem in which we determine individuals with the minimum loss function.

$$L = K(O - T)^2$$

With L loss function value, T target value, O objective value and K user parameter which permit to adapt each loss function to objective type.

### 3.4.3 Multi-criteria evaluation

Our problem is then to minimize the loss functions ensemble in order to obtain scenarios as near of the targets as possible. This evaluation must valorize the scenarios diversity too to allow us to suggest to the decision maker a wide range of solutions and not a group centered on the same scenario with only little variations. To realize this, we have chosen to use a method inspired by the Strength Pareto Evolutionary Algorithm. This technique presented in 1998 by E. Zitzler and L. Tiele ([Zit88] and [Zit89]) put down on the determination of the Pareto front associated to the problem and allows us to reach ours objectives of solution quality and population diversity.

During a mono-criterion evaluation, it's easy to compare two individuals by comparing a scalar fitness. In a multi-criteria optimization case, relations between individuals are more complexes. We can use the dominance notion. In a minimization problem, considering two objective vectors *v* and *u*. If all *v* components are less or equal to *u* components, with at least one component strictly less, so *v* vector correspond to a bester solution than *u*. In this case, we tell *v* dominate *u* on Pareto sense. On formal way, we can write:

$$v \overset{p}{<} u \text{ if } v \overset{p}{<} u \Leftrightarrow \forall i \in [1;c], v_i \leq u_i \text{ and } \exists j \in [1;c] : v_j < u$$

The whole of objective vectors which couldn't be dominated constitutes problem optimal values in Pareto sense. These values belong to the Pareto front. The Pareto-optimal whole is defined like unit which contain solutions in the search space with values are into the Pareto front.

We work with two sets of individuals. P, the population, and P', which contain Pareto front individuals. Individual fitness determination is decomposed in two steps:

*Step 1:* at each P' individual is associated a value representing there strength equal to the number of solutions dominate by i in population P divided by P height plus one (1).

*Step 2:* fitness $f_i$ of all individual appertaining to P is equal to the inverse of the sum of P' individual strength which dominate it plus one (2).

$$s_i = \frac{n}{\mu + 1} \ (1) \qquad\qquad f_i = \frac{1}{1 + \sum_{i, i < j}^{p} s_i} \ (2)$$

So, one individual is as less performing than it is dominated by individuals of P'. One selection method like roulette wheel is used after in order to favorite the good fitness individual. Figure 7 illustrate performances calculation.

With this technique, Pareto front individuals are valorized compared to others individuals. The firsts' one have a fitness equal at one and the seconds' inferior at one, so the Pareto front individuals have more chances than the other to be present into the next generation. This point permits to obtain a convergence to good scenarios.

For the second objective of the evaluation, valorize the population diversity, we can notice that a technique based on niches is implicitly effectuated by fitness calculation above. Each figure 7 rectangle is considered like a niche in Pareto dominance terms. If one niche contains a high number of solutions, its contribution to individual strength is strong. In return, this high strength implies a weak fitness for individuals belong to this niche. It's what we can notice in niche (1), in spite of this individuals aren't dominate only by a single other, they obtain a mediocre note. Inverse niches with few individuals will have dominants with weak strength which imply a high fitness for its. For example, niche (2) individuals obtain the best population fitness except Pareto front individuals. Thus we obtain a stabilization of the subpopulations height into niches.

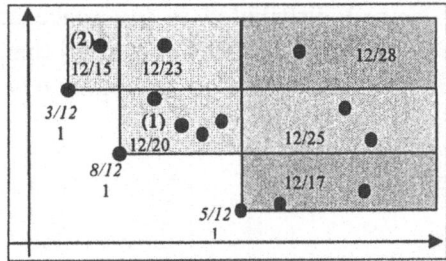

*Figure 7.* Fitness affectation

We can notice that actually, we use a clustering method in order to limit the number of individuals in the Pareto front.

## 4. RESULTS AND FUTURE EVOLUTIONS

### 4.1 Experimental results

Presently, to validate this tool we use a module to randomly generate problems. Tests on real problems from industry aren't still being considered but are envisaged in near future once the different tools (HILES, LORA and GESOS) linked. Results presented below have been obtained on middle size problem with 60 tasks with 15 options each. Fixed objectives were 5000 € for the project cost and 500 h for desired duration.

We use for the moment only these two criteria. Other criterion like risk associated to the project or product quality aren't yet implemented. Actually, during our experimentations, we voluntary use a high number of generations and this to verify the algorithm convergence and see the different algorithm phases.

On figure 8, we can note that average values of loss functions decrease before converge. In some cases, we note an increase of one of the criteria whereas the other decreases this translates simply the existing dependence between these two values. Of course, if we begin with a population very near of one of our objective but far to the second, the algorithm will reduce the quality on the first criterion to raise the second in order to obtain a best compromise. On figure 9, we can see the population (represented by the crosses) and Pareto front individuals (the points) repartition after research of the optimum. On this figure, we refund the classical Pareto front in minimization problem and we can notice that the population is good attracted on its borders. On figure 10, the individuals repartition is doing on a cross form centered on the fixed objectives values. In addition, we can see that the population is well distributed in the space of research and well covers a vast field of scenarios. It should be noted that, in this application, we could find a solution very close to the optimal with one duration to 500,7 h and a cost to 5003 €.

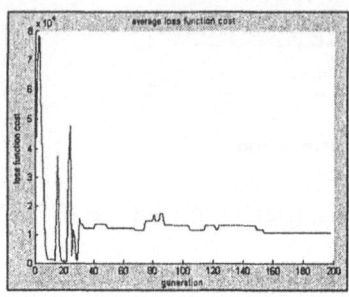 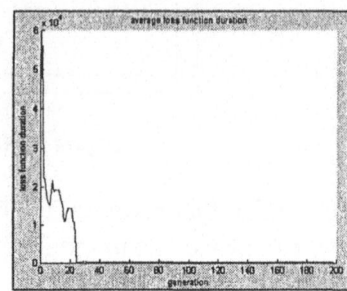

*Figure 8.* Average value of cost and duration loss function

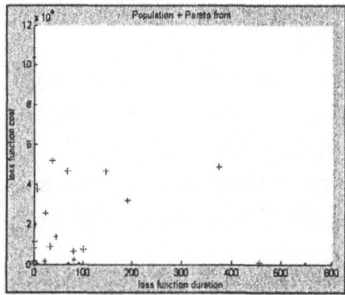 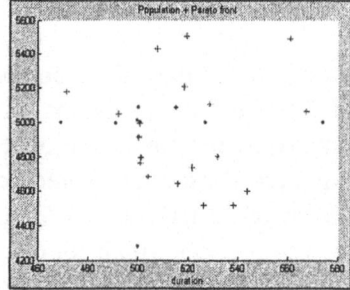

*Figure 9.* Repartition function of loss functions *Figure 10.* Repartition function parameters

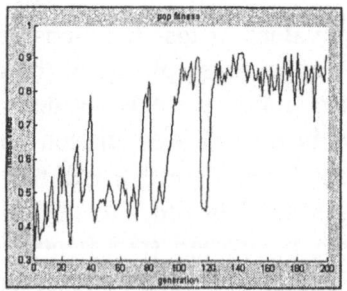 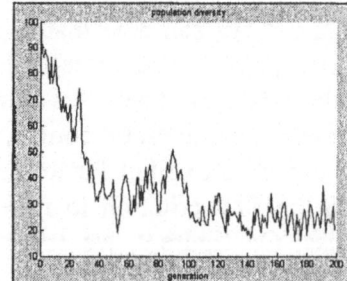

*Figure 11.* Average fitness value            *Figure 12.* Population diversity

In this example an optimal solution was obtained in less of 40 generations (figure 8). After, the fitness (figure 11) and its diversity (figure 12) variations are not related to the research of Pareto front individuals but to the second phase of the algorithm during which, once time the Pareto front established, population will tender to be distributed uniformly along the Pareto front. In this phase, it's no more the population which will push the performances of the Pareto front but the front which will attract the individuals of the population.

Results obtained in experiments are thus encouraging, since they show a rapid convergence of the face of Pareto towards the optimal solutions. Another advantage of this algorithm is its insensitivity to the distance between project objectives and limits. We can notice that even on problems with objectives very distant from those attainable, acceptable results are obtained from the viewpoint of the solution's quality. It is a considerable advantage; numerous other heuristic are very sensitive to this phenomenon and give in this case poor quality solutions.

## 4.2 GESOS prospects and evolutions

The use of evolutionary algorithms in this type of application is quite new because until now they were used in problems of scheduling where tasks are known but not the order in which they must be followed. Here, the problem is the opposite, the general order of the tasks is predetermined and we try to find which chain of tasks would lead us as close as possible to our objectives. It is thus a new problem that is posed. Thanks to the tool, we obtained encouraging results that validate our approach on examples elaborated for the purpose. In particular, we have shown that, when the genetic parameters are well-adjusted, convergence is obtained within few seconds, for quite complex problems (100 tasks with 100 options each [Bar04c]). Of course, the tool deserves to be improved, on several aspects which can be either relative to the management and design processes by taking into account more tasks parameters or relative to the genetic procedure (e.g. a more sophisticated stop criterion to elaborate, studying the impact of another chromosome coding, test multiple cut points and variants on mutation and crossover, realize a precise adjustment of algorithm parameters like mutation and crossover rates...).

## 5. CONCLUSION

Nowadays, project management is basically funded onto tasks scheduling and resources management considerations. It supervises product design tasks in the way that the decisions made determine the allocation of resources.

This situation is not totally satisfactory because it induces misunderstandings. In previous papers [Bar04a] [Bar04b], we have proposed the use of some models and tools. In this one, we focused on the selection and optimization methods and tools that can be envisaged. The paper showed that genetic techniques can be employed to reduce computation delays in order to help the project manager to quickly define project scenarios. This corresponds to a real industrial need. We exposed our strategy, justified its choice and presented the benefits that can be obtained on the case of a complex example, though our approach still merits improvements. In conclusion, GESOS seems to be a well-adapted tool for decision makers to manage their projects. Considering the whole project in witch we are involved, we determined ambitious objectives, and we are now in the phase of integrating the several research tools developed by our partners. We are now contemplating the possibility to use this platform and test it on real complex industrial applications.

# REFERENCES

[Bar04a] Baron C., Esteve D., "Towards a Shared Process for Product Design and Project", 14th Annual International INternational COnference on System Engineering (INCOSE), Toulouse, France, June 2004.

[Bar04b] Baron C., Esteve D., Rochet S. "How evolutionary computation can be introduced to select and optimize scenarii along a product design process", Transactions on Systems, N. Mastorakis Editor, World Scientific and Engineering Academy and Society Publishers, ISSN 1109-2777, pp. 888-893, issue 2, vol.3, April 2004.

[Bar04c] Baron C., Rochet S., Esteve D. "A genetic approach to support decision makers during project management", invited communication at 4th Int. Conf. on Soft Computing, Optimization, Simulation &Manufacturing Systems, Miami, Florida (USA), April 2004.

[Bri04] Briand C., Doucet J.-E., Esquirol P., Huget M.-J., Lopez P., "Projet de plate-forme logicielle LORA – specification 1.1 Représentation de problèmes d'ordonnancement de tâches et d'affectation de ressources", Rapport LAAS N°01551, December 2001, 24p, February 04.

[Gol94] Goldberg D., "Algorithmes génétiques", Addison-Wesley, 1994.

[Ham03] Hamon J.C., Esteve D, Pampagnin P., "HiLeS Designer: A tool for systems design". International Symposium Convergence 03: Aeronautics, Automotive & Space, Paris, December 2003.

[War89] Warner J.C., O'Connor J., "Molding Process is Improved by Using the Taguchi Method", Modern Plastics: 65-68, 1989.

[Zit99] Zitzler E., Thiele L., "Multiobjective Evolutionary Algorithms : A comparative Case Study and the Strength Pareto Approach". IEEE Trans. On Evolutionary Computation, tome 3, n°4, 257-271, 1999.

[Zit98] Zitzler E., Thiele L., "An Evolutionary Algorithm for Multiobjective Optimization : The Strength Pareto Approach", TIK report, N°43, May 1998.

# USING GENETIC ALGORITHMS AND TABU SEARCH PARALLEL MODELS TO SOLVE THE SCHEDULING PROBLEM

Pedro Pinacho*

ppinacho@diinf.usach.cl


Mauricio Solar*

msolar@usach.cl


Mario Inostroza*

minostro@diinf.usach.cl


Rosa Muñoz*

rmunoz@diinf.usach.cl
*(*) Departamento de Ingeniería Informática,*
*Universidad de Santiago de Chile,*
*Av. Ecuador 3659 Santiago, Chile.*

**Abstract**

This work presents a comparison between a Parallel Genetic Algorithm (PGA) and a Parallel Tabu Search (PTS) algorithm. Both are used for solving a scheduling problem on 45 tests based on the same parallel model, (Synchronous Network Concurrency Model) and testing sequential algorithms with 2, 4 and 8 processors. The results show that the PTS algorithm obtains better results, and covers a smaller portion of the solution space.

**Keywords:** Genetic Algorithms, Tabu Search, Parallelism, Scheduling.

## Introduction

One of the problems evidenced in an application that requires the computational power of a parallel machine is the assignment of tasks to the processors available with the purpose of reducing the total computational time utilized. This problem, referred to an instance of the *scheduling* problem, is represented by weighted Directed Acyclic Graphs (DAGs) also known as task graphs which configure a set of tasks in homogenous processors in order to minimize total required time. In its general form this is a NP-complete problem although there are polynomial solutions known for a few restricted cases [3], [7].

The representation of the tasks and assignment in a $DAG$ [8], in these graphs is defined by the tuple $G = (V, E, C, T)$, where $V = \{n_j, j = 1 : v\}$ is the set of task nodes and $v = |V|$ is the number of nodes, $E$ is the set of communication arcs, $e = |E|$ is the number of arcs, $C$ is the cost of the communication arcs and $T$ is the set of computation time of the nodes. The value $c_{i,j} \in C$ is the time of communication incurred throughout the arcs $e_{ij} = (n_i, n_j) \in E$, which is zero if both arcs are assigned to the same processor. The value $t_i \in T$ is the computation time of the node $n_i \in V$.

A task is an indivisible computation unit which may be an instruction, routine or an entire program. Additionally a task is considered non-preemtive due to the fact that once it is begun it must be completed without interruptions.

This article presents the context of the general scheduling problem in Section 2, defining the type of problem encountered, later in Section 3 the metaheuristics used are described. Section 4 shows how GA and TS have been parallelized, while Section 5 presents the tests carried out and the analysis of these. Finally, Section 6 presents the conclusions reached in this work.

## 1.    The Problem

The scheduling problem is defined as follows: given a number $v$ of tasks (where $t_i$ corresponds to the computation time of the $i$-th task) which must be carried out by $P$ processors (where $p_j$ corresponds to the $j$-th processor), it is required to know which tasks must be carried out on which processor, such that the total time to completion be as small as possible.

A few instances of the problem are described below:

Dependence among tasks: In order that task $i$ begin its execution, tasks $t_1, t_2, ..., t_k$, must have concluded, that is, a certain established order must be respected (where $k$ is the quantity of tasks that precede task $i$). In this respect, there are two possibilities:

- There is dependency between tasks.

- No task depends on the execution of another.

Duration of the task: This refers to the duration of the tasks. Two cases exist:

- All tasks have the same duration *(unitary)*.
- The tasks have different and arbitrary duration.

Communication Cost: Corresponds to the time required to communicate one task $t_k$ with its predecessors whose execution has finished. With respect to this, there are two different cases:

- Task $t_i$ must communicate with task $t_k$, to be carried out: if both tasks are executed on the same processor, the cost is considered to be zero or insignificant; if they are carried out on different processors there is a known associated cost $(c_{ij})$.
- Communication costs are not considered.

Number of Processors: Corresponds to the quantity of available resources to resolve a given problem. There are two alternatives:

- An unbounded number of processors is considered.
- The number of processors $(P)$ available for the problem is specified.

Processor Homogeneity: This has to do with the specific characteristics of the processors. There are two cases:

- The processors are identical.
- The processors do not have the same characteristics.

In the present work, the scheduling problem considered has the following characteristics (instance):

- There is dependency among tasks.
- Tasks differ in duration (arbitrary).
- Communication cost between tasks is taken into consideration.
- Processors are homogenous and limited.

Researchers in this area of study have devoted approximately forty years to develop various algorithms for this problem. A real alternative are Metaheuristic Algorithms. These are generally defined, and thus it is necessary to define their parameters in order to model the problem to be solved according to its nature. Their principal characteristic is that they do not ensure the finding of the optimal solution, but rather solutions that are close to the optimum. Some examples of these are Simulated Annealing [11], Genetic Algorithms [10], and Tabu Search [9].

## 2. Tabu Search and Genetic Algorithms

This work centers on the study of the effectiveness of the techniques of Genetic Algorithms and Tabu Search for the solution of a specific instance of the scheduling problem which are presented below.

## 2.1 Tabu Search (TS)

Tabu Search is a metaheuristic method introduced and developed in its present form by [9]. In General TS consists of generating, on the basis of a random and feasible initial solution, neighboring solutions from which the optimal solution is selected (or not) when compared to the initial solution. A Tabu List (L) is generated of the movements that are not allowed in the present iteration, (in this way movements that could result in the selection of a local optimum are excluded). There are different criteria for determining when it is possible to remove a movement from L. Intensification and diversification strategies define how close the generated solutions are to the initial solution.

The modeling used for this problem coincides with genetic algorithms in representation of individuals and in the evaluation function. The generation of a neighboring solution consists of changes in the positions of the elements of the initial solution. The criteria for functioning for a neighborhood were aspiration by default [9]. The search strategy is defined by the following parameters presented in [4]:

1 The size of L is 100.

2 The number of variations permitted is the average of the DAG input tasks, and the number of processors.

3 The size of the neighborhood is the sum of the previous.

When the number of iterations allowed in each cycle is completed, the search strategy is updated, and the number of differences between solutions is analyzed (Hamming distance). If it is larger than 50% of the size of a solution, the size of L is reduced as are the number of variations, and the size of the neighborhood is increased; if it is smaller, the size of L is increased as is the number of variations, and the size of the neighborhood is decreased.

## 2.2    Genetic Algorithms (GA)

Genetic Algorithms are metaheuristic methods [10], (of an evolutionary nature) that belong to the area of Artificial Intelligence, and make it possible to find solutions that are close to optimum for difficult optimization problems. GAs base their search on the mechanics of natural selection and genetics, where evolution operates directly on the chromosomes of living organisms by means of selection processes, crosses between individuals (thus generating offspring that are different to the parents), and mutations which allows adaptation to changes in the environment. According to this idea, GAs use an initial population of individuals (possible solutions for the modeled problem) that is random, finite and same size for each generation. The individuals are represented by binary strings in which a 1 represents a characteristic present in the chromosome of the individual (pure GAs). The initial population evolves from one generation to the next a fixed number of times by means of genetic operators. These select the best solutions according to a defined evaluation function, reproduce the individuals randomly changing the genetic information in two chromosomes, thus generating new individualism, and mutating some characteristic of the chromosome.

The model used in this work [12], corresponds to a hybrid representation of the chromosomes where the length of an individual is equal to the number of tasks plus the number of available processors. Each characteristic has a positive number between 1 and the number of tasks, (which represent the scheduled task in the DAG) or a negative number between 1 and the number of processors, (which represents the number of the processor where the assignments are being carried out). Reading the chromosome from left to right, the positive numbers next to negative numbers indicate what tasks are to be carried out, and in what order (Figure 1).

The evaluation function associated to this model determines the time that each individual requires per task, taking into consideration the associated computation and communication costs. The operators used in this modeling exercise as justified in [12], and whose parameters where tuned after a process of adjustment, are the following [6]:

*Mutation:* Two random positions for the individual are chosen and exchanged. Percent mutation: 1%.

*Crossover:* Elements from one of the parents are randomly selected $q$ and are stored in a row. Offsprings are created by copying each element from the other parent from left to right, if the element is in the row, the following element is copied. Percent crossover: 30%.

*Selection:* Individuals are selected randomly from a population, those that achieve the highest score by the evaluation function, have a higher probability of being selected. Selection percentage: 50%.

The size of the population in each generation is of 400 individuals.

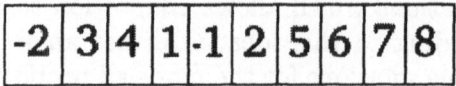

*Figure 1.* Chromosome representation of the GA

## 3. Parallel Tabu Search and Parallel Genetic Algorithms

Just as it is interesting to study the scheduling problem due to its application in the optimization of a parallel machine's resources, it is also interesting to apply parallel models to Meta-Heuristic techniques to extrapolate the improvements in process time allowed by parallelism. There are a variety of applicable parallel models [5], and different studies on the parallelization of specific methods [1]. Consequently, there is justification for the comparison of the parallel behavior between two known methods such as Genetic Algorithms [6], and Tabu Search [4].

## 3.1 Synchronous Network Concurrency Model

The parallelization of the metaheuristics used in this work is achieved through the *Synchronous Network Concurrency Model.* This parallel model uses $K$ processes executed independently, and with independent information. The best result is communicated to a master process which determines the best solution and communicates this to the concurrent processes [13].

The model uses coarse grain parallelization [1], in which the population is divided into sub-populations which are kept relatively isolated from each other. This model introduces the migration operator, which is used to send individuals of a sub-population to the master.

The most frequently used population models in the implementation of coarse grained genetic algorithms are the following: The *island* model, and the *stepping stone* model. In the *island* model the population is sub-partitioned into geographically isolated sub-populations and the individuals can migrate to any other sub-population. In the *stepping stone* model the population is partitioned in the same way, however migration is restricted to neighboring populations.

## 3.2    Parallel Genetic Algorithm *(PGA)*

The model used consists of a master GA and $K$ independent GAs (see Figure 2). The population is divided into equal parts for each GA. When one generation is finished, the GAs send their best individual to the master GA which determines the best of these sending it on to all the GAs according to the migration policy *best individual over random individual* (The best individual is copied over any solution for every GA [13]).

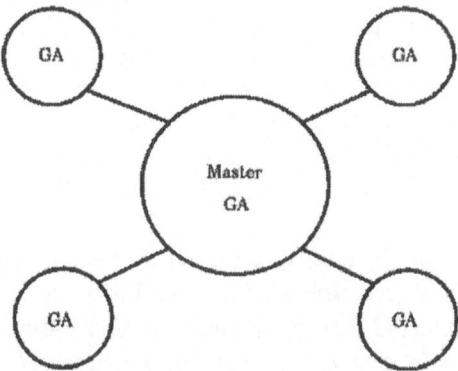

*Figure 2.*    Synchronous Network Concurrency Model applied to Parallel Genetic Algorithms

## 3.3    Parallel Tabu Search *(PTS)*

As with the parallel GA described above, Tabu Search has $K$ TSs with independent neighborhoods and tabu lists. Each sends its best solution to the master TS which copies the best of these to the rest of the TSs. The master process also takes care of initializing the parameters for the search strategy and the initial solutions for each TS.

## 4.    Tests Carried Out and Analysis of Results

The DAG test set presented is made up of 15 representative DAGs extracted from the study [14], and whose principal characteristics are detailed in Table 1. The scheduling problem used considers the assign-

*Table 1.* Test DAG characteristics

| DAG | $v$ | $e$ | $\sigma t_i$ | $\sigma c_{i,j}$ | Type of DAG |
|---|---|---|---|---|---|
| dag0000 | 8 | 8 | 8 | 8 | Unitary/Unitary |
| dag0001 | 9 | 9 | 90 | 23 | Arbitrary/Arbitrary |
| dag0002 | 9 | 9 | 9 | 23 | Unitary/Arbitrary |
| dag0003 | 10 | 9 | 43 | 22 | Arbitrary/Arbitrary |
| dag0004 | 8 | 9 | 8 | 9 | Unitary/Unitary |
| dag0007 | 9 | 12 | 9 | 12 | Unitary/Unitary |
| dag0008 | 10 | 9 | 10 | 22 | Unitary/Arbitrary |
| dag0009 | 20 | 19 | 85 | 52 | Arbitrary/Arbitrary |
| dag0011 | 20 | 19 | 20 | 19 | Unitary/Unitary |
| dag0012 | 21 | 20 | 21 | 20 | Unitary/Unitary |
| dag0014 | 21 | 20 | 48 | 20 | Arbitrary/Unitary |
| dag0026 | 14 | 13 | 14 | 13 | Unitary/Unitary |
| dag0027 | 13 | 17 | 13 | 17 | Unitary/Unitary |
| dag0029 | 13 | 18 | 25 | 64 | Arbitrary/Arbitrary |
| dag0033 | 6 | 6 | 6 | 6 | Unitary/Unitary |

ment of 15 DAGs for $P = 2, 4$ and 8 (45 tests). For each test, each algorithm is executed ten times: GA and TS with $K = 1, 2, 4$ and 8.

The tests were carried out on a machine with shared memory *Silicon Graphics*, with an Irix operating system, version 4.3 and C language.

The information evaluated for each test is the following: Mean Parallel Time *(PTmean)*, the size of the Mean Space Covered *(SCmean)* and the Minimum Parallel Time obtained during the 10 executions*(PTmin)*. Figures 3 and 4, show the graphs of the results obtained from *PTmean* and *SCmean* for the mentioned graphs itinerated over 2 processors ($P = 2$), with 2 parallel algorithms for GA and TS ($K = 2$).

The need for metaheuristics to approach the scheduling problem is justified upon inspection of the size of the search space [4] by means of the equation 1a [12], which establishes the number of possible methods for resolving a number of tasks $v$ over a number of processors $P$, while considering the dependency among tasks.

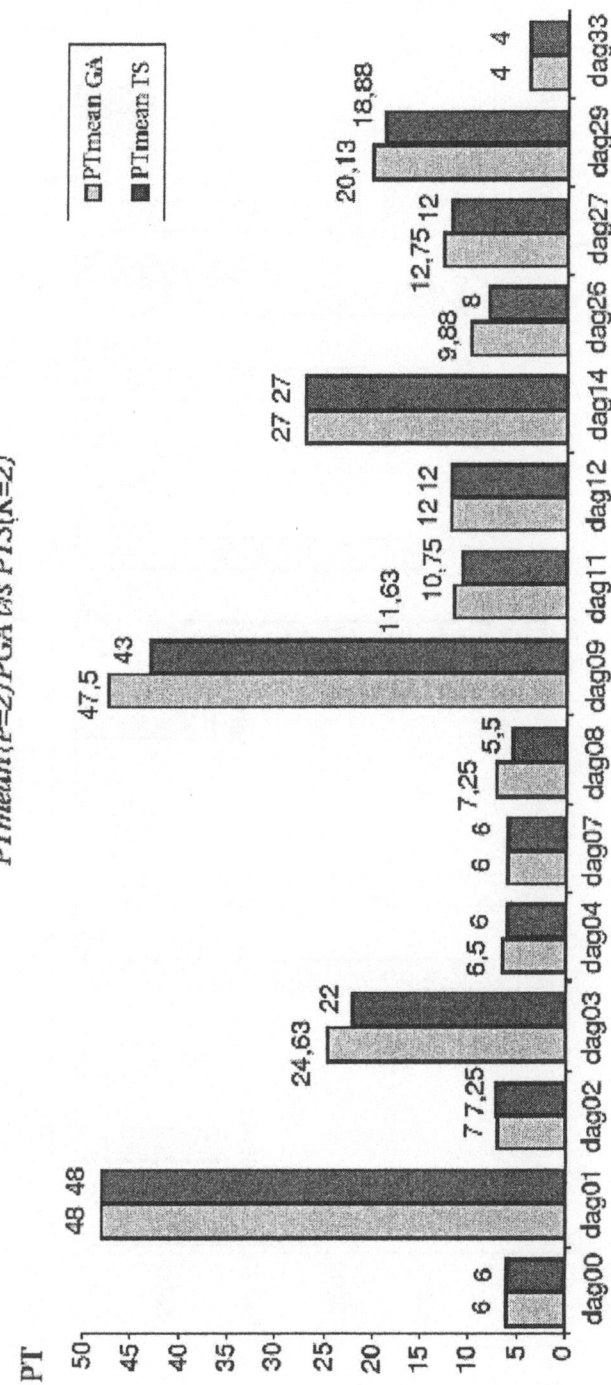

*Figure 3.* Mean Parallel Time between GA and TS with $K = 2, P = 2$.

352

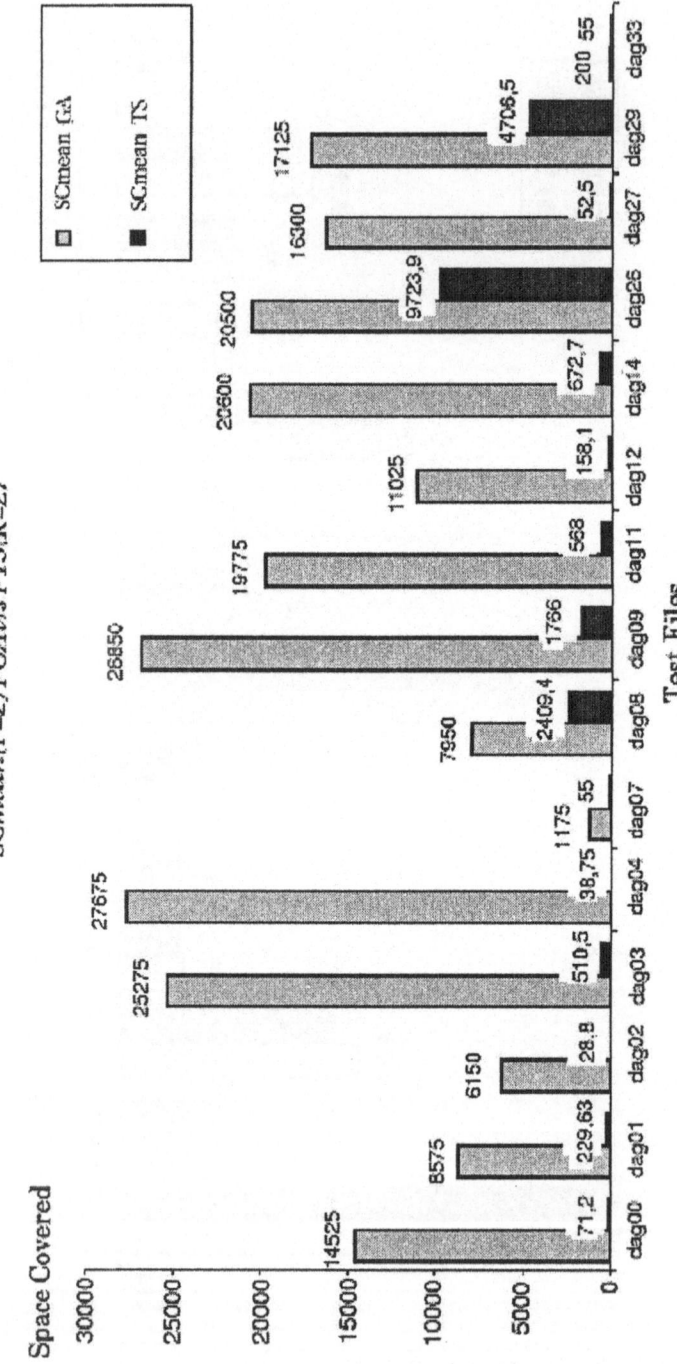

*Figure 4.* Mean Space Covered between GA and TS with $K = 2, P = 2$.

$$f(v,P) = \begin{cases} 1, & \text{if } v = 0 \wedge P = 0 \\ 1, & \text{if } v = 1 \wedge P = 0 \\ P, & \text{if } v = 1 \\ v!, & \text{if } P = 1 \\ \sum_{i=0}^{v}(v-i)!f(i,(P-1)) \begin{vmatrix} v \\ i \end{vmatrix}, & \text{O.C.} \end{cases} \qquad (1a)$$

With equation 1a table A.1 is deduced, with the sizes of the search spaces of the reviewed *DAGs*, thus highlighting the technical impossibility of obtaining solutions by exhaustive search in order to find an optimal solution because of the combinatorial explosion.

## 4.1  Analysis of Results

Figure 3 shows that the *Mean Parallel Time* of the TS based solutions, for scheduling with two processors ($P = 2$), are better than those achieved with the GAs. Additionally, upon reviewing the Figure 4, it can be seen that the *Mean Space Covered* for the GAs with two processors, is greater than TS.

Of the 45 tests carried out, the most representative of the behavior of the algorithms, are those carried out on the graphs assigned for $P = 8$. From the 15 tests selected, in 7 cases GA and TS obtained equal results for parallel time. Additionally, there are 4 cases in which TS obtained equal results independently of the degree of parallelism used, while the *Mean Parallel Time* increased.

As can be seen in Figure 5, *PTS* showed a better performance than *PGA* for all the configurations tested ($K = 1, 2, 4, 8$).

In terms of the *Mean Space Covered* for the mentioned DAGs with 8 processors ($P = 8$) (Figure 6), the PGAs decrease their exploration in the measure that the degree of parallelism increases confirming the results shown in [13]. For their part the PTS show a similar performance, although for *Mean Space Covered* always less, and a slower decrease in the measure that the degree of parallelism increases.

## 5.  Conclusions

According to the results obtained, it can be seen that the *PTS* shows better results than the *PGA*. This can be deduced from the observation that for similar quality solutions *(Mean Parallel Time)*, the *Mean Space Covered* for PTS is significantly less and is in fact a fraction of that used by PGAs. In practice, there is an obvious decrease in required processor time in order to find a good solution to the problem of scheduling multiprocessor machines.

354

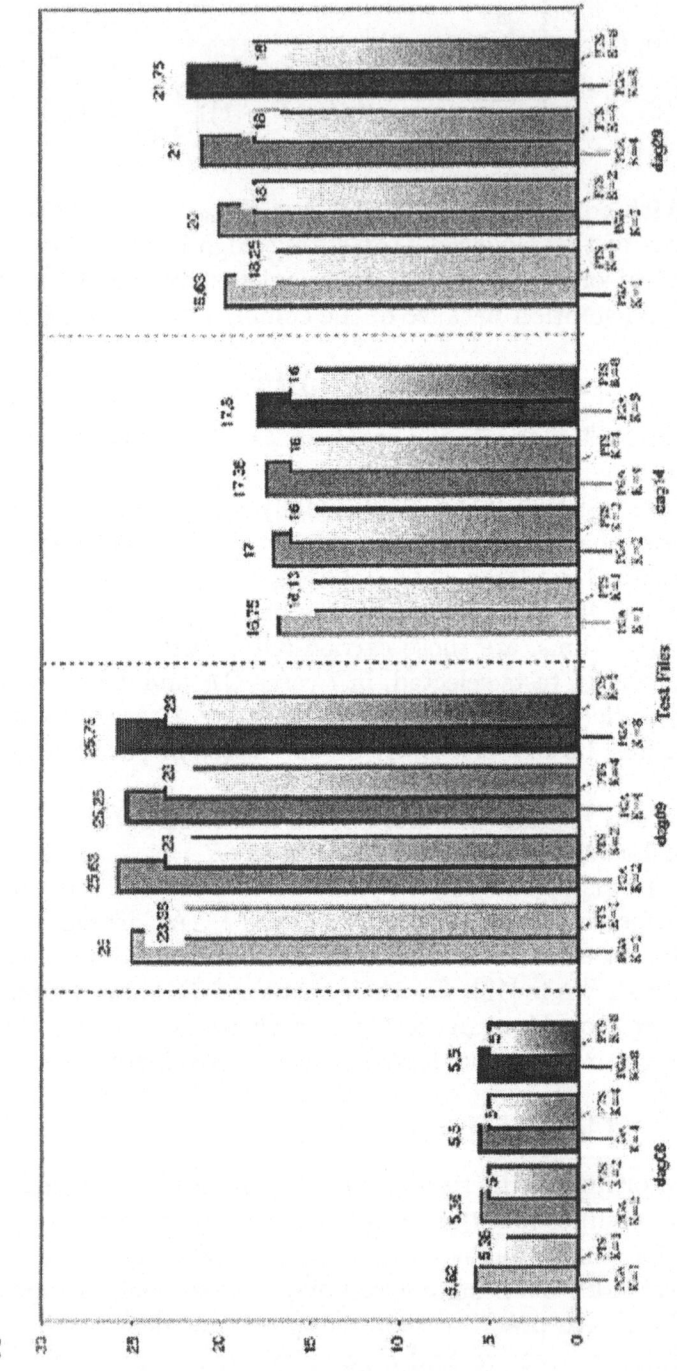

*Figure 5.* Mean Parallel Time between GA and TS with $K = 1, 2, 4, 8$ where $P = 8$.

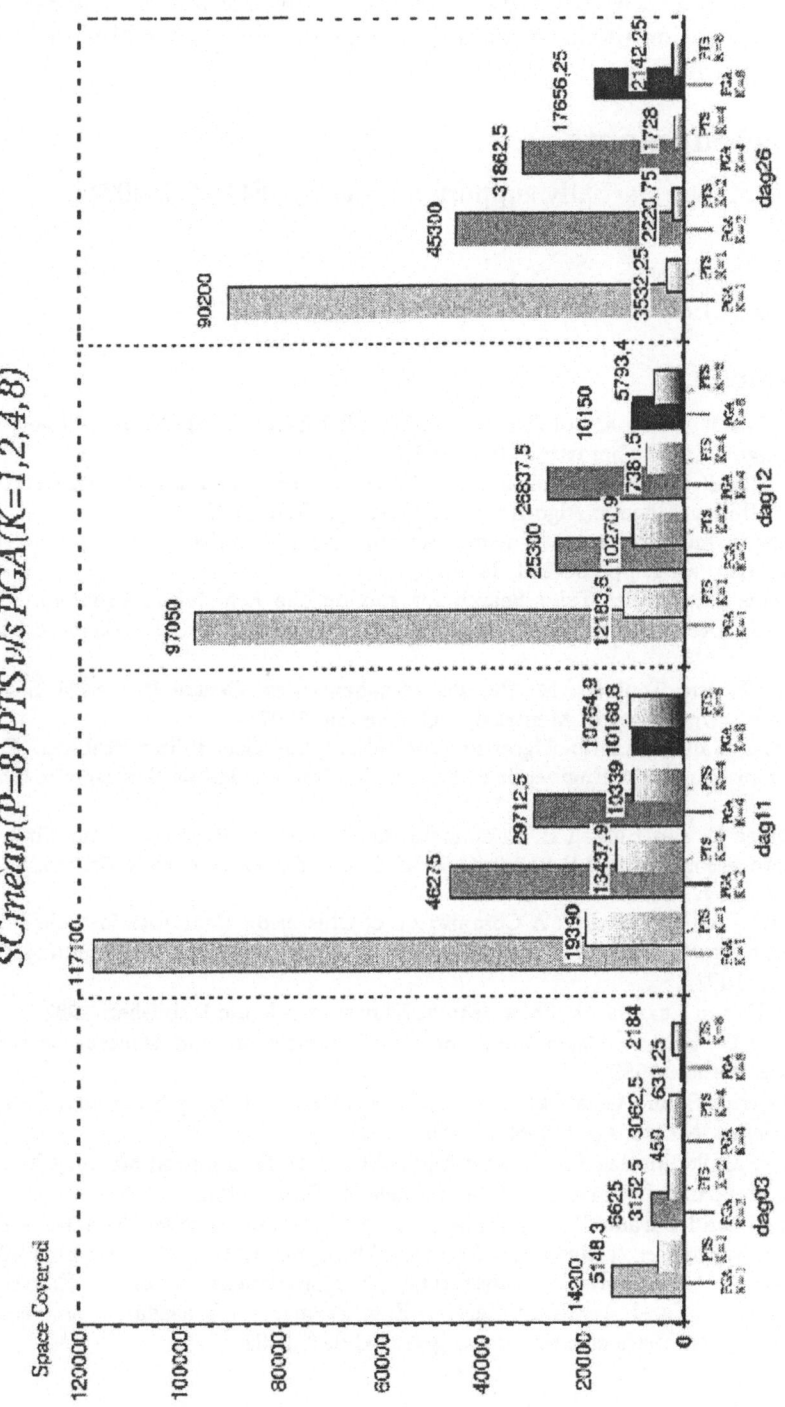

*Figure 6.* Mean Space Covered between GA and TS with $K = 1, 2, 4, 8$ where $P = 8$ .

The PTS and PGA can be used to solve other instances of the scheduling problem, perhaps with similar results. As future works we are studying the application of these parallel models to solve other kinds of combinatorial problems.

## Acknowledgments

This work was partially supported by FONDECYT 1030775.

## Appendix

See Table A.1 on next page.

## References

[1] Cantu Paz E. Summary of Research on Parallel Genetic Algorithms. Illinois Genetic Algorithms Laboratory, USA, 1995.

[2] Cantu Paz E. Migration Policies and Takeover Times in Parallel Genetic Algorithms, Illinois Genetic Algorithms Laboratory, USA, 1999.

[3] Coffman E. and Graham R. Optimal Scheduling for Two-Processor Systems. *Acta Informática*, vol.1, pp 200-213, 1972.

[4] Contreras P. Parallel Tabu Search for solving the Scheduling Problem. Final Project in Computer Engineering [in spanish]. Universidad de Santiago de Chile, 2002.

[5] Crainic T. and Toulouse M. Parallel Metaheuristics. Centre Recherche Sur les Transport, University of Montreal, QC, Canada, 1997.

[6] Díaz S. Parallel Genetic Algorithm for solving the Scheduling Problem. Final Project in Computer Engineering [in spanish]. Universidad de Santiago de Chile, 2002.

[7] Fernandez E. and Bussell B. Bounds on the Number of Processors and Time for Multiprocessor Optimal Schedules. *IEEE Trans. Computers*, vol C-22, no. 8, pp. 745-751, Aug. 1973.

[8] Gerasoulis A. and Tang T. A Comparison of Clustering Heuristics for Scheduling DAGs on Multiprocessors. *Journal on Parallel and Distributed Computing*, Vol. 16, N 4., 1992.

[9] Glover F. and Laguna M. *Tabu Search*, Kluwer Academic Publisher, 1997.

[10] Golberg D. *Genetic Algorithms in Search, Optimization, and Machine Learning*, Addison-Wesley, 1989.

[11] Kirkpatrick S. and Gelatt C. and Vecchi M. Optimization by Simulated Annealing, *Science*, N. 220, pp. 671-680, 1983.

[12] Kri F. Parallel Models for Genetic Algorithms with Distributed Memory. Master Thesis [in spanish], Universidad de Santiago de Chile, 1996.

[13] Solar M. and Parada V. A parallel genetic algorithm to solve the set-covering problem, *Computer & Operation Research*, 29(1), pp. 1221-1235, November 2002.

[14] Waseda. Kasahara Laboratory, Department of Electrical, Electronics and Computer Engineering, Waseda university, http://www.kasahara.elec.waseda.ac.jp/schedule/, 2002.

Table A.1. Test DAG characteristics

| DAG | v | P | Solution | GA | | | | SCmean | | | TS | | | |
|---|---|---|---|---|---|---|---|---|---|---|---|---|---|---|
| | | | | $K=1$ | $K=2$ | $K=4$ | $K=8$ | $K=1$ | $K=2$ | $K=4$ | $K=8$ | | | |
| 0 | 8 | 2 | 362880.0 | 7.2 | 4.0 | 3.4 | 2.5 | $1.1*10^{-2}$ | $2.0*10^{-2}$ | $1.7*10^{-2}$ | $1.4*10^{-3}$ | | | |
| 1 | 9 | 2 | $3.6*10^6$ | 0.6 | $2.4*10^{-1}$ | $1.3*10^{-1}$ | $5.010^{-2}$ | $1.5*10^{-2}$ | $6.3*10^{-3}$ | $1.1*10^{-2}$ | $7.4*10^{-3}$ | | | |
| 2 | 9 | 2 | $3.6*10^6$ | 0.2 | 0.2 | 0.2 | 0.1 | $2.0*10^{-3}$ | $7.9*10^{-4}$ | $2.0*10^{-3}$ | $2.2*10^{-3}$ | | | |
| 3 | 10 | 2 | $4.0*10^7$ | 0.1 | 0.1 | $4.0*10^{-2}$ | $2.0*10^{-3}$ | $2.4*10^{-3}$ | $1.0*10^{-3}$ | $8.3*10^{-4}$ | $4.4*10^{-4}$ | | | |
| 3 | 10 | 8 | $7.*10^{10}$ | $0.2*10^{-4}$ | $9.4*10^{-6}$ | $6.4*10^{-7}$ | $8.9*10^{-7}$ | $7.2*10^{-6}$ | $4.5*10^{-6}$ | $4.3*10^{-6}$ | $3.1*10^{-6}$ | | | |
| 4 | 8 | 2 | $3.6*10^5$ | 10.9 | 7.6 | 2.4 | 2.5 | 0.1 | $0.1*10^{-1}$ | $9.3*10^{-3}$ | $0.2*10^{-1}$ | | | |
| 7 | 9 | 2 | $3.6*10^6$ | 0.1 | $0.3*10^{-1}$ | $0.2*10^{-1}$ | $0.1*10^{-1}$ | $1.6*10^{-3}$ | $1.5*10^{-3}$ | $3.2*10^{-3}$ | $3.4*10^{-3}$ | | | |
| 8 | 10 | 2 | $4.0*10^7$ | $4.1*10^{-2}$ | $2.0*10^{-2}$ | $1.6*10^{-2}$ | $9.7*10^{-3}$ | $3.3*10^{-3}$ | $26.1*10^{-3}$ | $6.8*10^{-3}$ | $4.0*10^{-3}$ | | | |
| 8 | 10 | 8 | $7.1*10^{10}$ | $1.4*10^{-4}$ | $7.9*10^{-5}$ | $1.1*10^{-5}$ | $8.5*10^{-6}$ | $9.1*10^{-6}$ | $9.2*10^{-6}$ | $9.4*10^{-6}$ | $5.5*10^{-6}$ | | | |
| 9 | 20 | 2 | $5.1*10^{19}$ | $1.1*10^{-13}$ | $5.3*10^{-14}$ | $2.7*10^{-14}$ | $1.6*10^{-14}$ | $5.9*10^{-15}$ | $3.4*10^{-15}$ | $2.4*10^{-15}$ | $2.4*10^{-15}$ | | | |
| 9 | 20 | 8 | $2.2*10^{24}$ | $8.1*10^{-18}$ | $4.4*10^{-18}$ | $1.7*10^{-18}$ | $1.1*10^{-18}$ | $8.6*10^{-19}$ | $8.7*10^{-19}$ | $6.8*10^{-19}$ | $5.3*10^{-19}$ | | | |
| 11 | 20 | 2 | $5.1*10^{19}$ | $1.0*10^{-13}$ | $3.9*10^{-14}$ | $1.7*10^{-14}$ | $8.9*10^{-15}$ | $3.3*10^{-15}$ | $1.1*10^{-15}$ | $2.3*10^{-15}$ | $3.2*10^{-15}$ | | | |
| 11 | 20 | 8 | $2.2*10^{24}$ | $5.4*10^{-18}$ | $2.1*10^{-18}$ | $1.4*10^{-18}$ | $4.7*10^{-19}$ | $9.0*10^{-19}$ | $6.2*10^{-19}$ | $4.8*10^{-19}$ | $5.0*10^{-19}$ | | | |
| 12 | 21 | 2 | $1.1*10^{21}$ | $2.2*10^{-15}$ | $9.8*10^{-16}$ | $7.0*10^{-16}$ | $3.9*10^{-16}$ | $2.7*10^{-17}$ | $1.4*10^{-17}$ | $1.0*10^{-17}$ | $1.6*10^{-17}$ | | | |
| 12 | 21 | 8 | $6.0*10^{25}$ | $1.6*10^{-19}$ | $4.1*10^{-20}$ | $4.4*10^{-20}$ | $1.7*10^{-20}$ | $2.0*10^{-20}$ | $1.7*10^{-20}$ | $1.2*10^{-20}$ | $9.6*10^{-21}$ | | | |
| 14 | 21 | 2 | $1.1*10^{21}$ | $2.0*10^{-15}$ | $1.8*10^{-15}$ | $7.8*10^{-16}$ | $5.3*10^{-16}$ | $4.7*10^{-17}$ | $6.0*10^{-17}$ | $4.4*10^{-17}$ | $6.5*10^{-17}$ | | | |
| 14 | 21 | 8 | $6.0*10^{25}$ | $1.9*10^{-19}$ | $1.1*10^{-19}$ | $4.2*10^{-20}$ | $3.3*10^{-20}$ | $2.8*10^{-20}$ | $2.1*10^{-20}$ | $1.7*10^{-20}$ | $1.1*10^{-20}$ | | | |
| 26 | 14 | 2 | $1.3*10^{12}$ | $2.4*10^{-6}$ | $1.6*10^{-6}$ | $7.5*10^{-7}$ | $4.0*10^{-7}$ | $3.4*10^{-7}$ | $7.4*10^{-7}$ | $4.0*10^{-7}$ | $2.0*10^{-7}$ | | | |
| 26 | 14 | 8 | $1.0*10^{16}$ | $8.9*10^{-10}$ | $1.2*10^{-10}$ | $3.1*10^{-10}$ | $1.7*10^{-10}$ | $3.5*10^{-11}$ | $2.2*10^{-11}$ | $1.7*10^{-11}$ | $2.1*10^{-11}$ | | | |
| 27 | 13 | 2 | $8.7*10^{10}$ | $2.8*10^{-5}$ | $1.9*10^{-5}$ | $9.3*10^{-6}$ | $5.9*10^{-6}$ | $6.7*10^{-8}$ | $6.0*10^{-8}$ | $6,5*10^{-8}$ | $1.2*10^{-7}$ | | | |
| 27 | 13 | 8 | $4.8*10^{14}$ | $1.3*10^{-8}$ | $6.4*10^{-9}$ | $3.8*10^{-9}$ | $2.8*10^{-9}$ | $5.7*10^{-11}$ | $3.3*10^{-11}$ | $3.4*10^{-11}$ | $7.2*10^{-11}$ | | | |
| 29 | 13 | 2 | $8.7*10^{10}$ | $2.6*10^{-5}$ | $2.0*10^{-5}$ | $1.3*10^{-5}$ | $5*10^{-6}$ | $1.4*10^{-6}$ | $5.4*10^{-6}$ | $1.3*10^{-6}$ | $1.9*10^{-6}$ | | | |
| 29 | 13 | 8 | $4.8*10^{14}$ | $3.6*10^{-8}$ | $1.4*10^{-8}$ | $1.2*10^{-8}$ | $3.0*10^{-9}$ | $1.1*10^{-9}$ | $1.1*10^{-9}$ | $10.0*10^{-10}$ | $7.4*10^{-10}$ | | | |
| 33 | 6 | 2 | $5.0*10^3$ | 7.9 | 4.0 | 2.0 | 1.0 | 1.1 | 1.1 | 1.9 | 2.0 | | | |

# MODELLING DOCUMENT CATEGORIES BY EVOLUTIONARY LEARNING OF TEXT CENTROIDS

J.I. Serrano, M.D. Del Castillo
*Instituto de Automática Industrial, CSIC. Ctra. Campo Real, km.0,200. La Poveda. Arganda del Rey. 28500 Madrid. Spain*

**Abstract:** This paper deals with a supervised learning method devoted to producing categorization models of text documents. The goal of the method is to use a suitable numerical measurement of example similarity to find centroids describing different categories of examples. The centroids are neither abstract nor statistical models, but rather consist of bits of examples. The centroid-learning method is based on a genetic algorithm, the GAT. The categorization system using this genetic algorithm infers a model by applying the genetic algorithm to the set of preclassified documents belonging to a category. The models thus obtained are the category centroids that are used to predict the category of a new document. The application of this system is the task of classifying incoming documents.

**Key words:** similarity function, centroid, genetic learning, text classification

## 1. INTRODUCTION

There are well-known methods for automating the building of clusters and descriptive models of text documents[6]. Most such methods are included in the machine learning paradigm, where the categorization problem is envisioned as a process of learning supervised by the knowledge of the categories and of the training instances that belong to them. Documents manually classified are the key resource in such a paradigm, and a general inductive process automatically builds a text classification model for every category by extracting the main features from preclassified documents.

Two other example-driven techniques that infer no classification model are the k-nearest neighbour (K-NN)[2] and textual case-based reasoning (TCBR)[3]. Systems using these techniques start with a set of documents associated by hand with a kind of "solution". According to the terminology employed in these methods, when a new example is entered to be solved, the method compares the new example to the stored examples and retrieves the most similar ones. Then, the "solutions" associated with these similar examples are used to provide the solution to the new example. When examples are text documents, the "solution" associated with each document is the category the document belongs to. These methods employ no learning stage, and the only task that precedes the comparison of documents, very time- and storage space-consuming, is the allocation of preclassified documents.

## 2.      DOCUMENT CLASSIFICATION TASK

This paper deals with text supervised learning where text documents are the only information available. The goal of the method is to find the centroids that describe the different given document categories. Every centroid is neither an abstract nor a statistical model but rather consists of the set of words selected from the category documents that, when used for document categorization, yields the highest effectiveness of the model. The proposed centroid-learning stage is based on a genetic algorithm (GAT).

An important requirement of the supervised centroid-learning is to use a small amount of training examples for building a categorization system taking the right classification decisions in any text domain regardless of the domain characteristics. There are many specific thematic domains in which it is very difficult to obtain significant samples of training documents. Most of current exampled-based systems need exhaustive training sets implying high download and store costs for obtaining a final, reliable classification system[6].

The centroids learned can be used later for organizing tasks like classification and summarization[8]. The application of the GAT-based system focuses on the task of classifying incoming documents in several non-disjoint categories.

The following section describes the text preprocessing step. The details of the newly developed genetic algorithm and the proposed similarity function are discussed in Section 3. Sections 4 and 5 describe the generalization of the genetic algorithm and the classification application, respectively. Section 6 reviews the experimental settings and results. Last sections contain the conclusions.

# 3. GENETIC ALGORITHMS FOR TEXTS (GAT)

The information contained in text documents is often expressed in a natural language that must be mapped to a representation understandable by the classifier algorithm. The preprocessing step used here is comprised within the *bag of words* approach commonly used in most text applications[8]. The task of the system is to scan the text of documents in every category and to turn that text into lists of words, together with their occurrence frequency. Next, words belonging to a stop list or words without semantic contents are removed, and several stemming procedures are applied[4]. A preprocessed document is a list of pairs, each pair consisting of a word and its occurrence frequency.

Genetic algorithms are an optimization technique that simulates the natural evolution process[1]. Beginning with an initial population of individuals or chromosomes representing tentative solutions to a problem, a new generation is created by combining or modifying the best individuals of the previous generation. The process ends when the best solution is achieved.

The problem proposed is to obtain a centroid document representing the documents of a class. The central notion is a measure of similarity among documents, so documents in a class show a high intra-class similarity and a low inter-class similarity. One possible solution to this problem could be generated by taking a random set of words from the documents in a class and measuring the similarity between that random set and every document. Due to the huge search space and the lack of good heuristics based on the semantics of the words, there are many potential initial sets of words.

The initial population designed here to lead the search for centroids consists of the preprocessed documents of every class, since every document is the most similar to itself and one possible centroid with regard to the other documents in its class. After applying the GAT method, the centroid of every category is a document composed of different portions of every labelled document belonging to the category.

## 3.1 Text Representation and Genetic Operators

Every chromosome symbolizes a possible centroid document. The chromosomes of the initial population are the documents obtained after preprocessing. The genes of a chromosome are pairs consisting of a word and its occurrence frequency. Since documents are of a variable size, the length of chromosomes is also variable.

The genetic algorithm for texts uses three operators: copy, crossover and mutation.

**Copy Operator.** This operator selects some of the best chromosomes of a population and duplicates them in the next generation. Since the evolution of a population over time can produce worse chromosomes than the original set, this operator provides a mechanism for remembering chromosomes that were previously useful.

**Two-Point Crossover Operator.** Typically, a simple crossover operator generates a new offspring from selected parent chromosomes by swapping all the genes between a randomly selected position and the length of the chromosome less one. The version used by this GAT selects at random two positions in each parent chromosome.

There are two reasons for using a random multiple-point crossover operator. The first crossover point must belong to each parent because of the different length of chromosomes. The second random crossover point in each parent allows the number of exchanging genes to be smaller than the number of exchanging genes with a simple crossover operator. The resulting offspring may therefore turn out to be modified to a lesser degree.

**Mutation Operator.** This operator selects one gene of a chromosome and modifies its value. In the proposed algorithm, there are two ways of modifying a gene. One way lies in replacing the selected gene by another randomly selected from the full current set of words present in the documents of a category. This option enables all the words to contribute fairly. The other way to mutate a gene lies in increasing or decreasing the value of the occurrence frequency of the gene. This latter kind of mutation is justified by the design of the fitness function, as discussed in the following subsection.

## 3.2    Population Fitness Function

The objective of the fitness function is to compute some measurement of the profit or goodness a chromosome would have as a centroid document of a class. According to the assumptions, every chromosome of a concrete population is a centroid. The closer to every preprocessed document the centroid is, the better it will be.

Obviously, the chromosome taking the highest fitness value will be the best centroid. The main point of the fitness function is to find the measurement of similarity or, inversely, the measurement of distance among documents. The more similar a document is to another, the less distance will exist between them.

There are many studies about how to characterize the similarity between any two texts; some are statistics-based, and others are word semantics-based[5]. In this paper, similarity is calculated by a statistical function that takes into consideration the number of times words occur within the compared texts. Eq. 1 reflects the similarity function.

$$\text{Similarity } (X,Y) = \Sigma nx_i \cdot ny_j \; (\forall I, j \,/\, x_i \in X \; \& \; y_j \in Y \; \& \; xi = y_j) \qquad (1)$$

where $nx_i$ is the number of appearances of word $x_i$ in document $X$, and $ny_j$ is the number of appearances of word $y_j$ in document $Y$. This function calculates the similarity between document X and document Y. The degree of similarity between two documents is obtained by multiplying the number of occurrences of the words that are common to both documents. Thus, if a centroid contains many relevant words that are present in many documents, the centroid will take a high average similarity value with every document and therefore a low average distance value.

The fitness function value of a chromosome is the average similarity between all documents and that chromosome (see Eq. 2).

$$\text{Fitness(Chr)} = \frac{\Sigma_i^{\,N} \text{Similarity}(i, Chr)}{N} \qquad (2)$$

where $i$ is document $i$ from the initial set, $N$ is the number of initial documents, and $Chr$ is the chromosome evaluated.

In order for a genetic algorithm to be applied, certain other parameters must be determined as well, such as the maximum number of generations, the stop fitness value, the probability of application of operators and the operator workspace. The sizes of the workspace for the Copy, Two-Point Crossover and Mutation operators have been set to 30%, 65% and 80%, respectively. The optimal values of the application probabilities of the Copy, Two-Point Crossover and Mutation operators were 0.4, 0.65 and 0.8, respectively. All these values have been determined experimentally.

## 4. APPLYING GAT TO DOCUMENT CLASSIFICATION

The application of the GAT to text web pages or hypertext implies taking into account certain additional issues regarding the presence of often ungrammatical text in web pages. First, in the preprocessing step, the frequency of word occurrences is increased for some word formats in an experimental way.

Four different types of information can be found in web pages explicitly: URL, META keywords, hyperlinks and plain text. Words can assume a different semantic power depending on their placement. Based on this division of documents, the preprocessing step will generate four lists of word/occurrence frequency pairs, one each for the four types of information.

The GAT can consider a web page as a whole text or as four parts of text. When the web page is to be processed as a whole, the GAT will apply the crossover operator only to a part chosen at random for every two parent chromosomes selected to be crossed. If the web page is considered as consisting of four parts, then the chromosomes handled by the GAT are divided into four parts and the genetic operators will be applied to the four parts in a parallel manner. Therefore, the fittest chromosomes (and the text categories) can be modelled by as many centroids as different types information exist in the web pages belonging to the categories. Thus, the application of the GAT can be generalized to include grammatical texts and hypertexts, because any kind of document can be mapped onto the described web representation; and therefore use can be made of the information that web page authors give when they place a word in some special position and/or format.

The classification process begins when the system receives an unlabeled document. First, the similarity between the document and every learned centroid according to Equation 1 is calculated. Next, the document is classified as belonging to the category or categories whose centroid or centroids are closest to the document. In each category a threshold value of the similarity is set so that any document with a similarity less than the threshold is not classified into the category. An interesting advantage of the similarity measurement is that the values it takes for a document with respect to each centroid can be seen as degrees of membership in each category.

When the categorization system classifies web pages, it takes into account the existence of centroids composed of four centroids. Therefore, when a new web page is being classified, the similarity between every type of information on the page and the corresponding centroid is calculated. The final similarity between a web page and a category is given by the average of at most four similarity measurements.

## 5.     EMPIRICAL TESTS

The system described has been evaluated on two text collections. The first experiment allowed to set up the influence of the number of generations and the number of centroids per category to the system performance. Once these parameters were determined, the second experiment intended to evaluate two issues involved in the genetic centroid-based approach: 1) differences in classification performance, checked by considering the web documents as a whole or as four separate types of information (URL, META, TEXT, LINKS); 2) the results obtained with a two-point crossover operator instead of a simple crossover operator.

The first experiment was carried out on the Reuters-21578 collection. A subset of this collection was selected consisting of 1,987 documents belonging to eight categories. These documents were divided into two groups, a training set of 240 examples and a test set of 1,747 examples. The GAT method was applied to the training set, and the centroids thus obtained were used to classify the test set. Table 1 shows the classification performance for each category in the rows and the results for different values of the number of generations in the columns.

*Table 1.* Average results from five runs of the genetic algorithm on Reuters test set for classification with different maximum numbers of generations

|  | 20 Generations | | | 50 Generations | | | 100 Generations | | | 175 Generations | | |
|---|---|---|---|---|---|---|---|---|---|---|---|---|
|  | *Pr* | *Rc* | *F* | *Pr* | *Rc* | *F* | *Pr* | *Rc* | *F* | *Pr* | *Rc* | *F* |
| **ACQ** | 69.91 | 64.6 | 67.15 | 93.88 | 61.4 | 74.24 | 84.68 | 79.6 | 82.06 | 99.5 | 70 | 82.15 |
| **COF** | 49.18 | 93.75 | 64.51 | 56.86 | 90.62 | 69.87 | 50.81 | 96.87 | 66.66 | 37.03 | 93.75 | 53.09 |
| **EAR** | 96.33 | 72.37 | 82.65 | 97.82 | 78.62 | 87.17 | 99.85 | 87.87 | 93.48 | 98.40 | 87.5 | 92.59 |
| **GOL** | 90.9 | 80 | 85.1 | 99.99 | 88 | 93.61 | 95.65 | 88 | 91.66 | 79.16 | 76 | 77.55 |
| **NAT** | 88.23 | 44.11 | 58.82 | 78.26 | 52.94 | 63.15 | 74.99 | 44.11 | 55.55 | 99.99 | 52.94 | 69.23 |
| **MON** | 99.99 | 77.77 | 87.49 | 80.64 | 55.55 | 65.78 | 99.99 | 71.11 | 83.11 | 99.99 | 77.77 | 87.49 |
| **SUG** | 99.99 | 70.73 | 82.85 | 99.99 | 73.17 | 84.5 | 99.99 | 75.6 | 86.11 | 99.99 | 73.17 | 84.5 |
| **TRA** | 99.99 | 49.6 | 66.31 | 99.99 | 57.6 | 73.09 | 99.99 | 64 | 78.04 | 98.79 | 59.2 | 74 |
| **Avg.** | 86.81 | 69.11 | 76.95 | 96.93 | 59.5 | 73.73 | 92.33 | 71.8 | 80.78 | 99.14 | 64.6 | 78.22 |

Classification performance is based on calculating three different measurements: precision or percentage of correct predictions, recall or percentage of documents that have been correctly classified, and F-measure as a combination of the precision and recall measurements, *F-measure=(2\*precision\*recall)/(precision+ recall)*.

The greater the number of generations, the better the results are. Although the best results depend on the category, it seems that the best macroaveraged value of the maximum number of generations is 100.

A similar analysis was carried out to determine the influence of the number of centroids to the classification performance. The results showed the more centroids there are, the worse the results. Using more than two centroids is not a good option, because although the precision value is kept the remaining performance values are decreased.

The second experiment was carried out using a collection of web pages called BankSearch. This data set is jointly provided by BankSearch

Information Consultancy Ltd. and the Computer Science Department at the University of Reading. The collection consists of 10,000 web documents classified into ten categories of equal size, each containing 1,000 web pages[7]. A subset of this collection was selected, consisting of 4,625 examples equally distributed into five categories (Commercial Banks, Java, Astronomy, Soccer, Sport). All the categories were divided into four disjoint sets: one training set with 50 examples to learn the category centroids and three test sets with 250, 125 and 500 examples, respectively, to validate them. In this experimental setting, GAT was run for 100 generations and only one centroid per category was selected from the last generation.

The issue of considering web pages as a whole or as four separate types of information (URL, META, TEXT, LINKS) was explored using the first test set. The different performance between a two-point crossover operator and a simple crossover operator was explored using the second test set.

Table 2 and Table 3 show the classification performance for Test Set I and Test Set II, respectively.

*Table 2.* Average results from five runs of the genetic algorithm on Test Set I

| Categories TEST SET I | Full Document Two-Point Crossover | | | Four Information Types Simple Crossover | | | Four Information Types Two-Point Crossover | | |
|---|---|---|---|---|---|---|---|---|---|
| | *Pr* | *Rc* | *F* | *Pr* | *Rc* | *F* | *Pr* | *Rc* | *F* |
| COMMERCIAL | **95.45** | 8.4 | 15.441 | 89.28 | 60 | 71.770 | 90.53 | **95.6** | **92.996** |
| JAVA | **80.83** | 54 | 64.748 | 79.23 | **99.2** | **88.099** | 77.18 | 98.8 | 86.666 |
| ASTRONOMY | 98.03 | 40 | 56.818 | 93.13 | **76** | **83.700** | **99.41** | 68.4 | 81.042 |
| SOCCER | 53.57 | **98.8** | 69.47 | 89.64 | 90 | 89.820 | 91.86 | 90.4 | **91.129** |
| SPORT | **100** | 5.6 | 10.606 | **100** | 67.6 | 80.668 | **100** | 72 | **83.720** |
| Average | 85.57 | 41.36 | 55.765 | 90.26 | 78.56 | 84.004 | 91.79 | 85.04 | 88.286 |

*Table 3.* Average results from five runs of the genetic algorithm on Test Set II

| Categories TEST SET II | Full Document Two-Point Crossover | | | Four Information Types Simple Crossover | | | Four Information Types Two-Point Crossover | | |
|---|---|---|---|---|---|---|---|---|---|
| | *Pr* | *Rc* | *F* | *Pr* | *Rc* | *F* | *Pr* | *Rc* | *F* |
| COMMERCIAL | 93.33 | 11.2 | 20 | **95.23** | 64 | 76.555 | 91.79 | **98.4** | **94.980** |
| JAVA | **82.60** | 60.8 | 70.046 | 77.63 | **100** | **87.412** | 78.70 | 97.6 | 87.142 |
| ASTRONOMY | 98.33 | 47.2 | 63.783 | 94.73 | 72 | 81.818 | **100** | **76.8** | **86.877** |
| SOCCER | 53.44 | **99.2** | 69.467 | **95.72** | 89.6 | **92.560** | 92.06 | 92.8 | 92.430 |
| SPORT | **100** | 5.6 | 10.606 | **100** | 77.6 | 87.387 | **100** | 80 | **88.888** |
| Average | 85.54 | 44.8 | 58.803 | **92.62** | 80.64 | 86.215 | 92.51 | **89.12** | **90.783** |

The columns in Table 2 and Table 3 show the values of these measurements with three different GAT configurations: web pages as a whole text and web pages consisting of four types of information with simple and two-point crossover operators. All the numerical values given in the tables are the average result of five runs of the genetic algorithm.

As the results show, when the GAT is configured to consider four different kinds of information in web documents, it gives a better average performance than when it processes documents as a whole. The two-point crossover yields a slightly better performance than the simple crossover in both test sets. The best configuration for the algorithm therefore seems to be the configuration that considers the types of information in each document separately and employs the two-point crossover operator.

*Table 4*. Average results from five runs of the genetic algorithm on Test Set III

| Categories TEST SET III | Four Information Types | | |
|---|---|---|---|
| | *Pr* | *Rc* | *F* |
| COMMERCIAL | 71.69 | 98.8 | 83.095 |
| JAVA | 78.55 | 76.2 | 77.360 |
| ASTRONOMY | 96.15 | 75 | 84.269 |
| SOCCER | 89.76 | 91.2 | 90.476 |
| SPORT | 100 | 71.6 | 83.449 |
| Average | 87.23 | 82.56 | 84.830 |

This configuration was used to test classification performance in Test Set III, the test set with the largest number of web documents. Table 4 shows that the system performed very well in some categories, and, on average, the values of the performance measurements are quite high in all three test sets with only 50 training examples per category.

*Table 5*. Performance results of the GAT model and the Naïve Bayes classifier

| Categories TEST SET III | Four Information Types Two-Point Crossover | | | Naïve Bayes | | |
|---|---|---|---|---|---|---|
| | *Pr* | *Rc* | *F* | *Pr* | *Rc* | *F* |
| COMMERCIAL | 71.69 | 98.8 | 83.095 | 87.4 | 98 | 92.39 |
| JAVA | 78.55 | 76.2 | 77.360 | 95.6 | 77.2 | 85.02 |
| ASTRONOMY | 96.15 | 75 | 84.269 | 97.7 | 71.4 | 83.21 |
| SOCCER | 89.76 | 91.2 | 90.476 | 75.44 | 84.8 | 79.84 |
| SPORT | 100 | 71.6 | 83.449 | 69.52 | 84.4 | 76.24 |
| Average | 87.23 | 82.56 | 84.830 | 85.13 | 83.16 | 84.13 |

Table 5 shows a comparison between the GAT model and a Naïve Bayes classifier on the BankSearch collection. The training set was composed of 50 examples and the test set of 250 examples (Training Set and Test Set I). Due to the high dimensionality of the word space, a dimensionality reduction technique selecting 20% of the best ranked words was used before applying the Naïve Bayes classifier. Scoring words was carried out by the gain information statistical measurement. The results obtained strengthen the successful classification performance of the genetic-based model working on few training documents.

## 6. CONCLUSIONS

A genetic algorithm for texts has been proposed for obtaining centroid documents that describe text categories by learning those centroids and using them to classify documents. This technique consumes little time in the classification stage. The system requires no computations to find the similarity between new documents and the documents stored in the repository or the case base, but only to find the similarity with learned centroids. The classification results have shown that the technique works quite well using very few training documents and at most two centroids per category. The classification results can even be improved by fine-tuning the algorithm parameters and perhaps by selecting more representative training examples.

## REFERENCES

1. D. Goldberg, *Genetic Algorithms in Search, Optimization & Machine Learning* (Addison-Wesley Publishing Company, Inc, 1989)
2. S. Han Eui-Hong, G. Karypis and V. Kumar, Text Categorization Using Weight Adjusted k-Nearest Neighbor Classification, PAKDD'2001 (2001).
3. M. Lenz, A. Hubner and M. Kunze, Textual CBR, in *Case-Based Reasoning Technology*, edited by M. Lenz, B. Bartsch, H.D. Burkhard and S. Wess ( Springer. LNAI 1400, 1998).
4. M.F. Porter, An algorithm for suffix stripping, *Program*, **14**(3), 130-137 (1980).
5. M.M. Ritcher, The Knowledge Contained in Similarity Measures. Invited Talk at ICCBR-95 (1995).
6. F. Sebastiani, Machine Learning in Automated Text Categorization, *ACM Computing Surveys*, **34**(1), 1-47 (2002).
7. M.P. Sinka and D.W. Corne, A Large Benchmark Dataset for Web Document Clustering, in *Soft Computing Systems: Design, Management and Applications*, edited by A. Abraham, J. Ruiz-del-Solar, and M. Koeppen (Volume 87 of Frontiers in Artificial Intelligence and Applications, 2002), pp. 881-890.
8. K. Zechner, A Literature Survey on Text Summarization. Paper for Directed Reading (Fall 1996), *Computational Linguistics* (1997).

# ODEVAL: A TOOL FOR EVALUATING RDF(S), DAML+OIL, AND OWL CONCEPT TAXONOMIES

Óscar Corcho, Asunción Gómez-Pérez, Rafael González-Cabero and M. Carmen Suárez-Figueroa

*Laboratorio de Inteligencia Artificial. Facultad de Informática. Universidad Politécnica de Madrid. Campus de Montegancedo sn. Boadilla del Monte, 28660. Madrid, Spain*

Abstract:     Ontologies implemented in RDF(S), DAML+OIL, and OWL should be evaluated from the point of view of knowledge representation before using them in Semantic Web applications. Several language-dependent ontology validation tools and ontology platforms, such as OilEd with FaCT, can be used in order to evaluate RDF(S), DAML+OIL and OWL ontologies. This paper offers two main contributions. The first of these exams whether previous ontology tools detect knowledge representation problems in RDF(S), DAML+OIL, and OWL concept taxonomies. Indeed, such tools do not focus on detecting inconsistencies and redundancies in concept taxonomies. The second contribution is ODEval, a language-dependent tool for evaluating, from the point of view of knowledge representation, concept taxonomies in ontologies implemented in such languages. ODEval complements previous ontology tools when we want to evaluate RDF(S), DAML+OIL, and OWL concept taxonomies.

Key words:    Ontology Evaluation; Ontology Tools; Concept Taxonomies

## 1.     INTRODUCTION

Like any other resources used in software applications, ontology content needs to be evaluated before (re)using it in other ontologies or applications. Moreover, content evaluation as well as evaluation of the software environments used to build ontologies are critical processes before ontologies can be integrated in final applications.

Ontology evaluation is a crucial activity, which needs to be carried out during the whole ontology life-cycle. The goal of this evaluation is to determine what the ontology correctly defines, does not define at all, or even incorrectly defines. Few domain-independent methodological approaches (Fernández-López et al., 1999; Gómez-Pérez et al., 2003) have been reported for building ontologies, nevertheless all of them identify the need for ontology evaluation, but the evaluation is performed differently in each one.

The first work on ontology content evaluation started in 1994 and in the past three years the interest on this topic has grown. The principal efforts were made by Gómez-Pérez (2001) and by Guarino and Welty (2000).

Along with the increasing number of ontologies implemented in the ontology languages RDF(S)[1, 2], DAML+OIL[3], and OWL[4], certain specialized ontology parsers, namely Validating RDF Parser[5], RDF Validation Service[6], DAML Validator[7], DAML+OIL Ontology Checker[8], OWL Ontology Validator[9], and OWL Validator[10], and import services within ontology platforms, namely OilEd (Bechhofer et al., 2001), OntoEdit[11], Protégé-2000[12], and WebODE[13] have been built. These ontology tools must be studied in order to analyze whether they detect, from the point of view of knowledge representation, possible taxonomic problems, like inconsistencies and redundancies, in ontologies implemented in such languages.

In (Gómez-Pérez and Suárez-Figueroa, 2003, 2004) we describe how several ontology tools evaluate RDF(S) and DAML+OIL concept taxonomies. In this paper we detail our study with 41 ontologies, which are well-built from a syntactic point of view, but have inconsistencies and redundancies in their concept taxonomies. We have parsed these ontologies with the previous ontology parsers and have imported them into OilEd using its import service and connecting it to the reasoning engine FaCT (Horrocks et al., 1999). It has been discovered that, in the majority of the experiments, these ontology tools do not detect the taxonomic problems identified in

---

[1] http://www.w3.org/TR/PR-rdf-schema
[2] http://www.w3.org/TR/REC-rdf-syntax/
[3] http://www.daml.org/2001/03/daml+oil-walkthru.html
[4] http://www.w3.org/TR/owl-ref/
[5] http://139.91.183.30:9090/RDF/VRP/
[6] http://www.w3.org/RDF/Validator/
[7] http://www.daml.org/validator/
[8] http://potato.cs.man.ac.uk/oil/Checker
[9] http://phoebus.cs.man.ac.uk:9999/OWL/Validator
[10] http://owl.bbn.com/validator/
[11] http://www.ontoprise.de/products/ontoedit_en
[12] http://protege.stanford.edu/
[13] http://babage.dia.fi.upm.es/webode/

(Gómez-Pérez, 2001). For this reason, we have built ODEval[14] as a complement to the previous ontology tools. ODEval performs syntactic evaluation of RDF(S), DAML+OIL, and OWL ontologies, and evaluates their concept taxonomies from the point of view of knowledge representation using the ideas proposed in (Gómez-Pérez, 2001).

This paper is organized as follows: section two briefly presents possible anomalies that can appear in taxonomic knowledge; section three presents a brief description of the RDF(S), DAML+OIL, and OWL tools used in our experiments; section four includes our comparative study; section 5 describes ODEval; and finally, we conclude with further work on evaluation.

## 2. EVALUATING TAXONOMIC KNOWLEDGE IN ONTOLOGIES

Figure 1 presents a set of possible problems that can appear when ontologists model taxonomic knowledge in ontologies (Gómez-Pérez, 2001).

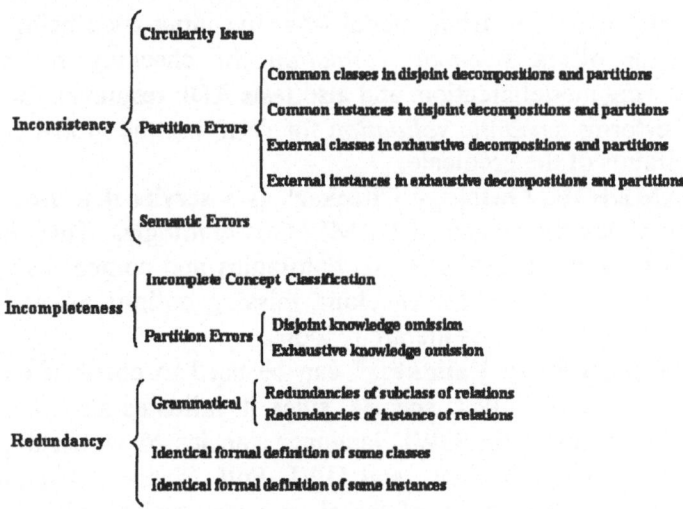

*Figure 1*. Potential problems that might appear in taxonomies

In this paper we focus on the automatic detection of inconsistencies (circularity issue and partition errors) and redundancy grammatical problems. We postpone the analysis of the others for further works.

---

[14] http://minsky.dia.fi.upm.es/odeval

## 3. RDF(S), DAML+OIL, AND OWL ONTOLOGY TOOLS

Currently, there are several ontology parsers and ontology platforms which can be used in order to evaluate RDF(S), DAML+OIL, and OWL ontologies. In this paper, we focus on the following ontology tools:

The ICS-FORTH **Validating RDF Parser** (VRP v2.5)[15] analyzes, validates and processes RDF schemas and resource descriptions. This parser offers *syntactic validation* for checking if the input namespace conforms to the updated RDF/XML syntax proposed by W3C, and *semantic validation* for verifying constraints derived from RDF Schema Specification (RDFS).

The W3C **RDF Validation Service**[16] is based on HP-Labs Another RDF Parser (ARP[17]), which currenlty uses the version 2-alpha-1. This service supports the Last Call Working Draft specifications issued by the RDF Core Working Group, including datatypes. It offers *syntactic validation* for checking if the input namespace conforms to the updated RDF/XML syntax proposed by W3C. However, this service does not do any RDFS validation.

The **DAML Validator**[18] uses the ARP parser from the Jena (1.6.1) toolkit to create an RDF triple model from the input code being validated. This validator offers *syntactic validation* for checking for namespace problems during model creation, and also tests RDF resources for existence. This tool performs *semantic validation* for verifying the global domain and range constraints of the predicate.

The **DAML+OIL Ontology Checker**[19] is a servlet that uses the OilEd codebase to check the syntax of DAML+OIL ontologies. This checker is a web interface to check DAML+OIL ontologies and content using Jena. It offers *syntactic validation* for checking missing definitions, and *semantic validation* for verifying class hierarchy loops.

The **OWL Ontology Validator**[20] can be used to check if an ontology conforms to a specific OWL species, since it validates an OWL ontology and reports as a result the OWL language species to which the ontology belongs: OWL Lite, OWL DL, and OWL Full. Besides, if requested, the validator returns a description of the classes, properties and individuals in the ontology in terms of the OWL Abstract Syntax.

---

[15] http://139.91.183.30:9090/RDF/VRP/index.html
[16] http://www.w3.org/RDF/Validator/
[17] ARP was created and is maintained by Jeremy Carroll at HP-Labs in Bristol
[18] http://www.daml.org/validator/
[19] http://potato.cs.man.ac.uk/oil/Checker
[20] http://phoebus.cs.man.ac.uk:9999/OWL/Validator

The **OWL Validator**[21] is based on the DAML Validator[22] (it uses a modified version of the Jena Toolkit). This tool is not a simple parser in the sense that it checks OWL ontologies not only for problems related to simple syntax errors, but also for other potential errors. The OWL Validator does not aim at perfoming full reasoning or inferencing, but only at checking these kinds of problems.

**OilEd**[23] (Bechhofer et al., 2001) was initially developed as an ontology editor for OIL ontologies, in the context of the European IST OntoKnowledge Project. However, OilEd has evolved and now is an editor of DAML+OIL and OWL ontologies. The current version is 3.5.

OilEd can connect to any DL reasoner that uses the interface described in the DL Implementation Group (DIG) reasoner interface (Bechhofer, 2002). Currently, it can connect to reasoning engines such as FaCT (Horrocks et al., 1999) to detect inconsistencies in class taxonomies.

OilEd can import ontologies implemented in RDF(S), OIL, DAML+OIL, OWL, and the SHIQ XML format.

# 4. COMPARATIVE STUDY OF RDF(S), DAML+OIL, AND OWL ONTOLOGY TOOLS

As we said before, the first goal of this paper is to analyse whether tools presented in section 3 detect problems presented in section 2.

We have built a testbed of 41 ontologies (7 in RDF(S), 17 in DAML+OIL, and 17 in OWL), each of which implements one of the problems presented in section 2. In the case of RDF(S) we have only 7 ontologies because partition knowledge cannot be defined in this language. These ontologies and the results of their evaluation can be found at http://minsky.dia.fi.upm.es/odeval. Any user can also evaluate its ontologies in that URL, since the ODEval[24] tool is publicly available there.

We have parsed our 41 ontologies using the ontology tools presented in section 3. All these tools recognised the code as well formed code, but the majority had problems detecting most of the knowledge representation problems that these ontologies contained.

The results of analysing and comparing these ontology tools are shown in table 1, and the symbols used in this table are the following:

---

[21] http://owl.bbn.com/validator/
[22] http://www.daml.org/validator/
[23] http://oiled.man.ac.uk
[24] http://minsky.dia.fi.upm.es/odeval

✓: The ontology tool detects the problem in this language

×: The ontology tool does not detect the problem in this language

--: The problem cannot be represented in this language

☑: The problem can be inserted in the ontology tool, which detects it when the ontology is verified

As we can see in table 1[25]:

- *Circularity problems* are detected by some of the ontology tools studied in this experiment. In particular, VRP is able to detect circularity at any distance in RDF(S) ontologies, indicating that there is a semantic error with the following message "loop detected". The DAML+OIL Ontology Checker identifies circularity at any distance in DAML+OIL ontologies, throwing the following warning "cycles in class hierarchy". And OilEd warns in its log that there are loops (circularity problems at any distance) in RDF(S) and DAML+OIL ontologies using this message "Cycles in class hierarchy!". However, OilEd imports the ontology and shows the inconsistency.

- Regarding *partition errors*, they have only been studied for DAML+OIL and for OWL, since they cannot be represented in RDF(S). None of the ontology parsers have detected partition errors with the DAML+OIL and OWL ontologies. Common classes in disjoint decompositions and partitions can be inserted in OilEd, but when we use FaCT, OilEd marks in red the wrong class and shows this message "Class$_i$ is an unsatisfiable class".

- As for *grammatical redundancy problems*, they are not detected by any of the ontology tools studied.

---

[25] In table 1 we use the following abbreviation:

VRP: Validating RDF Parser; RDF V. S.: RDF Validation Service; DAML V.: DAML Validator; DAML+OIL O. C.: DAML+OIL Ontology Checker; OWL O. V.: OWL Ontology Validator; OWL V.: OWL Validator;

R: RDF(S); D+O: DAML+OIL; O: OWL;

d. d.: disjoint decompositions; e. d.: exhaustive decompositions; p.: partitions; s-o: subclass-of; i-o: instance-of; Dir.: Direct; Ind.: Indirect

*Table 1.* Results of the analysis of the RDF(S), DAML+OIL, and OWL ontology tools

| | | | VRP | RDF V. S. | DAML V. | DAML +OIL O. C. | OWL O. V. | OW LV. | OilEd + FaCT | | |
|---|---|---|---|---|---|---|---|---|---|---|---|
| | | | R | R | D+O | D+O | O | O | R | D+O | O |
| **Inconsistency: Circularity Problems** | At distance 0 | | ✓ | ✗ | ✗ | ✓ | ✗ | ✗ | ✓ | ✓ | ✗ |
| | At distance 1 | | ✓ | ✗ | ✗ | ✓ | ✗ | ✗ | ✓ | ✓ | ✗ |
| | At distance N | | ✓ | ✗ | ✗ | ✓ | ✗ | ✗ | ✓ | ✓ | ✗ |
| **Inconsistency: Partition Errors** | Common classes in d. d. | Dir. | -- | -- | ✗ | ✗ | ✗ | ✗ | -- | ☑ | ☑ |
| | | Ind. | -- | -- | ✗ | ✗ | ✗ | ✗ | -- | ☑ | ☑ |
| | Common classes in p. | | -- | -- | ✗ | ✗ | ✗ | ✗ | -- | ☑ | ☑ |
| | Common instances in d. d. | Dir. | -- | -- | ✗ | ✗ | ✗ | ✗ | -- | ✗ | ✗ |
| | | Ind. | -- | -- | ✗ | ✗ | ✗ | ✗ | -- | ✗ | ✗ |
| | Common instances in p. | | -- | -- | ✗ | ✗ | ✗ | ✗ | -- | ✗ | ✗ |
| | External classes in e. d. | | -- | -- | ✗ | ✗ | ✗ | ✗ | -- | ✗ | ✗ |
| | External classes in p. | | -- | -- | ✗ | ✗ | ✗ | ✗ | -- | ✗ | ✗ |
| | External insts. in e. d. | | -- | -- | ✗ | ✗ | ✗ | ✗ | -- | ✗ | ✗ |
| | External instances in p. | | -- | -- | ✗ | ✗ | ✗ | ✗ | -- | ✗ | ✗ |
| **Redundancy: Grammatical Problems** | Redundancies of 's-o' relations | Dir. | ✗ | ✗ | ✗ | ✗ | ✗ | ✗ | ✗ | ✗ | ✗ |
| | | Ind. | ✗ | ✗ | ✗ | ✗ | ✗ | ✗ | ✗ | ✗ | ✗ |
| | Redundancies of 'i -o' relations | Dir. | ✗ | ✗ | ✗ | ✗ | ✗ | ✗ | ✗ | ✗ | ✗ |
| | | Ind. | ✗ | ✗ | ✗ | ✗ | ✗ | ✗ | ✗ | ✗ | ✗ |

# 5.    ODEVAL: A FRAMEWORK TO EVALUATE CONCEPT TAXONOMIES

As we can see in section 4, only a few ontology tools are able to detect loops in concept taxonomies in RDF(S), DAML+OIL, and OWL ontologies. Furthermore, only OilEd (connecting to the reasoning engine FaCT) is able to identify a few of partition errors in concept taxonomies. And regarding grammatical redundancy problems, none of the ontology tools detect themConsequently, we have decided to build ODEval[26], a tool for evaluating RDF(S), DAML+OIL, and OWL ontologies from a knowledge representation point of view using the ideas proposed in (Gómez-Pérez, 2001). ODEval is a complement to the previous ontology tools when we want to evaluate RDF(S), DAML+OIL, and OWL concept taxonomies, from a knowledge representation point of view.

In this section, we describe the algorithms, based on graph theory, used in ODEval to detect possible problems in ontology concept taxonomies. The concept taxonomy will be considered as a directed graph $G(V,A)$, where $V$ is a set of nodes (vertex) and $A$ is a set of directed arcs. The elements included in the sets $V$ and $A$ will be different depending on each language and on each type of problem that we want to detect.

## 5.1    RDF(S) Evaluation in ODEval

In RDF(S), the only primitive that can be used to express specialization/generalization between classes is *rdfs:subClassOf*. We cannot define disjoint nor exhaustive knowledge with any of the primitives of the language. Consequently, the only problems that can exist in RDF(S) ontologies are circularity and redundancy.

### 5.1.1    Circularity Problems

In order to detect circularity problems, the graph $G(V,A)$ will contain in $V$ the set of named and anonymous classes of the ontology, and in $A$ the set of all the *rdfs:subClassOf* relations between classes in the ontology. To detect these problems, ODEval looks for cycles in the graph $G$.

---

[26] http://minsky.dia.fi.upm.es/odeval

## 5.1.2    Redundancy Problems

In this case, the graph $G(V,A)$ will contain in $V$ the set of named and anonymous classes and instances of the ontology, and in $A$ the set of all the *rdfs:subClassOf* relations and "instance-of" relations. To detect grammatical redundancy problems in concept taxonomies, we define the predicate *reachablesFrom(G,v,R)* as the adjacent elements of the vertex $v$ in the transitive closure of the graph $G$ using the arcs that belong to the relation types set $R$. In other words, all the vertices $v_i$ for which we are able to find a path of arches of a type that belongs to R that begins in the vertex $v$ and ends in each vertex $v_i$. For each class *class_A* in the set $V$, and for each arc $r_i$ in the set $A$ whose origin is *class_A*, we take $r_i$ out of the set $A$ and check whether this change affects the set of elements that are reachable from the *class_A*. If there is no change, this means at least one of the $r_i$ is dispensable.

Formally, this can be defined as:

$$\forall r_i \in \{r_1 ... r_N\} \left| \begin{array}{l} reachables\,From(G, class\_A, R) \supset reachables\,From(\widetilde{G}_i, \\ class\_A, R) \end{array} \right.$$

where $\widetilde{G}_i$ is the graph $G$ without the arc of the relation we want to check,

$$\widetilde{G}_i \equiv G_i(\widetilde{V}_i, \widetilde{A}_i) = \left\{ \begin{array}{l} \widetilde{A}_i \equiv A - \{r_i\} \\ \widetilde{V}_i \equiv V \end{array} \right.$$

## 5.2    DAML+OIL Evaluation in ODEval

In DAML+OIL, the set $V$ of the graph $G(V,A)$ will contain both named and anonymous classes, and instances (in the case of partition errors and redundancy problems). Regarding the arcs to be included in the set $A$, we will distinguish between the specialization/generalization primitives (*rdfs:subClassOf*, *daml:disjointUnionOf*, *daml:intersectionOf*, and *daml:unionOf*), class equivalence primitives (*daml:sameClassAs* and *daml:equivalentTo*) and the "instance-of" relations between instances and classes. We have not considered the primitive *daml:complementOf*.

## 5.2.1    Circularity Problems

To detect circularity problems, the set $A$ of the graph $G(V,A)$ will contain specialization/generalization and class equivalence primitives. The direction of each arc is the same as the direction of the relation, except for *daml:unionOf* and *daml:disjointUnionOf*, where it is the opposite.

ODEval looks for the following types of cycles in the graph *G*:

- *Mixed cycles*. The arcs of these cycles contain class equivalence relations and specialization/generalization relations. In this case, we have found a circularity.
- *Equivalence cycles*. All the arcs of the cycle are class equivalence relations. In this case, we have found a redundancy problem, that is, one of the class equivalence relations could be removed.

### 5.2.2    Partition Errors

#### 5.2.2.1    Common classes and common instances in disjoint decompositions and partitions

ODEval uses the same evaluation algorithm for these partition errors. Detecting these errors is not as straightforward as only searching common direct classes or instances of the concepts that form the partition, but also recursively checking it in their subclasses.

The set *V* of the graph *G* will contain the classes (named and anonymous) and instances defined in the ontology. The set *A* will not only contain the specialization/generalization and class equivalence relations, but also arcs that connect each instance with the class to which it belongs.

We define the predicate *reachablesTo(G,v,R)*, which is the reverse of *reachablesFrom*, that is, it changes the directions of the arcs of the directed graph and looks for paths in the opposite direction. To know whether an element *element* (class or instance) of the ontology belongs to more than one path of a disjoint decomposition or a partition, composed by {*Class_P₁ⁱ*, *Class_P₂ⁱ*,..., *Class_Pₙⁱ*}, we must check that we can only reach one of the classes of the decomposition through the set of relations *A*. This is formally defined as follows:

$$
card\left\{ x \left| \begin{array}{l} x \in reachablesFrom(G, element, R) \land x \in \\ \{Class\_P_1^i,...,Class\_P_N^i\} \end{array} \right. \right\} = 1
$$

If we are interested in checking whether this error occurs in a disjoint decomposition or a partition, formed by the classes {*Class_P₁, Class_P₂,..., Class_Pₙ*}, we must check that there are no common elements in two or more branches of the partition. This can be expressed as follows:

$$\forall class1, class2 \in \{Class\_P_1, ..., Class\_P_n\}$$

$$\left| (class1 \neq class2) \rightarrow \begin{pmatrix} reachablesTo(G, class1, R) \\ \cap (reachablesTo(G, class2, R)) = \phi \end{pmatrix} \right.$$

### 5.2.2.2 External classes and external instances in exhaustive decompositions and partitions

As in the previous case, ODEval uses the same algorithm for both types of errors and the same information is included in the sets $V$ and $A$ of $G$.

The problem that arises here, is the existence in DAML+OIL of class equivalence relations. If the class *Class_A* to be checked has equivalent classes, then each of them must be checked separately. $E$ contains the set of classes equivalent to the base class:

$$E = reachablesTo(G, Class\_A, \{equivalentTo, sameClassAs\})$$

We call *Class_A'ᵢ* to each of the classes that belong to this set

$$E = \{Class\_A'_1, Class\_A'_2, ..., Class\_A'_M\}$$

We also define $A'$ as $A$ minus the class equivalence relations.
We can conclude that a base class *Class_A* has not external elements if:

$$\bigcup_{i=1}^{M} reachables\ To(G, Class\_A'_i, R') \subseteq \bigcup_{i=1}^{N} reachables\ To(G, Class\_P_i, R)$$

The following two errors can be found with this algorithm:

- *Partition error*. If the element is only reachable from the base class (or its equivalents) and it is not reachable from the classes of the decomposition. Depending on the type of the element, class or instance, we have an external class or external instance.
- *Redundancy problem*. If the element is reachable both from the base class (or its equivalents) and from one of the classes of the decomposition.

### 5.2.3 Redundancy Problems

Apart from the redundancy problems described in the previous sections, we can find redundancy in the same way described with RDF(S) (section 5.1.2), using the predicate *reachablesFrom(G,v,R)* and detecting whether removing an arc from the set $A$ implies any change in the set of elements reachable from a vertex.

## 5.3    OWL Evaluation in ODEval

In OWL, the set $V$ of the graph $G(V,A)$ will contain both named and anonymous classes, and instances (in the case of partition errors and redundancy problems). Regarding the arcs to be included in the set $A$, we will consider the following primitives: *rdfs:subClassOf*, *owl:intersectionOf*, *owl:disjointWith*, *owl:unionOf*, and the "instance-of" relations between instances and classes.

### 5.3.1    Circularity Problems

To detect circularity problems, the set $A$ of the graph $G(V,A)$ will contain specialization/generalization primitives. The direction of each arc is the same as the direction of the relation, except for *owl:unionOf*, where it is the opposite. ODEval looks for cycles in the graph $G$.

### 5.3.2    Partition Errors

#### 5.3.2.1    Common classes and common instances in disjoint decompositions and partitions

In these cases, ODEval uses the evaluation algorithm explained in section 5.2.2.1. The set $V$ of the graph $G$ will contain the classes (named and anonymous) and instances defined in the ontology. The set $A$ will not only contain the specialization/generalization, but also arcs that connect each instance with the class to which it belongs.

### 5.3.3    Redundancy Problems

We can find redundancy in the same way described with RDF(S) (section 5.1.2), using the predicate *reachablesFrom(G,v,R)* and detecting whether removing an arc from the set $A$ implies any change in the set of elements reachable from a vertex.

## 6.    CONCLUSIONS AND FURTHER WORK

In this paper we have shown that, in general, current ontology tools are unable to detect possible anomalies, from a knowledge representation point of view, in concept taxonomies in RDF(S), DAML+OIL, and OWL.

Taking into account that: (a) only a few ontology tools are able to detect loops in concept taxonomies in RDF(S), DAML+OIL, and OWL ontologies, (b) only OilEd (connecting to FaCT) is able to identify a few of partition errors in concept taxonomies, and (c) none of the ontology tools detect redundancy problems; we considered that it was necessary to create more advanced evaluators in order to be complement to the ontology tools studied.

Consequently, we have developed ODEval, which is a tool that evaluates RDF(S), DAML+OIL, and OWL concept taxonomies from a knowledge representation point of view. This tool is meant to help ontology developers in designing ontologies, without anomalies, in such ontology languages.

We will go on working in ontology evaluation from the knowledge representation point of view. We will extend ODEval so as to capture more problems in concept taxonomies (such as checking that the "subclass-of" relationships are defined between classes), relation taxonomies, etc.

## ACKNOWLEDGEMENTS

This work has been supported by the Esperonto project (IST-2001-34373), by several research grants from UPM ("Becas asociadas a proyectos modalidad A y B") and by a research grant from MEC (AP-2002-3828).

## REFERENCES

Bechhofer S (2002) *The DIG Description Logic Interface: DIG/1.0.* Technical Report. http://potato.cs.man.ac.uk/dig/interface1.0.pdf

Bechhofer S, Horrocks I, Goble C, Stevens R (2001) *OilEd: a reason-able ontology editor for the Semantic Web.* In: Baader F, Brewka G, Eiter T (eds) Joint German/Austrian conference on Artificial Intelligence (KI'01). Vienna, Austria. (LNAI 2174) Springer-Verlag, Berlin, Germany, pp 396–408.

Fernández-López M, Gómez-Pérez A, Pazos-Sierra A, Pazos-Sierra J (1999) *Building a Chemical Ontology Using METHONTOLOGY and the Ontology Design Environment.* IEEE Intelligent Systems & their applications 4(1) (1999) 37-46.

Gómez-Pérez A (2001) *Evaluating ontologies: Cases of Study.* IEEE Intelligent Systems and their Applications. Special Issue on Verification and Validation of ontologies. March 2001, Vol 16, N° 3. Pag. 391 – 409.

Gómez-Pérez A, Suárez-Figueroa MC (2004) *Evaluation of RDF(S) and DAML+OIL Import/Export Services within Ontology Platforms.* 3rd Mexican International Conference on Artificial Intelligence (MICAI 2004) Mexico City, Mexico. PP: 109-118.

Gómez-Pérez A, Suárez-Figueroa MC (2003) *Results of Taxonomic Evaluation of RDF(S) and DAML+OIL Ontologies using RDF(S) and DAML+OIL Validation Tools and Ontology Platforms Import Services.* Evaluation of Ontology-based Tools (EON2003) 2nd International Workshop located at the 2nd International Semantic Web Conference (ISWC 2003) Sundial Resort, Sanibel Island, Florida, USA. PP: 13-26.

Gómez-Pérez A, Fernández-López M, Corcho, O (2003) *Ontological Engineering*. November 2003. Springer Verlag.

Guarino N, Welty C (2000) *A Formal Ontology of Properties* In R. Dieng and O. Corby (eds.), Knowledge Engineering and Knowledge Management: Methods, Models and Tools. 12th International Conference, EKAW2000, LNAI 1937. Springer Verlag: 97-112.

Horrocks I, Sattler U, Tobies S (1999) *Practical reasoning for expressive description logics.* In: Ganzinger H, McAllester D, Voronkov A (eds) 6th International Conference on Logic for Programming and Automated Reasoning (LPAR'99). Tbilisi, Georgia. (Lecture Notes in Artificial Intelligence LNAI 1705) Springer-Verlag, Berlin, Germany, pp 161–180.

# AIR - A PLATFORM FOR INTELLIGENT SYSTEMS

Dragan Djuric[1], Dragan Gasevic[1], Violeta Damjanovic[2]

[1]*University of Belgrade, FON-School for Business Administration, POB 52, Jove Ilića 154, 11000 Belgrade, Serbia and Montenegro, dragandj@mail.ru, gasevic@yahoo.com, 2Postal Savings Bank, 27.marta 71, vdamjanovic@posted.co.yu*

**Abstract:** This paper presents AIR - a platform for building intelligent systems. Current IS platforms either are narrowly specialized (ontologies, expert system shells, etc.) or have complex extension mechanisms (i.e. do not use benefits of Model Driven Development). Based on OMG's Model Driven Architecture and its standards, AIR core consists of various MOF-based metamodels. Presented metamodels are mainly intended, but not limited, to support emerging standards related to the Semantic Web. Basing its architecture on MDA, AIR can support metamodels of almost any domain, including non-AI related. AIR also includes an integrated development environment for building such systems, which is based on Eclipse. Presented platform is intended to be an integration point of various intelligent systems and mainstream software technologies.

**Key words:** AI Tools, Intelligent Systems Engineering, Software Architecture, Model Driven Architecture, Metamodeling, XML, Eclipse

## 1. INTRODUCTION

The basic problem of existing environments for intelligent systems development is their narrow specialization. Most of them are implemented to support only initially envisioned functionalities – most often knowledge representation and reasoning. It is perfectly right from the intelligent systems point of view. But, real world applications and their development are rarely clearly bordered in their scope; that's why these applications are not enough. It is, therefore, necessary to integrate applications that are used for intelligent systems development into mainstream software platforms. This topic is going to gain more and more attention with the development of the Semantic Web [1] and increased integration of intelligent techniques in common information systems.

AIR is a Model Driven Architecture (MDA)-based [2] platform for building intelligent systems. It is based on various metamodels that model intelligent systems related domains. One of such metamodels is Ontology Definition Metamodel (ODM) [3]. An extensible integrated development environment based on Eclipse plug-in architecture [4] that equips AIR with powerful base for tools with rich GUI is also included. This platform is a part of Good-Old-AI (goodoldai.org.yu) effort in developing a platform that will enhance intelligent systems development using Model Driven Development (MDD) [5].

After the introduction, in section two the paper gives an overview of the related work. Section three explains the basic idea of AIR. The importance of metamodel as a conceptual unit in AIR is explained in section four. Section five and six describe implementation details of metamodel-based architecture and plug-in based architecture, respectively. Final section contains conclusions.

## 2.     RELATED WORK

Loom and Parka are previous well-known intelligent system development platforms. Loom was designed to support the construction and maintenance of "model-based" applications—Loom's model specification language facilitates the specification of explicit, detailed domain models, while Loom's behavior specification language provides multiple programming paradigms that can be employed to query and manipulate these models [6]. Parka and Parka-DB are frame-based AI languages/tools that enable scaling knowledge bases up to extremely large-size applications, and use DBMS technologies to support inferencing and data management [7]. Protégé tool is initially developed as an ontology editor, but it is act as an extensible knowledge- and rule-based platform that integrates ontological engineering techniques and languages (e.g. RDF, OWL) with rule-based expert system shells (e.g. tabs for Jess, CLIPS, Algernon, Prolog, JadeJess) [8].

The idea of developing the AIR platform emerged along with other important research activities and results achieved by the GOOD OLD AI group – many of the group's activities are closely related to intelligent system technology. Devedžić and Radović [9] have proposed a multi-layered framework for building intelligent systems, called *OBOA*, which incorporates a number of intelligent system techniques. More recently, a number of fuzzy logic tools have been developed in accordance with the OBOA framework; they make the basis of the more specific *Fuzzy OBOA* framework [10]. *Code Tutor* is a Web-based intelligent tutoring system for fast students' briefing in the area of radio-communication [11]. A unified MDA-based ontology infrastructure has been defined in order to integrate software and ontology engineering techniques [3]. *JessGUI* is a user-friendly Jess-based and XML-supported environment for developing frame and rule-based intelligent systems [12].

## 3. UNDERLYING SOLUTION OF AIR – THE BASIC IDEA

In order to integrate intelligent technologies with common information system technologies, and take such systems out of laboratories, we must develop appropriate tools. These tools must be easy to use and powerful enough to support creation of demanding applications. The best solutions for such demands are tools that employ mainstream software technologies that users are familiar with, and expand them with new functionalities. That is the idea that is in the roots of AIR. AIR is an integrated software environment for developing of intelligent systems that:

- Is based on open standards (OMG, W3C...),
- Uses existing mainstream software tools and architectures,
- Is extendable and adaptable.

We could itemize more characteristics, but these three are good examples of what AIR tries to achieve. It is clear that today's tools must be built according to standards if they want to succeed, so the OMG or W3C standard compliance is a must whenever it is possible. Regarding the fact that AIR is academic project, it is illusory to expect that it can become serious environment if it does not use existing solutions as its base. Such approach would depart it from its scope and route it to reinventing the wheel. Therefore, AIR should use any existing solution that fits into its puzzle. As it is intended to support work with new technologies that are still extremely changeable, AIR must support easy and seamless addition of new functionalities or replacing of existing parts with improved versions. Many of technologies that it aims to support are still in early phase, which means that they are frequently exposed to changes. AIR must be able to follow these changes.

The basic structure of AIR is depicted in the block diagram shown in Figure 1. The central part of AIR is a model base. First of all, it includes models of intelligent systems domains, but also models of any domain that is of interest. Currently, model base is implemented as a Meta-Object Facility (MOF)-based metadata repository [13] [14]. It contains MOF-based metamodels and models that are the core of AIR. AIR must have a mechanism that enables the exchange of contained data with other applications. This is achieved through MOF XML Metadata Interchange (XMI) format, based on XML. Such format also enables easier integration into Web.

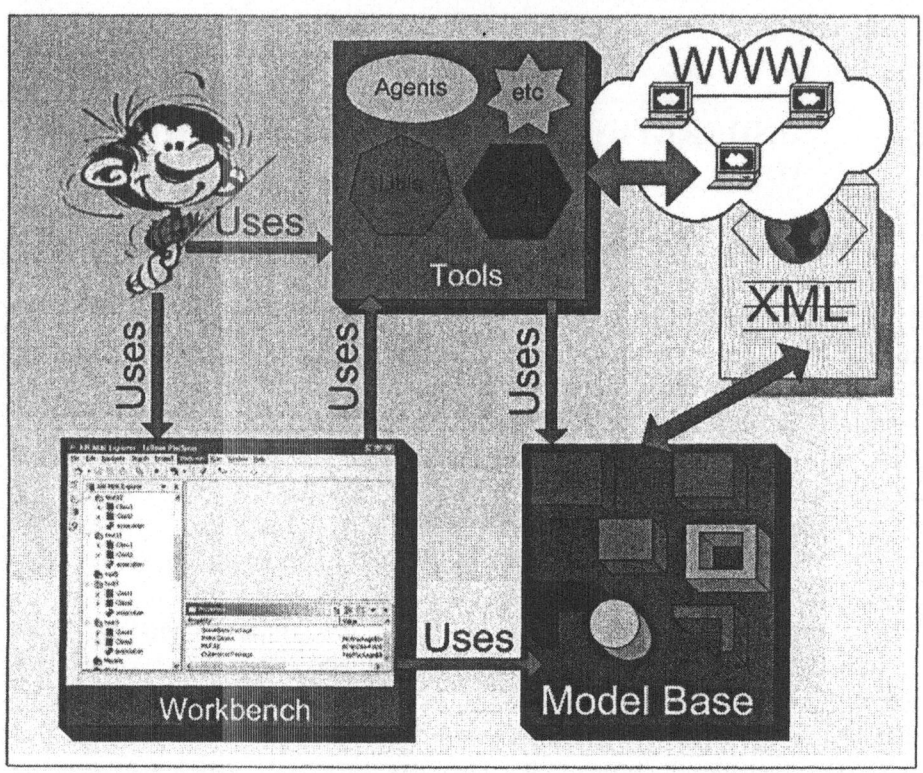

*Figure* 1 - Basic structure of AIR

The other important part of AIR is an integrated development environment that provides a rich GUI for manipulation with models – AIR Workbench. This part of AIR implementation is based on Eclipse platform. Model base can be also reached from numerous tools that are not a part of GUI – agents, analysis tools, utilities, etc.

# 4. METAMODEL - THE CONCEPTUAL BUILDING BLOCK OF AIR

AIR should be able to model a large number of domains. The real world consists of infinite number of concepts and facts that we are trying to describe using some models. Models are described using metamodels, models of models [15]. Modeling and metamodeling are well-known terms in software engineering, and standardization in that field recently started to gain more attention. AIR uses four-layer MOF-based metamodeling architecture according to OMG's MDA standards. Basic metamodels that AIR uses and their place in this architecture are shown in Figure 2.

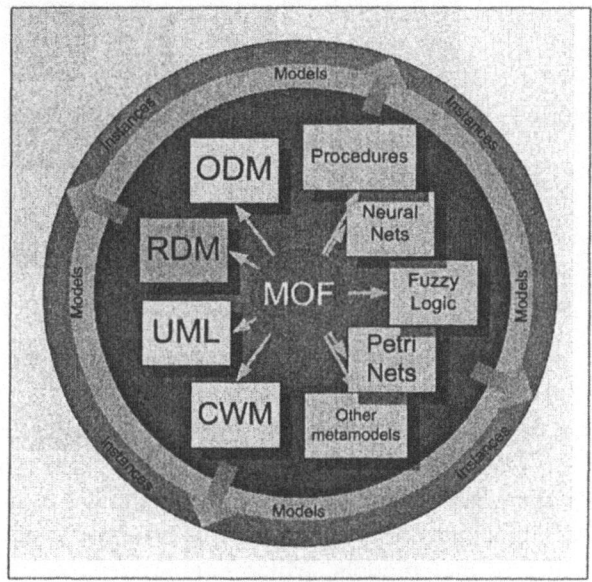

*Figure 2* - AIR Metamodels

In the center of this architecture is Meta Object Facility (MOF), a meta-metamodel used for modeling of all metamodels. Beside Unified Modeling Language (UML) and Common Warehouse Metamodel (CWM), metamodels usual in such architecture, important metamodels are Ontology Definition Metamodel (ODM) and Rule Definition Metamodel (RDM). For more specific purposes, such as Petri nets, fuzzy logic, neural nets, specialized metamodels can be included. Such metamodels should be added only if existing, models, ODM for instance, lack support for some of wanted features.

The basic building block of AIR is a metamodel. Metamodel enables some problem domain to be described, e.g. it supports creation of models that describe certain specific problems in that domain. The place of certain metamodel in four-layer MDA architecture and accompanying elements are shown in figure 3.

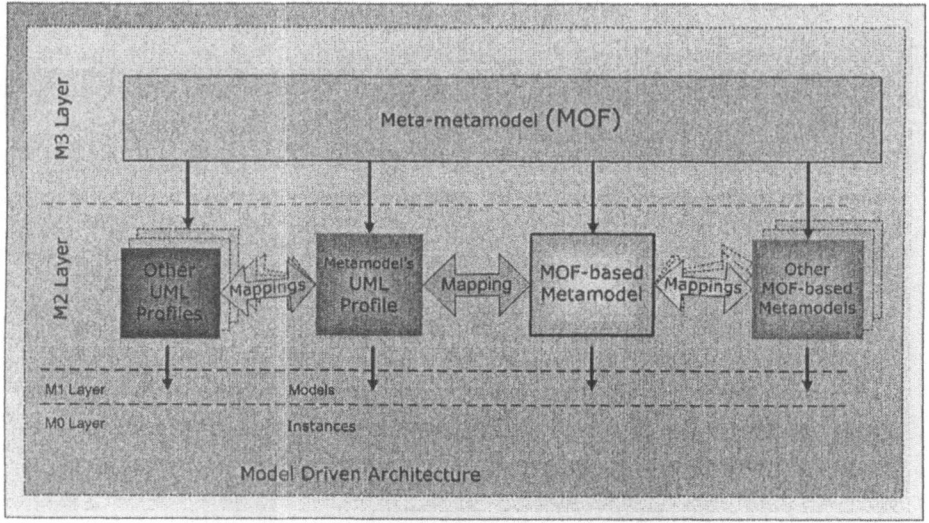

*Figure 3* - Custom Metamodel and UML Profile

Metamodel is described by MOF, and it is on M2 (metamodel) layer. To utilize widespread UML tools support, corresponding UML profile can be added. UML Profile is an expansion of UML metamodel in a standard way that enables UML to support new concepts. It is possible to add mappings to other UML profiles or metamodels, which enables several kinds of models to be used to model one problem, where each model kind is capable of capturing some specific details of that problem.


# 5.    IMPLEMENTATION OF MOF-BASED ARCHITECTURE

The MOF Specification [13] defines an abstract language and a framework for specifying, constructing, and managing technology neutral metamodels. It also defines a framework for implementing repositories that hold metadata (e.g., models) described by metamodels. Standard technology mappings are used to transform metamodels into metadata API, giving the framework an implementation. Figure 4 shows an overview of a MOF repository and its implementation in Java platform.

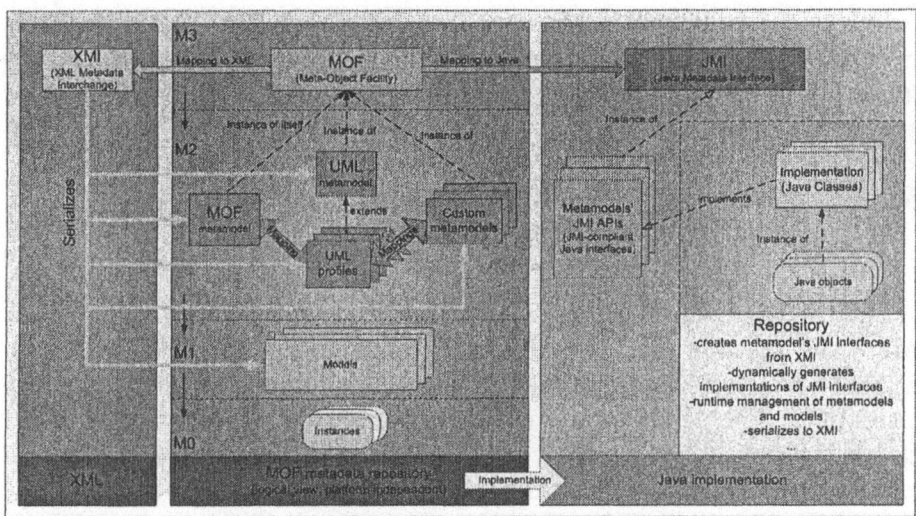

*Figure* 4 - Repository implementation on Java platform

A conceptual view of a MOF-based repository is shown in the center of Figure 4. It reflects MDA four-layer MOF-based architecture [2]. The MOF metamodel is used as a meta-metamodel, which describes all other metamodels (including MOF itself and UML). Custom metamodels can define mappings to UML, supported by UML profiles, which enables them to use UML tools support.

OMG (Object Management Group) defines a standard format for platform independent metadata interchange XML Metadata Interchange (XMI). It serializes MOF-based metamodels and models into plain text (XML), which enables such data to be exchanged in a standard way, and to be read by any platform-specific implementation.

Java repository implementation is based on Java Metadata Interchange (JMI) [14], a Java metadata API. Based on any MOF-based metamodel (serialized to XMI), JMI-compliant metamodel-specific JMI interfaces can be generated. These interfaces are used to access Java metadata repository, which is implemented by Java classes. All data from repository can be serialized into XMI and then exchanged with other repositories, regardless of their implementation. It is only required that they support MOF-based metadata (i.e. that they can "understand" MOF XMI format).

The reference implementation for JMI metadata repository is Unisys' CIM (www.unisys.com), but it seems that it has not been updated recently.

The other implementation is NetBeans MDR (mdr.netbeans.org), a part of open source NetBeans project. It is used by AIR as a metadata repository due to its generic implementation of JMI interfaces and frequent improvements and development. NetBeans MDR implements JMI interfaces in a generic way, so any metamodel can be loaded from XMI and instantly implemented using Java reflection.

# 6.    IMPLEMENTATION OF PLUG-IN ARCHITECTURE

AIR Workbench should provide various tools with rich GUI that makes AIR user friendly. This workbench is built on top of Eclipse plug-in architecture and Eclipse IDE (www.eclipse.org), today's leading extensible platform [4]. The main difference between Eclipse and other extensible IDEs is that Eclipse consists entirely of plug-ins that work on a tiny platform runtime, whereas other IDEs are monolithic tools with some extensions. Thus, Eclipse core plug-ins are of equal importance as any other plug-in, including AIR plug-ins. Figure 5 depicts Eclipse-based AIR plug-in architecture.

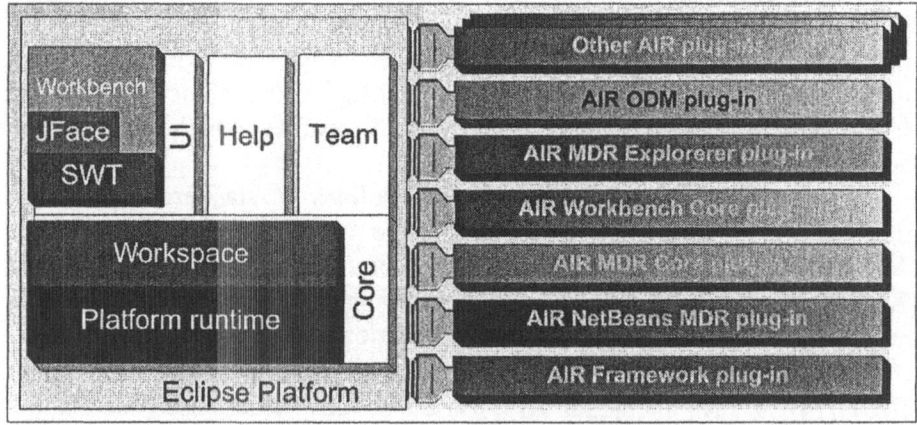

*Figure 5* - Eclipse-based AIR plug-in architecture

The ground of this architecture is Eclipse platform. Although only the Eclipse Core is mandatory, there is no reason not to utilize Eclipse UI (SWT, JFace, and Workbench), help and team support, so they are not discarded. Using the whole Eclipse IDE, AIR adds MDR and Intelligent Systems related plug-ins. Some of basic AIR plug-ins include those that are related to generic MDR support (AIR Framework, AIR NetBeans MDR, AIR MDR

Core), particular metamodel support (ODM, RDM, UML, CWM, etc.), or GUI-related (AIR MDR Explorer). These plug-ins are added as extensions to extension points defined by plug-ins that are part of Eclipse IDE. Being equalitarian with Eclipse plug-ins, AIR plug-ins also extend each other and offer future plug-ins to extend them. MOF Model package appearance in AIR MDR Explorer is shown in picture 6.

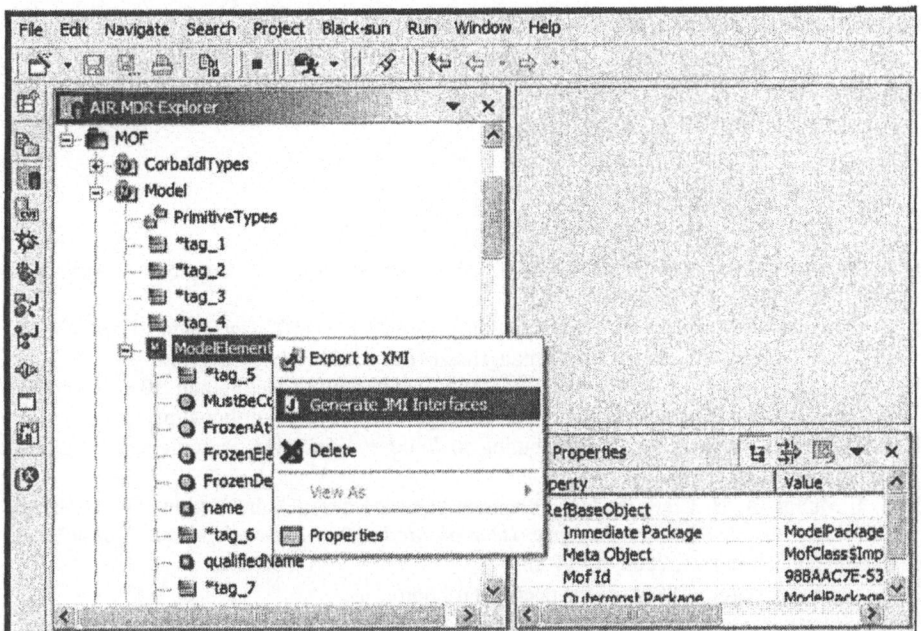

*Figure* 6 MOF Model in AIR MDRExplorer

This Explorer depicts MOF-based models and metamodels and serves as a starting point for model manipulation. Selecting any element, user can reach menus specific for that element and raise various actions. These actions span from usual actions (instantiating, deleting, viewing properties etc.) to more specific (opening various metamodel specific editors, starting transformations etc.). According to Eclipse architecture, these menus can be easily extended with new items that raise new actions.

# 7.    CONCLUSIONS

The platform for building intelligent systems defined in this paper is in accordance with the OMG's Model Drive Architecture. Its core is based on various MOF-based metamodels that enable modeling of many domains related to intelligent systems, but not limited to them. An implementation of metadata repository is based on NetBeans MDR. To provide an extensible user-friendly GUI, AIR includes an Extensible IDE based on Eclipse. Due to the fact that AIR is based on open standards and mainstream software technologies, it can bring intelligent systems closer to common users and applications.Future developments of proposed platform include defining of various metamodels that are of interest for intelligent systems and corresponding tools that use them. Parts of AIR that support metadata repository and extensible IDE should be also improved to offer better stability and richer functionality.

# REFERENCES

1  T. Berners-Lee, J. Hendler, O. Lassila, "The Semantic Web," *Scientific American*, Vol. 284, No. 5, 2001, pp 34-43.
2  J. Miller and J. Mukerji, eds, "MDA Guide Version 1.0," *OMG Document: omg/2003-05-01*, 2003. http://www.omg.org/mda/mda_files/MDA_Guide_Version1-0.pdf
3  Djurić, D., Gašević, D., & Devedžić, V. (2005). Ontology Modeling and MDA. Accepted for publication in *Journal on Object Technology*, Vol. 4, No.1. Forthcoming.
4  Erich Gamma, Kent Beck, "Contributing to Eclipse: Principles, Patterns and Plug-Ins", Addison-Wesley, 2003.
5  S. J. Mellor, A. N. Clark, and T. Futagami, "Guest Editors' Introduction: Model-Driven Development," *IEEE Software (spec. issue on Model-Driven Development)*, Vol. 20, No. 5, September/October, 2003, pp 14-18.
6.  Robert MacGregor, (1999), Retrospective on Loom. http://www.isi.edu/isd/LOOM/papers/macgregor/Loom_Retrospective.html
7  Hendler, J., Stoffel, K., Taylor, M., Rager, D., & Kettler, B. (1997). PARKA-DB: A Scalable Knowledge Representation System - Database PARKA. http://www.cs.umd.edu/projects/plus/Parka/parka-db.html, last visited February 14th, 2004
8  Fridman-Noy, N., et al: Creating Semantic Web Contents with Protégé-2000, IEEE Intelligent Systems, Vol. 16, No. 2 (2001) 60-71
9  Devedžić, V., & Radović, D. (1999). A Framework for Building Intelligent Manufacturing Systems. *IEEE Transactions on Systems, Man, and Cybernetics, Part C - Applications and Reviews*, 29(3), 402-419.
10 Šendelj, R. & Devedžić, V. (2004). Fuzzy systems based on component software. Accepted for publication in *Fuzzy Sets and Systems*. Forthcoming.
11 Šimić, G., & Devedžić, V. (2003). Building an intelligent system using modern Internet technologies. *Expert Systems with Applications* 25(3), 231-246.
12 Jovanović, J., Gašević, D., & Devedžić, V. (2004). A GUI for Jess. Accepted for publication in *Expert Systems with Applications*. Forthcoming.
13 MOF Spec 2002, Meta Object Facility (MOF) Specification v1.4, OMG Document formal/02-04-03, http://www.omg.org/cgi-bin/apps/doc?formal/02-04-03.pdf, April 2002.
14 Ravi Dirckze (spec. lead), "Java Metadata Interface (JMI) Specification Version 1.0", http://jcp.org/aboutJava/ communityprocess/final/jsr040/index.html, 2002
15  E. Seidewitz, "What Models Mean," *IEEE Software (spec. issue on Model Driven Development)*, Vol. 20, No. 5, 2003, pp 26-32.

# SWISSANALYST
*Data Mining Without the Entry Ticket*

O. Povel[1] and C. Giraud-Carrier[2]

*[1] Portia SA, Lausanne, Switzerland; [2] ELCA Informatique SA, Lausanne, Switzerland*

Abstract: This paper introduces SwissAnalyst, a complete Data Mining environment powered by Weka. SwissAnalyst was developed as an intuitive process layer, which offers all necessary features to place it on par, in terms of functionality, with most major commercial Data Mining software packages. As GNU GPL software, SwissAnalyst offers a license-free platform to develop both proofs of concept for potential business users and complex process-driven solutions for researchers.

Key words: Data Mining, KDD Process, GNU software, Graphical User Interface

## 1.     INTRODUCTION

Data Mining techniques, especially machine learning, have only recently come out of the research labs and the past few years have seen a proliferation of commercial Data Mining (DM) software packages. These packages, for the most part, essentially wrap a varying number of public domain (i.e., freely available) components or algorithms (sometimes re-implemented with rather small proprietary extensions) in an user-friendly graphical interface.

Although such tools seemingly make DM technology more readily available to non-expert end-users, they tend either to provide only limited functionality (e.g., few pre-processing facilities, only decision tree induction, etc.) or to come with a non-negligible price-tag, which is generally perceived as an expensive entry ticket for those "would-be adopters" who might just wish to first "peek through the fence" before committing more seriously to the technology.

The challenge with having high DM functionality at low cost, however, is in the expertise required to use and orchestrate the heterogeneous set of raw, public domain versions of algorithms. One of the most significant attempts at meeting this challenge is the recent development (and continuous improvement) of the Weka tool (Witten and Frank, 2000). Under its GNU General Public License (GPL), Weka makes freely available a large collection – probably the richest of its kind – of DM algorithms (pre-processing, classification, association, clustering and visualization). The success of Weka is evident in a recent survey, which suggested that it was the second most regularly used DM tool, after SPSS Clementine and before SAS Enterprise Miner (KDnuggets Poll, 2002a).

Satisfied with this popularity, we wanted to leverage Weka's rich functionality while extending it with a process-supporting tier to facilitate the development of more complex data mining projects, and offer an intuitive platform to develop real case studies or proofs of concept for potential industrial users, with no license fees.

The resulting system, SwissAnalyst – powered by Weka, thus addresses both the needs of business users who want to explore/demonstrate DM technology, as well as those of researchers wishing to have more support for the overall *process* of DM.

Although not currently as graphically-rich, SwissAnalyst includes most features necessary to offer as much functionality and process support as the best available commercial packages (Giraud-Carrier and Povel, 2003). As GNU GPL software written in Java, it is distributed freely and can easily be extended. This short paper details and illustrates the key features of SwissAnalyst.

## 2.    RELATED WORK

Although most data mining algorithms belong to the public domain, there are ironically very few freeware (i.e., GNU GPL) DM tools or packages. To the best of our knowledge, there are only three (with the exclusion of Weka itself) at the time of this writing:

YALE (Ritthoff, 2001; Fischer, 2002)

XELOPES (Thess and Bolotnikov, 2003)

Orange (Zupan and Demsar, 2003)

YALE is similar in essence to SwissAnalyst, in that it was also designed to specify and execute (although with a somewhat different approach) complex learning chains for pre-processing as well as multi-strategy learning. In addition, the latest version of YALE comes with an "interface" to Weka thus allowing users to leverage all of Weka's algorithms. There are two main differences, however, between YALE and SwissAnalyst. On the one hand, YALE lifts the requirement that all data fit in main memory, thus ensuring scalability, whilst SwissAnalyst inherits that limitation of Weka. On the other hand, YALE has no graphical user interface and all projects must be specified directly in XML, whereas SwissAnalyst produces XML from (semi) "graphical specifications," thus increasing usability.

XELOPES is a rich, PMML-compliant, open library for embedded data mining. It has a connector to Weka and is easily extensible with custom-defined classes. XELOPES does include a graphical user interface, but its purpose is "not to provide a professional Data Mining tool but to explore the usage of the XELOPES library." (Thess and Bolotnikov, 2003, p. 210). The interface organizes information around a static schema for creating and applying algorithms, and does not directly support the notions of process flow and learning streams, as does SwissAnalyst.

Much like XELOPES, Orange is component-based, making available for integration in other applications a number of data mining techniques. Although currently far more restricted in functionality than SwissAnalyst, the work on Orange, with its Widgets, is another attempt at offering explicit DM process support.

Finally, we note that concurrent to, but independent of, the development of SwissAnalyst, the Weka team has also been improving its software (Version 3.4.1 at the time of writing), particularly with respect to visualization capabilities and an attractive "Knowledge Flow GUI" for graphical programming. This latter addition to Weka is very much in the same spirit as SwissAnalyst.

## 3.     KEY FEATURES OF SWISSANALYST

This section gives a short account of the most practitioner-relevant features of SwissAnalyst:
- Process-oriented view
- Support for multiple streams
- XML save/reload
- Enhanced data exploration
- Improved results section
- Model pre-selection
- Enhanced pre-processing

Wherever applicable, illustrative screenshots are included. Familiarity with Weka is assumed.

## 3.1    Process-oriented View

Since Data Mining is a *process*, it seems only natural that DM software should explicitly support that process. Several process models, such as CRISP-DM (SPSS, 2000) and SEMMA (SAS, 1998), have recently been developed. Although each sheds a slightly different light on the DM process, their basic tenets are the same. A recent survey suggests that the most widely used methodology is CRISP-DM (KDnuggets Poll, 2002b).

SwissAnalyst organizes information on the screen in such a way that the entire process, inspired by CRISP-DM, is set out clearly and that it supports naturally the flow of activities within this process, as shown in Figure 1.

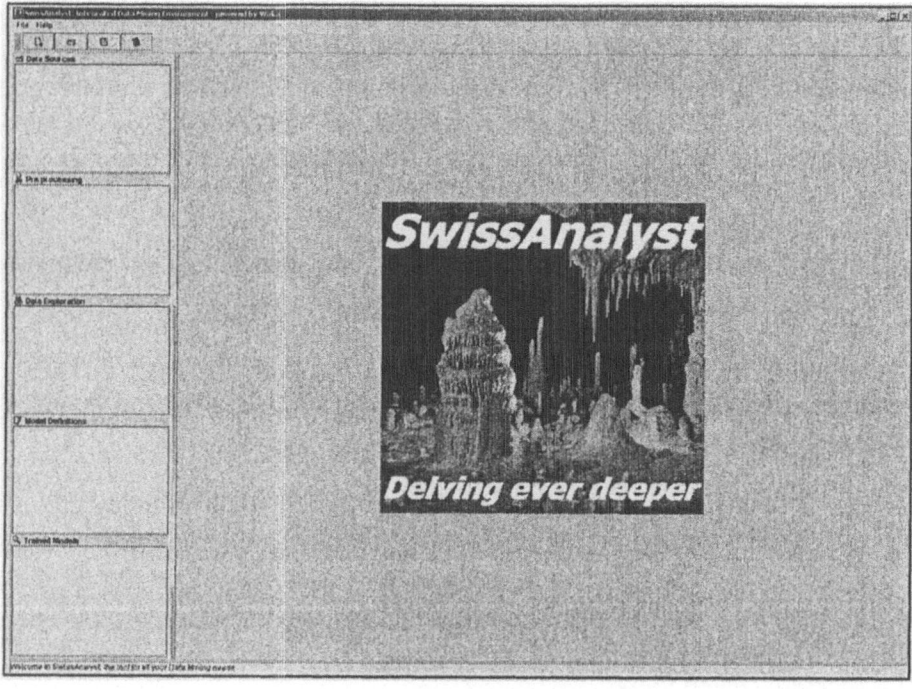

*Figure 1.* SwissAnalyst's Screen Layout

The five panels on the left-hand side correspond roughly to the standard activities of the DM process comprised between Business Understanding and Deployment:
- <u>Data Sources</u>: locating, loading and browsing datasets
- <u>Pre-processing</u>: defining and applying various transformations to the data
- <u>Data Exploration</u>: statistics, warnings and data visualization
- <u>Model Definition</u>: defining and executing various mining models

- Trained Models: evaluating models and applying them to new data

All menus are context-sensitive and accessible through right-mouse clicks over any object in the interface. For each section or object selected in a section, right-clicking presents the list of operations available for that section or object, as illustrated in Figures 2 and 3.

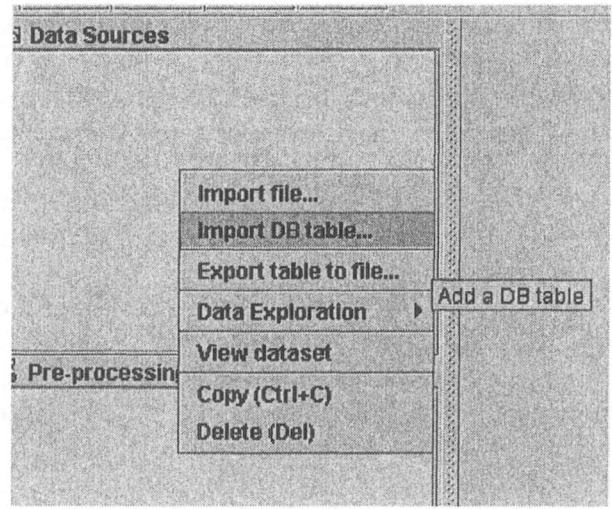

*Figure 2.* Context-sensitive Menus – Data Sources

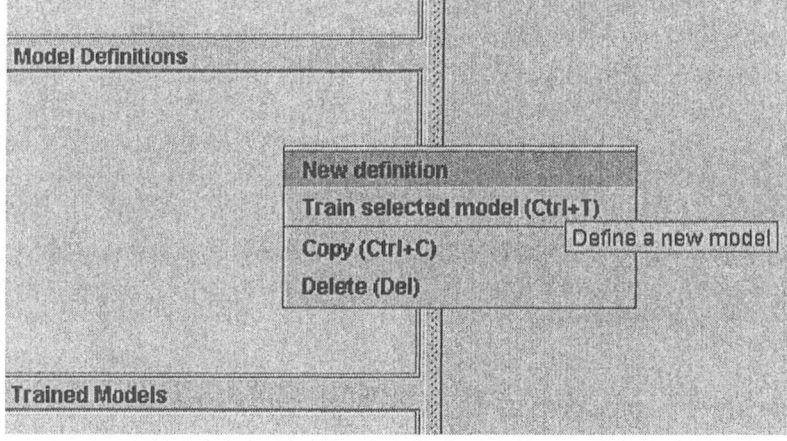

*Figure 3.* Context-sensitive Menus – Model Definitions

This simple design decision ensures that the interface consistently shows the right information at the right time, and applies the selected operation to the intended object. A similar result is achieved in Weka's new Knowledge Flow GUI, where sets of operations are listed as icons under context-sensitive tabs.

## 3.2    Support for Multiple Streams

Typical DM projects are experimental in nature and thus require the ability to support multiple data or execution flows for analysis and comparison. SwissAnalyst allows complex projects to be defined that incorporate many data sources and operations, and various process flows between them.

Streams (or learning chains) thus defined are context-sensitive so that whenever any component of a stream is selected, the entire stream is highlighted on screen as shown in Figure 4.

Stream highlighting provides the user with a simple visual cue as to the overall process. Note also that although default unique names are automatically created by SwissAnalyst for objects (see, for example, the Data Exploration panel in Figure 4), these can easily be changed by double-clicking the objects.

Furthermore, comments may be attached to all steps, thus allowing the user to record specific insight or clarification. Comment fields are absent from most DM software, yet they often prove essential in documenting the DM process, facilitating maintenance (changes to models, etc.) and knowledge transfer.

A small note on streams involving more than one pre-processing step is worth making. Although one is indeed able to apply pre-processing to a pre-processed step (i.e., some object in the Pre-processing panel), one should avoid doing so as only one object can be highlighted in the top-level stream. Hence, only one (here, the last one) of the pre-processing steps will be highlighted. Instead, one should use a single pre-processing step and edit it at will since each pre-processing step is essentially a sub-stream. There is nothing to be gained in functionality in having more than one pre-processing steps, since they are linked sequentially anyway, which can be handled at the sub-stream level (see Section 3.7).

## 3.3    XML Save / Reload

Complete projects, including induced mining models, are saved in XML format for ease of re-use and communication with other applications. Hence, models can be defined, trained and saved for later application to new datasets (e.g., unlabeled data to produce predictions).

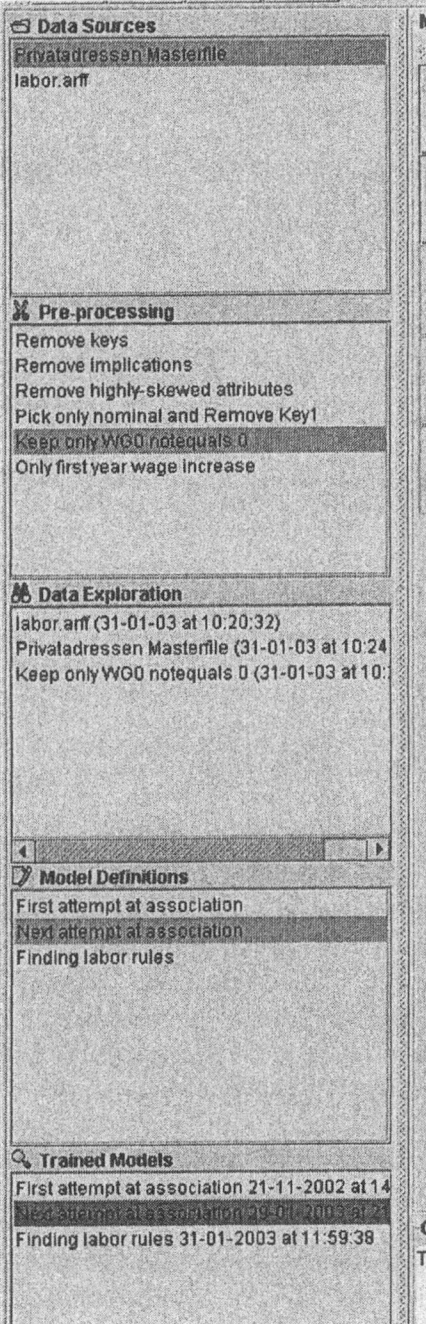

*Figure 4*. Data Mining Streams

The following is an excerpt from a sample XML project file.

```
<xml version="1.0" encoding="utf-8">
  <CommonInfo>
    <Value ProjectName="Project 1.xml"></Value>
    ...
  </CommonInfo>
    <Section name="Datasets">
      </Dataset>
      <Dataset name="contact-lenses.arff">
    <value FileName="contact-lenses.arff"></value>
    ...
      </Dataset>
    </Section>
    <Section name="PreProcesses">
      <PreProcess name="Keep only WG0 notequals 0">
    <value Parameter="SourceType">PreProcess</value>
    ...
      </PreProcess>
    </Section>
    <Section name="Statistics">
      <Statistic name="labor.arff (31-01-03 at 10:20:32)">
    <value Parameter="SourceType">DataSet</value>
    ...
      </Statistic>
    </Section>
    <Section name="ModelDefinitions">
      <MiningModel name="First attempt at association">
    <value Parameter="SourceType">PreProcess</value>
    ...
      </MiningModel>
    </Section>
    <Section name="Trainingresults">
      <Training name="First attempt at association 21-11-2002 at 14:22:53">
    <value Parameter="SourceType">MiningModel</value>
    ...
      </Training>
    </Section>
</xml>
```

Once a model is trained/saved, it can be executed or applied to any compatible dataset. Such an execution produces a dataset (in the Data Sources panel) equivalent to the original one with two additional columns, one for the predicted values and one for the corresponding confidences in those predictions. Using the Pre-processing capabilities of SwissAnalyst, it is then easy to extract useful actionable data, such as: all records (or adequate projections thereof) predicted as some value with a confidence level above some threshold (e.g., names and addresses of all prospects predicted to respond with a confidence higher than 85%).

## 3.4    Enhanced Data Exploration

When a dataset is loaded into SwissAnalyst (and whenever it is later selected in the Data Sources panel), a "data dump" of about 50 instances/records is automatically displayed on screen (in tabular form) so that users may get a quick and intuitive feel for the data. It is also possible to view the entire dataset.

Further data exploration is accessible via a sub-menu when selecting any dataset, either in the Data Sources panel or the Pre-processing panel, and results are stored in the Data Exploration panel.

In addition to providing detailed data statistics and a simple bar-chart-like viewer for value distributions, SwissAnalyst can automatically warn the user of pathological attributes, such as single-valued attributes, keys, attributes with a high proportion of missing values, etc. This information, summarized on a single report, shown in Figure 5, is useful in the data preparation phase of the DM process for the correct handling of such attributes (e.g., ignore, fill-in missing values, etc.).

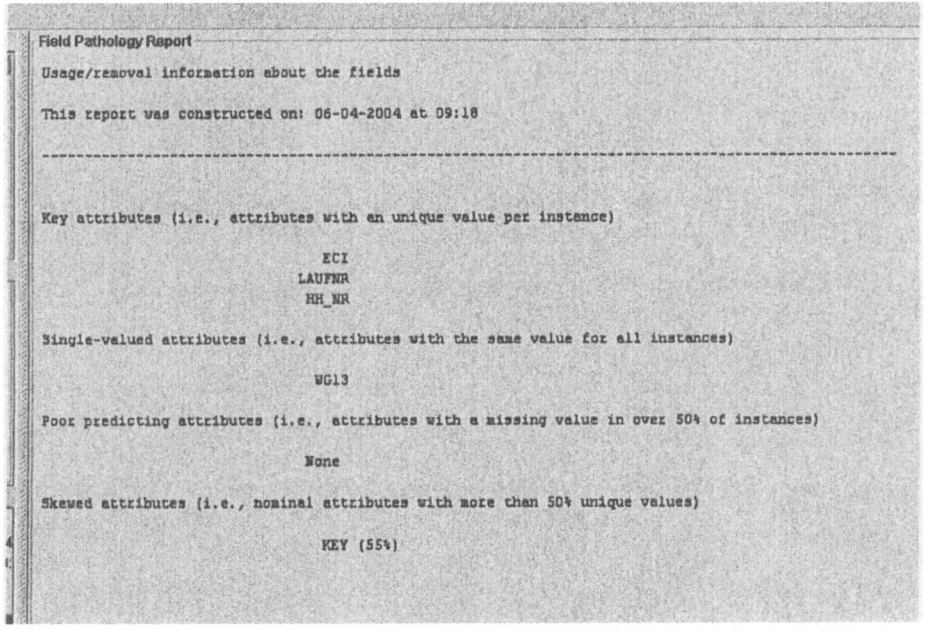

*Figure 5.* Field Pathology Report

## 3.5    Improved Results Section

The output/results section of Weka has been re-organised and enhanced. Results have been split into five categories:

- <u>Basics</u>: provides general information about the model, the data mining stream and any associated comments.

- Model: describes the induced model (e.g., text-based representation of decision tree, list of associations), including graphical representations when applicable (e.g., J4.8).
- Statistics: presents the model's statistics (i.e., confusion matrix, etc.).
- Graphs: displays response, lift and gain charts as well as ROC curves for all class values.
- Comparison: displays a 3-column table, which, for each instance of the test set, shows the actual class value, the predicted class value and the confidence in the prediction.

Some of these categories are disabled for certain types of mining algorithms (e.g., there are no graphs when performing clustering).

Figure 6 gives an illustration of the results section, with the graphs category selected. All graphs can be printed easily by right-clicking the mouse.

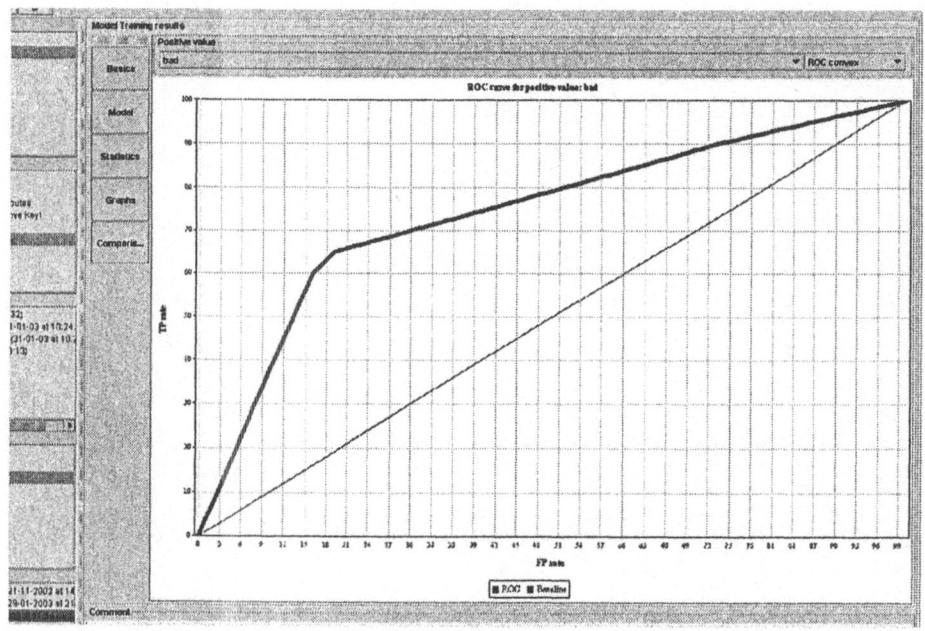

*Figure 6.* Results Section

Although Weka does offer support for some visualization/graphs (e.g., ROC curve), results are only displayed for one class value at a time, requiring the user to go back to the main window to select another class value, and opening a new window for the display. SwissAnalyst allows users to view the ROC curve of each class value simply by selecting the class value from a drop-down list in the graphs section.

Furthermore, from the same interface and with a similar drop-down list mechanism, SwissAnalyst displays response charts, as well as lift and gain charts.

## 3.6     Model Pre-selection

To assist novice users and avoid the unnecessary generation of error messages, SwissAnalyst implements a simple pre-selection scheme for classification algorithms.

Based on the features' types for a given data source, SwissAnalyst displays only those classification algorithms that are applicable (e.g., if the class attribute is continuous, then ID3 is not shown as an option). Figure 7 shows an example, where input features are of mixed types and the class is continuous.

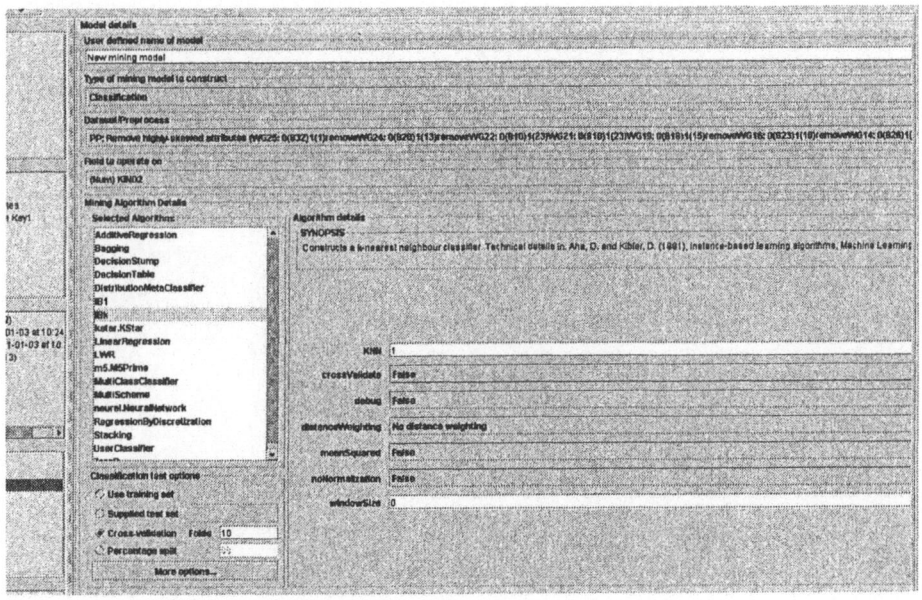

*Figure 7.* Model Pre-selection

Note that the pre-selection dynamically adapts as the user selects the type of mining model, the data source to operate on and the field to predict when applicable.

More sophisticated pre-selection mechanisms, such as the ontology-based approach of IDEA (Bernstein et al. 2002) or METAL's meta-learning approach (Farrand, 2002), both of which implemented in Weka, can easily be added. Such mechanisms further assist users in selecting and combining DM operators most suitable to a particular task and objective.

## 3.7    Enhanced Pre-processing

As in Weka, the pre-processing phase of the DM process in SwissAnalyst allows users to apply more than one pre-processing algorithms to the selected data source, thus creating a kind of pre-processing sub-stream. Elements of such substreams can not only be added and removed, but modified and re-ordered at will.

Figure 8 shows a simple sub-stream with two pre-processing tasks, an instance selection step, which filters instances based on some condition (generally based on the value of some attribute), and an attribute selection step, which removes specific attributes from the analysis.

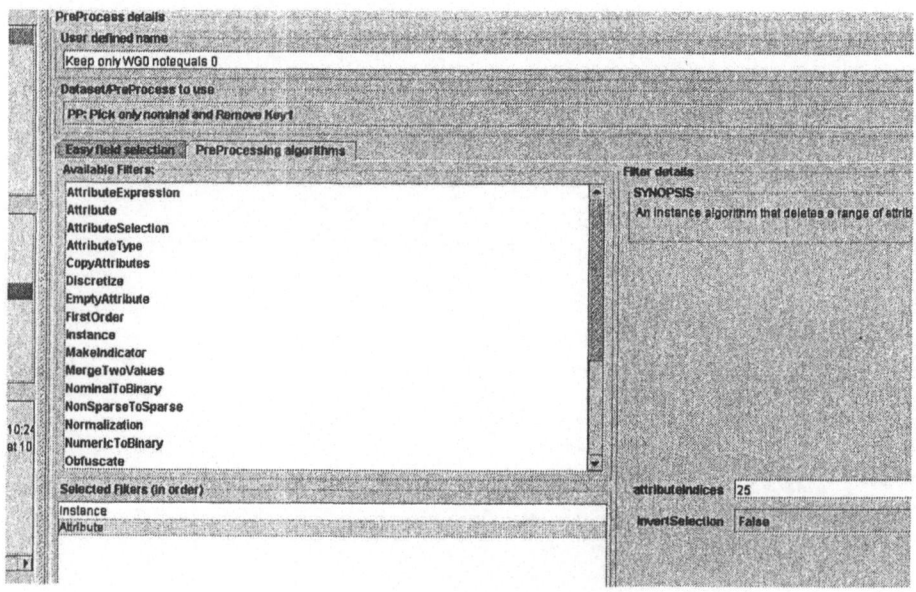

*Figure 8.* Pre-processing Sub-stream

Note that the "Easy Field Selection" tab allows users to quickly perform manual attribute selection (select/de-select) by clicking on individual attributes.

Pre-processing algorithms, known as filters in Weka, often apply to one or more attributes. These are specified by their index value. Historically, filters have been added to Weka from varying sources so that there is no standard indexing schemes, some filters assuming that index values start at 0 and others at 1. SwissAnalyst rectifies this by allowing uniform indexing, starting numbering at 1. Furthermore, to avoid confusion, all index values are automatically re-calculated when attributes are selected/de-selected by the user.

The AttributeSelectedClassifier and the FilteredClassifier of Weka have been purposely removed as they can be reconstructed more naturally and in line with the DM process by applying first a pre-processing task (i.e., attribute selection or an arbitrary filter) and then a mining algorithm.

## 4.      OBTAINING SWISSANALYST

Instructions to download SwissAnalyst may be obtained from datamining@elca.ch. Installation only requires the decompression of the archive to any directory and execution of the accompanying script file. SwissAnalyst has been successfully tested on both PC Windows and Unix platforms.

SwissAnalyst, powered by Weka, is also distributed as GNU GPL software. We will continue to improve it and encourage others to do likewise. No claim is made that the current version is either bug-free or DM panacea. It simply provides a clear process-oriented wrapper for Weka's functionality and offers a reasonable platform for further development.

## 5.      CONCLUSION

This short paper describes SwissAnalyst, a complete process-driven DM environment powered by Weka.

We contend that SwissAnalyst includes enough functionality and process support, with an intuitive graphical user interface, to make it attractive for (license-free) business proofs of concept as well as for advanced research purposes. Its open source character facilitates future enhancements, based on experience. Our own work will focus on:

- Extending data exploration with additional information, flexibility and advice.
- Improving user support by combining IDEA (Bernstein et al., 2002) and an incremental form of the METAL advice strategy (METAL, 2002).
- Adding further model visualization tools.

# ACKNOWLEDGEMENTS

Special thanks to our early beta-testers who provided valuable feedback on SwissAnalyst.

# REFERENCES

Bernstein, A., Hill, S. and Provost, F. (2002): Intelligent Assistance for the Data Mining Process: An Ontology-based Approach. New York University – Leonard Stern School of Business, Center for Digital Economy Research, *CeDER Working Paper # IS-02-02*.

Farrand, J. (2002). *WekaMetal*. Software available at www.cs.bris.ac.uk/~farrand/wekametal.

Fischer, S., Klinkenberg, R., Mierswa, I. and Ritthoff, O. (2002). *YALE: Yet Another Learning Environment – Tutorial*. CI-136/02, Collaborative Research Center 531, University of Dortmund, ISSN 1433-3325. Software available at /yale.cs.uni-dortmund.de.

Giraud-Carrier, C. and Povel, O. (2003). Characterizing Data Mining Software. *Journal of Intelligent Data Analysis*, 7(3): 181-192.

KDnuggets Poll (2002a). *Data mining tools you regularly use*. Full results available at www.kdnuggets.com/poll/data_mining_tools_2002_june2.htm.

KDnuggets Poll (2002b). *What main methodology are you using for data mining?* Full results available at www.kdnuggets.com/polls/methodology.html.

METAL (2002). *METAL: A Meta-Learning Assistant for Providing User Support in Machine Learning and Data Mining*. ESPRIT Project Nr 26.357. Official site at www.metal-kdd.org/.

Ritthoff, O., Klinkenberg, R., Fischer, S., Mierswa, I. and Felske, S. (2001). *YALE: Yet Another Learning Environment*. LLWA 01 – Tagungsband der GI-Workshop-Woche Lernen – Lehren – Wissen – Adaptivität, Forschungsberichte des Fachbereichs Informatik, Universität Dortmund, Nr. 763, ISSN 0933-6192.

SAS (1998). *From Data to Business Advantage: Data Mining, The SEMMA Methodology and SAS Software*. Available as a SAS Institute White Paper at www.sas.com.

SPSS (2000). *CRISP-DM 1.0: Step-by-step data mining guide*. Available as an SPSS White Paper at www.spss.com.

Thess, M. and Bolotnikov, M. (2003). XELOPES Library Documentation, Version 1.1.7, prudsys AG. Software available at www.prudsys.com.

Witten, I.H. and Frank, E. (2000). *Data Mining: Practical Machine Learning Tools and Techniques with Java Implementations*, Morgan Kaufmann. Software available at www.cs.waikato.ac.nz/ml/weka/index.html.

Zupan, B. and Demsar, J. (2003). *Orange*. Software available at magix.fri.uni-lj.si/orange.

# DATA MINING BY MOUCLAS ALGORITHM FOR PETROLEUM RESERVOIR CHARACTERIZATION FROM WELL LOGGING DATA

Yalei Hao[1], Markus Stumptner[1], Gerald Quirchmayr[1,2], Qing He[3]
[1] *Advanced Computing Research Centre, University of South Australia, SA5095, Australia,*
[2] *Institut für Informatik und Wirtschaftsinformatik, Universität Wien, Liebiggasse 4, A-1010 Wien, Austria,* [3] *Institute of Computing Technology, Chinese Academy of Sciences, Beijing 100080, China*

**Abstract:** Petroleum reservoir characterization is one of the most difficult and challenging tasks of the exporation of petroleum industry and usually a long and costly procedure. This paper proposes a novel kind of patterns for the classification over quantitative well logging data, which is called *MOUCLAS* (MOUntain function based CLASsification) Patterns, based on the concept of the fuzzy set membership function which gives the new approach a solid mathematical foundation and compact mathematical description of classifiers. It integrates classification, clustering and association rules mining to identify interesting knowledge in the well logging database. The aim of the study is the use of *MOUCLASS* patterns to interpret the pay zones from well logging data for the purpose of reservoir characterization. This approach is better than conventional techniques for well logging interpretation that require a precise understanding of the relation between the well logging data and the underlying property of interest.

**Keywords:** Data Mining, MOUCLAS Pattern, Petroleum Reservoir Characterization

## 1. INTRODUCTION AND MOTIVATION

Well logging data analysis, a geophysical prospecting technique, plays an essential role in petroleum exploration and exploitation. It is used to identify the pay zones of gas or oil in the reservoir formations[1]. The techniques of processing the huge databases such as well logging data is one of the main paths to increase and optimize production of oil and gas reservoirs. Accurate reservoir characterization through data analysis of well logging is an essential step in reservoir modeling & management and production optimization.

Three main types of well logging quantitative data, which are electrical, nuclear and acoustic data, can be collected by specific instruments lowering in the well borehole at different depth intervals. Then, the well logging interpreter analyzes the acquired data in order to recover the petrophysical parameters of formations across the borehole, such as porosity, permeability, lithology, grain size, amount of clay, water saturation, etc. Next, all these above findings are used for reservoir characterization so as to evaluate the reservoir formation[2]. A large number of techniques have been introduced in order to establish an adequate interpretation model for the petrophysical parameters of formations over the past fifty years, such as the determination of permeability[3].

In recent years the petroleum industry has witnessed a massive explosion in the volume and dimensions of data. It is caused by increased sampling rate, longer record acquisition, multi-component surveys, 4-D seismic, etc[4]. Thus we need efficient techniques to process such large databases. Beside the above conventional empirical and statistical techniques, data mining techniques have gained much attention since they can be an innovative option for well logging data analysis for the purpose of reservoir characterization and help identify the most information rich part of the large and high dimensional data sets.

Data mining based classification aims to build accurate and efficient classifiers not only on small data sets but more importantly also on large and high dimensional data sets, while the widely used traditional statistical data analysis techniques are not sufficiently powerful for this task[5, 6]. With the development of new data mining techniques on association rules, new classification approaches based on concepts from association rule mining are emerging. These include such classifiers as ARCS[7], CBA[8], LB[9], CAEP[10], etc., which are different from the classic decision tree based classifier C4.5[11] and k-nearest neighbor[12] in both the learning and testing phases.

ARCS[7] demonstrated the successful application of concepts of clustering for the purpose of classification. However, ARCS is limited to 2D-rules based classifiers of the format $A \wedge B \Rightarrow Class_i$, where A and B are two predicates. It uses the method of "Binning" to discretize the value of quantitative attributes. Consequently, the accuracy of ACRS is strongly related to the degree of discretization used. A non-grid-based technique[13] has been proposed to find quantitative association rules that can have more than two predicates in the antecedent. The authors noticed that the information loss caused by partitioning could not be ignored and have tried to employ a measure of partial completeness to quantify the information lost, but the measure is still constrained by the framework of binning. Though there are several excellent discretization algorithms[14, 15], a standard approach to discretization has not yet been developed. Different approaches could lead to different collections of large itemsets even with respect to the same support threshold in a given data set. ARCS and the non-grid-based technique lead to research question 1 addressed: "Is it possible that an association rule based classifier can be developed for quantitative attributes by the concepts of clustering which can overcome the limitation caused by the discretization method? " CBA[8] gives us an interesting indication that the idea of apriori property can be applied to a set of predicates (itemsets) for classification. Suppose an association rule based classifier in the form of $A_1 \wedge A_2 \wedge \ldots \wedge A_l \Rightarrow C_i$, where $A_j$ ($j$=1, ..., l) are predicate variables, $C_i$ is the class label, the antecedent of the rule is a frequent itemset. This raises question 2: "If an association rule based classifier can be built based on the concept of clustering, is it possible that a link between CBA and ARCS can be found so that an association rule based classifier with any number of predicates in the antecedent can be setup by clustering? "

The above research issues establish a challenge that comes within our research focus. In this paper, we present a new approach to the classification over quantitative data in high dimensional databases, called *MOUCLAS* (MOUntain function based CLASsification), based on the concept of the fuzzy set membership function. It aims at integrating the advantages of classification, clustering and association rules mining to identify interesting patterns in selected sample data sets.

## 2.    PROBLEM STATEMENT

We now give a formal statement of the problem of *MOUCLAS* Patterns (called *MPs*) and introduce some definitions. The *MOUCLAS* algorithm, similar to ARCS, assumes that the initial association rules can be agglomerated into clustering regions, while obeying the anti-monotone rule constraint. Our proposed framework assumes that the training dataset $D$ is a normal relational set, where transaction $d \in D$. Each transaction $d$ is described by attributes $A_j$, $j$ = 1 to $l$. The dimension of $D$ is $l$, the number of attributes used in $D$. This allows us to describe a database in terms of volume and dimension. $D$ can be classified into a set of known classes $Y$, $y \in Y$. The value of an attribute must be quantitative. In this work, we treat all the attributes uniformly. We can treat a transaction as a set of (attributes, value) pairs and a class label. We call each (attribute, value) pair an item. A set of items is simply called an itemset.

Since CBA indicates the feasibility of setting up a link between association rule and classification and ARCS proves that the idea of designing a classification pattern based on clustering can work effectively and efficiently, we design a *MOUCLAS* Pattern (so called *MP*) as an implication of the form:

$Cluster(D)_t \rightarrow y$,

where *Cluster(D)*$_t$ *is a cluster of D, t* = 1 to *m*, and *y* is a class label. The definitions of *frequency* and *accuracy* of *MOUCLAS* Patterns are defined as following: The *MP* satisfying minimum support is *frequent*, where *MP* has support s if s% of the transactions in *D* belong to *Cluster(D)*$_t$ and are labeled with class *y*. The *MP* that satisfies a pre-specified minimum confidence is called *accurate*, where *MP* has confidence c if c% of the transactions belonging to *Cluster(D)*$_t$ are labeled with class *y*.

Though framework of support – confidence is used in most of the applications of association rule mining, it may be misleading by identifying a rule $A \Rightarrow B$ as interesting, even though the occurrence of A may not imply the occurrence of B. This requires a complementary framework for finding interesting relations. Correlation[16] is one of the most efficient interestingness measures other than support and confidence. Here we adopt the concept of reliability[17] to describe the correlation. The measure of reliability of the association rule $A \Rightarrow B$ can be defined as:

$$\text{reliability} \quad R(A \Rightarrow B) = \left| \frac{P(A \wedge B)}{P(A)} - P(B) \right|$$

Since R is the difference between the conditional probability of B given A and the unconditional of B, it measures the effect of available information of A on the probability of the association rule. Correspondingly, the greater R is, the stronger *MOUCLAS* patterns are, which means the occurrence of *Cluster(D)*$_t$ more strongly implies the occurrence of *y*. Therefore, we can utilize reliability to further prune the selected *frequent and accurate and reliable MOUCLAS* patterns (*MPs*) to identify the truly interesting *MPs* and make the discovered *MPs* more understandable. The *MP* satisfying minimum reliability is *reliable*, where *MP* has reliability defined by the above formula.

Given a set of transactions, *D*, the problems of *MOUCLAS* are to discover *MPs* that have support and confidence greater than the user-specified minimum support threshold (called *minsup*)[18], and minimum confidence threshold (called *minconf*)[18] and minimum reliability threshold (called *minR*) respectively, and to construct a classifier based upon *MPs*.

## 3. THE *MOUCLAS* ALGORITHM

The classification technique, *MOUCLAS*, consists of two steps:
1. Discovery of *frequent*, *accurate* and *reliable MPs*.
2. Construction of a classifier, called *De-MP*, based on *MPs*.

The core of the first step in the *MOUCLAS* algorithm is to find all *cluster_rules* that have support above *minsup*. Let $C$ denote the dataset $D$ after dimensionality reduction processing. A *cluster_rule* represents a *MP*, namely a rule:

$$cluset \rightarrow y,$$

where *cluset* is a set of itemsets from a cluster $Cluster(C)_i$, $y$ is a class label, $y \in Y$. The support count of the *cluset* (called *clusupCount*) is the number of transactions in $C$ that belong to the *cluset*. The support count of the *cluster_rule* (called *cisupCount*) is the number of transactions in $D$ that belong to the *cluset* and are labeled with class $y$. The *confidence* of a *cluster_rule* is (*cisupCount* / *clusupCount*) $\times$ 100%. The support count of the *class y* (called *clasupCount*) is the number of transactions in $C$ that belong to the class $y$. The *support* of a *class* (called *clasup*) is (*clasupCount* / $|C|$) $\times$ 100%, where $|C|$ is the size of the dataset $C$.

Given a *MP*, the *reliability* R can be defined as:

$$R(cluset \rightarrow y) = \mid (cisupCount / clusupCount) - (clasupCount / |C|) \mid \times 100\%$$

The traditional association rule mining only uses a single *minsup* in rule generation, which is inadequate for many practical datasets with uneven class frequency distributions. As a result, it may happen that the rules found for infrequent classes are insufficient and too many may be found for frequent classes, inducing useless or over-fitting rules, if the single *minsup* value is too high or too low. To overcome this drawback, we apply the theory of mining with multiple minimum supports[19] in the step of discovering the frequent MPs as following.

Suppose the total support is *t-minsup*, the different minimum class support for each class $y$, denoted as *minsup_i* can be defined by the formula:

$$minsup_i = t\text{-}minsup \times freqDistr(y)$$

where freqDistr($y$) is the function of class distributions. *Cluster_rules* that satisfy *minsup_i* are called *frequent cluster_rules*, while the rest are called *infrequent cluster_rules*. If the *confidence* is greater than *minconf*, we say the *MP* is *accurate*.

The first step of *MOUCLAS* algorithm works in three sub-steps, by which the problem of discovering a set of *MPs* is solved:

**Algorithm:** Mining *frequent* and *accurate* and *reliable* MOUCLAS patterns (*MPs*)

**Input:** A training transaction database, *D*; minimum support threshold (*minsup$_i$*); minimum confidence threshold (*minconf*); minimum reliability threshold (*minR*)

**Output:** A set of *frequent, accurate* and *reliable* MOUCLAS patterns (*MPs*)

**Methods:**

(1) Reduce the dimensionality of transactions *d*, which efficiently reduces the data size by removing irrelevant or redundant attributes (or dimensions) from the training data, and

(2) Identify the clusters of database *C* for all transactions *d* after dimensionality reduction on attributes *A$_j$* in database *C*, based on the Mountain function, which is a fuzzy set membership function, and specially capable of transforming quantitative values of attributes in transactions into linguistic terms, and

(3) Generate a set of *MPs* that are both *frequent, accurate* and *reliable*, namely, which satisfy the user-specified minimum support (called *minsup$_i$*), minimum confidence (called *minconf*) and minimum reliability (called *minR*) constraints.

In the first sub-step, we reduce the dimensionality of transactions in order to enhance the quality of data mining and decrease the computational cost of the *MOUCLAS* algorithm. Since, for attributes A$_j$, *j* = 1 to *l* in database, *D*, an exhaustive search for the optimal subset of attributes within $2^l$ possible subsets can be prohibitively expensive, especially in high dimensional databases, we use heuristic methods to reduce the search space. Such greedy methods are effective in practice, and include such techniques as stepwise forward selection, stepwise backward elimination, combination of forwards selection and backward elimination, etc. The first sub-step is particularly important when dealing with raw data sets. Detailed methods concerning dimensionality reduction can be found in some papers[20-23].

Fuzzy based clustering is performed in the second sub-step to find the clusters of quantitative data. The Mountain-climb technique proposed by R. R. Yager and D. P. Filev[24] employed the concept of a mountain function, a fuzzy set membership function, in determining cluster centers used to initialize a Neuro-Fuzzy system. The substractive clustering technique[25] was defined as an improvement of Mountain-climb clustering. A similar approach is provided by the DENCLUE algorithm[26], which is especially efficient for clustering on high dimensional databases with noise. The techniques of Mountain-climb clustering, Substractive clustering and Denclue provide an effective way of dealing with quantitative attributes by mountain functions (or influence functions), which has a solid mathematical foundation and compact mathematical description and is totally different from the traditional processing method of binning. It offers us an opportunity of mining the patterns of data from an innovative angle. As a result, question 1 presented in the introduction can now be favorably answered.

The observation that, a region which is dense in a particular subspace must create dense regions when projected onto lower dimensional subspaces, has been proved by R. Agrawal and his research cooperators in CLIQUE[27]. In other words, the observation follows the concepts of the apriori property. Hence, we may employ prior knowledge of items in the search space based on the property so that portions of the space can be pruned. The successful performance of CLIQUE has again proved the feasibility of applying the concept of apriori property to clustering. It brings us a step further towards the solution of problem 2, that is, if the initial association rules can be agglomerated into clustering regions, just like the condition in ARCS, we may be able to design a new classifier for the purpose of classification, which confines its search for the classifier to the cluster of dense units of high dimensional space. The answer to question 2 can contribute to the third sub-step of the *MOUCLAS* algorithm to the forming of the antecedent of *cluster_rules*, with any number of predicates in the antecedent. In the third sub-step, we identify the candidate *cluster_rules* which are actually *frequent* and *accurate* and *reliable*. From this set of *frequent* and *accurate* and *reliable cluster_rules*, we produce a set of *MPs*.

---

1 $X$ = reduceDim ($I$); // reduce the dimensionality on the set of all items $I$ of in $D$
2 $Cluster(C)_t$ = genCluster ($C$); // identify the complete clusters of $C$
3 for each $Cluster(C)_t$ do
    $E$ = genClusterrules(*cluset, class*); // generate a set of candidate *cluster_rules*
4    for each transaction $d \in C$ do
5        $E_d$ = genSubClusterrules ($E$, $d$); // find all the *cluster_rules* in $E$ whose *cluset* are supported by $d$
6        for each $e \in E_d$ do
7            $e.$ clusupCount++;
            // accumulate the *clusupCount* of the *cluset* of *cluster_rule* $e$
8            if $d$.class = $e$.class then $e.cisupCount$++
            // accumulate the *cisupCount* of *cluster_rule* $e$ supported by $d$
9    end
10 end
11  $F$ = {$e \in E$ | $e.cisupCount \geq minsup_i$ }; // construct the set of frequent cluster_rules
12  $MP$ = genRules ($F$);//generate $MP$ using the genRules function by *minconf* and *minR*
13 end
14 $MPs$ = □ $MP$; // discover the final set of $MPs$

---

*Figure 1: The First Step of the MOUCLAS Algorithm*

Let $I$ be the set of all items in $D$, $C$ be the dataset $D$ after dimensionality reduction, where transaction $d \in C$ contains $X \subseteq I$, a $k$-itemset. Let E denote the set of candidates of cluster_rules, where $e \in E$, *and* F denote the set of frequent cluster_rules. The first step of the *MOUCLAS* algorithm is given in Figure 1.

The task of the second step in *MOUCLAS* algorithm is to use a heuristic method to generate a classifier, named *De-MP*, where the discovered *MPs* can cover $D$ and are organized according to a decreasing precedence based on their confidence and support. Suppose $R$ be the set of *frequent, accurate* and *reliable MPs* which are generated in the past step, and $MP_{default\_class}$ *denotes* the default class, which has the lowest precedence. We can then present the *De-MP* classifier in the form of

$<MP_1, MP_2, ..., MP_n, MP_{default\_class}>$,

where $MP_i \in R$, $i = 1$ to $n$, $MP_a > MP_b$ if $n \geq b > a \geq 1$ *and* $a$, $b \in i$, $C \subseteq$ $\square$ *cluset of $MP_{i_s}$*.

The second step of the *MOUCLAS* algorithm also consists of three sub-steps, by which the *De-MP* classifier is formed:

**Algorithm:** Constructing *De-MP* Classifier

**Input:** A training database after dimensionality reduction, $C$; The set of *frequent and accurate and reliable MOUCLAS* patterns (*MPs*)

**Output:** *De-MP* Classifier

**Methods:**

(1) Identify the order of all discovered *MPs* based on the definition of precedence and sequence them according to decreasing precedence order.

(2) Determine possible *MPs* for *De-MP* classifier from $R$ following the descending sequence of *MPs*.

(3) Discard the *MPs* which cannot contribute to the improvement of the accuracy of the *De-MP* classifier and keep the final set of *MPs* to construct the *De-MP* classifier.

In the first sub-step, the *MPs* are sorted in descending order, which has the training transactions surely covered by the *MPs* with the highest precedence when possible in the next sub-step. The sort of the whole set of *MPs* is performed following the definition of *precedence*:

Given two *MPs*, we say that $MP_a$ has a higher precedence than $MP_b$, denoted as $MP_a > MP_b$,

if $\forall MP_a, MP_b \in MPs$, it holds that: the confidence of $MP_a$ is greater than that of $MP_b$, or if their confidences are the same, but the support of $MP_a$ is greater than that of $MP_b$, or if both the confidences and supports of $MP_a$ and $MP_b$ are the same, but $MP_a$ is generated earlier than $MP_b$.

In the second sub-step, we test the *MPs* following decreasing precedence and stop the sub-step when there is no rule or no training transaction. For each *MP*, we scan $C$ to find those transactions satisfying the cluset of the

*MP*. If the *MP* can correctly classify one transaction, we store it in a set denoted as *L*. Those transactions satisfying the cluset of the *MP* will be removed from *C* at each pass. Each transaction can be identified by a unique ID. The next pass will be performed on the remaining data. A default class is defined at each scan, which is the majority class in the remaining data. At the end of each pass, the total number of errors that are made by the current *L* and the default class are also stored. When there is no rule or no training transaction left, we terminate this sub-step. After this sub-step, every *MP* in *L* can correctly classify at least one training transaction in *C*.

In the third sub-step, though we would like to find as many *MPs* as possible to give good coverage of the training transactions in the second sub-step, we prefer strong *MPs* which have relatively high support and confidence, due to their characteristics of corresponding to larger coverage and stronger differentiating power. Meanwhile, we hope that the *De-MP* classifier, consisting of a combination of strong *MPs*, has a relatively smaller number of classification errors, because of greedy strategy. In addition, the reduction of *MPs* can increase the understandability of the classifier. Therefore, in this sub-step, we identify the first *MP* with the least number of errors in *L* and discard all the MPs after it because these *MPs* produce more errors. The undiscarded *MPs* and the default class corresponding to the first *MP* with the least number of errors in *L* form our *De-MP* classifier.

The second step of the *MOUCLAS* algorithm is shown in Figure 2.

---

1 $R$ = sort($R$); // sort MPs based on their precedence
2 **for each** $MP \in R$ in sequence **do**
3    $temp = \varnothing$ ;
4    **for each** transaction $d \in C$ **do**
5      **if** $d$ satisfies the cluset of *MP* **then**
6        store $d$.ID in *temp*;
7        **if** *MP* correctly classifies $d$ **then**
8          insert *MP* at the end of $L$;
9       delete the transaction who has ID in *temp* from $C$;
10      selecting a default class for the current $L$;
       // determine the default class based on majority class of remaining transactions in $C$
11   **end**
12   compute the total number of errors of $L$;
    // compute the total number of errors that are made by the current $L$ and the default class
13 **end**
14 Find the first MP in $L$ with the lowest total number of errors and discard all the *MPs* after the *MP* in $L$;
15 Add the default class associated with the above mentioned first MP to end of $L$;
16 *De-MP* classifier = $L$

---

*Figure 2: The Second Step of the MOUCLAS Algorithm*

In the testing phase, when we classify a new transaction, the first *MP* in *De-MP* satisfying the transaction is used to classify it. In *De-MP* classifier, *default_class*, having the lowest precedence, is used to specify a default class for any new sample that is not satisfied by any other *MPs* as in C4.5[11], CBA[8].

## 4.    EXAMPLE OF *MOUCLAS* APPLICATION IN RESERVOIR CHARACTERIZATION

Oil/gas formation identification is a vital task of reservoir characterization in the petroleum industry, where the petroleum database contains such records (or attributes) as seismic data, various types of well logging data and petrophysical property data whose values are all quantitative.

An illustration of using well logging date for purpose of oil/gas formation identification is illustrated in Figure 3. The well logging data sets include attributes (well logging curves) of GR (gamma ray), RDEV (deep resistivity), RMEV (shallow resistivity), RXO (flushed zone resistivity), RHOB (bulk density), NPHI (neutron porosity), PEF (photoelectric factor) and DT (sonic travel time). Since most of the reservoirs are horizontally and vertically heterogeneous, no depth information is used for training.

One transaction of the database can be treated as a set of the items corresponding to the same depth and a class label (oil/gas formation or not). A hypothetically useful *MP* may suggest a relation between well logging data and the class label of oil/gas formation since. In this sense, a selected set of such *MPs* can be a useful guide to petroleum engineers to identify possible drilling targets and their depth and thickness at the stage of exploration and exploitation.

*MOUCLAS* aims at deriving an explicit or implicit heuristic relationship between measured values (well logging data) and properties to be predicted (oil/gas formation or not). The *MOUCLAS* method is ideally suitable to establish such implicit relationships through proper training. The notable advantage of *MOUCLAS* over more traditional processing techniques such as model based well logging analysis is that a physical model to describe the relationship between the well logging data and the property of interest is not needed; nor is an very precise understanding of the physical phenomena of the well logging data. From this point of view, *MOUCLAS* provides a complementary and useful technical approach towards the interpretation of petroleum data and benefits petroleum discovery.

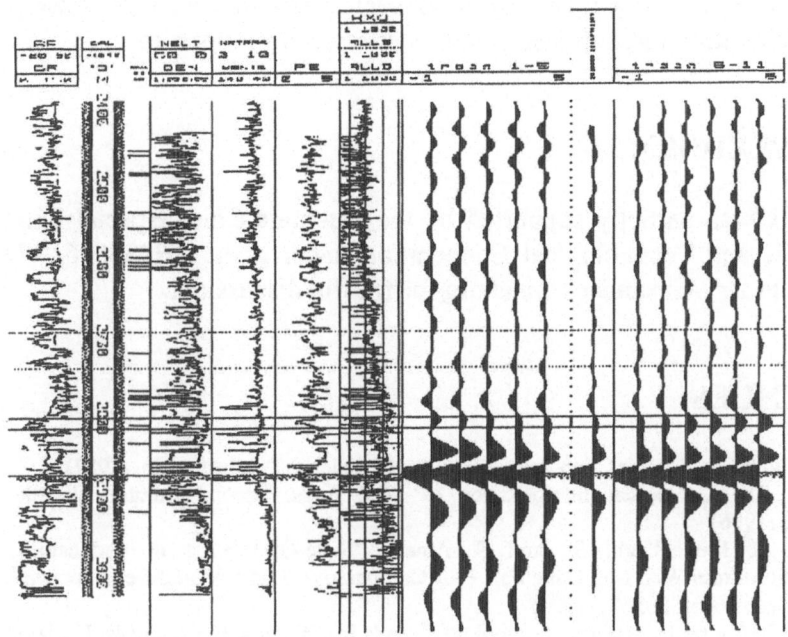

*Figure 3: Quantitative Petroleum Data for MOUCLAS Mining*

*( note: the dashed indicate the location of oil formation )*

# 5. CONCLUSIONS

A novel classification patterns, the *MOUCLAS* Pattern (*MP*) for quantitative data in high dimensional databases, is investigated in this paper for the cost effective and intelligent well logging data analysis for reservoir characterization. We also propose the algorithm for the discovery of the interesting *MPs* and construct a new classifier called *De-MP*. As a hybrid of classification and clustering and association rules mining, our approach may have several advantages which are (1) it has a solid mathematical foundation and compact mathematical description of classifiers, (2) it does not require discretization, as opposed to other, otherwise quite similar methods such as ARCS are strongly related to, (3) it is robust when handling noisy or incomplete data in high dimensional data space, regardless of the database size, due to its grid-based characteristic, (4) it is not sensitive to the order of input items and it scales linearly with the size of input. In the future research, we attempt to establish a relationship between different well logs, seismic attributes, laboratory measurements and other reservoir properties.

## ACKNOWLEDGEMENT

This work was partially supported by the Australia-China Special Fund for Scientific and Technological Cooperation under grant CH030086. We are grateful to Dr. Alexander Hinneburg for fruitful discussion.

## REFERENCES

1. D.V. Ellis, Well Logging for Earth Scientists, Elsevier Science Publishing Co. (1987)
2. M. Rider, The Geological Interpretation of Well Logs, Second Edition, Whittles Publishing, (1996)
3. B. Balan, S. Mohaghegh, S., and S. Ameri, "State-Of-The-Art in Permeability Determination From Well Log Data: Part 1 -A Comparative Study, Model Development," SPE Technical Report 30978, (1995)
4. F. Aminzadeh, Future Geoscience Technology Trends in, Stratigraphic Analysis, Utilizing Advanced Geophysical, Wireline, and Borehole Technology For Petroleum Exploration and Production, GCSEPFM pp 1-6, (1996)
5. Fayyad, U. M., Piatetsky-Shapiro, G., & Smyth, P. From data mining to knowledge discovery: An overview. Advances in knowledge discovery and data mining. AAAI/MIT Press. (1996) 1-34
6. Han, J., & M. Kamber. Data mining: concepts and techniques. Morgan Kaufmann Publishers. (2000)
7. B. Lent, A. Swami, and J. Widom. Clustering association rules. ICDE'97, (1997) 220-231
8. B. Liu, W.Hsu, and Y.Ma. Integrating classification and association rule mining. KDD'98. (1998) 80-86
9. Meretakis, D., & Wuthrich, B. Extending naive Bayes classifiers using long itemsets. Proc. of the Fifth ACM SIGKDD. ACM Press. (1999) 165-174
10. Dong, G., & Li, J. Efficient mining of emerging patterns: Discovering trends and differences. Proc. of the Fifth ACM SIGKDD. (1999)
11. Quinlan, J. R. C4.5: Programs for machine learning. San Mateo, CA: Morgan Kaufmann. (1993)
12. Cover, T. M., & Hart, P. E. Nearest neighbor pattern classification. IEEE Transactions on Information Theory, 13. (1967) 21-27
13. R. Skikant and R. Agrawal. Mining quantitative association rules in large relational tables. SIG-MOD'96, (1996) 1-12.
14. Fayyad, U., & Irani, K. Multi-interval discretization of continuous-valued attributes for classification learning. Proc. of the 13th Int'l Conf. on Artificial Intelligence. Morgan Kaufmann. (1993) 1022--1029
15. Dougherty, J., Kohavi, R., & Sahami, M. Supervised and unsupervised discretization of continuous features. Proc. of the Twelfth Int'l Conf. on Machine Learning pp. 94--202. Morgan Kaufmann. (1995)
16. Han, J., Pei, J., & Yin, Y. Mining frequent patterns without candidates generation. Proc. of the 2000 ACM-SIGMOD. ACM Press. (2000) 1-12

17. Khalil M. Ahmed, Nagwa M. El-Makky, Yousry Taha: A note on "Beyond Market Baskets: Generalizing Association Rules to Correlations". In The Proceedings of SIGKDD Explorations Volume1, Issue 2, (2000) 46-48

18. Agrawal, R., Srikant, R. Fast algorithms for mining association rules. Proc. of the 20th VLDB (1994) 487- 499

19. Bing Liu, Wynne Hsu, Yiming Ma, "Mining Association Rules with Multiple Minimum Supports" Proceedings of the ACM SIGKDD International Conference on Knowledge Discovery & Data Mining (KDD-99), August 15-18, San Diego, CA, USA (1999)

20. Dong, G., & Li, J. Feature selection methods for classification. Intelligent Data Analysis: An International Journal, 1, (1997)

21. H. Liu and H. Motoda, editors. Feature Selection for Knowledge Discovery and Data Mining. Boston: Kluwer Academic Publishers, (1998)

22. W.Sarawagi and M. Stonebraker. On automatic feature selection. Int'l J. of Pattern Recognition and Artificial Intelligence, 2, (1988) 197-220.

23. R. Kohavi and G. John. Wrappers for feature subset selection. Artificial Intelligence, (1997) 273-324

24. Yager, R. and D. Filev, "Generation of Fuzzy Rules by Mountain Clustering," Journal of Intelligent & Fuzzy Systems, Vol. 2, No. 3, (1994) 209-219

25. Chiu, S. L. Fuzzy model identification based on cluster estimation. Journal of Intelligent and Fuzzy System, 2(3), (1994)

26. A. Hinneburg and D. Keim. An efficient approach to clustering in large Multimedia dataset with noise. KDD'98, (1998) 58-65

27. R. Agrawal, J. Gehrke, D. Gunopulos, and P. Raghavan. Automatic subspace clustering of high dimensional data for data mining applications. SIGMOD'98. (1998)

# VERIFICATION OF PROCEDURAL REASONING SYSTEM (PRS) PROGRAMS USING COLOURED PETRI NETS (CPN)

Ricardo Wagner de Araújo
and Adelardo A. Dantas de Medeiros
*Federal University of Rio Grande do Norte - Brazil*
rwagner,adelardo@dca.ufrn.br

**Abstract**     PRS (a tool based on procedural reasoning) has inspired several works in Artificial Intelligence, mainly in embedded and industrial applications. This paper proposes a verification mechanism of PRS programs, based on equivalence rules with Coloured Petri Nets (CPN). This equivalence allows using existing analysis methods for coloured Petri nets to verify PRS programs.

## 1.     Introduction

One of the biggest difficulties in the project of expert systems for embedded or industrial applications is the real-time control of its execution. Many of the usual techniques of knowledge representation and inference in Artificial Intelligence do not have a guaranteed bounded response time. Purely procedural systems, in the other way, are not flexible enough to allow easily incorporating empirical or heuristic knowledge of human experts.

Declarative representations suffer from a lack of control on the execution of their rules, while imperative ones suffer from limited modularity. A promising trade-off for these situations is using Procedural Reasoning. Procedural Reasoning is particularly well suited for problems where implicit or explicit knowledge is already formalized as procedures or plans.

Procedural Reasoning [Georgeff and Lansky, 1986; Ingrand et al., 1992] is a set of tools and methods for representing and executing plans and procedures. These plans or procedures are conditional sequences of actions which can be run to achieve given goals or to react in particular situations. It differs from other usual knowledge representations because it preserves some flow information (i.e., the sequence of action and tests) associated to declarative aspects.

Some of the widely used implementations of procedural reasoning are Reactive Planning (RAP) [Firby, 1987] and PRS (Procedural Reasoning System)

system, originately developed at SRI International [SRI International, 1994]. In our work, we use PRS because it expresses very weel the trade-off between purely declarative and strictly imperative representations and it has good temporal properties and high expressive power. PRS has been used in practical situations as real-time applications – such as supervision and control of mobile robots [Ingrand and Despouys, 2001; Ingrand et al., 1996], failure detection in space shuttles [SRI International, 1994] as well as in the management of communication networks and alarm systems.

In complex knowledge-based systems, however, sometimes the real-time properties and the power of expression are not enough, and we also need verifying such systems as for correctness, reliabilitiy, performance and efficiency [Bench-Capon et al., 1993; Lee and O'Keefe, 1994]. PRS does not offer a verification mechanism. This work proposes some equivalence rules between programs written using a PRS subset and Coloured Petri Nets (CPNs). Thus, the existing methods to analyze CPNs can be used to validate the equivalent PRS program.

Petri nets are widely used to verify knowledge-based systems, as in the PRE-PARE [Zhang and Nguyen, 1993] and Task Structures [Lee and Lai, 2002] systems. We adopted Petri nets as the verification tool for modelling PRS programs because of their capability to model parallelism and non-determinism and also because it is possible to determine exact conversion rules between PRS structures and their equivalent in Petri nets.

## 2. PRS language

PRS main characteristics will be better explained in section 4. For now, we can say that a PRS agent consists of:

- Routine library: each routine, or KA (knowledge area), is a sequence of action and/or tests that can be executed to reach goals or to react to situations;
- Database: it contains the system current beliefs about the world;
- Current goals sets: in PRS, the goals describe desired tasks or behaviors. In the logic used by PRS, the goal to achieve a certain condition C is written as (! C); to test the condition, as (? C); to wait until the condition is true, as (θ C); to maintain C, as (# C); to assert the condition C in the database, as (=> C) and to retract it, as (Λ>C); and
- Intention graph: a dynamic set of routines, structured as a graph, where the system keeps information in real-time about the state of the routines chosen for execution and of their posted subgoals.

Each KA has a body and some invocation conditions. Figure 1 shows a KA that solves Tower of Hanoi. This KA is executed when an order to reach a goal is posted (as the INVOCATION field shows). It can be selected if the CONTEXT

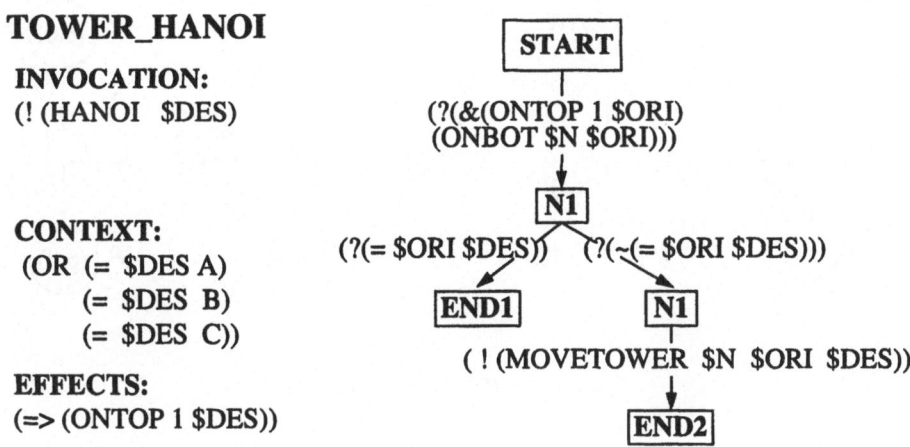

**TOWER_HANOI**

**INVOCATION:**
(! (HANOI  $DES)

**CONTEXT:**
(OR (= $DES A)
   (= $DES  B)
   (= $DES  C))

**EFFECTS:**
(=> (ONTOP 1 $DES))

*Figure 1.*    Tower of Hanoi KA.

field conditions are satisfied. Conditions contain variables to bound ($DES). There are two variable types in PRS: logical variables $var have the classic behavior of variables in logical programming (once bound, they do not change their value), while the program variables @var can be re-attributed.

The KA's body describes its execution. The execution initiates in START node and continues following the arcs through the net. If more than an arc leaves a node, any of them can be crossed. To cross an arc, the system must either test if the goal associated to the arc was already established in the database or launch a KA that reaches the goal associated to arc. This new goal will be incorporated to the intention graph and has to be satisfied before the current KA can be satisfied. If the system cannot satisfy any of the goals associateds to the arcs that leave a node, the entire KA fails. But when a terminal node (END node) is reached, the goal is considered satisfied and the facts listed in EFFECTS are concluded in the database.

## 3.    The Coloured Petri Net - CPN

The Coloured Petri Nets theory is widely known and can be found in the literature [Jensen, 1994]. A modeling example [Jensen, 1998] of an enabled transition for a resource allocation system by CPNs is shown in Figure 2.

Each place (circles that describe the system's states - B,C,S) contains a set of markers called tokens which carries a data value and belongs to type ($P$ and $E$, in this case). The place B has two tokens in the initial state of color (p,0), $P$ type. The place S has three tokens of color(e), $E$ type.

424

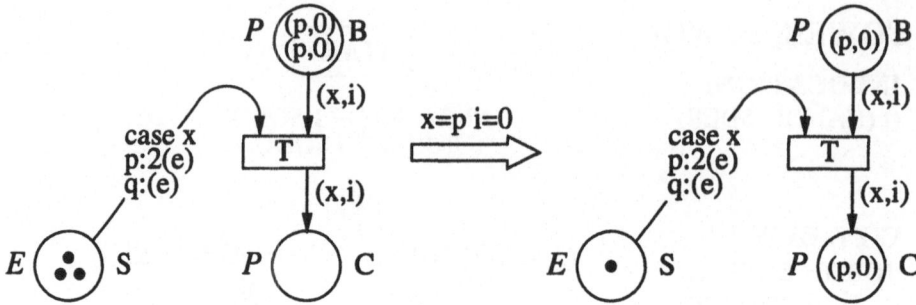

*Figure 2.* CPN - Transition Faring.


To be fired, a transition (rectangles that describe the actions) must have sufficient tokens on its input places, and these tokens must have values matching the arc expressions (arrows that describe how the CPN's state changes when the transitions occur). Consider the transition T. It has two arcs. The two arc expressions involve the variables x and i. To fire the transition, we have to bind these two variables to values in their types, in such a way that the arc expression of each incoming arc evaluates to a token value that is present on the corresponding input place.In this case, x=p and i=0. The right side of the Figure 2 shows the new state after the T transition fires.

## 4.    PRS and the Coloured Petri Nets

### Modeling Principle

To determine a CPN equivalent to PRS one associates network places to PRS nodes and transitions or sub-networks to the PRS arcs (see Figure 3). The token displacement models the evolution of the execution and its color contains the variables values currently defined. The number of colors has to be finite to generate a analyzable CPN: this implies we can only have "closed" variables (with a finite domain of values) in the PRS program we want to model.

To each arc we associate two branches in the CPN: one corresponding to case where the goal is reached (the token goes to the place that corresponds to the KA's following node) and the other corresponding to the case where the goal fails (the token's destination varies).

A necessary condition for a sub-net be a possible CPN model of a PRS arc is that it can be reduced to a token "dispatcher". If a sub net consumes a token in its input it has to produce a token in one of its two outputs: one models the attainment of the goal or the other one models its failure (indicated for T and F respectively, in the drawings).

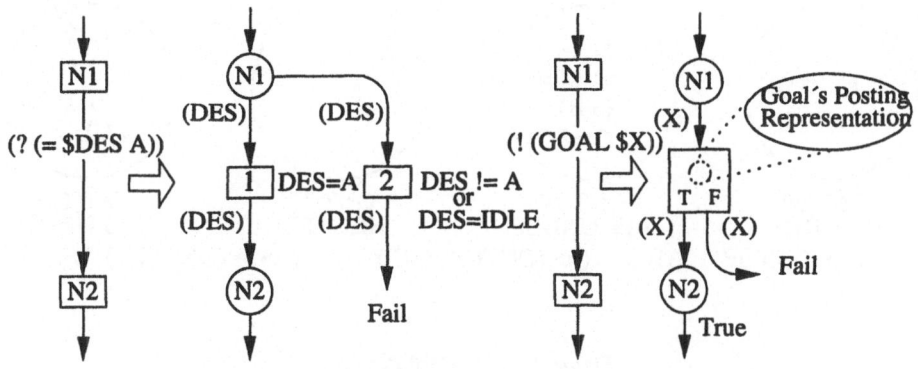

*Figure 3.* Two examples of equivalence between PRS and CPN.

## The Database

There are different predicates types in PRS. We will only present the representation of the standard predicates.

Each standard predicate is represented by four places, called AFF DEF and AFF UNDEF, NEG DEF and NEG UNDEF. The corresponding places DEF and UNDEF are complementary (the token that leaves a complementary place must return to the same place or goes to the other complementary place). The presence of one token of a certain color in a DEF place indicates that, for the corresponding value, the predicate was concluded affirmatively (AFF) or negatively (NEG). In a similar way, one token in an UNDEF place indicates that the predicate was not concluded (affirmatively or negatively) for this value. To use the technique of complementary places, some constraints are imposed:

- The places have to be bound (have a maximum number of tokens);
- The number of colors has to be finite;
- For each pair of complementary places, the initial marking guarantees the existence of a token of each color in one of the two places;
- In the initial marking, there are not tokens of the same color simultaneously in the AFF and NEG places.

Consider a predicate (ONTOP disc peg), where disc $\in$ {1,2,3}, peg $\in$ {A,B,C} and ONTOP is undefined in the beginning for all the combinations (disc peg). Figure 4 shows the predicate's representation after the conclusions ( => (ONTOP 1 A)), (=> (ONTOP 3 C)) and (=> ($\Lambda$ (ONTOP 3 B))).

The tests (? (...) ) on standard predicates are represented by CPN as shown in Figure 5. We only show the affirmation test model (? (PEG $ORI)); the

426

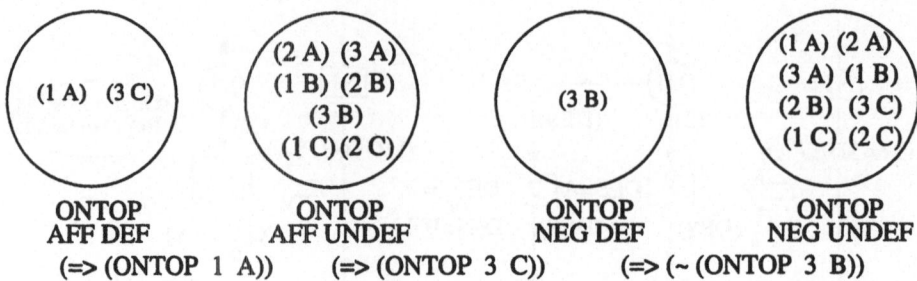

ONTOP AFF DEF     ONTOP AFF UNDEF     ONTOP NEG DEF     ONTOP NEG UNDEF

(=> (ONTOP 1 A))     (=> (ONTOP 3 C))     (=> (~ (ONTOP 3 B)))

*Figure 4.*    Standard Predicate.

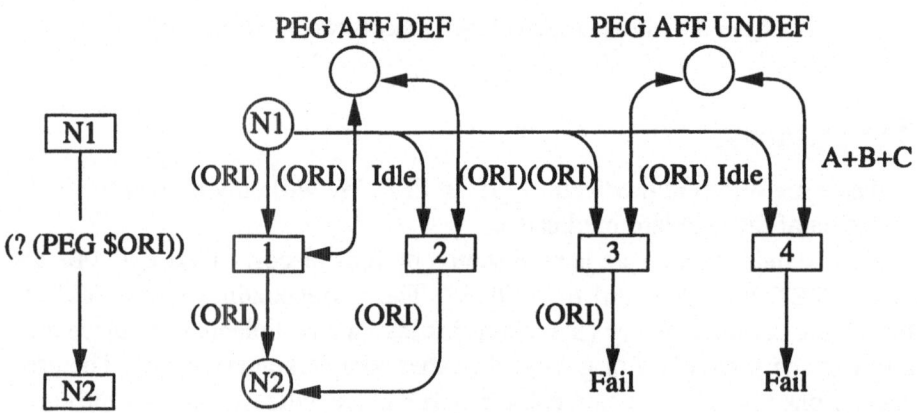

*Figure 5.*    Standard Predicate Test.

negative test model (? (Λ (PEG $ORI))) is identical, replacing PEG AFF DEF and PEG UNDEF by PEG NEG DEF and PEG NEG UNDEF, respectively.

Every token removed of one of the places that models PEG must be put in the same place, because a test does not modify the predicate value. The model of behavior of a test arc is different (different transitions are validated) according to predicate's argument. For example:

- The argument is already bound (has a precise value):
  - If for this value the predicate is defined, the test is successful (transition 1). If the predicate is undefined, the test fails (transition 3).
- The argument is not bound (IDLE):
  - If there is a value for which the predicate is defined, the test is successful and this value is transmitted (transition 2). This rep-

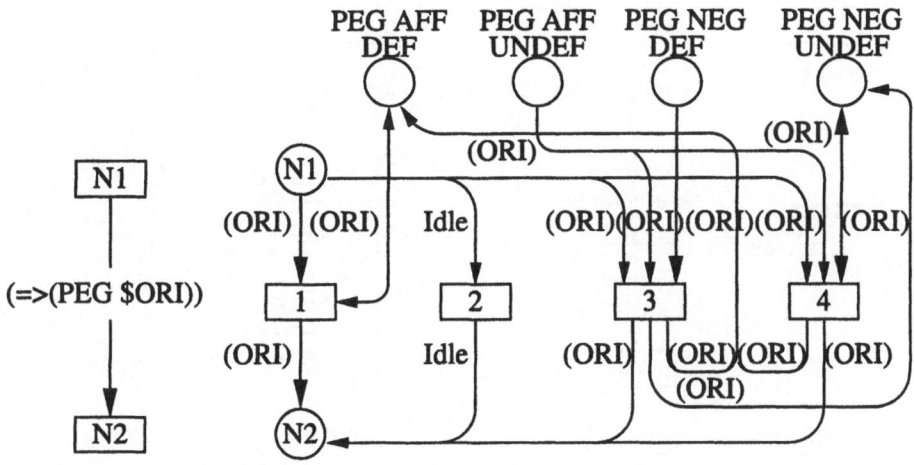

*Figure 6.* Standard Predicate Assert in Database.

resents unification mechanism of the variable. If PEG is undefined for all values, the test fails (transition 4).

We show in Fig. 6 the CPN equivalent to the assertive (=>(PEG $ORI))). For the conclusion of the negation, i.e., (=>(∧ (PEG $ORI), we have only to exchange the corresponding AFF and NEG places. We eliminate an eventual affirmation of the predicate when concluding its negation (transition 3). A conclusion with non-bound arguments (an error) does not change the predicate's state (transition 2).

## The Variables

Variables are carried by tokens, since their birth until the moment that they are not necessary anymore. Figure 7 shows an example of variables transmission modeling. Arc models are simplified because the KA's context field guarantees that the variables $X and $Y are bound.

The token will be a n-tuple with as many elements as PRS variables to preserve. Elements of the n-tuple will have as far possible values as the possible values for the PRS variables they represent, plus one (IDLE) to indicate that the variable is non-unified still.

## The Goals

When a goal is posted, it can be satisfied either by consulting the database or by calling a KA that satisfies this goal. For each predicate that can be posted, there must be, beyond the places that represent the predicate in the database

428

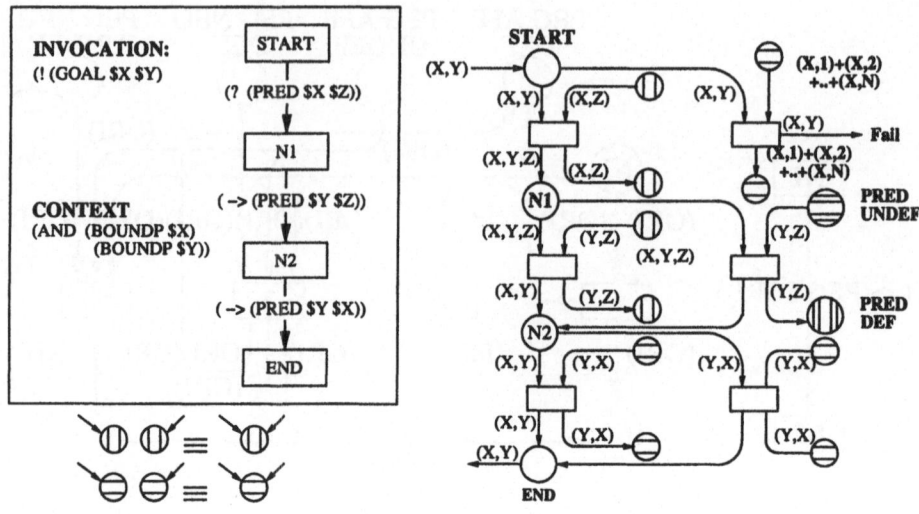

*Figure 7.*    Variables' Transmission Modeling.

(see section 4), three other specific places: POST, where the "client" routine indicates that the goal was posted, and SUCC and FAIL, where the "server" routine indicates the success or failure in attaining of the goal.

Figure 8 shows a goal posting complete model. At the moment of posting the goal, the CPN puts a token (with the goal's arguments colors) in the POST place and the execution of this branch enters in a wait state (place W) for a reply about the attainment of the goal. This reply will be materialized by the appearance of a token in either SUCC or FAIL place.

After the goal's posting, the model verifies if the predicate is not already satisfied in the database by a test (as in Figure 5). Otherwise, the system will look for a KA invoked by this goal. If one exists, the KAs will be activated and decide on the satisfaction or not of the goal, as presented in Figure 8.

## The Nodes

Normally, each PRS' node corresponds to a place in the CPN, except for the special type: the (IF-THEN-ELSE) condition node. The crossing of an arc that arrives at a condition node is always possible. If the goal associated with the arc is reached, the execution continues from the T half of the condition node; otherwise, from the F half. This node is represented by two places, one for each half. As each model of an arc must generate two possible exits for the token, we drive the branch that represents the success in the attainment of the goal to the T place and the branch that models the failure to the F place.

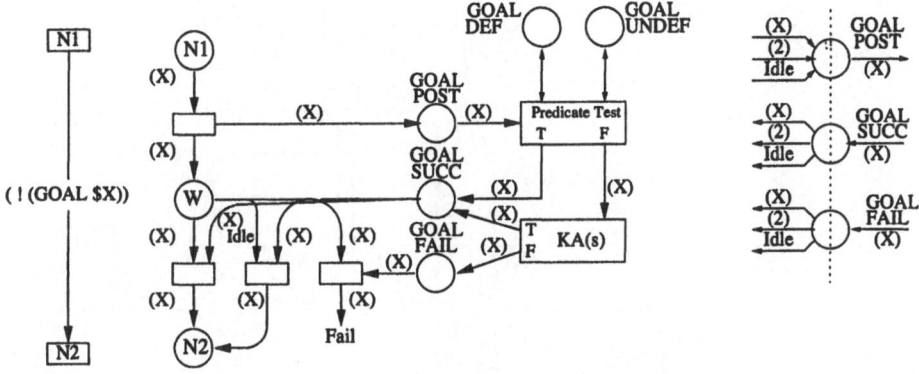

*Figure 8.* Goal Posting.

## The non determinism

In PRS when several arcs leave from the same node, the system chooses one arc at random to try to cross it. If it does not happen, it chooses one another arc and only considers that the KA failed after to have attempted all the arcs. PRS does not perform backtracking: if it gets to cross an arc, but it fails in the continuation of this branch it does not come back to the node in order to test the other unexplored arcs.

Given this behavior, it is necessary to conceive a structure to guarantee that the model tests all the arcs before designating an error. This structure is shown in Figure 9 for a case with two conflict arcs , but it is extensible for any arcs number.

Initially, the A place contains two numbered tokens, one for each arc. The only token in N1* guarantees the execution of only one arc at a time. If the execution of the arc that caught the token in N1* will have success, the model cleans the A and B places (it consumes all the tokens of the other branches) and the execution continues. In case of failure, the model replaces the token in N1*, authorizing another arc to be tested and puts the corresponding token to the arc that failed in B. If all the tokens are in B, the model indicates an error.

## The KAs

The CPN that models a KA has a start place called INIT. Between INIT and START there is a sub-net that tests if the KA's execution context (CONTEXT field) was satisfied. This is equivalent to add a supplementary arc in the KA to play the role of CONTEXT field, it does not modify the execution of the program (see Figure 10). In the same way, between the END place, that plays the role of

430

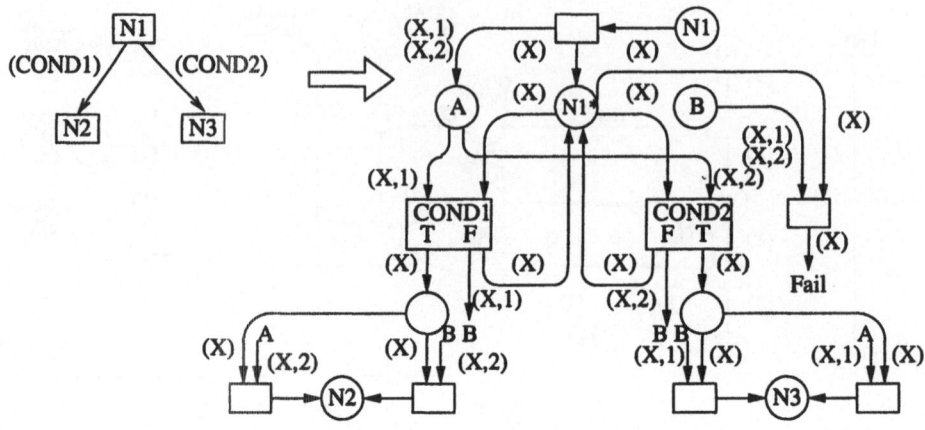

*Figure 9.* Node with some arcs that leave

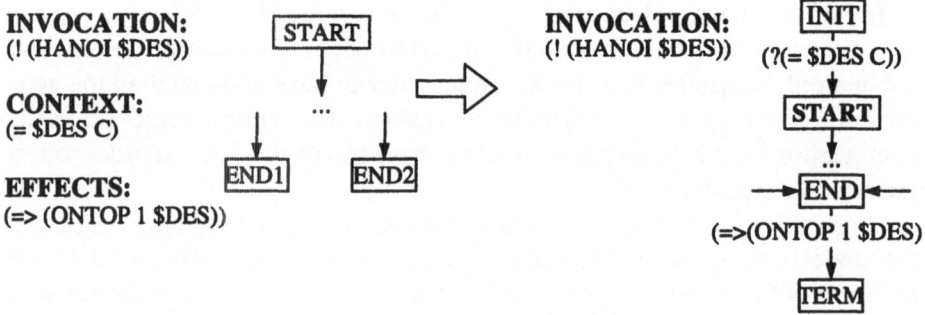

*Figure 10.* Equivalence between KAs' Fields and Arc.

all the terminals nodes of the KA, and the TERM place, that models successfully the KA execution ending, it has a sub-net that models the EFFECTS field.

The models in CPN of the KAs must also contain a FAIL place, where the appearance of one token indicates that the KA failed. The exit, in case of error (F), of all the arcs must be directed to this FAIL place, except for the special situations of the arcs that lead to a IF-THEN-ELSE node (section 8) and of the arcs that leave from a same node (section 8). Figure 11 shows a CPN equivalent to a generic KA. The arc models are not detailed and we assume that there is only one variable to transmit (DES) in the whole KA.

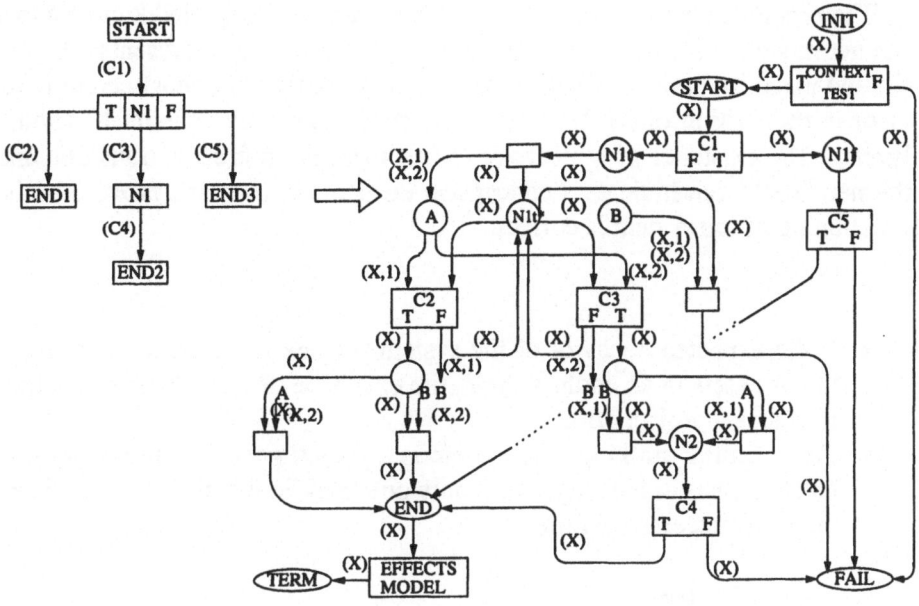

*Figure 11.* CPN Equivalence to KA.

# 5. Verification Methods

Summarily, we can say that the CPN can be analyzed in three main ways: by simulation, by acessibility graph (state space or occurrence graph) and by invariant methods (of place or transition).

Analysis methods allow to prove a number certain of Petri nets properties. These properties can be behavioral (for each initial marking) or structural (only depending on the structure of the net). The invariants establish certain structural properties and the accessibility graph allows, by inspection of the states, to determine all the net's properties, but only for a well accurate initial marking.

For the CPN of our model, the properties of interest are mainly the ones which were proved for a defined initial marking, for two reasons:

- There are complementary places in the net. So, the initial marking must guarantee the existence of the mandatory tokens in one of the complementary places.
- Normally, we are interested in guaranteeing the behavior of the system in specific situations, corresponding to well-defined initial markings.

The properties demonstrated for the CPN must be interpreted knowing that the net models a set of KAs and what the initial marking represents. A non-limited place in number of marks, for example, indicates almost certainly an error in the writing of the KAs (as a KA that recursively calls itself without limits). The existence of a blockage (when there is no fireable transition and the net "dies") can indicate a conception error or, in contrast, prove that the functioning of the system is correct:

- If the expected behavior of the system for one given initial marking is that it enters in an endless cycle, the existence of a blockage possibility indicates a project error.
- For an initial marking where there is a posted goal, it is necessary that CPN finishes in blockage, with only one mark in the places that indicate the goal success or failure.

## 6.    Conclusion

Because of space limitation, we presented only some of the equivalence rules between PRS programs and CPN that allows using the existing analysis tools, as CPN TOOL [Jensen, 2001], to verify PRS programs.

The main limitations of the proposed approach are the obligatory previous knowledge of the variable's finite domain and also the possible considerable size of the generated CPNs. The first limitation is not so restrictive in embedded or industrial applications, where usually the variables can only assume predefined values. The second one imposes the automatic generation and analysis of the Coloured Petri Nets.

The manual conversion between PRS and CPN can introduce errors. To avoid this, we are developing a (PRS to CPN) automatic converter in Common Lisp [Shapiro, 1992]. This is possible because all the equivalence rules presented here (and the other ones) follow generic laws and then can be translated into conversion rules able to be implemented by a conversion software to be used in practical situations.

Hence, we can use the CPN's analysis to investigate the main properties of the generated net and, consequently, indirectly to verify the PRS program that generated the net.

## Acknowledgment

The authors would like to thank the anonymous reviewers for their constructive comments as well the Professors Kurt Jensen and François Félix Ingrand by the use of CPN TOOLS and OpenPRS softwares and the Brazilian agency CAPES.

# References

Bench-Capon, T., Coenen, F., Nwana, H., and Paton, R. (1993). Two aspects of the validation and verification of knowledge-based systems. In *IEEE Expert*, pages 76–81.

Firby, James R. (1987). An investigation into reactive planning in complex domains. In *Proceedings of the 6th National Conference on Artifical Intelligence*, Seattle, WA, USA.

Georgeff, Michell P. and Lansky, A. L. (1986). Procedural knowledge. In *Proceedings of the IEEE*, volume 10, pages 183–198.

Ingrand, François Felix, Georgeff, Michael P., and Rao, Anand S. (1992). An architecture for real-time reasoning and system control. In *IEEE Expert*, volume 6, pages 34–44.

Ingrand, François Félix, Chatila, Raja, Alami, Rachid, and Robert, Frédéric (1996). PRS: A high level supervision and control language for autonomous mobile robot. In *ICRA - IEEE International Conference on Robotics and Automation*, volume 1, pages 43–49, Minneapolis, Minnesota, USA.

Ingrand, François Félix and Despouys, Olivier (2001). Extending procedural reasoning toward robot actions plannig. In *ICRA - IEEE International Conference on Robotics and Automation*, Seoul, South Korea.

Jensen, Kurt (1994). *Coloured Petri Nets - Analysis Methods*, volume 2. Springer Verlag, Aarhus, Denmark.

Jensen, Kurt (1998). A brief introduction to coloured petri nets. In Brinksma, E., editor, *Lecture Notes in Computer Science: Tools and Algorithms for the Construction and Analysis of Systems. Proceedings of the TACAS'97 Workshop*, pages 201–208, Enschede, The Netherlands. Springer-Verlag.

Jensen, Kurt (2001). CPN TOOLS. http://www.daimi.au.dk/∧cpntools.

Lee, J. and Lai, Lein F. (2002). A high-level petri nets-based approach to verifying task structures. In *IEEE Transactions on Knowledge and Data Engineering*, volume 14, pages 316–335.

Lee, J. and O'Keefe, R.M. (1994). Developing a strategy for expert system verification and validation. In *IEEE Transactions on Systems, Man, and Cybernetics*, volume 24, pages 643–655.

Shapiro, Stuart Charles (1992). *Common LISP - An Interactive Approach*. W.H. Freeman and Company, USA.

SRI International (1994). Shuttle malfunction handling. http://www.ai.sri.com/.

Zhang, D. and Nguyen, D. (1993). A tool for knowledge base verification. In Bourbakis, Nikolaos G., editor, *Knowledge Engineering Shells: Systems and Techniques*, volume 2 of *Advanced Series on Artificial Intelligence*, pages 455–486. World Scientific Pub Co, USA. ISBN: 9810210566.

# ON-LINE POSSIBILISTIC DIAGNOSIS BASED ON EXPERT KNOWLEDGE FOR ENGINE DYNO TEST BENCHES

O. de Mouzon,[1] X. Guérandel,[2] D. Dubois,[1] H. Prade,[1] and S. Boverie[3]

[1] *Institut de Recherche en Informatique de Toulouse*
*IRIT – UPS, 118 route de Narbonne, 31062 Toulouse Cedex 4, France*
{Olivier.deMouzon | Didier.Dubois | Henri.Prade}@irit.fr

[2] *Université Paul sabatier*
*DRT ISI, UPS, 118 route de Narbonne, 31062 Toulouse Cedex 4, France*
Xavier.Guerandel@free.fr

[3] *Siemens VDO Automotive S.A.S.*
*1 Avenue Paul Ourliac, BP 1149, 31036 Toulouse Cedex, France*
Serge.Boverie@siemens.com

**Abstract**      Car engine electronic control unit tuning is a tedious and difficult task. Engineers can no more check on-line the measurements validity: Control strategies are becoming more complex and measurements more numerous. A fault diagnosis approach relying on experts' qualitative and uncertain knowledge has been developed to identify whenever a malfunction is present. The theoretical framework - based on possibility theory and on consistency and abductive indices - is first explained. The latest results are then presented. Finally, the whole incremental development process of the prototypes is described, explaining the most difficult points and how they were handled.

**Keywords:**    Diagnosis, engine dynamometer, uncertainty, fuzzy sets, possibility theory.

## Introduction

The paper presents a prototype implementation part of a long term research and development project, which aims at improving the calibration of car engine Electronic Control Unit (ECU), on engine dyno test benches, by detecting malfunctions when they occur.

The approach is based on a fault diagnosis system (named *BEST*: Bench Expert System Tool) that makes use of expert's knowledge formalized with fuzzy sets. In fact, since [Sanchez, 1977], much work has been carried out in this field of fuzzy sets and diagnosis, and applied in different fields: E.g. in medical applications ([Buisson, 1999]) or industrial processes ([Ulieru, 2000]).

The paper is organized as follows: Section 1 describes the engine dyno context, the needs and expected benefits, and the architecture of BEST. The theoretical base on which it relies is presented in section 2. Then, section 3 presents the current prototypes and latest results. The discussion in section 4 points out the problems that were encountered and how they were solved. The conclusion indicates the last steps to be further developed.

## 1.    Context and framework

In oder to better understand the results and the choices made during the project, this section first presents the engine dyno test bench context and then gives the general architecture designed for BEST.

### Engine dyno test benches

Within one century, diesel and gasoline cars have gone from the carburettor to the electronic injection (ECU-controlled). More and more complex strategies have been implemented to answer to increasing constraints (pollutant regulations, vehicle behavior, new engine configuration: Direct injection, diesel common rail, variable valve timing, electric controlled throttle. . . ) and an increasing number of variables must be taken into account.

For each new engine or new version, the control strategy parameters have to be calibrated in order to fit the requirements. This is done through a large amount of testing and tuning, starting on engine dyno test benches.

**The calibration process.**    Figure 1 shows the ECU calibration process on an engine dyno, making use of a calibration tool. Basically, the ECU gets measurements from engine sensors (e.g., mass air flow, engine speed. . . ), computes other intermediate variables and finally tells the engine which amount of fuel should be injected and what the spark advance should be. The data used for this are recorded through the calibration tool. They are provided by engine sensors and ECU but also by the engine dyno sensors, as well as additionnal devices. So the *System* to diagnose through BEST is: engine, engine dyno, all sensor sets and additionnal devices.

**Data acquisition.**    Before doing any acquisition, the global conformity of the system has to be checked: Physical verification (sensors, fuel consumption measurements, gas analysis. . . ), but also system configuration (i.e. inhibited system functions). As sensors become more numerous and the strategies more complex, this global check requires more time and so the tuning engineer has

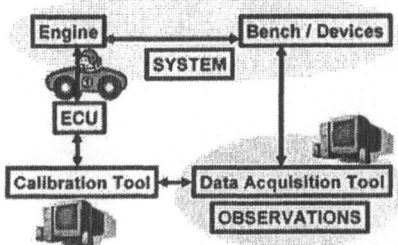

*Figure 1* The calibration process

less time for the testing itself and its methodology. Hence test duration is increasing while reliability is degraded.

Then, during the tests, an on-line verification must be done to guarantee the acquisition validity. Again the tuning engineers used to check the validity of measurements manually while running: Single-parameter raw thresholds, coherence of some parameters with standard values, and sometimes coherence between several parameters and previous tests. Today it is nearly impossible for engineers to ensure the global coherence on-line, due to the complexity raise of parameters and strategies. Most of the time, when there is a problem, it is discovered during post processing data treatment. Quite often the test has to be performed again.

**Needs and expected benefits.**   In fact, 10 to 20% of the manual tests must be reworked due to bad acquisitions, bad software configuration... Most of the time malfunctions are due to dyno bench environmental problems (gaz analysis, fuel balance...). So wrong acquisitions should be detected right away and the malfunction that occured should be identified as soon as possible in order to correct it quickly and make sound acquisitions again.

Some common and simple malfunctions are still identified by engineers. Yet others require time-consumming searches for their origin and symptoms whenever they occur. Indeed, engineers cannot keep in mind all the information and past experiences. Moreover they cannot watch in real time all the (numerous) measured channels.

In order to cope with such checkings, an expert system, BEST, has been considered. It has to perform global coherence checking, in the same way as for manual tests. It should also *detect* and *identify* malfunctions *as soon as* they appear: That is *on-line detection*.

## General architecture for BEST

BEST represents a huge amount of work and investment. It gathers several functionalities divided into different modules for step by step development and validation (a key point in the success of the implementation, as discussed in

438

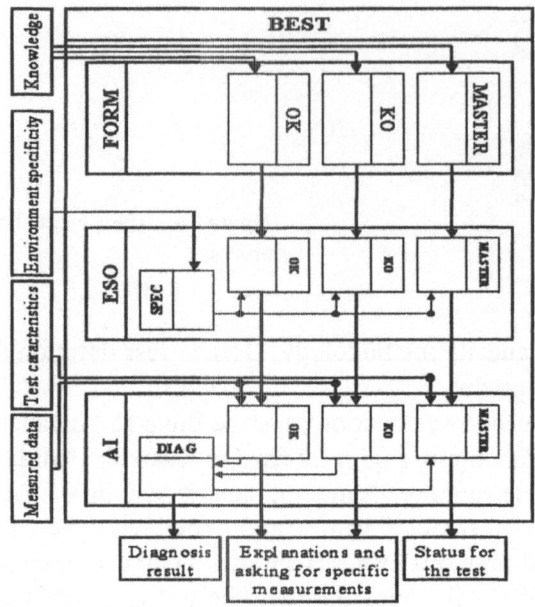

*Figure 2* The architecture of BEST

section 4). The general architecture of BEST and the part for which proto-types have been developed are explained below. Some of the ideas underlying this architecture can be found in other approaches to industrial diagnosis (e.g., [Cordier et al., 2000]).

Figure 2 presents the different modules:
• **FORM**: Enables the experts to formalize their knowledge, using fuzzy rules.
• **ESO**: Extracts, Sorts and Organizes the rules w.r.t bench/engine specificities.
• **AI**, which is the Artificial Intelligence part performing the diagnosis: It com-pares the extracted rules to the measurements made on the engine.

Each module, contains the 3 following submodules: OK (diagnosis based on models of normal behaviour), KO (diagnosis based on models of malfunc-tions) and MASTER (the supervision rules). In the AI module, OK and KO diagnosis are aggregated in DIAG. BEST_AI_OK gives the models of normal behaviour which are not reached and BEST_AI_KO tells which malfunctions have been identified. The use of two different diagnosis is safer in regard to incompleteness and possible inconsistency of some models. Besides, both di-agnosis (OK and KO) can give some feedback explaining why a model of nor-mal behaviour was not reached and why a malfunction was selected. They may also ask for other specific measurements in order to improve their diagnosis. Finally, MASTER decides wheather the test may continue, should use another computation for some variables, or should stop. This decision is taken accord-ing to the supervision rules, the test characteristics (necessary variables), the

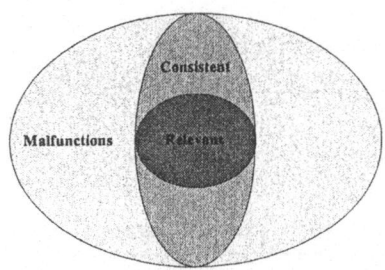

*Figure 3* Diagnosis process with $\mu_{cons}$ and $\mu_{rel}$

two diagnosis (pointing at the source faulty variables) and a dependency graph (which computes the induced faulty variables).

Prototypes has been developed for the whole KO part of this project, as the main objective was to build a demonstrative application which can detect and also *identify* malfunctions as soon as they appear on engine dyno test benches. This work is further described in the following sections.

## 2. Diagnosis fuzzy set based approach

This section presents the theoretical basis supporting the whole KO part of BEST. The knowledge relies on expert causal information. Possibility theory is used to capture the uncertainty pertaining to this kind of information. Observations may also be imprecise. Finally, the diagnosis makes use of two indices (see Figure 3). Refinements of these indices and ways to use them for more complex diagnosis (e.g. involving several malfunctions) can be found in [de Mouzon et al., 2001]. Here, only the basis is presented.

**Notations.** Let $\mathcal{M}$ be the set of all (known) possible malfunctions and $\mathcal{A}$ be the set of the $n$ observable attributes: $\{X_1, \cdots, X_n\}$. Let $m \in \mathcal{M}$ and $i \in \{1, \cdots, n\}$, then $\pi_m^i$ denotes the possibility distribution [Zadeh, 1978], that represents the (more or less) plausible values for attribute $X_i$ when malfunction $m$ (alone) is present. Let $U_i$ be the domain of $X_i$, so $\pi_m^i : U_i \longrightarrow [0, 1]$. $\mathcal{K}_m^i$ will be the fuzzy set corresponding to possibility distribution $\pi_m^i$.

The observations may also be imprecise (or uncertain). $\mu_{\mathcal{O}_i} : U_i \longrightarrow [0, 1]$ is the possibility distribution, which represents the (more or less) plausible values for the observed value of attribute $X_i$. $\mathcal{O}_i$ denotes the fuzzy set corresponding to possibility distribution $\mu_{\mathcal{O}_i}$.

$\mathcal{K}_m^i$ and $\mathcal{O}_i$ both express imprecision, when they contain more than one element. Yet, they model different types of imprecision:

- $\mathcal{O}_i$ imprecision can be "controlled" (in principle): Changing the sensors for more precise (usually more expensive) or less precise observations.

- Imprecision on $\mathcal{K}_m^i$, on the contrary, cannot be reduced (or changed) that easily: It depends on the available knowledge about the *System* only.

440

*Table 1.*   Main possibility distribution shapes for knowledge formalization

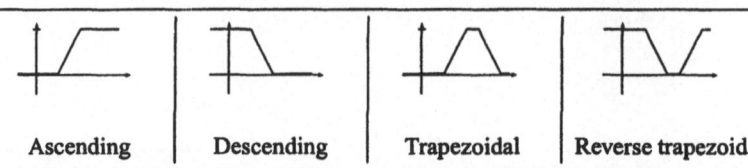

| Ascending | Descending | Trapezoidal | Reverse trapezoid |

When attribute $X_i$ is not yet observed, its value is not known, so it could be any value of $U_i$: $\forall u \in U_i$, $\mu_{\mathcal{O}_i}(u) = 1$. Similarly, when malfunction $m$ has no known effect on attribute $X_i$, all values are allowed: $\forall u \in U_i$, $\pi_m^i(u) = 1$.

In fact, for the knowledge representation, the experts are very often more comfortable in expressing their confidence in some values they consider highly possible or, on the contrary, totally impossible. So, for continuous attributes, the experts only need to tell what they know best (values of possibility 0 and 1). Then, $\pi_m^i$ is computed to follow the given information, be continuous and be piecewise linear. In the formalization process, the possibility distributions mainly used were increasing or decreasing ramp functions or trapezoidal ones, see Table 1. For discrete attributes, different levels of possibility (e.g., from 0 to 1 by step of 0.1 units) can be assessed.

**A consistency-based index.**   A consistency-based index has been defined: $\mu_{cons} : \mathcal{M} \longrightarrow [0, 1]$, which enables to discard observation-inconsistent malfunctions ($\mu_{cons}(m)$ close to 0).

The consistency between observations and knowledge on malfunction $m$ for a given attribute can be computed by $u \longmapsto \min(\mu_{\mathcal{O}_i}(u), \pi_m^i(u))$, which is the possibility distribution attached to $\mathcal{O}_i \cap \mathcal{K}_m^i$. The elements of highest possibility in this intersection give the *consistency degree between $\mathcal{O}_i$ and $\mathcal{K}_m^i$*: $\sup_{u \in U_i} \min(\mu_{\mathcal{O}_i}(u), \pi_m^i(u))$. The consistency degree of any malfunction $m$ and the observations is computed from those of $\mathcal{O}_i$ and $\mathcal{K}_m^i$ (for each attribute):

$$\mu_{\text{cons}}(m) = \min_{i=1}^{n} \sup_{u \in U_i} \min(\mu_{\mathcal{O}_i}(u), \pi_m^i(u)). \tag{1}$$

In case of too incomplete information (knowledge and/or observations), $\mu_{cons}$ might not be sufficient in order to select a small enough number of malfunctions. So, a second index is required in order to refine $\mu_{cons}$ and bring a better conclusion: find, among the undiscarded malfunctions, which one is most relevant to the observations.

**An abduction-based index.**   A malfunction is more relevant to the observations when its effects have been observed for sure. That is: $\mathcal{O}_i \subseteq \mathcal{K}_m^i$ (for crisp sets). In order to single out most relevant malfunctions, fuzzy inclusion of $\mathcal{O}_i$ in $\mathcal{K}_m^i$ has to be defined.

Inclusion can be defined by implication (for crisp sets, $A \subset B$ is equivalent to $\forall x, x \in A \Rightarrow x \in B$). So, several fuzzy implications ($\rightarrow$) have been checked for this purpose. Thus a second index is defined, which evaluates the relevance of a malfunction:

$$\mu_{\mathrm{rel}}(m) = \min_{i=1}^{n} \inf_{u \in U} \mu_{\mathcal{O}_i}(u) \rightarrow \pi_m^i(u). \tag{2}$$

The worst implication degree tells the extent to which the malfunction is relevant to the observations. Hence $\mu_{rel}$ selects the most relevant malfunctions ($\mu_{rel}(m)$ close to 1).

Dienes' strong implication ($a \rightarrow_D b \doteq \max(1 - a, b)$) was chosen because it is the most dicriminating and it keeps the following natural crisp property: If $\mathcal{O}_i \subseteq \mathcal{K}_m^i$, then $\mathcal{O}_i \cap \mathcal{K}_m^i \neq \emptyset$. That is: $\mu_{cons} \geq \mu_{rel}$.

This index is abductive in nature: It selects $m$ from the knowledge of the relation between cause $m$ and effects, and from the observation of these effects.

Note that $\mu_{rel}$ is useful because observations are imprecise. Indeed, $\mu_{rel} = \mu_{cons}$ in case of precise observations. But a totally precise observation is feasible only for discrete attributes. In case of continuous attributes (e.g., temperature, pressure), the observations given by sensors always have some imprecision (even if it can be made very small with high precision sensors).

Hence, the diagnosis is first based on $\mu_{cons}$ in order to discard and rank the malfunctions and then on $\mu_{rel}$ in case of ties, as schematically shown on Figure 3. See [de Mouzon et al., 2001] for a more complete discussion on the use of fuzzy sets in this diagnosis process and the extension to multiple-fault diagnosis (not yet implemented).

## 3. Actual application

This section describes the current complete prototypes which have been (incrementally) developed for the single fault diagnosis on engine dyno test benches, based on the framework presented above. They implement the KO-part (see Figure 2): The first prototype is off-line and integrates FORM and ESO modules. The second is on-line and corresponds to the AI-module.

## Off-line prototype: Knowledge formalization and selection

Knowledge is essential to diagnosis. Sometimes it can be computed from a database. None existed here, for reporting normal behaviour data and/or data under each specific malfunction. So, only expert knowledge could be considered. Hence a tool was needed to make both collecting and formalizing knowledge as easy and confortable as possible (BEST_KO_FORM module) for the engine dyno engineers. This creates a centralized knowledge base.

For ease of use, the same tool also enables to select from the knowledge base the pieces to be used, taking into account the state of the ECU calibration, the tests to make, and the test bench specificities. This generates the corresponding formalized knowledge file (BEST_KO_ESO module) directly used by the on-line diagnosis tool.

First, the FORM part contains friendly windows to express the knowledge step by step:

1) Express the malfunction definition: the user has to enter a unique definition with four characteristics: A group, a type, an identification and the nature of default (some choices are proposed for each). E.g., bench equipment [group] temperature sensor [type] 203 (inlet cylinder 3) [identification] dirty [default].

2) Give and structure the malfunction symptoms in an AND/OR tree.

3) Express each symptom through four elements: i) The attribute definition (function of the measurements and time). ii) A possibility distribution (as exemplified in Table 1). iii) Some conditions (engine running, ful load...). iv) An environment (bench and engine specificities).

Then the ESO part enables to easily select (or even modify) the knowledge to give to the diagnosis. When a new ESO file is created, the user has to parameter its environment. Only malfunctions of the knowledge base having compatible symptoms with this environment are automatically added into the file. For the incoherent symptoms, the user can choose to modify their environment in order to make them compatible or to remove them. The generated files are unreadable for the expert, which ensures that they will not be modified by hand. When necessary, modification can be done using this off-line application.

This tool has been a key point of the development of BEST, as knowledge is a root of diagnosis. The FORM part has enabled to express and formalize more than 250 malfunctions (about one third of the estimated total number) in 21 environments (about 75% of all). The ESO part not only supports knowledge selection for each specific environment, but also enables to test and validate knowledge immediately on the on-line diagnosis tool.

## On-line prototype: Diagnosis

This prototype is an on-line tool: it reads the data from the engine dyno test bench (through a Dynamic Data Exchange connection) while the calibration is runing, and warns as soon as possible when a malfunction is detected (in less than 3 minutes today). There are two levels of information:

i) An efficient diagnosis mode (a small icon sits in the system tray of Windows NT taskbar): While performing on engine dyno test, the prototype becomes active and works without human intervention. When an event occurs, i.e. detection of the possible presence of a malfunction, a popup window is

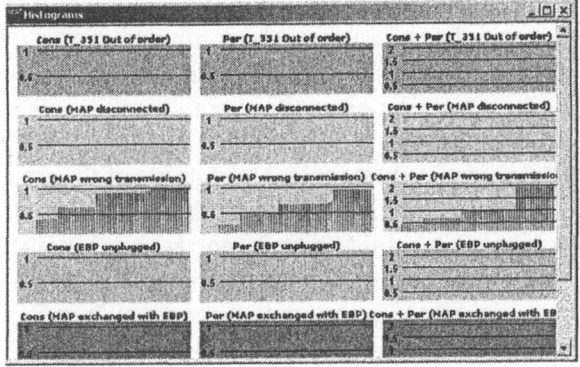

*Figure 4* Bargraphs for diagnosis indices ($\mu_{cons}$ [Cons] and $\mu_{rel}$ [Per]) trace in time for each malfunction ("debug" mode)

automatically opened and gives some information and advice on malfunctions and symptoms involved in the problem. In order to avoid blinking problems (with oscilating values near a single-limit), a malfunction is considered as appearing when $\mu_{rel}$ goes over 0.7 and disappearing when $\mu_{cons}$ goes under 0.3.

ii) A debug mode, displaying a bargraphs window (see Figure 4) and a console window where each event (attribute calculus, intermediate results, false alarms, ... ) is logged and can be saved on a text file.

The diagnosis application runs directly on the engine dyno test benches. Experiments have been conducted on-line on the benches in order to validate the method and the application. These experiments have been made on a representative case study involving 35 possible malfunctions (about 5% of all). Figure 4 gives an example for a few malfunctions where the one that occured is just being identified (here, "rel" reads "per").

The results of these experiments are satisfying: All malfunctions have been detected and identified on-line. Very little false alarms occurred: Only for temperature sensors during sharp transition phases. This was then corrected in the knowledge base. Hence, this diagnosis method has shown its usefulness. Some future steps are now given below, towards a complete industrial application.

## Future work

**Observation validity.** Some conditions might be necessary to compute the presence/absence of a symptom (e.g., engine stopped). Thus, at some moment only part of the information has been computed. In order to be able to make a diagnosis despite this problem, the easiest way is to make the hypothesis that former computations are still valid. This often holds and always does in demos (where the conditions to observe the changes are known). Yet, for a real on-line use, this hypothesis might not hold when a fault occurs.

A solution could be to have a validity index (for each piece of knowledge) that would depend on the time elapsed since the latest computation (of that piece of knowledge). Then a too old information would not be taken into account when it is contradictory to other more recently computed pieces of knowledge. On the contrary, if they still give the same information, this could also be taken into account as giving more support to the overall result.

**Observation errors.** For the moment, only a general evaluation of the error is computed. In fact, the real error (attached to each sensor) should be used.

This error is usually modelized by a probability distribution (as a gaussian). Yet, a possibility distribution like a fuzzy number (centered triangular distribution, with the maximum error as support) would be very convenient: It covers any symmetric probabilistic distribution on this support, [Dubois et al., 2002].

Besides, this solution is computationnally much more simple when it comes to computing the error of a complex attribute from the channels it combines.

## 4. Incremental development

The previous section presented the prototype complete version of BEST_KO. The current section explains the problems which had to be tackled and the development process which was adopted: A successful incremental approach. The first step was to analyse the type of knowledge accessible for the diagnosis. The second step was to test off-line the diagnosis method (see section 2). The third step was to test it on-line. The last step was to add a complete and more convenient tool for knowledge formalization, as presented in section 3. All prototypes were developed in Visual C++ V6, under Windows NT4.

### First step: Knowledge analysis – Towards formalization

BEST_AI_KO (Figure 2) is based on human beings' experience. Thus, recording and formalizing the available knowledge is a key step of this project, [Kahn et al., 1985]. So a preliminary standard form (Figure 5) had been defined to describe the malfunctions (under the assumption that it is present alone):

• Number (cell 4) – Name (cell 3): Identifying the direct source of observed anomalies). E.g., sensor out of order, badly calibrated sensor. . .

• Number (cell 6) – Environment (cell 5): For bench or engine environmental specific conditions. In some cases the same malfunction will generate different anomalies depending on the environment: E.g., a sealing defect in the intake system will have strongly different effects, depending on the sensor used on the engine: MAP (mass air pressure) or MAF (mass air flow).

• Description of symptoms of the malfunction may be added:

i) Attribute (cell 7, including observation conditions, if needed). Example for the "exhaust temperature sensor out of order" malfunction: Difference between this temperature and the other cylinder temperatures, when the engine is running. . . Note: Attributes may be as complex as needed.

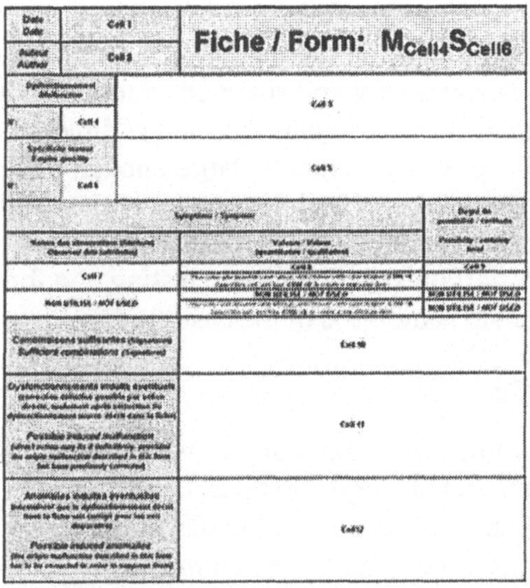
Fiche / Form: $M_{Cell4}S_{Cell6}$

NON UTILISE / NOT USED

*Figure 5* The first form

ii) Finally (cells 8 & 9), a possibility distribution is attached to each attribute, expressing to what extent a value is consistent (possibility 1) or not (possibility 0) with the presence of the malfunction. This makes it easier for the engineers to express which values they know possible, the ones they know impossible and the ones they are not sure about: In practice, engineers are asked for the core and the support of the possibility distribution. For the uncertain values, the possibility is calculated to be linear. The more the value is close to a possible value, the higher its possibility level. The more the value is close to an impossible value, the lower its possibility level (see Table 1).

• Last but not least, the form includes information about induced malfunctions ("in cascade", cell 11).

Of course, not all the knowledge on the malfunctions was asked for at that time, but at least a significant fragment of it was obtained in order to get an explicit structure concerning the type of information BEST would have to deal with. This first form made possible to collect knowledge on about 10% of all the malfunctions and 20% of all the environments. The knowledge cannot be exhibited here. But, the analysis of the filled-in forms led to these conclusions:

- Pieces of knowledge for a complex symptom may use connectors (and, or) between more elementary pieces of information.
- Those elementary pieces of information may also use any shape of function for representing the attribute value.
- Finally, there might be some conditions to be satisfied in order to be able to compute a valid result for presence/absence of a symptom (such as: engine cold, engine stopped, closed throttle, high engine speed...).

So, the knowledge collected from the forms could be formalized in a structured text file. Of course, not all the knowledge on the malfunctions was used at that time: This step is really time consumming and some basic tests about the diagnosis approach were first needed before going further in that direction. Efforts of formalization were first made on a case study, large enough to be representative of the kind of malfunctions to be taken into account in this field of application: The case study considered malfunctions that have an incidence in the engine gaz circulation. And to start on some real basic testing, the formalized knowledge was even restricted to some 15% of the case study.

## Second step: Off-line diagnosis

This first diagnosis prototype was implemented for a preliminary evaluation of this approach applied to ECU calibration on engine dyno test benches.

The knowledge was given through the structured text file discussed above. The data used for off-line tests were yet directly measured on the engine dyno test benches. They came from files where the measurements had been stored.

To reduce complexity for the first tests, data in each file had been collected at a stabilized running point. Transition phases were kept for later. Files were created for different running points, representative of the calibration process: engine speed and MAP table, and also richness and spark advance table.

Each file contained at least 131 measured channels during a 5 minute (or more) time period. The time frequency for measurements was every 100 ms. So each file contained at least 400 000 values (differents files for nominal behaviour and for each malfunction). The total number of files used for the tests was 181. For confidential resons, data are not given here (but the numbers given above give some indication on the complexity of the problem) and the results aim only at providing feedback on the implementation process.

Note that the first evaluation could not state whether this approach was good or not: The conclusion was that off-sets and noise (mainly 50 Hz) had first to be filtred. Then, the results of the tests were computed once more. As a general remark, too little knowledge was used for testing this diagnosis approach: 1) Some attributes were too complex to be included in the first tests. 2) Others needed special measurement equipment or conditions not possible at that time. 3) Too little knowledge had been collected. 4) Last but not least some pieces of knowledge turned out to be false. Nonetheless, some tests could be carried out. In fact, this situation is rather logical: Great efforts cannot be asked for with no clue on whether they will be worthwhile. Finally, the very first tests showed that this approach to BEST is all the more efficient as more formalized and validated (e.g. through some experiments) knowledge is provided. For instance, note that no false alarms were raised during normal behaviour and that they were all the less frequent as more specific symptoms were formalized.

# Third step: On-line diagnosis

The off-line evaluation not only was good enough to go forward for the on-line version, but also gave even more resons to do so: The necessary knowledge validation is much easier if it is possible to test/change right away pieces of knowledge. Besides, transitions phases had to be taken into account (as they are frequent on-line) and thus BEST would take advantage of observations gathered through out the whole calibration process, going from one running point to another. This is even more needed, as more knowledge is asked for, which means more symptoms that may need specific observations conditions.

In fact, the knowledge used took benefit from the important validation task pointed in the previous section and from the more numerous measurements accessible on-line. Besides, other functions had been implemented to take into account more complex attributes. Finally, transition phases were taken into account so that observation of several stabilized running points was possible, as well as the transition phases themselves. Hence, the previous malfunctions were described both more properly and in greater details.

But the main change in this prototype is that data are now read directly (using a Dynamic Data Exchange link) from the data acquisition tool (see Figure 1). As the acquisition tool has time priority, our prototype only reads data every 500 ms (formerly 100 ms) in order to keep enough time for $\mu_{cons}$ and $\mu_{rel}$ computations. All those operations are very little time consumming, but the constraints are very high. Time could also be gained with less feedback, but such a feedback (see Figure 4, for instance) is essential during the development process.

Another point to keep in mind is that only the measurements specified for the data acquisition tool are seen. In other words, there may be up to more than 200 measured channels or less than the 131 former ones. Thus, it may be necessary to add some channels during a calibration (that usually does not need them) for the sake of diagnosability.

An example of result is given in Figure 4. This section gives the main issues for a complete 20 minutes demo, testing the prototype on-line and even for some multiple malfunctions.

The results are better with this on-line prototype: Each malfunction is detected when it occurs and there are no false alarms for normal behaviour. This is mainly a benefit from knowledge validation. Besides some multiple (non-dependant) malfunctions were successfully tested. On top of that, all malfunctions are detected within 10 s time after they occur. Yet, this should be reconsidered, as, in the demo, the running points which are important to reach to observe the symptoms are known. It is very likely that a malfunction could be ignored for hours otherwise. This is one more point that asks for more knowledge, so that at least the presence/absence of one symptom may be computed for each malfunction, whatever the running point. Moreover, the malfunctions that still have too little knowledge provided, give some false alarms. More specific knowledge is needed to avoid them.

## 5. Conclusion

This paper has presented the prototyping results of a long term project in fault diagnosis applied to engine dyno test benches. Thus, it gives the whole evolution from the very first prototype to the actual. It takes into account not only the diagnosis process, but also all the necessary knowledge considerations for such a tool to be effective. It explains the results obtained at each stage, the problems we encountered and how they were solved.

This incremental process is one of the key of the success of this project. The begining of the project was quite unsure as huge amount of work had to be carried out, including promoting BEST inside the company. Today, a full prototype is implemented, from knowledge formalization to malfunction detection and the database contains about half of the malfunctions.

Some work still need be done, as implementing the real observation validity and errors. The extensions of the approach presented in [de Mouzon et al., 2001] should also be implemented to allow for multiple and cascading malfunction diagnosis.

## References

Buisson, J.-C. (1999). *Practical Applications of Fuzzy Technologies*, chapter Approximate reasoning in computer-aided medical decision systems, pages 337–361. The Handbooks of Fuzzy Sets Series. Kluwer Academic, Boston/London/Dordrecht.

Cordier, M.-O., Dague, P., Dumas, M., Lévy, F., Montmain, J., Staroswiecki, M., and Travé-Massuyès, L. (2000). AI and automatic control approches of model-based diagnosis: Links and underlying hypotheses. In *Proc. of the 4$^{th}$ IFAC Symp. on Fault Detection Supervision and Safety for Technical Processes (SAFEPROCESS'2000)*, volume 1, pages 274–279.

de Mouzon, O., Dubois, D., and Prade, H. (2001). Twofold fuzzy sets in single and multiple fault diagnosis, using information about normal values. In *Proceedings of the 10$^{th}$ IEEE International Conference on Fuzzy Systems (FUZZ-IEEE 2001)*, volume 3, Melbourne.

Dubois, D., Foulloy, L., Mauris, G., and Prade, H. (2002). Probability-possibility transformations, triangular fuzzy sets and probabilisitc inequalities. In *Proc. 9$^{th}$ Int. Conf. Info. Processing and Management of Uncertainty in Knowledge-based Syst.*, pages 1077–1083.

Kahn, G., Nowlan, S., and Mc Dermott, J. (1985). Strategies for knowledge acquisition. *IEEE Transactions on Pattern Analysis and Machine Intelligence (PAMI)*, 7(5):511–522.

Sanchez, E. (1977). Solutions in composite fuzzy relation equations: application to medical diagnosis in Brouwerian logic. In Gupta, M. M., Saridis, G. N., and Gaines, B. R., editors, *Fuzzy Automata and Decision Processes*, pages 221–234. North-Holland, Amsterdam.

Ulieru, M., editor (2000). *Intelligent Manufacturing and Fault Diagnosis (II). Soft computing approaches to fault diagnosis*, volume 127 of *Information Science*. Elsevier. Special issue.

Zadeh, Lofti Asker (1978). Fuzzy sets as a basis for a theory of possibility. *Fuzzy Sets and Systems*, 1(1):3–28.

# CBR AND MICRO-ARCHITECTURE ANTI-PATTERNS BASED SOFTWARE DESIGN IMPROVEMENT

Tie Feng[1,2], Jiachen Zhang[1], Hongyuan Wang[1], Xian Wang[1]
*[1]Institute of Computer Science and Technology, Jilin University, Changchun, 130012, China (fengtie@public.cc.jl.cn); [2]Key Laboratory of Symbolic Computation and Knowledge Engineering of Ministry of Education*

Abstract:     This paper presents a Case Based Reasoning (CBR) approach to identifying micro-architecture anti-patterns and replacing them with "good" patterns in order to improve the design of software system. The resulting system design benefits from better flexibility for adapting to future requirement change and expansion. In this approach, both problematic inflexible structures and their corresponding refactoring designs are formally defined and organized in a case base. The identification of anti-patterns is carried out through similarity measurement on class diagrams, sequence diagrams, OO quality metric and semantic constraints. A supporting system CBDIT was developed to aid this approach.

Key words:   Case Based Reasoning, Design Pattern, Anti-Pattern, Program Evolution, Refactoring.

## 1.      INTRODUCTION

Once a software product is delivered, the maintenance cycle begins, where continuous changes need to be made to the software product to accommodate further user requirements or adapt to new hardware or software environment. One of the barriers to enabling a smooth software maintenance cycle is the stiffness in the design of micro-architecture of many software systems. Identifying and removing the stiffness of these software design - so called "anti-patterns" will improve the effectiveness and efficiency of software maintenance.

Design pattern is commonly used in object-oriented design methodology to capture objects, collaborations and distribution of responsibility [1]. Anti-pattern is the next step to designing pattern research. Informally, an anti-pattern is a generalization of commonly occuring design solution to a problem that has negative consequence [2]. Most of existing work focuses on describing design pattern, especially anti-patterns, in natural language. We envisage that to be able to represent anti-patterns in formal language and provide a tool to automatically support the identification of anti-patterns and replace them with good quality design patterns will significantly advance the state of the art in this area.

Various attempts have been made in applying AI techniques to engineering practice. One of the most popular AI techniques is CBR that, in the context of software design improvement, can help capture experienced software design knowledge in an accumulated way. The captured software design can be used as big knowledge blocks to identify the problematic micro-architectures.

The following sections are organized as follows. Section 2 introduces the pattern language we use. Section 3 gives an example of anti-pattern and how it can be improved. Section 4 describes the framework of representing case. Section 5 illustrates the procedure of retrieving cases and provides an algorithm for identifying anti-patterns in software design. Section 6 presents an algorithm of applying cases through FACADE-oriented method. Section 7 introduces the architecture of CBDIT, CBR-Based Design Improvement Tools. The related work can be found in Section 8 and finally we reach conclusion.

## 2. SOFTWARE DESIGN PATTERN LANGUAGE

A software design can span across seven architectural levels, namely, global, enterprise, system, application, macro-component (framework), micro-architecture and object. Micro-architectural level contains a group of cooperative objects that inter-play with each other. The audience of micro-architectural design is normally programmers who implement the software system.

In our system, we adopt the following design language that contains class and relationships between classes. The class has the same meaning as that can be found in OO language. The relationships between classes can be classified into:

- Inh(C1, C2), where Class C2 inherits Class C1.
- Agg(C1, C2, m), where an object of Class C1 is aggregated by one or more objects of Class C2.

- Ini(C1, C2), where an object of Class C1 initiates an object of Class C2.
- Del(C1, C2), where an object of Class C1 delegates an object of Class C2 to fulfill some task.

Figure 1 shows an example of static design denoted in our design language.

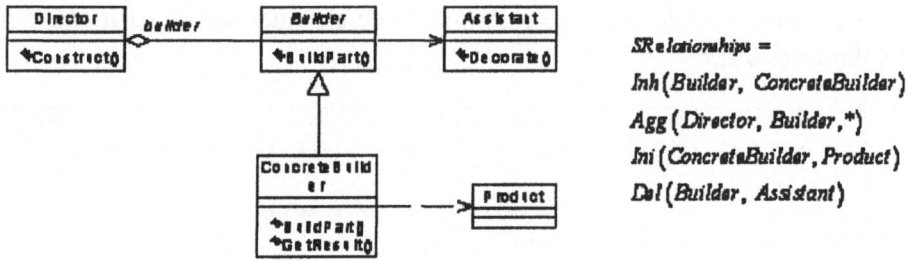

*Figure 1.* An Example for Static Design

In addition to static design, we also capture the dynamic behavior of software system. Similar to UML, where dynamic behavior is described by sequence diagram and collaboration diagram, we describe the interaction among objects using interaction sequence. An interaction sequence is represented as a list of tuples with three elements: initiating object, response object and message signature. Formally, we have

$IS = (io, ro, msg)^*$, $io \in S_1$, $ro \in S_1$, $msg \in S_2$, where IS is the interaction sequence; $S_1$ is the set of objects interact with each other at runtime; $S_2$ is the set of messages between two objects; io is the initiating object and ro is the response object. Figure 2 shows an example of dynamic behavior of system design.

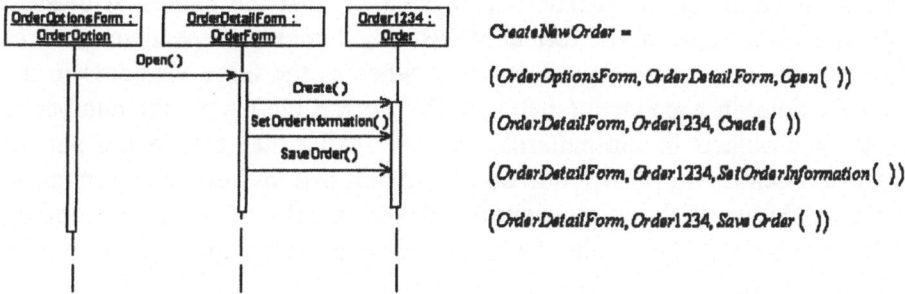

*Figure 2.* An Example of Dynamic Behavior of System Design

The interaction sequence is important for identify occurrence of problematic behavior, such as over-frequent interaction with database.

# 3.     AN EXAMPLE OF PATTERN AND ANTI-PATTERN

In this section we give an example of an anti-pattern instance using the denotation of the previous section and, in comparison, an improved pattern. First we have the following definition:

An architecture D is called micro-architecture anti-pattern, if it satisfies the three conditions:

(1)

```
D  = < StaticStructure > | < StaticStructure > < DynamicBehavior >
StaticStructure = < SClasses > < SRelationships >
SClasses = Class *
Class = < ClassName > | < Attribute > * < Method > *
SRelationship = Relation *
Relation = < Inh > | < Agg > | < Ini > | < Del >
Inh = " Inh(" < ClassName > , < ClassName > ")"
Agg = " Agg(" < ClassName > , < ClassName > , < Multiple > ")"
Ini = " Ini(" < ClassName > , < ClassName > ")"
Del = " Del(" < ClassName > , < ClassName > ")"
DynamicBehavior = < IS > *
IS  = "(" < io > "," < ro > "," < msg > ")"
io = < ObjectName >
ro = < ObjectName >
msg = < ReturnType > < MsgName > "(" FormalParameterList ")"
```

(2) D caused, in practice, quality problems in performance and extensibility for at least 3 times. (3) There are more than eight classes and objects in D.

Anti-pattern is an abstraction of a family of anti-pattern instances. Anti-pattern and anti-pattern instance is different in that the names of classes, objects and messages in the former are usually domain-independent (such as abstract product, concrete product, etc.), whereas the those elements in the latter are domain-dependent (such as staff, toolbar, etc.) Also, the number of classes and objects in anti-patterns is much smaller than that in anti-pattern instances because the classes and objects in anti-pattern have comprehensive typicality. Figure 3 shows an example of Anti-pattern and its corresponding XML expression. The result of expected design after improvement can be found in Figure 4.

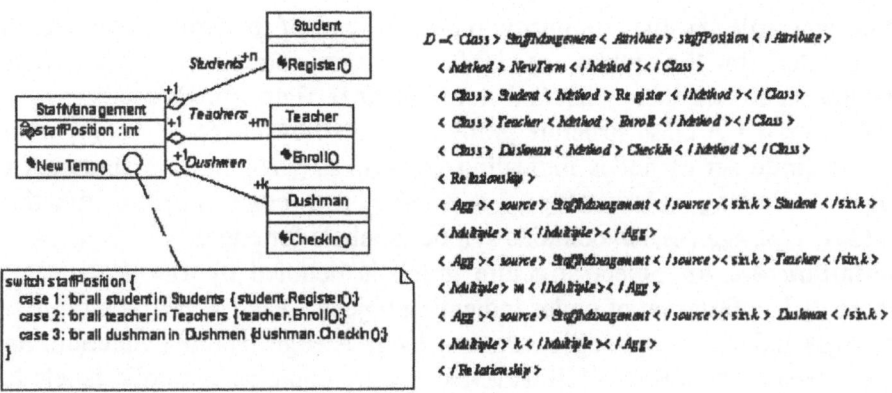

*Figure 3.* An Example of Anti-pattern and Its Corresponding XML Expression

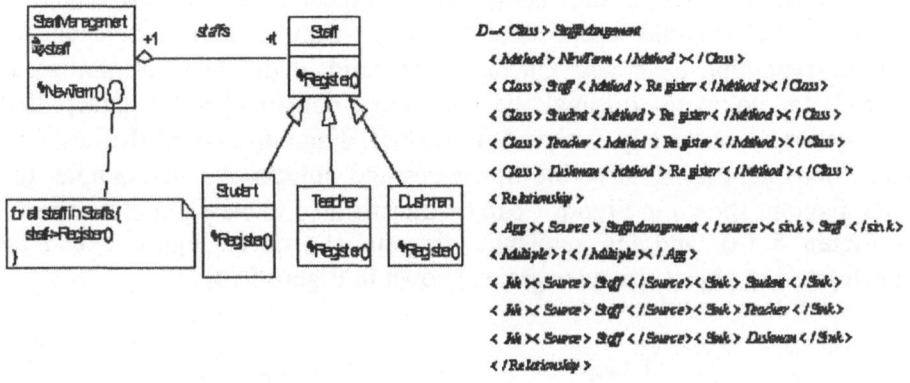

*Figure 4.* Result of Improved Design using Our Approach

## 4. REPRESENTING CASE

In our design improvement process, we have cases that capture five attributes, namely, Anti-Pattern Description (APD), Semantic Constraints (SC), Quality Metrics Before Improvement (QMBI), Pattern Description (PD) and Quality Metrics After Improvement (QMAI).

## 4.1 Describing Anti-pattern and Pattern

Both APD and PD contain four sub-attributes: name, effect, static structure and dynamic behavior. Static structure and dynamic behavior play important role in the similarity measurement of patterns; they can be represented in the forms of UML diagram, structure graphs, XML documents and adjacency list and stored in XML files or SQL databases.

**Definition 4.1** A class structure graph is denoted by $G = (N_c, E_r, \beta, L_\beta)$, where $N_c$ is a finite set of nodes indicating classes, $E_r \subseteq N_c \times N_c$ is a finite set of edges indicating relationships, $\beta: E_r \to L_\beta$ is a edge labeling function, and $L_\beta \subseteq \{Inh, Agg, Del, Ini\}$ contains symbolic labels for edges.

**Definition 4.2** An object structure graph is denoted by $G = (N_o, E_m, \beta, L_\beta)$, where $N_o$ is a finite set of nodes indicating objects, $E_m \subseteq N_o \times N_o$ is a finite set of edges indicating messages, $\beta: E_m \to L_\beta$ is a edge labeling function, and $L_\beta \subseteq PosInt$, where $PosInt = \{x \mid x \text{ is a integer} \wedge x > 0\}$, contains symbolic labels for edges.

It is obvious that both class structure graph and object structure graph are special examples of directed labeled graph in which symbolic label for node and node labeling function are ignored. The symbolic label for node and node labeling function are deliberately neglected in our approach to guarantee that original design could be equivalent to domain-independent case by renaming its nodes. On the other hand, if detailed information is needed to compare original design with domain-specific case, that information can be easily retrieved from UML diagrams and XML files. Our main focus here is the structure of classes and objects. As an example, the class diagram shown in Figure 1 can be transformed to class structure shown in Figure 5 (a), and the sequence diagram shown in Figure 2 can be transformed to object structure graph, shown in Figure 5 (b).

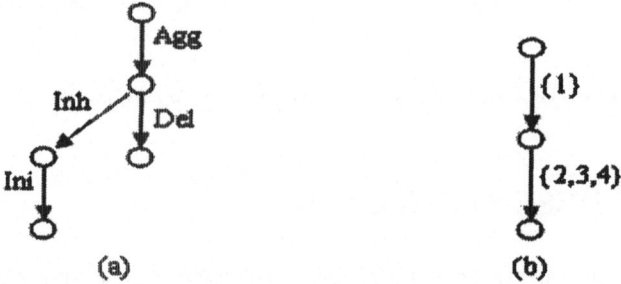

*Figure 5.* Simplified Class Structure Diagram and Object Structure Diagram

**Definition 4.3** Let $G_t = (N_t, E_t, \beta_t, L_{\beta t})$, $G_s = (N_s, E_s, \beta_s, L_{\beta s})$ be two class structure graphs or two object structure graph, the map from $G_t$ to $G_s$ is denoted by $\eta: G_t \to G_s$ which satisfies:

- $\forall n_t \in N_t$, $n_t$ maps to one and only one $n_s \in N_s$, denoted by $\eta(n_t) = n_s$;

- $\forall e_i = (n_{i1}, n_{i2}) \in E_i$, if $\eta(n_{i1}) = n_{s1}$, $\eta(n_{i2}) = n_{s2}$ and $e_s = (n_{s1}, n_{s2}) \in E_s$, then $e_i$ maps to $e_s$, denoted as $\eta(e_i) = e_s$.

From above definition, it is obvious that if there is a map from $G_i$ to $G_s$, $\eta: G_i \to G_s$, the number of nodes in $G_i$ is equal to or less than that of $G_s$. In the context of anti-pattern identification, if we can find a map between an anti-pattern and a trunk of graph in the original design, the anti-pattern is thereby identified and the case attached to the anti-pattern can be retrieved and applied to the original design, for instance, the anti-pattern is replaced with a good design pattern.

It is also noted that different relationships in a class diagram contribute differently to describing the static structure of a case. Thereby, every edge in the class structure graph in APD is assigned with a weight to denote that contribution. The weight can be adjusted by domain experts. Similarly, every edge in the object graph in APD is also assigned with a weight value.

Let NEC be the number of edges in class structure graph representing class diagram in APD, the default weight of each edge is assigned as 0.3*(1/NEC).

Let NEO be the number of edges in object structure graph representing sequence diagram in PD, the default weight of each edge is assigned as 0.2*(1/NEO).

## 4.2 QMBI and QMAI

QMBI and QMAI each contain eight sub-attributes: Weighted Methods per Class (WMC), Number of Children (NOC), Depth of Inheritance Tree (DIT), Response for a Class (RFC), Coupling Between Objects (CBO), Lack of Cohesion in Methods (LCOM), Number of Abstract Class (NOAC) and Number of Relation with Abstract Class (NRWAC). The definition of the first six sub-attributes can be found in [3]. In addition, we believe that the last two sub-attributes, in the micro-architecture context, implies the rate of application of polymorphism mechanism in OO design – an indicator of extensibility of an OO system, and thereby also need to be included. As an example, the NOAC and NRWAC for the designs in Figure 3 and Figure 4 are listed in Table 1.

*Table 1.* Changes in NOAC and NRWAC before and after Design Improvement

|  | Design in Figure 3 | Design in Figure 4 |
|---|---|---|
| NOAC | 0 | 1 |
| NRWAC | 0 | 4 |

## 4.3      Semantic Constraints

Structural information alone is not sufficient to decide whether change can be made to the original design. Take the following case for example, although there exists a structural mapping between the design on the left-hand side in Figure 6 with that in Figure 3, the two are not referred to the same design pattern because of the mismatch of the semantic information here. As a result, we need to incorporate semantic information into the matchmaking process.

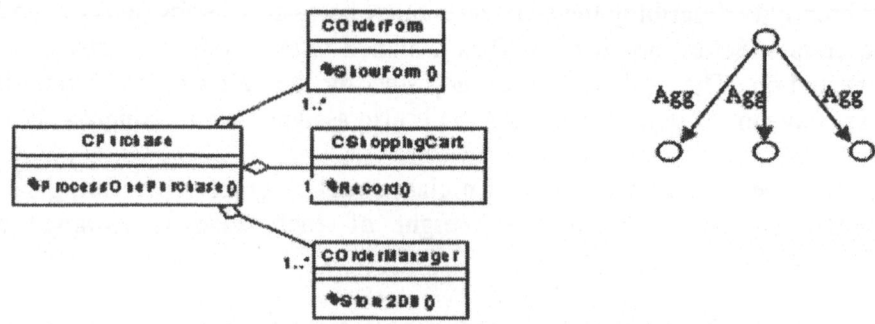

*Figure 6.* An Example for Structually-Matched while Semantically-Not-Match Design

Semantic constraints are represented by weighted logic predicates that describe design knowledge. For example, the semantic constraints in the design improvement case shown in Figure 3 and Figure 4 are given as below:

- MeaningSimilar (Class$_{i1}$.Function$_{i1}$, Class$_{i2}$.Function$_{i2}$, ..., Class$_{im}$.Function$_{im}$)  [$\omega 1$]
- Invoke (Class$_z$.Function$_y$, Class$_{j1}$.Function$_{j1}$, ..., Class$_{jm}$.Function$_{jm}$)  [$\omega 2$]
- Class$_{i1}$.Function$_{i1}$ = Class$_{j1}$.Function$_{j1}$, ..., Class$_{im}$.Function$_{im}$ = Class$_{jm}$.Function$_{jm}$  [$\omega 3$]

  The facts that satisfies the above predicates are:

*MeaningSimilar(Student.Register, Teacher.Enroll, DushMonCheckin)*          [$\omega 1$]

*Invoke(StaffManagement.NewTerm, Student.Register, Teacher.Enroll, DushMonCheckin)*  [$\omega 2$]

*Student.Register = Student.Register, Teacher.Enroll = Teacher.Enroll, DushMonCheckin = DushMonCheckin*  [$\omega 3$]

Let NSC is the number of semantic constraints, the default weight of each predicate is assigned as 0.3*(1/NSC). For example, default weight of MeaningSimilar, Invoke and equations are both 0.3*(1/3) = 0.1.

Synonym library can be consulted to judge the value of predicates, such as MeaningSimilar. Synonym library are indexed by domain name and part of speech. In our system, 8 domains are considered: Manufacturing, Telecommunications, Health care, Insurance, Financial services, Professional services, Travel and E-Commerce Models. Our survey suggests that complete data model resource has been explored, however very few work on domain application model resource has been explored [4]. With the application of the system, more domain catalogs and synonyms can be added by the domain experts.

# 5. RETRIEVING CASES

Case retrieval consists of 4 parts: class structure graph match, object structure graph match, quality metric data match and semantic constraints match. In our approach, the maximal values of degree of similarities ($DS_c$, $DS_o$, $DS_q$ and $DS_s$) of above 4 parts are guaranteed as 0.3, 0.2, 0.3 and 0.2 according to our calculation method of degree of similarity. That is Max $(DS)=Max (DS_c + DS_o + DS_q + DS_s)=0.3+0.2+0.2+0.3=1$.

## 5.1 Similarity Measure of Structure Graphs

After designs are transformed into directed labeled graphs (class structure graph and object structure graph), algorithms for matching class diagrams and for matching sequence diagrams are similar. Matching problem is equivalent to a sub-graph isomorphism detection problem. Although sub-graph isomorphism detection problem has been shown to be NP-complete [5], graphs transformed from diagrams of APD are very small ones usually only with less than 8 nodes. Furthermore, there exist techniques, such as tabu search [6], which use domain specific knowledge for graph-structured case retrieval, and decomposition approach [7].

Taking class structure graph as example (the algorithm for object structure graph is similar), to measure degree of similarity of two graphs, we first represent class structure graph as adjacency list. An adjacency list is a representation for a directed graph that has n vertexes and an array of n lists of vertexes. List i contains vertex j if there is an edge from vertex i to vertex j. Adjacency list records information of node index, some marks indicate node counterpart, edge label, weight of edge, whether a node or an edge has been successfully checked, and so on. The algorithm for matching between two adjacency lists is listed in Figure 7.

*Input:* two adjacency lists, one represents class structure graph of APD (adjAPD), the other one represents original design (adjOD); a threshold of degree of similarity (TDS).

*Output:* adjacency lists, each represents a sub-graph of class structure graph of original design which have a higher DS than TDS.

---

(1) *Create an ordered list SeqAPD including all different nodes in adjAPD,*

  *the order of which is given arbitrarily (but once the order is det er min ed,*

  *it is not allow to change in process). Suppose there are M elements in adjAPD.*

(2) *Create a set setOD including all different nodes in adjOD;*

(3) *Calculate all subsets, set₁, set₂, ..., setₖ, of setOD that have exactly M elements.*

  *Let subSetOD = { set₁, set₂, ..., setₖ };*

(4) *For every elements in subSetOD setᵢ, accoding to edges given in two adjacency*

  *lists of input, compare adjacency lists of all possible forms of setᵢ (totally M !*

  *possibilities) with that of SeqAPD. Suppose the ordered list, including all setᵢ that*

  *equal SeqAPD, be preSeq = {seq₁, seq₂, ..., seqₗ};*

(5) *For every seqᵢ, calculate* $DS_a = \sum_{j=1}^{l} V_j$, *where l is the total number of edges of seqᵢ,*

  $V_j = \omega_j$, *if* $\beta\left(edge_j \ of \ seq_i\right) = \beta'\left(edge_j \ of \ seqAPD\right)$, *otherwise,* $V_j = 0$. *If* $DS_a \geq TDS$

  *, output adjacency list of seqᵢ.*

---

*Figure 7.* Algorithm for Matching between Two Adjacency Lists

## 5.2    Similarity Measure of Quality Metric Data

$DS_q = 0.2 \times \left[ \sum_{i=1}^{8}\left(1 - \frac{|VI_i - VC_i|}{VC_i}\right) \times \frac{1}{8} \right]$, where $VI_i$ and $VC_i$s' meaning are

listed in Table 2. It is obvious that $DS_q$ obtains its maximum 0.2 when All $VI_i = VC_i$ (i=1, .., 8).

*Table 2.* Meaning of $VI_i$ and $VC_i$

|  | 1 | 2 | 3 | 4 | 5 | 6 | 7 | 8 |
|---|---|---|---|---|---|---|---|---|
| VI (Value of Initial design) | WMC | NOC | DIT | RFC | CBO | LCOM | NOAC | NRWAC |
| VC(Value of Case) | WMC | NOC | DIT | RFC | CBO | LCOM | NOAC | NRWAC |

## 5.3    Similarity Measure of Semantic Constraints

$DS_s = \sum_{i=1}^{n} M_i$, where n is the total number of semantic constraints; $M_i = \omega_i$ if the ith semantic constraint is satisfied; $M_i = 0$ otherwise. It is obvious that the maximum value of $DS_s = \sum_{i=1}^{n} \omega_i = 0.3$.

## 6.    FACADE-ORIENTED CASE APPLICATION

```
i = 2 ;
While ( S_ccu ≠ Φ ) Do
    D_t = D_1 ;  Get one Case ∈ S_ccu ; Let S_ccu = S_ccu − Case ;
    Let S_c1 = {class | class ∈ D_1 ∧ class ∉ Case.APD}
    Let S_c2 = {class | class ∈ Case.APD}
    Remove all classes ∈ S_c2 from D_1 ;
    Add a class FACADE to D_1 ; Add all classes ∈ Case.PD to D_1 ;
    Remove all relationships ∈ Case.APD from D_1 ;
    Add all relationships ∈ Case.PD ;
    While ( S_c1 ≠ Φ ) Do
        Get one C_1 ∈ S_c1 ; Let S_c1 = S_c1 − C_1 ;
        While ( S_c1 ≠ Φ ) Do
            Get one C_2 ∈ S_c1 ; Let S_c1 = S_c1 − C_2 ;
            If (∃R ∈ {Inh, Ini, Del} in D_1 ∧ R(C_1, C_2)) Then
                Remove R(C_1, C_2)from D_1 ; Add R(C_1, FACADE) to D_1 ; EndIf ;
            If (∃R ∈ {Inh, Ini, Del} in D_1 ∧ R(C_2, C_1)) Then
                Remove R(C_2, C_1)from D_1 ; Add R(FACADE, C_1) to D_1 ; EndIf ;
            If (∃Agg(C_1, C_2, k) in D_1) Then
                Remove Agg(C_1, C_2, k)from D_1 ; Add Agg(C_1, FACADE, k) to D_1 ; EndIf ;
            If (∃Agg(C_2, C_1, k) in D_1) Then
                Remove Agg(C_2, C_1, k)from Di ; Add Agg(FACADE, C_1, k) to Di ; EndIf ;
        EndWhile ;
    EndWhile ;
```

*Figure 8.* Algorithm of FACADE-Oriented Case Application

Case application is the procedure to replace the problematic micro-architecture. The algorithm for FACADE-oriented case application is listed in Figure 8.

*Input:* a set of selected cases which will be applied into original design, original design $D_1$.

*Output:* a sequence of improved designs, each one of which is obtained by appling one case.

## 7.     CBDIT: A CBR-BASED DESIGN IMPROVING TOOL

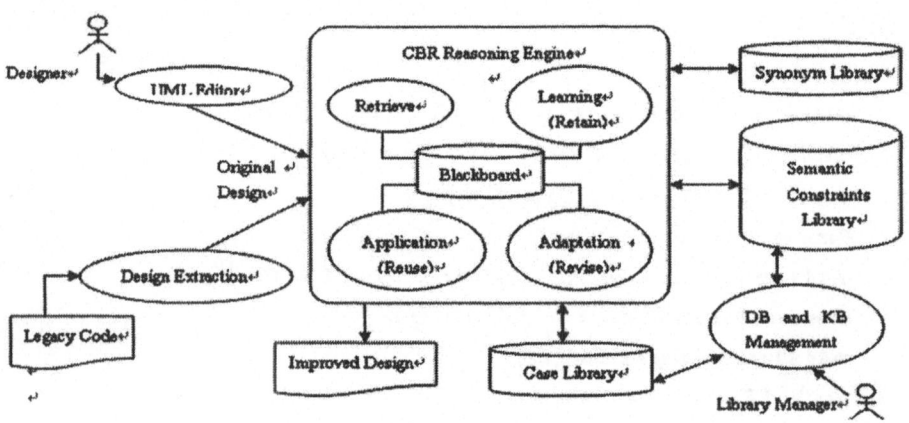

*Figure 9.* Architecture of CBDIT

The architecture of CBDIT, which is shown in Figure 8, includes four sub-systems.

- UML Editor sub-system is designed to visually draw class diagram and sequence diagram.
- Design Extraction sub-system is designed to extract design information from legacy code with incomplete design documentation.
- DB and KB Management sub-system is designed to create, delete, modify and search data and knowledge stored in databases and knowledge bases.
- CBR Reasoning Engine is the heart of CBDIT whose working mechanism has been explained in previous sections.

## 8. RELATED WORK

Paulo Gomes [8] presented a method of using CBR for automating software design patterns and implemented it into a system called REBUILDER. Differences can be identified between Gomes's method and ours:

- The cases in REBUILDER are used to capture similar design pattern across applications, whereas our cases are specifically designed to describe anti-patterns.
- REBUILDER uses WordNet to help retrieve design cases. In Wordnet, single terms are interconnected through simple relations. However, a single word is insufficient in describing and matching case. In our approach, we use context information, such as combined graph and semantic information, to help identify cases.

Alexandre L. Correa [9] described an approach that uses heuristics, design patterns and anti-patterns to reusing object oriented design expertise and a tool called OOPDTool. In their method, OO design constructions are identified by meta-model predicates and rule-based reasoning.

Richard C. Gronback [10] introduced a mechanism of using audits, metrics and refactoring in Boland Together ControlCenter to remodel software. This method is driven by the automated measurement of quality factors, such as CBO (Couplings Between Objects), RFC (Response For Classes), and audits, such as NOIS (Negation Operator on 'if'). Unfortunately, only conversation based manual refactoring interface is provided.

Jirapun Daengdej [11] attempts to use CBR for design reuse. However, their method doesn't address design pattern or anti-pattern issue. Instead, they search similar E-R diagram in design library given some domain specific key words.

There is also some other research work on applying design patterns to legacy code analysis [12][13][14]. However, their focus on design patterns is to improve the understandability of legacy system.

## 9. CONCLUSION

This paper describes an approach to improving software design for increased flexibility, expansibility, and maintainability of object-oriented system. Based on CBR technique, this approach is capable of identifying micro-architecture anti-patterns in original design and substituting it with high quality designs.

The future work includes efficiently addressing the variation of micro-architecture anti-patterns, extending knowledge base to cover more application domains and design knowledge, and developing powerful reengineering tool to help extract more precise design information.

# REFERENCES

[1] Erich Gamma, Richard Helm, Ralph Johnson, and John Vlissides, Design Patterns: Elements Of Object-Oriented Software Architecture, Addison-Wesley, Reading, MA, 1995

[2] William J. Brown, Raphael C. Malveau, Hays W. "Skip" McCormick III, Thomas J. Mowbray, Antipatterns: Refactoring Software, Architectures, And Projects In Crisis, Wiley Computer Publishing, 1998

[3] Chidamber, S.R., and C.F. Kemerer, "A Metrics Suite for Object-Oriented Design", IEEE Transactions on Software Engineering, 20(6), pp.476-493, 1994.

[4] Len Silverston, The Data Model Resource Book Revised Edition Volume2: a Library of Universal Data Models by Industry Types, John Wiley&Sons, Inc. New York, 2001

[5] Garey, M.R., and Johnson, D.S., Computers and Intractability a Guide to the Theory of NP-Completeness. W.H.Freeman, 1977.

[6] Sanja Petrovic, Graham Kendall, and Yong Yang, "A Tabu Search Approach for Graph-Structured Case Retrieval", In Proc. STAIRS 02, volume 78 of Frontiers in Artificial Intelligence and Applications, pp. 55-64. IOS Press, 2002.

[7] Messmer, B.T., and Bunke,H., "Efficient Subgraph Isomorphism Detection: A Decomposition Approach", IEEE transactions on knowledge and data engineering, 12-2, pp.307-323, 2000.

[8] Paulo Gomes, Francisco C. Pereira, Paulo Paiva, Nuno Seco, Paulo Carreiro, José Ferreira, Carlos Bento, "Using CBR for Automation of Software Design Patterns", in Proc. of the European Conference on Case-Based Reasoning (ECCBR'02), Aberdeen, Scotland, UK, September, 2002, LNAI 2416, pp. 534-548, Springer-Verlag Berlin Heidelberg, 2002

[9] Alexandre L. Correa, Cláudis M.L. Werner, Gerson Zaverucha, "Object Oriented Design Expertise Reuse: an Approach Based on Heuristics, Design Patterns and Anti-Patterns", URL: http://citeseer.nj.nec.com/439618.html

[10] Richard C. Gronback, "Software Remodeling: Improving Design and Implementation Quality", A Borland White Paper, January, 2003.
http://www.togethersoft.com/events/webinars/archive/software_remodeling_whitepaper.pdf

[11] Jirapun Daengdej, Peerapol Moemeng, and Supawat Charoenvikrom, "Toward the Use of Case-Based Reasoning for Design Reuse", 2002.
http://citeseer.nj.nec.com/534321.html

[12] Niere, W.Schafer, J.Wadsack, L.Wendehals, and J.Welsh. "Towards Pattern-based Design Recovery", In Proc. of the 24th International Conference on Software Engineering, Orlando, Florida, USA, pp. 338-348, May, 2002.

[13] Dirk Heuzeroth, Thomas Holl, Gustav Hogstrom, Welf Lowe, "Automatic Design Pattern Detection", In Proc. of the 11th IEEE International Workshop on Program Comprehension (IWPC'03), Portland, Oregon, May 10 - 11, pp.94-104, 2003, USA.

[14] Herve Albin-Amiot, Pierre Cointe, Yann-Gael Gueheneuc and Narendra Jussien. "Instantiating and detecting design patterns: Putting Bits and Pieces Together", In Proc.

of the 16<sup>th</sup> IEEE International Conference on Automated Software Engineering (ASE'01), San Diego, California, pp.166-173, November 26-29, 2001.

# A DECISION SUPPORT SYSTEM (DSS) FOR THE RAILWAY SCHEDULING PROBLEM*

L. Ingolotti[1],P. Tormos[2] ,A. Lova [2],F. Barber [1],M.A. Salido [3] and M. Abril[1]

[1]*DSIC, Universidad Politecnica de Valencia,Spain;* [2]*DEIOAC, Universidad Politecnica de Valencia, Spain;* [3] *DCCIA, Universidad de Alicante, Spain*

**Abstract**    The recent deregulation occurred in the public railway sector in many parts of the world has increased the awareness of this sector of the need for quality service that must be offered to its customers. In this paper, we present a software system for solving and plotting the Single-Track Railway Scheduling Problem efficiently and quickly. The problem is formulated as a Constraint Satisfaction Problem (CSP), which must be optimized. The solving process uses different stages to translate the problem into mathematical models, which are solved to optimality by means of mixed integer programming tools. The Decision Support System (DSS) we present allows the user to interactively specify the parameters of the problem, guarantees that constraints are satisfied and plots the optimized timetable obtained.

**Keywords:**    Planning and Scheduling, Railway Scheduling Problems, Industrial Application of AI

## 1.    INTRODUCTION

The recent deregulation in the public railway sector in many parts of the world has increased the awareness of this sector of the need for quality service that must be offered to its customers. Under pressure for improvement, computer tools have been developed to help planners do their work more efficiently and quickly. In this context, the timetable planning plays a fundamental role in the management and operation of a public transport system. Nowadays, software tools offer effective support for the construction of schedules. Many of the proposed tools are of the form of an interactive *what-if* application, in which the goal is to obtain feasible solutions quickly rather than obtaining an optimized solution. Information on network topology, engine properties as well as user requirements are stored in databases. Graphical user interfaces allow schedule planners to build and edit schedules interactively based on

---

*This work has been supported by a join contract RENFE-UC/UPV

time space diagrams that contain lines representing trains serving each route. However, the automatic generation of feasible schedules still remains too time-consuming. In particular, currently implemented algorithms are still too slow for networks of real-world size. In fact, existing software tools such as HAS-TUS, FBS, BERTA, MICROBUS, VISUM ÖV 7.0, ptv interplan, and solutions by TLC GmbH, Berlin, D are limited to only modifying an already existing timetable [4]. Although the use of such tools can be valuable, a train scheduling tool that is also capable of finding optimal solutions for the problem within a reasonable computational time is equally desired.

In this paper, a computer tool that is able to obtain optimized railway running maps[1] is presented. The running map will contain information regarding the topology of the network and the schedules of the trains; that is, arrival and departure times of trains at each station, frequency, stops, etc. The resulting optimized running map combines user requirements and deals with a wide variety of the complex constraints encountered in practical train scheduling.

## 2. THE TRAIN SCHEDULING PROBLEM

Planning of train schedules is a part of the general planning process of traffic systems and is traditionally broken down into several stages that have to be completed before a train schedule can be created. These stages are: Network Planning, Line Planning, Train Schedule Planning and Stock and Crew Planning. Planning rail traffic problems are basically optimization problems that are computationally difficult to solve as they belong to the NP-hard class of problems. Hence, efforts in the development of new, powerful, exact and heuristic algorithms are justified. The models and methods applied to solve these problems have been analyzed in [1], [3].

The majority of the papers published in the area of periodic timetabling in the last decade are based on the Periodic Event Scheduling Problem (PESP) introduced by [9]. Schrijver and Steenbeek in [8] developed a constraint programming based solver called CADANS to solve the feasibility problem. Nachtigall was the first to consider the objective function to be to minimize the passenger waiting time [5]. In [6] they developed a genetic algorithm to solve the problem in a context with two criteria taking into account investments in infrastructure over improvements in passenger waiting time. Odijk in [7] developed a cutting plane algorithm to solve the feasibility problem. His objective was to quickly generate a set of feasible timetables in order to be able to evaluate infrastructure projects. Recently, Caprara, Fischetti and Toth have proposed a graph formulation for the problem using a directed multigraph in which

---

[1]We consider a running map as an association between trains and the arrival and departure times at/from each location in their paths.

nodes correspond to departures/arrivals at a certain station at a given time instant [2]. This formulation is used to derive an integer linear programming model that is relaxed in a Lagrangian way. In their formulation, the objective is to maximize the sum of the benefits based on the differences between actual traversal times and ideal timetables, of the scheduled trains.

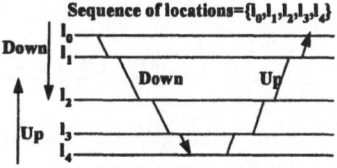

*Figure 1.* Each oblique line represents the position of a train depending on the time (axis x).

## 3. DESCRIPTION OF A SINGLE-TRACK RAILWAY SCHEDULING PROBLEM (STRSP)

Consider a STRSP problem defined by:

1 a set of ordered locations $L=\{l_0,l_1,...,l_m\}$ that must be visited by each train. Each $l_i$ is a place to stay or pass through. A pair of adjacent locations is joined by a single-way track.

2 a set of trains for each direction ($T_D$ and $T_U$). Given the sequence of locations L, $T_D=\{t_0,t_2,...,t_d\}$ visits the locations in the order given by the sequence (down direction), and $T_U=\{t_1,t_3,...,t_u\}$ visits the locations in the opposite order (up direction). The variable $t_i$ represents the ith train that starts the journey in a given direction (see Figure 1).

3 a journey for trains $T_U$ and $T_D$ in L specifies the traversal time for each section of track and each direction in L ($R_{i\rightarrow i+1}$ and $R_{i\rightarrow i-1}$), and the minimum stop time ($S_i$) for commercial purposes in each $l_i$.

Considering $t_y dep\_l_x$ and $t_y arriv\_l_x$ as the departure and arrival times of train $t_y$ from/at location $l_x$, the STRSP consists in finding the optimal running map (with minimum average traversal time) that satisfies all the following constraints[2]:

- Time Intervals to start the journey by the first train in each direction, $[min_D,max_D]$ and $[min_U,max_U]$,

$$min_D \leq t_0 dep\_l_0 \leq max_D \wedge min_U \leq t_1 dep\_l_m \leq max_U$$

---

[2]The constraints are related to railway infrastructure, parameters of trains to be scheduled and traffic rules.

- Frequency Constraint specifies the period ($F_U/F_D$) between departures of two consecutive trains in each direction at the same location,

$$\{\forall t_i, l_k / t_i \in T_D - \{t_d\} \wedge l_k \in L - \{l_m\}\}, t_{i+1}dep\_l_k = t_i dep\_l_k + F_D$$
$$\{\forall t_i, l_k / t_i \in T_U - \{t_u\} \wedge l_k \in L - \{l_0\}\}, t_{i+1}dep\_l_k = t_i dep\_l_k + F_U$$

- Stopover Constraint: a train must stay in a location $l_k$ at least $S_k$ time units,

$$\{\forall t_i, l_k / t_i \in T_D \cup T_U \wedge l_k \in L - \{l_m + l_0\}\}, t_i dep\_l_k \leq t_i arriv\_l_k + S_k$$

- Exclusiveness Constraint: a single-way section of track must be occupied by only one train at the same time,

$$\{\forall t_j, t_i, l_k / t_j \in T_D \wedge t_i \in T_U \wedge l_k \in L - \{l_m\}\},$$
$$t_i dep\_l_{k+1} \geq t_j arriv\_l_{k+1} \vee t_j dep\_l_k \geq t_i arriv\_l_k$$

A *conflict* occurs when two trains going in opposite directions require the same section of track at the same time. We denote $C_{ijk} \equiv\, <t_i, t_j, s_{k\_k+1}>$ when $t_i \in T_D$ and $t_j \in T_U$ compete for the section track $l_k, l_{k+1}$. The crossing of two trains going in opposite directions can be performed only at locations where one of the two trains has been detoured from the main track. This operation requires a reception and expedition time for the detoured train.

- Reception Time Constraint: At least are required $R_k$ time units at location $l_k$ between the arrival times of two trains going in the opposite direction (Figure 2),

$$\{\forall t_j, t_i, l_k / t_j \in T_D \wedge t_i \in T_U \wedge l_k \in L\},$$
$$t_j arriv\_l_k \geq t_i arriv\_l_k + R_k \vee t_i arriv\_l_k \geq t_j arriv\_l_k + R_k$$

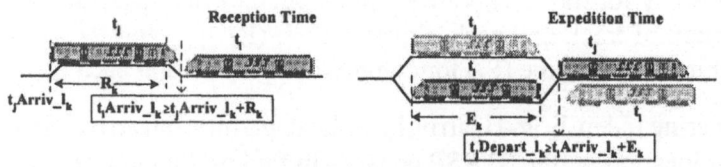

*Figure 2.* Reception and Expedition time constraint

- Expedition Time Constraint: At least are required $E_k$ time units at location $l_k$ between the arrival and departure times of two trains going in the opposite direction (Figure 2),

$$\{\forall t_j, t_i, l_k / t_j \in T_D \wedge t_i \in T_U \wedge l_k \in L\},$$
$$t_j dep\_l_k \geq t_i arriv\_l_k + E_k \vee t_i dep\_l_k \geq t_j arriv\_l_k + E_k$$

- Precedence Constraint: each train employs a given time interval ($R_{k \to k+1}$ or $R_{k \to k-1}$) to traverse each section of track ($l_k \to l_{k+1}$ or $l_k \to l_{k-1}$) in each direction,

$$\{\forall t_i, l_k / t_i \in T_D \wedge l_k \in L - \{l_m\}\}, t_i arriv\_l_{k+1} = t_i dep\_l_k + R_{k \to k+1}$$

$$\{\forall t_i, l_k / t_i \in T_U \wedge l_k \in L - \{l_0\}\}, t_i arriv\_l_{k-1} = t_i dep\_l_k + R_{k \to k-1}$$

The complexity of the problem lies mainly in the number of conflicts that can appear during the generation of the running map. In each conflict, one of two trains must wait for the release of the section of track (priority assignment). This problem is a well known NP-hard problem which makes exploring all possibilities for optimality complex and inefficient. In the DSS system, the search space is drastically reduced by means of a pre-processing stage before applying CSP techniques to solve the problem.

## 4. THE SOLVING TOOL: A DEPENDENT-DOMAIN CSP

The architecture of our system is shown in Figure 3. First, the user gives the parameters of a required running map (L1): which journeys, number of trains, time interval to start the journey and frequency. All parameters are stored in a common database and used by the solver process (L2). Finally, the solution is shown graphically to the user (L3), who can interact with the system.

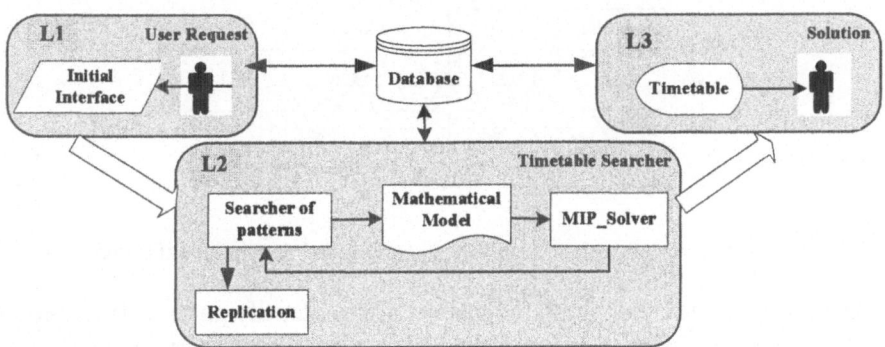

*Figure 3.*    General System Architecture

The main module is the solver process, which obtains an optimized running map (L2 in Figure 3). This process is efficiently performed by identifying, solving, and replicating a given pattern.

## 4.1 Identification of replication patterns

The identification of replication patterns to reduce complexity in order to solve STRSP is based on the concept that we have named *Equivalent Conflicts*:

470

Two conflicts $C_{mek}$ (conflict between $t_m$ and $t_e$ for the section of track $k, k+1$) and $C_{ojh}$ (conflict between $t_o$ and $t_j$ for the section of track $h, h + 1$) are equivalents if and only if:

- they occur in the same section of track (i.e.: $k = h$);

- for each conflict $C_{mm'v}$ (i.e.: each conflict of $t_m$ with another train $t_{m'}$ for a section track $v, v + 1$) there exists one conflict $C_{oo'v}$ (conflict between $t_o$ and another train $t_{o'}$ for a section track $v, v + 1$) or vice versa;

- for each conflict $C_{e'ew}$ , a conflict $C_{j'jw}$ exists or vice versa.

For instance, in Figure 4, $C_1$ and $C_2$ (which represent to $C_{mek}$ and $C_{ojh}$ respectively) are equivalent conflicts due to the following:

- They occur in the same section of track.

- all conflicts between $t_m$ and any other $t_{m'}$ ($C_3$, $C_5$) occur in the same section of track that all conflicts between $t_o$ and $t_{o'}$ ($C_4$, $C_6$), respectively.

- all conflicts between $t_e$ and any other $t_{e'}$ ($C_7$) occur in the same section of track as all conflicts between $t_j$ and $t_{j'}$ ($C_8$), respectively.

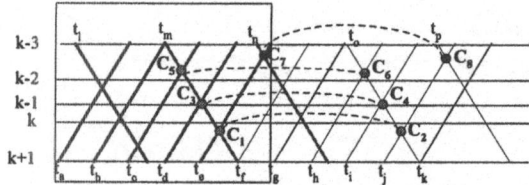

*Figure 4.* An example for equivalent conflicts and pattern identification

The concept of equivalent conflicts allows us to identify patterns in a running-map. A pattern is a part of the whole running map, where only non equivalent conflicts exist (Figure 4). Each possible start departure time in each direction gives rise to a set of non-equivalent conflicts and a consequent pattern. Solving a pattern implies solving the complete running map, because if the related set of non-equivalents conflicts is solved, all equivalent conflicts may be solved similarly. That is to say, the complete running map can be obtained by replicating the solved pattern. Finding and replicating the pattern with minimum cost produces the optimal running map. Thus, the basic process consists in identifying and solving the patterns for each possible start departure time in each direction (Figure 5 shows how a pattern for a given start departure time is identified and solved), and choosing the pattern with minimum cost and replicating it along the running map. It is important to remark that once a pattern is identified, increasing the number of trains does not increase the problem complexity.

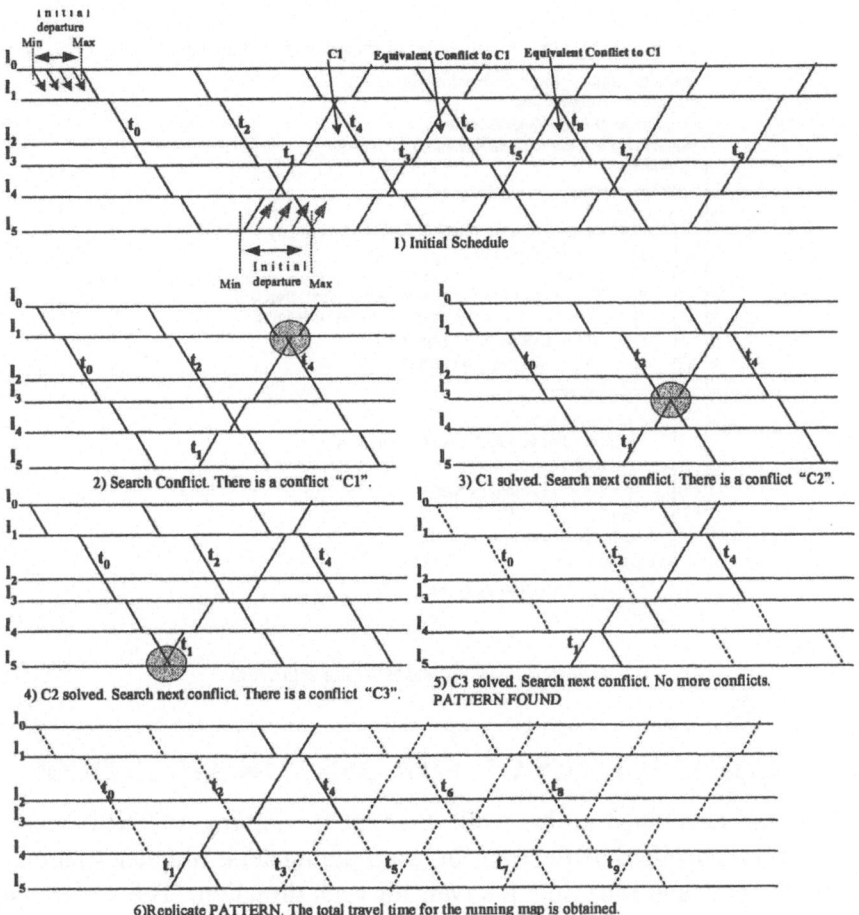

*Figure 5.* Outline of the algorithm

## 4.2 Algorithm for Single-Track Railway Scheduling

The pattern to be solved and replicated depends on the set of non-equivalent conflicts which in turn depends on the initial departure of the trains. The algorithm to identify and to solve patterns has three nested loops (Figure 6): *Loop 1* explores departure times for the first trains in each direction, *Loop 2* explores assignment of priorities for trains and *Loop 3* identifies the set of non-equivalent conflicts. Constraints are generated only for the subset S of trains implied in the current set of non-equivalent conflicts, and solved (if possible) according to the assignment of priorities given by the second loop.

Once all possible sets of non-equivalent conflicts (patterns) are identified and solved, the best solution is replicated to obtain the optimal running map.

```
C ← ∅               //Set of conflicts that are not equivalent among them
best ← -1           //best is a variable to save the best found cost
RM ← feasible       //RM is a running map
c_s ← Search start conflict
Assignment of beginning schedule
While there is some feasible RM and c_s is not NULL
    priority ← 0
    While priority < 2ⁿ or priority = 0
        n ← 0
        While there is a conflict c non-equivalent to any
        conflict belonging to C
            n ← n+1              //R' is the set of generated constraints taking into
            S ← subset of trains  account only the subset S
            R' ← instance of the problem constraints for S
            RM ← Call to MIP Solver (R')
            Search next conflict in RM
        End While
        Compute cost cst
        If (cst < best and RM is feasible) or best = -1
            best ← cost
            Save provisionally RM
        End If
        priority ← priority +1
    End While
    c_s ← Move c_s to next section track
End While
```

*Figure 6.*    Main steps in the algorithm

## 5.    CAPABILITIES OF THE DSS FOR THE STRSP

The DSS developed in this work is a tool for solving a STRSP according to the values specified by the user for given parameters: frequency, number of trains, journey, and start time interval, for each direction. The system considers the set of parameters with their corresponding values as a request. Once the problem has been parameterized, the system solves it, saving the obtained running map in a database for its later graphical display. Figure 7 shows an example of a request solved by the DSS. In this example, for each direction the user composes his request choosing: a frequency (1 hour), a journey, a number of trains (100) and a time interval to start the journey (6:00-6:30 for DOWN and 8:00-8:30 for UP). The system took 25 seconds to solve this problem using an Intel Pentium 4 1,6 GHz processor. The user interface of the DSS allows the parameters to be easily modified obtaining a solution for each request. This makes the DSS an appropriate tool application for what-if analysis. The number of trains that could be allocated in one day in the running map with a given frequency, or the best departure time to start a given journey, in order to obtain the minimum average traversal time, etc, are some examples of useful information for the final operator. The graphical interface through the space-time diagrams shows the topology of the solution in a clearer way.

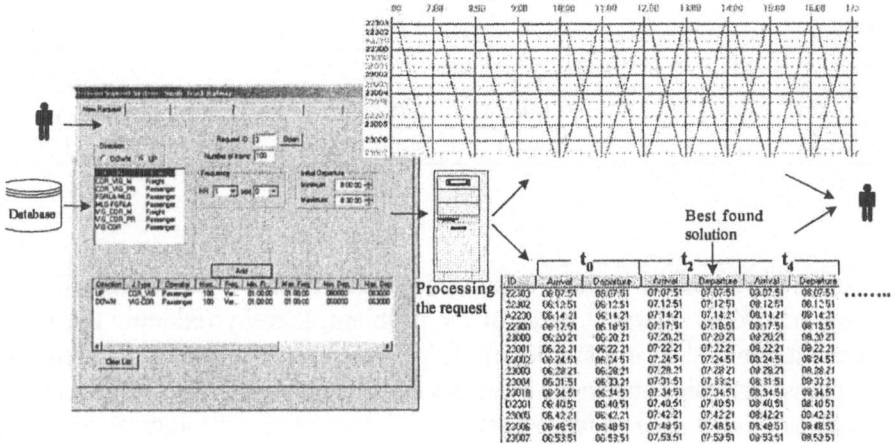

*Figure 7.* An example using the application

# 6. RESULTS

In this section we evaluate some problems, whose value parameters can be applied to practical cases. Each constraint satisfaction problem is defined by the pair $< n, f >$, where $n$ is the number of trains and $f$ is the frequency between consecutive trains. In Table 1, we present the execution time in problems solved with DSS and general constraint solvers (LINGO, CHEEP, CPLEX, etc), where the number of trains was increased from 10 to 50 while the frequency was fixed to 60 and problems where the frequency was increased from 60 to 120 and the number of trains was fixed to 20. In both cases, the number of locations was 40 and the departure time was [06:00:00 - 06:30:00] in down direction and [05:30:00 - 06:30:00] in up direction. The problems were solved with an Intel Pentium 4 1,6 GHz processor.

In Table 1, we observe that DSS reduces considerably the execution time in all cases due to it reduces the search space using the heuristic described in previous sections while general solvers provide the optimal schedule without preprocessing and they must study the complete problem.

# 7. CONCLUSIONS AND FUTURE RESEARCH

In this paper, a DSS to solve the Single Track case of this problem has been developed. The system provides the user with an interface to parameterize the

*Table 1.* Execution time in problems $< n, 60 >$ and $< 20, f >$.

| Problems | DSS - Run Time (sc) | Solvers - Run Time (sc) | Problems | DSS - Run Time (sc) | Solvers Run Time (sc) |
|---|---|---|---|---|---|
| <10,60> | 3 | 9 | <20,60> | 5 | 313 |
| <16,60> | 4 | 46 | <20,75> | 1 | 4200 |
| <20,60> | 5 | 313 | <20,90> | 1 | 95 |
| <36,60> | 6 | 1487 | <20,105> | 1 | 34 |
| <50,60> | 7 | >4800 | <20,120> | 1 | 147 |

problem . It solves the request in an optimal and efficient way using CSP guided by the proper characteristics of the problem, thereby reducing the search space and hence the computational effort. The user can obtain different running maps for easier and more effective decision making. The current system is being validated by a railway company. Future work will address to the extension of the method in order to deal with double tracks and networks already occupied by other trains.

# References

[1] Bussieck, M.R., Winter, T., and Zimmermann, U.T., 'Discrete optimization in public rail transport', *Math. Programming*, **79(1-3)**, 415–444, (1997).

[2] Caprara, A., Fischetti, M., and Toth P., 'Modeling and solving the train timetabling problem', *Operations Research*, **50**, 851–861, (2002).

[3] Cordeau, J.F., Toth, P., and Vigo, D., 'A survey of optimization models for train routing and scheduling', *Transportation Science*, **32(4)**, 380–404, (1998).

[4] Liebchen, C., and Möhring, R., 'A case study in periodic timetabling', *Electronic Notes in Theoretical Computer Science*, *66*, **6**, (2002).

[5] Nachtigall, K., 'Periodic network optimization with different arc frequencies',*Discrete Applied Mathematics 69*, **1-2**, 1–17, (1996).

[6] Nachtigall, K., and Voget, S., 'Minimizing waiting times in integrated fixed interval timetables by upgrading railway tracks', *European Journal of Operational Research*, (1997).

[7] Odijk, M.A., 'A constraint generation algorithm for the construction of periodic railway timetables', *Transportation Research, 30*, **6**, 455–464, (1996).

[8] Schrijver, A., and Steenbeek, A., 'Timetable construction for railned', Technical Report, *CWI, Amsterdam, The Netherlands (in Dutch)*, (1994).

[9] Serafini, P., and Ukovich, W., 'A mathematical model for periodic scheduling problems', *SIAM Journal on Discrete Mathematics*, **2(4)**, 550–581, (1989).

# AN INTERACTIVE MULTICRITERIA OPTIMISATION APPROACH TO SCHEDULING

Martin Josef Geiger, Sanja Petrovic
*Automated Scheduling, Optimisation & Planning Research Group*
*School of Computer Science & IT, University of Nottingham, UK*
mjg@cs.nott.ac.uk, sxp@cs.nott.ac.uk

**Abstract**  Scheduling problems overall assume that it is possible to identify stable criteria definitions measuring the quality of alternatives. In real world problems however, this does not necessarily have to be the case. Situations may change over time or even within the decision making process, and so may criteria and preferences of the decision maker.

The paper presents an interactive multicriteria guided optimisation framework for production scheduling. The methodology enables the decision maker to successfully change the definitions of optimality criteria and his/her preferences. The methodology was tested on a real-world scheduling problem faced by the Sherwood Press Ltd, a printing company based in Nottingham, UK.

**Keywords:**  Planning and Scheduling, Evolutionary Systems, Genetic Algorithms

## 1. Introduction

Scheduling in real-world manufacturing environments is a complex problem with a considerable amount of research activities in the fields of operations research, computer science and artificial intelligence, going back several decades (Brucker, 2001). The general problem of scheduling can be described to be a problem of assigning resources to tasks over time subject to a set of side constraints (e.g. resource capacity constraints, etc.) with the goal of optimising one or more objectives.

Over the years, various classes of scheduling problems have been investigated, and consequently different methods have been developed (Pinedo, 2002). Nevertheless, the impact of scheduling research on the real world problems has been limited. One of the reasons is that scheduling algorithms usually employ a single objective function which often fails to reflect preferences of the decision maker.

Multicriteria approaches to scheduling allow the integration of several, usually conflicting aspects or 'points of view' (Roy, 1996) that have to be con-

476

sidered simultaneously. Due to the complexity of most problems heuristic and metaheuristic techniques have been used for their solving with increasing popularity (Coello Coello et al., 2002).

This paper presents a methodology which enables the decision maker to change the set of optimality criteria and his/her preferences during the search process. The paper is organised as follows. Some concepts of multiobjective optimisation relevant for this paper are given in Section 2. Section 3 describes the production scheduling problem that was studied. Section 4 proposes a novel framework for interactive multicriteria optimisation, overcoming restrictions. The proposed methodology was tested on real-world data provided by Sherwood Press, a printing company based in Nottingham, UK, and the results are presented in Section 5. Conclusions are given in Section 6.

## 2. Concepts from multiobjective optimisation

The multicriteria decision making (MCDM) process involves four phases shown in Figure 1: formulation of a model which includes identification of optimality criteria and identification of the alternatives (the search space), search for the alternatives, the choice of the most preferable alternative and the execution of the selected solution. With each schedule $S \in S$ a vector of objective functions $G(S) = \big(g_1(S), \ldots, g_z(S)\big)$ is associated.

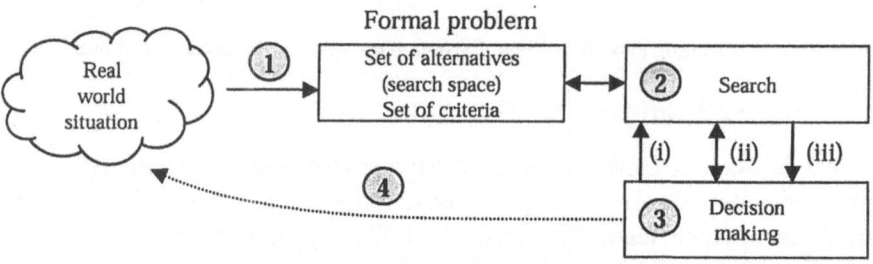

*Figure 1.* Multicriteria model building, search, and decision making process.

As criteria may be conflicting, the notion of optimality is interpreted in the sense of *Pareto optimality* (see e.g. Van Veldhuizen and Lamont, 2000), which is based on the concept of dominance relations among objective vectors. Without loss of generality, we assume in the further descriptions the minimisation of objective values.

DEFINITION 1 (PARETO DOMINANCE RELATION) *A vector of objective functions $G(S)$ is said to dominate an vector $G(S')$ if and only if $\forall i\ g_i(S) \leq g_i(S') \wedge \exists i \mid g_i(S) < g_i(S')$. We denote the dominance of a vector $G(S)$ over a vector $G(S')$ with $G(S) \preceq G(S')$.*

Using the dominance relation, the definition of Pareto optimality is derived as follows.

DEFINITION 2 (PARETO OPTIMALITY) *A solution S is said to be Pareto optimal if and only if* $\neg \exists S' \in \mathcal{S} \mid G(S') \preceq G(S)$. *The set of all Pareto optimal solutions is called the Pareto set P for which* $P \subseteq S$ *holds.*

As visualised in steps 2 and 3 in Figure 1, the solving of the scheduling problem can now be seen in identifying a most preferred schedule $S^* \in P$, which itself is twofold. First, a Pareto optimal schedule is computed, which is $\mathcal{NP}$-hard if the scheduling problem for at least one criterion definition is $\mathcal{NP}$ (Ehrgott, 2000). Second, an element $S^* \in P$ has to be selected. Three general strategies are possible.

(i) *A priori.* The preferences of the decision maker are obtained before the search.

(ii) *Interactive.* The problem solving alters between search and decision making, successively revealing preferences.

(iii) *A posteriori.* After identifying the Pareto set $P$, the decision problem is solved using multicriteria decision aiding techniques (Vincke, 1992).

While a few approaches combine the set of criteria to an overall evaluation function (Allahverdi, 2003), most existing applications to multicriteria scheduling are a posteriori approaches of Pareto optimisation (Bagchi, 1999). Interactive applications are however comparably scarce (Hapke et al., 1998).

## 3. Problem statement

### Machine environment

We investigated the scheduling problem faced by the Sherwood Press printing company which may be best characterised as a flexible job-shop problem with release dates and due dates (Błażewicz et al., 2001). The machine environment is characterised by a set $\mathcal{M} = \{M_1, \ldots, M_m\}$ of machines organised into disjunct working centres. Seven working centres have been identified to be of relevance for scheduling: printing, cutting, folding, cards insertion, embossing/debossing, gathering/stitching/trimming, and packaging.

As processing times depend on both the machine and the particular task, the working centres may be regarded as consisting of unrelated parallel machines. The availability of the machines changes over time. Some machines may also be operated on Saturdays while others are only available from Monday till Friday. Compared with problems known from literature, in the described problem shifts of the job floor have to be respected, allowing the assignment of tasks to machines only within a specific time window on each day.

## Job characteristics

Scheduling in the investigated problem has to deal with a set $\mathcal{J} = \{J_1, \ldots, J_j, \ldots, J_n\}$ of jobs, each of them consisting of a set $J_j = \{T_{j1}, \ldots, T_{jk}, \ldots, T_{jt}\}$ of tasks. The tasks are ordered with respect to a technically required processing sequence which is known in advance. Associated with each job $J_j$ is a release date $r_j$, a due date $d_j$, and a nonnegative weight $w_j$ reflecting its relative importance for the decision maker. While the release date must not be violated, the due date constraints are desirable to satisfy but is is often impossible to find a solution which violates none of them.

Each task $T_{jk}$, being able to be processed on one or several machines of a certain working centre, has a quantity $q_{jk}$ indicating the size of the task, e.g. the amount of sheets that have to be printed. Furthermore, processing times $p_{ijk}$, setup times $s_{ijk}$ and cleanup times $c_{ijk}$ for each task $T_{jk}$ on machine $M_i$ are given.

It has to be noticed that some tasks are not processed as a whole as they would exceed the capacity of the processing machine on a certain day. These tasks are split into smaller processing units called lots. In a general formulation, for each task $T_{jk}$ exists a set of lots $\mathcal{L}_{jk} = \{L_{jk1}, \ldots, L_{jku}, \ldots, L_{jkl}\}$, $l \geq 1$. Here, a lot $L_{jku}$ has a quantity $q_{jku}$ such that

$$\sum_{u=1}^{l} q_{jku} = q_{jk} \quad j = \{1, \ldots, n\}, \quad k = \{1, \ldots, t\} \tag{1}$$

While setup- and cleanup times are not dependent on the quantity of the lot, the processing time $p_{ijku}$ of lot $L_{jku}$ on machine $M_i$ can be computed as

$$p_{ijku} = \frac{q_{jku}}{q_{jk}} p_{ijk} \tag{2}$$

In the studied problem, the decision about how to split tasks with longer processing times is not treated separately from the problem of finding a schedule, and the lot quantities $q_{jkl}$ are additional decision variables.

## Optimality criteria

Meeting the agreed due dates is an important goal. Taken the completion time $C_j$ of job $J_j$, we are able to obtain the total weighted tardiness:

$$g_1(S) = \sum_{j=1}^{n} w_j T_j \tag{3}$$

where

$$T_j = \max\{0, C_j - d_j\} \tag{4}$$

Although the splitting of tasks into lots may enable a parallel processing and a possible earlier completion, setup- and cleanup times are together with the organisational overhead accordingly increased. The second objective is the minimisation of the number of lots.

$$g_2(S) = \sum_{j=1}^{n} \sum_{k=1}^{t} |\mathcal{L}_{jk}| \tag{5}$$

Given the defined objective functions $g_1$ and $g_2$, the problem can now be treated as a vector optimisation problem.

$$\text{minimise } G(S) = \left( g_1(S), g_2(S) \right) \tag{6}$$

However, the definition of optimality criteria cannot be regarded as exhaustive due to two reasons:

1 In practice, the general objective functions aggregate tardiness and number of lots over a large number of jobs, implying the possibility that different schedules might have similar or even identical evaluations.

2 It may not be possible to formulate all desired objectives in the phase of the model construction, meeting the formal requirement of exhaustiveness of the set of criteria (Bouyssou, 1990). Some information might not be present from the very beginning but are discovered during the search and decision making process.

As a result, it may occur that none of the Pareto optimal solutions given a certain definition of criteria is preferred by the decision maker.

While existing multicriteria approaches already consider the problem of possibly changing preferences during search in interactive techniques, a methodology for changing optimality criteria, to our knowledge has not been proposed yet.

## 4. A novel framework for interactive multicriteria optimisation

In the proposed framework, the decision maker is allowed to redefine the set of criteria interactively during the search process in order to refine the notion of optimality according to the specific situation. Three cases are possible:

1 A new objective function is introduced.

2 An existing objective function is removed from the objective vector $G(S)$.

3 An existing evaluation function is altered. As an example, the weights $w_j$ of the jobs may be changed during the search.

```
[1] Create initial population of solutions POP
[2] If no change in criteria definition is detected
[3]      Select schedule S ∈ POP
[4]      Create neighbouring solution S^nh using S
[5]      Update population with S^nh with respect to nondominance
[6] Else
[7]      Recompute weak nondominance relations in POP
[8]      Return to [2]
```

*Figure 2.* Multicriteria guided evolutionary algorithm.

Obviously, changes within the objective vector have an impact on the evaluation of the alternatives. A closer investigation reveals that the concept of Pareto optimality may not be sufficient to anticipate possible changes of the set of criteria. We therefore propose the concept of *weak nondominance* to be used.

DEFINITION 3 (WEAK NONDOMINANCE) *An objective vector $G(S)$ is said to be weakly nondominated if and only if $\neg \exists S' \in S \mid \forall i \ g_i(S') < g_i(S)$.*

With respect to Definitions 2 and 3, a Pareto optimal solution is also weakly nondominated but not vice versa. However, weakly nondominated solutions may become Pareto optimal if the definition of criteria is altered such that a criterion for which inequality within the objective vector holds is removed.

During the search, all weakly nondominated solutions are kept in an archive, which is successively updated. The introduction of conflicting criteria accordingly results in an archive having a larger cardinality.

## An evolutionary algorithm for interactive scheduling

The proposed framework is based on an evolutionary algorithm. A population oriented approach has been chosen for implementation as a whole set of weakly nondominated solutions should be found simultaneously. As the pseudo code for the algorithm in Figure 2 shows, in the case of occurring changes of the optimality criteria the weakly nondominance relations among the individuals of the population are updated, resulting possibly in a removal of alternatives that do not meet Definition 3.

## Lot-sizing

The splitting of larger tasks is crucial for the further assignment to the machines. Numerous small lots should be avoided, while tasks with longer processing times have to be devided such that they meet the availability time windows of the machines. A probabilistic decision rule has been used to decide

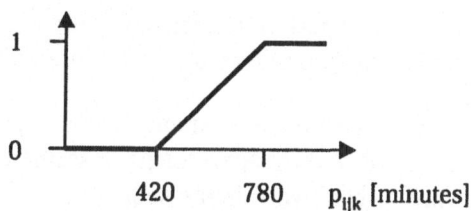

*Figure 3.* Probabilistic splitting of tasks depending on their processing time $p_{ijk}$.

whether tasks should be split into smaller processing units. For each task $T_{jk}$, a probability of splitting is derived depending on its processing time $p_{ijk}$ on machine $M_i$. With respect to the known daily capacity of the machines and the duration of the shifts, tasks are not split if their processing time is lower or equal to 7 hours (shift is 8 hours). Starting with 7 hours, the split probability is monotonically increasing up to a maximum value of 1 being reached at 13 hours which is depicted in Figure 3.

In the case of a splitting, a uniform number of splits between $\lceil \frac{p_{ijk}}{780} \rceil$ and $\lceil \frac{p_{ijk}}{420} \rceil$ is chosen.

## Representation and decoding

The schedule encoding of the evolutionary algorithm consists of a set of job permutations, one for each machine. At the beginning of the optimisation procedure, lots are assigned randomly to technically possible machines and their sequences are randomly generated. As different assignments are possible, the permutations of the machines can have different elements (lots) and consequently can be of different length.

To obtain a schedule with start and end dates for the lots, the permutational representation is decoded using the approach of (Giffler and Thompson, 1960) for constructing active schedules avoiding cycles within the precedence graph of the schedule. Here, all lots are subsequently scheduled while conflicts for processing on the same machine are resolved with respect to the sequence in the permutation, giving leftmost occurring lots priority. An example of this representation is given in (Mattfeld and Bierwirth, 2004).

## Operators

As different schedules might have different chromosome lengths, existing crossover techniques of combining two encodings are not applicable. Instead, a set of mutation operators is used, and at each iteration a neighbourhood solution is generated by applying one of the following operators with equal probability:

1 *Resplitting.* One of the splitted tasks is randomly chosen and the number of defined splits is changed within the given interval.

2 *Resequencing.* The position of a single lot on a particular machine is changed by means of a shift operator as described in (Reeves, 1999), shifting it forward of backward in the sequence.

3 *Reassignment.* A lot is removed from a machine and reassigned to a different machine from the set of machines appropriate for the task.

## 5. Results

The algorithm has been tested on a real world data set from Sherwood Press, containing the workload of four weeks (18 machines, 64 jobs, 218 tasks). In total 50 test runs have been performed starting with different initial populations, each containing 50 individuals, leading to an overall approximation of the Pareto set $P$ as shown in Figure 4. In each test, 100,000 schedules have been computed, keeping the best found alternatives from generation to generation.

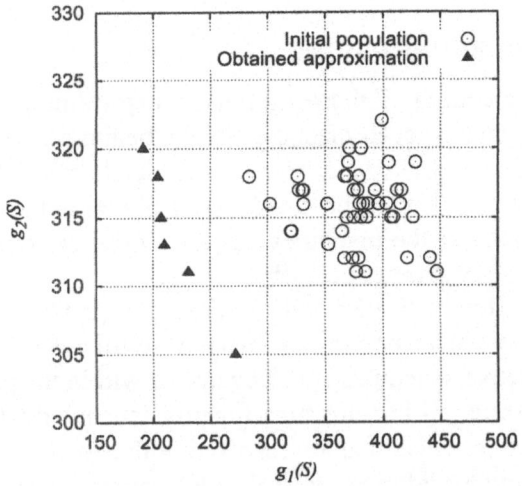

*Figure 4.* Results for the problem instance.

As suspected, the results show a tradeoff between the number of lots defined by the splitting procedure and the weighted tardiness. Numerous smaller lots are easier to schedule with respect to the total weighted tardiness. However, it has to be taken into consideration, that $g_1(S)$ does not discriminate between individual jobs but aggregates over their whole set, therefore allows a compensation of tardiness of different jobs.

In order to improve the quality of the schedules further, an additional objective function $g_3$ measuring the tardiness of a specific, highly important but late job was introduced during the search. It can be seen in Figure 5 that similar schedules with respect to the criterion $g_1$ are more clearly distinguishable by criterion $g_3$. While this aspect of evaluating the schedules is added to the set of criteria, the existing information of $g_1$ and $g_2$ is kept.

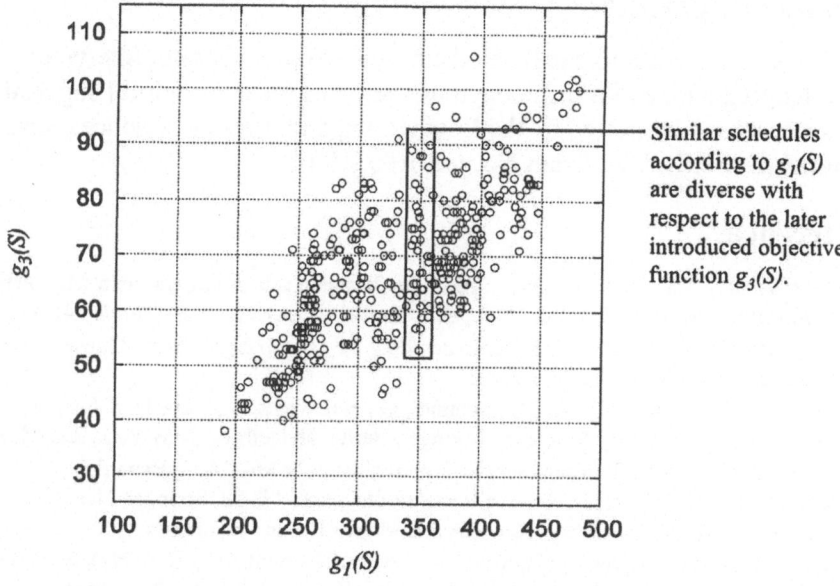

Similar schedules according to $g_1(S)$ are diverse with respect to the later introduced objective function $g_3(S)$.

*Figure 5.* Comparison of schedules according to their $g_1$ and $g_3$ values.

The introduction of an additional criterion is the most direct way of expressing the importance of the mentioned job. Another possible action could be changing the weight of the selected job. However, it would affect the relative importance of jobs, and it might not be easy for the decision maker in practical situations with numerous jobs to find a proper weight adaptation in order to obtain the intended results. Also, the introduction of a new criterion does not allow compensation of tardiness of jobs.

## 6.    Conclusions

A general approach for interactive multicriteria optimisation has been presented. An evolutionary algorithm has been proposed and applied to a problem from the printing industry. We believe that the successive introduction of criteria during the search is an important factor reflecting decision making in complex scheduling environments while guiding the search to preferred regions of the search space. Each 'point of view' is added or removed during the search

484

and decision making procedure in a step-by-step procedure while maintaining transparency for the decision maker.

Apart from the application for scheduling in the printing industry, the methodology is of general use for complex decision problems where the relevant criteria are changing over time and have to be developed interactively by the decision maker.

## Acknowledgments

The authors would like to thank their industrial collaborator Sherwood Press Ltd., Nottingham, and three anonymous referees for their helpful suggestions. This research is supported by the Engineering and Physical Sciences Research Council (EPSRC), UK, Grant No. GR/R95319/01.

## References

Allahverdi, Ali (2003). The two- and $m$-machine flowshop scheduling problem with bicriteria of makespan and mean flowtime. *European Journal of Operational Research*, 147:373–396.

Bagchi, Tapan P. (1999). *Multiobjective scheduling by genetic algorithms*. Kluwer Academic Publishers, Boston, Dordrecht, London.

Błażewicz, J., Ecker, K. H., Pesch, E., Schmidt, G., and Węglarz, J. (2001). *Scheduling Computer and Manufacturing Processes*. Springer, Berlin, Heidelberg, New York, 2nd edition.

Bouyssou, Denis (1990). Building criteria: A prerequisite for MCDA. In Bana E Costa, Carlos, editor, *Readings in Multiple Criteria Decision Aid*, pages 58–80. Springer, Heidelberg.

Brucker, Peter (2001). *Scheduling Algorithms*. Springer, Berlin, 3rd edition.

Coello Coello, Carlos A., Van Veldhuizen, David A., and Lamont, Gary B. (2002). *Evolutionary Algorithms for Solving Multi-Objective Problems*. Kluwer Academic Publishers.

Ehrgott, Matthias (2000). *Multicriteria Optimization*. Springer, Berlin, Heidelberg, New York.

Giffler, B. and Thompson, G. L. (1960). Algorithms for solving production-scheduling problems. *Operations Research*, 8:487–503.

Hapke, Marciej, Jaszkiewicz, Andrzej, and Słowiński, Roman (1998). Interactive analysis of multiple-criteria project scheduling problems. *European Journal of Operational Research*, 107:315–324.

Mattfeld, Dirk C. and Bierwirth, Chrstian (2004). An efficient genetic algorithm for job shop scheduling with tardiness objectives. *European Journal of Operational Research*, 155:616–630.

Pinedo, Michael (2002). *Scheduling: Theory, Algorithms, and Systems*. Precentice Hall, Upper Saddle River, NJ, 2nd edition.

Reeves, Colin R. (1999). Landscapes, operators and heuristic search. *Annals of Operations Research*, 86:473–490.

Roy, Bernard (1996). *Multicriteria Methodology for Decision Aiding*. Kluwer Academic Publishers, Dordrecht.

Van Veldhuizen, David A. and Lamont, Gary B. (2000). Multiobjective evolutionary algorithms: Analyzing the state-of-the-art. *Evolutionary Computation*, 8(2):125–147.

Vincke, Philippe (1992). *Multicriteria Decision-Aid*. John Wiley & Sons, Chichester, New York, Brisbane, Toronto, Singapore.

# Erratum to: Artificial Intelligence Applications and Innovations

## Max Bramer and Vladan Devedzic (eds.)

This book was originally published with a copyright holder in the name of the publisher in error, whereas IFIP International Federation for Information Processing holds the copyright.

--------------------------------------------------------------------------

The updated original online version for this book can be found at
DOI 10.1007/978-1-4020-8151-4

--------------------------------------------------------------------------

M. Bramer, et al. (eds.), *Artificial Intelligence Applications and Innovations*,
DOI 10.1007/978-1-4020-8151-4_41, © IFIP International Federation for Information Processing, 2017   E1